MALABAR MANUAL

MALABAR MANUAL

WILLIAM LOGAN

VOL. 2

IN TWO VOLUMES

GYAN

Published by

Gyan Publishing House
5, Ansari Road
Daryaganj, New Delhi-110002
Phone: 011-47034999, 9811692060
E-mail: books@gyanbooks.com

Distribution Network
gyanbooks.com
India, USA, Canada, UK, Australia, France

ISBN : 978-81-212-4535-7 (Set)
ISBN : 978-81-212-5014-6 (HB)
First Published, Madras 1887

2nd Impression 2020

Printed at: Gyan Press, Delhi.

MALABAR.

BY

WILLIAM LOGAN, M.C.S.

COLLECTOR AND MAGISTRATE OF THE DISTRICT, AND
FELLOW OF THE UNIVERSITY OF MADRAS.

IN TWO VOLUMES.

VOL. II.

MADRAS:
PRINTED BY R. HILL, AT THE GOVERNMENT PRESS.

1887.

FRONTISPIECE TO VOL. I

" നിങ്ങൾ ചത്തും കൊന്നും അടക്കിക്കൊൾക."

CHERAMAN PERUMAL'S SWORD GIVEN TO THE ZAMORIN WITH THE ADVICE TO DIE AND KILL AND ANNEX

(ENGRAVED FROM AN ORIGINAL SKETCH)

Reg. No. 75/'81 503

Photo-Zinco Press, C. S. O., Madras.

CONTENTS OF VOL. II.

APPENDICES.

APPENDIX I.—STATISTICS.

No. 1.—*Statement showing the number of amsams and dēsams in the district of Malabar as they stood in Fasli* 1291.

Taluks.	Area in square miles.	Government.				Zemindaries.				Inam.				Total.					
		Inhabited.		Uninhabited.		Inhabited.		Uninhabited.		Inhabited.		Uninhabited.		Inhabited.		Uninhabited.		Total.	
		Number of amsams.	Number of dēsams.	Number of amsams.	Number of dēsams.	Number of amsams.	Number of dēsams.	Number of amsams.	Number of dēsams.	Number of amsams.	Number of dēsams.	Number of amsams.	Number of dēsams.	Number of amsams.	Number of dēsams.	Number of amsams.	Number of dēsams.	Number of amsams.	Number of dēsams.
1	2	3	4	5	6	7	8	9	10	11	12	13	14	15	16	17	18	19	20
Chirakkal ..	*683	43	274	..	..	..	..	..	..	..	..	..	..	43	274	..	..	43	274
Kottayam ..	460	28	220	..	..	..	..	..	..	..	..	..	..	28	220	..	..	28	220
Kurumbranad ..	527	57	322	..	..	..	..	..	..	..	..	..	..	57	322	..	..	57	322
Wynad ..	891	13	57	..	..	..	..	..	..	..	..	..	..	13	57	..	..	13	57
Calicut ..	360	41	225	..	..	..	..	..	..	..	..	..	..	41	225	..	..	41	225
Ernad	997	52	298	..	..	..	..	..	..	..	..	..	..	52	298	..	..	52	298
Walluvanad ..	932	64	501	..	..	..	..	..	..	..	..	..	..	64	501	..	..	64	501
Palghat ..	681	56	177	..	..	..	..	..	..	..	..	..	..	56	177	..	..	56	177
Ponnāni ..	450	73	510	..	..	..	..	..	..	..	..	..	..	73	510	..	..	73	510
Cochin	3	1	1	..	..	..	..	..	..	..	..	..	..	1	1	..	..	1	1
Total ..	5,984	428	2,585	..	..	..	..	..	..	..	..	..	..	428	2,585	..	..	428	2,585

* Inclusive of Laccadive Islands, which measure 6¼ square miles.

Note.—The area in square miles does not correspond with the census statement. The talukwar census statements give the area in *acres*, which when reduced come to 8,000 and odd square miles. The area shown above is taken from a statement submitted to the Board from the Collector's office on 13th December 1871.

No. 2.—*Statement of population arranged with reference to caste, according to the census of* 1881.

Nationality.	Caste.	Population.		
		Males.	Females.	Total.
Hindus.	Brahmans	24,571	23,112	47,683
	Rajputs	277	85	362
	Agamadayan	111	73	184
	Ambalakáran	15	12	27
	Ambattan	4,141	4,206	8,347
	Balija	770	696	1,466
	Besta or Valayan	8,141	7,883	16,024
	Dévángulu	4	6	10
	Golla or Idaiyar	1,533	1,356	2,889
	Gouda	741	321	1,062
	Lingadhári	59	12	71
	Kaikálar	10,048	10,417	20,465
	Kallan	33	14	47
	Kamsala or Kammalan	24,606	26,947	51,553
	Komati	595	501	1,096
	Kumara or Kushavan	5,826	5,944	11,770
	Kurumbar	1,065	997	2,062
	Kuruba Golla	11	5	16
	Madiga	89,588	92,026	181,614
	Maravan	66	70	136
	Mutratcha	5	1	6
	Náyar	155,163	166,511	321,674
	Oddar	811	871	1,682
	Padayachchi	506	502	1,008
	Palli	20,137	20,672	40,809
	Parayan	44,918	48,694	93,612
	Reddi	73	46	119
	Sale	10,702	10,887	21,589
	Seniyan	265	221	486
	Shanan or Idiga	277,772	281,945	559,717
	Shembadavan	87	80	167
	Shetti	10,551	10,394	20,945
	Telugalu or Vadugar	3,794	4,017	7,811
	Upparavan	1	..	1
	Vaniyar or Gondla	21,251	21,530	42,781
	Vannan	18,331	19,225	37,556
	Vanniyan	696	563	1,259
	Vellalan	3,787	3,738	7,525
	Yadavalu	9	15	24
	Others	82,525	79,650	162,175
	Not Stated	818	623	1,441
	Total	824,403	844,868	1,669,271
Muhammadans.	Arabs	229	17	246
	Lubbai	159	159	318
	Mappilla	248,192	247,056	495,248
	Moghal	1	..	1
	Pathan	1,466	1,450	2,916
	Said	67	57	124
	Shaikh	41	3	44
	Others	9,646	9,447	19,093
	Not Stated	67,819	66,389	134,208
	Total	327,620	324,578	652,198

No. 2.—*Statement of population arranged with reference to caste, according to the census of* 1881—(Continued).

Nationality.	Caste.	Population.		
		Males.	Females.	Total.
Christians and others.	British-born subjects	1,008	130	1,138
	Other British subjects	107	97	204
	Other Europeans or Americans ..	168	148	216
	Eurasians	944	580	1,524
	Natives	10,155	10,017	20,172
	Not Stated	9,650	10,292	19,942
	Total ..	22,032	21,164	43,196
	Grand Total ..	1,174,274	1,190,761	2,365,035

No. 3.—*Statement showing the population arranged with reference to occupation, according to the census of* 1881.

Major heading.	Minor heading.	Number of males employed.	Number of females employed.
Professional.	Officers of National Government	4,328	20
	Do. of Local Government	2,847	36
	Do. of Independent Government and Native States.	31	1
	Army	2,274	..
	Clergy	11,490	13,249
	Lawyers and law stationers	840	..
	Physicians, &c.	4,155	642
	Authors and literary persons	2,793	227
	Artists	5	..
	Musicians	1,469	93
	Actors	1,514	225
	Teachers	3,828	139
	Scientific persons	1,563	13
	Total ..	37,137	14,645
Domestic.	Persons engaged in boarding and lodging ..	480	560
	Attendants, servants, &c.	5,313	5,441
	Wife of specified occupations	..	401
	Other wives	..	465
	Total ..	5,793	6,867
Commercial.	Mercantilemen	6,489	903
	Other general dealers	10,479	1,401
	Carriers on railway	320	1
	Do. on roads	4,711	44
	Do. on canals and rivers	2,964	14
	Do. on seas and rivers	3,755	17
	Engaged in storage	131	4
	Messengers and porters	20,418	2,053
	Total ..	49,267	4,437
Agricultural.	Agriculturists	343,969	227,852
	Arboriculturists	45	33
	Horticulturists	2,854	746
	Persons engaged about animals	13,082	3,948
	Total ..	359,950	232,579
Industrial.	Workers in books	206	2
	Do. in musical instruments	5	..
	Do. in carving and figures	9	..
	Do. in tackle for sports, &c.	2	2
	Do. in watches, &c.	9	..
	Do. in arms	19	..
	Do. in machines and tools	569	31
	Do. in carriages	2,414	..
	Do. in harness	3	..
	Do. in ships	179	..
	Do. in houses and buildings	15,977	363
	Do. in furniture	5	..
	Do. in chemicals	276	19
	Do. in wool and worsted	2	..
	Do. in silk	3	6
	Do. in cotton and flax	12,247	9,904
	Do. in dress	14,592	13,656

No. 3.—*Statement showing the population arranged with reference to occupation, according to the census of* 1881—(Continued).

Major heading.	Minor heading.	Number of males employed.	Number of females employed.
Industrial—(*Continued*).	Workers in hemp and other fibrous materials ..	3,253	38,407
	Do. in animal food	10,201	4,295
	Do. in vegetable food	19,235	44,386
	Do. in drinks and stimulants	43,196	4,317
	Do. in grease, horn, ivory, &c.	117	1,547
	Do. in skins, feathers, quills, &c.	588	52
	Do. in gums and resins	8,582	3,272
	Do. in wood	11,359	2,052
	Do. in bark	160	478
	Do. in cane, rush, and straw	7,713	8,228
	Do. in paper	16	..
	Miners	32	..
	Workers in stone and clay	48,642	2,768
	Do. in earthenware	3,697	2,438
	Do. in glass	25	11
	Do. in salt	972	413
	Do. in water	25	10
	Do. in gold, silver, &c.	5,149	85
	Do. in copper	276	10
	Do. in tin and quicksilver	25	
	Do. in lead and antimony	28	5
	Do. in brass and other mixed metals ..	1,146	109
	Do. in iron and steel	5,691	893
	Total ..	216,645	137,759
Indefinite and non-productive.	General laborers	27,850	18,081
	Other persons of indefinite occupations	1,216	27
	Persons of rank or property not returned under any occupation.	31	30
	Persons of no specified occupation	476,385	776,336
	Total ..	505,482	794,474
	Total population ..	1,174,274	1,190,761

No. 4.—*Statement showing the number of houses, population, and cattle in each taluk.*

Taluks.	Number of houses.					Population.			Agricultural stock.						
	Terraced.	Tiled.	Thatched.	Unspecified.	Total.	Males.	Females.	Total.	Tilling cattle.	Cows.	She buffaloes.	Sheep.	Ploughs.	Horses.	Ponies.
Chirakkal ..	..	..	..	..	..	132,715	139,954	272,669	35,119	51,534	6,505	5,595	10,405	..	..
Kottayam ..	..	..	..	..	..	81,345	84,430	165,775	18,227	21,827	626	2,210	6,077	..	..
Kurumbranad ..	..	..	..	..	..	129,394	131,630	261,024	39,020	53,539	1,156	3,886	12,009	..	..
Wynad	..	..	..	..	..	49,661	38,430	88,091	47,957	15,332	17,711	465	10,583	..	..
Calicut	..	..	..	..	..	103,669	102,293	205,962	27,221	32,604	1,027	2,747	8,524	..	..
Ernad	..	..	..	..	..	148,521	147,622	296,143	69,807	57,208	3,545	5,667	25,129	..	..
Walluvanad ..	..	..	..	..	..	153,236	154,866	308,102	92,491	73,596	6,798	16,086	36,246	..	..
Palghat	..	..	..	..	..	165,311	177,143	342,454	74,904	45,274	5,489	10,713	30,070	..	..
Ponnani	..	..	..	..	..	194,150	198,504	392,654	54,309	40,467	6,096	10,984	22,345	..	..
Cochin	..	..	..	..	..	11,142	10,218	21,360	102	498	..	238	..	..	..
Laccadive Islands.	..	..	..	..	..	5,130	5,671	10,801	..	..	..	..	..	..	..
Total ..	...	..	..	..	..	1,174,274	1,190,761	2,365,035	459,157	391,879	48,953	58,591	161,388	..	..

No. 5.—*Statement of rent roll for Fasli* 1291.

Pattas.	Single pattas.		Joint pattas.		Total pattas.	
	Number.	Assessment.	Number.	Assessment.	Number.	Assessment.
		RS.		RS.		RS.
Below Rs. 10	141,272	3,73,393	4,090	13,007	145,362	3,86,400
Above Rs. 10 and below Rs. 30.	21,054	3,54,492	927	15,696	21,981	3,70,188
Do. Rs. 30 ,, 50.	5,336	2,00,471	260	10,201	5,596	2,10,672
Do. ,, 50 ,, 100.	3,894	2,63,414	151	10,257	4,045	2,73,671
Do. ,, 100 ,, 250.	1,956	2,89,671	73	9,980	2,029	2,99,651
Do. ,, 250 ,, 500.	393	1,32,887	8	2,508	401	1,35,395
Do. ,, 500 ,, 1,000.	98	65,834	4	2,892	102	68,726
Do. ,,1,000	28	42,518	1	1,144	29	43,662
Total ..	174,031	17,22,680	5,514	65,685	179,545	17,88,365

No. 6.—*Statement showing the rainfall for a series of ten years in the district of Malabar.*

Faslis.	Official years.	July.	August.	September.	October.	November.	December.	January.	February.	March.	April.	May.	June.	Total.
		INCH.	INCH.	INCH.	INCH.	INCH.	INCH.	INCH.	INCH.	INCH.	INCH.	INCH.	INCH.	INCH.
1282 ..	1872-73	30·88	15·72	15·30	3·89	3·36	1·98	..	3·02	0·08	5·14	11·54	29·71	120·62
1283 ..	1873-74	37·12	8·60	6·53	7·85	0·41	0·75	..	0·19	0·05	3·25	21·60	44·25	130·60
1284 ..	1874-75	30·46	12·69	8·93	10·23	2·56	1·90	0·06	..	0·46	2·98	4·80	34·15	109·22
1285 ..	1875-76	29·65	11·59	4·73	6·29	1·99	0·43	..	0·08	1·81	1·90	2·46	22·27	83·20
1286 ..	1876-77	35·64	11·82	5·07	2·25	1·18	0·08	..	0·15	0·61	2·71	5·00	38·12	102·63
1287 ..	1877-78	10·93	24·26	15·10	20·14	4·23	2·15	0·01	..	0·82	3·63	7·70	36·28	125·25
1288 ..	1878-79	22·19	32·83	23·71	12·61	4·48	1·54	0·17	0·30	1·53	1·93	23·01	17·96	142·26
1289 ..	1879-80	25·08	15·22	7·12	10·17	3·96	1·69	0·02	0·24	0·34	5·21	10·26	30·19	109·50
1290 ..	1880-81	25·36	7·60	5·26	4·81	7·78	0·99	0·12	..	0·65	0·97	5·17	10·65	69·36
1291 ..	1881-82	18·34	22·12	7·53	4·01	7·86	0·12	1·36	..	0·19	1·55	14·82	42·37	120·27

No. 7.—*Statement showing the prices of grain for a series of ten years in the district of Malabar.*

Faslis.	Official years.	Rice, 1st sort, per garce.	Rice, 2nd sort.	Paddy, 1st sort.	Paddy, 2nd sort.	Cholum.	Cumboo.	Raggy.	Varagoo.	Horse-gram.	Ulundoo.	Wheat.	Salt.
		RS.	RS.	RS.	RS.	RS.	RS.	RS.	RS.	RS.	RS.	RS.	RS.
1282 ..	1872-73 ..	392	360	185	168	174	178	203	360	237	413	528	357
1283 ..	1873-74 ..	416	377	183	167	..	..	194	..	292	456	458	364
1284 ..	1874-75 ..	441	399	201	180	..	..	209	..	305	431	460	384
1285 ..	1875-76 ..	428	391	200	178	..	..	220	..	282	408	447	389
1286 ..	1876-77 ..	549	499	251	230	..	..	351	..	429	453	518	391
1287 ..	1877-78 ..	612	564	272	247	..	..	485	..	507	460	487	366
1288 ..	1878-79 ..	577	538	259	244	..	..	309	..	381	410	533	376
1289 ..	1879-80 ..	475	430	218	198	..	..	259	..	332	417	496	354
1290 ..	1880-81 ..	383	354	180	162	..	..	222	..	249	421	500	344
1291 ..	1881-82 ..	372	347	171	158	..	..	212	..	211	411	515	330

No. 8.—*Statement showing the collections under the several heads of revenue in the district of Malabar for a series of ten years.*

Faslis.	Official years.	Land revenue.	Forest revenue.	Abkári.	Income and License taxes.	Sea customs.	Land customs.	Salt.	Stamp.	Total.
		RS.	RS.	RS.	RS.	RS.	RS.	RS.	RS.	RS.
1282	1872-73 and 1873-74 ..	17,72,824	45,812	2,81,449	29,117	1,33,634	11,524	11,06,642	5,29,951	39,10,953
1283	1873-74 and 1874-75 ..	17,74,901	27,924	2,81,561	209	1,14,018	12,154	10,40,923	6,19,592	38,71,282
1284	1874-75 and 1875-76 ..	17,73,907	21,788	2,74,666	6	1,40,216	4,292	11,05,766	6,75,403	39,96,044
1285	1875-76 and 1876-77 ..	17,75,081	39,062	2,53,760	18	43,370	2,031	8,43,529	6,73,820	36,30,671
1286	1876-77 and 1877-78 ..	17,69,521	62,617	2,21,472	..	43,855	6,582	4,65,978	7,31,018	33,01,043
1287	1877-78 and 1878-79 ..	18,18,822	30,551	2,35,618	..	63,219	6,048	2,06,157	7,31,750	30,92,165
1288	1878-79 and 1879-80 ..	18,25,428	48,053	2,89,000	57,400	47,983	7,116	3,70,311	7,41,839	33,87,130
1289	1879-80 and 1880-81 ..	18,37,861	37,728	2,59,038	26,113	38,570	5,338	5,96,670	8,07,887	36,09,205
1290	1880-81 and 1881-82 ..	18,25,895	1,01,055	2,43,018	22,244	42,088	4,205	3,58,770	7,66,803	33,64,078
1291	1881-82 and 1882-83 ..	18,02,693	68,375	2,38,467	26,491	45,722	7,271	35,853	7,35,654	29,60,526

No. 9.—*Statement showing the particulars of the several tenures, other than ryotwari.*

Names of zemindaries and inam villages.	The entire beriz of the estate.	Peishcush or quit-rent.
Zemindary.	RS. A. P.	RS. A. P.
Town Cannanore and islands under Ali Rája of Cannanore	30,000 1 10	15,000 0 11
Inam villages	....	....

No. 10.—*Agricultural statistics, acreage of principal crops, &c., in the district of Malabar for Fasli* 1291.

Name of taluks.	Number of acres under nunjah cultivation.	Number of acres under punjah cultivation.															
	Paddy.	Garden coco-nut, areca-nut, and jack topes.	Modru.	Ponam.	Gingelly seed.	Raggy.	Chama.	Chollum.	Peas.	Horse-gram.	Dholl.	Cumboo.	Beans (puliya-mara).	Castor-oil seeds.	Coffee.	Pepper.	Ginger.
1. Chirakkal ..	44,509	28,254	1,775	11,824	416	..	..	..	..	..	..	..	..	..	..	2,513	..
2. Kottayam ..	16,384	25,155	598	8,295	14	17	180	5	37	57	62	..	..	..	17	3,939	..
3. Kurumbranad.	34,682	69,080	1,118	2,501	305	69	1,973	7	465	164	..	..	..	..	124	551	17
4. Wynad ..	26,945	..	207	10	..	1,745	87	..	2	7	2	..	..	3	35,241	1	5
5. Calicut ..	17,342	32,819	2,351	761	605	54	1,127	..	107	35	8	..	..	..	..	10	34
6. Ernad	45,483	30,546	7,188	909	1,373	..	1,650	..	90	105	75	..	..	..	1,773	..	1,600
7. Walluvanad ..	54,021	21,058	14,204	..	3,567	600	901	..	223	129	700	..	..	..	203	71	75
8. Palghat ..	83,938	13,595	5,102	..	3,152	996	4,239	445	2,123	576	138	26	43	185	..	..	57
9. Ponnani ..	71,978	45,487	2,295	..	875	1,000	2,300	..	3,700	1,800	..	..	..	..	..	10	2,700
10. Cochin ..	320	532	..	..	..	..	..	..	..	..	..	..	..	..	..	..	..
Total ..	395,602	266,526	34,838	24,300	10,307	4,481	12,457	457	6,747	2,873	985	26	43	188	37,358	7,095	4,488

No. 11.—*Statistics of cultivation, &c., for the past ten years in the district of Malabar.*

Fasli.	Cultivable area.	Area under cultivation.						Deduct remissions.	Balance.
		Punjah.		Nunjah.		Water-cess.	Total assessment.		
		Extent.	Assessment.	Extent.	Assessment.				
1	2	3	4	5	6	7	8	9	10
	ACRES.	ACRES.	RS.	ACRES.	RS.	AS.	RS.	RS.	RS.
1282 ..	3,799,891	397,267	6,17,672	387,426	11,65,750	..	17,83,422	5,137	17,78,285
1283 ..	3,799,891	394,388	6,22,029	388,171	11,66,998	..	17,89,027	12,023	17,77,004
1284 ..	3,799,891	398,346	6,24,419	388,566	11,67,045	..	17,91,464	6,630	17,84,834
1285 ..	3,799,891	400,273	6,28,476	388,285	11,66,746	..	17,95,222	4,728	17,90,494
1286 ..	3,686,047	407,644	6,38,033	389,303	11,68,468	..	18,06,501	35,579	17,70,922
1287 ..	3,686,047	414,372	6,38,088	386,497	11,65,747	..	18,03,835	9,982	17,93,853
1288 ..	3,686,047	403,875	6,34,351	388,035	11,66,777	..	18,01,128	12,619	17,88,509
1289 ..	3,686,047	383,317	6,18,518	388,599	11,67,775	..	17,86,293	6,479	17,79,814
1290 ..	3,686,047	390,322	6,28,774	395,537	11,69,165	..	17,97,939	7,883	17,90,056
1291 ..	3,686,047	389,455	6,28,669	395,602	11,69,338	..	17,98,007	12,205	17,85,802

Fasli.	Miscellaneous.	Total ryotwar demand.	Assessment on land permanently cultivated.	Jodi.	Total land revenue demand.	Balance of former years.	Total annual demand.	Total collection.	Balance at the close of the fasli.
	11	12	13	14	15	16	17	18	19
	RS.	RS.	RS.	RS.	RS.	RS.	RS.	RS.	RS.
1282 ..	46,031	18,24,316	15,000	2,552	18,41,868	74,851	19,16,719	18,25,176	91,543
1283 ..	51,510	18,28,514	15,000	2,552	18,46,066	91,543	19,37,609	18,17,852	1,19,757
1284 ..	37,381	18,22,215	15,000	2,552	18,39,767	1,19,757	19,59,524	18,35,791	1,23,733
1285 ..	35,121	18,25,615	15,000	2,552	18,43,167	1,23,733	19,66,900	18,35,515	1,31,385
1286 ..	36,258	18,07,180	15,000	2,552	18,24,732	1,31,385	19,56,117	18,33,221	1,22,896
1287 ..	40,064	18,33,917	15,000	2,552	18,51,469	1,22,896	19,74,365	19,24,781	49,584
1288 ..	40,821	18,29,330	15,000	2,552	18,46,882	49,584	18,96,466	18,48,172	48,294
1289 ..	42,430	18,22,244	15,000	2,552	18,39,796	48,294	18,88,090	18,45,371	42,719
1290 ..	36,334	18,26,390	15,000	2,552	18,43,942	42,719	18,86,661	18,29,036	57,625
1291 ..	37,139	18,22,941	15,000	2,552	18,40,493	57,625	18,98,118	18,27,102	71,016

No. 12 (a).—*Statement showing the number and value of suits, &c., disposed of in civil and revenue courts in North Malabar for a series of ten years.*

Years.	Number of suits, &c., disposed of in different courts.										
	Ordinary suits.								Appeals from decisions of		
	Village munsifs.	Revenue courts.	District munsifs' courts.	Subordinate judges.	Judges of small cause courts as subordinate judges.	Civil judges.	Total number of suits.	Total value in rupees.	Village munsifs.	Revenue courts.	District munsifs.
1	2	3	4	5	6	7	8	9	10	11	12
								RS. A. P.			
1873-74	2	..	2,011	91	..	9	2,113	5,41,345 7 9	..	1	273
1874-75	59	..	2,420	45	..	4	2,528	23,89,782 13 10	..	..	357
1875-76	319	..	2,975	30	..	5	3,329	19,64,264 6 5	..	..	462
1876-77	193	..	2,905	29	..	6	3,133	8,19,508 1 7	..	..	680
1877-78	163	..	2,802	48	..	..	3,013	7,43,959 3 0	..	..	813
1878-79	129	..	3,602	26	..	..	3,757	6,02,186 14 4	..	..	865
1879-80	263	..	3,756	46	..	4	4,069	7,56,363 11 9	..	..	720
1880-81	283	..	3,702	34	..	2	4,021	6,36,707 4 7	..	..	919
1881-82	329	..	3,465	36	..	4	3,834	6,24,484 6 8	..	..	954
1882-83	178	..	3,149	45	..	1	3,373	5,37,603 14 5	..	..	796
Total ..	1,918	..	30,787	430	..	35	33,170	96,16,206 4 4	..	1	6,839

No. 12 (a).—*Statement showing the number and value of suits, &c., disposed of in civil and revenue courts in North Malabar for a series of ten years*—(Continued).

Years.	Number of suits, &c., disposed of in different courts—(*Continued*).									
	Appeals from decisions of—(*Continued*).				Small causes.					
	Subordinate judges.	Judges of small cause courts as subordinate judges.	Civil judges.	Total number of suits.	District munsifs.	Subordinate judges.	Judges of small cause courts.	Civil judges.	Total number of small causes.	Total value in rupees.
	13	14	15	16	17	18	19	20	21	22
										RS. A. P.
1873-74	17	..	..	291	8,126	1,345	..	..	9,471	3,58,155 6 11
1874-75	11	..	..	368	7,857	1,245	..	..	9,102	3,68,508 3 8
1875-76	9	..	..	471	8,323	1,451	..	..	9,774	3,85,918 11 0
1876-77	3	..	..	683	10,435	1,784	..	..	12,219	4,57,992 5 9
1877-78	7	..	..	820	9,037	1,690	142	..	10,869	4,37,994 13 11
1878-79	7	..	..	872	9,808	1,728	171	..	11,707	4,58,127 8 2
1879-80	8	..	..	728	9,822	1,769	140	..	11,731	4,76,642 2 8
1880-81	10	..	..	929	9,467	1,722	103	..	11,292	4,16,855 10 5
1881-82	18	..	..	972	8,830	1,593	111	..	10,534	4,07,856 5 0
1882-83	11	..	..	807	8,550	1,575	122	..	10,247	3,99,543 13 8
Total ..	101	..	..	6,941	90,255	15,902	789	..	106,946	41,67,594 11 2

No. 12 (b).—*Statement showing the number and value of suits, &c., disposed of in civil and revenue courts in South Malabar for a series of ten years.*

Years.	Number of suits, &c., disposed of in different courts.										
	Original suits.								Appeals from decisions of		
	Village munsifs.	Revenue courts.	District munsifs.	Principal sadr amins.	Judges of small cause courts as principal sadr amins.	Civil judge.	Total number of suits.	Total value in rupees.	Village munsifs.	Revenue courts.	District munsifs.
1	2	3	4	5	6	7	8	9	10	11	12
								RS. A. P.			
1873-74	381	..	4,671	89	..	..	5,141	9,14,712 8 2	..	..	525
1874-75	422	..	5,058	128	..	3	5,611	12,58,261 3 6	..	..	493
1875-76	373	..	6,519	172	..	..	7,064	12,59,136 10 11	..	..	513
1876-77	617	..	7,006	142	..	2	7,767	12,74,352 1 7	..	..	655
1877-78	503	..	8,032	82	..	3	8,620	23,81,266 11 2	..	..	783
1878-79	1,070	..	7,441	127	..	2	8,640	18,04,166 14 3	..	..	757
1879-80	1,118	..	8,220	200	..	7	9,545	17,94,609 3 11	..	..	831
1880-81	1,357	..	8,401	216	..	1	9,975	17,15,926 15 4	..	..	907
1881-82	1,231	..	7,664	137	..	1	9,033	14,65,732 5 1	..	..	1,001
1882-83	1,219	..	7,922	118	..	4	9,263	14,37,372 7 3	..	..	1,075
Total ..	8,291	..	70,934	1,411	..	23	80,659	1,53,05,567 1 2	..	..	7,540

No. 12 (b).—*Statement showing the number and value of suits, &c., disposed of in civil and revenue courts in South Malabar for a series of ten years*—(Continued).

Years.	Number of suits, &c., disposed of in different courts—(*Continued*).											
	Appeals from decisions of—(*Continued*).				Small causes.							
	Principal sadr amins.	Judges of small cause courts as principal sadr amins.	Civil judge.	Total number of appeals.	District munsifs.	Principal sadr amins.	Judges of small cause courts.	Civil judge.	Total number of small causes.	Total value in rupees.		
	13	14	15	16	17	18	19	20	21	22		
										RS.	A.	P.
1873-74	25	..	..	550	8,280	1,313	..	..	9,593	3,70,351	2	2
1874-75	16	..	..	509	9,082	1,332	..	..	10,414	3,75,824	15	1
1875-76	7	..	..	520	8,579	540	..	..	9,119	3,36,045	10	11
1876-77	8	..	..	663	9,398	576	..	..	9,974	2,53,627	5	1
1877-78	18	..	..	801	8,995	435	..	..	9,430	2,54,675	8	7
1878-79	20	..	..	777	8,559	667	..	..	9,226	2,85,001	15	1
1879-80	25	..	..	856	9,059	812	..	..	9,871	3,13,558	2	1
1880-81	53	..	..	960	9,333	775	..	..	10,108	3,05,165	1	6
1881-82	31	..	..	1,032	8,038	792	..	..	8,830	2,86,015	9	5
1882-83	19	..	..	1,094	7,940	693	..	..	8,633	2,36,640	13	3
Total ..	222	..	..	7,762	87,263	7,935	..	..	95,198	30,16,906	3	2

No. 13.—*Statement of persons tried, convicted, and acquitted, and of property lost and recovered for a series of ten years, ending with the 31st December 1882, in the district of Malabar.*

Nature of offences.	1873.						1874.						1875.		
	Number of persons tried during the year.	Acquitted or discharged.	Convicted.	Remaining under trial.	Property Stolen.	Property Recovered.	Number of persons tried during the year.	Acquitted or discharged.	Convicted.	Remaining under trial.	Property Stolen.	Property Recovered.	Number of persons tried during the year.	Acquitted or discharged.	Convicted.
					RS.	RS.					RS.	RS.			
1. Murder	31	16	15	6	..	..	29	21	8	6	204	49	13	5	8
2. Culpable homicide	11	6	5	..	..	..	6	2	4	3	..	..	8	2	6
3. Rape	6	..	6	..	..	..	..	..	..	..	..	..	..	..	..
4. Hurts and assaults	3,947	2,314	1,631	..	..	..	2,970	1,677	1,293	..	..	..	3,307	1,805	1,502
5. Other offences against person.	192	106	86	6	..	..	111	53	58	2	..	..	113	77	36
6. Dacoity	24	14	10	11	2,161	59	38	16	22	5	3,236	162	90	30	60
7. Robbery	11	6	5	..	940	265	23	5	18	3	1,103	144	15	1	14
8. House-breaking	166	51	115	9	26,875	3,138	276	124	152	2	40,143	4,874	214	49	165
9. Theft	1,197	650	547	25	29,700	10,605	1,499	784	715	34	34,099	9,971	1,315	546	769
10. Other offences against property	2,212	1,632	580	11	4,757	1,006	1,947	1,361	586	6	6,490	1,109	2,327	1,583	744
11. Other offences against Penal Code	1,034	332	702	22	..	..	1,102	407	695	58	..	..	1,126	345	781
Total ..	8,831	5,129	3,702	90	64,433	15,073	8,001	4,450	3,551	119	85,275	16,309	8,528	4,443	4,085
12. Offences under special and local laws	4,276	579	3,697	5	78	53	3,992	427	3,565	7	84	64	3,808	487	3,321
Grand total ..	13,107	5,708	7,399	95	64,511	15,126	11,993	4,877	7,116	126	85,359	16,373	12,336	4,930	7,406

No. 13.—*Statement of persons tried, convicted, and acquitted, and of property lost and recovered for a series of ten years, ending with the 31st December* 1882, *in the district of Malabar*—(Continued).

Nature of offences.	1875—(*Continued*).			1876.							1877.						
	Remaining under trial.	Property		Number of persons tried during the year.	Acquitted or discharged.	Convicted.	Remaining under trial.	Property		Number of persons tried during the year.	Acquitted or discharged.	Convicted.	Remaining under trial.	Property	
		Stolen.	Recovered.					Stolen.	Recovered.					Stolen.	Recovered.
		RS.	RS.					RS.	RS.					RS.	RS.
1. Murder	15	396	46	24	4	20	5	1,500	26	40	3	24	13	..	..
2. Culpable homicide	6	..	..	4	..	4	2	..	..	21	6	15	..	..	..
3. Rape	..	..	..	2	..	2	..	..	..	..	..	..	..	..	..
4. Hurts and assaults	1	..	..	3,745	2,261	1,484	..	..	..	4,193	2,279	1,909	5	..	..
5. Other offences against person.	3	..	..	197	68	129	..	..	..	25	1	23	1	..	..
6. Dacoity	11	26,868	735	265	29	236	24	18,673	1,501	138	33	91	14	2,581	243
7. Robbery	2	569	3	20	6	14	..	792	139	18	6	11	1	967	94
8. House-breaking	21	43,527	4,583	245	46	199	23	1,64,532	31,470	545	54	455	36	73,382	6,807
9. Theft	22	24,332	8,166	1,251	371	880	25	26,163	9,250	1,723	298	1,357	68	41,085	11,298
10. Other offences against property	27	14,759	2,744	2,768	2,003	765	12	7,730	1,188	2,450	1,657	777	16	..	..
11. Other offences against Penal Code	48	..	..	1,113	271	842	46	..	..	908	261	617	30	..	..
Total ..	156	1,10,451	16,277	9,634	5,059	4,575	137	2,19,390	43,574	10,061	4,598	5,279	184	1,18,015	18,442
12. Offences under special and local laws	15	59	46	3,492	425	3,076	3	52	43	4,529	377	4,151	1	115	87
Grand total ..	171	1,10,510	16,323	13,126	5,484	7,642	140	2,19,442	43,617	14,590	4,975	9,430	185	1,18,130	18,529

No. 13.—*Statement of persons tried, convicted, and acquitted, and of property lost and recovered for a series of ten years, ending with the 31st December* 1882, *in the district of Malabar*—(Continued).

Nature of offences.	1878.						1879.						1880.		
	Number of persons tried during the year.	Acquitted or discharged.	Convicted.	Remaining under trial.	Property		Number of persons tried during the year.	Acquitted or discharged.	Convicted.	Remaining under trial.	Property		Number of persons tried during the year.	Acquitted or discharged.	Convicted.
					Stolen.	Recovered.					Stolen.	Recovered.			
					RS	RS.					RS.	RS.			
1. Murder	39	3	28	8	..	..	25	8	13	4	..	..	28	11	16
2. Culpable homicide	8	1	7	..	..	..	11	2	9	..	..	..	13	8	5
3. Rape	1	1	..	..	..	..	2	..	2	..	..	..	1	1	..
4. Hurts and assaults	3,884	1,994	1,887	..	..	..	3,679	1,902	1,757	20	..	..	3,870	2,173	1,691
5. Other offences against person.	13	1	12	..	..	..	27	1	23	3	..	..	158	75	81
6. Dacoity	32	6	26	..	330	16	10	4	6	..	105	19	26	11	15
7. Robbery	22	8	14	..	765	85	28	5	21	2	1,501	59	15	3	12
8. House-breaking	504	45	443	16	34,106	8,229	390	28	351	11	26,905	6,193	291	40	245
9. Theft	1,981	331	1,568	82	36,162	10,879	1,576	249	1,271	56	43,402	15,211	1,331	315	995
10. Other offences against property	2,586	1,569	1,001	16	..	..	781	318	459	4	..	..	558	236	314
11. Other offences against Penal Code	1,212	349	820	43	..	..	2,057	1,032	992	33	..	..	2,641	1,320	1,298
Total ..	10,282	4,308	5,806	168	71,363	19,209	8,586	3,549	4,904	133	71,913	21,482	8,932	4,193	4,671
12. Offences under special and local laws	4,287	513	3,773	1	132	97	5,473	442	5,024	7	121	79	7,074	574	6,500
Grand total ..	14,569	4,821	9,579	169	71,495	19,306	14,059	3,991	9,928	140	72,034	21,561	16,006	4,767	11,171

No. 13.—*Statement of persons tried, convicted, and acquitted, and of property lost and recovered for a series of ten years, ending with the 31st December* 1882, *in the district of Malabar*—(Continued).

Nature of offences.	1880—(*Continued*).			1881.						1882.					
	Remaining under trial.	Property		Number of persons tried during the year.	Acquitted or discharged.	Convicted.	Remaining under trial.	Property		Number of persons tried during the year.	Acquitted or discharged.	Convicted.	Remaining under trial.	Property	
		Stolen.	Recovered.					Stolen.	Recovered.					Stolen.	Recovered.
		RS.	RS.					RS.	RS.					RS.	RS.
1. Murder	2	..	..	* 25	6	16	2	..	..	22	9	11	2	..	..
2. Culpable homicide	..	..	..	17	10	6	1	..	..	13	3	9	1	..	..
3. Rape	..	..	..	1	..	1	..	..	..	..	..	..	..	..	..
4. Hurts and assaults	6	..	..	4,092	2,465	1,627	..	..	..	4,479	2,831	1,648	..	..	..
5. Other offences against person.	2	..	..	861	292	564	5	..	..	* 617	265	343	8	..	..
6. Dacoity	..	407	30	27	13	14	..	927	59	18	..	18	..	243	105
7. Robbery	..	3,476	1,551	27	7	17	3	640	68	22	9	12	1	356	173
8. House-breaking	6	18,922	4,424	396	129	259	8	29,399	2,190	401	73	317	11	25,280	7,661
9. Theft	21	27,492	7,208	1,559	654	891	14	36,618	7,050	* 1,395	415	948	30	32,816	16,204
10. Other offences against property	8	..	..	264	115	140	9	..	..	313	94	209	10	..	..
11. Other offences against Penal Code	23	..	..	2,640	1,631	994	15	..	..	2,920	1,859	1,033	28	..	..
Total ..	68	50,297	13,213	9,909	5,322	4,529	57	67,584	9,367	10,200	5,558	4,548	91	58,695	24,143
12. Offences under special and local laws	..	122	83	8,009	618	7,383	8	74	53	* 9,324	770	8,542	11	341	310
Grand total ..	68	50,419	13,296	17,918	5,940	11,912	65	67,658	9,420	19,524	6,328	13,090	102	59,036	24,453

* Four men died and one man was transferred to Coimbatore district.

No. 14.—*Statement showing the expenditure on public works from imperial and provincial funds for the last five years in the Malabar district.*

Years.	Imperial.				Provincial.			
	Military.	Civil buildings.	Irrigation.	Total.	Civil buildings.	Communications.	Miscellaneous public improvements.	Total.
	RS.	RS.	RS.	RS.	RS.	RS.	RS.	RS.
New works.								
1878-79 ..	8,100	..	..	8,100	6,895	..	2,057	8,952
1879-80 ..	2,984	806	..	3,790	15,067	7,109	..	22,176
1880-81 ..	6,732	2,663	..	9,395	16,382	..	..	16,382
1881-82 ..	1,365	..	..	1,365	17,204	..	..	17,204
1882-83 ..	12,981	..	..	12,981	35,398	..	4,612	40,010
Repairs.								
1878-79 .	17,295	471	2,038	19,804	4,535	..	..	4,535
1879-80 ..	13,066	193	2,253	15,512	5,867	..	..	5,867
1880-81 ..	20,887	174	..	21,061	710	..	..	710
1881-82 ..	23,963	467	1,564	25,994	1,680	..	781	2,461
1882-83 ..	25,610	839	1,748	28,197	2,792	..	1,777	4,569

No. 15.—*Statement showing receipts and expenditure of special funds for the last five years.*

—	1877-78.					1878-79.			1879-80.			1880-81.			1881-82.		
	Balance at the beginning of the year.	Receipts during the year.	Total.	Expenditure during the year.	Balance at the end of the year.	Receipts during the year including balance.	Expenditure during the year.	Balance at the end of the year.	Receipts during the year including balance.	Expenditure during the year.	Balance at the end of the year.	Receipts during the year including balance.	Expenditure during the year.	Balance at the end of the year.	Receipts during the year including balance.	Expenditure during the year.	Balance at the end of the year.
1	2	3	4	5	6	7	8	9	10	11	12	13	14	15	16	17	18
	Rs.	Rs.	Rs.	Rs.	Rs.	Rs.	Rs.	Rs.	Rs.	Rs.	Rs.	Rs.	Rs.	Rs.	Rs.	Rs.	Rs
1. Jungle conservancy fund ...	4	7	11	...	11	23	...	23	23	23	...	...	...	...	...	...	...
2. Nanal grass do. ...	...	...	...	...	...	...	...	...	...	...	...	...	...	...	...	...	...
3. Cattle pound do. ...	699	3,344	4,043	3,774	269	4,322	3,775	547	3,966	3,252	714	3,920	3,279	641	3,760	2,507	1,253
4. Public bungalow do. ...	...	...	...	...	...	...	...	...	...	...	...	...	...	...	...	...	...
5. Endowment do. ...	...	...	...	...	...	...	...	...	...	...	...	...	...	...	...	...	...
6. Village service do. ..	46,540	91,067	1,37,607	86,230	51,377	1,46,860	86,504	60,356	1,51,667	89,684	61,983	1,52,429	91,696	60,733	1,51,996	91,927	60,069
7. Canal and ferry do. ...	...	...	...	...	...	...	...	...	27,911	941	26,970	82,683	82,683	...	68,954	68,954	...
8. Irrigation cess do. ...	...	...	...	...	...	...	...	...	...	...	...	...	...	...	...	...	...
Total ...	47,243	94,418	1,41,661	90,004	51,657	1,51,205	90,279	60,926	1,83,567	93,900	89,667	2,39,032	1,77,658	61,374	2,24,710	1,63,388	61,322

No. 16.—*Statement showing the different sources of irrigation belonging to Government in Malabar.*

Taluks.	Tanks. No. of tanks.	Tanks. Average extent of cultivation within the last five years.	Tanks. Assessment including all charges for water, &c.	Channels. No. of channels.	Channels. Average extent of cultivation within the last five years.	Channels. Assessment including all charges for water, &c.	Anicuts. No. of anicuts.	Anicuts. Average extent of cultivation within the last five years.	Anicuts. Assessment including all charges for water, &c.	Wells. No. of wells.	Wells. Average extent of cultivation within the last five years.	Wells. Assessment including all charges for water, &c.
		ACRS. AS. AMS.	RS. A. P.		ACRS. AS. AMS.	RS. A. P.		ACRS. AS. AMS.	RS. A. P.		ACRS. AS. AMS.	RS. A. P.
Chirakkal	...	...	...	...	...	...	...	...	...	...	...	...
Kottayam	...	...	...	...	...	...	...	...	...	...	...	...
Kurumbranad ...	...	...	...	...	...	...	...	...	...	...	...	...
Wynad	...	...	...	...	...	...	...	...	...	...	...	...
Calicut	...	...	...	...	...	...	...	...	...	...	...	...
Ernad	8	82 0 0	228 0 0	97	3,073 0 0	9,250 0 0	4	95 0 0	265 0 0	252	318 0 0	640 0 0
Walluvanad ...	174	1,467 10 0¾	7,668 13 0	61	4,347 13 5¼	31,942 6 7	...	...	...	55	496 15 10¾	974 15 9
Palghat	1,354	5,001 3 10¾	48,310 13 2	82	2,213 11 6¼	6,034 9 5	24	1,690 15 9¾	6,655 6 6	...	...	...
Ponnani	158	485 0 0	3,494 0 0	12	575 0 0	2,689 0 0	5	3,639 0 0	5,486 0 0	...	...	...
Cochin	...	...	...	...	...	...	3	172 8 15¾	* 1,892 4 0	...	...	...

* This includes a sum of Rs. 315 which is collected from ryots whose fields are affected by the influx of salt water, and on whose account protective works (embankments) are constructed on contract.

No. 17.—*Education—General statistics, Malabar, from* 1873-74 *to* 1882-83.

Description of schools.	1873-74.			1874-75.			1875-76.			1876-77.		
	No. of schools.	No. of pupils.		No. of schools.	No. of pupils.		No. of schools.	No. of pupils.		No. of schools.	No. of pupils.	
		Boys.	Girls.		Boys.	Girls.		Boys.	Girls.		Boys.	Girls.
1. Maintained from imperial or provincial funds. — Colleges ..	..	..	..	..	..	..	..	..	..	..	..	..
High ..	..	..	..	..	..	..	..	..	..	..	..	..
Middle ..	..	..	..	..	..	..	..	..	..	..	..	..
Primary ..	..	..	..	..	..	..	..	..	..	..	..	..
Normal ..	..	..	..	..	..	..	..	..	..	..	..	..
2. Maintained from local or municipal funds. — High ..	..	..	..	..	..	..	..	..	..	..	..	..
Middle ..	..	..	..	..	..	..	..	..	..	..	..	..
Primary ..	..	..	..	..	..	..	..	..	..	..	..	..
Normal ..	..	..	..	..	..	..	..	..	..	..	..	..
Total ..	..	..	..	..	..	..	..	..	..	..	..	..
B. Schools aided—												
1. By salary grants .. — High ..	..	..	..	..	..	..	..	..	..	..	..	..
Middle ..	..	..	..	..	..	..	..	..	..	..	..	..
Primary ..	..	..	..	..	..	..	..	..	..	..	..	..
2. By result grants .. — High ..	..	..	..	..	..	..	..	..	..	..	..	..
Middle ..	..	..	..	..	..	..	..	..	..	..	..	..
Primary ..	..	..	..	..	..	..	..	..	..	..	..	..
3. Combined salaries and result grants. — High ..	..	..	..	..	..	..	..	..	..	..	..	..
Middle ..	..	..	..	..	..	..	..	..	..	..	..	..
Primary ..	..	..	..	..	..	..	..	..	..	..	..	..
Total ..	..	..	..	..	..	..	..	..	..	..	..	..
C. Schools under inspection for results grants, but not aided. — Colleges ..	..	..	..	..	..	..	..	..	..	..	..	..
High ..	..	..	..	..	..	..	..	..	..	..	..	..
Middle ..	..	..	..	..	..	..	..	..	..	..	..	..
Primary ..	..	..	..	..	..	..	..	..	..	..	..	..
Total ..	..	..	..	..	..	..	..	..	..	..	..	..
Number of successful candidates for the Uncovenanted Civil Service examinations educated in the district.	..	..	..	..	..	..	..	..	..	..	..	..
Number of successful candidates for special tests.	..	..	..	..	..	..	..	..	..	..	..	..
Number of successful candidates for Matriculation and F.A. — Matriculation.	..	..	..	..	..	..	..	..	..	..	..	..
F.A. ..	..	..	..	..	..	..	..	..	..	..	..	..
Grand total ..	398	19,524		475	21,358		631	22,265		700	30,730	

No. 17.—*Education—General statistics, Malabar, from* 1873-74 *to* 1882-83 —(Continued).

Description of schools.	1877-78.			1878-79.			1879-80.		
	No. of schools.	No. of pupils.		No. of schools.	No. of pupils.		No. of schools.	No. of pupils.	
		Boys.	Girls.		Boys.	Girls.		Boys.	Girls.
1. Maintained from imperial or provincial funds. — Colleges ..	..	..	..	1	28	..	1	40	..
High ..	..	..	..	4	213	..	4	224	..
Middle ..	..	..	..	8	421	..	7	423	..
Primary ..	..	..	..	8	544	..	8	409	..
Normal ..	..	..	..	3	80	..	3	84	..
2. Maintained from local or municipal funds. — High ..	..	..	..	..	..	..	..	..	..
Middle ..	..	..	..	16	259	..	17	300	..
Primary ..	..	..	..	22	1,043	34	25	1,300	20
Normal ..	..	..	..	..	..	..	1	24	..
Total ..	..	..	..	62	2,588	34	66	2,804	20
B. Schools aided—									
1. By salary grants. — High ..	..	..	..	..	..	..	1	48	..
Middle ..	..	..	..	2	103	..	3	126	7
Primary ..	..	..	..	4	320	41	5	439	50
2. By result grants. — High ..	..	..	..	..	..	..	..	..	..
Middle ..	..	..	..	..	..	..	..	..	..
Primary ..	..	..	..	201	8,088	400	176	6,909	376
3. Combined salaries and result grants. — High ..	..	..	..	..	..	..	..	..	..
Middle ..	..	..	..	..	..	..	..	..	..
Primary ..	..	..	..	272	8,586	..	391	10,754	..
Total ..	..	..	..	479	17,097	441	576	18,276	433
C. Schools under inspection for results grants, but not aided. — Colleges ..	..	..	..	..	..	..	1	50	..
High ..	..	..	..	..	..	..	1	100	..
Middle ..	..	..	..	1	20	..	1	117	..
Primary ..	..	..	..	137	4,232	23	149	4,670	314
Total ..	..	..	..	138	4,252	23	152	4,937	314
Number of successful candidates for the Uncovenanted Civil Service Examinations educated in the district.	..	..	..	..	..	..	..	..	..
Number of successful candidates for special tests.	..	..	..	..	..	..	..	..	..
Number of successful candidates for Matriculation and F.A. — Matriculation.	..	..	..	..	..	..	..	..	..
F.A. ..	..	..	..	..	..	..	..	..	..
Grand total ..	738	28,877		679	24,435		794	26,784	

No. 17.—*Education—General statistics, Malabar, from* 1873-74 *to* 1882-83 —(Continued).

Description of schools.		1880-81. No. of schools.	1880-81. Boys.	1880-81. Girls.	1881-82. No. of schools.	1881-82. Boys.	1881-82. Girls.	1882-83. No. of schools.	1882-83. Boys.	1882-83. Girls.
1. Maintained from imperial or provincial funds.	Colleges ..	1	43	..	1	53	..	1	93	..
	High ..	4	198	..	4	230	..	4	290	..
	Middle ..	7	442	..	7	480	..	6	404	..
	Primary ..	8	468	..	7	453	..	4	138	..
	Normal ..	3	78	..	2	70	..	2	74	..
2. Maintained from local or municipal funds.	High ..	..	..	..	..	..	..	..	..	..
	Middle ..	13	235	..	12	252	..	12	306	..
	Primary ..	16	817	15	13	763	..	18	848	88
	Normal ..	1	17	..	2	32	..	2	46	..
	Total ..	53	2,298	15	48	2,333	..	49	2,199	88
B. Schools aided—										
1. By salary grants.	High ..	1	50	..	1	37	..	1	52	..
	Middle ..	4	257	11	7	284	15	5	221	22
	Primary ..	6	549	137	4	56	146	4	72	222
2. By result grants.	High ..	..	..	..	..	..	..	1	32	..
	Middle ..	2	20	..	4	135	..	7	169	34
	Primary ..	208	9,099	540	307	14,849	646	334	11,812	2,106
3. Combined salaries and result grants.	High ..	..	..	..	..	..	..	..	..	..
	Middle ..	..	..	..	..	..	..	3	40	..
	Primary ..	370	13,623	..	331	11,592	..	319	12,576	1,791
	Total ..	591	23,598	688	654	26,953	807	674	24,974	4,175
C. Schools under inspection for results grants, but not aided.	Colleges ..	1	90	..	1	86	..	1	56	..
	High ..	1	120	..	2	156	..	1	57	..
	Middle ..	2	136	7	5	254	21	2	235	..
	Primary ..	139	4,898	44	167	6,136	166	213	6,507	1,036
	Total ..	143	5,244	51	175	6,546	187	217	6,855	1,036
Number of successful candidates for the Uncovenanted Civil Service Examinations educated in the district.		..	..	..	..	..	..	..	218	3
Number of successful candidates for special tests.		..	..	..	..	..	..	..	..	..
Number of successful candidates for Matriculation and F.A.	Matriculation.	..	..	..	..	..	..	..	99	..
	F.A.	..	..	..	..	..	..	..	19	..
	Grand total ..	787	31,894		877	36,826		940	39,327	

No. 18.—*Statement showing receipts and expenditure*

Municipal towns.	Years.	Receipts.									
		Rate on houses and lands.	Trade tax.	Tolls.	Tax on carriages and animals.	Registration of carts.	Licenses.	Fines.	State contribution.	Arrears including balance.	Miscellaneous.
		RS.	RS.	RS.	RS.	RS.	RS.	RS.	RS.	RS.	RS.
Cannanore.	1878-79 ..	9,510	3,578	600	1,851	502	372	678	..	2,655	1,425
	1879-80 ..	8,191	3,541	700	1,581	502	136	..	..	1,466	2,192
	1880-81 ..	6,552	2,356	2,005	972	420	105	556	..	2,028	736
	1881-82 ..	11,579	2,609	2,500	988	442	181	831	74	570	565
	1882-83 ..	10,873	2,412	3,280	1,159	470	135	569	744	1,152	900
	Total ..	46,705	14,496	9,085	6,551	2,336	929	2,634	818	7,871	5,818
Tellicherry.	1878-79 ..	5,451	2,985	3,374	536	29	140	66	1,579	6,974	4,502
	1879-80 ..	7,970	2,889	2,990	366	23	60	181	1,508	5,109	4,674
	1880-81 ..	8,838	3,161	2,476	487	18	25	252	1,814	3,641	5,348
	1881-82 ..	10,173	3,777	2,390	959	98	211	498	1,838	4,897	4,709
	1882-83 ..	8,371	3,815	1,655	990	95	75	290	2,133	2,524	4,572
	Total ..	40,803	16,627	12,885	3,338	263	511	1,287	8,872	23,145	23,805
Calicut.	1878-79 ..	13,451	5,078	4,055	1,853	432	233	1,437	..	3,673	1,360
	1879-80 ..	18,801	4,710	3,424	1,739	328	107	637	..	2,063	2,282
	1880-81 ..	18,760	4,171	3,820	1,773	251	185	1,479	..	6,313	2,609
	1881-82 ..	19,632	3,714	3,950	2,067	441	739	2,176	..	13,239	3,219
	1882-83 ..	18,974	3,311	3,876	1,776	452	1,060	1,882	..	12,480	4,665
	Total ..	89,618	20,984	19,125	9,208	1,904	2,324	7,611	..	37,768	14,135
Palghat.	1878-79 ..	5,765	..	6,515	..	..	968	167	..	5,638	3,179
	1879-80 ..	6,798	..	5,990	..	..	732	140	..	7,187	3,671
	1880-81 ..	7,046	..	6,042	..	..	690	225	..	7,715	3,323
	1881-82 ..	7,045	..	5,720	..	..	847	402	..	4,243	2,794
	1882-83 ..	6,992	..	6,060	..	..	900	422	..	7,179	1,680
	Total ..	33,646	..	30,327	..	..	4,137	1,356	..	31,962	14,647
Cochin.	1878-79 ..	4,091	2,099	..	129	78	200	144	1,020	893	5,685
	1879-80 ..	5,423	2,208	..	146	76	150	196	1,020	1,050	4,840
	1880-81 ..	6,818	2,432	..	94	65	170	152	1,020	4,266	3,576
	1881-82 ..	7,145	2,540	..	56	70	160	148	520	3,991	3,645
	1882-83 ..	6,609	2,192	..	53	64	130	80	520	2,875	3,625
	Total ..	30,086	11,471	..	478	353	810	720	4,100	13,075	21,371

of the several Municipal commissions for a series of five years.

Other receipts and advances recovered.	Total.	Expenditure.							Balance.
		New works.	Repairs.	Conservancy.	Police.	Establishment.	Miscellaneous.	Total.	
RS.	RS.	RS.	RS.	RS.	RS.	RS.	RS.	RS.	RS.
455	21,626	..	1,995	5,228	..	1,308	11,630	20,161	1,465
2,406	20,715	..	829	2,499	..	3,379	13,625	20,332	383
627	16,357	..	892	2,160	..	3,168	9,567	15,787	570
1,690	22,029	..	826	4,194	..	2,745	13,112	20,877	1,152
885	22,579	..	1,267	6,563	..	2,407	9,989	20,226	2,353
6,063	1,03,306	..	5,809	20,644	..	13,007	57,923	97,383	5,923
133	25,769	..	6,133	4,423	..	1,973	9,412	21,941	3,828
416	26,186	2,553	4,546	4,136	1,121	1,983	10,745	25,084	1,102
183	26,243	2,765	5,455	4,484	476	2,368	92,001	24,749	1,494
225	29,775	898	4,154	4,190	3,826	2,833	11,787	27,688	2,087
281	24,801	177	3,520	5,725	157	2,267	12,246	24,092	709
1,238	1,32,774	6,393	23,808	22,958	5,580	11,424	53,391	1,23,554	9,220
8,622	40,194	1,525	9,461	6,809	..	6,738	14,564	39,097	1,097
9,795	43,885	3,685	6,228	5,143	2,832	6,122	16,141	40,151	3,734
10,184	49,545	1,509	7,762	3,744	4,370	6,202	15,354	38,941	10,604
9,531	58,708	2,995	10,480	4,558	4,190	7,951	18,369	48,543	10,165
10,710	59,186	1,811	12,378	5,994	1,078	9,512	20,797	51,568	7,618
48,842	2,51,518	11,525	46,309	26,248	12,470	36,525	85,225	2,18,300	33,218
4,417	26,649	508	5,621	2,391	..	2,292	9,817	20,629	6,020
5,297	29,815	1,583	5,030	2,684	1,233	2,081	9,870	22,481	7,334
4,586	29,627	4,508	4,652	2,368	1,844	2,111	9,909	25,392	4,235
7,356	28,407	1,425	3,161	3,148	1,697	2,187	10,347	21,965	6,442
8,974	32,207	3,057	4,051	3,711	..	2,130	13,735	26,684	5,523
30,630	1,46,705	11,081	22,515	14,302	4,774	10,801	53,678	1,17,151	29,554
..	14,339	16	704	713	..	7,680	4,783	13,896	443
..	15,109	173	1,698	602	2,038	6,963	3,286	14,760	349
82	18,675	428	2,386	295	3,093	6,155	4,126	16,483	2,192
452	18,727	2,173	2,336	529	2,733	5,958	3,330	17,059	1,668
4	16,152	538	1,756	904	..	7,520	4,272	14,990	1,162
538	83,002	3,328	8,880	3,043	7,864	34,276	19,797	77,188	5,814

No. 19.—*Statement showing the receipts and expenditure of local funds*

Receipts.	1878-79.	1879-80.	1880-81.	1881-82.	1882-83.
	RS.	RS.	RS.	RS.	RS.
1. Balance ...	— 64,908	6,967	68,301	93,604	1,06,364
2. Allotments from general reserve—					
(a.) Provincial funds. For schools ...	6,060	1,890	1,418	2,510	1,456
For roads ...	...	1,650	...	5,500	...
For general purposes ...	11,200	...	...	...	...
(b.) Special funds. Surplus pound fund ...	611	273	214	488	225
Ferry rents ...	57,123	60,973	52,499	53,344	80,491
Avenues ...	8,413	4,685	3,428	5,125	3,900
Miscellaneous ...	2,610	1,643	1,990	1,469	1,341
(c.) Savings and refunds ...	...	...	38	15	8
3. Rates and taxes—					
(a.) Cess on land ...	2,05,682	2,26,365	2,18,664	2,23,272	2,23,324
(b.) Tolls ...	71,291	77,664	75,992	55,209	62,216
(c.) House-tax ...	...	...	...	...	...
4. Moyan endowment ...	...	...	...	...	1,663
5. Fees in schools ...	2,807	3,482	3,747	3,721	4,835
6. Contributions from other circles and municipalities.	7,890	6,496	6,396	6,220	9,066
(a) For inspection ...	...	...	132	60	460
7. Receipts from endowments, contributions, &c.—					
(a.) Educational ...	12	38	251	13,687	...
(b.) Hospitals ...	253	242	322	337	237
(c.) Choultries ...	353	320	540	465	777
(d.) Miscellaneous ...	741	...	79	58	1
8. Miscellaneous—					
(a.) Sale of materials, tools, and plant ...	27	...	...	...	544
(b.) Sale of other property ...	...	...	...	30	26
(c.) Bungalow subscriptions and fees ...	990	1,094	1,012	941	755
(d.) Public work receipts and refunds ...	5,180	13,870	9,074	14,388	8,454
(e.) Loan under Act XIV of 1871 ...	23,098	...	...	...	...
(f.) Miscellaneous (bandy-pettah receipts)	49	781	424	258	275
(g.) Nuisance fines ...	505	11	32	27	42
(h.) Sale-proceeds of books, by book hawker	2,132	3,321	3,811	3,980	2,723
(i.) Advances recoverable ...	...	...	36	135	92
(k.) Cash recoveries ...	616	...	...	...	...
(l.) Permanent advance ...	...	...	15	25	35
(m.) Sale of medicines ...	...	...	...	90	...
(n.) Cheques payable ...	...	...	2,51,185	...	...
Grand total ...	3,42,735	4,11,767	6,99,600	4,84,978	5,08,330

under Act IV of 1871 *for the last five years in the district of Malabar.*

Expenditure.	1878-79.	1879-80.	1880-81.	1881-82.	1882-83.
GRANT I.	RS.	RS.	RS.	RS.	RS.
New works.					
1. Communications	14,934	14,209	22,886	23,610	5,063
Civil buildings	367	3,932	500	3,000	58
Miscellaneous public improvements ...	...	...	20	58	...
Repairs.					
2. Communications	1,66,494	1,62,611	1,72,123	1,80,636	1,17,868
Civil buildings	2,766	3,342	4,194	5,884	4,404
3. Establishments—					
(a.) Cost of local fund engineering establishment.	43,831	41,515	34,459	40,050	41,085
(b.) Contingencies	...	30	...	...	...
(c.) Tolls and ferries	364	1,313	1,682	683	809
(d.) Other charges	...	...	11	— 175	...
(e.) Tools and plant	348	4,264	4,813	4,600	2,007
(f.) Refund of receipts (cesses on revenue)	...	303	...	45	8
(g.) Tolls and ferry establishment ...	...	...	571	...	...
(h.) Compensation to land and toll contractors.	...	...	767	2,687	...
(i.) Refunds	...	...	11,245	13,581	5,317
(j.) Contributions	16,915	2,120	6,334	7,289	6,659
(l.) Interest on loan and payments ...	2,027	8,973	10,040	11,202	12,468
(m.) For adjustment of expenditure ...	...	10,448	...	...	...
(n.) Stock purchase	...	...	...	...	3,600
Total Grant I ...	2,48,046	2,53,060	2,69,645	2,93,150	1,99,356
GRANT II.—EDUCATION.					
1. Payment for inspection	6,448	5,917	6,174	6,505	6,033
2. Training schools	5,466	...	...	2,457	3,359
3. Local fund schools	9,516	12,402	13,561	11,089	10,743
4. Stipends to Hindu and Mappila schools ...	9,234	10,974	12,135	13,005	12,781
5. Result grants	11,243	14,681	13,118	22,359	20,108
6. Pay of book hawkers and purchase of books.	2,618	3,819	4,638	4,805	3,591
Total Grant II ...	44,525	47,793	49,626	60,220	56,615
GRANT III.—SANITATION, MEDICAL, &c.					
1. Hospitals and dispensaries	17,678	11,367	12,830	13,730	11,382
2. Vaccine establishment	2,828	3,228	4,747	5,559	6,134
3. Sanitary do.	2,054	1,797	2,103	2,115	1,855
4. Choultries and musaferkannas	1,223	1,206	2,349	1,268	1,340
5. Bungalows	1,702	1,664	1,078	1,767	1,700
6. Contribution	10,173	8,873	8,453	6,172	12,676
7. Miscellaneous	5	...	79	108	689
8. Moyan endowed establishment	...	...	...	...	587
Total Grant III ...	35,663	28,135	31,639	30,719	36,363
GRANT IV.—MISCELLANEOUS.					
Contribution to controlling establishment ...	...	233	1,743	2,402	2,645
Do. Collector's office	960	960	960	960	888
Do. Local Fund Board office ...	1,006	1,024	} 1,864	{ 796	570
Do. Audit office	...	...		1,419	1,009
Contingencies including travelling allowances of Local Fund Members and Clerks, &c.	1,146	1,413	1,206	2,318	6,672
Total Grant IV ...	3,114	3,630	5,773	7,896	11,784
Advances recoverable	...	...	...	135	92
Miscellaneous debt account	...	9	...	...	...
Permanent advance	...	10	33	...	35
Refund of cess	...	2	...	...	...
Cheques payable	...	...	2,49,280	...	...
Grand total expenditure ...	3,31,348	3,32,639	6,05,996	3,92,119	3,04,245
Balances ...	11,387	79,128	93,604	92,859	2,04,085
Total ...	3,42,735	4,11,767	6,99,600	4 84,978	5,08,330

No. 20.—*Statement showing the number and tonnage of vessels which arrived at, and departed from, the district of Malabar for a series of ten years.*

Official years.	Square rigged.				Native crafts.		Total.	
	Steamers.		Ships.					
	Number.	Tonnage	Number.	Tonnage	Number.	Tonnage	Number.	Tonnage
			Arrivals.					
1867-68 ..	219	105,138	242	63,978	8,977	240,801	9,438	409,917
1868-69 ..	224	120,631	299	91,266	9,540	296,251	10,063	508,148
1869-70 ..	563	242,912	324	106,844	8,384	291,777	9,271	641,533
1870-71 ..	551	253,343	278	97,671	8,069	266,056	8,898	617,070
1871-72 ..	522	278,536	271	92,455	8,895	287,297	9,688	658,288
1872-73 ..	413	265,806	263	88,391	8,398	295,777	9,074	649,974
1873-74 ..	269	242,422	194	55,140	9,368	296,757	9,831	594,319
1874-75 ..	357	405,516	177	56,452	9,600	323,743	10,134	785,711
1875-76 ..	469	579,892	218	52,700	8,771	288,568	9,458	921,160
1876-77 ..	480	536,054	333	101,402	13,365	766,870	14,178	1,404,326
			Departures.					
1867-68 ..	216	103,002	215	63,302	8,661	227,367	9,092	393,671
1868-69 ..	220	117,302	314	90,630	9,272	287,364	9,806	495,296
1869-70 ..	565	243,773	304	95,040	8,266	292,004	9,135	630,817
1870-71 ..	551	263,343	261	92,675	7,909	267,048	8,721	623,066
1871-72 ..	528	280,746	296	89,398	8,738	288,922	9,562	659,066
1872-73 ..	407	261,061	245	80,988	8,294	293,858	8,946	635,907
1873-74 ..	270	243,047	191	51,946	9,268	294,821	9,729	589,814
1874-75 ..	355	403,012	173	55,101	9,578	321,054	10,106	779,167
1875-76 ..	470	580,667	221	51,850	8,727	288,353	9,418	920,870
1876-77 ..	478	541,286	289	80,977	13,309	767,320	14,076	1,389,583

No. 21.—*Statement showing the value of import trade, with particulars of articles, in the district of Malabar for a series of ten years.*

Articles.	Official years.									
	1867-68.	1868-69.	1869-70.	1870-71.	1871-72.	1872-73.	1873-74.	1874-75.	1875-76.	1876-77.
	RS.	RS.	RS.	RS.	RS.	RS.	RS.	RS.	RS.	RS.
Millinery and wearing apparel ..	82,202	1,00,226	1,62,889	1,18,296	65,418	1,85,658	1,69,390	1,50,031	1,38,683	1,52,066
Gold and silver, lace and thread ..	657	2,419	187	43,057	..	..	..	..	..	5,439
Books and stationery	33,097	39,224	40,522	50,680	36,392	41,014	58,856	60,345	46,181	41,831
Twist and yarn	8,70,199	9,13,844	9,04,865	7,90,352	8,48,326	9,07,402	8,96,091	8,75,500	9,69,301	12,27,613
Piece goods, dyed and printed ..	2,94,285	3,91,150	2,61,804	1,04,742	3,02,036	3,41,745	5,85,078	3,02,491	3,22,055	4,00,367
Do. plain	16,42,844	16,42,489	13,52,146	15,59,528	17,48,245	18,88,155	17,05,115	14,97,538	16,56,389	18,64,379
Drugs	82,574	1,23,129	1,26,064	1,10,000	1,29,216	1,25,382	1,09,571	1,02,100	97,319	1,25,870
Dyes	45,000	30,380	31,859	19,726	21,227	24,497	23,959	20,939	16,721	31,741
Betelnut, boiled and raw	69,233	58,944	59,442	39,266	26,043	61,150	22,439	44,363	36,681	29,181
Glassware	25,603	56,943	26,674	28,559	27,166	29,133	26,347	42,361	42,934	45,763
Paddy	7,95,832	11,32,761	6,52,936	6,93,179	6,24,090	7,94,259	13,25,215	22,45,357	18,99,875	25,76,665
Rice	24,07,609	29,85,483	34,64,752	31,37,901	29,83,836	34,80,858	32,96,348	25,88,049	27,86,834	90,53,305
Grain of sorts	4,15,178	4,88,847	2,54,276	2,69,248	2,66,541	2,51,852	6,25,368	6,38,019	5,67,027	42,20,602
Gunnies and gunny bags	71,575	1,38,123	94,299	35,787	1,80,844	1,47,401	1,43,848	1,05,027	1,28,629	1,01,838
Jewellery	33,286	8,423	7,058	5,066	29,224	12,653	8,845	10,936	2,186	1,963
Machinery	4,16,327	21,540	52,551	5,69,783	87,752	49,721	1,02,436	79,871	43,768	43,845
Malt liquors	2,51,457	1,44,018	1,70,587	2,96,745	1,71,459	3,07,200	2,30,554	1,81,090	78.778	1,32,957
Metals	7,19,814	8,35,550	8,09,902	7,07,339	8,42,802	8,03,978	4,98,786	6,84,365	8,26,322	8,06,401
Naval stores	1,240	2,377	4,470	2,75,767	29,312	29,024	74,838	52,846	..	..
Oilman's stores	26,655	26,574	23,195	26,000	31,163	18,108	40,507	71,232	..	..
Porcelain and earthenware	31,428	25,134	32,057	48,302	65,455	60,178	10,648	47,722	53,241	57,300
Pipe staves and casks	1,01,870	1,29,307	2,03,778	1,42,946	2,29,178	2,69,522	1,49,762	1,33,418	..	..
Provisions	1,26,586	1,63,279	1,34,610	1,20,747	1,19,248	1,48,186	1,41,732	1,77,525	3,72,876	2,70,688
Railway stores	59,014	..	..	..	53,018	8,321	1,872	..	..	..
Seeds	1,63,604	1,97,105	1,65,838	1,92,311	2,16,867	1,75,262	2,37,418	2,44,610	1,87,091	3,58,278
Silk, raw	..	..	..	..	..	..	..	..	..	255
Do. piece goods	56,221	55,880	47,770	53,392	36,365	70,602	36,002	27,693	20,191	48,045
Spices	2,67,446	2,86,220	2,93,343	5,11,573	2,11,798	2,07,880	4,22,391	5,64,784	6,18,046	3,32,224
Spirits	60,964	61,044	67,107	89,773	1,18,605	91,322	1,01,041	70,789	1,03,892	89,205
Tea	11,480	15,344	12,334	8,439	12,222	11,171	13,416	9,323	188	8,712
Timber and planks	67,307	39,225	48,989	48,569	50,722	59,494	28,612	57,912	1,96,126	2,14,356
Wines	46,583	63,402	63,792	79,266	63,501	1,02,070	66.707	70,463	81,250	52,912
Woollen	92,209	1,07,399	94,220	79,528	1,23,429	96,374	1,02,680	1,11,725	66,870	1,23,818
Wool	..	..	135	458	653	430	342	97	120	596
Sundries	35,93,490	39,01,812	31,40,791	48,86,483	56,83,915	42,54,547	50,57,889	32,40,262	34,39,220	32,45,231
Total ..	129,62,869	141,87,595	128,05,242	151,42,808	155,36,068	150,54,549	163,14,103	145,08,784	147,98,794	256,63,446

No. 22.—*Statement showing the value of export trade, with particulars of articles, in the district of Malabar for a series of ten years.*

Articles.	Official years.									
	1867-68.	1868-69.	1869-70.	1870-71.	1871-72.	1872-73.	1873-74.	1874-75.	1875-76.	1876-77.
	RS.	RS.	RS.	RS.	RS.	RS.	RS.	RS.	RS.	RS.
Bones ...	...	...	...	...	5,295	...	656	263	7,726	29,224
Coffee ...	54,93,189	76,87,061	61,79,455	75,26,634	96,05,938	98,88,578	126,54,513	109,75,433	110,86,736	95,70,306
Cotton, wool ...	1,78,301	6,14,802	4,27,113	1,96,938	2,30,448	3,12,497	68,340	41,333	99,128	6,550
Do. goods ...	4,78,003	6,81,996	4,72,133	7,13,053	5,62,053	6,12,494	6,69,770	6,89,050	8,45,963	10,43,565
Dregs of gingelly ...	...	...	...	...	...	...	...	...	...	4
Drugs ...	40,578	57,233	88,499	84,181	52,072	71,623	76,591	63,419	71,596	57,335
Indigo ...	14,967	187	20,897	650	...	...	128	51	...	53
Dyes of sorts ...	1,83,645	1,83,573	97,607	93,505	1,25,191	89,912	69,755	56,224	87,896	1,91,576
Emigrants' stores ...	...	...	...	...	...	...	...	...	...	...
Feathers ...	64	...	...	...	...	...	...	...	...	...
Fishmaws ...	13,983	16,776	37,789	26,109	37,232	63,443	32,851	28,641	63,895	49,613
Fruits and nuts ...	34,25,256	36,21,973	34,22,688	25,60,088	39,28,002	32,20,460	28,91,331	31,47,773	13,58,074	32,91,763
Paddy ...	38,547	36,374	19,947	84,173	46,404	1,22,830	1,22,159	15,716	1,04,541	2,70,946
Rice ...	2,65,678	1,55,484	3,10,518	3,93,256	8,97,136	11,39,219	7,40,869	4,89,532	68,049	16,91,939
Wheat ...	76,946	81,177	53,423	19,629	21,798	38,613	59,158	30,060	29,694	68,877
Grain of sorts ...	1,07,122	1,00,814	2,48,371	1,36,083	1,79,673	1,02,965	65,280	59,798	69,619	8,28,617
Hides ...	15,141	16,784	27,020	52,200	65,283	69,225	1,16,647	2,44,552	1,89,217	87,276
Horns ...	12,039	12,661	14,236	8,264	7,137	11,541	13,487	11,141	6,614	7,766
Ivory and ivoryware ...	6,476	3,913	8,712	3,078	2,814	3,943	...	2,817	7,670	7,258
Jewellery ...	11,710	842	28,153	21,761	5,880	3,950	6,884	5,320	6,340	14,275
Mats ...	22,689	36,690	45,294	24,727	28,494	29,156	38,844	26,293	50,982	1,48,369
Molasses ...	5,72,736	2,77,476	1,68,235	5,74,468	6,74,843	96,119	3,84,864	4,82,335	3,53,517	1,46,084
Coir and coir rope ...	11,87,650	17,42,020	17,26,418	13,21,998	14,11,849	17,34,617	16,94,404	23,22,453	17,55,562	25,67,287
Hemp ...	14,587	19,886	13,295	13,935	6,014	16,061	12,055	25,379	28,018	28,333
Naval stores of sorts ...	9,961	12,596	8,863	7,996	8,530	6,322	6,172	5,570	...	...
Oil ...	23,76,577	37,20,968	35,88,418	29,60,288	53,45,673	51,35,590	28,24,778	27,54,844	26,99,598	33,20,296
Perfumery ...	1,694	101	499	691	167	998	1,169	2,315	3,622	6,505
Precious stones ...	15,000	...	...	...	...	...	...	...	...	...
Salt ...	943	885	1,461	1,837	2,534	3,135	1,025	3,353	20,339	5,618
Saltpetre ...	2,306	950	1,663	2,455	6,310	2,367	5,017	3,765	175	8,677
Seeds ...	60,870	93,234	90,145	67,517	1,03,024	1,06,474	75,933	47,746	60,371	1,02,183
Shawls, cashmere ...	...	...	...	...	...	575	...	200	...	...
Silk piece-goods ...	2,295	3,541	2,182	2,981	5,378	24,907	861	10,723	2,492	3,801
Spices ...	19,51,053	20,78,107	22,66,042	24,43,158	28,00,480	19,16,185	23,39,715	31,89,542	28,56,599	23,61,636
Spirits ...	4,488	1,730	3,513	9,189	999	12,638	8,522	6,808	7,64,818	17,215
Sugar ...	34,519	10,902	18,655	30,400	26,827	38,531	24,908	34,175	298	38,889
Timber and wood ...	9,99,780	11,72,474	11,13,350	9,10,624	8,44,518	9,34,004	9,07,369	8,60,211	8,91,160	10,28,101
Tobacco ...	1,55,890	1,09,406	1,68,966	1,69,717	1,43,544	2,38,010	2,04,750	2,39,289	1,69,038	1,86,737
Wax and wax candles ...	5,816	17,360	12,447	8,806	11,783	8,709	10,754	7,295	16,694	24,928
Sundries ...	9,50,634	20,21,059	15,66,134	7,40,216	32,33,313	10,31,885	11,19,861	6,28,558	27,62,339	13,90,256
Total ...	187,31,133	245,91,054	222,52,161	212,10,606	306,24,636	270,88,576	272,49,415	265,11,977	265,38,380	286,01,858

APPENDIX II.

List of the Animals of Malabar.

Scientific name.	Author's name.	Habitat.	Trivial name.
Order PRIMATES.			
Fam. SIMIADÆ.			
Gen. Presbytis—			
P. priamus	Elliot ..	Eastern Ghats.	The Madras langur.
P. Johnii	....	Malabar Coast.	The Malabar langur.
P. jubatus	....	....	The Nilgiri langur.
Gen. Inuus	Geoffroy.		
I. silenus	....	....	The lion monkey.
Gen. Macacus—			
M. radiatus	....	....	The Madras monkey.
Fam. LAMURIDÆ.			
Gen. Loris—			
L. gracilis	....	....	The slender lemur.
Sub-order *CHEIROPTERA*			
Fam. PTEROPODIDÆ.			
Gen. Pteropus—			
P. Edwardsi	....	....	The large fox bat.
P. Leschenaultii	....	....	The fulvous fox bat.
Gen. Cynopterus—			
C. marginatus	....	....	The small fox bat.
Fam. VAMPYRIDÆ.			
Sub-fam. *Megadermatinæ*.			
Gen. Megaderma—			
M. lyra	....	....	The large-eared vampire bat.
Sub-fam. *Rhinolophinæ*.			
Gen. Rhinolophus—			
R. perniger	....	....	The large leaf bat.
R. Pearsoni	....	....	Pearson's leaf bat.
R. affinis	....	....	The allied leaf bat.
R. Rouxi	....	....	The rufous leaf bat.
Gen. Hipposideros ..	Gray.		
H. speoris	....	....	The Indian horse-shoe bat.
H. murinus	....	....	The little horse-shoe bat.
Gen. Rhinopoma	Geoffroy.		
R. Hardwickii	....	....	The long-tailed leaf bat.
Fam. NOCTILIONIDÆ.			
Sub-fam. *Taphozoinæ*.			
Gen. Taphozous	Geoffroy.		
T. longimanus	....	....	The long-armed bat.
T. melanopogon	....	....	The black-bearded bat.
T. saccolaimus	....	....	The white-bellied bat.
Sub-fam. *Noctilioninæ*.			
Gen. Nyctinomus	Geoffroy.		
N. plicatus	....	....	The wrinkled-lipped bat.

List of the Animals of Malabar—(Continued).

Scientific name.	Author's name.	Habitat.	Trivial name.
Order PRIMATES—(*Cont.*)			
Sub-ord. *CHEIROPTERA.* —(Continued).			
Fam. VESPERTILIONIDÆ			
Sub-fam. *Scotophilinæ.*			
Gen. Scotophilus—			
S. Coromandelianus ..	....	....	The Coromandel bat.
Gen. Nycticejus	Horsfield.		
N. Heathii	....	....	The large yellow bat.
N. lutens	....	....	The Bengal yellow bat.
N. Temminckii	....	....	The common yellow bat.
N. canus	....	....	The hoary bat.
Gen. Murina	Gray.		
M. formosa	....	....	The beautiful bat.
Gen. Kerivoula	Gray.		
K. picta	....	....	The painted bat.
Gen. Vespertilio—			
V. adversus	....	....	The Malayan bat.
Order INSECTIVORA.			
Fam. SORECIDÆ.			
Gen. Sorex—			
S. cærulescens	....	....	The common musk shrew.
S. murinus	....	....	The mouse-colored shrew.
S. serpentarius	....	....	The rufescent shrew.
S. Tytleri	....	....	The Dehra shrew.
S. soccatus	....	....	The hairy-footed shrew.
S. melanodon	....	....	The black-toothed pigmy shrew.
Fam. ERINACEIDÆ.			
Gen. Erinaceus—			
E. micropus	....	....	The South-Indian hedgehog.
Order CARNIVORA.			
Fam. URSIDÆ.			
Gen. Ursus—			
U. labiatus	....	....	The Indian black bear.
Gen. Mellivora	Storr.		
M. Indica	....	....	The Indian badger.
Fam. MUSTELIDÆ.			
Gen. Martes—			
M. flavigula	....	....	The Indian marten.
Sub-fam. *Lutrinæ.*			
Gen. Lutra	Ray.		
L. Nair	....	....	The common Indian otter.
L. vulgaris*	....	....	The hill otter.
L. species?	....	....	Nilgiri otter.
Fam. FELIDÆ.			
Gen. Felis	Linn.		
F. tigris	....	....	The tiger.
F. pardus	....	....	The pard.
F. Bengalensis	....	....	The leopard cat.
F. Jerdoni	....	....	The lesser leopard cat.

* Undescribed.

List of the Animals of Malabar—(Continued).

Scientific name.	Author's name.	Habitat.	Trivial name.
Ord. CARNIVORA-(*Cont.*)			
Fam. FELIDÆ—(*Cont.*)			
Gen. Felis—(*Cont.*)			
F. chaus	....	....	The common jungle cat.
Fam. VIVERRIDÆ.			
Sub-fam. *Hyæninæ.*			
Gen. Hyæna—			
H. striata	....	....	The striped hyæna.
Sub-fam. *Viverrinæ.*			
Gen. Viverra	Linn.		
V. civettina	....	....	The Malabar civet cat.
V. Malaccensis	....	....	The lesser civet cat.
Gen. Paradoxurus ..	F. Cuvier.		
P. musanga	....	....	The common tree cat.
Gen. Herpestes	Illiger.		
H. griseus	....	....	The Madras mungoos.
H. Smithii	....	....	The ruddy mungoos.
H. fuscus	....	....	The Nilgiri brown mungoos.
H. vitticollis	....	....	The stripe-necked mungoos.
Fam. CANIDÆ.			
Gen. Canis—			
C. aureus	....	....	The jackal.
Gen. Cuon—			
C. rutilans	....	....	The wild dog.
Fam. DELPHINIDÆ.			
Gen Delphinus	Linn.		
D. plumbeus	....	....	The plumbeous dolphin.
Gen. Globicephalus—			
G. Indicus	....	....	The Indian caing whale.
Fam. BALÆNIDÆ.			
Gen. Balænoptera—			
B. Indica	....	....	The Indian fin-whale.
Order RODENTIA.			
Fam. SCIURIDÆ.			
Gen. Sciurus—			
S. Malabaricus	....	....	The Malabar squirrel.
S. Elphinstonei	....	....	The Bombay red squirrel.
S. palmarum	....	....	The common striped squirrel.
S. tristriatus	....	....	The jungle striped squirrel.
S. Layardi	....	....	The Travancore striped squirrel.
S. sublineatus	....	....	The Nilgiri striped squirrel.
Gen. Pteromys—			
P. petaurista	....	....	The brown flying squirrel.
Gen. Sciuropterus—			
S. fuscocapillus	....	....	The small Travancore flying squirrel.
Gen. Gerbillus—			
G. Indicus	....	....	The Indian jerboa rat.

List of the Animals of Malabar—(Continued).

Scientific name.	Author's name.	Habitat.	Trivial name.
Ord. RODENTIA—(*Cont.*)			
Fam. SCIURIDÆ—(*Cont.*)			
Gen. Nesokia—			
N. Indica	....	....	The Indian mole-rat.
Gen. Mus—			
M. bandicota	....	....	The bandicoot rat.
M. rattus	....	....	The black rat.
M. decumanus	....	....	The brown rat.
M. brunneus	....	....	The tree rat.
M. rufescens	....	....	The rufescent tree rat.
M. oleraceus	....	....	The long-tailed tree mouse.
M. Nilagiricus	....	....	The Nilgiri tree mouse.
M. urbanus	....	....	The common Indian mouse.
M. homourus	....	....	The hill mouse.
M. terricolor	....	....	The earthy field mouse.
Gen. Platacanthomys—			
P. lasiurus	....	....	The long-tailed spiny mouse.
Gen. Golunda—			
G. Elliotti	....	....	The bush rat.
G. meltada	....	....	The soft-furred field rat.
Fam. HYSTRICIDÆ.			
Sub-fam. *Hystricinæ*.			
Gen. Hystrix—			
H. leucura	....	....	The Indian porcupine.
Fam. LEPORIDÆ.			
Gen. Lepus—			
L. ruficaudatus	....	....	The common Indian hare.
L. nigricollis	....	....	The black-naped hare.
Order UNGULATA.			
Fam. ELEPHANTIDÆ.			
Gen. Elephas—			
E. Indicus	....	....	The Indian elephant.
Fam. SUIDÆ.			
Gen. Sus—			
S. Indicus	....	....	The Indian wild boar.
Fam. CERVIDÆ.			
Gen. Rusa—			
R. aristotelis	....	....	The sambur stag.
Gen. Axis—			
A. maculatus	....	....	The spotted deer.
Gen. Cervulus—			
C. aureus	....	....	The rib-faced or barking deer.
Fam. MOSCHIDÆ.			
Gen. Memimna	Gray.		
M. Indica	....	....	The mouse deer.
Order EDENTATA.			
Fam. MANIDIDÆ.			
Gen. Manis	Linnagus.		
M. pentadactyla ..	....	....	The Indian scaly ant-eater.

APPENDIX III.

List of the Fishes of the Malabar District (from Dr. Day's "Malabar Fishes").

Scientific name.	Habitat.	Trivial name.
Sub-class **TELEOSTEI.**		
Order **ACANTHOPTERYGII.**		
Fam. *BERYCIDÆ.*		
Genus Holocentrum (Artedi)—		
H. rubrum	Seas	....
Fam. *PERCIDÆ.*		
Genus Lates (Cuv. et Val.)—		
L. calcarifer	Seas and estuaries ..	Nair fish.
Genus Serranus (Cuv. et Val.)—		
S. sexfasciatus	Seas	....
S. flavo-cœruleus	....	....
S. bontoo	Seas	....
S. erythrurus	....	....
S. lanceolatus	Seas	Kurupu, Mal.
S. diacanthus	Seas	Killi-meen, Mal.
S. formosus	Seas	....
Genus Genyoroge (Cantor)—		
G. cœruleopunctata	Seas	....
G. notata	Seas	Vella-chembolay.
G. rivulata	Seas	....
G. alboguttata	Malabar sea	....
Genus Mesoprion (Cuv.)—		
M. rangus	Seas	....
M. rubellus	Seas	....
M. Johnii	Seas	Chembolay, Mal.
M. sillaoo	Seas	....
M. fulviflamma	Seas	....
M. aurolineatus	Malabar sea	....
M. Madras	Malabar sea	....
Genus Ambassis—		
A. Commersonii	Fresh & brackish water.	....
A. nalua	Rivers and estuaries ..	....
A. Dussumieri	Seas and estuaries ..	....
Genus Therapon—		
T. trivittatus	Seas and estuaries ..	Kutcha.
T. servus	Seas and estuaries ..	....
T. theraps	Seas and estuaries ..	....
Genus Pristipoma—		
P. hasta	Seas	....
P. maculatum	Seas	....
P. guoraka	Seas and estuaries ..	Erruthum-corah, Mal.
P. Dussumieri	Coast and estuaries ..	....
Genus Diagramma; Plectorhynchus (Lacép)—		
D. nigrum	....	"Black rock fish."
D. griseum	Malabar	....
Genus Lobotes—		
L. Surinamensis	Seas	Parrandee, Mal.

List of the Fishes of the Malabar District—(Continued).

Scientific name.	Habitat.	Trivial name.
Sub-class TELEOSTEI—(*Cont.*)		
Order **ACANTHOPTERYGII**—(*Continued*).		
Fam. *PERCIDÆ*—(Continued).		
Genus Scolopsis (Cuv.)—		
S. Japonicus	Seas	....
Genus Dentex (Cuv.)—		
D. hasta	Malabar	....
Genus Synagris—		
S. grammicus	Cochin	....
Genus Upeneoides (Bleeker)—		
U. vittatus	Seas	Cheerul, Mal.
Genus Upeneus (Bleeker)—		
U. Malabaricus	Seas	....
U. Indicus	Seas	....
Genus Chrysophrys—		
C. hasta	Seas and estuaries ..	....
C. calamara	Seas and estuaries ..	Arnee, Mal.
Genus Chætodon (Artedi)—		
C. prætextatus	Malabar sea	....
Genus Heniochus (Cuv. et Val.)—		
H. macrolepidotus	Seas	Purroamee, Mal.
Genus Scatophagus (Cuv.)—		
S. argus	Estuaries and seas ..	Nutchar-char, Mal.
Genus Ephippus (Cuv.)—		
E. orbis	Seas	....
Genus Drepane—		
D. punctata	Seas	Piindthee, Mal.
Genus Toxotes (Cuv.)—		
T. jaculator	Seas	....
Genus Pterois (Cuv.)—		
P. volitans	Seas	Purrooah, Mal.
P. miles	Seas	....
Genus Tetraroge—		
T. Belengerii	(Mahé) Seas	....
Genus Prosopodasys (Cant.)—		
P. dracæna	Seas and estuaries ..	....
Genus Minous (Cuv. et Val.)—		
M. monodactylus	Seas	....
Genus Platycephalus—		
P. insidiator	Seas	Crocodile fish.
P. Malabaricus	Seas	....
P. suppositus	Seas	....
Genus Anema (Gunth.)—		
A. inerme	Seas	....
Genus Sillago (Cuv.)—		
S. sihama	Sens	....
Genus Umbrina (Cuv.)—		
U. Dussumieri	Seas	....
Genus Sciæna—		
S. maculata	Seas	Cutlah, Mal.
S. Dussumieri	Malabar	....
S. sina	Seas	....
Genus Corvina—		
C. semiluctuosa	Seas	....
C. carutta	Seas and rivers ..	....
C axillaris	Malabar	....
C. lobata	Malabar	....
C. Neilli	Malabar	....
C. albida	Seas	....

List of the Fishes of the Malabar District—(Continued).

Scientific name.	Habitat.	Trivial name.
Sub-class TELEOSTEI—(*Cont.*)		
Order **ACANTHOPTERYGII**—(*Cont.*)		
Fam. *PERCIDÆ*—(Continued).		
Genus Corvina—(*Continued*).		
C. Belengerii	Seas	....
Genus Otolithus—		
O. ruber	Seas	....
O. argenteus	Seas	....
Fam. *POLYNEMIDÆ*.		
Genus Polynemus—		
P. heptadactylus	Seas	....
P. sextarius	....	....
P. Indicus	....	....
P. tetradactylus	....	....
Fam. *SPHYRÆNIDÆ*.		
Genus Sphyræna—		
S. jello	Seas	Chelahoo, Mal.
S. obtusata	....	....
Fam. *TRICHIURIDÆ*.		
Genus Trichiurus—		
T. Malabaricus	Seas	....
T. haumela	Seas	....
T. savala	Seas	....
Fam. *SCOMBRIDÆ*.		
Genus Scomber—		
S. kanagurta	Seas	Ila, Mal.
Genus Cybium—		
C. Commersonii	Seas	....
C. lineolatum	Seas	....
C. guttatum	Seas	Arrakeeah, Mal. Seir fish.
Genus Naucrates—		
N. ductor	Seas	....
Genus Elacate—		
E. nigra	Seas	....
Genus Echeneis—		
E. naucrates	Seas	Putthoo-muday, Mal.
Genus Stromateus—		
S. sinensis	Seas	White pomfret.
S. argenteus	Seas	Silver pomfret.
S. cinereus	Seas	Grey pomfret.
S. niger	Seas	Black pomfret.
Fam. *CARANGIDÆ*.		
Genus Caranx—		
C. Rottleri	Seas	....
C. kurra	Seas	....
C. mate	Seas	Batta-parra.
C. kalla	Seas	....
C. melanostethos	Seas	....
C. speciosus	Seas	....
C. para	Seas	....
C. ekala	Seas	....
C. hippos	Seas	....
C. atropus	Seas	....

List of the Fishes of the Malabar District—(Continued).

Scientific name.	Habitat.	Trivial name.
Sub-class TELEOSTEI—(*Cont.*)		
Order **ACANTHOPTERYGII**—(*Cont.*)		
Fam. *CARANGIDÆ*—(Continued).		
Genus Caranx—(*Continued*).		
C. armatus	Seas	....
C. ciliaris	Seas	....
C. gallus	Seas	....
Genus Chorinemus—		
C. lysan	Seas	....
C. tol	Seas	....
C. tala	Seas	....
C. Sancti Petri	Seas	Pallagay.
C. tooloo	Seas	....
Genus Trachynotus—		
T. ovatus	Seas	....
T. Bailloni	Seas	Vella-oodoo and Parru-vu.
Genus Psettus—		
P. argenteus	Seas	....
P. falciformis	Seas	Purrandee.
Genus Platax—		
P. teira	Seas	....
Genus Equula—		
E. insidiatrix	Seas; also (said to be) fresh-water.	Paarl-coorchee.
E. edentula	Seas	....
E. splendens	Seas	....
E. Blochii	Seas	....
E. daura	Seas	....
E. oblonga	Seas	....
E. fasciata	Seas	....
Genus Lactarius—		
L. delicatulus	Seas	Parruwah.
Genus Pempheris—		
P. Molucca	Seas	....
Fam. *GOBIIDÆ* (Owen).		
G. giurus	Fresh-waters	Wartee-poollah and Pooan.
G. viridi-punctatus	Seas	....
G. criniger	Seas	....
G. Malabaricus	Rivers of Malabar ..	....
G. neglectus	Rivers of Malabar ..	....
G. acutipinnis	Seas and estuaries ..	....
Genus Apocryptes—		
A. rictuosus	Seas and estuaries ..	....
Genus Eleotris—		
E. butis	....	Kullahray.
E. fusca	Fresh-water	Poolan.
Genus Amblyopus—		
A. Hermannianus	Estuaries	....
A. cæculus	....	....
Genus Trypauchen—		
T. vagina	Seas and estuaries ..	....
Fam. *BATRACHIDÆ.*		
Genus Batrachus—		
B. grunniens	Seas and estuaries ..	....
B. trispinosus	Seas and estuaries ..	....
B. Dussumieri	Malabar	....

List of the Fishes of the Malabar District—(Continued).

Scientific name.	Habitat.	Trivial name.
Sub-class **TELEOSTEI**—(*Cont.*)		
Order **ACANTHOPTERYGII**—(*Cont.*)		
Fam. *PEDICULATI.*		
Genus Antennarius—		
A. marmoratus	Seas	....
A. nummifer	Seas	....
Fam. *BLENNIIDÆ.*		
Genus Salarias—		
S. fasciatus	Seas	....
Fam. *TEUTHIDIDÆ.*		
Genus Teuthis—		
T. vermiculata	Seas	Kuterah.
T. Java	Seas	....
Fam. *ACRONURIDÆ.*		
Genus Acanthurus—		
A. matoides	....	....
Genus Acronurus—		
A. melanurus	....	....
Fam. *NANDIDÆ.*		
Genus Nandus—		
N. marmoratus	Fresh-water	Mootahree.
N. Malabaricus	Hill streams	....
Genus Pristolepis—		
P. marginatus	Hill streams	....
Fam. *LABYRINTHICI.*		
Genus Anabas—		
A. scandens	Fresh-water	Undee-collee.
Genus Polyacanthus—		
P. cupanus	Fresh-water	Caringanah and Wunnettee.
Fam. *ATHERINIDÆ.*		
Genus Atherina—		
A. Forskalii	Seas	....
Fam. *MUGILIDÆ.*		
Genus Mugil—		
M. cunnesius	Seas	Mahlah.
M. subviridis	Seas	....
M. Sundanensis	Seas	....
M. engeli	Seas	....
M. poicilus	Seas	....
M. cunnumboo	Seas	....
M. parsia	Seas	....
M. suppositus	Seas	....
M. Waigiensis	Estuaries	Fresh-water Mullet.
M. carinatus	Seas	....
Fam. *OPHIOCEPHALIDÆ.*		
Genus Ophiocephalus—		
O. marulius	Rivers	Choaree-verarl and Cooravoo.

List of the Fishes of the Malabar District—(Continued).

Scientific name.	Habitat.	Trivial name.
Sub-class TELEOSTEI—(*Cont.*)		
Order **ACANTHOPTERYGII**—(*Cont.*)		
Fam. *OPHIOCEPHALIDÆ*-(Cont.)		
Genus Ophiocephalus—(*Continued*).		
O. diplogramme	Malabar	....
O. striatus	Fresh-water	Verarl or Wrahl.
O. gachua	Fresh-water	Kuravu.
O. punctatus	Fresh-water	....
Fam. *FISTULARIDÆ*.		
Genus Fistularia—		
F. serrata	Seas	....
Fam. *MASTACEMBELIDÆ*.		
Genus Mastacembelus—		
M. armatus	Fresh-water	....
M. Guntheri	Fresh-water	....
Order **PHARYNGOGNATHI**.		
Sub-order **Pharyngognathi Acanthopterygii.**		
Fam. *POMACENTRIDÆ*.		
Genus Glyphidodon—		
G. Cochinensis	Seas	....
Fam. *LABRIDÆ*.		
Sub-fam. JULIDINA.		
Genus Platyglossus—		
P. nigrescens	Seas	Kullaray, Mal.
Fam. *GERRIDÆ*.		
Genus Gerres—		
G. filamentosus	Seas	....
G. punctatus	Seas	....
G. limbatus	....	....
Fam. *CHROMIDES*.		
Genus Etroplus—		
E. Suratensis	Fresh-water	....
E. maculatus	Fresh-water	Pultattay.
Sub-order **Malacopterygii Pharyngognathi.**		
Fam. *SCOMBERESOCIDÆ*.		
Genus Belone—		
B. caudimaculata	Seas and estuaries ..	....
B. annulata	....	....
B. cancila	Fresh-water	Coalan and Marraloo.
Genus Hemiramphus—		
H. Reynaldi	Rivers and tanks ..	....
H. limbatus	Seas	....
H. xanthopterus	Seas	....
H. Georgii	....	....

List of the Fishes of the Malabar District—(Continued).

Scientific name.	Habitat.	Trivial name.
Sub-class TELEOSTEI—(*Cont.*)		
Order **ANACANTHINI.**		
Fam. *GADIDÆ.*		
Genus Bregmaceros—		
B. McClellandi	**Estuaries**	....
Fam. *PLEURONECTIDÆ.*		
Genus Pseudorhombus—		
P. Russellii	....	....
Genus Synaptura—		
S. foliacea	**Estuaries**	**Sappatte.**
Genus Plagusia—		
P. bilineata	....	....
Genus Coilia—		
C. Reynaldi	**Seas and estuaries** ..	....
C. Dussumieri	**Seas and estuaries** ..	....
Genus Chatœssus—		
C. chacunda	**Seas and estuaries** ..	....
C. altus	**Seas**	**Noonah, Mal.**
Sub-order **Physostomi Apodes.**		
Fam. *MURÆNIDÆ.*		
Sub-fam. ANGUILLOIDEI.		
Genus Muræna—		
M. maculata	**Fresh-water and estuaries.**	....
Sub-fam. CONGROIDEI.		
Group CONGRIFORMES.		
Sub-group *Murænesoces.*		
Genus Murænesox—		
M. telabon	**Seas and estuaries** ..	....
Sub-fam. OPHISUROIDEI.		
Group OPHISURI.		
Genus Ophichthys—		
O. ornatissimus	**Malabar**	....
Genus Pisoodonophis—		
P. boro	**Seas and estuaries** ..	....
Sub-fam. GYMNOTHORACOIDEI.		
Group MURÆNOPHIDES.		
Genus Gymnothorax—		
G. tile	**River and fresh-water** ..	....
G. favaginea	**Seas and estuaries** ..	....
Fam. *SYNBRANCHIDÆ.*		
Sub-fam. SYNBRANCHOIDEI.		
Group SYNBRANCHINI.		
Genus Synbranchus—		
S. Bengaliensis	**Estuaries and fresh-water.**	....

List of the Fishes of the Malabar District—(Continued).

Scientific name.	Habitat.	Trivial name.
Sub-class TELEOSTEI—(*Cont.*)		
Order **ANACANTHINI**—(*Cont.*)		
Sub-ord. **Physostomi Apodes**-(*Cont.*)		
Fam. *LEPTOCEPHALIDÆ.*		
Genus Leptocephalus—		
L. Malabaricus	Malabar	....
L. acuticaudatus	Malabar	....
L. Dussumieri	....	....
Order **PLECTOGNATHI.**		
Sub-order **Ostracionidæ.**		
Fam. *OSTRACIONOIDEI.*		
Genus Ostracion—		
O. nasus	Seas	....
O. tetragonus	Seas	....
Sub-order **Gymnodontidæ.**		
Fam. *TETRAODONTOIDEI.*		
Sub-fam. TETRAODONTIFORMES.		
Group Tetraodontini.		
Genus Tetraodon—		
T. lunaris	Seas and estuaries ..	....
Genus Crayracion—	....	....
C. fluviatilis	Seas and estuaries and salt marshes.	....
C. testudineus	....	Paattha.
C. Cochinensis	Cochin	....
Genus Leiodon—		
L. viridipunctatus	Cochin	....
Fam. *BALISTISIDÆ.*		
Genus Alutarius—		
A. lævis	Seas	Mullah-poorah.
Order **PHYSOSTOMI.**		
Sub-order **Siluridæ.**		
Fam. *SILUROIDEI.*		
Sub-fam. BAGRIFORMES.		
Genus Netuma—		
N. Netuma	Seas and estuaries ..	....
Genus Arius—		
A. subrostratus	Malabar	....
A. rostratus	Aleppy	....
A. cœlatus	Seas	....
A. gagora	Seas and estuaries ..	....
Genus Osteogeniosus—		
O. militaris	Seas and estuaries ..	....
Genus Batrachocephalus—		
B. mino	Seas	....

List of the Fishes of the Malabar District—(Continued).

Scientific name.	Habitat.	Trivial name.
Sub-class TELEOSTEI—(*Cont.*)		
Order PHYSOSTOMI—(*Cont.*)		
Sub-order Siluridæ—(*Continued*).		
Fam. *SILUROIDEI*—(Continued).		
Sub-fam. BAGRIFORMES—(*Cont.*)		
Sub-group *Bagri*.		
Genus Hara—		
H. Malabarica	Mountain streams ..	....
Genus Pseudobagrus—		
P. chryseus	Fresh-water	....
Genus Hemibagrus—		
H. oculatus	Rivers and fresh-water.	....
Genus Hypselobagrus—		
H. armatus	Malabar	....
H. cavasius	Fresh-water	....
H. montanus	Manantoddy river ..	....
H. Malabaricus	Mountain streams ..	....
H. tengara	....	....
Group PANGASINI.		
Sub-group *Pangasii*.		
Genus Pseudeutropius—		
P. Sykesii	....	....
Sub-fam. SILURIFORMES.		
Group SILURINI.		
Genus Wallago—		
W. attu	Fresh-water	Wahlah.
W. Malabaricus	Rivers	....
Fam. *CHACOIDEI*.		
Sub-fam. PLOTOSIFORMES.		
Genus Plotosus—		
P. Arab	Seas and estuaries ..	....
P. limbatus	Seas	....
Fam. *HETEROBRANCHOIDEI*.		
Sub-fam. HETEROBRANCHIFORMES.		
Genus Clarias—		
C. magur	Fresh-water	....
C. Dussumieri	Fresh-water	....
Sub-fam. SACCOBRANCHIFORMES.		
Genus Saccobranchus—		
S. singio	Fresh-water	Kebree-moen.
Fam. *SCOPELIDÆ*.		
Sub-fam. SAURINA.		
Genus Saurus—		
S. tumbil	Red Sea, seas of India, Malaysia, Western Pacific.	....

List of the Fishes of the Malabar District—(Continued).

Scientific name.	Habitat.	Trivial name.
Sub-class TELEOSTEI—(*Cont.*)		
Order PHYSOSTOMI—(*Cont.*)		
Sub-order Siluridæ—(*Continued*).		
Fam. *SCOPELIDÆ*—(Continued).		
Sub-fam. SAURINA—(*Continued*).		
Genus Harpodon—		
H. nehereus	Seas and estuaries of India, Burmah, Malaysia, China.	....
Sub-order Cyprinidæ.		
Fam. *COBITIOIDES*.		
Genus Nemacheilus—	Travancore hills ..	
N. rubripinnis	Malabar	....
Genus Platacanthus—		
P. agrensis	....	....
Genus Rohita—		
R. Dussumieri	Rivers of Malabar ..	....
Sub-fam. BARBINI.		
Group SYSTOMI.		
Genus Puntius—		
P. chrysopoma	Bombay, fresh-water, Malabar.	Minduttee.
P. pinnauratus	Fresh-water, Malabar ..	....
P. melanampyx	Hill ranges, Travancore.	....
P. parrah	Fresh-water Malabar ..	Parrah-perlee.
P. perlee	Malabar	....
P. Denisonii	Hills, Travancore ..	....
P. Hamiltonii	Fresh-water and Coromandel Coast.	Oolee-perlee.
Group CATLÆ.		
Genus Amblypharyngodon—		
A. Jerdoni	Malabar	Uremboo, Mal.
Genus Barilius—		
B. Bakeri	Hill ranges, Malabar ..	....
Group DANIONES.		
Genus Paradanio—		
P. aurolineatus	Malabar	....
Genus Rasbora—		
R. Malabarica	Malabar	Koka-metche.
Fam. *CYPRINODONTOIDES*.		
Sub-fam. APLOCHEILIFORMES.		
Genus Panchax—		
P. lineatum	Rivers, tanks, &c. ..	....
Sub-order Physostomi Abdominales.		
Fam. *CLUPEOIDÆ*.		
Genus Chirocentrus—		
C. dorab	Seas	....
Genus Chanos—		
C. pala	Seas, tanks, estuaries ..	....
Genus Dussumieria—		
D. acuta	Seas	Koorie, Mal.

List of the Fishes of the Malabar District—(Continued).

Scientific name.	Habitat.	Trivial name.
Sub-class TELEOSTEI—(*Cont.*)		
Order **PHYSOSTOMI**—(*Cont.*)		
Sub-ord. **Physostomi Abdominales**—(*Continued*).		
Fam. *CLUPEOIDÆ*—(Continued).		
Genus Elops—		
E. machnata	....	....
E. apalike	Fresh-water & estuaries.	Cunnay, Mal.
Genus Sardinella—		
S. Neohowii	Seas	Charlay, Mal. Oil sardine.
Genus Pellona—		
P. Dussumieri	Malabar	....
Genus Pristigaster—		
P. tartoore	Seas	....
Genus Spratella—		
S. fimbriata	Malabar	Cuttay, Charlay, or "Sardine."
Genus Meletta—		
M. lile	Seas	Cooba.
Genus Alausa—		
A. palasah	Seas and rivers ..	Sable fish.
A. melanura	Seas	....
Genus Engraulis—		
E. taty	Seas	....
E. Brownii	Seas	....
E. auratus	Seas	....
E. Hamiltonii	Seas	....
E. Malabaricus	Seas	Monangoo.
Genus Triacanthus—		
T. biaculeatus	Seas	....
Order **LOPHOBRANCHII**.		
Fam. *SYNGNATHIDÆ*.		
Group HIPPOCAMPINÆ.		
Genus Hippocampus—		
H. comes	Seas	Horse-fish, Coordameen.
Sub-fam. SYNGNATHIDÆ.		
Group SYNGNATHINA.		
Genus Ichthyocampus—		
I. Ponticerianus	Seas and estuaries ..	....
Genus Syngnathus—		
S. argyrostictus	....	....
Group NEROPHINÆ.		
Genus Microphis—		
M. Bleekeri	Seas and estuaries ..	....
M. cunculus	....	....
Sub-class SELACHII.		
Order **PLAGIOSTOMI**.		
Sub-order **Squali**.		
Fam. *SCYLLIÆ*.		
Genus Chiloscyllium—		
C. plagiosum	Seas	....

APPENDIX III.

List of the Fishes of the Malabar District—(Continued).

Scientific name.	Habitat.	Trivial name.
Sub-class **SELACHII**—(*Cont.*)		
Order **PLAGIOSTOMI**.—(*Cont.*)		
Sub-order **Squali**—(*Cont.*)		
Fam. *CARCHARIÆ*.		
Genus Scoliodon—		
S. acutus	Seas	....
Genus Prionodon—		
P. melanopterus	Seas	....
P. lamia	....	....
Fam. *CESTRACIONTES*.		
Genus Cestracion—		
C. zygæna	Seas	....
C. Leeuwenii	....	....
Sub-order **Rajæ**.		
Fam. *SQUATINORAIJOIDÆ*.		
Group Pristisidæ.		
Genus Pristis—		
P. semisagittatus	Seas	....
Group Rhamphobatides.		
Genus Rhyncobatus—		
R. Djeddensis	Seas	....
Group Rhinobatides.		
Genus Rhinobatus—		
R. obtusus	....	....
R. granulatus	Seas	....
Fam. *RAIÆ*.		
Group Torpedines.		
Sub-group (*with two dorsal fins*).		
Genus Narcine—		
N. Indica	Seas	....
Sub-group (*with one dorsal fin*).		
Genus Astrape—		
A. dipterygia	Seas	....
Group Trygones.		
Genus Trygon—		
T. uarnak	Seas	....
Genus Pteroplatea—		
P. micrura	Seas	....
Genus Hypolophus—		
H. sephen	....	....
Group Myliobatides.		
Genus Ætobatis—		
A. narinari	Seas	Therrundee.

APPENDIX IV.

List of abbreviations of Authors' names.

Scopoli	Scop.	Tunstall	Tunst.
Latham	Lath.	Shaw, G.	Shaw.
Tunstall	Tunst.	Müller	Müll.
Sundevall, C. J.	Sund.	Vigors	Vig.
Gray, J. E.	J. E. Gr.	Malherbe, Alf.	Malh.
Gray, G. R.	G. R. Gr.	Burton, E.	Burt.
Horsfield	Horsf.	Drapiez	Drap.
Daudin, W. M.	Daud.	Gould	Gould.
Linnæus	Lin.	Vahl. Mart.	Vahl.
Temminck	Tem.	Illiger	Ill.
Reinwardt	Rein.	Gmelin	Gm.
Vieillot, L. P.	Vieill.	Reichenbach, H. G. L.	Reich.
Hodgson	Hodgs.	Valenciennes, A.	Val.
Jerdon	Jerd.	Forster, J. Reinhold	Forest.
Pennant, T.	Penn.	Hermann, J.	Herm.
Boddært, M.	Bodd.	Hay Lord A. *	Hay.
Sykes	Sykes.	Cuvier	Cuv.
Desfontaines, R. L.	Desf.	Swainson	Sws.
Tickell	Tick.	Bechstein, J. M.	Bechst.
Lesson Revé, P.	Less.	Duméril, A. M. C.	Dum.
Pallas, P. S.	Pall.	Strickland	Strickl.
Franklin	Frankl.	Hemprich and Ebrenberg	Hemp. and Ebr.
Blyth	Bly.	Brooks	Brooks.
Raffles	Raff.	Savi, P.	Savi.
Sparrmann, A.	Sparrm.	Wagler, Dr. Joannes	Wagl.
Hume, A. O.	Hume.	Bonnaterre L'Abbe	Bonn.
Layard	Lay.	Kubl Heinrich	Kubl.
Jardine and Selby	Jard. and Selb.	?	Frenzl.
Pearson, Dr. J. T.	Pears.	Leisler, J. P. A.	Leisl.
Viscount Walden	Wald.	Naumann, J. A.	Naum.
Leach, William Elford	Leach.	Swinhoe, Robt.	Swinh.
Paykull, Gust.	Payk.	Radde, Prof. Gustav	Radde.
Buchanan Hamilton Fr. Ham.	B. Ham.	Legge, Capt. W. V.	Legge.
Van Hasselt	Hass.	Ljung Iven, I.	Ljung.
Bosc, L. A. G.	Bosc.	Kelaart, Dr.	Kel.
Montagu, Geo.	Mont.	Lafresnaye, Baron Frederic de.	Lafr.
Lichtenstein, Henrich	Licht.		
Stephens, J. F.	Steph.		

* Afterwards Lord Walden, then Marquis of Tweedale.

List of the Birds of Malabar.

Jerdon's No.	Scientific name.	Trivial name.	Author's name.
2	Otogyps calvus	The black vulture	Scop.
4	Gyps indicus	Long-billed brown vulture	Scop.
5	Pseudogyps bengalensis	The white-backed vulture	Gm.
6	Neophron ginginianus	The Indian scavenger vulture	Lath.
8	Falco peregrinus	The peregrine	Gm.
9	Do. peregrinator	The shaheen	Sund.
11	Do. jugger	The lagger	J. E. Gr.
14	Do. severus	The Indian hobby	Horsf.
17	Cerchneis tinnunculus	The kestrel	Lin.
18 bis.	Do. pekinensis	The eastern lesser kestrel	Swinh.
19 bis.	Do. amurensis	Eastern red-legged hobby	Radde.
21	Astur palumbarius	The goshawk	Lin.

List of the Birds of Malabar—(Continued).

Jerdon's No.	Scientific name.	Trivial name.	Author's name.
22	Astur trivirgatus	The southern crested goshawk ..	Tem.
23	Do. badius	The shikra	Gm.
24	Accipiter nisus	The sparrow hawk	Lin.
25	Do. virgatus	The besra	Rein.
27	Aquila mogilnik	The imperial eagle	Gm.
28	Do. clanga	The spotted eagle	Pall.
30	Do. hastata	The long-legged eagle	Less.
31	Hieraëtus pennatus	The booted eagle	Gm.
32	Neopus malayensis	The black eagle	Rein.
33	Nisaëtus fasciatus	Bonelli's eagle	Vieill.
? 35 bis.	Limnaëtus ceylonensis	The Ceylon crested hawk eagle ..	Gm.
37	Lophotriorchis kieneri ? ..	The rufous-bellied hawk eagle ..	Gerv.
38	Circaëtus gallicus	The common serpent eagle ..	Gm.
39	Spilornis cheela	The Indian harrier eagle	Lath.
39 bis.	Do. melanotis	The Southern Indian harrier eagle.	Jerd.
40	Pandion haliaëtus	The osprey	Lin.
41	Polioaëtus ichthyaëtus	The white-tailed sea eagle	Horsf.
43	Haliaëtus leucogaster	The white-bellied sea eagle ..	Gm.
44 bis.	Buteo desertorum	The African buzzard	Daud.
48 bis.	Butastur indicus	The eastern buzzard	Gm.
51	Circus macrurus	The pale harrier	Gm.
53	Do. melanoleucus	The pied harrier	Forst.
54	Do. aruginosus	The marsh harrier	Lin.
55	Haliastur indus	The brahminy kite	Bodd.
56	Milvus govinda	The pariah kite	Sykes.
57	Pernis ptilorhynchus	The crested honey buzzard ..	Tem.
58	Baza lophotes	The crested black kite	Cuv.
58 ter.	Do. ceylonensis	The Ceylon baza	Legge.
59	Elanus cæruleus	The black-winged kite	Desf.
60	Strix javanica	The eastern screech owl	Gm.
61	Do. candida	The grass owl	Tick.
63	Syrnium indranee	The brown owl	Sykes.
65	Do. ocellatum	The mottled wood owl	Less.
68	Asio accipitrinus	The short-eared owl	Pall.
69	Bubo bengalensis	The rock-horned owl	Frankl.
70	Do. coromandus	The dusky horned owl	Lath.
71	Do. nipalensis	The forest eagle owl	Hodgs.
72	Ketupa ceylonensis	The brown fish owl	Gm.
74	Scops pennatus	The Indian scops owl	Hodgs.
75 quat.	Do. malabaricus	The Malabar scops owl	Jerd.
76	Carine brama	The spotted owlet	Tem.
77	Glaucidium radiatum	The jungle owlet	Tick.
78	Do. malabaricum ..	The Malabar owlet	Bly.
81 bis.	Ninox scutellata	The southern hawk owl	Raff.
82	Hirundo rustica	The swallow	Lin.
83	Do. javanica	The brown-bellied swallow ..	Sparrm.
85	Do. erythropygia	The mosque swallow	Sykes.
90	Ptyonoprogne concolor	The dusky martin	Sykes.
91	Do. rupestris	The mountain martin	Scop.
92	Chelidon urbica	The house martin	Lin.
95	Chatura sylvatica	The forest spine-tail	Tick.
96	Do. indica	The large spine-tail	Hume.
98	Cypselus melba	The Alpine swift	Lin.
100	Do. affinis	The eastern swift	J. E. Gr.
102	Do. batassiensis	The palm swift	J. E. Gr.
103	Collocalia unicolor	The Indian edible-nest swiftlet ..	Jerd.
104	Dendrochelidon coronata ..	The Indian crested swift ..	Tick.
105	Batrachostomus moniliger ..	The Singalese frog-mouth	Lay.
108	Caprimulgus kelaarti	The Nilgiri night-jar	Bly.
111	Do. atripennis	The ghat night-jar	Jerd.
112	Do. asiaticus	The common Indian night-jar ..	Lath.

List of the Birds of Malabar—(Continued).

Jerdon's No.	Scientific name.	Trivial name.	Author's name.
113	Caprimulgus mahrattensis ..	Sykes' night-jar	Sykes.
114	Do. monticolus	Franklin's night-jar	Frankl.
114 ter.	Lyncornis Bourdilloni	Bourdillon's eared night-jar ..	Hume.
115	Harpactes fasciatus	The Malabar trogon	Forst.
117	Merops viridis	The Indian bee-eater	Lin.
118	Do. Philippinus	The blue-tailed bee-eater	Lin.
119	Do. leschenaulti	The Indian chestnut-headed bee-eater.	Vieill.
122	Nyctiornis athertoni	The blue-bearded bee-eater ..	Jerd. and Selb.
123	Coracias indica	The Indian roller	Lin.
126	Eurystomus orientalis	The broad-billed roller	Lin.
127	Pelargopsis gurial	The Indian stork-billed king-fisher.	Pears.
129	Halcyon smyrnensis	The white-breasted king-fisher ..	Lin.
130	Do. pileata	The black-capped purple king-fisher.	Bodd.
132	Do. chloris	The white-collared king-fisher ..	Bodd.
133	Ceyx tridactylus	The three-toed purple king-fisher..	Pall.
134	Alcedo bengalensis	The Indian king-fisher	Gm.
135 ter.	Do. asiatica	The malayan king-fisher	Sws.
136	Ceryle rudis	The pied king-fisher	Lin.
140	Dichoceros cavatus	The great pied-horn-bill	Shaw.
141	Hydrocissa coronata	The Malabar pied-horn-bill ..	Bodd.
144	Ocyceros birostris	The common grey horn-bill ..	Scop.
145	Tockus griseus	The jungle grey horn-bill ..	Lath.
147	Palæornis eupatria	The southern Alexandrine parroquet	Lin.
148	Do. torquatus	The rose-ringed parroquet ..	Bodd.
149	Do. purpureus	The western rose-headed parroquet.	Müll.
151	Do. columboides	The blue-winged parroquet ..	Vig.
153	Loriculus vernalis	The Indian lorikeet	Sparrm.
160	Picus mahrattensis	The yellow-fronted woodpecker ..	Lath.
164 bis.	Yungipicus gymnopthalmus ..	The southern pigmy woodpecker ..	Bly.
165	Hemicircus cordatus	The heart-spotted woodpecker ..	Jerd.
166 bis.	Chrysocolaptes strictus	The southern large gold-backed woodpecker.	Malh.
169	Thriponax hodgsoni	The Indian black woodpecker ..	Jerd.
171	Gecinus striolatus	The small green woodpecker ..	Bly.
175	Chrysophlegma chlorigaster ..	The southern yellow-naped woodpecker.	Jerd.
179	Micropternus gularis	The Madras rufous woodpecker ..	Jerd.
180	Brachypternus aurantius ..	The golden-backed woodpecker ..	Lin.
181	Do. puncticollis ..	The southern golden-backed woodpecker.	Malh.
183	Tiga shorei	The large three-toed woodpecker ..	Jerd.
184	Do. javanensis	The common three-toed woodpecker.	Ljung.
186	Viva innominata	The speckled piculet	Burt.
194	Megalaima viridis	The small green barbet	Bodd.
197	Xantholæma hæmacephala ..	The crimson-breasted barbet ..	Müll.
198	Do. malabarica	The crimson-throated barbet ..	Bly.
199	Cuculus canorus	The European cuckoo	Lin.
200	Do. striatus	The eastern cuckoo	Drap.
202	Do. sonneratti	The banded bay cuckoo	Lath.
203	Do. micropterus	The large-billed cuckoo	Gould.
205	Hierococcyx varius	The hawk cuckoo	Vahl.
207	Do. sparverioides ..	The great hawk cuckoo	Vig.
208	Cacomantis passerinus	The Indian plaintive cuckoo ..	Vahl.
210	Surniculus lugubris	The drongo cuckoo	Horsf.
212	Coccystes jacobinus	The pied crested cuckoo	Bodd.
213	Do. coromandus	The red-winged crested cuckoo ..	Lin.
214	Eudynamus honorata	The koel	Lin.
216	Rhopodytes viridirostris	The small green-billed malkoha ..	Jerd.

List of the Birds of Malabar—(Continued).

Jerdon's No.	Scientific name.	Trivial name.	Author's name.
217	Centrococcyx rufipennis	The coucal or crow-pheasant ..	Ill.
218	Do. bengalensis ..	The lesser coucal	Gm.
219	Taccocua leschenaultii	The southern sirkeer	Less.
224	Arachnothera longirostra ..	The little spider-hunter	Lath.
232	Cinnyris zeylonica	The amethyst-rumped honey-sucker.	Lin.
233	Do. minima	The tiny honey-sucker	Sykes.
234	Do. asiatica	The purple honey-sucker ..	Lath.
236	Do. lotenia	The large purple honey-sucker ..	Lin.
238	Dicæum erythrorhynchus ..	Tickell's flower-pecker	Lath.
239	Do. concolor	The Nilgiri flower-pecker ..	Jerd.
250	Sitta castaneoventris	The chestnut-bellied nuthatch ..	Frankl.
253	Dendrophila frontalis	The velvet-fronted nuthatch ..	Horsf.
254	Upupa epops	The hoopoe	Lin.
255	Do. ceylonensis	The Indian hoopoe	Reich.
257 bis.	Lanius caniceps	The southern rufous-backed shrike.	Bly.
260	Do. vittatus	The bay-backed shrike	Val.
261	Do. cristatus	The brown shrike	Lin.
264	Tephrodornis sylvicola	The Malabar wood-shrike	Jerd.
265	Do. pondicerianus ..	The common wood-shrike	Gm.
267	Hemipus picatus	The pied fly shrike	Sykes.
268	Volvocivora sykesi	The black-headed cuckoo-shrike ..	Strickl.
270 bis.	Grancalvus layardi	The southern cuckoo-shrike ..	Bly.
272	Pericrocotus flammeus	The orange minivet	Forst.
276	Do. peregrinus	The small minivet	Lin.
277	Do. erythropygius ..	The white-bellied minivet ..	Jerd.
278	Buchanga atra	The kingcrow	Herm.
280	Do. longicaudata	The long-tailed kingcrow ..	Hay.
281	Do. cærulescens	The white-bellied kingcrow ..	Lin.
282	Chaptia ænea	The bronzed drongo	Vieill.
285	Dissemurus paradiseus	The lesser racket-tailed drongo ..	Lin.
286	Chibia hottentotta	The hair-crested drongo	Lin.
287	Artamus fuscus	The ashy swallow-shrike	Vieill.
288	Muscipeta paradisi	The paradise fly-catcher	Lin.
290	Hypothymus azurea	The black-naped blue fly-catcher ..	Bodd.
292	Leucocerca aureola	The white-browed fantail ..	Vieill.
293	Do. leucogaster	The white-spotted fantail	Cuv.
295	Culicicapa ceylonensis	The grey-headed fly-catcher ..	Sws.
297	Alseonax latirostris	The southern brown fly-catcher ..	Raff.
300	Ochromela nigrorufa	The black and orange fly-catcher..	Jerd.
301	Stoporala melanops	The verditer fly-catcher	Vig.
302	Do. albicaudata	The Nilgiri verditer fly-catcher ..	Jerd.
304	Cyornis rubiculoides	The blue-throated red-breast ..	Vig.
306	Do. tickelli	Tickell's blue red-breast	Bly.
307	Do. ruficaudus	The rufous-tailed fly-catcher ..	Sws.
309	Do. pallipes	The white-bellied blue fly-catcher.	Swinh.
323	Erythrosterna albicilla	The white-tailed robin fly-catcher.	Pall.
339	Callene rufiventris	The rufous-bellied shortwing ..	Bly.
342	Myiophonus horsfieldii	The Malabar whistling thrush ..	Vig.
345	Pitta brachyura	The Indian ground thrush ..	Lin.
351	Cyanocinclus cyaneus	The blue rock thrush	Lin.
353	Petrophila cinclorhyncha ..	The blue-headed chat thrush ..	Vig.
354	Geocichla cyanotis	The white-throated ground thrush.	Jerd. and Selb.
357	Turdulus wardii	Ward's pied blackbird	Jerd.
359	Merula nigropilea	The black-capped blackbird ..	Lafr.
360	Do. simillima	The Nilgiri blackbird	Jerd.
360 bis.	Do. kinnisi	The Ceylon blackbird	Kel.
372	Oreocincla nilgirensis	The Nilgiri thrush	Bly.
385	Pyctorhis sinensis	The yellow-eyed babbler	Gm.
389	Alcippe poiocephala	The Nilgiri quaker thrush ..	Jerd.
390	Do. atriceps	The black-headed wren warbler ..	Jerd.
398	Dumetia albogularis	The white-throated wren babbler ..	Bly.

List of the Birds of Malabar—(Continued).

Jerdon's No.	Scientific name.	Trivial name.	Author's name.
399	Pellorneum ruficeps	Swainson's wren warbler ..	Sws.
404	Pomatorhinus horsfieldi	The southern scimitar babbler ..	Sykes.
409	Garrulax delesserti	Delessert's babbler	Jerd.
423	Trochalopteron cachinnans ..	The Nilgiri laughing thrush ..	Jerd.
424	Do. jerdoni	The Banasora laughing thrush ..	Bly.
433	Malacocircus griseus	The white-headed babbler ..	Lath.
434	Do. malabaricus ..	The jungle babbler	Jerd.
435	Do. somervillii ..	The rufous-tailed babbler	Sykes.
436	Argya malcolmi	The large grey-fronted babbler ..	Sykes.
437	Layardia subrufa	The rufous babbler	Jerd.
438	Chatarrhœa caudata	The striated bush babbler	Dum.
442	Schænicola platyurus ..	The broad-tailed reed bird ..	Jerd.
445	Hypsipetes nilgiriensis ..	The southern black bulbul ..	Jerd.
446	Do. ganeesa	The southern black bulbul ..	Sykes.
450	Criniger ictericus	The yellow-browed bulbul	Strickl.
455	Rubigula gularis	The ruby-throated bulbul	Gould.
456	Do. flaviventris	....	Tick.
457	Brachypodius poiocephalus ..	The grey-headed bulbul	Jerd.
460 bis.	Otocompsa fuscicaudata	The southern red-whiskered bulbul.	Gould.
462	Molpastes hæmorrhous	The Madras bulbul	Bly.
463	Phyllornis jerdoni	The green bulbul	Gm.
464	Do. malabaricus	The Malabar green bulbul ..	Gm.
467	Ægithina tiphia	The common dwarf bulbul ..	Lin.
469	Irena puella	The fairy bluebird	Sykes.
470	Oriolus kundoo	The Indian oriole	Jerd.
471	Do. indicus	The black-naped Indian oriole ..	Jerd.
472	Do. melanocephalus	The black-headed oriole	Lin.
475	Copsychus saularis	The magpie robin	Lin.
479	Thamnobia fulicata	The southern black robin	Lin.
481	Pratincola caprata	The pied-chat	Lin.
482	Do. bicolor	The hill pied-chat	Sykes.
497	Ruticilla rufiventris	The Indian red start	Vieill.
507	Larvivora superciliaris	The blue wood-chat	Jerd.
514	Erithacus cæruleculus	The artic blue-throated robin ..	Pall.
515 bis.	Acrocephalus orientalis	The eastern large reed-warbler ..	Tem. and Schl.
516	Do. dumetorum ..	The lesser reed-warbler	Bly.
517	Do. agricolus	The paddy-field warbler	Jerd.
530	Orthotomus sutorius	The Indian tailor-bird	Forst.
534	Prinia socialis	The ashy wren-warbler	Sykes.
536	Do. gracilis	Franklin's wren-warbler	Frankl.
539	Cisticola cisticola	The fantail-warbler	Temm.
540	Do. exilis	The red-headed fantail-warbler ..	Vig. and Horsf.
543	Prinia inornata	The earth-brown warbler	Sykes.
553	Hypolais rama	Sykes' warbler	Sykes.
556	Phylloscopus magnirostris ..	The large-billed tree-warbler ..	Bly.
559	Do. nitidus	The bright green tree-warbler ..	Bly.
560	Do. viridanus	The greenish tree-warbler	Bly.
560 bis.	Do. tytleri	Brook's tree-warbler	Brooks.
561	Do. affinis	Tickell's tree-warbler	Tick.
565	Reguloides superciliosus	The crowned tree-warbler	Gm.
589	Motacilla maderaspatensis ..	The river or large pied wagtail ..	Gm.
591 bis.	Do. alba	The grey-backed wagtail	Lin.
592	Calobates melanope	The grey and yellow wagtail ..	Pall.
593 ter.	Budytes flavus	The blue-headed wagtail	Lin.
594 bis.	Do. citreolus	The grey-backed yellow wagtail ..	Pall.
595	Limonidromus indicus	The forest wagtail	Gm.
596	Anthus maculatus	The Indian tree pipit	Hodgs.
598	Anthus montanus	The Nilgiri tree pipit	Jerd.
600	Corydalla rufula	The Indian tit-lark	Vieill.
603	Agrodroma similis	The rufous rock pipit	Jerd.
631	Zosterops palpebrosa	The white-eyed tit	Tem.

List of the Birds of Malabar—(Continued).

Jerdon's No.	Scientific name.	Trivial name.	Author's nam
645	Parus atriceps	The Indian grey tit	Horsf.
648	Machlolophus aplonotus	The southern yellow tit	Bly.
660	Corvus macrorhynchus ..	The Indian corby	Wagl.
663	Do. splendens	The Indian grey-necked crow	Vieill.
674	Dendrocitta rufa	The Indian magpie ..	Scop.
678	Do. leucogastra	The long-tailed magpie	Gould.
684	Acridotheres tristis	The myna	Lin.
686	Do. fuscus	The jungle myna	Wagl.
687	Sturnia pagodarum	The black-headed myna ..	Gm.
688	Do. malabarica	The grey-headed myna ..	Gm.
689	Do. blythi	The white-breasted tree myna	Jerd.
690	Pastor roseus	The rosy pastor	Lin.
692	Eulabes religiosa	The southern hill myna ..	Lin.
694	Ploceus philippinus	The Indian weaver bird ..	Lin.
697	Amadina malacca	The black-headed munia ..	Lin.
698	Do. rubronigra	The chestnut-bellied munia ..	Hodgs.
699	Do. punctulata	The spotted munia	Lin.
700	Do. pectoralis	The rufous bellied munia	Jerd.
701	Do. striata	The white-backed munia	Lin.
703	Do. malabarica	The plain brown munia	Lin.
704	Estrelda amandava	The red waxbill	Lin.
706	Passer domesticus	The sparrow	Lin.
711	Gymnoris flavicollis	The yellow-necked sparrow ..	Frankl.
716	Emberiza buchanani	The grey-necked bunting	Bly.
722	Euspiza luteola	The red-headed corn bunting ..	Sparrm.
738	Carpodacus erythrinus	The common rose-finch	Pall.
755	Mirafra affinis	The Madras bush-lark	Jerd.
760	Pyrrhulanda grisea	The black-bellied finch lark ..	Scop.
761	Calandrella brachydactyla ..	The short-toed or social lark ..	Leisl.
765	Spizalanda deva	The small crown-crest	Sykes.
765 bis.	Do. malabarica	The large crown-crest	Scop.
767	Alauda gulgula	The Indian sky-lark	Frankl.
773	Crocopus chlorigaster	The southern green pigeon ..	Bly.
774	Osmotreron bicincta	The orange-breasted green pigeon.	Jerd.
775	Do. malabarica	The grey-fronted green pigeon ..	Jerd.
780	Carpophaga ænea	The imperial green pigeon ..	Lin.
781 bis.	Do. cuprea	The southern bronzed imperial pigeon.	Jerd.
786	Palumbus elphinstonei	The Nilgiri wood pigeon	Sykes.
788	Columba intermedia	The Indian blue rock pigeon ..	Strickl.
792	Turtur pulchratus	The Indian turtle-dove	Hodgs.
793	Do. meena	The rufous turtle-dove	Sykes.
794	Do. senegalensis	The little brown dove	Lin.
795	Do. suratensis	The spotted dove	Gm.
796	Do. risorius	The eastern ring-dove	Lin.
797	Do. tranquebaricus	The ruddy ring-dove	Herm.
798	Chalcophaps indica	The emerald ground-dove ..	Lin.
803	Pavo cristatus	The pea-fowl	Lin.
813	Gallus sonneratii	The grey jungle-fowl	Tem.
814	Galloperdix spadiceus	The red spur-fowl	Gm.
815	Do. lunulatus	The painted spur-fowl	Val.
822	Ortygornis pondicerianus	The grey partridge	Gm.
826	Perdicula asiatica	The jungle bush-quail	Lath.
828	Microperdix erythrorhynchus ..	The painted bush quail	Sykes.
829	Coturnix communis	The quail	Bonn.
830	Do. coromandelica	The rain-quail	Gm.
831	Excalfactoria chinensis	The blue-breasted quail	Lin.
832	Turnix taigoor	The black-breasted bustard quail ..	Sykes.
834	Do. joudera	The larger button quail	Hodgs.
835	Do. dussumieri	The pigmy button quail	Tem.
839	Sypheotides aurita	The lesser florican	Lath.

List of the Birds of Malabar—(Continued).

Jerdon's No.	Scientific name.	Trivial name.	Author's name.
842	Glareola orientalis	The large eastern swallow-plover or the eastern pratincole.	Leach.
843	Do. lactea	The smaller swallow-plover	Tem.
844	Squatarola helvetica	The grey plover	Lin.
845	Charadrius fulvus	The eastern golden plover ..	Gm.
846	Ægialitis geoffroyi	The large sand-plover	Wagl.
847	Do. mongola	The lesser sand-plover	Pall.
848	Do. cætiana	The Kentish ring-plover ..	Lath.
849	Do. dubia	The common ring-plover ..	Scop.
855	Lobivanellus indicus ..	The red-wattled lapwing ..	Bodd.
856	Lobipluvia malabarica	The yellow-wattled lapwing	Bodd.
859	Œdicnemus scolopax ..	The stone-curlew	Gm.
860	Strepsilas interpres ..	The turnstove	Lin.
861	Dromas ardeola	The crab-plover	Payk.
862	Hæmatopus ostralegus ..	The fyster-catcher	Lin.
865	Grus communis	The common crane ..	Bechst.
866	Anthropoides virgo	The Numidian or Demoiselle crane.	Lin.
867	Scolopax rusticola	The wood cock	Lin.
868	Gallinago nemoricola	The wood snipe	Hodgs.
870	Do. sthenura	The pin-tail snipe	Kubl.
871	Do. cœlistis	The fan-tail or common snipe	Gm.
872	Do. gallinula	The jack snipe	Lin.
873	Rhynchæa bengalensis	The painted snipe	Lin.
874	Pseudoscolopax semipalmatus ..	The snipe-billed godwit ..	Jerd.
875	Limosa ægocephala	The small godwit	Lin.
876	Terekia cinerea	The avoset sand-piper ..	Gould.
877	Numenius lineatus	The eastern curlew	Cuv.
878	Do. phæopus	The whimbrel	Lin.
880	Machetes pugnax	The ruff	Lin.
882	Tringa subarquata	The curlew stint	Gould.
884	Do minuta	The little stint	Leisl.
885	Do. temmincki	The white-tailed stint ..	Leisl.
886	Limicola platyrhyncha	The broad-billed stint ..	Tem.
891	Rhyacophila glareola	The spotted sand-piper ..	Lin.
892	Totanus ochropus	The green sand-piper ..	Lin.
893	Tringoides hypoleucus	The common sand-piper ..	Lin.
894	Totanus glottis	The green shanks	Lin.
895	Do. stagnatilis	The lesser green shanks ..	Bechst.
896	Do. fuscus	The spotted red shanks ..	Lin.
897	Do. calidris	The red shanks	Lin.
898	Himantopus candidus	The stilt	Boun.
899	Recurvirostra avocetta	The avocet	Lin.
900	Parra indica	The bronze-winged jacana ..	Lath.
901	Hydrophasianus chirurgus ..	The pheasant-tailed jacana ..	Scop.
902	Porphyrio poliocephalus ..	The purple coot	Lath.
903	Fulica atra	The common or bald coot ..	Lin.
905	Gallinula chloropus	The water-hen	Lin.
907	Erythra phœnicura	The white-breasted water-hen ..	Penn.
909	Porzana maruetta	The spotted crake	Leach.
910	Do. bailloni	Baillon's crake	Vieill.
911	Do fusca	The ruddy crake	Lin.
912	Rallina euryzonoides	The banded rail	Lafr.
913	Hypotœnidia striata	The blue-breasted banded rail ..	Lin.
914	Rallus indicus	The Indian water rail	Bln.
915	Leptoptilus argalus	The adjutant	Lath.
916	Do. javanicus	The black adjutant or hair-crested stork.	Horsf.
917	Xenorhynchus asiaticus ..	The black-necked stork	Lath.
918	Ciconia nigra	The black stork	Lin.
920	Dissura episcopa	The white-necked stork ..	Bodd.
923	Ardea cinerea	The heron	Lin.
924	Do. purpurea	The purple heron	Lin.

List of the Birds of Malabar—(Continued).

Jerdon's No.	Scientific name.	Trivial name.	Author's name.
925	Herodias torra	The large white egret	B. Ham.
926	Do. intermedia	The lesser white egret	Hass.
927	Do. garzetta	The little egret	Lin.
928	Demiegretta gularis	The white-throated reef heron	Bosc.
929	Bubulcus coromandus	The cattle egret	Bodd.
930	Ardeola grayi	The pond heron	Sykes.
931	Butorides javanica	The little green bittern	Horsf.
932	Ardetta flavicollis	The black bittern	Lath.
933	Do. cinnamomea	The chestnut bittern	Gm.
934	Do. sinensis	The yellow bittern	Gm.
937	Nycticorax griseus	The night heron	Lin.
938	Tantalus leucocephalus	The pelican ibis	Forst.
940	Anastomus oscitans	The shell ibis	Bodd.
941	Ibis melanocephala	The white ibis	Lath.
942	Inocotis papillosus	The warty-headed ibis	Tem.
943	Falcinellus igneus	The glossy ibis	Gm.
944	Phœnicopterus antiquorum	The flamingo	Tem.
950	Sarcidiornis melanonotus	The comb duck	Penn.
951	Nettopus coromandelianus	The cotton teal	Gm.
952	Dendrocygna javanica	The whistling teal	Horsf.
953	Do. fulva	The large whistling teal	Gm.
954	Casarca rutila	The ruddy shell drake	Pall.
957	Spatula clypeata	The shoveller	Lin.
959	Anas pæcilorhyncha	The spot bill or grey duck	Forst.
961	Chaulelasmus streperus	The gadwall	Lin.
962	Dafila acuta	The pintail	Lin.
964	Querquedula crecca	The common teal	Lin.
965	Do. circia	The garganey	Lin.
967	Fuligula rufina	The red-crested pochard	Pall.
968	Do. ferina	The pochard or dunbird	Lin.
969	Do. nyroca	The white-eyed pochard	Gould.
971	Do. cristata	The tufted pochard	Lin.
975	Tachybaptes fluviatilis	The little grebe or dabchick	Tunst.
979	Larus ichthyactus	The great black-headed gull	Pall.
980	Do. brunneicephalus	The brown-headed gull	Jerd.
981	Do. ridibundus	The laughing gull	Lin.
983	Sterna anglica	The gull-billed tern	Mont.
984	Hydrochelidon hybrida	The small marsh tern	Pall.
987	Sterna melanogastra	The black-bellied tern	Tem.
988 ter.	Do. saundersi	Saunders' little tern	Hume.
989	Do. bergii	The large sea tern	Licht.
990	Do. media	The lesser sea tern	Horsf.
992	Do. anæstheta	The panayan tern	Scop.
992 bis.	Do. fuliginosa	The sooty tern	Gm.
993	Anous stolidus	The common noddy	Lin.
995	Rhynchops albicollis	The Indian skimmer	Sws.
996	Phaëton rubricaudus	The bed-tailed boatswain bird	Bodd.
996 bis.	Do. indicus	The short-tailed boatswain bird	Hume.
1000 bis.	Fregata minor	The lesser frigate bird	Gm.
1004	Pelecanus manillensis	The spotted billed pelican	Gm.
1004 bis.	Do. roseus	The eastern white pelican	Gm.
1006	Phalacrocorax fuscicollis	....	Steph.
1007	Do. pygmæus	The little cormorant	Pall.
1008	Plotus melanogaster	The Indian snake-bird	Penn.

APPENDIX V.

List of some of the Butterflies of Malabar and the Western Ghāts.

No.	Author's name.	Scientific name.	Remarks.
1	Boisduval	Danais (Parantica) grammica.	
2	Moore	Do. (Chittira) Nilgiriensis.	
3	Cramer	Do. (Tirumala) limniace.	
4	Butler	Do. (Do.) septentrionis.	
5	Linnæus	Do. (Salatura) chrysippus.	
6	Cramer	Do. (Do.) genutia.	
7	Do.	Euplæa core.	
8	Hewitson	Mycalesis (Virapa) anaxias.	
9	Linnæus	Do. (Calysisme) mineus.	
10	Guèrin	Do. (Telinga) Adolphei.	
11	Butler	Do. (Nissanga) junonia.	
12	Moore	Lethe todara.	
13	Guèrin	Do. Nilgiriensis.	
14	Hewitson	Do. Ceylonica.	
15	Guèrin	Ypthima chenni.	
16	Moore	Melanitis bela, variety.	
17	Cramer	Do. ismene.	
18	Butler	Elymnias caudata.	
19	Fabricius	Telchinia violæ.	
20	Do.	Cirrhochroa thais.	
21	Drury	Messaras erymanthis.	
22	Do.	Atella phalanta.	
23	Linnæus	Acidalia niphe.	
24	Drury	Vanessa charonia.	
25	Hübner	Pyrameis callirhoë.	
26	Linnæus	Do. cardui.	
27	Do.	Junonia lemonias.	
28	Do.	Do. ænone.	
29	Do.	Do. asterie.	
30	Do.	Do. orithyia.	
31	Cramer	Precis iphita.	
32	Moore	Kallima Wardii.	
33	Westwood	Ergolis Taprobana.	
34	Linnæus	Do. Ariadne.	
35	Boisduval	Cyrestis thyodamas.	
36	Linnæus	Hypolimnas bolina.	
37	Do.	Do. misippus.	
38	Moore	Limenitis canniba.	
39	Do.	Neptis varmona.	
40	Do.	Do. jumba.	
41	Do.	Do. nandina.	
42	Do.	Rahinda plagiosa.	
43	Linnæus	Athyma leucothoë.	
44	Stoll	Dophla Evelina.	
45	Forster	Symphædra nais.	
46	Westwood	Charaxes psaphon.	
47	Drury	Do. athamas.	
48	Moore	Libythea lepita.	
49	Godart	Do. myrrha.	
50	Westwood	Spalgis epius.	
51	....	Pithecops species.	
52	Drury	Curetis thetys.	
53	Horsfield	Cyaniris puspa.	
54	Do.	Do. akasa.	

List of some of the Butterflies of Malabar and the Western Ghâts—(Continued).

No.	Author's name.	Scientific name.	Remarks.
55	....	Cyaniris species.	
56	Kollar	Zizera maha.	
57	Fabricius	Tarucus Plinius.	
58	Do.	Castalius rosimon.	
59	Moore	Do. hamatus.	
60	Cramer	Jamides bochus.	
61	Moore	Nacaduba ardates.	
62	....	Do. species.	
63	Fabricius	Catochrysops Strabo.	
64	Linnæus	Polyommatus bæticus.	
65	Fabricius	Lampides ælianus.	
66	Godart	Do. elpis.	
67	Guèrin	Talicada nyseus.	
68	Druce	Calapæcilma elegans.	
69	Fabricius	Rathinda amor.	
70	Moore	Dendorix epijarbas.	
71	Do.	Rapala lazulina.	
72	Cramer	Aphnæus etolus.	
73	....	Do. species.	
74	....	....	
75	....	Pratapa species.	
76	Cramer	Loxura atymnus.	
77	Horsfield	Bindahara sugriva.	
78	Moore	Surendra quercetorum.	
79	....	Do. species.	
80	Moore	Amblypodia naradoides.	
81	....	Hypolycæna species.	
82	Fabricius	Nychitona xiphia.	
83	Linnæus	Terias hecab.	
84	Horsfield	Do. drona.	
85	Cramer	Catopsilia catilla.	
86	Do.	Do. crocale.	
87	Fabricius	Do. gnoma.	
88	Linnæus	Do. pyranthe.	
89	Butler	Ixias latifasciata.	
90	Cramer	Do. Marianne.	
91	Linnæus	Hebomoia glaucippe.	
92	Butler	Callosime purus.	
93	Do.	Do. pernotatus.	
94	Do.	Do. pseudevanthe.	
95	Wallace	Idmais fulvia.	
96	Felder	Colias Nilgiriensis.	
97	Boisduval	Catophaga neombo.	
98	Cramer	Do. Paulina.	
99	Moore	Hiposcritia narendra.	
100	Fabricius	Appias libythea.	
101	Do.	Huphina phryne.	
102	Sparrman	Mancipium canidia.	
103	Cramer	Belenois mesentina.	
104	Moore	Nepheronia pingasa.	
105	Drury	Delias eucharis.	
106	Felder	Papilio (Dalchina) teredon.	
107	Do.	Do. (Zetides) doson.	
108	Linnæus	Do. (Do.) Agamemnon.	
109	Cramer	Do. (Orpheides) erithonius.	
110	Fabricius	Do. (Harimala) crino.	
111	Cramer	Do. (Hiades) polymnestor.	
112	Linnæus	Do. (Charus) Helenus.	
113	Do.	Do. (Laertias) pammon.	
114	Do.	Do. (Menelaides) Hector.	
115	Fabricius	Do. (Do.) aristolochiæ.	
116	Linnæus	Do. (Chilasa) clytia.	
117	Moore	Do. (do.) tamilana.	

List of some of the Butterflies of Malabar and the Western Ghâts—(Continued).

No.	Author's name.	Scientific name.	Remarks.
118	Cramer	Papilio (Ornithoptera) minos.	
119	Fabricius	Badamia exclamationis.	
120	Guèrin	Choaspes Benjamini.	
121	Fabricius	Parata Alexis.	
122	Cramer	Do. œromus.	
123	....	Baracus species.	
124	Butler	Astictopterus stellifer.	
125	Moore	Baoris kimara.	
126	Do.	Parnara narvoa.	
127	Fabricius	Chapra Mathias.	
128	Moore	Telicota bambusæ, variety.	
129	....	Padraona species.	
130	Butler	Do. mæsoides.	
131	Hewitson	Taractrocera coramus.	
132	Do.	Halpe beturia, variety.	
133	Cramer	Hyarotis adrastus.	
134	Fabricius	Tagiades Atticus.	
135	Mabille	Do. obscurus, variety.	
136	Cramer	Udaspes folus.	
137	Moore	Plesioneura ambareesa.	
138	....	Do. species.	
139	Fabricius	Caladenia Dan.	
140	Moore	Do. indrani.	
141	Felder	Abaratha Ransonneti.	
142	Moore	Do. agama.	
143	Fabricius	Hesperia galba.	
144	....	Unnamed.	
145	....	Isoteinon species.	

APPENDIX VI.

List of Timber Trees.

Scientific name.	Habitat.	Elevation.
Order II.—MANGOLIACEÆ.		
MICHELIA, *Linn.*		
M. Nilagirica	Western Ghats ..	....
M. champaca	Wynaad Plateau ..	....
Order III.—ANONACEÆ.		
GONIOTHALAMUS, *Blume.*		
G. Wightii	Palghat Hills ..	3,000 to nearly 5,000 feet.
G. Wynadensis	Wynaad	....
CYATHOCALYX, *Champ.*		
C. Zeylanicus	Malabar	1,000 to 3,000 feet.
UNONA, *Linn. F.*		
U. pannosa	Western Ghat ..	Up to 3,500 feet.
U. Lawii	Malabar	....
POLYALTHIA, *Bl.*		
P. coffeoides	Wynaad	1,000 to about 3,500 feet.
PHÆANTHUS.		
P. Malabaricus	Malabar	....
MILIUSA, *Lesch.*		
M. montana	Western Ghats ..	....
M. Indica	....	....
M. Nilagirica	....	....
OROPHEA, *Blume.*		
O. Thomsoni	....	1,000 to 4,000 feet.
O. uniflora	North Canara Ghats ..	....
BERBERIDACEÆ.		
Berberis, L.		
B. Nepalensis	Nilgiris and Western Ghats.	5,000 feet and upwards.
CAPPARIDACEÆ		
Cratæva. Linn.		
C. nurvala	Malabar	....
MORINGACEÆ.		
Moringa.		
M. pterygosperum	Malabar	....

List of Timber Trees—(Continued).

Scientific name.	Habitat.	Elevation.
Order III.—ANONACEÆ—(*Contd.*)		
BIXINEÆ.		
Flacourtia, Commers.		
F. Ramontchi	Malabar	....
F. cataphracta	Malabar	....
HYDNOCARPUS, *Gærtn.*		
H. Wightiana	Malabar	About 2,000 feet.
H. inebrians	Malabar	Up to 2,000 feet.
PITTOSPOREÆ.		
Pittosporum, Banks.		
P. floribundum	Western Ghâts ..	Up to 4,000 feet.
Order X.—POLYGALEÆ.		
XANTHOPHYLLUM, *Roxb.*		
X. Arnottianum	Malabar	....
X. Angustifolium	....	....
Order XI.—TAMARISCINEÆ.		
TAMARIX, *Linn.*		
T. ericoides	Malabar	...
Order XII.—GUTTIFERÆ.		
GARCINIA, *Lam.*		
G. purpurea	Wynaad	....
G. Morella	Western Ghâts ..	2,000 feet.
G. conicarpa	....	....
XANTHOCHYMUS, *Roxb.*		
X. ovalifolius	Malabar	....
CALOPHYLLUM, *Linn.*		
C. inophyllum	Malabar	....
MESUA.		
M. speciosa	Malabar	Up to nearly 5,000 feet.
M. ferrea, *Linn.*	....	....
Order XIII.—TERNSTRŒMIACEÆ.		
Eurya Japonica	Malabar	....
SHOREA, *Roxb.*		
S. laccifera	Wynaad	....
HOPEA.		
H. parviflora	Malabar and South Canara.	....

List of Timber Trees—(Continued).

Scientific name.	Habitat.	Elevation.
Order XIII.—TERNSTRŒMIACEÆ —(*Continued*).		
VATERIA, *L.*		
V. Malabarica	Malabar	3,000 to 4,000 feet.
V. Indica	....	....
Order XV.—MALVACEÆ.		
Kydia calycina	Malabar	3,000 to 5,500 feet.
HIBICUS, *Linn.*		
H. tiliaceus	Western Coast ..	....
THESPESIA, *Cav.*		
T. populnea	Malabar	....
BOMBAX.		
B. Malabaricum	Malabar	....
ERIODENDRON, *D.C.*		
E. enfractuosum	Malabar	....
CULLENIA, *Wight.*		
C. excelsa	Wynaad	Up to 4,000 feet.
STERCULIA, *Linn.*		
S. Balanghas	Wynaad	....
S. villosa	Malabar	....
HERITIERA, *Ait.*		
H. littoralis	Malabar	....
HELLICTERES, *Linn.*		
H. isora	Malabar	....
PTEROSPERMUM, *Schreb.*		
P. Ruberifolium	....	Over 2,500 feet.
P. Heyneanum	Malabar	....
P. Glabrescens	Wynaad	....
ERIOLÆNA, *D.C.*		
E. Hookeriana	Malabar	To about 4,000 feet.
E. Quinquelocularis	Wynaad	....
Order XVII.—TILIACEÆ.		
PITYRANTHE, *Thw.*		
Grewia tiliæfolia	Malabar	4,000 feet.
G. Asiatica	Malabar	....
G. lævigata	Malabar	....
ELÆOCARPUS, *Linn.*		
E. oblongus	Malabar	....
E. seratus	Western Ghâts ..	....
E. Glandulifera	Wynaad	2,500 to 6,000.

List of Timber Trees—(Continued).

Scientific name.	Habitat.	Elevation.
Order XVII.—TILIACEÆ—(*Contd.*)		
ERYTHROXYLON.		
E. Indicum	Malabar	....
Order XIX.—GERANIACEÆ.		
AVERRHOA, *Linn.*		
A. bilimbi	....	....
A. carambola	Malabar	....
Order XX.—RUTACEÆ.		
Melicope Indica	Western Ghâts ..	....
EVODIA.		
E. triphylla	Wynaad	....
GLYCOSMIS, *Core.*		
G. pentaphylla	Malabar	To 5,000 feet.
MURRAYA, *Linn.*		
M. exotica	....	....
M. Konighii	Malabar	....
CLAUSENA.		
C. Willdenowii	Wynaad	3,000 feet.
LIMONIA, *Linn.*		
L. alata	Western Ghâts ..	6,000 feet.
ATALANTIA, *Corp.*		
A. monophylla	Malabar	
A. racemosa	Malabar	....
A. Missionis	Malabar	2,000 feet.
Order XXI.—SIMARUBEÆ.		
A. Malabarica	....	....
A. excelsa	Malabar	....
SAMADERA, *Gærtn.*		
S. Indica	Malabar	....
GOMPHIA, *Schreb.*		
G. Angustifolia	Western Ghâts ..	3,000 feet.
Order XXIII.—BURSERACEÆ.		
CANARIUM, *Linn.*		
C. strictum	Malabar	4,000 to 4,500 feet.
Order XXIV.—MELIACEÆ.		
MELIA, *Linn.*		
M. Azadirachta	Malabar	....

List of Timber Trees—(Continued).

Scientific name.	Habitat.	Elevation.
Order XXIV.—MELIACEÆ—(*Contd.*).		
DYSOXYLUM, *Bl.*		
D. macrocarpum	Wynaad	....
D. sp.	....	....
BEDDOMEA.		
B. simplicifolia	Wynaad	2,000 to 4,000 feet.
B. Indica	Western Ghats ..	3,500 to 4,000 feet.
SWIETENIA, *Linn.*		
S. mahogani	Nilambur	(Exotic.)
SOYMIDA, *A. Juss.*		
S. febrifuga	Pâlghât	....
CHICKRASSIA, *A Juss.*		
C. tabularis	Malabar	....
CEDRELA, *Linn.*		
C. toona	Malabar	....
Order XXV.—CHAILLETIACEÆ.		
CHALLETIA, *D.C.*		
C. gelonioides	Western Ghats ..	4,000 feet.
OPILIA, *Roxb.*		
O. amentacea	Malabar	....
GOMPHANDRA, *Wall.*		
G. axillaris	Western Forests ..	4,000 feet.
G. coriacea	Western Forests ..	3,000 to 7,000 feet.
Order XXVII.—ILICINEÆ.		
ILEX, *Linn.*		
I. Malabarica	....	....
I. Wightiana	Western Ghats ..	6,000 to 8,000 feet.
Order XXVIII.—CELASTRINEÆ.		
EUONYMUS.		
E. dichotomus	Western Forests ..	4,000 to 4,500 feet.
E. Goughii	Malabar	3,000 to 4,000 feet.
E. angulatus	Western Ghats ..	....
E. serratifolius	Wynaad	3,000 feet.
GLYPTOPETALUM.		
G. grandiflorum	Wynaad	2,500 to 3,000 feet.
MICROTROPIS, *Wall.*		
M. ramiflora	Western Ghats ..	6,000 to 7,000 feet.
M. densiflora	Western Slopes ..	6,000 to 7,000 feet.
M. Wallichiana	Western Ghats ..	5,000 feet.

List of Timber Trees—(Continued).

Scientific name.	Habitat.	Elevation.
Order XXVIII.—CELASTRINEÆ —(*Continued*).		
PLEUROSTYLIA.		
P. Wightii	Malabar	....
Order XXIX.—RHAMNEÆ.		
ZIZYPHUS, *Juss.*		
Z. jujuba	....	....
Z glabrata	Western Forests ..	....
Z. nummularia	Malabar	....
COLUBRINA, *Linn.*		
C. Asiatica	Malabar	....
RHAMNUS, *Linn.*		
R. hirsutus	Western Ghats ..	5,000 to 6,000 feet.
Order XXX.—SAPINDACEÆ.		
SCHLEICHERA, *Willd.*		
S. trijuga	....	....
SAPINDUS, *Linn.*		
S. emarginatus	Malabar	....
NEPHELIUM, *Linn.*		
N. erectum	Malabar	2,000 to 3,000 feet.
DODONÆA, *Linn.*		
D. viscosa	Malabar	8,000 feet.
Order XXXI.—SABIACEÆ.		
MELIOSMA.		
M. pungens	Malabar	5,000 feet.
M. simplicifolia	....	....
Order XXXII.—ANACARDIACEÆ.		
MANGIFERA.		
M. Indica	Malabar	4,000 feet.
ANACARDIUM.		
A. occidentale	Malabar	....
NOTHOPEGIA.		
N. Colebrookiana	Malabar	....
BUCHANANIA.		
B. latifolia	Malabar	4,000 feet.
ODINA.		
O. Wodier	Malabar	....,

List of Timber Trees—(Continued).

Scientific name.	Habitat.	Elevation.
Order XXXII.—ANACARDIACEÆ —(*Continued*).		
SEMECARPUS.		
S. anacardium	Malabar	....
S. Grahami	Malabar	2,000 to 3,000 feet.
SPONDIAS.		
S. mangifera	....	....
Order XXXIII.—CONNARACEÆ.		
ROUREA.		
R. santaloides	Mercara	....
CONNARUS.		
C. pinnatus	Malabar	....
C. monocarpus	....	....
Order XXXIV.—LEGUMINOSÆ.		
MUNDULEA.		
M. suberosa	Malabar	....
SESBANIA.		
S. grandiflora	Malabar	....
S. Ægyptiaca	Malabar	....
Tribe HEDYSAREÆ.		
Ougeinia. Benth.		
O. dalbergioides	Western Ghats ..	4,000 feet.
DESMODIUM.		
D. cephalotes	Malabar	....
D. umbellatum	....	....
Tribe PHASEOLÆ.		
Erythrina. Linn.		
E. Indica	Malabar	....
Tribe DALBERGIEÆ.		
Dalbergia, Linn.		
D. latifolia	Malabar	....
D. paniculata	Malabar	....
PTEROCARPUS, *Linn.*		
P. marsupium	Malabar	....
PONGAMIA.		
P. glabra	....	....
Sub-Order II.—*CÆSALPINIEÆ*.		
Tribe EUCÆSALPINIEÆ.		
Cæsalpinia.		
C. sappan	Nilambur and all Malabar.	Up to 2,500 feet.

List of Timber Trees—(Continued).

Scientific name.	Habitat.	Elevation.
Order XXXIV.—LEGUMINOSÆ—(*Continued*).		
Sub-Order II.—*CÆSALPINIEÆ*—(Continued).		
Acrocarpus.		
A. fraxinifolius	Wynaad	4,000 feet.
Poinciana.		
P. elata	....	....
P. regia	Malabar	....
Tribe Cassieæ.		
Cassia.		
C. florida	....	....
C. Roxburghii	Palghat	....
C. fistula	Malabar	....
Tribe Bauhinieæ.		
Bauhinia.		
B. Malabarica	Malabar	4,000 feet.
B. purpurea	Malabar	....
Tribe Amherstieæ.		
Humboldtia.		
H. Brunonis	Malabar	....
Tamarindus.		
T. Indica	Malabar	....
Tribe Cynometreæ.		
Cynometra.		
C. ramiflora	....	....
Sub-Order *MIMOSEÆ.*		
Tribe Adenanthereæ.		
Adenantheræ.		
A. pavonina	....	....
Xylia.		
X. dolabriformis	....	....
Tribe Acacieæ.		
Acacia, Wild.		
A. Arabica	Malabar	3,000 or 3,500 feet.
A. Catechu	Malabar	3,000 or 4,000 feet.
A. sundra	Malabar	....
A. Farnesiana	Malabar	5,000 feet.
Tribe Ingeæ.		
Albizzia, Surazzini.		
A. Lebbek	Malabar	50 feet.
A. odoratissima	Malabar	3,000 feet.

List of Timber Trees—(Continued).

Scientific name.	Habitat.	Elevation.
Order XXXIV—LEGUMINOSÆ —(*Continued*).		
Sub-Order *MIMOSÆ*—(Continued.)		
Tribe INGEÆ—(*Continued*).		
Albizzia—(Continued).		
A. Wightii	Malabar	....
A. procera	Malabar	....
Order XXXV.—ROSACEÆ.		
PHOTINIA, *Lindl.*		
P. Lindleyana	Western Ghâts ..	5,000 to 6,000 feet.
Order XXXVI.—RHIZOPHOREÆ.		
RHIZOPHORA.		
R. mucronata	Western Coast ..	....
R. conjugata	....	....
CERIOPS, *Arnt.*		
C. Candolleana	Western Coast ..	....
KANDELIA, *Arnt.*		
K. Rheedii	Malabar	....
BRUGUIERA, *Lam.*		
B. Rheedii	....	....
B. cylindrica	Malabar	....
CARALLIA, *Roxb.*		
C. integerrima	....	4,000 to 5,000 feet.
BLEPHARISTEMMA, *Wall.*		
B. corymbosa	Malabar	2,500 feet.
Order XXXVII.—COMBRETACEÆ.		
TERMINALIA, *Linn.*		
T. tomentosa	Malabar	3,000 or 3,500 feet.
T. paniculata	Malabar	2,000 or 3,000 ,,
T. Arjuna	Malabar	3,500 or 4,000 ,,
T. Bellerica	Malabar	....
T. catappa	Malabar	....
T. chebula	....	4,000 feet.
ANOGEISSUS, *Wall.*		
A. acuminatus	Pâlghât	....
LUMNITZERA, *Willd.*		
L. racemosa	Balasore (Malabar) ..	....

List of Timber Trees—(Continued).

Scientific name.	Habitat.	Elevation.
Order XXXVIII.—MYRTACEÆ.		
EUGENIA, *Linn.*		
E. jambolana	....	....
E. nervosa	Malabar	3,000 feet.
E. calophyllifolia	Malabar	5,000 to 6.000 feet.
E. Arnottiana	Malabar	6,000 to 7,000 feet.
E. montana	Malabar	....
E. Malabarica	....	....
E. caryophyllæa	Malabar	3,000 feet.
E. lanceolata	Western Ghâts ..	....
E. Wightii	Western Ghâts ..	....
E. Munroii	Western Ghâts ..	....
E. bracteata	Malabar	5,000 feet.
E. Willdenovii	....	....
E. Mooniana	Western Ghâts ..	4,000 feet.
E. Wynadensis	Wynaad	2,000 to 3,000 feet.
E. Argentea	Wynaad	3,000 feet.
BARRINGTONIA, *Forst.*		
B. racemosa	Malabar	....
Order XL.—LYTHRARIEÆ.		
WOODFORDIA, *Salisb.*		
W. tomentosa	Malabar	....
PEMPHIS, *Forst.*		
P. acidula	Malabar	....
LAWSONIA, *Linn.*		
L. alba	Malabar	....
LAGERSTRŒMIA, *Linn.*		
L. Reginæ	Malabar	2,000 feet.
L. microcarpa	Malabar	....
SONNERATIA, *Linn.*		
S. acida	Malabar	....
PUNICA, *Linn.*		
P. granatum	Malabar	....
CASEARIA, *Linn.*		
C. Wynadensis	Malabar	2,000 to 3,000 feet.
Order XLIII.—ARALIACEÆ.		
ARALIA, *Linn.*		
A. Malabarica	Wynaad	....
HEPTAPLEURUM, *Gærtn.*		
H. obovatum	Western Ghâts ..	2,000 to 6,000 feet.

List of Timber Trees—(Continued).

Scientific name.	Habitat.	Elevation.
Order XLVI.—RUBIACEÆ.		
ANTHOCEPHALUS, *A. Rich.*		
A. Cadambus	....	....
ADINA, *Salisb.*		
A. cordifolia	....	....
NAUCLEA.		
N. elliptica	Malabar	2,000 feet.
HYMENODICTYON, *Wall.*		
H. excelsum	....	....
H. Utile	Palghat	....
WENDLANDIA, *Bartl.*		
W. Notoniana	....	....
MUSSÆNDA, *Linn.*		
M. frondosa	Malabar	....
GARDENIA, *Linn.*		
G. latifolia	Palghat	3,500 feet.
PLECTRONIA, *Linn.*		
P. Rheedii	Wynaad	5,000 feet.
P. Leschenaultii	Malabar	....
IXORA, *Linn.*		
I. parviflora	....	....
I. barbata	Malabar	4,500 feet.
I. polyantha	Malabar	....
I. coccinea	....	....
PAVETTA.		
P. Indica	Malabar	....
COFFEA, *Linn.*		
C. Bengalensis	....	....
MORINDA, *Linn.*		
M. bracteata	Malabar	....
M. umbellata	Western Forests ..	4,000 feet.
SAPROSMA, *Blume.*		
S. Wightii	Western Ghats ..	6,000 feet.
S. glomerata	Western Ghats ..	2,000 to 4,000 feet.
Order XLVII.—COMPOSITÆ.		
VERNONIA, *Schreb.*		
V. volkameriæfolia	....	5,000 feet.

List of Timber Trees—(Continued).

Scientific name.	Habitat.	Elevation.
Order XLVIII.—ERICACEÆ.		
VACCINIUM, *Linn.*		
V. Neilgherrense	Wynaad	2,000 to 3,000 feet.
Order XLIX.—MYRSINEÆ.		
EMBELIA, *Burm.*		
E. robusta	Wynaad	....
ARDISIA, *Linn.*		
A. pauciflora	Malabar	....
A. paniculata	Malabar	....
A. elliptica	Western Forests ..	....
ÆGICERAS, *Gærtn.*		
Æ. majus	Malabar	....
Order L.—SAPOLACEÆ.		
BASSIA, *Linn.*		
B. latifolia	Malabar	60 feet.
B. Malabarica	Malabar	4,000 feet.
Section ISONANDRA.		
Bassia Wightiana	Western Forests ..	2,000 to 6,000 feet.
MIMUSOPS, *Linn.*		
M. Roxburghiana	Malabar .. .	....
Order LI.—EBENACEÆ.		
DIOSPYROS, *Linn.*		
D. sylvatica	Western Forests ..	4,000 feet.
D. ovalifolia	Wynaad	1,000 to 4,000 feet.
D. Candolliana	Wynaad	....
D. Nîlagirica	Western Ghats ..	3,000 to 4,000 feet.
D. paniculata	Wynaad	2,000 to 3,000 feet.
D. pruriens	Wynaad	3,000 feet.
D. microphylla	Wynaad	3,000 feet.
MABA, *Forst.*		
M. buxifolia	Malabar	6,000 feet.
Order LII.—STYRACEÆ.		
SYMPLOCOS, *Linn.*		
S. spicata	Malabar	7,000 feet.
S. nervosa	Nîlgiri	....
S. pulchra	Nîlgiri	3,000 to 4,000 feet.
S. acuminata	Wynaad	5,000 feet.
Order LIII.—JASMINEÆ.		
LIGUSTRUM, *Linn.*		
L. robustum	Malabar	....

List of Timber Trees—(Continued).

Scientific name.	Habitat.	Elevation.
Order LIII.—JASMINEÆ—(*Continued*).		
CHIONANTHUS, *Linn.*		
C. Malabarica	Western Ghâts ..	....
Order LIV.—APOCYNEÆ.		
CARISSA, *Linn.*		
C. carandas	....	....
CERBERA, *Linn.*		
C. odallum	Western Coast ..	....
TABERNAMONTANA, *Linn.*		
T. coronaria	Malabar	....
WRIGHTEA.		
W. tomentosa	Wynaad (Malabar) ..	....
W. Wallichii	Wynaad (Malabar) ..	4,000 feet.
ALSTONIA.		
A. scholaris	....	....
A. venenata	Malabar	3,000 to 4,500 feet.
Order LV.—LOGANIACEÆ.		
STRYCHNOS, *Linn.*		
S. nux-vomica	....	....
S. potatorum	Malabar	3,000 feet.
FAGRÆA.		
F. obovata	Malabar	....
Order LVI.—BORAGINEÆ.		
CORDIA.		
C. Wallichii	....	....
C. myxa	Malabar	
C. monoica	Travancore	2,000 feet.
C. Rothii	Western Forests ..	....
C. Perottetii	Western Forests ..	....
C. fulvosa	Western Forests ..	....
EHRETIA.		
E. buxifolia	Malabar	....
Order LVIII.—BIGNONIACEÆ.		
BIGNONIA.		
B. Indica	Malabar	3,000 feet.
SPATHODEA.		
S. falcata	....	....
S. Rheedii	Tellicherry (Malabar).	....
S. crispa	Malabar	....
S. arcuata	Palghât	....

List of Timber Trees—(Continued).

Scientific name.	Habitat.	Elevation.
Order LVIII.—BIGNONIACEÆ—(*Continued*).		
STEREOSPERMUM.		
S. suaveolens	Malabar	....
PAJANELIA.		
P. Rheedii	Malabar	Up to 2,000 feet.
Order LIX.—VERBENACEÆ.		
VITEX, *Linn.*		
V. pubescens	Malabar	....
PREMNA, *Linn.*		
P. purpurascens	Wynaad	....
CALLICARPA, *Linn.*		
C. lanata	Malabar	Up to 4,000 feet.
CLERODENDRON, *Linn.*		
C. infortunatum	Malabar	Up to 5,000 to 6,000 feet.
TECTONA, *Linn.*		
T. grandis	Malabar	....
AVICENNIA, *Linn.*		
A. officinalis	Malabar	....
Order LXI.—MYRISTICEÆ.		
MYRISTICA, *Linn.*		
M. laurifolia	....	....
M. Malabarica	....	....
LASIOSIPHON, *Fresen.*		
L. eriocephalus	Malabar	Up to 5,000 feet.
Order LXVI.—SANTALACEÆ.		
SANTALUM.		
S. album	Malabar	....
Order LXVII.—SALICACEÆ.		
SALIX.		
S. tetrasperma	....	....
Order LXVIII.—LAURINEÆ.		
PHŒBE, *Nees.*		
P. lanceolata	Wynaad	3,000 feet.
CINNAMOMUM.		
C. Zeylanicum	Malabar	....

List of Timber Trees—(Continued).

Scientific name.	Habitat.	Elevation.
Order LXVIII.—LAURINEÆ—(*Continued*).		
TETRANTHERA, *Jacq.*		
T. tomentosa	....	....
T. laurifolia	....	....
T. ligustrina	....	....
T. venulosa	....	....
T. (Cyclodaphne) sebifera	....	....
ACTINODAPHNE, *Nees.*		
A. angustifolia	Malabar	4,000 to 5,000 feet.
Order LXIX.—EUPHORBIACEÆ.		
Tribe I.—PHYLLANTHEÆ.		
Actephila, Blume.		
A. excelsa	Malabar	Up to 5,500 feet.
Phyllanthus, Linn.		
P. emblica	Malabar	....
P. juniperinoides	Wynaad	....
P. distichus	Malabar	....
P. Indicus	Wynaad	Up to 3,000 feet.
Glochidion, Forst.		
G. littorale	Malabar	....
G. nitidum	Malabar	....
G. lanceolarium	Malabar	....
G. tomentosum	Malabar	....
G. Hohenackeri	Malabar	....
G. asperum	Malabar	....
G. diversifolium	Malabar	....
G. Malabaricum	Malabar	....
G. velutinum	Malabar	Up to 4,000 feet.
G. Heyneanum	Malabar	....
Breynia, Forst.		
B. rhamnoides	Malabar	....
Securiega, Juss.		
S. obovata	Malabar	....
S. leucopyrus	Malabar	....
Baccaurea, Lour.		
B. sapida	Wynaad	....
Bischoffia.		
B. Javanica	....	....
Hemicyclia, Wight and Arnt.		
H. sepiaria	Malabar	Up to 3,000 feet.
H. venusta	Western Ghats ..	2,000 to 4,000 feet.
Cyclostemon.		
C. Indicus	Malabar	....

List of Timber Trees—(Continued).

Scientific name.	Habitat.	Elevation.
Order LXIX.—EUPHORBIACEÆ —(*Continued*).		
Tribe I.—PHYLLANTHEÆ—(*Continued*).		
Antidesma.		
A. Ghæsembilla	Malabar	....
A. Bunius	Western Ghâts ..	Up to about 4,000 feet.
A. Diandrum	Malabar	....
Tribe BRIEDELIEÆ.		
Briedelia, Willd.		
B. stipularis	Malabar	....
Cleistanthus, Hook.		
C. Malabaricus	Malabar	....
Tribe CROTONEÆ.		
Croton, Linn.		
C. oblongifolium	Malabar	....
C. Malabaricum	Malabar	Up to 4,000 feet.
Tribe ACALYPHEÆ.		
Aleurites, Forst.		
A. Moluccana	....	....
Agrostistachys, Dalzell.		
A. Indica	Malabar	3,000 to 5,000 feet.
Sarcoclinium, Wight.		
S. longifolium	Western Ghâts ..	2,000 to 4,000 feet.
Mallotus.		
M. albus	Western Forests ..	Up to 4,000 feet.
M. muricatus	Western Ghâts ..	....
M. Lawii	Malabar	....
M. Philippinensis	Malabar	....
Macaranga.		
M. Indica	Malabar	....
Homonoya, Lour.		
H. riparia	Malabar	....
H. ritusa	Malabar	....
Codiæum, Rumph.		
C. umbellatum	Western Ghâts ..	Up to 3,000 feet.
Excœcaria, Linn.		
E. insignis	Malabar	....
E. Cochinensis	Malabar	Up to 5,000 feet.
E. Indica	Malabar	....
E. oppositifolia	Malabar	....
E. agallocha	Malabar	....

List of Timber Trees—(Continued).

Scientific name.	Habitat.	Elevation.
Order LXIX.—EUPHORBIACEÆ —(*Continued*).		
Tribe EUPHORBIEÆ.		
E. nivulia	Malabar	....
E. antiquorum	Malabar	....
E. trigona	Malabar	....
Sarcococca, Lindley.		
S. saligna	Malabar	....
Order LXX.—URTICEÆ.		
ULMUS, *Linn.*		
U. integrifolia	Wynaad	....
CELTIS, *Tourn.*		
C. serotina	Wynaad	At 2,500 feet.
SPONIA, *Comm.*		
S. Wightii	Malabar	....
S. Velutina	Malabar	....
S. Orientalis	Malabar	....
ARTOCARPUS, *Linn.*		
A. hirsuta	Malabar	....
A. integrifolia	Malabar	Up to 4,000 feet.
A. incisa	Malabar	....
PLECOSPERMUM, *Trecul.*		
P. spinosum	Malabar	....
STREBLUS, *Lour.*		
S. aspera	Malabar	....
TAXOTROPHIS, *Blume.*		
T. Roxburghii	Malabar	....
FICUS, *Linn.*		
F. religiosa	....	....
F. infectoria	Malabar	....
F. Wightiana	Malabar	....
F. Bengalensis	Malabar	....
F. tomentosa	Malabar	....
F. Mysorensis	Malabar	....
F. laccifera	Malabar	....
F. Tsiela	Malabar	....
F. retusa	Malabar	....
F. Benjaminea	Malabar	....
F. nervosa	Malabar	....
F. asperrima	Malabar	....
F. parasitica	Malabar	....
F. hispida	Malabar	....
F. glomerata	Malabar	....
LAPORTEA, *Gandich.*		
L. crenulata	Western Ghâts ..	....

List of Timber Trees—(Continued).

Scientific name.	Habitat.	Elevation.
Order LXX.—URTICEÆ—(*Contd.*)		
BŒHMERIA, *Jacq.*		
B. Travancorica	Wynaad	Up to 4,500 feet.
MONOCARPUS.		
M. longifolius	Malabar	Up to 7,000 feet.
Order LXXI.—CASUARINACEÆ.		
CASUARINA, *Linn.*		
C. equisitifolia	Malabar	....
Sub-class IV.—**Gymnospermæ.**		
Order LXXII.—CYCADACEÆ.		
CYCAS, *Linn.*		
C. circinalis	Malabar	Up to 500 feet.
Class II.—**MONOCOTYLEDONS.**		
Order LXXIV.—PALMEÆ.		
Caryota urens	Malabar	....
Corypha umbraculifera	Malabar	....
Areca concinna	Malabar	....
Order LXXV.—PANDANACEÆ.		
PANDANUS, *Linn.*		
P. odoratissimus	Malabar	....
P. furcatus	Malabar	....
Order LXXVI.—GRAMINEÆ.		
Tribe BAMBUSACEÆ.		
Arundinaria, Michaux.		
A. Wightiana	Western Ghats ..	6,000 feet.
Bambusa, Schreb.		
B. arundinacea	Malabar	3,000 feet.
Oxytenanthera, Munro.		
O. Thwaitesii	Western Ghats ..	....
Section III.—BACCIFERÆ.		
Teinostachyum, Munro.		
T. Wightii	Western Ghats ..	Up to 3,000 to 4,000 feet.
Beesha, Rheede.		
B. Rheedii	Malabar	....
Dendrocalamus, Nees.		
D. strictus	Wynaad	Up to 3,000 feet.

APPENDIX VII.

List of Roads in the district of Malabar.

N.B.—The spelling of the names of places is, to facilitate reference, that to be found in sheets Nos. 44, 61 and 62 of the Indian Atlas.

District No.	Name of roads.	Situated in the following taluks.	Length in miles in each taluk.	Total length in district.	Deduct: Lengths kept up by Municipalities or French Government.	Deduct: Length outside Municipal limits common to a line previously entered in this list.	Length actually maintained by the Local Fund Board.	Remarks.
1	2	3	4	5	6	7	8	9
	Main lines consecutively numbered from North to South.		M. F.	M. F.	M. F.	M. F.	M. F.	
1	Coast road from Beypoor railway station to Canara frontier near Peyrncotha *viâ* Calicut, Tellicherry, Cannanore, and Tullipurmbu.	Calicut .. Kurumbranad. Kottayam .. Chirakkal ..	14 5 30 2 7 7 44 2	97 0	15 1	..	81 7	Of the entry in col. 6, Calicut Municipality maintains 6 miles in Calicut taluk; French Government maintains 1 mile in Kurumbranad taluk; Tellicherry Municipality maintains $3\frac{3}{8}$ miles in Kottayam taluk; and Cannanore, Military cantonment, $4\frac{3}{4}$ miles in Chirakkal taluk. This line includes trace north of Tullipurmbu, viz., 15 miles, which is unopened.

2	Cannanore Fort *viâ* Perambady ghaut, to Coorg and Mysore *viâ* Coodally, Mattanur, Ulleyil, and Gunnoth.	Chirakkal .. Kottayam ..	12 5 21 6	34 3	..	3 4	30 7	Of the entry in col. 7, part is "Military," part coast road No. 1.
3	Tellicherry *viâ* Pariah ghaut, to Mysore frontier (Bawally bridge) *viâ* Coothpurmbu, Canooth, Pariah, and Manantawaddy.	Kottayam .. Wynad ..	22 7 38 5	61 4	1 6	..	59 6	The entry in col. 6 relates to Tellicherry Municipality in Kottayam taluk.
4	Calicut *viâ* Tamaracherry ghaut, to Mysore frontier near Pongolycottah *viâ* Tamaracherry, Pudupaddy, Vyteery, Culpetta, and Gunapuddyvuttum.	Calicut .. Wynad ..	35 0 37 3	72 3	3 2	..	69 1	The entry in col. 6 relates to Calicut Municipality in Calicut taluk.
5	Calicut *viâ* Carcoor ghaut, to Nilagiris and Mysore *viâ* Coondoty, Arreacode, Nellumboor, and Yeddakurra.	Calicut .. Ernad ..	6 3 53 5	60 3	3 0	..	57 3	Do. do.
6	Calicut *viâ* Coondoty, Mullapuram, Munaur, Palghat railway station, and Palghat, to Coimbatoor frontier at Walliar.	Calicut .. Ernad .. Walluvanad .. Palghat ..	6 6 25 6 39 0 29 4	101 0	7 2	13 6	80 0	Of the entry in col. 6, Calicut Municipality in Calicut taluk maintains 3 miles; Palghat Municipality in Palghat taluk maintains 4[illegible] miles; common to No. 5; 13[illegible] miles in Calicut and Ernad taluks.
7	Palghat to Ponnani *viâ* Purley, Puttamby, and Tritala.	Palghat .. Walluvanad .. Ponnani ..	14 4 24 0 16 5	55 2	1 2	..	54 0	The entry in col. 6 relates to Palghat Municipality in Palghat taluk.
	Branch lines and Railway feeders consecutively numbered from North to South.							
8	Peyrncotha on No. 1 to Yedanaad on No. 9 *viâ* Wudawudur and Allakatu.	Chirakkal ..	11 1	11 1	..	..	11 1	
9	Kuvoy to Bimlipatam on No. 1 *viâ* Kunjamunglum and Maudoy.	Do. ..	19 3	19 3	..	..	19 3	

List of Roads in the district of Malabar—(Continued).

District No.	Name of roads.	Situated in the following taluks.	Length in miles in each taluk.	Total length in district.	Deduct: Lengths kept up by Municipalities or French Government.	Deduct: Length outside Municipal limits common to a line previously entered in this list.	Length actually maintained by the Local Fund Board.	Remarks.
1	2	3	4	5	6	7	8	9
	Branch lines and Railway feeders consecutively numbered from North to South—(Continued).		M. F.	M. F.	M. F.	M. F.	M. F.	
10	Kunjamunglum on No. 9 to Tullipurmbu on No. 1.	Chirakkal ..	5 6	5 6	..	..	5 6	
11	Kunjamunglum on No. 9 to Kuthur.	Do. ..	7 4	7 4	..	..	7 4	
12	Tullipurmbu on No. 1 to Irrity bridge on No. 2 *vià* Nedwullur, Surrukundapurum, and Eroocur.	Do. ..	27 6	27 6	..	..	27 6	
13	Eroocur on No. 12 to Calliaud ..	Do. ..	2 6	2 6	..	..	2 6	
14	Billipatam on No. 1 to Cannanore *vià* Chalautu.	Do. ..	5 5	5 5	2 3	..	3 2	The entry in col. 6 relates to Cannanore Military cantonment in Chirakkal taluk.
15	Iyecode to Chalautu on No. 14 ..	Do. ..	4 6	4 6	..	..	4 6	
16	Cheracul on No. 1 to Katampully.	Do. ..	1 7	1 7	..	..	1 7	
17	Cannanore fort to Kakaud backwater.	Do. ..	3 5	3 5	2 7	..	0 6	The entry in col. 6 relates to Cannanore Military cantonment in Chirakkal taluk.
18	Aychoor at 8th mile on Coorg road No. 2 to junction with No. 19.	Do. ..	1 1	1 1	..	..	1 1	

19	Chuviel on No. 1 to Mattanur on No. 2 *viâ* Anjeracundy.	Chirakkal .. Kottayam ..	7 5 6 0	13 5	..	..	13 5	
20	Chuviel on No. 1 to Coothpurmbu on No. 3 *viâ* Mambram ferry.	Chirakkal .. Kottayam ..	7 7 4 4	12 3	..	..	12 3	
21	Coothpurmbu on No. 3 to Mattanur on No. 2.	Do. ..	8 1	8 1	..	..	8 1	
22	Tellicherry to Eroocur on No. 12 *viâ* Pinroy and Anjeracundy.	Kottayam .. Chirakkal ..	13 2 6 0	19 2	..	..	19 2	
23	Nittur on No. 22 to junction with No. 3 at Peirce, Leslie and company's coffee works.	Kottayam ..	2 1	2 1	..	..	2 1	
24	Irrity bridge on No. 2 to Nedimpoya (foot of Pariah ghaut) on No. 3.	Do. ..	12 1	12 1	..	..	12 1	
25	Kotayem to Perinkulatur on No. 27 *viâ* Paunur.	Do. ..	7 3	7 3	..	..	7 3	
26	Kudarur on No. 3 to Paunur on No. 25.	Do. ..	5 1	5 1	..	..	5 1	
27	Loop line from Tellicherry to Manantawaddy on No. 3 *viâ* Perinkulatur, Nadapuram, Kuttiadi ghaut, and Corote Angaddy.	Do. ..* Kurumbranad. Wynad ..	6 2 23 1 19 5	49 0	0 2	..	48 6	The entry in col. 6 relates to Tellicherry Municipality in Kottayam taluk.
28	Aumanny on No. 3 to Coorg frontier *viâ* Vagoor.	Wynad ..	9 5	9 5	..	..	9 5	
29	Tirunelly valley to junction with No. 28.	Do. ..	10 4	10 4	..	..	10 4	
30	Pariah on No. 3 to Corote Angaddy on No. 27.	Do. ..	9 4	9 4	..	..	9 4	
31	Vyteery on No. 4 to Manantawaddy on No. 3 *viâ* Turrioterrah and Kuthirapandi ferry.	Do. .. Do. ..	8 7 18 5	27 4	..	6 4	21 0	Common to No. 27 in Wynad taluk.
32	Branch from Talapoya bridge on No. 4 to Vyteery lodge on No. 31.	Do. ..	1 1	1 1	..	..	1 1	
33	Branch from No. 31 near Kundoth to No. 35 near Kellur Angaddy.	Do. ..	1 0	1 0	..	..	1 0	
34	Old loop line from Manantawaddy *viâ* Pullikul Angaddy to Arricurrah on No. 27.	Do. ..	8 0	8 0	..	..	8 0	

List of Roads in the district of Malabar—(Continued).

District No.	Name of roads.	Situated in the following taluks.	Length in miles in each taluk.	Total length in district.	Deduct: Lengths kept up by Municipalities or French Government.	Deduct: Length outside Municipal limits common to a line previously entered in this list.	Length actually maintained by the Local Fund Board.	Remarks.
1	2	3	4	5	6	7	8	9
	Branch lines and Railway feeders consecutively numbered from North to South—(Continued).		M. F.	M. F.	M. F.	M. F.	M. F.	
35	Manantawaddy *viâ* Punnamurthcotah and Gunapuddyvuttom (Sultan's battery) on No. 4 to Nilgiri boundary near Molapilly.	Wynad .. Do. ..	12 1 24 7	37 0	..	11 5	25 3	4 miles and 2 furlongs common to No. 27, and 7 miles and 3 furlongs common to No. 4; both in Wynad taluk.
36	Old loop line from Manantawaddy *viâ* Veetoyary to Punnamurthcotah on No. 35.	Do. ..	8 0	8 0	..	..	8 0	
37	Punnamurthcotah on No. 35 to Culpetta on No. 4.	Do. ..	9 3	9 3	..	2 5	6 6	Common to No. 4 in Wynad taluk.
38	Chundale on No. 4 by Maypady to Nilagiri boundary near Mooppyenad.	Do. ..	19 0	19 0	..	..	19 0	
38(a)	Kulpathi to junction with No. 38.	Do. ..	3 4	3 4	..	..	3 4	
39	Gunapuddyvuttum (Sultan's battery) on No. 4 to Nilagiri boundary near Chulicod on road to Cherambadi.	Do. ..	6 4	6 4	..	..	6 4	

40	Junction with No. 1, two miles north of Wuddakurray (Badagara) to Nadapuram on No. 27.	Kurumbranad ..	7 1	7 1	..	..	7 1	
41	Junction with No. 1 at Wuddakurray (Badagara) to termination of canal.	Do. ..	0 5	0 5	..	..	0 5	
42	Coolyaddy (mis-spelt for Kuttiadi) on No. 27 *viâ* Melnoniam and Neddavenur to Ulliary on No. 44.	Do. ..	16 0	16 0	..	..	16 0	
43	Junction with No. 1, five miles south of Wuddakurray (Badagara) *viâ* Pyolli to Melnonian on No. 42.	Do. ..	10 7	10 7	..	..	10 7	
44	Coilandy on No. 1 to Tamaracherry on No. 4 *viâ* Ulliary.	{ Do. .. { Calicut ..	15 1 3 6	} 18 7	..	..	18 7	
45	Pudiangaddy on No. 1 to junction with No. 46 near Kokotri bridge.	Do. ..	2 5	2 5	..	..	2 5	
46	Calicut *viâ* Karaparamba to Kokolur on No. 44.	Do. ..	15 1	15 1	3 0	..	12 1	The entry in column 6 relates to Calicut Municipality in Calicut taluk.
47	Junction with No. 46 near Karaparamba to toll-gate on No. 4.	Do. ..	1 2	1 2	..	..	1 2	
48	Tamaracherry on No. 4 to junction with No. 49.	Do. ..	8 2	8 2	..	..	8 2	
49	Mokoth on No. 4 to Arreacode on No. 5.	Do. ..	17 0	17 0	..	..	17 0	
50	Calicut by Chowoyur to Moppurom	Do. ..	16 0	16 0	0 6	..	15 2	The entry in column 6 relates to Calicut Municipality in Calicut taluk.
51	Toll-gate on No. 4 to Chowoyur on No. 50.	Do. ..	2 3	2 3	..	..	2 3	
52	Arreacode on No. 5 to junction with No. 57.	Ernád ..	10 0	10 0	..	0 7	9 1	Common to No. 5 in Ernád taluk.
53	Eddamunnah (Eddawanna) on No. 5 *viâ* Wundoor, Wallaghaut, and Sissapara to Nilagiri boundary at Nadgani.	Do. ..	29 0	29 0	..	..	29 0	

List of Roads in the district of Malabar—(Continued).

District No.	Name of roads.	Situated in the following taluks.	Length in miles in each taluk.	Total length in district.	Deduct: Lengths kept up by Municipalities or French Government.	Deduct: Length outside Municipal limits common to a line previously entered in this list.	Length actually maintained by the Local Fund Board.	Remarks.
1	2	3	4	5	6	7	8	9
	Branch lines and Railway feeders consecutively numbered from North to South—(Continued).		M. F.	M. F.	M. F.	M. F.	M. F.	
54	Puttamby railway station *viâ* Parunthallamunna (Angadipuram), Pandikad, and Wundoor to junction with No. 5 near Cherupoya bridge.	Walluvanad .. Ernad ..	23 3 15 0	38 3	..	..	38 3	
55	Munjary on No. 57 to Munaur on No. 6 *viâ* Pandikad and Malauttoor.	Ernad .. Walluvanad ..	10 7 17 7	28 6	..	2 6	26 0	Common to No. 6 in Walluvanad taluk.
56	Munjary on No. 57 to Mangoth on No. 6.	Ernad ..	5 4	5 4	..	..	5 4	
57	Tiroor railway station *viâ* Mullapuram on No. 6 and Munjary to Eddamunnah (Eddawanna) on No. 5.	Ponnani .. Ernad ..	5 0 25 2	30 2	..	..	30 2	
58	Junction line between No. 53 and No. 57 near Tirculluncotur.	Do. ..	4 4	4 4	..	..	4 4	
59	unction line between No. 57 and No. 6 *viâ* Anakayam bridge and Mungadda.	Do. .. Walluvanad ..	0 6 8 4	9 2	..	..	9 2	

60	Beypoor railway station to Tritala on No. 7 *viâ* Pudiangaddy and Cootipooram railway station.	Ernad .. Ponnani	.. ..	10 6 26 2	37 0	..	2 1	34 7	Common to No. 7 in Ponnani taluk.
61	Purpenangady railway station to Mullapuram on No. 57 *viâ* Tiruangaddy.	Ernad ..	..	18 3	18 3	..	1 2	17 1	Common to No. 6 in Ernad taluk.
62	Coondoty on No. 5 to Tiruangaddy on No. 61.	Do.	..	9 5	9 5	..	1 0	8 5	Common to No. 71 in Ernad taluk.
63	Pilamanthole bridge on No. 54 to Nuradi iron girder bridge on No. 57 *viâ* Collatore.	Walluvanad	..	14 4	14 4	..	..	14 4	
64	Mooliarchy on No. 54 to Malauttoor on No. 55.	Do.	..	5 5	5 5	..	..	5 5	
65	Cootipooram railway station *viâ* Collatore to Bugavuddykavu on No. 6.	Ponnani Walluvanad	.. ..	8 5 8 3	17 0	..	0 2	16 6	Common to No. 63 in Walluvanad taluk.
66	Loop line from Parunthallamunna (Angaddypooram) on No. 6 *viâ* Cherpelcherry to Mundoor on No. 6.	Do. Palghat	.. ..	20 4 8 2	28 6	..	0 6	28 0	Common to No. 54 in Walluvanad taluk.
67	Goondiar (near Munaur) on No. 6 to Triallicode on No. 66.	Do.	..	9 0	9 0	..	..	9 0	
68	Tanoor railway station to Tanoor.	Ponnani	..	1 2	1 2	..	..	1 2	
69	Tannaloor on No. 60 *viâ* Wakatoor and Kawoo to Coopum on No. 54.	Do. Walluvanad	.. ..	16 3 5 2	21 5	..	..	21 5	
70	Tiroor railway station to Ponnani *viâ* Pudiangaddy on No. 60.	Ponnani	..	10 1	10 1	..	..	10 1	
71	Tiroor railway station to Ponnani on No. 7 *viâ* Pulliendavoo.	Do.	..	10 0	10 0	..	0 6	9 2	Common to No. 70 in Ponnani taluk.
72	Pudiangaddy on No. 60 to Perony.	Do.	..	3 2	3 2	..	..	3 2	
73	Cootipooram railway station to Eddapal on No. 7.	Do.	..	5 3	5 3	..	0 3	5 0	Common to No. 60 in Ponnani taluk.
74	Tritala on No. 7 to Chowkaad ..	Do.	..	9 7	9 7	..	..	9 7	The total length of this road which begins and ends in British Territory is 17 miles 4 furlongs of which 7 miles 5 furlongs lie in Cochin Territory.
75	Ferry on No. 7 between Puttamby railway station and Tritala to Coopum on No. 54.	Walluvanad	..	4 6	4 6	..	..	4 6	

List of Roads in the district of Malabar—(Continued).

District No.	Name of roads.	Situated in the following taluks.	Length in miles in each taluk.	Total length in district.	Deduct: Lengths kept up by Municipalities or French Government.	Deduct: Length outside Municipal limits common to a line previously entered in this list.	Length actually maintained by the Local Fund Board.	Remarks.
1	2	3	4	5	6	7	8	9
	Branch lines and Railway feeders consecutively numbered from North to South—(Continued).		M. F.	M. F.	M. F.	M. F.	M. F.	
76	Puttamby railway station to Kutnaad.	Walluvanad .. Ponnani ..	0 1 3 0	3 1	..	..	3 1	
77	Puttamby railway station to Cherpelcherry on No. 66.	Walluvanad ..	11 1	11 1	..	..	11 1	
78	Junction with No. 7 *viâ* Shoranoor railway station to the iron girder bridge.	Do. ..	2 7	2 7	..	..	2 7	
79	Shoranoor railway station to (Padinjar) Angady on No. 7 *viâ* Kutnaad.	Ponnâni ..	12 0	12 0	..	..	12 0	The total length of this road which begins and ends in British Territory is 19 miles 2 furlongs; of which 7 miles 2 furlongs lie in Cochin Territory.
80	Wauniancolumcurra on No. 7 to Kothakurishi, 5 miles on No. 81.	Walluvanad ..	3 6	3 6	..	..	3 6	
81	Wootapollium railway station to Cherpelcherry on No. 66.	Do. ..	11 2	11 2	..	0 5	10 5	Common to No. 77 in Walluvanad taluk.
82	Luckady railway station feeder from No. 7.	Do. ..	1 6	1 6	..	..	1 6	

83	Purley railway station on No. 7 to Mundoor on No. 6.	Palghat	4 1	4 1	..	1 0	3 1	0-2 common to No. 7 in Palghat taluk, and 0.6 common to No. 66 in Palghat taluk.
84	Palghat on No. 6 to Coimbatoor boundary near Meengairy *viâ* Poodoonagrum and Colungode.	Do. ..	20 2	20 2	2 1	..	18 1	The entry in column 6 relates to Palghat Municipality in Palghat taluk.
85	Loop line from Palghat on No. 6 to Muncurray on No. 7 *viâ* Poadoor and Chembracolum.	Do. ..	11 0	11 0	1 0	..	10 0	Do. do.
86	Palghat *viâ* Allatoor and Wurrakunchairy to Cochin frontier at Vaniampara.	Do. ..	24 5	24 5	2 1	..	22 4	Do. do.
87	Palghat on No. 6 *viâ* Yellapooly to Cochin frontier at Erratakulam.	Do. ..	10 4	10 4	..	3 0	7 4	Common to No. 6 in Palghat taluk.
88	Palghat on No. 6 to Cochin frontier near Chittur.	Do. ..	8 0	8 0	1 2	..	6 6	The entry in column 6 relates to Palghat Municipality in Palghat taluk.
89	Loop line from Palghat on No. 6 *viâ* Kodowayoor on No. 92 to Koonishairy on No. 90.	Do. ..	10 5	10 5	1 4	..	9 1	Do. do.
90	Palghat on No. 6 *viâ* Koonishairy to Cochin frontier near Vullangy.	Do. ..	10 7	10 7	1 4	..	9 3	Do. do.
91	Conjecode railway feeder from No. 6.	Do. ..	0 2	0 2	..	..	0 2	
92	Poodoonagrum on No. 84 *viâ* Kodowayoor to Muncurray on No. 7.	Do. ..	17 0	17 0	..	..	17 0	
93	Colungode on No. 84 to Allatoor on No. 86 *viâ* Koonishairy on No. 90.	Do. ..	12 0	12 0	..	2 0	10 0	
94	Colungode on No. 84 to Cochin frontier near Vullangy.	Do. ..	3 7	3 7	..	..	3 7	
95	Munbalom bridge on No. 86 to Cochin frontier near Vullangy.	Do. ..	7 3	7 3	..	..	7 3	
96	Ponnani *viâ* Veleankode, Chaitwye, and Muddoolokathoo to Cochin frontier near Kodungaloor.	Ponnani ..	42 6	42 6	..	..	42 6	
97	Chowkaad to Yennamakkal dam ..	Do. ..	8 6	8 6	..	..	8 6	
		Total ..	..	1,568 5	..	..	1,463 4	

APPENDIX VIII.

Port Rules, &c., of the major ports.

CANNANORE.

Boat fees at Cannanore.

	RS.	A.	P.
1. Boats of 2 tons and under, laden or unladen—			
To all vessels in 3 fathoms	0	6	0
Do. 5 and under	0	14	0
Do. 7 and over according to agreement	1	8	0
For every ton or fraction of a ton beyond 2 ..	One-half of these rates additional.		
2. Transhipping trip and return trip	Half the above rates.		
3. Trip between 6 P.M. and 5 A.M. in monsoon, and on Sundays and close holidays.	Double the above rates.		
4. Detention alongside of vessels more than three hours.	Do. do.		
5. With an awning	Four annas additional.		

NOTE.—This scale prevails also at Tellicherry.

Scale of fees for measuring vessels.

	RS.
Under 50 tons	7
50 tons and under 100 tons	11
100 do. 150 do.	15
150 do. 200 do.	19
200 do. 250 do.	23
250 do. 300 do.	27
300 tons and upwards	30

NOTE.—This scale prevails at all the ports.

Port rules for Cannanore.

RULE 1.—All vessels within the port of Cannanore shall be bound to take up such berth as may be appointed for them by the conservator, and shall change their berths or remove when required by such authority.

RULE 2.—All vessels taking in or discharging ballast, or any particular kind of cargo within the port of Cannanore, shall take up such berth as the conservator may direct.

RULE 3.—A free passage shall be kept to piers, jetties, landing places, wharves, quays, docks, and moorings; and all vessels shall be bound to move when required by the conservator to clear such passages.

RULE 4.—All vessels within the port of Cannanore shall anchor, moor, and unmoor, when and where required by the conservator.

RULE 5.—The cargo boat rules published by Government, under date the 30th September 1867, shall be in force at the port of Cannanore.

RULE 6.—No vessels within the limits of the port of Cannanore shall boil any pitch or dammer on board, or shall draw off spirits by candle or other artificial lights.

RULE 7.—All vessels in the roadstead of Cannanore shall, when at anchor between sunset and sunrise, have a good light hoisted at the starboard foreyard arm; and all vessels under weigh at night, shall show a good light at the foreroyal or upper foremast head, and when under weigh in tow of a steamer, shall, in addition, show a light at each foreyard arm; the steamer showing the usual light prescribed by the Admiralty Regulations.

N.B.—An infraction of rules 2 and 6 renders a commander liable to a penalty of 200 rupees, and an infraction of any of the other rules to a penalty of Rs. 100.

TELLICHERRY.

The port rules for Tellicherry are the same as those in force at Cannanore, except that rule 7 runs as follows:—

RULE 7.—All vessels in the roadstead of Tellicherry whether steam-ships or sailing vessels, shall, when at anchor between sunset and sunrise, exhibit at the starboard foreyard arm, but at a height not exceeding 20 feet above the hull, a white light in a globular lantern of eight inches in diameter and so constructed as to show a clear, uniform, and unbroken light visible all round the horizon, and at a distance of at least one mile.

CALICUT.

Rate of boat-hire at Calicut, Beypore.

1. Boats conveying 1 ton and under, laden or unladen—

	RS.	A.	P.
To all vessels under 3 fathoms	0	6	0
Do. in 3 and under 5 fathoms ..	0	14	0
Do. in 5 and under 7 fathoms ..	1	8	0

In and beyond 7 fathoms, the rate to be at the option of parties contracting.

For every quarter ton over one ton ..	One quarter of the above rates additional.
2. Transhipping trip and return trip ..	Half the above rates.
3. Trip between 6 P.M. and 5 A.M. in monsoon, and on Sundays and close holidays.	Double the above rates.
4. Detention alongside of vessels more than three hours.	Do. do.
5. With an awning	Four annas additional.

The port rules at Calicut are the same as at Cannanore, except that rules 5 and 7 run as follows:—

RULE 5.—The cargo boat rules published by Government, under date the 23rd April 1847, shall be in force at the port of Calicut.

RULE 7.—All vessels in the roadstead of Calicut, whether steam-ships or sailing vessels, shall, when at anchor between sunset and sunrise, exhibit at the starboard foreyard arm, but at a height not exceeding 20 feet above the hull, a white light in a globular lantern of eight inches in diameter and so constructed as to show a clear, uniform, and unbroken light visible all round the horizon, and at a distance of at least one mile.

BEYPORE.

The port rules for Beypore are similar to those in force at Cannanore,[1] except in regard to the following:—

RULE 2.—All vessels within the entrance of the backwater shall, if required by the conservator, rig in their jib and driver-booms, and strike their masts and yards.

RULE 3.—All vessels within the entrance of the backwater shall remove any anchor or spar, or other substance projecting from her side, if required to do so by the conservator.

RULE 5.—A free channel shall be kept for ships moving up and down the backwater, and also free passage to piers, jetties, landing places, wharves, quays, docks, and moorings, and all vessels shall be bound to remove, when required by the conservator, to clear such channels or passages.

RULE 7.—All vessels within the entrance of the backwater shall be moored or warped from place to place as required by the conservator, and no vessel shall cast of a warp that has been made fast to her to assist a vessel in mooring without being required to do so by the conservator or officer in charge of the vessel mooring.

RULE 10.—Every vessel, whether a steamer or a sailing vessel, when riding at anchor, shall exhibit, where it can best be seen, but at a height not exceeding 20 feet above the hull, a white light in a globular lantern of eight inches in diameter, and so constructed as to show a clear, uniform, and unbroken light visible all round the horizon, and at a distance of at least one mile.

N.B.—An infraction of any of the above rules renders a commander liable to a penalty of 100 rupees under Section 9 of Act XXII of 1855.

COCHIN.

Instructions to commanders of vessels entering the port of Cochin.

SIR,—I am desired by the Master Attendant, Administrative Department, at Madras, to request that you will, without delay, fill up the accompanying report and return it by the bearer, the hour of whose departure from your vessel should be noted on the report.

2. Your *immediate* and most particular attention is requested to the imperative necessity of your entering in the report herewith forwarded *the state of health* of your *crew and passengers*, and whether any *infectious and malignant or other disease* has appeared on board during the voyage. *In the event of any such sickness having occurred*, you are hereby ordered and directed to prevent all communication with other vessels in the roads or with the shore, until the Port and Marine Surgeon shall have duly reported such

[1] Rules 1, 4, 6, 8 and 9 are identical with rules 1, 2, 4, 5 and 6 respectively of those in force at Cannanore.

intercourse to be free from objection. If sickness has appeared and still prevails, you are required to hoist the flag R of the Commercial code by day, or two lighted lanterns one over the other at the fore by night. On either of these signals being hoisted, the commander or other person in charge of such vessel shall consider himself in quarantine. No dead bodies are to be thrown overboard in the roadstead.

NOTE.—No boats to be allowed alongside until the ensign is hoisted at some mast-head in token that the commander accepts the responsibility of the preceding caution.

3. Your attention is particularly directed to the following rules.

4. The best anchorage in the roads is with the following bearings:—

Flagstaff E. $\frac{1}{2}$ N. to E. N. E. in $5\frac{1}{2}$ to $6\frac{1}{2}$ fathoms, soft ground, about 2 to $2\frac{1}{2}$ miles off shore.

5. All post office packets and letters are to be delivered to the post office peon who is sent for them.

6. Commanders are requested to fill up and return the accompanying paper relative to the port light, and the Master Attendant, Administrative Department, at Madras, invites them to forward to him any observations they may wish to offer regarding this or any other light along the coast which they may have passed.

7. Commanders are required to report themselves in person on landing at the Master Attendant's office, and to bring with them the ship's register, with two lists of the officers, ship's company and passengers; and no vessel will be admitted to entry at the custom-house without producing a certificate from the Master Attendant that the provisions of this article have been complied with. In the case of certain vessels arriving in port to load part cargo for foreign ports, although the goods to be exported in them may be afloat, commanders must come on shore immediately after anchoring for the purpose of entering their vessels at the marine and customs offices, and if any of the export cargo afloat is taken on board before permission is obtained by signal from the flagstaff, they will be liable to a penalty of 1,000 rupees under Sections 61 and 136 of the Sea Customs Act of 1878.

8. Commanders are also required, previous to clearing out, to deliver to the Master Attendant two lists of the officers, crew, and passengers proceeding by the vessel, together with notification of all casualties which may have occurred during her stay in port, whether by death, discharge, or desertion. No vessel will be granted port clearance until the production of a certificate from the Master Attendant that the port rules have been complied with.

9. Commanders requiring a pilot to enter the inner harbour are to hoist the union jack at the foreroyal mast-head. Applications for pilots inwards and outwards are to be made to the Master Attendant in writing.

10. No cargo is to be landed in ship's boats under a penalty of 50 rupees and confiscation of the boat.

11. No ballast is to be thrown overboard in less than 9 fathoms; nor is any to be discharged on the beach, or elsewhere, from which it would be liable to be washed into the port. The penalty for infringing this rule is 500 rupees.

12. Commanders of vessels having more than 50 lb. of gunpowder or other combustibles on board are, under a penalty of 200 rupees for default,

to report the same to the conservator, who will arrange, if necessary, for landing and storing the excess.

13. When the surf is so high as to render communication with the shore dangerous, a red and white chequered flag will be hoisted at the Master Attendant's flagstaff. When the surf is impassable the first distinguishing pendant will be displayed under that flag.

14. Should a boat be urgently required during the night, three lights should be hoisted horizontally, and in case of danger from fire or other causes, blue lights should be burnt and guns fired.

15. No boats are to be detained alongside after 6 P.M. The detention of a boat during the day for more than three hours will entail double hire. Commanders and officers are particularly requested to abstain from ill-using boatmen or other natives. All complaints will be promptly inquired into.

16. In the event of boisterous weather having been experienced, commanders are requested to report the same to the Master Attendant for the information of the Marine Superintendent, forwarding, if likely to be useful copy of the log detailing the circumstances.

17. No vessel of 200 tons and upwards is to be moved in the inner harbour without having a pilot or the conservator on board; and no vessel exceeding 100 tons and less than 200 tons is to be moved without a pilot, except under the authority of the conservator, under penalty in each case of 100 rupees.

18. All vessels in the inner harbour shall have their jib and driver booms rigged in, and their yards and top masts struck, unless otherwise permitted by the conservator. All projections from the ship's side must be removed.

19. All vessels moored in the stream shall keep a clear hawse.

20. No vessel anchored between the buoys and inner harbour shall have lights exhibited aloft or above the deck.

21. No warps are to be made fast to the fairway buoys.

22. A free passage of half a cable's length or 120 yards shall be kept between the wharves, jetties, landing places, and dockyards, and the position of the vessels moored in the inner harbour.

23. The Madras Ports Acts can be seen at the Master Attendant's office, and copies of them can be had at six annas each.

24. Schedules of the boat-hire, pilot, and other charges of the port are hereto annexed.

NOTE.—Similar instructions to the above are sent to commanders of vessels entering the other ports of the district.

SCHEDULE A.

Boat-hire to the outer roads.

	RS.	A.	P.
Boats carrying 6 large pipes of oil, or 7 small pipes or 12 puncheons or 20 hogsheads.	2	8	0
Boats carrying 50 bales yarn or fibre, or 50 cases of coffee or 12 bales hides.	3	0	0
Boats carrying 100 bags rice, coffee, pepper, &c. ..	3	12	0

	RS.	A.	P.
Boats carrying 100 cwt. coir yarn in dholls or ballasts, or 100 cwt. coir rope.	3	8	0
One cargo boat measuring not less than 8 tons, carrying general cargo or ballast or passengers.	3	8	0
One cargo boat measuring less than 8 tons and above 3 tons carrying general cargo or ballast or passengers.	2	8	0
Return trip, loaded from same vessel—Half the above rates.			
Return trip, loaded from another vessel—Three-quarters of the above rates.			
Transhipping from one vessel to another	2	0	0
Ordinary trip, passenger or Quilon boat, to or from the roads.	1	8	0
Return trip, passenger or Quilon boat	0	12	0

Boats carrying more than the above quantities of specified cargo, to be paid proportionately for the excess.

Double the above rates in foul weather, in going to and from vessel in and beyond 7 fathoms and at night.

Boat-hire in the inner harbour.

	RS.	A.	P.
For 1 boat load of cargo to or from a vessel ..	1	0	0
Return trip from same vessel—Half the above rates.			
Do. another vessel—Three-quarters the above rates.			
Passenger or Quilon boat to or from a vessel ..	0	2	0

In cases of extraordinary service, as proceeding to a vessel beyond the limits of the port, or rendering aid to a vessel in distress, under circumstances of peril, &c., the Master Attendant shall adjudge to be paid such additional hire as the service may seem to warrant, reporting the same for the confirmation of the Collector.

Schedule B.

Pilot Charges.

I.—For every vessel of any burden exceeding 100 tons, but not exceeding 200 tons—

						Per foot. RS.	A.	P.
(*a.*)	Drawing	4	feet and over	3	feet of water ..	0	10	0
(*b.*)	Do.	5	do.	4	do. ..	0	11	0
(*c.*)	Do.	6	do.	5	do. ..	0	13	0
(*d.*)	Do.	7	do.	6	do. ..	0	15	0
(*e.*)	Do.	8	do.	7	do. ..	1	4	0
(*f.*)	Do.	9	do.	8	do. ..	1	9	0

	Per foot. RS. A. P.
(*g.*) Drawing 10 feet and over 9 feet of water ..	1 14 0
(*h.*) Do. 11 do. 10 do. ..	2 8 0
(*i.*) Do. 12 do. 11 do. ..	3 2 0
(*j.*) Do. 13 do. 12 do. ..	3 12 0

(The draft of water will be calculated upon a whole foot, *e.g.*, a vessel drawing 3½ feet will be charged at 4 feet or Rs. 2-8-0; and one drawing less than 3½ at 3 feet or Rs. 1-4-0.)

	RS.
II.—(*a.*) For every vessel whose burden exceeds 200 tons, but does not exceed 400 tons	30
(*b.*) For every vessel whose burden exceeds 400 tons, but does not exceed 600 tons	40
(*c.*) For every vessel whose burden exceeds 600 tons.	50

Schedule C.

	RS.	A.	P.
For the use of the anchor boat from 8 A.M. to sunset per diem	20	0	0
For the use of a hawser (besides making good any injury it may sustain per diem)	5	0	0
Transporting a vessel from one position to another after she has been moored, of 300 tons and upwards ..	7	0	0
Do. do. do. under 300 tons ..	3	8	0

Schedule D.

Scale of fees for measuring vessels.

The same as at Cannanore.

The port rules for Cochin are identical with those in force at Beypore, except that rule 8 runs as follows:—

Rule 8.—The cargo boat rules published by Government in G.O., No. 317, dated 16th December 1873, shall be in force at the port of Cochin.

NARAKAL.

Directions for vessels bound to the roads of Narakal.

1. The port of Narakal is situate about 5 miles to the north of Cochin, and its flagstaff is in latitude 10° 2′ N. and longitude 76° 13′ 36″ E.

2. Owing to a mud flat extending off the place, and breaking the force of the ocean swell, the usual sea existing in an open roadstead is barely felt in a depth of five fathoms; but under three fathoms the water is perfectly

smooth. A first-class red buoy is moored on the flat in 18 feet water and bears from the Narakal flagstaff W. by N. ½ N.

3. In consequence of the total absence of surf on the beach abreast, a free and easy communication with the shore can be maintained at all periods of the year, and in all weathers, by boats of every description.

4. Vessels intending to seek this anchorage during the south-west monsoon, or in bad weather, should take up a berth with the Narakal flagstaff bearing from E. b. S. to E. by S. ½ S.—the Cruz Milagre gap S.E. to S.E. ½ E. and the Cochin light-house, which is distinctly visible, S.E. ¾ S. to S.E. by S. distance off shore about 3 miles in 4 to 5 fathoms.

5. Cruz Milagre is a conspicuous opening formed in the belt of coconut trees which fringes the coast, and is clearly discernible from a ship's deck either when approaching from the northward, or from the offing abreast of Narakal. But coming from the southward, the gap is not open to view until abreast of it.

6. Close attention should be paid to the lead while approaching the flat, as from the extreme softness of the mud, the contact with the bottom is scarcely felt, and an error may lead vessels into shallow water.

7. Vessels unable to remain in the roads of Cochin from stress of weather, or bound to that port during the south-west monsoon, will find Narakal, a perfect safe anchorage, and can ride securely and communicate with Cochin either by land or backwater, in less than two hours.

8. Ships intending to leave the roads of Cochin for Narakal should steer a N. W. b. N. course until abreast of the place, and then run in for the anchorage according to the bearings given. In the event of the wind being scant, vessels should endeavour to leave Cochin during the ebb tide, as the flood is likely to sweep them in shore.

9. An ordinary light, visible about 8 miles, is exhibited from the flagstaff at Narakal during the prevalence of the south-west monsoon from the 10th May to the 30th September, which is a good guide to ships wishing to make for that anchorage during the night.

10. Boats intending to communicate from ships in the anchorage to the shore at Narakal in bad weather, should make direct for the flagstaff where they can safely be hauled up on the beach, which is free of surf to the extent of two miles; but should avoid going far to the north or south before making for the shore, as heavy breakers prevail in the outer surf line during the prevalence of a heavy monsoon.

11. Provisions and water can easily be obtained, and to vessels navigating this part of the western coast during the south-west monsoon, and receiving any damage or loss, Narakal affords a very desirable place of resort where such injuries can be remedied by the facilities which Cochin offers.

12. At the first burst of the monsoon, previous to which the surrounding sea is calm and quiet, there is always a sea prevailing in Narakal roads and on the shore; but after the lapse of about a week, when the surrounding sea is much disturbed by the violence of the weather, the waters at Narakal subside into their normal serenity which continues till the end of the year.

APPENDIX IX.

Port Rules, &c., of the minor ports.

In the exercise of the power conferred by Section 7 of the Indian Ports Act No. XII of 1875, the Governor of Fort St George in Council hereby prescribes the following port rules for each of the undermentioned ports * :—

Port rules.

RULE 1.—All vessels within the port shall be bound to take up such berths as may be appointed for them by the conservator, and shall change their berths or remove therefrom when required by such authority.

RULE 2.—All vessels within the entrance of the backwater shall, if required by the conservator, rig in their jib and driver-booms and strike their masts and yards.

RULE 3.—All vessels within the entrance of the backwater shall remove any anchors, spars or other things projecting from their sides if required to do so by the conservator.

RULE 4.—All vessels taking in or discharging ballast or cargo or any particular kind of cargo within the port shall, whilst so engaged, occupy such stations respectively as the conservator may from time to time direct.

RULE 5.—Free passages of such width as the conservator shall from time to time direct shall be kept for ships moving up and down the backwater and also along or near to the piers, jetties, landing places, wharves, quays, docks, and moorings in or adjoining the port.

RULE 6.—All vessels within the port shall anchor, moor, and unmoor as may from time to time be required by the conservator.

RULE 7.—All vessels within the entrance of the backwater shall be moved or warped from place to place in such manner as may from time to time be required by the conservator, and no vessel shall cast off a warp that has been made fast to her to assist a vessel in mooring without being required to do so by the conservator or the officer in charge of the vessel mooring.

RULE 8.—The cargo boat rules published by Government under date the 30th September 1867, as modified by notification of Government under the Ports Act XII of 1875 of this date, and, by Madras Act I of 1881, in ports to which that Act shall be extended, shall be in force at the said ports.

RULE 9.—No pitch or dammer shall be boiled nor shall any spirits be drawn off by candle or other artificial light on board any vessel within the limits of the port.

RULE 10.—Every vessel, whether a steamer or a sailing vessel, when riding at anchor, shall exhibit, where it can best be seen, but at a height not exceeding 20 feet above the hull, a white light, in a globular lantern of eight inches in diameter, and so constructed as to show a clear, uniform, and unbroken light, visible all round the horizon, at a distance of at least one mile.

* The minor ports mentioned at p. 80 of the text.

APPENDIX X.

Proverbs.

1. If you put anything inside, it will surely be known outside.
2. Inwardly malicious, but pious outwardly.

2. Literally, Dagger within, plaster without.

3. Call one passing afar and you lose one-eighth of a pice.
4. Want of ingenuity finds fault with any material.

4. Cf. "A bad workman quarrels with his tools."

5. The man on the opposite bank rolled the boat.

5. Alluding to false accusation.

6. Why starest thou at me for being duped by Akkara Māvilon?

6. A kūran or mouse-deer is caught in a trap laid by A. B̀ says to the deer "why starest," &c.

7. Why blamest thou thy mother for thy defeat in market?
8. How to dig out the root of Angillapongu (a rootless plant floating on water)?

8. Alluding to attempting impossibilities.

9. Why should you remove your shoes when water flows far off?
10. If the father be a *Mahout* (elephant-keeper), will the son also have a callosity on his hinder parts?
11. If there are five buffaloes to milk, the neighbourhood will come to know it. If you strain and drink the conjee (boiled rice with water) your breast will know it.
12. You can keep a betel-nut in your lap, but not a betel-nut tree.
13. The drum gets beaten, but the drummer gets the money.
14. Brothers should never get the length of blows.
15. Even an elephant will fall down if its foot slips.

16. Would you catch a leech and put it abed?

17. The roof, if broken, will fall inside: a bridge falls into the current.

18. If eyes are given to the leech no chatty can be hung up from the roof.

19. A miry pit suits a leech.

20. A god will be recognized only if clad accordingly.

21. Though I hurt my throat, I will not renounce my share.

22. "The best can do no more."

22. A squirrel does what it can.

23. No mirror is necessary to see one's brother's foot.

24. Short life for being overwise.

25. Covetousness will lead to unusual labour.

26. The thirteenth constellation, royal anger, bilious complaint, and paternal curse, cease not until they produce their effect.

27. Danger follows avarice.

28. If my food could give me good strength and God gives me a long life, you will see me in the battle-field called Mannattāl.

29. Spoken of a time-server.

29. Put oil to the sword that is used daily.

30. Applies to artisans and others who have to take their labour to the market daily.

30. Do not benight yourself with a piece of work that cannot be done in one day.

31. If love fails, right fails also.

32. A gift made with a good heart is nectar.

33. Will not you be satisfied with eating the bread? Why should you count the air-holes in it?

34. If you practice you can carry an elephant.

35. A door is a morsel (lit. *pappatam*) to him who devours a temple.

36. In practising, a good many arrows are lost and a good many cadjans used as *copy-books*.

36. He who has lost a great many arrows becomes a good archer: he who has spoiled a great many cadjans, a good writer.

37. A Dutchman's anchor ?

37. The arrow is at Kumbalath, the bow at Sekkalath, but the Nāyar who uses them has reached Pannangāt gateway.

38. If the mother is a harlot, the daughter is also one.

39. Mother in the ഉറി (net-work for suspending pots), sister below it, and the wife in mortar (rice-pounding).

40. If mother is beaten, father should enquire about it; and if sister is beaten, brother-in-law should enquire about it.

41. In allusion to a story wherein the "uncle" and the cow are put *in statu quo* by an umpire. Is repeated by a man when he stops a quarrel, &c.

41. Let uncle stand where he used to stand, and the cow where she used to stand.

42. If you take more than your share, the sky will fall down on your head.

43. She who leaves her husband, falling in love with a king, gets neither.

44. Is there war after the king is slain ?

45. Instant death results from the biting of a salamander.

46. It is said that the reptile forgets a thing ere its tail (while creeping) has reached where its head was.

46. Forgetfulness is with salamander.

47. Borrowed from the weaver; meaning, with reference to any difficulty, that there is as much of it as there is in disentangling half a pallam of yarn.

47. Difficulty of half a pallam weight of thread.

48. Half a pallam weight will waste away when any one goes by side of another.

49. The dog ate the rice and bit the carpenter woman, and yet it snarls.

50. A thousand crows will come if you throw rice.

51. If you (devour) subdue your anger, it will turn out nectar; but if you devour (fail to use?) your weapon, you will not keep up your manliness.

	52. One in infirmity cannot be ceremonious, nor can one in destitution make presents.
53. For the operation cannot improve the substance.	53. What has been ground should not be pounded.
54. Is the complaint of a patient who has to swallow, unassisted, what the doctors compound.	54. Many are there to grind, but there is only one to drink.
	55. Riches (are) ruin.
	56. A mean fellow becoming rich will cause an umbrella to be held up for him even at midnight.
	57. Do half yourself and leave the other half to Providence.
	58. Every clump of bushes is an elephant to an ignorant man.
	59. One need not explain to men of understanding, nor should one explain to men of ignorance.
	60. If you can give a thousand to be butchered, why cannot you give one to be reared?
61. Said of one in extreme agony.	61. Like a cock that struggles having its head cut off.
62. Said of one hard-worked.	62. Like a washerman's donkey.
	63. Do not speak to a distressed Pulayi woman about a jungle full of firewood.
	64. He is a bed or mattress to ten persons.
65. Said of a dying man.	65. If all the gods come, it can be managed.
	66. In the treatment of those who are not versed in Ashtanga Hridayam, turmeric is used as orris root and camphor as *Plumbago Ceylanica*.
67. Cf. "A worm will turn."	67. Even a rat-snake will bite if attacked in its hole.
	68. There will be no pulp in a jack-fruit that looks beautiful.
69. Deprecates overcrowding.	69. A plantain tree that grows in a cluster of several others will produce no bunch.
	70. Put on the chains and log as soon as you see that an elephant is *mast*.
	71. Will a goat know anything of the merchandise in a bazaar?

72. Dress supplies what merit lacks.

72. To the Chakkiyar who does not know how to dance, dress and ornaments are everything.

73. Like a jungle where goats are allowed to graze.

74. The proximity of kings was dreaded in former days.

74. Goats spoil a jungle just as a wandering king a country.

75. "Out of one's element."

75. How will an oil-monger behave if told off to weave?

76. Give an elephant rather than give rise to hopes.

77. The innermost part of a plantain tree that has brought out its bunch has a "heart" resembling ivory in colour, &c.

77. Are ivory and the heart of the plantain tree equal to each other?

78. The walking of an elephant and the running of a horse are equal.

79. "Hamlet, Prince of Denmark, without the part of Hamlet."

79. How can it be a procession if there is no elephant?

80. When a dog barks at an elephant-keeper on the back of his elephant, how much will he be frightened?

81. When elephants fight, the ants are crushed to death.

82. To an elephant a horse is only a footstool.

83. A palm-tree is sugar to an elephant.

84. An elephant needs no decoration.

84. Do not hang bells on the neck of an elephant.

85. Alludes to people prone to find fault with anything and everything.

85. One so careful that he looks to see if a worm has bitten a gold mohur.

86. Spoken of a stupid fellow.

86. None but senseless words will be uttered, though thousands of instructions are poured into the ear.

87. He holds a thousand gardens on rent, but has only oil-cakes to make curry with at night.

88. A man will be called only half a physician if he has made a thousand men blind.

89. One dose of arsenic is sufficient to kill a thousand crows.

90. Having borne it a thousand leagues, do not drag it half a league.

91. Better to see one sovereign than a thousand ministers.

92. A thousand proverbs are not injurious to life, but a thousand curses are.

93. He who pretended to possess a thousand senses, has now a rock on his breast; and the other who pretended to possess a hundred, is strung on the rib of a cocoanut leaf; but I who am said to possess only one sense may now leap off free.

93. Not quite clear, but is probably spoken by a tiny fish, and has reference to its own escape through the meshes of the net, while the turtle is caught and placed on its back with a stone upon it and the larger fish are strung on an "īkkil."

94. A thousand words have not the weight of half a pallam (one quarter pound).

95. If grown there will be a thousand coconuts (tengnga), otherwise the loss is but a thousand shells (tongna).

95. The words of a person about to plant a thousand nuts.

96. However fondly you may bring up a stranger, he will ever remain a stranger.

97. The Vāriyan is blamed for another's fault.

97. Is commonly repeated when one is blamed for another's fault.

98. You may a thousand times kiss another's child, but not once slap it.

99. Better (more serviceable) our own gums than the teeth of other people.

100. If there is nobody else, then give me a Paṭṭar. If there is nothing else to eat, then give me *Tāl* (edible plant).

100. A Paṭṭar (foreign Brahman) gets a Nāyar girl when no one else will have her. Tāl is eaten only when nothing else is procurable.

101. A hundred languages in half a dozen districts.

102. Even if you spill it in a stream, it should be measured.

102. Teaches the importance of accounts.

103. Like Ali's going to Nágapuram.

103. In allusion to a stupid errand-boy who, as soon as he was told he must run an errand to a certain place, went thither without waiting to receive the message and returned.

104. If you drink milk at the cattle-pen you will not have butter-milk at home.

	105. You should not strike a cow on its muzzle when it is coming to the pen.
106. "When you are at Rome do as the Romans do."	106. When one flying-fox visits another, the one takes one branch, the other another.
	107. The result of your deeds during the prime of your life will be seen at the time of your death.
	108. Avaricious men will fall into great danger.
109. In Malabar a carpenter begins life by making cocoanut-shell spoons; in old age he earns a scanty livelihood by making the same description of useful articles.	109. Drudgery at the beginning of life and the end, like (the career of) a carpenter.
110. "Necessity knows no law."	110. When necessity compels, a temple is a mere compound.
111. Precious stones are not unfrequently valued according to the worth of the wearer.	111. The worth of the gem depends on the worth of the man who wears it.
112. "If you want a thing done, do it yourself."	112. Better go yourself than send many.
	113. What the root is to a tree, such is help to a man (who needs it).
	114. A long pole for a deep pit.
115. "Grasp your nettle."	115. There is no chilliness if you plunge deep (into water).
116. "Distance lends enchantment to the view."	116. When seen from this side, the opposite side looks green.
	117. "Itala" (a fast-burning wood) is not suitable for cremation: nor is a Sudra (for the purpose now in hand).
	118. Like a snake that heard thunder.
	119. Like a tree struck down by lightning.
	120. Do not associate with one that has no friend.
	121. If you associate with one that has no friend, you will lose all your nine friends and at last yourself.
	122. Children brought up by a beggar will not leave off mendicancy.

123. Fit for no work.

123. Like a snake that has devoured its prey.

124. Probably in allusion to constant calls the maid has to attend to.

124. Like the door of a room in which a maid-servant sleeps.

125. Do not stretch out your legs before you are seated.

126. The would-be donor is certainly liberal.

126. When the rock at Iringath becomes gold, half of it will be given to Dēvar.

127. Improvements should never begin at the wrong end.

127. Do not thatch your gate-house till after you have thatched your dwelling.

128. Spoken of things that have found their way to people's hands and never will return.

128. Will (red-hot) iron belch the water it has drunk?

129. A grave wrong is not counteracted by a slight act of the opposite kind.

129. If you swallow an iron bar, will drinking ginger-water enable you to digest it?

130. The horse knows the taste of iron and the elephant the weight of a chain.

131. Iron and skill will go bad if not used.

132. Falling between two stools.

132. If you put your feet in two boats you will find yourself in the middle (of the stream).

133. If you cut down a tree on which you are seated, the tree will come uppermost and you undermost.

134. An idle fellow will not know what appetite is, but he will who digs hard.

135. Probably meaning that when there is a greater man present, a lesser one should not make much ado.

135. When flesh is present, the feathers should not struggle.

136. The man who went for meat died of shivering (having been benighted in the jungle), and the man who sent for it died of greediness.

137. Meat is eaten, but the horns are not strung up and hung around the neck.

138. If there is want in the Brahman's house, you need not expect to find anything in the King's palace.

	139. He that can be useful at home, will not go abroad as a serving man.
	140. A man with plenty at home finds plenty abroad.
141. The birth of a daughter is to a Brahman the beginning of anxiety and expense.	141. Why do you look like a Brahman to whom a daughter has been born?
	142. Homeward a man will carry even seventy-five (measures) [an extraordinarily heavy load].
143. An emaciated child certainly does not indicate plenty at home.	143. The circumstances of the family can be guessed from the child's hip.
144. Has access to all parts of the house (?)	144. Like the cat in a Brahman's house.
	145. *Āmāta* (superfine gold) is to the poor the same as common gold.
	146. A wife, if not liked, is found fault with in whatever she does.
	147. Money is a hatchet for severing friendship.
	148. Do not plant (a tree) head downwards.
	149. A young deer does not know the jungle tracks; an old deer is not strong enough to run.
150. Making a deal of noise (with the feet).	150. Like a dog on a heap of cockle-shells.
	151. Like a monkey who has got a lump of bread.
152. Both are apt to take advantage and worry you.	152. Do not show your sore to a fly nor your toothless gums to a child.
153. Some mishap (to an enemy) in the nick of time.	153. Sore-mouth to crows when dates ripen.
	154. Is a louse to be the wages for removing a nit?
	155. What the miser Māyan had acquired, the prodigal Māyan consumed.
	156. She that went to act as a midwife brought forth twins.
157. The reason is not known; possibly because intercourse with the island was forbidden to Brahmans, or because the trip thither was attended with danger.	157. The Brahman who sees Ceylon will never see his home again.

	158. Is that stump of the stalk for me and the coconut for Mullappalli (a Nambūtiri)?
159. For fear of hurting himself (?)	159. Will a man who has a sore on his hip pass through a narrow stile?
	160. How can a man who has no clothes to wear, use a clothes line?
	161. A child that has eaten well will jump and play about, but a child that has not, will play seated in one place.
	162. We should not put pebbles in rice left over after meals.
	163. A man who has taken his meals will not know the hunger of a man who has not taken it.
	164. The man who has taken his meals wants a mat; but the man who has not done so wants a plantain leaf (off which to eat).
	165. You should not wish to make an attachment (distraint) in a house where you have lived as a boarder.
166. *Vide* 143.	166. The appearance of a child tells the distress prevailing.
	167. No presents at meals and no ceremonies in sleep.
	168. If destitute of any other things, take rice made of seed paddy, and if no clothing, wear silk.
169. As their "luck" so the crops.	169. The good luck of the people who are to eat, can be seen at the place ploughed.
	170. If you are industrious you can have your dinner.
171. Real merit alone will retain its place.	171. If you force anything up it will slide down of itself.
	172. Better to be drowned in a well with a stone hung on our neck, than to be mounting both ends of a pestle (rice-pounder) for which there is no use (rice to be pounded).
	173. Nothing salted will be more saltish than salt.
	174. If any one eat salt, he will drink water.

	175. If salt is saltish, then the Māpp̣illa (shopkeeper) will cheat.
176. Underwent hardship in a useless occupation.	176. He was exposed to smoke while pounding paddy husks.
177. *I.e.*, You must allow for wastage. *Tuḍi* and *ural* are alike in shape, but the latter is several times larger than the former.	177. A small drum (*tuḍi*) will be formed of it even if you make it as large as a mortar (*ural*).
	178. One must expect to get blows if seated at the foot of a mortar.
179. The former is operated upon on one side only, while the latter is beaten on both sides (at least in Malabar).	179. A mortar (for pounding rice) complains to a finger-drum.
180. See 177.	180. Being cut for a pestle, turned out a short stick.
	181. Even an *uṛi* (a network for suspending household pots) will laugh if the truth is spoken.
	182. A poor man's iron bar is required for stealing a rich man's gold.
	183. If you jump up without knowing your strength, you are sure to break your hip.
184. The former hastens to the feast. The pig, frightened at the sound of the "horn," runs for its life.	184. A Paṭṭar (foreign Brahman) who has heard of a rice choultry and a pig that has heard of a chase (runs equally fast).
	185. In eating and bathing be first, and in war, umbrella, and mud, take the middle.

APPENDIX XI.

Vocabulary of the language--Mahl—spoken in the Island of Minicoy. Taken down from Āli Mālikhān, Āmīn (Headman) of the Island.

English.	Mahl.
Man	Piriheṇu.
Woman	Aṃgaheṇu.
Child	Kudi.
Boy	Piriheṇ Kudi.
Girl	Aṃgaheṇ Kudi.
Young	Kuṭa.
Old	Bōḍu.
Husband	Phirimihā.
Wife	Abimihā.
Son	Piriheṇ Darivu.
Daughter	Aṃgaheṇ Darivu.
Marriage	Kāvini Kuṛam.
House	Ge Gōti.
Room	*No word.*
Door	Dōṛu.
Window	Kudi Dōṛu.
Roof	Timi.
Earth	Binmatti Bimkā.
Sky	Uḍu.
Fire	Aliphāng.
Water	Phēng.
Air	Vē Maḍu.
Wind	Vē Gada.
Cloud	Vilā.
Sun	Iru.
Moon	Hadu.
Star	Taṛi.
Rain	Pār.
Light	Havali.
Darkness	Antiri.
Morning	Hentuṇu.
Noon	Menturugam.
Evening	Havīṛu.
Day	Duvālu.
Night	Rēgam.
Week	*No word.*
Month	Mastuvass.
Year	Ahari.
Sunday	Āditta.
Monday	Ōmā.
Tuesday	Aṃgārā.
Wednesday ..	Budā.
Thursday	Buraswati.
Friday	Hukkuru.
Saturday	Oṇihiru.
One	Ĕkkē.
Two	Dē.
Three	Tinē.
Four	Hattaṛi.
Five	Pahē.
Six	Hayē.
Seven	Hatti.
Eight	Aṛēg.
Nine	Nuvē.
Ten	Dihē.
Eleven	Egārā Ekluss.
Twelve	Doḷōss.
Thirteen	Doḷōss ēkkē.
Fourteen	Doḷōss Dē.
Fifteen	Doḷōss Tinē.
Sixteen	Doḷōss Hattaṛi.
Seventeen	Doḷōss Pahē.
Eighteen	Doḷōss Hayē.
Nineteen	Doḷōss Hatti.
Twenty	Doḷōss Aṛēg.
Twenty-one ..	Doḷōss Nuvē.
Twenty-two ..	Doḷōss Dihē.
Twenty-three ..	Doḷōss Eklus.
Twenty-four ..	Phasihi.
Twenty-five ..	Phasihi Ĕkkē.
Twenty-six ..	Phasihi Dē and so on.
Thirty-six	Tintōḷōss.
Thirty-seven ..	Tintōḷōss Ĕkkē an so on.
Forty-eight ..	Phaṇass.
Sixty	Phattoḷōss.
Seventy-two ..	Phāhitti.
Eighty-four ..	Haidoḷōss.
Ninety-six ..	Hiyā.
One hundred ..	Hiyā Hattaṛi, s Satts kā.

English.	Mahl.
One hundred and one.	Sattikā ēkkē.
Two hundred ..	Dwi Satta.
Three hundred ..	Tin Sattikā.
Four hundred ..	Hattaṛi Sattikā and so on.
One thousand ..	Hā Hē.
Ten thousand ..	Dihāss.
One hundred thousand.	Sattika Hāss.
Quarter	Kāl.
Half	Bē.
Three-quarters ..	Mukkāl.
East	Iṛumatti.
West	Oḷakumatti.
North	Utturu.
South	Dekkunu.
Hair	Ittaṛi.
Head	Bö.
Eye	Lō.
Nose	Nēphai.
Mouth	Aṃkā.
Tooth	Dai.
Face	Mūṇu.
Neck	Kharu, Khanturā.
Ear	Kampai.
Arm	Ai.
Hand	*No word.*
Belly	Baḍu.
Leg	Phē.
Foot	Daphē.
Finger	Iṃgili, Atu-iṃgili.
Toe	Phē-iṃgili.
Skin	Haṃg.
Heat	Hūṇu.
Hot	Hūṇuvē.
Cold	Iha.
Thunder	Guguṛi.
Lightning	Vidum.
Tree	Gass.
Dog	Pirihēṇ Laṭi.
Bitch	Aṃgahēṇ Laṭi.
Cat	Bulō.
Bull	Pirihēṇ Gēri.
Cow	Aṃgahēṇ Gēri.
Rat	Mīdau.
Fish	Mass.
Flesh	Mass.
Sea	Khaḍu.
Ship	Ṇau.
Boat	Baṛkāss.
God	Khalāṃki, Dēvatāṃki.
Idol	Bhuddhu.
Mosque	Missakkuyi (? Mosque).
Father	Baphu.
Mother	Ama.
Island	*No word.*[1]
Leper	Bōḍu Bali.
Far	Duṛu.
Near	Gāhi.
New	Au.
Sick	Bali Nukaṛē.
Fever	Hum Hattavē.
Small-pox	Khaṛi Vadili.
Cholera	Hoḍē Baḍē lāgatti.
Love	Lobīvē.
Fear	Biṛu Gaṇi.
Anger	Ṛuḷi Hatuvē.
Friend	Ṛahu Mattiri.
Foe	Jussman.
Good	Hēvu.
Bad	Nubē.
Black	Khaḷu.
White	Dōm.
Red	Ṛēyi.
Blue	Nu.
Yellow	Ṛīntu.
Green	*No word.*
Dry	Hikki.
Milk	Kiṛu.
Rice (boiled) ..	Bai.
Blood	Lē.
Cloth	Pheli.
Iron	Dagaḍu.
Silver	Ṛihi.
Gold	Ṛain.
Copper	Lō.
Brass	Hudulō.
Lead	Timaṛā.
Tin	Tuttiyā.
To walk	Higaṇi.
To do	Kuṛaṇi.
To sit	Ittaṇi.
To see	Phēṇē.
To hear	Ivē.

[1] They use the word for "country"—"rahrum."

English.	Mahl.
To smell	Vassduvē
Lie (down)	Ottaṇi.
Speak	Vāhakadakkaṇi.
Ask	Ahaṇi.
Dig	Koṇṇaṇi.
Plough (to)	*No word.*
Plough (noun)	*Do.*
Horse	Ass.
Eat	Khaṇi.
Beat (strike)	Thaḷaṇi.
Kill	Maṛaṇi.
Bury	Vaḷulaṇi.
To call	Bāṇikā.
To cook	Bai Kakkaṇi.
To cut	Khaṭaṇi.
To stab	Thoṛu Phēli.
Salt	Lōṇu.
Chilly	Oṇu.
Mustard	*No word.*
Oil	Thēvu.
Butter	Veṇṇē.
Mat	Kuṇan.
Pillow	Khaṇṇi.
Doubt	Uṛappanai.
Certainty	Uṛapp.
Path	Magu (S. Mārga).
Hedge	Phuḷa.
Paper	Khaṛudass.
To write	Liyāṇi.
Read	Hiyāṇi.
Right	Thēdu.
Wrong	Hamaṇuvi.
Owner	Oṇi.
Property	Mutal.
Money	Ṛuppiyā.
Right	Kaṇāyi.
Left	Vāyi.
Front	Kuṛimatti.
Back	Phuṛagass.
Above	Mati.
Below	Tiri.
Grass	Hūyi.
Stone	Gau.
Sand	Dōmvēli.
Sin	Phāp.
Large	Bōḍu.
Small	Kuṭa.
Fowl	Kukkuḷu.
Egg	Biss.
Lamp	Vvō.
Cot (bedstead)	Entu.
Pot	Ṗhuphē.
Spade	Hutali.
Axe	Phuṛu.
Chisel	Vaṭankari.
Knife	Kuṛaphai.
Needle	Thinōss.
Cap	Thākhiya.
Shoe	Phevaṃg.
Sail (of a ship)	Ṛiyan.
Tail	Phintu.
Box	Phōṛi.
Gun	Baḍi.
Gunpowder	Baḍi Bēss.
Bullet	Bōḍu Uṇṭa.
Shot	Kudi Uṇṭa.
Net	Dau.
Hook (fishing)	Buḷi.
Deep	Phum.
Long	Digu.
Short	Kuṛu.
Broad	Phuḷau.
High	Ussmiṃg.
Narrow	Phuḷaumi, Haṇivi.
You	Tha Khalīg.
I	Aphuṛiṃg Ma.
We	Aphuṛimiṃg.
He	Eyi.
She	Eyā.
They	Eyimiṃg.
That	Eyuti.
This	Miyuti.
Yours	Thagē.
Mine	Aphuṛiṃg Ma.
His	Eyi.
Hers	Eyā.
Their	Eyiṃimg.
Whose	Khāgi.
When	Kōṃg Ṛegu.
Where	Kontāka.
Why	Kēvu Gantē.
Which	Kōṇch.
Me	Ma.
Him	Esōṛu.
Her	Egoyyā.
Them	Eyimiṃg.
You (objective)	Thā.
Complainant	Saṛiyai Kuṛāmiyā.

English.	Mahl.
Defendant ..	.. Prati.
Witness ..	.. Sākshi.
Document ..	.. Ādāram.
Trial ..	.. Sariyai Kuṛaṇi.
Decision ..	.. Vidhi.
Fine ..	.. Phēsā.
Imprisonment	.. Taṭavu.
Medicine ..	.. Bēss.
Physician ..	.. Bēss Kuṛāmiyā.
Dish ..	.. Thaṛhi.
Copper vessel	.. Lō.
Wooden vessel	.. Tharagi.
Chair ..	.. Adaṛāda Gōnṭi.
Spoon ..	.. Samusā.
Ink-bottle ..	.. Davādu.
Price ..	.. Agu.
Body ..	.. Harigaṃg.
To sleep ..	.. Nidaṇi.
To drink ..	.. Bōṇi.
To bathe ..	.. Eṛaṇi.
To steal ..	.. Vakkan Kuṛaṇi.
Tank ..	.. Vaḷu.
Well ..	.. Phempuvaḷu.
River ..	.. Koru.
To laugh ..	.. Hīgōṇi.
To cry ..	.. Ṛōṇi.
Pain ..	.. Thadu.
Pleasure ..	.. Ohā.
Sorrow ..	.. Hittadu.
I speak ..	.. Aphuṛiṃg Buṇaṇi; Ma Buṇaṇi.
You speak	.. Khalīg Buṇaṇi.
He speaks ..	.. Ēyi Buṇaṇi; Esōṛu Buṇaṇi.
They speak	.. Eyimiṃg Buṇaṇi.
I do ..	.. Aphuṛiṃg Kuṛaṇi Ma Kuṛaṇi.
You do ..	.. Khalīg Kuṛaṇi.
He does ..	.. Eyi Kuṛaṇi; Esōṛu Kuṛaṇi.
They do ..	.. Eyimiṃg Kuraṇi.
I go ..	.. Aphuṛiṃg Higādaṇi Ma Higādaṇi.
He goes ..	.. Eyi Higādaṇi; Esōṛu Higādaṇi.

English.	Mahl.
You go ..	.. Khalīg Higādaṇi.
They go ..	.. Eyimiṃg Higādaṇi.
I see ..	.. Aphuṛiṇa Phēṇē; Ma Phēṇē.
He sees ..	.. Esōṛu Phēṇē.
You see ..	.. Khalīgayā Phēṇē.
They see ..	.. Eyimiṃg Phēṇē.
Eye-brow ..	.. Bumā.
Moustache ..	.. Mattimass.
Beard ..	.. Tumpuḷi.
Tears ..	.. Lōlu Phāṃg.
Nails ..	.. Nīvati.
Ring ..	.. Mudi.
Lip ..	.. Tumpai.
Tobacco ..	.. Dumpai.
Snuff ..	.. Vāhi.
Betel-leaf ..	.. Bilēyi.
Areca-nut ..	.. Phuvā.
Coat ..	.. Libass.
Stick ..	.. Asā.
Sugar ..	.. Ussakkuṛu.
Honey ..	.. Māmuyi.
Sea-beach ..	.. Attiri.
Plantain ..	.. Khēvu.
Emergent ..	.. Vōhē Avākka.
Book ..	.. Phoyi.
Koran ..	.. Tiriss.[1]
School ..	.. Kiyavāggē.
Teacher ..	.. Kiyavādē Mīha.
Student ..	.. Kiyavā Kudī.
Dream ..	.. Huva Phiṃg.
Firewood ..	.. Daṛu.
Who are you? ..	Tha Sibahāri Kākutē.
What is your name?	Khalīk Namakki Kēkati.
What is your age?	Kitaṃg Ahaṛu Vejjatē.
When did you leave your country?	Ṛaṛum Phuṛi Kōntu vāhā Kutē.
I left my country on last Friday.	Diyā Hukkuṛu Duvāhu Ṛaṛum Phuṛi.
How do you know that?	Thaṛāg Enguni Kīna Kuntē.

[1] The Hindustani word (corrupted) for 30, because in the big copy of the Koran it is written on 30 ജുസ് (*jūs*) of 12 leaves (പൈഗം—*pheigam*) each, or 360 leaves in all. A *jūs* does not take heed of where the Sūras begin and end. The Islanders are without exception Muhammadans.

English.	Mahl.	English.	Mahl.
I came in an Odam.	Ma Oḍiyaggē Ayi.	Bring that goat ..	Oyō Bakkaṛi Giṇṇa-haṛi.
How long were you at sea?	Khaḍugē Gīnadu-vass Viyāṇg.	Shut my box ..	Aphuṛiṃg Phoṛi Thaḷu Lahāṛi.
Where did you land?	Hontākattē Phēbi.	Send this to him ..	Mi Geṃkuss Dēhērē.
What things have you brought?	Khalīk Kōnch Ginai.	Ask him what he wants.	Thaṛa Kōnchaṃgahe Bēṇumi Ēha Ba-lahaṛi.
I have brought (1) coir, (2) cocoanuts, (3) cowries, (4) tortoise-shell, and (5) jaggery.	Ma (1) Rōṇu, (2) Kāhaṛi, (3) Boli, (4) Kāmpuphai, (5) Hakkuṛu, Ma-giṇai.	He says he has a "*Sankadam*" (grievance).	Essuṛā Saṃkaṭam Ebūtti.
Was there any sickness in your country when you left it?	Tha Ṛaṛum Phuṛ Iṛuge Balimaḍu Khami Uḷaiaṃg.	I have no time to-day; come to-morrow or the day after it.	Mihintakku Nuphe-ṇeveṇe Māta Mak-ku Nu Enadupa-hu Āṇantahare.
What do you wish to buy here?	Mitaṇu Thaṛaphi Tugē Oti Kōnch Gaṇanti.	Can you climb that tree?	Khalīg Yēg Egāhia Aṛam Kēṛeṇahē.
		He fell down ..	Esuṛu Gāhum Veṭij.
		He got a wound ..	Esuṛu Aibuṛivejji.
Are your accounts ready?	Khalīg Khaṇakku Gaṇass Obiyya.	He is a fool ..	Esuṛu Muyāki.
		No, he is very clever	Ṇu-Esuṛu Ṛaṃkuḷu Gulākki.
How many peons have you got? ..	Khalīg Gātuge Kitā Siphai Ebāṛutē.	Yes, you speak truth.	Khalīg Thēdu Bu-ṇaṇi.
Who draws toddy in your country?	Khalīg Ṛaṛugē Ṛā Ṇagaṇi Kōmpētti.	Where do you live?	Khalīg Kontāku Thē Uḷuṇi.
When do you go back?	Kalīg Kōm Iṛakuntē Higādaṇi.	In a shop ..	Phiyāṛāgeyā.
I want a barber ..	Aphuṛiṇa Bobālā Mihē Beṇumē.	I remember it ..	Maṛā Hautaṃg Obōyi.
Can he shave? ..	Tha Bobālā Daṇehē.	I will see you next year.	Nagā Ahaṛu Khalīgē Maphiṇṇāṇi.
Look at me ..	Magāyi Balahaṛe.		
Run after him ..	Maphahattuga Āna Haṛe.		

APPENDIX XII.

COLLECTION OF DEEDS.

No. 1.

a. Hail! Ṣri—The King who has taken the supreme rule, King (Perumāl (Sri Bhāskara Ravi Varman, wielding the sceptre and ruling for many 100,000 years, in his time, in the thirty-sixth year against[1] the second cycle (literally, year), on the day when he was pleased to sit in Muyirikodu, he was pleased to grant this favor.

[*N.B.*—The Jewish translation, particularly incorrect in the rendering of this sentence, deserves, perhaps, to be listened to in its translation of Muyirikodu "residing in Kranganūr or Kodungalūr." Perhaps the Musiris of the ancients is to be sought so far south. The calculation of the thirty-sixth year against the second cycle, which Mr. Whish has attempted, guided by the authority of other documents of considerable age, I am not prepared to criticize, as I am doubtful of the signification of "*Etir*" against (before?).]

b. We have given to Joseph Rabban (the principality) Anjuvaṇṇam, along with the 72 Janmi[2] rights, such as (going) with elephants and (other) conveyances, tribute from subordinate landholders, and the possession (or revenue) of Anjuvaṇṇam, the light by day, the spreading cloth, the litter, the umbrella, the Vaḍuca drum (Jews' transl.: "drum beaten with two sticks"), the trumpet, the gateway with seats, ornamental arches, and similar awnings and garlands (charawu, *i.e.*, T. சாவை) and the rest.

[*N.B.*—Here the name of Anjuvaṇṇam has been mistaken by the Jewish and other translators. The Jews translate it "five colours," and the revenue of Anjuvaṇṇam is converted by them into a right to convert from the five castes. But the language of the document forbids to take "*anju*" for the numeral 5: it would have been "*aintu*" as in the later document, II*a*.[3] The present translation of *vīḍu pēru*, generally mistaken for a gift of houses, or even for a gift to 72 families is fully secured by document II[3] in several places; *vīḍu* (*cf. II, k*[3]) is the verbal noun of *viḍu*, "to leave," signifies "remittance, freedom," hence in ancient T. synonymous with *S. mocsha*; the derived meaning is "freehold, Janmam," hence the modern signification "gardens house." Some of the privileges are not quite determined;

---

[1] Compare a similar use of the word "*Etir*" in Deed No. 4. "The date of this deed cannot be later than the eighth century A.D." Nor can the deed be "older than the beginning of the eighth century." Burnell *in Ind. Ant. III*, 334: "Probably not later than the ninth century A.D., nor earlier than the seventh." Caldwell, *Grammar of Dravidian Languages, Introdn.*; 89, *Edn.* 1875, "About 750." *Burnell, South Indian Palæography*, 2*nd Edn.* 140.

[2] See the note which follows: the word used is *Vīḍupēṛ*.

[3] No. 3 in this collection.

pācudam (T. tribute) is, in the Jewish translation, the right of calling from the corners of the street that low castes may retire. After "umbrella" the Jews have inserted a word of which they do not know the meaning.]

c. We have remitted to him the tribute to the Supreme Government (literally, the world-bearing-hire of II[1] *l.*).

[*N.B.*—The Jews translate literally, but ungrammatically, "and the revenue of the land and balances their hires he remitted."]

And we have enacted with this copper-deed that when the other town inhabitants pay taxes to the (Perumāl's) palace, he shall not have to pay; when they receive, he shall also receive.

[*N.B.*—Nothing of the Jewish version can here be of any use; they are quite misled by the word *Cōyil*, which they take for synagogues, and hence conclude the sense to be this: "and he shall be chief to the rest of the cities in which there are synagogues and Jewish inhabitants," without any attention to the structure of the sentence. But the sentence is difficult on account of the (antiquated) double *aru*, which I take for "time, term;" of Beschi's அறுவரி "tax paid at fixed times;" and the derivative *āru*, used in Malayāḷam and Canarese for "*when*." From a comparison of this and the first[2] document, it appears that the residence of the Jewish and Christian chieftains was not in the little principality given to them, but that they remained in the metropolis as the seat of commerce. The Jewish translation may give confirmation to the tradition that there were Jews and synagogues in many cities, and that naturally enough their naturalized Emir had jurisdiction over the whole nation, which he represented in the system of Government then established.]

d. (Given) to Joseph Rabban, the owner of Anjuvaṇṇam, and to his posterity, sons and daughters, nephews and sons-in-law—a hereditary appendage for the time that earth and moon exist—Anjuvaṇṇam, a hereditary appendage. Sri.

[*N.B.*—*Pracriti* "what is natural, essential to." I take it for synonymous with *janmam*, which also first signifies "birth," then in Malayaḷām "hereditary property." Different is the use of *pracriti* in II*a.* The Jews translate it here with "standing."]

e. Thus do I know Gōvardhana Mārttāndan, owner of Vēṇāḍu (or Travancore). Thus do I know Kotei Sri Candan, owner of the Vēnavāli province (perhaps Bembali, wherein now Cottayam. May it not be the older name of Odunādu, I[2].)

[*N.B.*—These are the two southern vassals.]

f. Thus do I know, Māna Vēpala Māna Vīyan, owner of Erāla province (the name of the Tamutiri, changed by the Jewish version, according to the current tradition, into Māna Vicrama, *vulgo* Māna Vikkiran), thus do I know Rāyaran Chāttan, owner of Valluwa province.

[*N.B.*—These are the two northern vassals, as[3] I.]

g. Thus do I know, Cotei Ravi, owner of Neḍumpureiyūr district (Jewish version corrupted by the writers, but the tradition that this is the Palacāḍu Rāja seems correct. Neḍumpureiyūr is an old temple on the Pālghatcheri road, from which Mr. Whish obtained some inscriptions).

---

[1] Deed No. 3, Clause (*l*).

[2] No. 2 in this collection.

[3] No. 3 in this collection.

Thus do I know Mūrkhan Chāttan, commanding the Eastern Army. The Jews take Kīḷpadei for a proper name. It seems these two are the great eastern vassals on the road which leads through the Coimbatoor gap to the old fields of battle between the Pāndi, Chōla and Chēra princes. I conclude from Document[1] I, that in a later period the Chēra country, properly speaking, had been taken from the Chēramāns).

[According to Ellis it was divided among the great vassals as early as A.D. 389, and finally, though at what period is uncertain, was reduced to a province of the Pāndyan government. (Trans. Madras Lit. Society, p. 19.)]

h. Candan of Great Taleicheri Kil-way ("under-mouth," eastern commander or viceroy, *i.e.*, dhalawa, "army-mouth" or general); the mountain-splitter. The writing of Kēlappa.

[*N.B.*—It is open to question whether these persons are two or three. The Jewish version has only the first and the last, leaving out the middle altogether. If Kil-way be the name of a place, we must render "the writing of Kil-way Kelappan, the mountain-splitter," and the latter appellation may be taken for a title given to the writer because he deals in metals (compare the grand-goldsmith of the I[1] document). But as Buchanan says the Jews find in the names of the subscribing Rājas the Colattiri and the Curumbenāḍu rulers, we may find it possible to recognize in the Candan of Taleicheri a family member or vassal of Colattiri, who with this sea-town recognized the rule of the Perumāl, and in the mountain-splitter the chieftain of the Curumbar or jungle-dwellers, so called either from his mines at Tamracheri or from a pass he opened through the ghats. It does not seem that in the time of these three documents the northern Malabar or Colatirri did belong to the Perumāls; for if it did, its Rājas would certainly have obtained as high and conspicuous a place in the line of witnesses as their relations of Venadu, to whom in old times they appear certainly superior. They recognized[2] perhaps a Tulu or Maisūr dynasty as supreme lords.]

["Perimpadappu, who is now the Rāja of Cochin, is here not mentioned, because (the Perumāl) made him his heir and successor." There is certainly some truth in this remark, from what is said[1] I, about the name Vira Kēraḷa, now the standing appellation which the Perimpadappu assumes on his accession to the throne].

Note.—This translation of the Cochin Jews' deed was published by Dr. Gundert in the *Madras Journal Lit. Sc., XIII, Part I*, p. 137. Other translations by Ellis and Burnell are to be found in *Madras J. L. S. XIII, II*, and *Ind. Ant. III*, 34; also by K. Kēḷu Nāyar in *M.J., L.S., N.S., V.* 42.

No. 2.

Hari Ṣrī. Adoration to Gaṇapati.

The blessed rule having devolved from the earth-ruler Man-lord Chacravarti Vīra Kēraḷa[3] (the first of the line), through regular succession, upon Sri Vīra Rāghava Chacravarti, now wielding the sceptre for many 100,000

[1] No. 2 in this collection.

[2] It is suggested in the text that *Kēraḷam* was at this time more or less under the Western Chalukya kings and that the northern Kōlattiri family had not at this time been founded.

[3] This is, so far as known, the earliest instance of the use, *within Malabar itself*, of this dialectic (Canarese) form of the ancient name, *Chēra*, of the country.

years, (in the year) Jupiter[1] in Capricornus, the 21st of[1] the Mīna month, Saturday, Rōhaṇi[1] asterism, the following grant was made in the royal palace (of the Perumāl). We have given to Iravi Corttan of Mahōdēver-pattṇam [henceforth to be called Grand Merchant of the Chēramān world (Kēraḷa)], the lordship of Maṇigrāmam. We also have given to him (the right of) the feast-cloth (?), house-pillars (or pictured rooms ?), all the revenue, the curved[2] sword (or dagger), and in (or with) the sword the sovereign merchantship, the right of proclamation, the privilege of having forerunners, the five musical instruments, the conch, the light (or torch burning) by day, the spreading cloth, litter, royal umbrella, Vaḍuca drum (drum of the Telugu's or of Bhairava ?), the gateway with seats and ornamental arches, and the sovereign merchantship over the four classes[3] (or streets), also the oilmakers and the five kinds of artificers[4] we have subjected to him (or given as slaves to him). We have given as eternal (literally, "water"[5]) possession to Iravi Corttan, the lord of the town, the brokerage and due customs of all that may be measured[6] by the paṛa, weighed[6] by the balance, stretched[6] by the line, of all that may be counted[6] or carried, contained within salt, sugar, musk, and lamp-oil, or whatever it be, viz., within the river-mouth of Coḍungalur and the tower, or between the four Talis (temples of the deputy Brāhmans) and the grā-mams belonging to them. We have given it by an unreserved[7] tenure to Iravi Corttan, Grand Merchant of the Chēramān world, and to his sons and sons' sons in proper succession.

Witnesses are :—

With the knowledge of the two Brāhman[8] divisions of Panniyūr and Chowaram village have we given it ; with the knowledge of the Vēṇāḍu and Ōdunāḍu (rulers) have we given it ; with the knowledge of the Eṛānāḍu and Vaḷḷuwanāḍu (rulers) have we given it ; given for the time that sun and moon shall last ; with the knowledge of the above, written by Nambi Chaḍayan, grand goldsmith of the Chēramān world.

Note.—The above is one of the deeds belonging to the Syrian Christians of the Cochin and Travancore States. This translatiou, by Dr. Gundert, appeared in the Madras "*Journal of Literature, &c.," Vol. XIII, Part I,* p. 118.

No. 3.

The following is the translation, as far as it can be made out, with short remarks in brackets.

a. Hail ! In the time (literally, year) of Perumāl (Cō, king, or Gō) Sthānu Ravi Gupta, who now rules gloriously for many 100,000 years,

---

1 "A.D. 774 is the only possible year."—Dr. Burnell in *Indian Antiquary* I, p. 229.

2 The knife variously styled the war-knife, Nayar knife, Māppiḷḷa knife, &c., is probably referred to. See *Koḍungakatti* in Glossary. The possession of this weapon is now illegal.

3 *Chēri*—probably foreign settlers—as corporate bodies.

4 1, Goldsmith ; 2, Carpenter ; 3, Founder ; 4, Ironsmith ; 5, Coppersmith.

5 In the case of the Jews' grant there was no transfer by "water." Did this part of the ceremony come into the country with the Vedic *Brāhmans* ? See Deed No. 38.

6 "*Quæ pondere, numero, mensuráve constant.*" Is there here a relic of the Roman trade with Muziris ? *i.e.*, the Coḍungallur of this grant ?

7 This grant is chiefly of privileges and dignities of sorts, though made with "water."

8 See pages 272–76 of the text.

treading under foot hostile heads, in his fifth[1] year, this year under the concurrence of His Excellency the Ayyan Adigal, governing the Vēṇāḍu (the Travancore king is still called Vēṇād Adigal, "the adorable feet of Vēṇādu") of Anjuwaṇṇam (the Jewish principality of Deed No. 1) and of Punnattala's Lord[2] (the next neighbour, *vide d*), the following grant of a freehold[3] has been given by His Excellency the Ayyan Adigal to the Tarisā[4] church (and community), established (or built) by Isodāta Virāi of Curakkeni Collam. (The name Tarisā is perhaps to be recognized in the Dariaygal of the Syrian tradition.)

b. (This sentence is the most difficult of the whole, first, on account of the many antiquated terms of country customs; secondly, on account of the construction, *perār* being the negative verb which gives no plausible translation. I prefer to read *pērār*, and take it as the nominative for the genitive.) And I also (one of the above lords or Maruwān Sapīr Īsō or the church, *vide n*), who formerly had the possession of the share[5] staff (வாரக்கோல், feudal tenure ?) of the four families of Īlawar ("Simhalese, also Tīyar, · Dwīpar, Islanders," now palm-tree cultivators), and of the eight families of Īlakeyar (Sīhala low castes or slaves ?) belonging to them, and one family of washermen coming from the same stock as these—all these being entitled to the fetter-right[6] (தளை the foot-rope for mounting coconut trees ?) and ladder-right[6] (for reaping pepper ?), to the tax for the elephant feeder, and to the wash gold ("*eri*," perhaps *ari*), which the Chāndān ("great person ? sun ?") is wont to get (*māttu*, "hook in" T., "get by ruse" M.), as well as to the harvest gold ("*polipon*," gold of interest ? shining gold ?), to the nightly meal of rice and to the pot measure—I, possessed of this share-staff, and of the Cavvān (or *cappam* ? "tribute"), and of those five Kandis (pieces of ground or shares ?), have given them by a free and unrestricted transfer.

c. Maruwān Sapīr Īsō (Maruwān, the Syrian lord ?), who has received the water (hereditary possession) of this town, having arranged that these four families of Īlawar (with their servants and washerman), two families of—,[7] one family of carpenters, and four families of Vellāler (Tamil agriculturists)—the latter being Cārālar (T. ploughmen, M. temple-servants, used, *Clause m*, for trustees, hence *Clause i*, the noun *Cārānmei*, "trusteeship") of the Alavē (or *Aladeiya*) land— that all these may do their duty[8] to the God, the planter by planting (rice, &c.), the setter by setting (trees, or by building, offering ?), so that the required ceremonies, such as the oil for

---

[1] Probably fifty years later than Deed No. 2. "Ninth Century" (Haug).—*Burnell in Ind. Ant. III*, 315.

[2] பதி (*pati*).

[3] பெறு (peru).

[4] Dr. Burnell thinks *Tarisā* is of Semitic origin, signifying study. In modern Persian *Tarsā* means prayer.—*Ind. Ant. III*, 310. Other scholars have found in this word the Biblical "Tarshish."—*Madras Journal of Literature and Science, XIII, Part I.*

[5] The shares of produce, &c., due to the *Kō* (king) and to the *Pati* (over-lord) were styled *vāram* (see *i*). The possession of the *vārakkōl* probably gave the holder authority to collect those dues.

[6] கணம் (kaṇam).

[7] *Sic.*

[8] The various members of the community were evidently told off to perform various junctions; those customary functions were hereditary: hence caste. See pages 109-113 of the text. The community was evidently organized on the model of a well-ordered household.

the church, suffer no diminution, has enacted and given to the Tarisā church the land now to be described.

d. Decreed with the sanction of the Palace-major (Koyilatikārikal) Vyarāka Dēvar (probably Commissioner of the Perumāl, since he is repeatedly mentioned before the Travancore vassal), and power given with (the ceremony of) water [1] drops for seizing and possessing, under the concurrence of His Excellency the Ayyan Adigal, His Excellency the second Rāja Rāma (brother of the former and next heir), his officers and ministers, and of the 600 [2] (a local authority, *vide f*); also of the (neighbouring) lords of Punnattala ("place of Calophyllum trees") and Pūlacudi ("dwelling of silk cotton trees"), the land bounded so that the east border be Vayalcādu (open waste plain) and the backwater included; the south-east border be the wall near the little door-gate? (*Chiru wātil cāl matil*); the west border the sea; the north border the Tōrana garden; the north-east border the garden of the unapproachable (*andilan*) of Punnattala; the land enclosed within these four borders I have empowered to take, and by executing this copper-deed have given, for the days that earth, moon and sun exist.

e. And it has farther been settled with the concurrence of His Excellency the Ayyan Adigal, His Excellency Rāma, and the Palace-major, that the church people (Palliyār, probably heads of the Tarisā citizens) alone have power to punish the (heathen) families of this land for any offence [3] whatsoever, and receive the fines expenses, head-price and breast-price (probably the right of selling males and females for serious caste offences);

f. mine own relations, whoever they be, whatever the charges be, shall never have the right there to speak as heads of the land dealing with subjects. Let the 600 [4] (see *d*), the Anjuwaṇṇam [4] and Maṇigramam [4] (Jewish and Christian principalities) be the protectors.

g. Let them, even Anjuwaṇṇam and Maṇigramam, act both with the church and the land according to the manner detailed in this copper-deed for the times that earth, moon and sun exist.

h. Ordered with the sanction of the Palace-major Vyarāka Dēvar, and with the sanction of His Excellency the Ayyan Adigal, and His Excellency Rāma, and free [5] tenure granted to these (Palliyār) as follows:—

---

[1] See note to Deed No. 2. In this case the transfer was of land and other things; the things transferred by Deed No. 2, with "water," were privileges of sorts.

[2] Compare the notice of the "Six Hundred" in Deed No. 4. It is almost certain that the *Kāraṇavar* of all the *Taras* (Nayar villages) in the *Nād* constituted the "Six Hundred;" but Dr. Gundert in the translation of Deed No. 4 says, though with some doubt, "Body-guard." See pp. 87-90 and 132-33 of the text and the word "*Kūṭṭam*" in the Glossary, *App. XIII*.

[3] Among the privileges recited in a "Malabar Jenmum" deed granted by the Kōlattiri Raja to the Honorable Company's linguist at Tellicherry in October 1758 are the following: "Penalties or condemnations and customs, beginning with one principal and ending with all other things," which was explained to the Joint Commissioners (Diary 15th February 1793) as meaning "the power of administering justice, both civil and criminal, even to the cutting off the hands of a thief."

[4] The deed, it will be observed, makes no allusion here to the headmen of the Jewish and Christian communities, although it is known from Deeds Nos. 1 and 2 that such headmen had been appointed. The conclusion is, therefore, that the power of protection here assumed resided not in the headmen, but in the communities *as corporate bodies*. This strengthens the view in the note to para. (*d*) that the "Six Hundred" were really the *Kūṭṭam* (see Appendix XIII) of the *Kāraṇavar* of the *Nād*.

[5] *Viduper*.

(Again a difficult sentence. I take *Ulaku*, *i.e.*, lōka for the official name of the citizens, Christian freemen formed into a corporation [1] and distinguished both from the Paḻḻiyār, who are their headmen, and from the Cuḍi or Heathen families, who live on their grounds as farmers or slaves.) There being 61 citizens, the number not to be increased nor to be diminished; no personal tax to be received for the slaves they buy (or, "the person tax to be received" if you read pērār); for admitting any conveyances or letting them out they are to receive 8 coins (Kāchu-*wāyinam* is vāhanam, understand horses, waggons); in the case of (female) elephants and of boats, whether for letting in or letting out, they are to receive 4 coins; merchandise belonging to the citizens to be disposed of (or removed) by them with the cognizance of the above (the Paḻḻiyār? or the protecting lords?); and that they (the Paḻḻiyār) do all the business (rights and duties) of a lord (swāmi) on the place of packing the wares (or on spots where poles with leaves are set up as signs of prohibition) and elsewhere, only after deliberation with the above-mentioned (Anjuwaṇṇam and Maṇigrāmam?); that Anjuwaṇṇam and Maṇigrāmam protect the citizens in every coming generation; [2] that in the space within the four gates (or in the four public offices?) and on the spot where land for sale (or "under prohibition") is given in trust, the palace (or Supreme Government) having received the king's tithe [3] (Kō-pata-wāram), Anjuwaṇṇam and Maṇigrāmam receive the Lord's tithe [3] (Pati-ppata-wāram),

k. with the sanction of the Palace-major Vyarāka Devar, who has given to these (the Paḻḻiyār) the 72 janmi [4] rights (*viduperu*), such as for marriages (or processions), the elephant's back, the earth, the water, &c. (or "earth and water on the elephant," at all events, marks of nobility), and with the concurrence of His Excellency the Ayyan Adigal, His Excellency Rāma, the ministers and officers, the 600, and the Lords of Punnattala and Pūlacudi, let Anjuwaṇṇam and Maṇigrāmam carry out this unrestricted possession right in the manner described by this copper-deed for the time that earth, moon and sun exist.

l. If any injustice be done to these (the Paḻḻiyār? or Anjuwaṇṇam and Maṇigrāmam?), they may withhold the tribute ("world-bearing hire") and remedy themselves the injury done to them. Should they themselves commit a crime, they are themselves [5] to have the investigation of it.

---

[1] This and the succeeding para. (*k*) prove conclusively that Dr. Gundert's position here is correct. The Jews and Syrians were organized in guilds or corporations precisely similar to the Nāyars, the *Paḻḻiyār* corresponding to the *Taṛavāḍ* (*Taṛa-pāḍ*) *Kāraṇavar*, and *Anjuwaṇṇam* and *Maṇigrāmam* to the "600" of the *Nād.*

[2] நாலு வாதிலகத்தும் விலை (*or* ல்) க்கும் (? viḷakkum = for cultivation) பூமியாக காராண்மை கொடுக்குமெடத்தும் கொப்பதவாரங் கொயில்கொண்டு பதிப்பதவாரம் அஞ்சுவண்ணமும் மணிக்கிராமவுங் கொள்வதாக.

[3] There is here the earliest intimation of what "*Pāṭṭam*" was originally. See the Glossary. The king (*Kō-pād*) and the over-lord (*Pati-pād*) had each a share (*vāram*) of the produce, not necessarily of the land alone. Is it too far-fetched to derive *pāṭṭam* from *pāṭṭa-vāram?*

[4] See note to Deed No. 1.

[5] The Muhammadan community in Malabar does not seem to have possessed this privilege.—*Tahafut-ul-Mujahideen*" by Rowlandson, pp. 72, 73.

m. And let whatever the two chieftains[1] in Anjuwaṇṇam and Maṇigrāmam, who have taken the water (possession) as trustees for this town (*Cārāḷar*, see *c*), may do in unison be counted for one act.

n. And let Maruwān Sapīr Īsō, who took the water for this town, since he acquired (or transferred? *peruttu*) the share-staff (*Vārakōl* of *b*), and those 5 pieces (or *Anjacandi*) which formerly were the property of the Paḷḷiyār, pay for it the full price to the church. This also I have given over by unrestricted transfer.

o. I have ceded to the Tarisā church people, by full and unrestricted tenure, every kind of revenue by this copper-deed for the time that earth, moon and sun do last.

p. Those Ilawar[2] are permitted to follow out their occupations (?) in the bazar and on the wall. The washerman[2] may come and do his work in the bazar[3] and on the wall.

q. Nor have the Island[4] ruler (or Tīyar headman) and the Wall officer, or whoever it be, any power to stop them on any charges whatsoever. Though they should commit a trespass, the Paḷḷiyār alone have to try them.

r. I have given this in the manner detailed in the copper-deed, for the time that earth, moon, and sun do last, by full, free and unrestricted tenure.

s. The person who made this full, free and unrestricted transfer to the Tarisāpaḷḷi through His Excellency the Ayyan Adigal, is Maruwān Sapīr Īsō.

t. To those who keep this and care to see it observed let God himself be gracious (what is *anugramam* or *anucrāmam?*). The writing of Ayyan; and may this benefit (*vel*, or is it a compound word?) be equal to Cula Sundara's (Vishnu?). Rule victoriously!

Note.—The above is one of the deeds belonging to the Syrian Christians of the Cochin and Travancore States. This translation, by Dr. Gundert, appeared in the *Madras "Journal of Literature, &c.*" Vol. XIII, Part I., p. 130.

No. 4.

Svasti Ṣri.—In the year that runs for the Kōlavāḷan[5] (or Kēraḷavāḷan?) Rāmar the fourth, opposed[6] to the fourth year, in this year has the ruler of Rāma-vala-nāḍu, Kannankandan of Vāli (or Valiyattu), and his officers and the 600[7] (body-guard?), in concert with the house-gods (ancestors? Brāhmans?), performed the following act:—Chellan, the father (or stay? lord) of Kanayapalli, wanted to purchase Tirumunnūr, the Paḍārar's[8]

---

[1] The allusion here to the headmen (see Deeds 1 and 2) shows that their respective corporate bodies or guilds *acted* through them, though the real power (see Note to paragraph *f*) rested with the community. So too must it have been in the Nayar organization by *Nāds*.

[2] Presumably these were some of the families of the land conveyed along with it in paragraph (*c*).

[3] Presumably outside the limits of the land conveyed by paragraph (*d*).

[4] See Glossary under *Tīyan*, &c.

[5] The first part of this word is not very clear in the original, but there is little doubt that it is not *Kēralavāḷan*. It may be either *Kōlavāḷan* or *Chēravāḷan*.

[6] *Etir*, the same word that occurs in the Jews' *Deed No.* 1.

[7] See notes to Deed No. 3.

[8] *Paḍarar* unīl.

domain, and, finding the gold required for it not forthcoming, delayed the purchase. (Here the verb പൊഴിക്കുക seems plain, but its meaning is obscure. Can it be Tamil ചുഴിക്കുക, revolve in mind?). The purchase of this domain[1] of the Paḍārar, with all[2] that belongs to it, has then been made by the ruler of Chēranāḍu (or Chara?) and his officers, and the image of the god of the Paḍārars, with their sovereignty (*prabhutvam*), has been subjected[3] to the 600, and is possession[4] (*Kāṇam* or mortgage?) held under[4] the king (*Irān*). They may burn a lamp of joy (*nanda viḷakku*, an old privilege, see Curian's Essay, 1872, p. 12). The Ūrāḷan is to be the hand of the Paḍārar. The 600 ought to make the Paḍārar perform the service with one Naḻi rice. Let them also look after Tirukkunam, the property of these (or this) Paḍārar and protect[5] (*ilaxikkā = raxikka*) it for them, even the 600, and the agreeing party furnish them for this purpose with good liquor (madhu), fire and water (or holy ashes?). When the agreeing party (mortgagor?) maintains the temple offerings, then the Potuvāl has to go and hand to them what they order. It is not the 600 that have thus to serve (different meaning, if വിട്ടി should have to be read). (Follows something, which I cannot read, about the expense at the fane of Tirukkunam. The last line is readable, except the end.) The Ūrāḷan, if he be guilty of embezzlement (?), shall be fined 25 Kaḻanju gold.

Note.—This translation of an inscription on stone in old Vaṭṭeḻuttu characters is by Dr. Gundert. The stone was found at Tiruvannūr (the "Tirumunnūr" of the inscription), one of the residences of the Zamorin Mahārāja Bahādūr in Calicut town.

No. 5.

Kumbha Vyāḻam, on the 5th of Karkitakam solar month (ഞായറ്), in the dignified presence (തിരുമുമ്പ) of our Kallē Kuḷangarē Ēmūr Bhagavati, in the northern entrance of the temple (വടക്കെനട), Sēkhari Varma *alias* Tekkunāthan,[6] with the knowledge (അറിവ) of the four immediate successors[7] (നാല്ക്കൂറവാഴ്ച്ചയും) of the two Tamburāṭṭis (രണ്ട തമ്പുരാട്ടിയും = two

---

[1] *Paḍarar mēl.* [2] *Eppēreppaṭṭatum.*

[3] *Ārunuṟṟuvarkkum Kiḻpaṭṭu.*

[4] *Irānukku Kiḻiṭṭu Kāṇam.* This is the earliest instance excepting Clause (*b*) of No. 3, of the use of this impoitant word *Kāṇam*. The "600" were evidently appointed to be the *Kāṇakkārar* (overseers or protectors) of the Paḍarar's estate. *Conf.* p. 133 of the text.

[5] See note to paragraph (*f*) of Deed No. 3. This sentence, taken in connection with the use of the word *Kāṇam* above, shows that the duty [see note to paragraph (*e*) of Deed No. 3] of the *Kāṇakkārar* was to supervise and protect. The collection of the *pāṭṭam* [see notes to paragraphs (*b*) and (*i*) of Deed No. 3] on behalf of the *Kō-pād* would naturally be part of that duty. The share of the *pāṭṭam* due to the *Patipād* went into their own exchequer as a corporate body, or into the exchequer of their headman, or perhaps partly into the one and partly into the other. Compare notes to paragraphs (*i*) and (*m*) of Deed No. 3, and the word *Kāṇam* in the Glossary as to the derivation of the word *Kāṇam*. *Conf.* also p. 132 of the text.

[6] *Tekku-nāthan* (literally, southern lord), that is, the Southern *Nāyakkan* of Pālghat, the ruler of *Temmalapuram*.

[7] *Kūṟvāḻcha*, from Dravidian *kūṟu* (= part, share) and Dravidian *vāḻcha* (= living prosperously, reigning, governing). The immodiate successors of a Rāja had a share in the administration.

queens, ladies), of the two Anantiravars in the female line (രജ്ജപെൺ വഴി അനന്തിരവന്മാരും), of the Kūṛūr Nambūripād (കൂരനമ്പൂരിപാട്ടും), of the inhabitants (നാട്ടുകാര) of Rāyirinallara and Kumarapuram (രായിരിനല്ലരകമരപുരം), of townspeople (നഗരക്കാരും) of Yōgakkār (യോഗക്കാരും), of Koppaṇa Mannāḍi (കൊപ്പുണമന്നാടി), and of two Koḍakarttākkanmār[1] (കൊടകത്താക്കന്മാർ), our Ēmūr Bhagavati Dēvasvam nilam, called Koṭṭapaḍi (കൊട്ടപടി), and lands (ഉഭയം) sowing 242 kalams (കലം = a Tamil measure of 12 marcals) of seed, (comprised) in the 14 Chērikkal[2] (ചേരിക്കല്ല) under (the place called) Kunnumpāṛa (കുന്നംപാറ), with the paṛambas (പറമ്പ) and tanks by their (lands) banks (തൻകര), and lands (ഉഭയം) sowing 1,200 kalams (കലം = 12 marcals) of seed, including nanja and punja (നഞ്ചപുഞ്ച), (comprised) in the 42 Chērikkal (ചേരിക്കൽ) (extending) from Chembana (ചെമ്പന) to Kāchanaḍa (കാച്ചനട) at the ghat (മലയകം = literally, within the hill), and the Akamala[3] (അകമല = valley), Puṛamala[3] (പുറമല), Chiṛamala[3] (ചിറമല), and Kīḻamala[3] (കീഴമല) of the ghat (മലയകം); these are given as Mānyam[4] (മാന്യംവിട്ടുക), to last till stones (കല്ല), and Cāvēry (കാവേരി), and grass (പുല്ല), and the earth (ഭൂമി) exist, in order that with the income (വരുമാനം) derivable from them the expenses of Pūja (പൂജ), and of feeding (ഊട്ട = generally feeding of Brāhmans), and of songs (പാട്ട = probably songs at temple), and of the subjects (പ്രജകൾ) may be met without any distinction (?) (ഏറവരികയും ഇല്ലാമൽ). Besides this, with the pāṭṭam[5] (പാട്ടം) of 411 kalams (കലം) sowing seeds special ceremonies (വിശേഷ അടിയന്തരം) will go on (നടക്കം). Whoever does harm (ദോഷം) to these, will merge (പോകുന്നവർ) in those who murder Brāhmans (ബ്രഹ്മഹത്തി) on the banks of the Ganges (ഗംഗകര). With the knowledge of the witnesses Vaḍakkunāthan[6] (വടക്കുംനാഥൻ) and Vilvādrināthan (വില്വാദ്രിനാഥൻ).

Note.—Translated from a copy received from Nellissēri Śiva Rāmayyan of Pālghat town. The document is in places barely intelligible.

No. 6.

Letter (തീട്ട) from Kandan Dāmōdaran. To be read over by Mangāt Menon (മേനവൻ = accountant) and communicated (തിരുമനസ്സു ഉണർത്തിക്ക = awaken the blessed mind) to Triśśivapērur (Trichūr) Natuvilē Matattil Kakkōte Tirumanassu (തിരുമനസ്സു = blessed mind, a term applied to Nam-

---

1 Probably intended for *Kōṭṭa-Karttākkanmār* = literally, fort lords. Perhaps the same as the *Cotual* (*Kōṭṭavāḻi*) of the Portuguese.

2 Lands set apart for the support of Rajas.

3 These four words probably denote "the valleys and mountain spurs."

4 *Mānyam* (Sanskrit) = deserving of honor or regard, and lands nearly or altogether exempt from tax. Note that this is the case of a Raja parting with a portion of the lands set apart for his own use (Chērikkal).

5 See note to paragraph (*i*) of Deed No. 3. It is to be inferred that this *pāṭṭam* was derived from other land than that conveyed as *Mānyam*. Probably it was from land of which the temple had already obtained the "water right" and the *Pati-pāṭṭa-vāram* or *pāṭṭam* of which was now also given up.

6 See above. This was the head (Northern Nayakkan) of the other branch of the Palghat Raja's family.

būtiris, &c.), who looks after the affairs of Tiruvālattūr Bhagavati, our household goddess (പരദേവത); the object (കാൎയ്യം), than, is that, with a view that prosperity may come to us (നമുക്ക ശ്രേയസ്സവരേണ്ടതിന്ന) by removing the displeasure (തിരുവെള്ളക്കേട contracted from തിരുവുള്ളക്കെട, a particular term for the displeasure of Nambūtiris, Rājas, &c.) of the Bhagavati, incurred by our having done something (ചിലകൈക്കാൎയ്യംചെയ്തു = did some deeds by the hand) to Chūvath Nambi from Sankētam (സങ്കേതം = an asylum or holy refuge exempt from war and profanation), we have made a gift (ദാനം ചെയ്തു). by way of atonement (പ്രായശ്ചിത്തമായി), of our property (സ്വന്തം) Mēlētattakku, bounded on the east by Elayachchāpāra, Ariyampāka and Pārakkatavu, on the south by river (പുഴ), on the west by Pantillottumākku, and on the north by Pantittōḍu (തോട = canal), lands for 12 (പന്തിരു) kaḷams (കളം, a Tamil measure = 12 marcals) of seed, and paṛambas situated within these boundaries, Etavantikāvil Ayyan (അയ്യൻ or അയ്യപ്പൻ = deity of hunting), the Ayyappan Vāriyam (വാരിയം = Variyar's house), Kambu kuḷam (കുളം = tank), Kula nilam (നിലം = land), and 20 paṛas of paddy as Mēlvāram (മേൽവാരം), out of the Michāram due to us on account of Oravan Kandam, 60 paṛas lands demised (ചാൎത്തിയ) to Kottavaḷi (Nambūtiri). Thus Kārtikanyāyar (കാൎത്തികഞായററിൽ = in the solar month of Kārtika) of Bahudhāniya[1] Varsham (ബഹുധാന്യവൎഷം). May Kārtiyāyini (കാൎത്ത്യായിനി = female deity) be pleased and become protectress. With the knowledge of Tiruvālattūr Potuval Chūtanārayanan Vādamūli Kumaran Kandan, the witness to this.

Note.—Translated from a copy received from Nellissēri Siva Rāmayyan of Pālghat town. The language of this deed is ordinary modern Malayāḷam. It is placed here in the list because its date is, like the dates of those that precede it, not referable to the Kollam or Putuveppu era, but it is an ordinary modern deed.

No. 7.

In the month of Makaram of the year 465,[2] Vayalmanakkal Shangara Nārāyaṇan, the proprietor[3] (ഉടയ) of Parayāt Dēsam, has conveyed (എഴുതി കൊടുത്തു = literally, wrote (and) gave] for 48,101 old fanams[4] to Ayikkarē, Iṭṭikōta, and Itichakki, by a copper-plate (ചെപ്പേട) executed by Shangara Nārāyaṇan in the blessed (തിരു) presence of Villiyār Vāṭṭa Svarūpam,[5] his lands (ഉൾപാറികൾ) and paṛambas (പറമ്പുകൾ) in the Parayāt Dēsam, (which are) bounded on the east by Aynārikkal channel (തോട), on the south by Kotatha ferry, on the west by Kuttiruthi channel (തോട), and on the north by Kayanutti channel (തോട), as well as the Sthānamānangal (സ്ഥാനമാനങ്ങൾ = literally, rank and honors; but per Gundert "rank and emoluments

[1] The twelfth year in the Brihaspati (60 years) Cycle.

[2] A.D. 1290.

[3] This is the same phrase as that used in Deeds Nos. 1 and 2 to express the connection between a ruling chief and his naḍ.

[4] It will be seen in subsequent deeds that the price paid is never stated.

[5] The "Beliartes" of the Portuguese, the Koḍungallūr (Cranganore) dynasty.

of office"), Yekku[1] (ഒയക്കം sic ?), Chollu (ചൊല്ലു = command), Kuttu (കുത്തു = probably authority over transactions, such as signing deeds), Viḷakku[2] (വിളക്കു = lamp), right of digging and splitting (വെട്ടുകയുംപിളക്കുകയും), cows having five nipples to the udder (അഞ്ചുമുല), Chelli (ചെല്ലി = a sort of grass in the fields, ചെല്ലുകയുക = to stray as cattle. *Gundert*, Chelli = ? stray cattle), fighting bull (ചെങ്കൊമ്പ = literally, red horn), dramatic ornaments or religious festival (വെലയാട്ടസാധനം), enjoyment of crops (വിളപൊടുക്കങ്ങൾ),[3] the fish known as Caṇṇan[4] in the tank (കുളത്തിൽകണ്ണൻ), the hog that has fallen into a well (കിണറ്റിൽപന്നി), and civet cat (പെരു = probably മെരു) and tigress (പുലി), abnormal jackfruit (കൊമ്പചക്ക)[5] and bunch of plantains with tree (കലവാഴ), and all similar rank and honors (സ്ഥാനമാനങ്ങൾ). Thus Ayikkarē, Iṭṭikōta, and Itichakki have taken by writing (എഴുതിച്ചുകൊണ്ടാർ) from Shangara Nārāyaṇan, in the blessed presence (തിരുമുമ്പ) of Villiyār Vāṭṭa Svarūpam, his lands (ഉൽപത്തികൾ) and paṛambas (പറമ്പുകൾ) specified in Parayāt Dēṣam, as well as the rank and honors (സ്ഥാനമാനങ്ങൾ),[6] Yekku (ഒയക്കം sic), Chollu (ചൊല്ലു = command), Kuttu (കുത്തു, see notes above), Viḷakku (lamp), the right of digging and splitting (വെട്ടുകയും പിളക്കുകയും), cows having five nipples to the udder (അഞ്ചുമുല), Chelli (ചെല്ലു, see above), the fighting bull (ചെങ്കൊമ്പ), dramatic ornaments (വെലയാട്ട സാധനം, see above), the fish known as Caṇṇan in the tank (കുളത്തിൽകണ്ണൻ), the hog that has fallen into a well (കിണറ്റിൽപന്നി), civet cat (പെരു = probably മെരു), tigress (പുലി), abnormal jack (കൊമ്പചക്ക) and bunch of plantains with tree (കലവാഴ), and all similar ranks. Thus Iṭṭikōta and Itichakki got by writing the Dēṣam (ദേശം അടക്കി എഴുതിച്ചുകൊണ്ടാർ), by paying 48,101 old fanams; the witnesses who know this being Tiriwālu Paṭṭēri, Talāppu of Paḷutinēpalli, Vaykōt Kamal and Katammāt Menon.

Note.—It is not known whether the boundaries specified are the boundaries of the Dēṣam, or only of a portion of it. The copy from which this translation was made was obtained from the Dewan of Cochin State.

No. 8.

In the year 640,[7] Vrischika Vyāḷam, solar month (ഞായർ) Kanni, under the orders of Iṭṭikōmbi and Anantiravars (അനന്തിരവർ), and of Kalpātti Mukkālvaṭṭams (മുക്കാൽവട്ടങ്ങൾ = the oracles of *Vēḷichapāḍu*), the land bounded on the east by the paṛamba north of the Chiṛa (ചിറ = tank or embankment) and Tekka Telava, on the south by Maravalli Tōḍu (തോട = stream), on the west by patti Kaḍavu (കടവ = ferry), and on the north by

1 ഏക്കം (Ekkam) means turning for fight.—*Gundert.*

2 കുത്തുവിളക്കു, if taken together, means "lamp with a long handle" used as insignia.

3 First-fruits would probably better express the meaning.

4 *Varāl—pirāl* (North Malabar)—*prāl* = *Maral.*

5 Jackfruit with a horn, abnormal growth.

6 Some of these "ranks" (*Sthānam*) and "honors" (*Mānam*) are (see Glossary under "Revenue") privileges supposed to appertain exclusively to ruling Rājas.

7 A.D. 1464.

the Kalpātti Kaḍavu (കടവ = ferry), is made a gift of with water[1] (ധാരാ ദത്ത) to the temple (കോവിൽ), with the very superior (മെച്ചമെച്ച = superior and superior) use of protection[2] (രക്ഷാമുള്ളഉപഭോഗം), to the Brāhmans living therein, and with the upper and lower produce (മേൽഫലവും കീഴ്ഫലവും), retainers and slaves (ആളടിയാർ), cattle (ഏര), and iron (ഇരിമ്പു = ploughshare), seed and valli (വിത്തുംവള്ളിയും), oil-mill (ചക്ക), and Mukkālvaṭṭam (മുക്കാൽവട്ടം = also applied to the temples of Bhagavati, where the oracles were consulted), 130 Brāhman houses existing therein, 132 fanams given to Tiranda Mana with interest of 132 fanams, the gold, silver, and copper vessels belonging to the temple, and every such thing. Nephew[3] (മരുമകൻ) Iṭṭikōmbi and Anantiravars and these Mukkālvaṭṭam (മുക്കാൽവട്ടം), are witnesses[4] (to this) (സാക്ഷിക്കടവർ); the support to this (ഇതിനാശ്രയധാരമാകുന്നത) is Chokkanāthan (Ṣiva), Ēmūr Bhagavati and Mēlkāraṇavan (chief administrator). Written to this effect by Rāyiramkandatt Pangi.

Note.—The copy from which this translation was made was obtained from Nellissēri Ṣiva Rāmayyan of Pālghat town.

No. 9.

Aṭṭipettōlakaruṇam (അട്ടിപ്പെറോലകരണം), executed in Mēḍam Nyāyar (solar month), Makara Vyāḷam, of the year 699.[5] Pulāvaḷi Nākan Nārāṇan[6] has given, with water, the Aṭṭippēr of his Chennapuram Dēṣam (ദേശം), and Dēṣādhipatyam (ദേശാധിപത്യം), and Chennapuratt[7] Ambalam (അമ്പലം = temple), and Ambalapaḍi Ūrāyma (അമ്പലപ്പടിഊരായ്മ), and the Dēvasvam lands (ഉഭയങ്ങൾ), and paṛambas, and Cheṛumars (വള്ളി ചാത്തന്മാർ), and Kolapuratt Taṛavād,[8] and the lands (ഉൽപ്പത്തി), and paṛambas, and Cheṛumars (വള്ളിചാത്തന്മാർ), and Kuḍiyiruppus (കുടിയിരുപ്പ) belonging to the said Taṛavād, to Vāḷayūr[9] Kuriyetat Viyatan Mānichan, after receiving from his hands (കയ്യാൽ) the current market value thereof (അന്നപ്പെറുംഅർത്ഥം)[10] = literally, the then breeding money, *i.e.*, the then market value.

---

[1] Transfers of the "water right" required formerly the sanction of the *Perumāl*, as well as of the local chief, and his heir, and the "six hundred," and neighbouring lords (Deed 3). Here the transfer is made by the local chief with the concurrence, however, of the people, whose mouth-piece was the *Veḷichapād* or oracle. The *Perumāl* or *Kōn* of Kēraḷam was now extinct. Each ruling chief of a nād had probably set himself up as *Kōn*.

[2] This deed adheres to the old line of providing for the "protection" of the inhabitants. Compare Deed 3.

[3] "Nephew," that is of the Pālghat Rāja. He was probably at the time the ruling chief, for the head of the house did not always possess executive functions.

[4] The copy is to this effect, but *sākshi* (witness) has probably been mistaken for *sūkshi*, which gives the more intelligible meaning, that these individuals would "take care" the deed of gift was carried out.

[5] A.D. 1523.

[6] Both parties to this deed are *Sāmandar*, the caste of the Zamorin Rājas.

[7] Also called Keitodika temple, situated in the Cheṛuppuḷḷaṣṣēri Amṣam of Waḷḷuvanād Taluk.

[8] See Glossary and Note to Deed No. 22.

[9] Also called Viṇākunnatt.

[10] "The price it will then fetch; so much as it is worth."—*Gundert*. Compare the second note to Deed No. 7. This phrase occurs frequently in subsequent deeds.

Thus Vālayūr Kuriyetat Viyatan Mānichan has received, with water, the Aṭṭippēr of the above-said Chennapuram Dēṣam (ദേശം), and Dēṣādhipatyam (ദേശാധിപത്യം), and Chennapuratt Ambalam (അമ്പലം = temple), and Ambalapaḍi Ūrāyma (അമ്പലപ്പടി ഊരാണ്മ), and the Dēvasvam lands (ഉഭയങ്ങൾ), and paṛambas, and Cheṛumars (വല്ലിആളർ), and Kolapuratt Taṛavād, and the lands (ഉല്പത്തി), and paṛambas, and Cheṛumars (വല്ലിആളർ), and Kuḍiyiruppus (കടിയിരുപ്പ) belonging to the said Taṛavād, after paying the current market value thereof (അന്നപെറും അൎത്ഥം). Thus Pulāvaḻi Nākan Nārāṇan has given, with water, the Aṭṭippēr of the four boundaries (നാലതിർ), and paṛambas, and nilams, and produce (ഫലം = fruit), and all of these, &c., comprised in the said Dēṣam (ദേശം), lands (ഉൽപത്തി), paṛambas and Kuḍiyiruppus (കടിയിരുപ്പ), as also everything, of whatever[1] description (എപ്പേർപ്പെട്ടത), included in them, after receiving the current market value (അന്നപെറും അൎത്ഥം). Thus Viyatan Mānichan has received, with water, the Aṭṭippēr of the four boundaries, and paṛambas, and nilams, and phalams, and all of these and everything else included in the said Dēṣam, and in the lands (ഉൽപത്തി), and paṛambas, and Kuḍiyiruppu after paying the market value (പെറും അൎത്ഥം). That the Aṭṭippēr is given with water and that the Aṭṭippēr is received with water, is witnessed by Kandikundatt Nambūtiri and Patinharē Kūr.[2] Written by Chāttu.

Note.—The copy from which this translation was made was obtained from Kīḻepāṭṭ Teyyan Menon of Waḷḷuvanād Taluk, Malabar.

No. 10.

Veppōlakaruṇam (വെപ്പോലകരണം), executed in the solar month (ഞായർ) of Chingam, 725,[3] towards the end of Karkaḍaka Vyāḻam (കൎക്കടകവ്യാഴംപോകന്ന). Elaya Nambi Vīṭṭil Chāttan Rāman and heirs (തമ്പിമാർ) received 111½ new fanams from (the hands of) Mūttanambiar Vīṭṭil Kelan Kandan and heirs (തമ്പിമാർ) in this manner. Now the object of receiving the above 111½ fanams is that Elaya Nambi Vīṭṭil Chāttan Rāman and heirs (തമ്പിമാർ) grant (literally, write and give) Nambukkotil Kandam 2 plots, Pantārattil Kandam 1 plot, Kundu Kandam 1 plot, and Pulikkunnat compound (വളപ്പ്). Mūttanambiar Vīṭṭil Kelan Kandan and Anantiravars accordingly obtain *Veppu*[4] (വെപ്പ്) right on payment of the said sum. Thus written by the grantee, with the knowledge of Ayikkara Kandan Chāttan, witness for the parties granting and obtaining Veppu (വെപ്പ്) right for the said amount.

Note.—Translated from a copy received from Kīḻepāṭṭ Teyyan Mēnon of Waḷḷuvanād Taluk.

---

[1] The same phrase occurs in Deed No. 4.

[2] The branch of the reigning family, probably Zamorin of Calicut.

[3] A.D. 1550.

[4] *Veppu* signifies a deposit, hence a pledge for the sum advanced. It is equivalent to *Oṭṭi*. See Glossary.

No. 11.

Aṭṭippeṭṭōlakaraṇam (അട്ടിപ്പേറോലകരണം), executed in Kumbham Nyāyar (ഞായർ = solar month) of the year (which has) advanced (ചെന്ന) to 762.[1] Kiḻakke Kūṭṭattil[2] Chandu of Kannanuriyatt Ūr (ഊര = village) granted Aṭṭippēr and water (അട്ടിപ്പേരുംനീരുംകൊടുത്താൻ) of his Nirattu house,[3] granted Aṭṭippēr and water of Kannanuriyatt Kisaliyakat Nirattu house,[3] Kannanuriyatt Kisaliyakat Kūṭṭattil[4] Chandu granted Aṭṭippēr and water of his Nirattu[3] house by settling the price (വിലമുറിച്ചു). Kisaliyatt Chandu granted Aṭṭippēr and water by settling the price (വിലമുറിച്ചു) and receiving the full value in gold (പൊന്നാറ). In this way (ഇന്നാക്കൈ) the Ūrāḷan, in the blessed name (തിരുനാമം) of Nallātat Pērillātta,[6] fixed the price (വിലമുറിച്ചു) and obtained Aṭṭippēr and water (അട്ടിപ്പേറുംനീരുംകൊണ്ടാം) of the said Nirattu house. In this way the witness[6] (സാക്ഷി), knowing (this transaction) on behalf of the party who fixed the price and granted Aṭṭippēr and water of the said house, and of the party who obtained (the same), is Talavaṭṭatt[7] Kiḻakke Viṭṭil Nambādi Kanakkampalli Kaṇṇan. Written in the hand of Kanakkam Valli.

Note.—Translated from a copy received from the Huzur Sheristadar, Malabar Collector's Office.

No. 12.

Aṭṭippettōlakaraṇam (അട്ടിപ്പേറോലകരണം), executed in Tulu Nyāyar (ഞായർ) = solar month) of the year (which has) advanced to (ചെന്ന) 793.[8] Kunimal Micheri Kunhāmu of Putuppaṭṭaṇatt Ūr (ഊര = village) received the current market value (അന്നപെറുംവിലഅർത്ഥംവാങ്ങി) of the Ottakandam land (ഒറ്റകണ്ടം) at the north-western extremity (മൂല) of Valayala land in a way extinguishing the water (right) (നീരറ) and extinguishing the price (വിലയറ). The Ūrāḷars of Nallatat Nerillat Tiru nāmam [തിരുനാമംവയരാ (?) = blessed name] joining the nearest Anantiravars for the time being, and with the knowledge of the neighbours (അയല) and of the over-lord (പതി = lord, or master), and in the presence of the Kōvil (കോവിൽ = literally, palace, hence king) of that Nād,[9] paid the full value in gold

---

[1] A.D. 1587.

[2] Literally, *Chandu* of the Eastern *Kūṭṭam* (see Appendix XIII), belonging to the village of *Kannanuriyatt*.

[3] See note to Deed No. 20.

[4] Literally *Chandu* of the Eastern *Kūṭṭam* (see p. 132 of the text), belonging to the village of *Kannanuriyatt*.

[5] Literally, *nameless*.

[6] Neither *Kō* nor *pati* was present at the execution of this deed apparently. The circle of the Taṛas did, however, probably witness its execution. See following note.

[7] Probably intended for *Taṛa-vaṭṭatt*. See notes to Deeds Nos. 13, 14 and 20.

[8] A.D. 1617.

[9] In Deeds Nos. 1, 2 and 3 the *Kō* was the *Perumāl* or Emperor (*Chakravarti*) of Malabar. Here the *Kō* is merely king of a *nād*. In fact the *Nāḍuvāḻi* has by this time become the *Kō*.

(പൊന്നറകൊടുത്തു), settled the price (വിലമുറിച്ചു), and obtained Aṭṭippēr with water for full value (അട്ടിപ്പേറുംനീരുംകൊണ്ടാന്റ). In the blessed name (തിരുനാമംചാർത്ത) of Urulleri Nallatat Pērillātta paid the current market value (അന്നപെറുംവിലഅത്ഥവുംകൊടുത്തു), with the knowledge of the neighbours (അയല), of the over-lord (പതി), and of the Kōvil (കോവിൽ = palace, hence king) of that Nād, settled the price (വിലമുറിച്ചു), and obtained Aṭṭippēr with water (അട്ടിപ്പേറുംനീരുംകൊണ്ടാൻ) of the Ottakandam[1] land (ഒററകണ്ടം) for 60[2] Iḍangaḻis of paddy at the north-western extremity of Valayala Kandam (കണ്ടം = piece of land), belonging to the Putuppaṭṭaṇatt Kunimal Muvailacheri Kunhāmu. In this way written in the hand of Nallatat Perillat Taye Kanakkam[3] Valli, witness knowing (this transaction) on behalf of parties who granted and who obtained Aṭṭippēr with water of what is contained within these boundaries of the said piece of land — ദൈവത്തിന്റെകണ്ടം (God's land) on the east, Āmat Kōṭṭa (കോട്ട = fortress) on the south, അടിയോടിന്റെകണ്ടം (Aḍiyōḍi's land) on the west, and Akkam-vīṭṭil Nāyar's Korappalli on the north.

Note.—Translated from a copy received from the Huzur Sheristadar, Malabar Collector's Office.

No. 13.

Aṭṭippettōlakaraṇam (അട്ടിപ്പേറോലകരണം), executed in Chinga Nyāyar (ഞായർ = solar month) of the year (which has) advanced to (ചെന്ന) 795.[4] Putiyavīṭṭil Kunnummal Kandumalacheri Tāye Chandu Kuṛup, Kora Kuṛup and Tāye Kunhan Kuṛup of Putuppaṭṭanatt[5] Ūr (ഊര = village), received the current market value (അന്നപെറുംവിലഅത്ഥവുംവാങ്ങി) of their Kunnummal house,[6] and having received the full value in gold (പൊന്നറ), in a way extinguishing the water (right) and extinguishing the price, granted the Aṭṭippēr and water (അട്ടിപ്പേറുംനീരും), after settling the price (വിലമുറിച്ചു), by joining the nearest Anantiravars for the time being (അന്നടുക്കം അനന്തിരവരെയുംകൂട്ടി), and with the knowledge of the neighbours (അയല) and of the over-lord[7] (പതി = lord or master). In this way (ഇന്നാകരെ), in the blessed name (തിരുനാമം വയരാൽ) (?) of Nallātat Pērillātta[8] Tāye, Kuruḻḻēri Ūrāḷars, sitting inside (കരുള്ളേരി ഊരാളര ഉള്ളിരിക്കെ), paid the current market value of the Kunnummal house belonging to (തങ്ങളുടെ),

---

[1] It should be noticed that though the usual modern meaning of *Kandam* is *rice-field*, its original meaning is a *piece* or *fragment* or *share* of anything. When the Nāyar "600" were breaking up their communal rights in land, this word probably meant share.

[2] This means the seed required to sow the land was 60 Iḍangaḻis.

[3] Probably *Kaṇakkapiḷḷa* = writer, accountant of the temple.

[4] A.D. 1620.

[5] *Putuppaṭṭaṇam* (new town) was at one time the seat of the Southern Regent of Kōlattunād.

[6] See note to Deed No. 20.

[7] The *Kō* (king) is not here mentioned, but see Deed No. 14.

[8] Literally, *nameless*.

the said Kandumalacheri Tāye Chandu Kuṛup, Kora Kuṛup and Kunhan Kuṛup, settled the price (വിലമുറിച്ച) and obtained the Aṭṭippēr and water (അട്ടിപ്പേറുന്നീരുംകൊണ്ടാൻ). In this way (ഇന്നമക്കമെ) the good and bad stones (കല്ലുംകരടും), stump of *Nux vomica* (കാഞ്ഞിരകുററി) the front side and back side (മുമ്പുംപിമ്പും) ? thorns (മുള്ള), cobras (മൂൎക്കൻപാമ്പ), hidden treasure and the vessel in which it is secured (വെപ്പും ചെപ്പും), and water included in the four boundaries of the said house (വീട) are granted as Aṭṭippēr and water by settling the price. In behalf of the grantor, and in behalf of the purchaser of Aṭṭippēr with water, the wiṭnesses (അച്ചി) knowing (this) are Taṛavaṭṭam [1] Tekkum Talaṣṣēri (തറവാട്ടംതെക്കും തലശ്ശേരി), Kēḷu Kuṛup and Kilēriye Karuṇākara Kuṛup. Written by the god's accountant (ദൈവത്തിന്റെ കണക്കപിള്ള) with due publicity (കെട്ടുകെൾപ്പിച്ച = literally, heard and caused to be heard), in the blessed name (തിരുനാമംവയരം) (?) of Nallātat Pērillātta (nameless) god, with the Ūrāḷars sitting inside (ഊരാള ചിരുന്ന).

Note.—Translated from a copy received from the Huzur Sheristadar, Malabar Collector's Office.

No. 14.

Aṭṭippettōlakaraṇam (അട്ടിപ്പെററൊലകരണം), executed in Chinga Nyāyar (ഞായർ = solar month) of the year (which has) advanced (ചെന്ന) to 795.[2] Kuruvayilātt Tāyatt Puttalatt Nambiar of Putupaṭṭaṇatt Ūr (ഊര = village) received the current market value (അന്നപെറും വിലത്തരം), and with the knowledge of the neighbours (അയൽ), and of the over-lord (പതി = lord [3] or master), and in the presence (മുമ്പാകെ) of the king [4] (കോവിൽ = palace, put for king) ruling (വാഴും) that Nāḍu (അന്നാട), received full value in gold (പൊൻനിറിപ്പാഞ്ഞി), and granted Aṭṭippēr (അട്ടിപ്പെർ) and water (നീർ) by settling the price (വിലമുറിച്ച) in a way extinguishing the price (വിലയറമുറിച്ച) of his share [5] (കതി corruption of ഓഹരി = share) of his Mīttalapavuttil,

---

[1] *Taṛavaṭṭam* means "circle of Taṛas." The witnesses were evidently Karaṇavar of the Taṛas of the nad. See pp. 88 and 132 of the text. The *Pati* also knew of the transaction. See above. Who was this *Pati*? Paragraph (*i*) to Deed No. 3 seems to make it clear that at that time the *Pati* was the "600" of the nad, the body that corresponded in the Jews' and Christians' organizations to Anjuvaṇṇam and Maṇigrāmam in their corporate capacities. Whether the "600" had by this time divided the common property (the *Pati-paṭṭa-vāram*) among all the Taṛavads represented in the "600" it is difficult to say. On the whole, it is probably correct that the *Pati-paṭṭam* was divided among all the *Taṛavād* families (see the items included under *Taṛavād* in Deed No. 9) and that the individual known as the *Pati* was either the hereditary military commandant of the *Dēṣam* or the *Nāḍuvāḷi*, or perhaps some temporarily influential man in the nad.

[2] A.D. 1620.

[3] Compare the note to Deed No. 13.

[4] This deed is exactly similar to No. 13, and comes from the same part of the country. The omission of attestation by the *Kō* in No. 13 is therefore curious.

[5] Compare the note to Deed No. 35. Were the original *vīḍus*—manors—held *jointly* by the Taṛa? Does not this deed and No. 35 also afford evidence of the "gradual disentanglement of the separate rights of individuals from the blended rights of a community?"—*Maine Anc. Law*, pp. 269-70.

house.[1] Pallikkara Viṭṭil Ūrāḷan, in the blessed name (തിരുനാമം) of Pērillātta[2] Tayē (god) of Nallātatt Ūr (ഊര് = village), purchased Vayara and Nīr [വയറും നീരും = perhaps, including grass and water (?)] by settling the price (വിലമറിച്ച). In this way the boundaries of this house are, east Mēkkombatt house, south as far as Mekkalam, west as far as Tāyatt Puttillam, and north as far as Tirinnātt Kandi; the Kanynyra kuyi paramba and field (വയൽ), Chembu (ചെമ്പു = inferior yellowish soil ?), and water (നീർ) included in the above four boundaries; of these the Aṭṭippēr and water (അട്ടിപ്പേരുംനീരും) are granted after settling the price (വിലമറിച്ച). In behalf of him who granted the Aṭṭippēr and water (അട്ടിപ്പേരുംനീരും വിലമറിച്ചുകൊടുത്തമെയക്കം), and in behalf of him who purchased the Aṭṭippēr and water (അട്ടിപ്പേരും നീരും വിലമറിച്ചുകൊണ്ടമെയക്കം), the witness (താച്ചി corruption of സാക്ഷി) who knows this is Talavattutt[3] Putiya Paṭṭaṇatt Nānikkott Nambiar. Written by Mēkkanattokam Palli.

Note.—Translated from a copy received from the Huzur Sheristadar, Malabar Collector's Office.

No. 15.

Aṭṭippettōla Kāryam (അട്ടിപ്പെറോലകാര്യം), executed in the month (മിസം) of Kanni, 281, Putuvaypa[4] (പുതുവപ്പു). The Cochin Rājas (പെരുമ്പടപ്പ) Gangādhara (ഗംഗാധര), Vīra (വീര), Kēraḷa (കേരള), Trikkōvil (തൃക്കോവിൽ) Adhikārikal (അധികാരികൾ = Sarvādhikāryakār), granted on receipt of the market Aṭṭippēr value (പെറുംവില അട്ടാപ്പേരത്തിം), found then by four people (അന്നനാലരകണ്ട), a *Nīrmutaludakamare*[5] *Aṭṭippēr* (നീർമുതലുദകമറെ അട്ടിപ്പെറ) of their Dēṣam (ദേശം) to the north of the bar[6] (അഴി), and Pāliyat Rāman Iravi and heirs (തമ്പിമാർ) accordingly obtained, on payment of the market Aṭṭippēr value (പെറുംവില അട്ടിപ്പേരത്തിം), found then by four people (അന്നനാലരകണ്ട), a *Nīrmutaludakamare* Aṭṭippēr of the Dēṣam to the north of the bar. The boundaries[7] of the Dēṣam included in the Aṭṭippēr are Kaḻukutta[8] (കഴുകുത്ത = probably the depth of a pole) in the river (കായൽ) on the east, Kaḻukutta in the sea (കടൽ) on the west, the bar on the south, and the Captain's Cross (കപ്പിത്താൻ കുരിശികലെ) tōḍu (channel) on the north. Everything[9] contained within the said four boundaries (എന്നിനാല തൃക്കകത്ത

---

1 See note to Deed No. 20.

2 Literally, *nameless*.

3 *Taravattatt* (?). See note to No. 13.

4 *Putuvaypu* or *Putuveppu* (literally, new deposit) is an island formed between the mouths of the Cranganore and Cochin rivers. The deposit was formed in A.D. 1341. The date of the deed is therefore A.D. 1622.

5 From *Nīr* (Drav.) = water; *mutal* (Drav.) = property; *udakam* (Sansk.) = water; *varē* (Drav.) = as far as, up to.

6 Cochin bar.

7 This Dēṣam must have formed the southern extremity of what is now called the Island of Vypeen, part of which is now British territory inherited from the Dutch.

8 Meaning the boundary extends so far into the river as can be sounded by a bamboo pole used in propelling boats.

9 Compare Deed No. 21 and the note thereto.

അകപ്പെട്ട എപ്പേർപ്പെട്ടതും), such as stones (കല്ലു), charcoal (കറികട്ട), stumps of *Strychnos nux vomica* (കാഞ്ഞിരക്കുററി), thorn-clump (മുള്ളുമുരിട), cobras (മൂർഖപാമ്പ), holes (അള), mounds[1] (തറ), treasure (നിധി), wells (കിണറ) skies (ആകാശം), underground (പാതാളം), watercourses (നീരുവീതി), boundaries (അതിര), field ridges (വരമ്പ), canals (തോട), washing-places (തുറ), roads used by persons (ആൾപോകംവഴി), streams, (നീരപോകം ചാൽ), forests having deer (മാൻപ്പെട്ടംകാട), shady places having honey (തേൻപ്പെട്ടംചോല,), Dēsam[2] (ദേശം), Dēsādhipatyam [2](ദേശാധിപത്യം), Amṣam [3](അംശം), Sthānam (സ്ഥാനം), battle wager (അങ്കം), customs duty (ചുങ്കം), and everything else (മററ എപ്പേർപ്പെട്ടതും) was sold and purchased respectively. Written in the hand of Itti.

Note.—Translated from a copy received from the Dewan of Cochin.

No. 16.

Aṭṭipettōlakaraṇam (അട്ടിപ്പെററൊല കരണം), executed in Karkaḍaka Nyāyar (ഞായർ = solar month) of the year (which has) advanced to (ചെന്ന) 800.[4] The blessed name of Nallātat Ūrāḷan of Kuruvalleri Ūr (ഊര = village). The Ūrāḷan of the god paid the current market value (അന്നപെറും വില അത്ഥവും കൊടുത്ത), joined the nearest Anantiravars for the time being (അന്നടുക്കം അനന്തിരവാരെയുംക്കൂടി), paid the full value in gold (പൊന്നെരകൊടുത്ത), settled the price (വിലയറുറിച്ച), obtained Aṭṭippēr and water (അട്ടിപ്പെറും നീരും കൊണ്ടേൻ) of the Karumani house[5] belonging to (തന്റെ) Perunkinillāt Pilārat Chāttu Nambiyār. In this way the boundaries are south as far as the fields (വയൽ), west as far as Kātakandam, north as far as Aviyāram Kandi (eastern boundary not given); thorns (മുള്ള), good and bad stones (കല്ലുംകരടും), the stump of *Nux vomica* (കാഞ്ഞിരകററി), thorns (മുള്ള), and cobras (മൂർക്കൻപാമ്പ), included in the circle (വട്ടം) of the above four boundaries, are granted on Aṭṭippēr and water, after fixing the price (വിലമുറിച്ച). The witness (സാക്ഷി) in behalf of the grantor and grantee is....... Written by Valli.

Note.—Translated from a copy received from the Huzur Sheristadar, Malabar Collector's Office. The deed is incomplete, and, to some extent, unintelligible.

No. 17.

Pāṭṭōlakaruṇam (പാട്ടോലകരണം), executed in the solar month (ഞായർ) of Kumbham, of the year 822.[6] Mūkkachāttil Kandar Kandar and Karumattil Ponnan Chāttu received 121 new fanams from Chembil Parangodan Kandar; the object, then, of receiving the said 121 fanams is that our

---

[1] *Taṛa* is probably correctly translated here as "mounds," its original meaning.

[2] This deed is very interesting as it shows that Rajas were in the habit of occasionally selling the over-lordships (*Pati*) of territory. See note to Deed No. 13.

[3] *Amṣam* (Sansk.) = share, part; probably synonymous here with *vdram*, *i.e.*, the *Kō's* or *Pati's* share of produce.

[4] A.D. 1625. [5] See note to Deed No. 20. [6] A.D. 1627.

Talappalli Tirutt Kandam [1] 6 plots (കണ്ടം), Pulakkura Kandam [1] 2 plots, making a total of 8 plots, are a *pāṭṭam*, [2] together with the Kāvalpalam (കാവൽപലം or കാവൽഫലം = remuneration for protection [3] of land claimed by the chief inhabitants), on an annual [2] *pāṭṭam* of 5 potis (പൊതി) of paddy, as per the Eḍappāl Peru-nāḻi (പെരുനാഴി = big nāḻi); out of this deduct 2 potis and 8 tūnis (തുണി) as interest on the amount at 5 per cent., and commutable at 4 paṛas per fanam (നാലുപറവിലയും), and 12 tūnis (തുണി) for Kāvalpalam (കാവൽഫലം). May the balance of 2 potis (പൊതി) be paid annually. Thus written by Eḷēdatt Eḷayad.

Note.—Translated from a copy received from Kiḻepātt Teyyan Menon of Waḷḷuvanād Taluk.

No. 18.

Aṭṭippēṭṭōlakaruṇam (അട്ടിപ്പെറ്റോലകരണം), executed at Nallēppaḷḷi Mannam [4] (മന), of Ankavēṇātkaṭavūr (അങ്കവേണാട്ടകടവൂർ) Keirētatt (കൈരെടത്ത), in the solar month (ഞായർ) of Mithunam Eḍava vyāḻam, 831.[5] Chambattil Chāttan Chāttan and heirs (തമ്പിമാർ) received the market value (പെറുമതിം) from Iswara Paṭṭar, son of Ellappa Paṭṭar, residing at Nallēppaḷḷi. Thus the object of the said market value is that Chambattil Chāttan Chāttan and heirs, by pouring water granted as Nīrmutal (നീർമുതൽ = literally, water property) Nīraṭṭippēr (നീരട്ടിപ്പേർ = Aṭṭippēr with water) of 2 pieces of land sowing 20 paṛas and lying above the Vākappātat Arayākka Chiṛa lands sowing 45 paṛas down from Eḻuvat Potta in Kalayam Koḷumbu and above (മേലുട) Ankarāt Nilam, others sowing 20 paṛas above Ṭaḻatteturu Nilam, and others sowing 20 paṛas above Kāṛakkātan Chiṛa in Kosavan Kuḻi, making a total of (ആകെ) lands sowing 105 paṛas, and paṛambas on both sides, together with the upper and lower produce (മേൽഫലവും കീഴ്ഫലവും). Iswara Paṭṭar and heirs accordingly paid the said market value (പെറുമതിം), and by receiving water poured out obtained as Nīrmutal (നീർമുതൽ = water property) Nīraṭṭippēr (നീരട്ടിപ്പേർ = Aṭṭippēr with water) of the said lands sowing 20 paṛas at Vākappatom, sowing 45 paṛas at Kalayam Kolumbil, 20 paṛas of Tāḻatte, and 20 paṛas at Kosavankuḻi, making a total of (ആകെ) lands sowing 105 paṛas, and the paṛambas on both sides, together with the upper and lower produce (മേൽഫലവും കീഴ്ഫലവും). Written in the hand of Ponnachatat Pannochan, with the knowledge of Vettiyil Chāttan Chāttan and Tēvūr Teyyan Raman witnesses knowing this.

Note.—Translated from a copy received from Nallēpaḷḷi Ankarātta Valiya Mannādiyār of Cochin State.

---

[1] Here again *Kandam* occurs in a way to suggest that it originally meant the Taṛavād's share of the communal rights. See Deed No. 12.

[2] *Pāṭṭamāyi pāṭṭamāndu.*

[3] The duty of the *Kāṇakkārs* (Nayar headmen) was protection. See note to Deed No. 4. It is a significant fact that in this, the earliest *Kāṇam* deed, the duty of protection is thrown on the Kāṇakkar.

[4] *Vide* note to Deed No. 24.

[5] A.D. 1656.

No. 19.

Tīṭṭu (തീട്ട) of Yōgiyātiri (യോഗിയാതിരി), addressed to (കണ്ടുകൊൾവും) our Elavathūr Vānchi Tāyamman and heirs (തമ്പിമാര). In consideration of what we have enjoyed (നമുക്കവേണ്ടി അനുഭവിച്ചതിന്ന) from your Kārṇavan Chittalapalli Nambidi, we have given to you at the Rishabha Yōgam (ഋഷഭയോഗം = council of that name), for your hereditary enjoyment (വംശപരമ്പരയായി അനുഭവിച്ചുകൊള്ളുമാറും), the following: the Pallipuratta Pāṭṭam [1] (പാട്ടം), to be enjoyed as Kārām pāṭṭam[1] ? (കാരാംപാട്ടം-കാരായ്മപാട്ടം = perpetual pāṭṭam), and the Velakkora land sowing 62 paṛas, and Kāramata sowing 7 paṛas, which were given to you for 36 years, and 2 nārāyams of boiled rice (ചോറ) at Pilakkōd in Madilagam. From the solar month of Makaram, 842,[2] what is here written under orders may be enjoyed in hereditary succession (വംശപരമ്പരയായി).

Note.—Translated from a copy of a copper-plate deed received from the Nallēpaḷḷi Ankarātta Valīya Mannāḍiyar of Cochin State. The deed is barely intelligible in places.

No. 20.

Aṭṭippeṛṛōlakaraṇam (അട്ടിപ്പേറോലകരണം), executed in Mēta Nyāyar (ഞായർ = solar month) of the year (which has) advanced (ചെന്ന) to 845.[3] Putiyaparambatt Tachchōli [4] Emma Kuṛup and Rayiru Kuṛup of Meppayil Ūr (ഊര = village) having received (വാങ്ങികൊണ്ടു) the current market value (അന്നപെറും വില അർത്ഥം) of their Malamal house, [5] and joining (with them) the nearest Anantiravars for the time being (അന്നടുക്കം അനന്തിരവരെകൂടി), and having received (വാങ്ങി) full value in gold (പൊന്നിരവാങ്ങി), granted Aṭṭippēr and water (അട്ടിപ്പേറുനീരും), after settling the price (വിലമുറിച്ച), in a way to extinguish the price (വിലയറ) and water (right) (നീരറ), with the knowledge of the neighbours (അയൽ) and the over-lord (പതി = lord or master), and in the presence (മുമ്പാകെ) of the Kōvil (കോവിൽ = palace, hence king) of that Nād. Putiyaparambatt Tachchōli Dēvan Yamma Kuṛup and Rayiru Kuṛup having paid (കൊടുത്തു) the current market value (അന്നപെറുംവിലഅർത്ഥം), and having paid (കൊടുത്തു) the full value in gold (പൊന്നിറ), purchased the Aṭṭippēr by settling the price (വിലമുറിച്ച) of his (തന്റെ) Malamal house, by joining (with them) the nearest Anantiravars for the time being (അന്നടുക്കം അനന്തിരവരെയുംകൂടി), and with the knowledge of the neighbours (അയല) and of the over-lord (പതി = lord, master), and in

---

[1] Compare note to paragraph (*i*) of Deed No. 3.

[2] A.D. 1666.

[3] A.D. 1670.

[4] Apparently the family of the hero of the തച്ചോളിപാട്ട, the Robin Hood of North Malabar. *Conf.* p. 96 of the text.

[5] *Vīḍu* (Drav.) ordinarily means a house, but it had a meaning more ancient and more approximate to the verb [*viḍuka* (Drav.) = to part, let go, untie, discharge, abandon] from which it is derived. The *vīḍupēr*, 72 of which were conferred on the Jews by Deed No. 1, were items which were "given up" to them by the Perumal. The meaning of *vīḍu* in this deed would probably be more precisely represented by the word "manor." Compare the note on Taṛavād in Deed No. 22, and the note on *Purayiḍam* in Deed No. 26.

the presence (മുമ്പെ) of the king of that Nād (അന്നാടകൊവിൽ), in a way extinguishing the water (right) (നീരറ) and extinguishing the price (വിലയറ). In the blessed name of Perillātta (പെരില്ലാത്തതിരുനാമംവയരാം) of Nallādath Ūr (ഊര =village), the Ūrāḷars, by sitting inside (ഊരാളരുള്ളിരിക്കെ), got the Malamal house surrendered (വെപ്പിച്ചകൊണ്ടാൻ = liṭerally, caused to be laid down) by paying the current market value (അന്നപെറും വിലയത്ഥം), and by joining the nearest Anantiravars for the time being (അന്നുള്ളം അനന്തിരവരെയും കൂടി), and with the knowledge of the neighbours and the over-lord (അയല്വും പതിയും അറിയ), the Aṭṭippēr and water (അട്ടിപെറുംനീരും) were got surrendered (വെപ്പിച്ചകൊണ്ടാൻ) in the blessed name of the god (ദൈവം തിരുനാമം വയരാം ?) (by) the Ūrāḷars sitting inside (ഊരാളരുള്ളിരിക്കെ). In this way (ഇമ്മാക്കമെ) the boundaries of the said house are east as far as the god's swamp (പടന്ന), south as far as the river, west as far as the hill (മല), and north as far as the hill cultivated with chōḷam (ചൊളംവെച്ച), by Kiḻalam Kuṛup, the good and bad stones (കല്ലും കരടും), the stump of *Nux vomica* (കാഞ്ഞിരകററി), thorns (മുള്ള), cobras (മൂർക്കൻപാമ്പ), hidden treasure (വെപ്പ), the vessel in which it is secured (ചെപ്പ), water (നീര), included (അടങ്ങിട്ടുള്ള) in these four boundaries (are) given as Aṭṭippēr with water (നീരൊട്ടുകൂടി അട്ടിപ്പെറും നീരും), by settling the price (വിലമുറിച്ച); in behalf of the giver (കൊടുത്തമെയക്കം) and in behalf of him who purchased the Aṭṭippēr and water by settling the price, the witnesses (സാച്ചി) knowing (this) are Taṛavaṭṭam[1] Kaikanda (തറവാട്ടും കൈകണ്ട = literally, influential in the circle[1] of Taṛas), Malachchēri Kunka Kuṛup and Chellattan Karunakara Kuṛup; written by the god's accountant (ദൈവത്തിന്റെ കണക്കപിള്ള) with due pùblicity (കെട്ടുകേൾപ്പിച്ച = literally, heard and caused to be heard).

Note.—Translated from a copy received from the Huzur Sheristadar, Malabar Collector's Office. The document is in one place very obscure. There is an apparent inconsistency in the beginning, where the vendors are first said to sell the house by receiving the price and then to buy the same house by paying the price.

No. 21.

Aṭṭippettōla Kāryam (അട്ടിപ്പെററൊലകാരിയം), executed in the month (ധനം) of Dhanu, 853.[2] The Cochin Rājas (പെരുമ്പടപ്പ) Lekshmikōvil Adhikārikal (അധികാരികൾ = Sarvādhi-kāryakār), on receipt of the market Aṭṭippēr value, then found by four people (അന്നനാലരകണ്ട പെറുംവില അട്ടിപ്പെരത്ഥം) granted an Aṭṭippeṛa (അട്ടിപ്പെറ) of their Pilavattara paṛamba[2] (പറമ്പ), and Pāliyat Rāman Ittikkumaran and heirs (തമ്പിമാര) accordingly obtained, on payment of the market Aṭṭippēr value, then found by four people, an Aṭṭippeṛa of Pilavattara paṛamba. The boundaries of the paṛamba sold are Nambulikat paṛamba on the east, Vayikkat paṛamba on the south, Vayal on the west, and Vatakkera paṛamba on the north. Everything[3] of what-

---

[1] See note to Deed No. 13. [2] A.D. 1677-78.

[3] By this deed the Cochin Rāja disposed of a piece of garden. Compare with this the Deed No. 15.

ever description,[1] that is contained (അകപ്പെട്ട എപ്പേർപ്പെട്ടതും) within the said boundaries, including stones (കല്ല്), charcoal (കരിക്കട്ട), stump of *Strychnos nux vomica* (കാഞ്ഞിരക്കുററി), thorn-clump (മുള്ളുമുരിട), cobras (മൂർഖപാമ്പ), holes (അള), mounds (തറ), treasure (നിധി), wells (കിണറ), skies (ആകാശം), the underground (പാതാളം), water-course (നീരൊഴിധി), and everything else (മററ എപ്പേർപ്പെട്ടതും), were sold and purchased, as witness Kotamangalat Baṭṭatiri and Uḻutaral Baṭṭatiri. Written in the hand of Vaṭṭakkumcheri Uṇikkumaran.

Note.—Translated from a copy received from the Dewan of Cochin.

No. 22.

Tīṭṭu (തീട്ടു = letter from a superior to an inferior) from Karunnukki Tattan Nārāyaṇan to the Fifteen[2] (പതിനഞ്ചു) of Iriṇyālakuḍa[2] and to the Mūttatu (മൂത്തത) of Kolamanna. As the anger (കോപം) of Kūḍalmāṇikkam (കൂടൽമാണിക്കം = probably an evil spirit) was found in our Taṛavād, we have this day, according to the remedy suggested (ഒഴികഴിവിരിക്കുന്നപ്രകാരം) by an astrological calculation (പ്രശ്നം), surrendered (ഒഴിഞ്ഞു) by a document (എഴുതിവെച്ചു = literally, wrote and placed) laid on the blessed door (തൃപ്പടി) = door of temple) the lands (നിലം) and paṛambas (പറമ്പ) which are our Taṛavād[3] Janmam[4] (തറവാടജന്മം) in Allūr Dēṣam, in the country (നാട) of Chūndal, and Poymalē temple (ക്ഷേത്രം), Turutti temple, and Ālu Bhagavati temple out of (our) temples (ക്ഷേത്രം), and the property (വസ്തുവക), and retainers (ആൾ), and slaves (അടിയാർ) and others (മുതലായതും) of the above temples (ഈ ക്ഷേത്രങ്ങളിലെ), and in addition to this (ഇതുകൂടാതെ) the property (വസ്തുക്കൾ) in the interior Dēṣams (ഉൾദേശം) of Poravur, Perumannai and Kandiyūr, and the Kārāyma and Samudāyam (കാരായ്മസമുദായം) of the Kandiyūr temple (ക്ഷേത്രം), as perpetual (ശാശ്വതം) enjoyment (അനുഭോഗം), with water (ഉദകമായി), in order that (they) may be enjoyed for ever and ever (എന്നെന്നേക്കും) as Dēvaswam (property); all the above-written property

---

[1] In No. 15 the following were also named:—1, Boundaries; 2, Field ridges; 3, Canals; 4, Washing-places; 5, Roads; 6, Streams; 7, Deer forests; 8, Shady places for honey; 9, Dēṣam; 10, Dēṣādhipatyam; 11, Amṣam; 12, Sthānam; 13, Angam; and 14, Chungam. If all these important privileges had been conveyed by this deed, it is hardly possible that they would have been all lumped together under the general head at the end. Moreover, Deed No. 15 has likewise a general head for privileges not mentioned.

[2] *Iriṇyālakuḍa* is one of the original 64 Nambūtiri Grāmams (villages). The "Fifteen" probably constituted the council of the *Grāmam*, just as the *Kāraṇavar* of the Nayar *Taṛa* represented the *Taṛa* in the *Kūṭṭam* in the nad, or the *Paḷḷiyar* (literally, church people) the various communities of Christians under the protection of *Maṇigrāmam*. See Deed No. 3.

[3] The use of this word here by a Brahmaṇ family marks a change in the constitution of society. The *Taṛa* was the Nayar village or guild (so to speak); *Taṛavād* is *Taṛa-pāḍu*, that is, authority in the Taṛa. How could a Nambūtiri family have obtained authority in the Taṛa? The answer seems to be supplied by Deed No. 9 and also by Deeds Nos. 11, 13, 14, 16 and 20. The *viḍu* is, probably, equivalent to Taṛavad, and both alike, it will be seen, were frequently sold.

[4] This deed was executed by a Nambūtiri family in favor of the elders of a Nambūtiri village. This is the earliest instance as yet found of the use of the Sanskrit word *Janmam* in a Malayāḷi deed.

(മേലെഴുതിയവക സകലവും) may be enjoyed by the Dēvaswam in the same manner as we are enjoying them. (This is) executed voluntarily (മനപ്പൂർവ്വമായി), with gift of water Janmam [1] (ജന്മനീരുദകം), by Karumukka Illath Tattan Nārāyaṇan, Chumaran, and Saraswati and Nanganeli out of the females (അന്തർജ്ജനങ്ങൾ), on the 14th of Chittari month, in the year 856,[2] on the auspicious day, (ശുഭദിനം) of Tuesday (മംഗലവാരം) and written by Uṇikkandan Viṭṭil Rāman. Witnesses: Kōvūr Vāsudēvan and Nallūrpilli Paramēswaran.

Note.—Translated from a copy received from the Dewan of Cochin.

No. 23.

Pāṭṭōlakaruṇam (പാട്ടോലകരണം), executed in the solar month (ഞായർ) of Karkaḍakam, of the year 868.[3] Tirumalaṣṣēri Nārāṇan Nārāṇan having received 240 new fanams from (literally, from the hands of, കയ്യാൽ) Tekkēt Rāman Kumaran; now the object (കാര്യം) of receiving the said 240 fanams is that the lands at the northern end of Potiyapuram are a pāṭṭam [4] on a pāṭṭam of 24 paṛas of paddy, exclusive of an allowance for damage (കേട) and inclusive of Vāṣi (വാശി = allowance for difference of measures); let the net pāṭṭam of 12 paṛas of paddy, after deducting 12 paṛas for interest on the amount (advanced) at 5 per cent., and commutable at 1 paṛa per fanam, be paid annually to my Poḻattikkārar (പൊഴത്തിക്കാരർ = Pravarttikkār). Thus written by Ambāḻāt Kēlu.

Note.—Translated from a copy received from Kiḻepātt Teyyan Mēnon of Waḷḷuvanād Taluk.

No. 24.

Aṭṭippettōlakaraṇam (അട്ടിപ്പേറോലകരണം), executed in Chingam Nyāyar (ഞായർ = solar month), Karkiḍaka Vyāḻam, of the year 881,[5] at the Chittūr Mannatt [6] (മന്നത്തിരുന്ന = literally, sitting at the Mannatt) of the Kiḻap-pālayūr Nād (നാട). Kotakarē Kumaran Kandan received from (കയ്യാൽ = literally, from the hands of) Ambāt Rāman Mānchu the market value (പെരുവാരിതം); thus the object (കാര്യം) of this market value (പെരുവാരിതം) is that Kotakarē Kumaran Kandan has given, with water as Aṭṭippēr, his land (തൊറവ) sowing 80 paṛas, and bounded on the north by Otachirayil Mātampalli Vatti Kandam (field), on the south by the high road (പെരുവഴി), on the east by Pārikkāt Paru Nilam, and on the west by the hill; together with its upper produce (മേൽഫലം) and lower produce (കീഴ്ഫലം), as well as Vellayan and his two children, Kuṭṭi Kaṇṇan and his four children, and Tambi (തമ്പി) and his two children, making a total of five (adults) and six

---

1 *Vide* note above. Compare the phrase frequently repeated in the preceding and subsequent deeds, namely, Aṭṭippēr nīr, &c. *Janma nīr udakam* is merely the Sanskritised form of the ancient phrase.

2 A.D. 1681.

3 A.D. 1693.

4 *Paṭṭamāyi pāṭṭamāndu.*

5 A.D. 1706.

6 A place of judgment or assembly, or a place for transacting business. For the three kinds of Mannatt, *vide* Gundert's Dictionary under മന at page 788. The Chittūr Taluk of Cochin State lies east of Palghat.

children, and making a grand total of eleven Cheṛumars (വല്ലിചാത്തന്മാര), out of his (Kumaran Kandan's) slave Cheṛumars (അടിയാൻ വല്ലിചാത്തന്മാർ). In this way Ambāt Rāman Mānchu and heirs (തമ്പിമാര) have taken with water as Aṭṭippēr, after paying the above market value (പെരുവത്തം), the abovesaid land sowing 80 paṛas, and bounded on the north by Otachirayal Mātampalli Vatti Kandam (കണ്ടം = field), on the south by the high road (പെരുവഴി), on the east by Pārikkāt Paru Nilam, and on the west by the hill; together with the jungles (കാട) and embankment (കര) on both sides (ഇരുകര), as also Vellayan and his children, Kuṭṭi Kaṇṇan and his children, Tambi and his children, making a total of five adults and six children, and making a grand total of eleven Cheṛumars (വല്ലിചാത്തന്മാർ) out of the slave Cheṛumars (അടിയാര വല്ലിചാത്തന്മാർ). The witnesses who know this (transaction) are Ilamulē Chennan Rāman and Chennāḻikkote Chātta Rāman. Written by Mēlōḍatt Menon.

Note.—Translated from a copy received from the Nallēpaḷḷi Ankarātta Valiya Mannāḍiyār of Cochin State.

No. 25.

Aṭṭippettōlakaraṇam (അട്ടിപ്പെറോലകരണം), executed in Dhanu Nyāyar (ഞായർ = solar month), Chinga Vyāḻam, of the year 882,[1] at the Chittūr. Mannatt[2] (മന്നത്തിരുന്ന = literally, sitting at the Mannatt) of the Kiḻpapālayūr Nād (നാട). Mātampalli Korissan and heirs (തമ്പിമാർ) received from the hands of (കയ്യാൽ) Eḻuvatt Chāttan Malayan the market value (പെറുവത്തം). The object (കാര്യം), then, of this market value is that the Otasara land (ഉഭയം) I obtained from Kotukarē Nāyar, and sowing 500 Nāḷi (നാഴി) seeds, the boundaries whereof are these: below the Ambāt Nilam and above the Porayattavar's Nilam, west of Aṇṇāyi Kāṇam (അണ്ണായികാണം) and east of the public road. The land comprised within these (boundaries), and sowing 50 paṛas seed, and Vellanan, son of Cheṛuman (വല്ലിചാത്തൻ) Tambi, obtained[3] (നേടി) by me, and the original document (മുതൽകരണം) thereon, and the jungle (കാട), the hillock or margin (കര), channel (തോട), fees (ഇറ),[4] and the upper and lower produce (മേൽഫലവും കീഴ്ഫലവും) comprised within the abovesaid boundaries, are given with water as Aṭṭippēr by Mātampalli Korissan and heirs (തമ്പിമാർ). Thus having paid the said market value (പെറുവത്തം), the abovesaid Otasara land (നിലം), sowing 50 paṛas seed, and Cheṛuman (വല്ലിചാത്തൻ) Vellanan, with the original document (മുതൽകരണം) thereof, as well as the upper and lower produce comprised within the said boundaries, are taken with water as Aṭṭippēr by Eḻuvatt Chāttan Malayan and heirs (തമ്പിമാര). Thus the witnesses who know this (transaction) are Ilamulē Chēnnan Rāman and Chennāḻikkotē Chātta Rāman. Written by Nerayath Teyān.

Note.—Translated from a copy received from the Nallēpaḷḷi Ankarātta Valiya Mannāḍiyār of Cochin State.

---

[1] A.D. 1707.

[2] *Vide* note to Deed No. 24.

[3] Probably before this transaction regarding the land.

[4] Ancient meaning, tribute, taxes.

No. 26.

Aṭṭippeṭṭōla Kāryam (അട്ടിപ്പെറൊലകാര്യം), executed in the Kanni Nyāyar (solar month) of the year 888.[1] Kuḻikkāt Kārumukkil Nārāṇan Memman and heirs (തമ്പിമാര) conveyed (എഴുതികൊട്ടുത്തൻ = literally, wrote and gave), as Nīrmutalaṛuti,[2] Aṭṭippēr (നീരുമുതലറുതി അട്ടിപ്പേരാകെ), their Kārumattara Dēṣam (ദേശം) by receiving the market Aṭṭippēr value (പെറും വിലഅട്ടിപ്പെരത്ഥം), as then found by four people (നാലരകണ്ട), to Pāliyatt Mānnan Kōmmi, in the blessed name (തിരുനാമം) of Puṭiya (പുതിയ = new; probably newly-built) Peruntiracōvil Tēvar (പെരുന്തിരകൊവിൽതേവര = god of Peruntira temple, or god of that name). The boundaries of the Purayiḍam[3] (പുരയിടം = the site of a habitation, compound) thus purchased on Aṭṭippēr at Karumattara Dēṣam, are Otikkam Tōḍu (തോട = stream) on the east, the river on the south, Angāḍi Kaḍaivu (അങ്ങാടികടവ = shop ferry) on the west, and Rāmanchira (രാമൻചിറ = a tank or embankment of that name) on the north. Everything, of whatever[4] description (എപ്പെട്ടുത), included in the above four boundaries, has been purchased (എഴുതിച്ചുകൊണ്ടാൻ = literally, wrote and took or brought) by Pāliyatt Mānnan Kōmmi, as Nīrmutalaṛuti Aṭṭippēr (നീർമുതലറുതിഅട്ടിപ്പേറാകെ), in the blessed name of Puṭiya Peruntiracōvil Tēvar (പുതിയപെരുന്തിരകൊവിൽതേവര). The witnesses who know this (transaction) are Chēkolli Nambūtiri and Kūtampiḻḻi Nambiḍi.

Note.—Translated from a copy received from the Dewan of Cochin.

No. 27.

Aṭṭippeṭṭōlakaruṇam (അട്ടിപ്പെറൊലകരുണം), executed in the solar month (ഞായർ) of Kumbham, 888,[5] Kumbha Vyāḻam. Mātattil Ōtanyil Mūkkan and heirs (തമ്പിമാർ) received the current market value (അന്നപെറുംഅത്ഥം) from Nāmbaḻe Nārāṇan Chinnaran, and granted (വെച്ചുകൊട്ടുത്താൻ) him the Aṭṭippēr, with water (നീരുതകമായി), of the Adhipatyam (ആധിപത്യം = sovereignty) of his Kīḻē-Ōtani Taṛavād[6]..................[7]............ in Vellōtt Kuriṣṣi Dēṣam, along with the said Dēṣam and Dēṣādhipatyam (ദേശാധിപത്യം = supreme authority in the Dēṣam), and Ūrāyma (ഊരായ്മ), and Ama[8] [ആമ = turtle (?)] and hill (മല), and Malapuṛam (മലപ്പുറം =

---

[1] A.D. 1712.

[2] *Nīr* (Drav.) = water; *mutal* (Drav.) = property; *aṛuti* (Drav.) = end, utmost limit.

[3] This word is probably used here in a wider sense than ordinary. As the sale was of a *Dēṣam*, the proper rendering of *pura* (= house), *iḍam* (= place, mansion), should probably be *manor*. Compare the note on *vīḍu* in Deed 20.

[4] It is impossible to say from this whether the official dignities of *Dēṣavāḻi* were included in the rights conveyed.

[5] A.D. 1713.

[6] Here the word *Taṛāvāḍ* (*Taṛa-pāḍu*, see Glossary) bears its original meaning. Compare notes on *vīḍu* in Deed No. 20 and on *Purayiḍam* in Deed No. 26.

[7] Words gone here owing to age of document.

[8] Perhaps the seat shaped like a turtle, or perhaps *Ambalapaḍi*, the seat of honor in a temple. The *Āma*, however, was probably portable, while the *Ambalapaḍi*, was fixed in the outer side of the wall of the sanctuary.

hill side), and Nanya (നഞ്ഞ = a poison used in fishing), and hunting (നായാട്ട), and everything, of whatever description (ഏപ്പേർപ്പെട്ടതും). Thus Nārāṇan Chumaran and heirs (തമ്പിമാർ) obtained (ചെപ്പിച്ചുകൊണ്ടാൻ), by paying the current market value (പെരുംഅർത്ഥം), the Kiḻē-Ōtani Taṛavād, Dēṣam, Dēṣādhipatyam, Ambalapaḍi[1] (അമ്പലപ്പടി), Ūrāyma, hill (മല), Malapuṛam (hill-side), Nanya (നഞ്ഞ), and hunting. Mūkkan and heirs (തമ്പിമാർ) accordingly granted Aṭṭippēr with water, after receiving the current market value, and Nārāṇan Chumaran and heirs (തമ്പിമാർ) obtained Aṭṭippēr with water after paying the current market value, as witnessed on behalf of both grantor and grantee by the Sabhavaṭṭam (സഭാവട്ടം = circle of assembly). Written in the hand of Putiyētat Komunni.

Note.—The original is in Vaṭṭeḻuttu charactor. A clause near the end is imperfect, and has been omitted. The copy from which this translation has been made was obtained from Kiḻēppāṭṭ Teyyan Mēnon of Waḷḷuvanād Tāluk, Malabar.

No. 28.

Aṭṭippettōlakaraṇam (അട്ടിപ്പെറ്റോലകരണം), executed in the month (മാസം) of Karkiḍakam of the year 898.[2] Samudāyattiri Paṇikkar and heirs (തമ്പിമാർ) have given, with water (നീരട്ടി), the Aṭṭippēr of the land (നിലം) called Vellātt oḻuva, sowing 12 paṛas and belonging to the three Paṇikkars of Vellātt Samudāyam (വെള്ളാട്ടസമുദായത്തിൽ പണിക്കാക്കന്മൂവൃക്കും), after receiving[3] the market Aṭṭippēr gold (പെരുംഅട്ടിപ്പെറുപൊന്ന), then found by four people (അന്നനാലരകണ്ട). In this way Pāliyatt Mānnen Komi and heirs (തമ്പിമാർ) have bought with water the land (നിലം) called Vellātt oḻuva, sowing 12 paṛas, after paying (മാവറുതലററ) the market Aṭṭippēr gold then found by four people. The witnesses who know this are Mangalassa Nambūtiri and Kiḻāni Nambūtiri. Written by Pattatt Rāman.

Note.—Translated from a copy received from the Dewan of Cochin.

No. 29.

Aṭṭippettōlakaruṇam (അട്ടിപ്പെറ്റോലകരണം), executed in the solar month of Karkiḍakam, 898,[2] Dhanu Vyāḻam. Kolappurat Nōkan Nārāyaṇan and heirs (തമ്പിമാർ) received the current market value (അന്നപെരുംഅർത്ഥം) from Pālayūr Viyatan Mānichan, and granted him the Aṭṭippēr with water of Mūrkankandi Nilam, Kodunga Nilam, Telākka Nilam, Ataṁban Nilam, Patinhārē Vellakunnu paṛamba, and Namban Pallimanyāyal (പള്ളിമയ്യാൽ),

---

[1] Here *Ambalapaḍi* seems to be the equivalent of *Āma*, *vide* above.

[2] A.D. 1723.

[3] Receiving and paying are qualified by the phrase മാവറുതലററ, which cannot be clearly made out. If മാവർ is a corruption of മൂവര, then the clause may mean "in a way extinguishing the right of the three," *i.e.*, three Paṇikkars. But if മാവര stands for മാവൻ, then the clause may mean "in a way extinguishing the right of Mavan, a deity of Nayars." The Paṇikkars being called Samudāyam favors this interpretation. Finally the word may mean that the right extinguished was "as far as the mango tree," *i.e.*, the timber right. On this last point compare Deed No. 43.

situated in Irimbālaṣṣēri Dēṣam. Thus Pālayūr Viyatan Mānichan paid the current market value and obtained the Aṭṭippēr with water of the said Mūrkankandi Nilam, Kodunga Nilam, Telākka Nilam, Atamban Nilam, Patinhārē Vellakunnu paṛamba and Namban Pallimanyāyal (പള്ളിമഞ്ഞായൽ). The boundaries (അതിൎത്തികൾ) of the said lands are east Vellātkunnu, south Nambankalam Nilam, west Ayyappantēpanatiri Nilam, and north Vellarākku Nilam. Everything, of whatever description (എപ്പേൎപ്പെട്ടതും), contained within the said boundaries is given (as) Aṭṭippēr with water. The boundaries of Mūrkankandi Nilam are east Mātāna Nilam, south Atamāri Nilam, west the embankment of the tank, and north the canal; everything, of whatever description (എപ്പേൎപ്പെട്ടവയും), included within the said boundaries, including the planting space of seedlings (ഞാറ്) and the interval between them (ഞാറിയിടപ്പുഴുത), was obtained on Aṭṭippēr with water; as witnessed on behalf of both grantor and grantee by neighbours (അയല്ലും), the over-lord[1] (പതിയും), and the Sabhavaṭṭam (circle of assembly). Written in the hand of Vellōt Rāman.

Note.—The original is in Vattēḻuttu character. The copy from which this translation was made was obtained from Kiḻēpāṭṭ Teyyan Mēnon of Waḷḷuvanād Tāluk, Malabar.

No. 30.

Aṭṭippettōlakaruṇam (അട്ടിപ്പെറോലകരണം), executed in the solar month of Makaram of the year 898,[2] Dhanu Vyāḻam. The Ūrāḷars of Īswaramangalam sitting inside [ഉള്ളിരുന്ന = sitting inside (probably of temple)] in the sacred name (തിരുനാമക്കെപ്പേരാൽ) of the god (ദേവർ), received the current market value (anna peṛum artham) from Valayūr Kuriyētat Viyatan Mānichan, and granted him the Aṭṭippēr with water, *Nīrudakamāyi*, of their Veṭṭan Nilam in Kiḻatrikkōvil Dēṣam. Thus Valayūr Kuriyētat Viyatan Mānichan paid the current market value (അന്നപെറുമൎത്ഥം) and obtained the Aṭṭippēr with water of the Veṭṭan Nilam in Kiḻatrikkōvil Dēṣam. The Ūrāḷars of Īswaramangalam sitting inside (ഉള്ളിരുന്ന = sitting inside, perhaps of temple), in the sacred name (തിരുനാമക്കെപ്പേരാൽ) of the god (ദേവർ), granted the Aṭṭippēr with water, of everything, of whatever description (എപ്പേൎപ്പെട്ടതും), comprised within the four boundaries of the said Veṭṭan Nilam in Kiḻatrikkōvil Dēṣam. Thus witnessed by the Sabhavaṭṭam[3] (സഭാവട്ടം = circle of assembly) on behalf of the parties granting and obtaining, for current value, the Aṭṭippēr with water of Veṭṭan Nilam in Kiḻatrikkōvil Dēṣam, together with everything, of whatever description, contained within its four boundaries. Written in the hand of Panku.

Note.—The original is in Vaṭṭēḻuttu characters. The copy from which this translation was made was obtained from Kiḻēpāṭṭ Teyyan Mēnon of Waḷḷuvanād Tāluk, Malabar. A clause near the end is imperfect and has been omitted.

---

[1] Here the Pati and the circle of assembly attest the deed.

[2] A.D. 1723.

[3] The circle of assembly represented authority.

No. 31.

Pāṭṭōlakarunam (പാട്ടോലകരണം), executed in the solar month (ഞായർ) of Kanni, 899.[1] Tirumalaśśēri Nārāṇan Nārāṇan received 840 new fanams from (the hands of) Mūlayil Kummiṇi Tāyi; the object (കാര്യം), then, of receiving the said 840 fanams is that the land called Ekaram in Īswaramangalam Pāṭṭam[2] (പാട്ടം) is a pāṭṭam[3] on a pāṭṭam of 56 paṛas of paddy, as per my Nārāyappaṛa;[4] out of this deduct 11 paṛas on account of damage (കേടുപിഴ) and 42 paṛas on account of interest on the amount (advanced); let the balance of 3 paṛas of pāṭṭam, which with Vāśi (വാശി = allowance for difference of measure) becomes 3 paṛas and 3 tūṇis (തൂണി = a measure about 1½ Iḍangāḻi), be paid to my Poḻuttikkārar (പൊഴുത്തിക്കാരര = Pravarttikkar). Thus written by Atiyārat Krishnan.

Note.—Translated from a copy received from Kiḻēpāṭṭ Teyyan Mēnon of Waḷḷuvanād Tāluk.

No. 32.

Pāṭṭōlakaraṇam (പാട്ടോലകരണം), executed in the solar month of Kanni, 899.[1] Tirumalaśśēri Nārāṇan Nārāṇan received 101 fanams and 125 paṛas of paddy from Mūlayil Kummiṇi Tāyi; the object, then, of receiving the said 101 fanams and 125 paṛas of paddy is that the land which formerly belonged to Kundanūr Perumpilāvil people of Cheṛumarutūr Dēśam is a pāṭṭam[3] on a pāṭṭam of 48 paṛas, as per my Nārāyappaṛa (നാരായപറ), exclusive of an allowance for damage (കേട). Out of this deduct 10 paṛas as interest on the amount at 5 per cent., and commutable at 4 paṛas per fanam, and let the balance of 38 paṛas be paid to my Poḻuttikkārar (പൊഴുത്തിക്കാരര) annually. Thus written by Atiyārat Teyyan.

Note.—Translated from a copy received from Kiḻēpātt Teyyan Mēnon of Waḷḷuvanād Tāluk.

No. 33.

Aṭṭippettōlakaraṇam (അട്ടിപ്പെറ്റോലകരണം), executed in the solar month (ഞായർ) of Mithunam of the year 900.[5] Having received from (കയ്യാൽ = from the hands of) Āṭayur Rāman, Samudāyam (സമുദായം) (of) the Ūrāḷars who sit inside (ഉള്ളിരുന്ന = sitting within, perhaps the temple), in the blessed name (തിരുനാമം) of the Pallimal Tēvar (തേവർ = god), the current market value (അന്നുപെറും അർത്ഥം), Patavarkōte Nārāyaṇan Dēvan granted

---

[1] A.D. 1724.

[2] The sense in which the word *pāṭṭam* is here used, that is, as an aggregation of lands, points to yet another mode in which the "Six Hundred" broke up their communal rights. The *Nād* was assessed with a certain quantity of produce as the *Kō's* share, that is, as *Kō-pāṭṭa-vāram.* Note (i) to Deed No. 3. The *Taṛavād Kāraṇavar* in distributing the land would have to assign liability to pay a certain portion of the *Kō's pāṭṭam* to each piece of land made over to each *Taṛavād* as its share of the common property. Each piece of land would then come to be known as so and so's or such and such *pāṭṭam.* The use of the word in this sense is still adhered to in British Cochin inherited from the Dutch.

[3] *Pāṭṭamāyi pāṭṭamāndu.*

[4] നാരായം = a certain measure.

[5] A.D. 1725.

[എഴുതിവെച്ചുകൊടുത്താൻ = literally, wrote and gave by laying (on the ground)] Aṭṭippēr (അട്ടിപ്പേർ) with pouring of water (നീരടകമായി), of Arangatodi land (നിലം) of 12 paṛas, Mutayan Chattamili of 12 paṛas, Pullānimuri of 6 paṛas, the land above it (അതിന്നമേലെ), of 5 paṛas, and Kunnachcheri Kandam[1] of 12 paṛas, aggregating (കൂടി) lands sowing 47 measures (വടിപ്പൻ = a measure) of seed, possessed by him (തനിക്കുള്ള) in Valia Kundanūr Dēśam. Thus paying the current market value (അന്നവെ വംത്തം), Atayur Rāman Samudāyam (of) the Ūrāḷars who sit inside (ഉള്ളിരുന്ന = see note above), in the blessed name (തിരുനാമം) of the Pallimal Tēvar (തേവർ), obtained [എഴുതിവെപ്പിച്ചുകൊണ്ടാൻ = literally, wrote and caused to be laid (on the ground)] Aṭṭippēr (അട്ടിപ്പേർ) with pouring of water (നീരടകമായി), of Arangatodi land (നിലം) of 12 paṛas, Mutayan Chāttamili of 12 paṛas, Pullānimuri of 6 paṛas, the land above it (അതിന്നമേലെ) of 5 paṛas, and Kunnachcheri Kandam of 12 paṛas, aggregating lands sowing 47 measures (വടിപ്പൻ) of seed, (situated) in Valia Kundanūr Dēśam. Thus Patavarkōte Nārāyaṇan Dēvan having received the current market value, granted (എഴുതിവെച്ചുകൊടുത്താൻ) Aṭṭippēr with pouring of water (നീരടകമായി), of the lands sowing 47 paṛas of seed which he possesses (തനിക്കുള്ള) in Valia Kundanūr Dēśam. Thus Atayur Rāman obtained (എഴുതിവെപ്പിച്ചുകൊണ്ടാൻ = see note above) the said lands (as) Aṭṭippēr with pouring of water (നീരടകമായി). Thus the witness who knows this on behalf of the grantor (എഴുതിവെച്ചുകൊടുത്തമെയ്യും) and grantee (എഴുതിവെച്ചുകൊണ്ടമെയ്യും) is Rāru Paṭṭēri (Bhaṭṭatiri). Written by Kēlachchātil Rāman.

Note.—Translated from a copy received from the Dewan of Cochin.

No. 34.

Dēśapāttōlakaruṇam (ദേശപാട്ടോലകരുണം), executed in the solar month (ഞായർ) of Karkaḍakam 906[2] Chinga Vyāḻam Kūḍallūr Yōgiyātiri Tiruvaḍi (കൂടല്ലൂരയൊഗിയാതിരിതിരുവടി) in the name of Triśśivapērūr Appan [തൃശ്ശിവപേരൂർഅപ്പൻ = Trichur god (?)] received 14,000 old fanams from Kūttalē Anantanārāyaṇan Tayamma. The object of receiving the above 14,000 fanams is that subsequent to the former document, lands sowing 420 paṛas of Kanimangalam Chērikkal[3] (ചേരിക്കൽ), 120 paṛas of Utiyal, 360 paṛas of Manniti Chērikkal (ചേരിക്കൽ), 620 paṛas of Mattūr Chērikkal, 120 paṛas of Ayinampāṭṭam,[4] and 120 paṛas of Mangalūr Vengattara and 18 Cheṛumars (വല്ലിയാൾ) are a pāṭṭam to you[5] on a pāṭṭam of 5,000 paṛas of paddy including the 1,000 paṛas payable by Kayarādi[6] Pattillattavar and the 120 paṛas payable from Veḷḷāmkūṛ [വെള്ളാംകൂറ (?)]. The net annual puṛapād is 1,500 paṛas after deducting 1,050 paṛas for interest on the amount (advanced),

---

[1] See note to Deed No. 12. [2] A.D. 1731.

[3] Lands belonging to Rajas or temples.

[4] See note to Deed No. 31 on *pāṭṭam* used in this way.

[5] *Pāṭṭamāyi pāṭṭamāndu.*

[6] കയരാടിപത്തില്ലത്തവർ = the ten Illam people of Kayarāti (?).

2,240 paras for Changngātam[1] (ചങ്ങാതങ്ങളും) and Palisa [പലിശകളും = persons rendering service as guards bearing (palisa) shields] and 210 paras for പ്രവൃത്തിക്കാരന്[2] (?) പ്രോത്തിയാവന് (different kinds of agents, servants), making a total deduction of 3,500. The above purapād of 1,500 paras with one Chōtana (ചോതന = a measure) of oil should be annually[3] paid regularly on the 1st of every Chingam, and you may enjoy വഴിപിഴ (fines) for infringing old customs. Written in the hand of Kuruppat Chēnnan.

Note.—Translated from a copy of a copper-plate deed received from the Nallāpaḷḷi Ankarātta Valiya Mannādiyār of Cochin State.

No. 35.

Valiyōlakaranam (വലിഓലകരണം, corruption of വിലയോലകരണം = bill of sale), executed in the solar month (ഞായര്) of Karkaḍakam of the year 914.[4] Kurikkalōtē Pālakkal Mīttalevīṭṭil Ummanga and Uchchira of Cherukunnatt village (ഊര) sold as far as their share (തങ്ങൾക്കുള്ള ഓഹരി ഒഴുവും) of the Tara[5] (തറ) Kandam (കണ്ടം = field) and swamps (കൈപ്പാട) below their house (വീട). Tāyatt Vīṭṭil Rairu Koran and heirs (തമ്പിമാര്) purchased (the same) by paying the current market[6] value (അന്നപെറുംഅര്ത്ഥം). The boundary of the land (കണ്ടം) for which this price was paid is east as far as the river, south as far as the Pālakkal paramba (പറമ്പ), west as far as the Pālakkal paramba, and north as far as the Pātikkarantē Kandam (land). The land (നിലം) produce (ഫലം = fruit) hidden treasure (ഓപ്പു) and the vessel in which it is secured (ചെപ്പു) and thorns (മുള്ള), and cobras (മൂര്ഖൻപാമ്പ) included in the said four boundaries are purchased (വിലകൊണ്ടവൻ) by paying the price (വിലകൊടുത്ത). The witness[7] who knows this (transaction) is Kuppadākkal Kaṇṇan Kammāran and the witness who knows the house[8] (കുടിഅറിയുംസാക്ഷി) is Valliyotan Chingan Kelu. Written with the knowledge of the neighbours[9] (കേട്ടുകേൾപ്പിച്ചു) in the hand of Talavil Ṣankaran.

Note.—Translated from a copy received from the District Munsif of Kavai, Chirakkal Tāluk. The original is in Tamil (*Kōleluttu*) characters.

---

[1] See Glossary. [2] Probably for പ്രവൃത്തിയാവൻ.

[3] This deed cannot be clearly understood, as the previous deed is not forthcoming. So far as can be made out it is a Kāṇam deed (see Glossary under "Kāṇam" and notes to Deed No. 4) of a whole *Dēsam* or of the whole of the demisor's interest in land, &c., in the *Dēsam*. It is of interest because the *Kāṇakkār* had evidently to take upon himself the protection of the territory. See Deed No. 4.

[4] A.D. 1739.

[5] The fact that the vendors sold their share of the *Tara* field or *Tara* portion (*Kandam*, see Deed No. 12) looks as if the *Tara* (Nāyar village or guild) had held property in its corporate capacity in this part of the country (Northern Kōlattunad). See Deed No. 4 and Deed No. 14.

[6] Literally, *Anna* = that day; *Perum* = which will produce; *Artham* = the money, wealth.

[7] The attestation of the neighbours and of two special witnesses was alone considered necessary in this case.

[8] (?)

[9] Literally "heard and caused to be heard." Keṭṭu-Keḷpichu.

No. 36.

Aṭṭippeṭṭōlakaraṇam (അട്ടിപ്പെറൊലകരണം), executed in Eḍavam Nyāyar (solar month) Karkaḍaka Vyāḻam of the year 917 [1] at the Chittūr Mannatt [2] (മന്നത്ത) of the Kiḻappalayur Nād (നാട). Vārikkōt Rāman and heirs (തമ്പിമാർ) received the market value (പെറുവത്ഥം) from the hands of Ambāt Rāman Mānchu. The object of this market value is that Vārikkāt Rāman and heirs have given with water as Aṭṭippēr his (Rāman's) property (തൊന്മ) the field [3] (കണ്ടം) sowing 10 paṛas (and situated) above the Ambāttē field by the side (ഓരം) of the hill (മല) and below the field belonging to the Ayam house, together with its adjoining hillock or margin (കര) and upper and lower produce (മെൽഫലവുംകീഴ്ഫലവും). Thus having paid the said market value the abovesaid land (നിലം) which is above the Ambāt field by the side of the hill and below the field belonging to Ayam house, and sowing 10 paṛas, together with its adjoining hillock or margin and the upper and lower produce has been taken with water as Aṭṭippēr by Ambāt Mānchu and heirs (തമ്പിമാർ). Thus the witnesses who know this (transaction) are Ilamulē Chennan Rāman and Chennāḻikkote Chātta Rāman. Written by Kuttikāt Itti Korappen.

Note.—Translated from a copy received from the Nallēpaḷḷi Ankarātta Valiya Mannāḍiyar of Cochin State.

No. 37.

Aṭṭippeṭṭōlakaraṇam (അട്ടിപ്പെറൊലകരണം), executed at Nallaypaḷḷi Mannatt [2] (മന്നത്ത) in Angavēnāt (അങ്കവെണാട്ടു) (?) Kaḍavūr (കടവൂർ) (?) Kayariyaḍath (കയരിയടത്ത) (?) in the solar month (ഞായർ) of Tulām 924 [4] Makara Vyāḻam. Karutta Mannāṭṭil Iravi Itarachan and heirs (തമ്പിമാർ) received from (the hands of) Tottatt Malayan Itti Chāttar the current market value (പെരുവത്ഥം). The object of receiving the market value is that Karuttamannāṭṭil Iravi Itarachan and heirs have given by pouring water as Nīrmutal (നീർമുതൽ = water property) the Nīr Aṭṭippēr (നീർഅട്ടിപ്പെർ) of his (Itarachan's) land (തൊന്മ) [5] situated on the south of the Kaḷaparamba (കളപറമ്പ) and Pūḷa (പൂള = silk-cotton tree) which are above the embankment (ചിറ) lying below that (land) demised on Kāṇam [6] (കാണംചാത്തിയ) by them (Itarachan and heirs) at Kottamangalam (കൊററമങ്ങലം) and (situated) on the north of the Koḷachira (കൊളചിറ = big tank); the plots (കണ്ടം) included within these (limits) sowing 70 paṛas and Kuḻi (കുഴി = an excavated ground) and the three Kuḻi parambas (കുഴിപറമ്പ) with their upper and lower produce (മെൽഫലവും കിഴ്ഫലവും) together with Atiyān Valli Chāttanmār (അടിയാൻവള്ളിചാത്തന്മാർ = slave Cheṛumars) Kaṇṇan's son Karuttapulli and Rangayan. Thus Tōdatt Malayan Itti Chāttan and heirs

---

[1] A.D. 1742.

[2] *Vide* note to Deed No. 24.

[3] *Kandam*. See note to Deed No. 12.

[4] A.D. 1748.

[5] *Tonma*, a corrupt form of *Svanma*, which occurs in Deed No. 6.

[6] The land demised on *Kāṇam* was not sold.

(തമ്പിമാർ) by giving the abovesaid market value (പെറുവത്തം) obtained as water property (നീർമുതൽ) the Nīr Aṭṭippēr (നീരട്ടിപ്പേർ) of the abovesaid lands with their upper and lower produce (മേൽഫലവും കീഴഫലവും) and Kuḻi (കുഴി) and the three Kuḻi parambas together with two Cherumars (വള്ളിയാൻ). Witnesses hereof are Vaḍavannūr Veḷḷāḷars (വടവന്നൂർവെള്ളാളർ) and Kiḻillatt Anantiravars (കീഴില്ലാത്ത അനന്തിരവർ). Written in the hands of the vendor (കൊണ്ടാൻ).

Note.—Translated from a copy received from the Nallēpaḷḷi Ankarātta Valiya Mannāḍiyar of Cochin State.

No. 38.

Baliyōlakaraṇam (ബലിയോലകരണം, corruption of വിലയോലകരണം = sale-deed), executed in the solar month (ഞായർ) of Makaram of the year 925.[1] Kāliyatt Vīṭṭil Kunyan Nambi and heirs (തമ്പിമാര) having received (വാങ്ങി) the current market[2] value (അന്നപെറും പൊൻകാണം വില) sold (വിലകൊട്ടത്താർ) the Kurikkalōtt Pālakkal Kōliyatt Putiyavīttilē Vaḷappa (വളപ്പ = paramba) in Cherukunnatt village (ഊര = village) Pālakkal Mittalēvīṭṭil Kammāran Otēnan having paid (കൊടുത്ത) the current market[2] value (അന്നപെറും പൊൻകാണം വില) purchased (വിലകൊണ്ടാൻ) (the same). The boundaries of this paramba (പറമ്പ) are, east as far as the Canal (തോട), south as far as the Chettire Kāranma Kandam[3] (കണ്ടം = field), west as far as the eastern wall (മതിൽ) of Kāliyatt Mittalē house, and north as far as the Bhagavati Ammēre Kandam[3] (കണ്ടം = field). Kāliyatt Vīṭṭil Kunyan Nambi and heirs having received the current market value sold[4] the lands (നിലം) and produce (പലം = fruit), including (അടക്കി) the hidden treasure (വെപ്പി) and the vessel in which it is secured (ചെപ്പ) comprised within the said four boundaries. Pālakkal Mittalēvīṭṭil Kammāran Otēnan purchased[5] (the same) by paying the current market value. The witness (താച്ചി corruption of സാക്ഷി) who knows this (transaction) is Kuppāḍakkal Kaṇṇan Kammāran and the witness who knows the house (?) [കടിഅറിയുംതാച്ചി (?)] is Vellyodan Chindan Kōran. With the knowledge of these, written in the hand of Talavil Nārāyaṇan Ṣankaran.

Note.—Translated from a copy received from the District Munsif of Kavai, Chirakkal Tāluk. The original is in Tamil (*Kōleḻuttu*) characters.

---

[1] A.D. 1750.

[2] Literally, *Anna* = that day; *Perum* = which will produce; *Pon* = gold; *Kāṇam* = *kāṇam*, possession; *Vila* = price.

[3] See note to Deed No. 12.

[4] The use of the word *Kāṇam* above proves, that what was sold was the *Kāṇam* right (compare Deed No. 4). If so, it is important to observe exactly the things so conveyed, viz., lands, produce and hidden treasure. *Veppum Cheppum* are two of the best known incidents of the water birthright.

[5] It is suggested in a note to Deed No. 2 that possibly the transfer of freehold "by water" came into the country with the Vēdic Brahmans, whose influence was never so great in this part of the country (North Kōlattunad, Chirakkal Tāluk) as it was further south. Possibly, therefore, this deed and, perhaps, No. 35 also were meant to be freehold deeds. They were certainly handed in as copies of so-called Janmam deeds.

No. 39.

Aṭṭippeṭṭōlakaraṇam (അട്ടിപ്പെറ്റോലകരണം), executed in the solar month (ഞായർ) of Dhanu of the year 932.[1] Nechchikkōt Rāman Kiṭṭaṇan (കിട്ടണൻ = vulgar form of Krishnan) and heirs (തമ്പിമാർ) received from (കയ്യാൽ = from the hands of) Kuṛuppatt Chīrukōta and heirs (തമ്പിമാർ) the current market value (അന്നുപെറും അത്ഥം). Thus having received the current market value, Nechchikkōt Rāman Kiṭṭaṇan and heirs granted (എഴുതികൊടുത്താൻ = literally wrote and gave) the Aṭṭippēr (അട്ടിപ്പേർ) as water property (നീർമുതൽ) with water (ഉദകം) of his Kotumanna land (നിലം) sowing 6 paṛas in Kurichchikkare Dēṣam. Thus having paid the current market value, Kuṛuppatt Chīrukōta and heirs obtained [എഴുതിച്ചുകൊണ്ടാൻ = literally had or got (it) written] the Aṭṭippēr as water property (നീർമുതൽ) with water of the Kotumanna land sowing 6 paṛas in Kurichchikkare Dēṣam. Thus Nechchikkōt Rāman Kiṭṭaṇan and heirs granted the Aṭṭippēr as water property with water of the Kotumanna (land) of 6 paṛas. Thus having paid the current market value, Kuṛuppatt Chīrukōta and heirs obtained (എഴുതിച്ചുകൊണ്ടാൻ, see note above) the Aṭṭippēr as water property with water of Kotumanna (land) of six paṛas in Kurichchikkare Dēṣam. Thus Rāman Kiṭṭaṇan and heirs granted (എഴുതികൊടുത്താൻ) the said land. Thus Chīrukōta and heirs obtained (എഴുതിച്ചുകൊണ്ടാൻ) the said land. The witnesses who know this in behalf of the grantor (എഴുതികൊടുത്തതമെയ്യും) and of the grantee (എഴുതിച്ചുകൊണ്ടതമെയ്യും) are Koravankuḻi Nāyar and Āttittrē Kora Māppiḷḷa. Written in the hand of Chīrāman.

Note.—Translated from a copy received from the Dewan of Cochin.

No. 40.

Aṭṭippeṭṭōlakaraṇam (അട്ടിപ്പെറ്റോലകരണം), executed in the solar month (ഞായർ) of Mithunam of the year 934.[2] Having received the current market value (അന്നുപെറും അത്ഥം) from (കയ്യാൽ = from the hands of) the Ūrāḷar in the blessed name (തിരുനാമത്തപേരാൽ) of Kurichchikkare Tēvar (തേവർ = god) Techchikkot Chakkan Rāmar and heirs (തമ്പിമാർ) granted (എഴുതികൊടുത്താൻ = wrote and gave) the Aṭṭippēr (അട്ടിപ്പേർ) with pouring water (നീരുദകമായി) of his Pati paṛamba of 7 paṛas in the Mūti Dēṣam. Thus having paid the current market value (the Ūrāḷars) obtained [എഴുതിച്ചുകൊണ്ടാൻ = literally had or got (it) written] the Aṭṭippēr with pouring water of Pati paṛamba of 7 paṛas in the Mūti Dēṣam. Thus Chakkan Rāmar and heirs granted (എഴുതികൊടുത്താൻ, see note above) the said land. Thus having paid the current market value, the Ūrāḷar in the blessed name of Kurichchikkare Tēvar obtained (എഴുതിച്ചുകൊണ്ടാൻ, see note above) the said land. The witnesses who know this in behalf of the grantor (എഴുതികൊടുത്തതമെയ്യും) and grantee (എഴുതിച്ചുകൊണ്ടതമെയ്യും) are Koravankuḻi Nāyar and Malamavatiyil Mākkachār. Written in the hand of Kōyat Kōndu.

Note.—Translated from a copy received from the Dewan of Cochin.

---

[1] A.D. 1756-57. [2] A.D. 1759.

No. 41.

Aṭṭippeṭṭōlakaraṇam (അട്ടിപ്പേറോലകരണം), executed at Chittur Mannatt [1] (മന്നത്ത) in Kiḻappalayūr Nād in the solar month (ഞായർ) of Mīnam 938 [2] Eḍavam Vyāḻam. Eḻuvatt Rāman Chāttan and heirs (തമ്പിമാർ) received from Ambāt Mānchu Rāman the current market value (പെരുവത്തം). The object of receiving the said market value is Eḻuvatt Rāman Chāttan and heirs give as water property (നീർകൂത്തൽ) by pouring water the Nīr Aṭṭippēr (നീരട്ടിപ്പേർ) of the land (തൊറമ) called Otasera above the Porayatta Nilam and below the Ālukkan Chiṛa, comprising plots sowing 60 paṛas of paddy and the paṛambas (പറമ്പ) on both sides (ഇരുകര) and the upper and lower produce (മേൽഫലവും കീഴ്ഫലവും) and the Nuri (നുരി = space required for planting seedlings) and the Nuriyiḍa Paḻuta (നുരിയിടപഴുത = interval between the planting of seedlings). Thus Ambāt Rāman and Mānchu and Rāman and heirs (തമ്പിമാർ) by giving the current market value obtained as water property (നീർകൂത്തൽ) the Nīr Aṭṭippēr with the pouring of water of the said land Otasera above the Porayatta Nilam and below the Ālukkan Chiṛa, comprising plots sowing 60 paṛas of seed and the paṛambas on both sides, and the Nuri (നുരി = the space required to plant seedlings) and Nuriyiḍa Paḻuta (നുരിയിടപഴുത = interval between the planting of seedlings). Thus Rāman Chāttan and heirs receiving the current market value have executed this, and likewise Mānchu Rāman and heirs paying the current market value have got this executed. Thus the witnesses to this are Elamally Chēnur Rāman and Chennalikāt Chāttan Rāman. Written in the hand of Achatt Kandu.

Note.—Translated from a copy received from the Nallēpaḷḷi Ankarātta Valiya Mannāḷiyār of Cochin State.

No. 42.

To the Adhikāri (അധികാരി) of Tirumala Dēvara (ദേവര) in Cochin. Heard from Cochin Ṣangara Pillay that boundaries were fixed (അതൃത്തിതി രിച്ചു) to the compounds [3] (പുറയിടങ്ങൾ = literally the site of a habitation) and lands [4] (കണ്ടങ്ങൾ) belonging to Tirumala Dēvasam in the tracts (പ്രദേശ ങ്ങൾ) included in Turavūr and Manakkottuttu (subject to) Chērttala Mandavattum [5] Vātukkal [5] and that copies were brought and deposited [അടവെച്ചി ച്ചു(?)] at the Mandavattum Vātukkal (മണ്ടപത്തുംവാതുക്കൽ) of documents (പ്രമാണങ്ങൾ) relating to property held on Eṛakkārāyma [6] (ഏറാക്കാരായ്മ) and Janmam (ജന്മം). Therefore I have relinquished (ഒഴിഞ്ഞുതന്നു) in behalf of

---

[1] See note to Deed No. 24. [2] A.D. 1763.

[3] Probably *manors* would be more correct. See note to Deed No. 26.

[4] See note to Deed No. 12 regarding Kandam.

[5] *Manḍapam* (Sansk.) = open shed or hall, and *Vātil* (Drav.) = door, gate, chief entrance. Taken together they mean a Tahsildar's office.

[6] A right by which a small puṛapad is paid to the Janmi by the name of Eṛa-Micharam. It is not generally renewed, but of late it is renewed on payment of Oppu and Tuṣi *alone*. It is now recognised as redeemable.

the Dēvasvam the Mupra[1] (മുപ്ര) and ⅛ of what is Janmam (ജന്മം) and Eṛakārāyma (എറക്കാരായ്മ) documents whereof have been found. Enjoying (them) thus the Michavāram[2] of Eṛakārāyma should be paid annually to the Mandavattum Vātukkal and receipts (ചീട്ട) taken. Thus to this effect written on the 10th of the month (മാസം) of Makaram of the year 945[3] under the orders of His Highness (തിരുവുള്ളമുണ്ടായിട്ടിനിനവ്വ) by Anancha Perumāl Anancha Perumāl, the Valia Mēleḻuttu Kaṇakku (വലിയമെലെഴുത്ത കണക്ക = an office of that name).

Note.—Translated from a copy received from the Dewan of Cochin State.

No. 43.

Aṭṭipper ōla karaṇam (അട്ടിപ്പെറൊലകരണം), executed on the closing (പൊകന്ന) solar month (ഞായര) of the Chingam of the year 951.[4]

Pilāparambil Kēlan Kōman and heirs (തമ്പിമാര) having received the current market Aṭṭippēr value (പെറുംവില അട്ടിപ്പെററത്ഥം) as found at the time by four people (അന്നനാലരകണ്ട) granted (എഴുതികൊടുത്താൻ = literally wrote and gave) the Aṭṭippēr with pouring of water (നീരടകമായി) of the plot (കണ്ടം) lying east to west on the northern slope (വടക്കെ എറക്കിൽ) of the hill in the western Oḍi (ഒടി = division or range of fields) of Karaka Akathūtta belonging to them (തങ്ങൾക്കുള്ള) in Kutuvūr Dēṣam, so as to extinguish the (right in) mango tree (മാവരെ)[5] the (right in) sand (മണലരെ) and the right in water (ഉടകമരെ) and to convey the right of ceremony (കമ്മംമടക്കി)[6] without any dispute respecting this and touching that (ഒന്നതൊട്ടൊന്ന ചൊല്ലി ചൊതിയംകൂടാതെ). In this way Iḻuvan Tharayolil Kalavan Māman and heirs (തമ്പിമാര) obtained the Aṭṭippēr with pouring of water (നീരടകമായി) of the plot (കണ്ടം) lying east to west on the northern slope of the western hill and belonging to Kēlan Kōman and heirs, in a manner to extinguish the (right in) mango tree (മാവരെ), the (right in) sand (മണലരെ), and the (right-in) water (ഉടകമരെ), and to convey the right of ceremony (കമ്മംമടക്കി) and without any dispute respecting this and

---

[1] *Literally*, three (*Mūnnu*) *paṛas* (bushels), *i.e.*, 3 paṛas per 10 paṛas, the State share of the net produce.

The *Mupra* assessment in the Native States of Travancore and Cochin is perhaps the relic of the ancient *Kō-Pāṭṭāvaram* (see note to paragraph (*i*) of Deed No. 3). It is certainly noteworthy that if a Nambūtiri in Travancore sells his freehold land to any one but a Nambūtiri, an obligation to pay *Mupra* (in the case of wet lands, and *Eṭṭayil onnu* (1 in 8 in the case of garden lands) immediately attaches to the land.—(Ward and Connor's Survey Memo., p. 63. Trevandrum Ed.). The Brāhman hierarchy had evidently prior to the execution of Deed No. 2 (A.D. 774) been admitted to privileges equal or perhaps superior to those conferred on the Jews and Syrians. Those privileges were probably hereditary, but not assignable to any one but Nambūtiris.

[2] *Micha* (Drav.) = height, above, and *Vāram* (Drav., perhaps from *varavu*, income) = share in general.

[3] A.D. 1770.

[4] A.D. 1776.

[5] These seem to indicate that the timber-right, the earth-right, and the water-right were given up.

[6] It is not clear what this means.

touching that (ഒന്നതൊട്ടൊന്ന ചൊല്ലി ചൊതിയം കൂടാതെ). Thus the witness who knows this is Otaparambatt Kiṭṭaṇan Nāyar. Written by Poringelil Chennan.

Note.—Translated from a copy received from the Subordinate Judge of British Cochin.

No. 44.

This is *Aṭṭippettōlakaraṇam* (അട്ടിപ്പെറൊലകരണം) written in the solar month (ഞായര്) of Tulām of the year 954.[1] Talikokkāt Paramēswaran Trivikraman and heirs (തമ്പിമാര്) have given, by receiving the market (പെറും[2] = literally, born[2] or produced) Aṭṭippēr[2] value (അട്ടിപ്പെറർത്ഥം) as then found (കണ്ടു) by four people (നാലര്) the Aṭṭippēr[2] with pouring of water (നീരടകമായ) and accompanied by Janmam[2] right (ജന്മഫലം = literally, born[2] fruit) over their (lands) in Talikolangara Dēṣam and bounded on the east by (the land called) Totu-pata, west of Pāngolam and Kunnatōtupata, on the west . . . . on the south by Puḻi Kandam and Manakkāṭṭilavan's dwelling compound (മണക്കാട്ടിലവൻ ഇരിക്കുന്നപറമ്പ) . . . . north . . . . field and Pilākkāt paṛamba, on the west . . . . on the east by the Patinhārē Dēvasvam Totuva, on the south by . . . . jungle (കാട), (*Note.*—Here more boundaries follow which owing to omission of words are unintelligible) ; (the lands) included in the above four boundaries (നാലതിര) and sowing 18 paṛas, Erinhēri (lands) of 8 paṛas, Nālpatinām land, Karuvannūr Punja (പുഞ്ച) (land) of 9 paṛas, making a total of punja lands (പുഞ്ചനിലം) of 38 paṛas and wet lands (ഉൽപ്പത്തി) and paṛambas (പറമ്പ) Netumpalli Tarana Nellūr Nārāyaṇan Paramēswarán and heirs (തമ്പിമാര്) take the abovesaid lands (ഉൽപ്പത്തി) and paṛambas (പറമ്പ) and the waste (കാട) Chulliparamba in the east and west (കിഴമെല്) with flowing water (നീരടകമായി) and water caused to come into contact (നീരട്ടിച്ച) along with the Janmam right (ജന്മഫലം, see note above) . . . . Witnesses knowing (this) are Pōnnallūr, Kūttampilli, Kataluramallūr, Kiḻakkiniyedatt Kokka.

Note.—Translated from a copy received from the Dewan of Cochin State.

No. 45.

Aṭṭippettōlakaruṇam (അട്ടിപ്പെറൊലകരണം), executed at Tatta Mangalam Mannatta[3] (മന്നത്ത) in Pālayūr Nād (നാട) in the solar month of Kumbham in the year 957.[4] Dhanu Vyāḻam, Shippi Ammiyār, daughter of Thoppa Paṭṭar,[5] a Paradēṣi (പരദെശി = foreigner) and heirs (തമ്പിമാര്) residing at Kākuriṣṣi Akaram (അകരം = a Brāhman house) received from Ambāṭ Rāman Iṭṭuṇṇi Rāman the current market value (പെറുവർത്ഥം). Thus the object of receiving the said market value is that Shippi Ammiyār and heirs (തമ്പിമാര്) give by pouring water as water property (നീർക്കൂറ്) the Nīr

---

[1] A.D. 1778.

[2] Here the close connection between the Drav. *Pēru* and the Sanskritised form of it *Janmam* is sufficiently obvious.

[3] See note to deed No. 24. [4] A.D. 1781-82. [5] East Coast Brāhman.

Aṭṭippēr (നീർഅട്ടിപ്പേർ) of 2 kandams (plots) sowing 120 nāḻis (നാഴി) of paddy and situated below your land (തൊന്മ)[1] called Otaṣira nilam of Chamba (?) and above our Pārakkal Kandam (plot) and the paṛambas (പറമ്പ) on both sides (ഇരുകര) of it together with the upper and lower produce (മേൽഫലവും കീഴ്ഫലവും). Thus Ambāt Rāman Iṭṭuṇṇi Rāman and heirs (തമ്പിമാർ) obtained with the pouring of water as Nīrmutal (നീർമുതൽ = water property) the Nīr Aṭṭippēr (നീരട്ടിപ്പേർ) of the abovesaid two plots of land below the Otaṣira land of Chambatt (ചമ്പത്ത) and above the Pārakkal Kandam and sowing 12 paṛas of seed, and the paṛambas on both sides of it with the upper and lower produce (മേൽഫലവും കീഴ്ഫലവും). Thus the witnesses who know this are Kiḻatti Arangan Chāttan and Mānikatt Kandan Teyyan. Written in the hand of Eḻuvatt Thoppu.

Note.—Translated from a copy received from the Nallēpaḻḻi Ankarātta Valiya Mannāḍiyār of Cochin State.

No. 46.

Aṭṭippettōlakaruṇam (അട്ടിപ്പെറൊലകരുണം), executed at Chittūr Mannatt[2] in the solar month (ഞായർ) of Eḍavam in the year 959[3] Kumbham Vyāḻam. Porayatt Rāman and heirs (തമ്പിമാര) received the current market value (പെറുവത്തം) from Ambāt Rāmαn Iṭṭuṇṇi Rāman. The object (കാര്യം) of receiving the said market value is that Porayatt Rāman and heirs give (കൊടുത്താർ) with pouring water as water property (നീർമുതൽ) the Nīr Aṭṭippēr (നീരട്ടിപ്പേർ) of the Kandams (കണ്ടം = plot) sowing 12 paṛas seed, bounded on the north by your (തന്റെ) land (തൊന്മ) called Otaṣira Aṇṇākoṇath (ഒടശിര അണ്ണാകൊണത്ത) and on the south by our (ഞങ്ങടെ) Nilam, east by Tiruttillatt Nilam, and on the west by the slope (വെള്ളചരു) of the paṛamba, together with the (right of) guarding[4] (പാരാവു or പാറാവു = sentry or guard) and Kārāyma[4] (കാരായ്മ) as well as the upper and lower produce (മേൽഫലവും കീഴ്ഫലവും) and everything of whatever description (എപ്പെർപ്പെട്ടതും) comprised within these four boundaries. Ambāt Rāman Iṭṭuṇṇi Rāman and heirs (തമ്പിമാര) obtain with the pouring of water as water property (നീർമുതൽ) the Nīr Aṭṭippēr (നീരട്ടിപ്പേർ) by giving the said market value of the Kandam (plot) sowing 12 paṛas and bounded on the north by the Otaṣira Aṇṇākoṇath Nilam, on the south by their (തങ്ങടെ) Nilam, on the east by Tiruttillatt Nilam, and on the west by the slope of the paṛamba together with the right of guarding (പാരാവും) and Kārāyma as well as the upper and lower produce and everything of whatever description (എപ്പെർപ്പെട്ടതും) comprised within these four boundaries. Thus the witnesses who know this are Chāttan Rāman and Chennāḻikot Teyyan Rāman. Written in the hand of Tatchāt Kandu.

Note.—Translated from a copy received from the Nallēpaḻḻi Ankarātta Valiya Mannāḍiyār of Cochin State.

---

[1] *Tonma.* See note to Deed No. 37.

[2] See note to deed No. 24. [3] A.D. 1784.

[4] Compare notes to paragraphs (*c*) and (*f*) and (*m*) of Deed No. 3; also notes to Deed No. 4.

No. 47.

Aṭṭippeṭṭōlakaraṇam (അട്ടിപ്പെറോലകരണം), executed in the solar month (ഞായർ) of Karkaḍakam of the year 963.[1] Chirakkal Panayānullil Nārāyaṇan Chumaran and heirs (തമ്പിമാര) having received the market Aṭṭippēr value (പെറും അട്ടിപ്പെറെത്ഥം) as found at the time by four people (അന്നനാല പെർകണ്ടു) granted (എഴുതികൊടുത്താൻ) the Aṭṭippēr with water flowing (നീരു തകമായി) and water coming into contact (നീരട്ടിച്ച) of their (തങ്ങൾക്കുള്ള) Kaḻimpuṛam Dēṣam (കഴിമ്പുറം ദേശം). Thus Ayirūr Nārāyaṇa Rāma Varma Avatiri Kōvilatikārikal and heirs (തമ്പിമാര) having paid the market Aṭṭippēr value (പെറും അട്ടിപ്പെററത്ഥം) as found then by four people (അന്നനാലപെർകണ്ടു) obtained (എഴുതിച്ചുകൊണ്ടോൻ) the Aṭṭippēr with water flowing (നീരുദകമായി) and water coming into contact (നീരട്ടിച്ച) of the said Kaḻimpuṛam Dēṣam. Thus the boundaries of this Dēṣam are east Edamuttam Dēṣam, south Ramallūr Dēṣam, west Mēppuṛatta Paṛamba (which is), west of Tirunilam, and north Kuruvetti Paṛamba. The lands (ഉൽപത്തികൾ) and paṛambas (പറമ്പുകൾ) and everything else of whatever description (മററും എപ്പെപ്പെട്ടതും) included (അകപ്പെട്ട) within the above four boundaries and the Dēṣam,[2] Dēṣādhipatyam,[2] Ambalappaḍi[2] and Ūrāyma[2] have been given and received with water flowing (നീരുദകം). The witnesses who know this are Kuttumpilli Mūtta Nambūtiri, Kuṇampilli Nambūtiri, Edatiruttu Pattāli, and Kutāykkal Ṣankaran Kammal. Written by Chemmāppallil Ṣankaran Shollampenambiyath Ṣankaran.

Note.—Translated from a copy received from the Subordinate Judge of British Cochin.

No. 48.

Vilayōlakaraṇam (വിലയോലകരണം = deed of sale), executed in the solar month (ഞായർ) of Mithunam of the year 983.[3] Pālakkal Patinhārē Vīṭṭil Rayiru Chandu and heirs (തമ്പിമാർ) of Cheṛukunnatt village (ഊര) sold by receiving the current market value (അന്നപെറും വിലയറുതാം) the paṛamba (പറമ്പ) known as Kallinga Vaḷappa which is the Janmam (ചെന്മം corruption of ജന്മം) of Payangōte Pālakkal Patinharē Vīṭṭil Chandu of Cheṛukunnatt village (ഊര). The said paṛamba was purchased by paying the current market value[4] (അന്നപെറും വിലഅറുതാം) by Karippatt Palli Kūlakatt Chiṛakkal Kūlakatt Ravi Varma Rāja (രാച). The boundary of this paṛamba (പറമ്പ) is east as far as the Cheṛukunnatt Dēvasvam (ദേവസ്വം) Kandam (field), south as far as Kalattil Kolaṇgakote Paṛamba, west as far as Udayammāḍatt Pālakkal Kandam (land), and north as far as the land (കണ്ടം)

---

[1] A.D. 1788.

[2] Incidents attached to the rank of a Dēṣavaḻi. See Glossary.

[3] A.D. 1808.

[4] No mention here of water, though *Janmam* would seem to mean the water birthright. The deed is called merely a deed of sale—not an *Aṭṭippēr*. There are only three deeds in this collection, Nos. 35, 38, and 48, in proof of the fact, but it is not improbable that neither *Aṭṭippēr* nor *Janmam* was in general. use in North Kōlattunād (Chiṛakkal Taluk until after the British occupation.

of Chiṛakkal Kōvilakam and Cheṛukunnu Dēvasvam (തേവസ്വം). The lands (നിലം) produce (ഫലം = fruit), stones (കല്ല), thorns (മുള്ള), hidden treasure (നിധി), and other things of whatever description (എപ്പേർപ്പെട്ടതും) included in the said boundaries were purchased by paying the current market value by Karippatt Palli Kūlakattil Chiṛakkal Kūlakatt Ravi Varma Rāja Tamburan to Pālakkal Patinhāre Vīṭṭil Rayiru Chandu and heirs. Thus the witnesses (സാക്കി corruption of സാക്ഷി) are Chenicheri Chāttu and (കൂടി അറിയും ?) Puliyankotan Kaṇṇan. Written in the hand of Katankōtan Chandu Koran with the knowledge of the neighbours (കെട്ടുകേൾപ്പിച്ചു).[1]

Note.—Translated from a copy received from the District Munsif of Kavai, Chiṛakkal Tāluk.

No. 49.

Aṭṭippettōlakāryyam (അട്ടിപ്പെറോലകാര്യം), executed in the solar month (ഞായർ) of Makaram of the year 985.[2] Mēḍabyāḻam at Mitrānannapuram Mukkālvaṭṭam (മുക്കാൽവട്ടം = temple of Bhagavati). Payyur Paramēswaran Nārāyaṇan and heirs (തമ്പിമാർ) granted (എഴുതികൊട്ടത്താൻ = literally wrote and gave) to Ennūr Nandiyār Valli Nārāyaṇan Nārayaṇan and heirs (അമ്പിമാർ) by receiving the current market value (പെറുംവില അത്ഥം) as then found by four people (അന്നനാലരകണ്ട) the Aṭṭippēr (അട്ടിപ്പേർ) with pouring of water (ഉദകപൃർവ്വം) in such a manner that (the transaction) might not in future (മേലിൽ) be questioned (ചോദ്യയം) by us, our heirs (ശേഷമാര = descendants) or anybody else (മറെറാരുത്തരാലും), their (തങ്ങൾക്കുള്ള) Puttūr Dēṣam[3] (പുത്തൂരദേശം) Dēṣādhipatyam[3] (ദേശാധിപത്യം) two temples (ക്ഷേത്ര ങ്ങളും) (called) Mitrānannapuram (മിത്രാനന്ദപുരം) and Tekkiniyammakāva, the Ambalappaḍi[3] (അമ്പലപ്പടി) Urāyma[3] (ഊരായ്മ) and other temple dignities (മറ്റുംക്ഷേത്രാധിപത്യങ്ങളും) the lands (ഉല്പത്തി) and paṛambas (പറമ്പ) the retainers[4] (ആള) and slaves (അടിയാർ) the dues (പോകങ്ങൾ corruption of ഭോഗങ്ങൾ = enjoyments) of Dēṣavāḻi (ദേശവാഴി) and everything else of whatever description (മറ്റുമെപ്പേർപ്പെട്ടതും) included (അകപ്പെട്ട) within (അകത്ത) this Dēṣam. Thus Ennūr Nandiyar Valli Nārāyaṇan and Anantiravars obtained (എഴുതിച്ചകൊണ്ടാർ = literally, had or got written) by paying the current market value (പെറുവില അത്ഥം) as then found by four people (അന്ന നാലരകണ്ട) the Aṭṭippēr with pouring of water (ഉദകപൃർവ്വം) in such a manner that (the transaction) might not in future (മേലിൽ) be questioned (ചോദ്യയം) by Paramēswaran Nārāyaṇan, heirs (തമ്പിമാര) descendants (ശേഷക്കാര) or anybody else, (മറെറാരുത്തരാലും) Paramēswaran Nārāyaṇan's and heirs (തമ്പി മാർ) Puttūr Dēṣam,[5] Dēṣādhipatyam,[5] the two temples (called) Mitrānannapuram and Tekkiniyammakāva, the Ambalappaḍi[5] and Ūrāyma[5] and

---

[1] Keṭṭū Kelpichu = heard and caused to be heard. [2] A.D. 1810.

[3] Incidents attached to the dignity of a Dēṣavāḻi. See Glossary.

[4] The conveyance of rights in free retainers after the introduction of British rule is to be noted as it explains the relations which have all along subsisted between the *Janmi* and those beneath him.

[5] "C.D. was anciently *Dēṣavāḻi* of the Dēṣams of—— in your division, but as the present family is disqualified from poverty (or want of respectability or other cause) you will exercise in these Dēṣams the duties of head of Police, of Village Munsif, and of Tax-

other temple dignities (മററും ക്ഷേത്രാദിപത്യങ്ങൾ), the lands and paṛambas (ഉല്പത്തികളും പറമ്പുകളും), the retainers and slaves (ആളടിയാർ), the dues (ഭോഗങ്ങൾ, see note above) of Dēṣavāḻi, and everything else of whatever description included within this Dēṣam. Thus the witnesses for this Aṭṭip-pettōla (അട്ടിപ്പെററോല) in behalf of the grantors (എഴുതികൊടുത്തവരെയും) and the grantees (എഴുതിച്ചുകൊണ്ടവരെയും) are Vennarattūr Okki, Tekkiniyētam and Nantiyārvalli. Written in the hand of Kollikandara Govindan.

Note.—Translated from a copy received from Mr. H. Wigram, District Judge of South Malabar.

No. 50.

Royal letter addressed to Cheruvattur Nambūtiri. Eḷētat Ullannūr Illam in Perumpilleṣṣēri Dēṣam of Urakam Pravirtti having become extinct that Taṛavad [1] together with the property (വസ്തു) rice-lands (ഉല്പത്തി), persons (ആൾ = probably retainers, guards), slaves (അടിയാര), chest of documents (പെട്ടിപ്രമാണം) and all Ambalapaḍi and Ūrāyma rights and everything of whatever description (എപ്പേർപ്പെട്ടതും) with the exception of the Ūrāyma of Changarayil Kshētram (temple), are hereby granted [2] to you Cheruvattur Nambūtiri for exclusive enjoyment (മറെറാരുത്തരാലും ചോദ്യംകൂടാതെ = literally without any question from any one). Written in the month of Vrischikam 1020 [3] M.E. in the hand of Pavvattil Krishnan, in the presence and under the orders of Kaṇayannūr Kōvilakam Rāja.

Note.—Translated from a copy received from Nelliṣṣēri Ṣiva Rāmayyan of Pālghat Town.

No. 51.

ROYAL LETTER ADDRESSED TO CHUNDAYKĀT OTALŪR (NAMBŪTIRI).

Whereas there being no male members in the two Illams of Kandiyūr Natuvattunnu Natuvat and Kandāṇaṣṣeri Pālaykāt in Ālūr Muri of Chundal Pravirtti, Sridēvi and Sāvitri, two females of Natuvat Illam,[4] have executed a document authorizing [5] Otalūr Nambūtiri to marry [5] in the said Taṛavād,[4] to hold and enjoy the property, movable and immovable (വസ്തുവ

---

collector, but you will not interfere with the *Dēṣavāḻi Sthānamāna Avakāṣam* (or such ancient privileges belonging to him as *Dēṣavāḻi*) as the Government may deem it advisable to permit to be enjoyed, and as the inhabitants may voluntarily offer in conformity with old customs." Extract from Mr. Græme's form of sanad appointing Adhikaris of Amṣams. Special Commissioner to Principal Collector, 20th May 1823. *Conf.* p. 89 of the text.

[1] See note to Deed No. 22.

[2] This illustrates one mode in which Nambūtiri inheritances are passed on in the Native States.

[3] A.D. 1844.

[4] *Illam* is a Dravidian, not a Sanskrit word. It is now almost exclusively applied to Nambūtiri family houses, but anciently the *il* was the king's house. See the use of *Kōvil* (properly *Kōyil*) in Deed No. 12 and others. The Nambūtiris, in right of the princely privileges which seem to have been conferred on them, in common with Jews and Syrians, probably assumed the right, among their other privileges, of styling their dwellings royal houses. There is a strong contrast in this deed between *Illam* and *Taṛavād*—See note to Deed No. 22.

[5] This illustrates another mode in which Nambūtiri inheritances are passed on in the Native States.

ങ്ങൾ), including the slaves and the Ambalapaḍi, Ūrāyma and other titles and honors (സ്ഥാനമാനങ്ങൾ) attached to the pagodas of Ariyannūr, Kandiyūr and Plākkāt, and to maintain the females: and whereas that document has now been presented before us, we hereby direct that Otalūr (Nambūtiri) do marry in the said Taṛavād, hold and enjoy the property, movable and immovable, slaves and chest of documents (പെട്ടിപ്രമാണം) belonging to the two Illams of Natuvat and Pālaykāt, and the Ambalapaḍi, Ūrāyma, titles and honors, and everything else pertaining to the abovementioned three pagodas and maintain the females. Written in the month of Mithunam 1026 [1] M.E. in the hand of Pavvattil Krishnan, in the presence and under the orders of Trichur Vatakkechira Kōvilakam Rāja.

Note.—Translated from a copy received from Nellissēri Ṣiva Rāmayyan of Pālghat Town.

No. 52.

ROYAL LETTER ADDRESSED TO CHŌLAYKARA (NAMBŪTIRI).

Whereas the document executed on the 8th Mithunam 991 by Tāmaraṣṣēri Nambūtiri of Kariyannūr Muṛi, in Chengaḻikkōt Pravirtti, authorizing [2] Cholaykara Nambūtiri to hold and [2] enjoy, in the capacity of Anantiravan,[2] the Tāmaraṣṣēri Taṛavād and the property, movable and immovable, slaves, chest of documents (പെട്ടിപ്രമാണം), Dēṣam, Dēṣādhipatyam, Ambalapaḍi, Ūrāyma, and everything else belonging to that Taṛavād [3] has been produced before us: and whereas Tāmaraṣṣēri Nambūtiri and the female members are dead and Chōlaykara has married in that Taṛavād and has been enjoying the property and titles pertaining to the same; and whereas Chōlaykara has communicated the matter to us by a letter, we hereby direct that Chōlaykara do hold and enjoy the said Tāmaraṣṣēri Taṛavād and the property, movable and immovable, slaves, chest of documents (പെട്ടിപ്ര മാണം), Dēṣam, Dēṣādhipatyam, Ambalapaḍi, Ūrāyma, and everything else attached to the Taṛavād. Written in the month of Vrischikam 1031[4] M.E. in the hand of Pavvattil Krishnan, in the presence and under the orders of Kaṇayannūr Kōvilakat Tamburan.

Note.—Translated from a copy received from Nellissēri Ṣiva Rāmayyan of Pālghat Town.

No. 53.

ROYAL LETTER ADDRESSED TO PATIYUR (NAMBŪTIRI).

Whereas the document executed by Nangayya and Nangeli, the only members (female) of Pattallūr Illam in Etakkulam Muṛi of Arippālam Pravirtti, authorizing [5] Patiyūr Nambūtiri to hold and [5] enjoy the property,

---

[1] A.D. 1851.

[2] This illustrates another mode of passing on Nambūtiri inheritances in the Native States.

[3] See note to deed No. 22.

[4] A.D. 1855.

[5] Illustrative of another mode of passing on Nambūtiri inheritances in the Native States.

movable and immovable, slaves, chest of documents (പെട്ടിപ്രമാണം), Ambalapaḍi, Ūrāyma, titles and honors attached to Vellinattan Pagoda, Dēṣam, Dēṣādhipatyam, and everything else belonging to that Taṛavād[1] has been produced before us and Pattallur Nangeli is dead, we hereby direct that Patiyūr Nambūtiri do hold and enjoy, as he has hitherto done, by virtue of the document aforesaid, the Pattallūr Taṛavād, and the property, movable and immovable, slaves, chest of documents (പെട്ടിപ്രമാണം) belonging to the same, Ambalapaḍi and Ūrāyma of Vellittat Pagoda, Dēṣam and Dēṣādhipatyam, and everything else connected with the said Taṛavād, and maintain the female Nangayya. Written in the month of Dhanu 1031[2] M.E. in the hand of Pavvattil Krishnan, in the presence and under the orders of Iringātakkūte Kōvilakat Tamburan.

Note.—Translated from a copy received from Nellissēri Ṣiva Rāmayyan of Pālghat Town.

No. 54.

Janmam[3] *deed* (ജന്മാധാരം) executed by 1, Erēchchan *alias* Chekkuṇṇi Nāyar; 2, Chandu Nāyar; 3, Chāttu Nāyar, sons of Koletuttakuriyēttina Cherātammaḷ; and 4, Erēchchan Nāyar, son of Peṇṇuṭṭi Amma in Nedungōṭṭūr Dēṣam, Kōṭṭūḷi Amṣam, Calicut Tāluk, to Rāma *alias* Uṇṇippera Kuṛup, son of Matiravana Cherukōṭṭu Cherunni Amma of the above Dēṣam, on the 12th Chingam of the year (കൊല്ലം) 1056, corresponding to 26th August 1881. Whereas Rs. 300 was fixed (നിശ്ചയിച്ച) as the Janmam value (ജന്മവില) of 1, Vaḍakkēmūlakkandam (വടക്കെമൂലകണ്ടം = northern corner land) in the eastern division (കടി) of Kiḻakkē (eastern), Māntayār Nilam (നിലം = land); and 2, Vaḍakku Paḍinyārē Mūlakkandam Paṛamba (north-western corner portion of the paṛamba) in Veḷuttūr Paṛamba, specified in the schedule below, which are our Janmam, we have this day granted (തന്നിരിക്കുന്നു) the Janmam of the property (വകകൾ), with everything of whatever description (എപ്പേർപ്പെട്ടതൊട്ടുകൂടി);[4] out of the Janmam value of Rs. 300 due to us (ഞങ്ങൾക്കുവരെണ്ടും = literally, that ought to come to us) we have reserved (നിർത്തി) Rs. 103, being the Kāṇam and loan (കടം വായ്പ), including interest (പലിശകൂടി), due by us the first and second executants to Chemmalaṣṣēri Patinyārayil Kōru Kuṛup on land No. 1, and Rs. 166-10-0, being the Kāṇam and loan (കടംവായ്പ), including interest (പലിശകൂടി), due to you on the paṛamba No. 2, making under the two heads (വകരണ്ടിൽ) Rs. 270-10-0, and the balance of Rs. 29-6-0 we have received in cash (റൊക്കം) from you, and we are satisfied as to the Janmam value of Rs. 300; we have therefore no claim (അവകാശം) and concern (ചെച്ച്) about your possessing (അടക്കി) and enjoying (അനുഭവിക്ക) the property (വകകൾ) as Janmam (ജന്മമായി) under this (deed) (ഇതിനാൽ).

---

[1] See note to Deed No. 22. [2] A.D. 1855-56.

[3] This phrase has come into general use throughout the district within the last few years only.

[4] *Eppērpeṭṭatu*, the same word used in Deed No. 4.

Where property is situated.							Per 6-feet Kōl.		Boundaries.				Possession.	
District.	Sub-District.	Taluk.	Amsam.	Dēsam.	Number.	Name of Property.	East to West.	North to South.	East.	South.	West.	North.	Former.	Present.
Malabar.	Calicut.	Calicut.	Koṭṭuḷi.	Nedungōttūr.	1	Kiḻakkē Māntayār Nilath, Kiḻakke Oḍiyil Vaḍakkē, Mūlakkandam Nilam.	15	18	Paḍinyāṛē Natuvakuni Nilam.	Kiḻakkē Māntayār Nilam.	Kiḻakkē Māntayar Nilam.	Pathway	Kuriyēttina Chattu Nayar.	Kuriyēttina Chattu Nayar.
					2	Vaḻattūrparambil Vaḍakkepaḍinyāṛē, Mūlakkandam Nilam.	16	14	Vaḻattūr Paṛamba.	Vaḻattūr Paṛamba.	Penapuṛath Paṛamba.	Otikkōt Paṛamba and Paḍinyāṛē Kuriyēttina Paṛamba.	Uṇṇippera Kuṛup.	Uṇṇippera Kurup.

Written in the hand of Kakkāḍan Imbichchi Āndi with Matirapanapennapurat Iṭṭirārappa Kuṛup and Mannil Arikkōtparambat Kēlu Aḍiyōḍi as witnesses to this—

1. CHEKKUṆṆI NĀYAR (signed).
2. CHANDU NĀYAR („).
3. CHĀTTU NĀYAR („).
4. ERŌMAN NĀYAR („).

Witnesses
1. IṬṬIRĀRPPA KUṚUP („).
2. KĒLU AḌIYOḌI („).

Note.—Translated from a copy received from the Registrar of Malabar.

No. 55.

KŌVILAKAM No. 10 OF 1057.

Royal letter (തീട്ടു), written jointly by Waḷḷuvanāṭṭudaya [1] Kaḍannamūttayil Waḷḷuvanāṭṭukare Mankadakōvilakat Vēdapurāṭṭi Valiya Tamburāṭṭi of Mankaḍa Amṣam, Waḷḷuvanād Tāluk, and Srivallabhan Valiya Tamburan Avarkal of the said Kōvilakam, to Māmbee Āli, son of Moidu of Valambūr Amṣam, of the said tāluk. The object (കാര്യം) is that, whereas one item of Kuḍiyirippu (കുടിയിരിപ്പു), being the Janmam of Mankaḍa Kōvilakam Chērikkal, purchased (തീറാധാരം) on the 13th Vrischikam 1052 from Avaṛānkuṭṭi and his brother Sāid Āli, sons of Kaḷattiltoḍiyil Pari, and specified in the schedule below, has this day been demised to you on a pāṭṭam of 3 fanams and a Kānam [2] of Rs. 4-9-2, equal to 16 new fanams, you should

---

[1] One of the families which attested Deeds Nos. 1 and 2.

[2] There is here no mention of any fine on entry. It is not usual to mention it or state its amount.

pay within the 30th Makaram of each year from 1057, Annas 6, being the michchāram payable annually, after deducting the interest on the Kāṇam amount and the Government assessment from the aforesaid pāṭṭam, as well as 2 annas for Ōṇavāḷakkula (ഓണവാഴക്കുല = bunch of plantains presented during the Ōṇam festival) and Annas 2 on account of Nei Viḷḷakku (നെയ്‌വിളക്ക = lamp lighted with ghee) in Mankaḍa temple from your pocket (കയ്യാൽ = literally, from the hand) and obtain receipt (നിരമുറി); and if the michchāram is left in arrears without being paid at the prescribed time, you should pay the same, with interest at 12 per cent.; you should also surrender, on receipt of the Kāṇam, the Kuḍiyirippu mentioned in the schedule on demand.[1]

Situation of Property.							Per 6-feet Kōl.		Boundaries.				Possession.	
District.	Sub-District.	Taluk.	Amṣam.	Dēṣam.	Number.	Name of Property.	East to West.	North to South.	East.	South.	West.	North.	Former.	Present.
Malabar.	Perintalmaṇṇa.	Waḷḷuvanad.	Valambūr.	Arimbra.	1	Paṇaratodika Kuḍiyirippu	38	21	Mulakkanchēri Paḷḷi Manyayal.	Taḷatte-paṇaratodika Kuḍiyirippu.	Puliyakōd Paḷḷimanyayal.	Karimpanatodika Kuḍiyirippu.	Moitu.	Āli.

Written in the hand of Pulāppullimadattil Venkidēswara Paṭṭar on the 6th December 1881, corresponding to the 22nd Vrischikam 1057, with the undersigned witnesses.

Note.—Translated from a copy furnished by the District Registrar.

No. 56.

Paṇaya pāṭṭa kuḷikkāṇa[2] *kuḍiyirippu* deed (പണയപ്പാട്ടകുഴിക്കാണകുടിയിരിപ്പ), executed on the 9th Dhanu 1057 by Naḍuvilakat Māmukkōya, son of Māyan Kōya of Nagaram Amṣam, Calicut Tāluk, to Ayyappan, Mundakkutti Imbichchi and Sāmi, sons of Puvvattinkal Tannikunnat Chekku, residing in Vaḷappil Paṛamba in Veliyanchēri Dēṣam, Kasba Amṣam of the said tāluk. Whereas I have this day granted you a renewed lease (പൊളിച്ചെഴുതിചാൎത്തി തന്നു) of the Vaḷappil Paṛamba, the boundaries and extent of which are specified in the schedule below, being my Janmam, and included in the property assigned to me as my share in execution of the Appeal decree No. 282 of 1880, against the decree of the Subordinate Court of South

[1] This is the innovating clause which is so much objected to by tenants, particularly by those who have paid fines on entry or renewal fees. See Mr. Holloway's decision in South Malabar Subordinate Court case No. 398 of 1854 in Glossary under "*Kāṇam.*"

[2] *Paṇayam* = pledge; *pāṭṭam* = rent; *kuḷi* = pit, excavation; *Kāṇam* = money claim; *kuḍiyirippu* = house-site, meaning a deed embracing in its conditions some elements of a mortgage, a lease, an improving lease, and a building lease.

Malabar in Regular Suit No. 329 of 1879 of the District Munsif's Court of Calicut, which was transferred to the former Court, on an annual pāṭṭam of Rs. 17-8-0, equal to 70 fanams, on a Kāṇam of 144 fanams and 12 vīṣams (വീശം), the Kāṇam already due to your father Chekku, *plus* 38 fanams and 8 vīsams, the improvement value with Aḻi (അഴി) = customary deduction in paying for improvements under Kuḻikkāṇam when the Janmi has not to pay for the tenth plant) of 15 cocoanut and 8 areca trees, this day paid for, *plus* 516 fanams and 12 vīṣams, equal to Rs. 129-3-0, received this day in cash (ഇന്നറൊക്കംവാങ്ങിയ), making under the three heads a total Kāṇam of 700 fanams, equal to Rs, 175, and on a Puṛappād pāṭṭam of Rs. 8-12-0, deducting Rs. 8-12-0 for interest on the money advanced (അത്തിപ്പലിശ); you should enjoy the lease (പാട്ടംനടന്ന) of the paṛamba and pay annually from Vrischikam 1058 Rs. 8-12-0, being the Puṛappād pāṭṭam after deducting the interest on the Kāṇam amount, and obtain receipt (ശീട്ടി). Keikkūli Avakkāṣam (കൈക്കൂലിഅവകാശം = fine upon a lease and its renewal) equal to the amount of the pāṭṭam has been collected. Aḻikuḻikkāṇam (അഴികഴി കാണം = customary improvement value subject to Aḻi), according to local custom (ദേശമര്യാദ), for trees already planted but not paid for, and for those that may be planted hereafter, excepting the 38 cocoanut and 8 areca trees and miscellaneous trees (പട്ടമരം) included in the lease, along with those which have been paid for, and the Kāṇam amount of Rs. 175 will be paid on eviction when the term expires. It has also been stipulated that if the paṛamba is not properly taken care of, or if the pāṭṭam is allowed to fall into arrears, the property should be surrendered on demand after settlement of accounts, irrespective of the term of the lease (കാലനിയമംപറയാതെ = literally, without speaking about the term), and that as the Government tax (ശിമനികതി) and the Municipal tax of the paṛamba stand in your name, the amount of Government tax, if paid by you, will be allowed out of the pāṭṭam payable by you; but the Municipal tax must be paid by you. Written in the hand of Putiyakōvilakam Paṛambil Sankaralinkam Piḷḷa on the 21st December 1881 with the undersigned as witnesses to this :—

Where Property is situated.					Name of Property.	Per 6-feet Kōl.		Boundaries.				Possession.	
Registration District.	Taluk.	Amṣam.	Dēṣam.	Number.		East to West.	North to South.	East.	South.	West.	North.	Former.	Present.
Malabar.	Calicut.	Kasba.	Veliyancheri.	1	Vaḷappil Paṛamba.	18	19½	Western portion of Parayil Taḷam Nilam.	Taṛaparamba Parayil Taḷam Nilam Kandam.	Western portion of Parayil Taḷam Nilam.	Western portion of Parayil Taḷam Nilam.	Do. Ayyappan and 3 others.	Do. Ayyappan and 3 others

Witnesses— MĀMUKKŌYA (signed).

* * *

***Note.*—Translated from a copy furnished by the District Registrar.**

No. 57.

Kāṇam[1] *deed*, executed by Chekku Paṇikkar, son of Puliyoṣṣēri Mittalē Vīṭṭil Iṭṭu Amma of Cheṛuvaṇṇūr Amṣam and Dēṣam, Calicut Tāluk, to Govindan Nāyar, son of Chellāt Imbichchi Amma of the above Dēṣam. Whereas I have granted you, for the period included within 12 years (12 കൊല്ലത്തിന്നകമായ) Dhanu Nyāyar (ഞായർ = solar month) of this year 1057, a renewal of Kuḻikkāṇakuḍiyirippu (കുഴിക്കാണകുടിയിരിപ്പിന്നപൊളിച്ചെഴുതിചാർത്തി)[2] of Vaṭṭakandi Paṛamba and two others items of property, which are my Taṛavād Janmam[3] in the above Dēṣam, and the boundaries and extent of which are described in the schedule below, on a pāṭṭam of 14 fanams for Paṛambas 1 and 2, and 4 paṛas of paddy per Nānāḻiyan paṛa (നാനാഴിയൻപറ), worth 10 annas, for land No. 3, and on a Kāṇam of 12 fanams, being the amount for which a lease was granted in 1046 after payment of the improvement value of (കുഴിക്കൂറതീർത്ത ചാർത്തിയ) 2 coconut and 1 jack tree in Paṛamba No. 2 *plus* 4 fanams, being the improvement value with Aḻi (അഴി or അഴിവു = customary deduction in paying for improvements under കുഴിക്കാണം when the Janmi has not to pay for the tenth plant) of two coconut trees now grown in the said paṛamba, making a total under the two heads of 16 fanams, from which deduct fanams 5 for arrears of rent, leaving a balance of 11 fanams as present Kāṇam and on a Puṛappād pāṭṭam of 13½ fanams and 4 paṛas of paddy, half a fanam being deducted for interest on the Kāṇam[4] amount; you should from this (day) ഇതമുതൽ enjoy the lease (പാട്ടംനടന്ന) of these lands annually (കാലംതോറും), and pay me annually 13½ fanams and 4 paṛas of paddy, being the Puṛappād pāṭṭam (പുറപ്പാടപാട്ടം) due to me after deducting the interest on your Kāṇam (amount) and obtain receipt (പൃക്കമുറി). Customary improvement value, subject to Aḻi (അഴി, see above) മരമര്യാദഅഴികുഴിക്കാണം will be paid[5] for young trees (ഇളംഫലം) already planted but not paid for (മുമ്പവെച്ചതിൽതീരാതെയുള്ള), and for trees which may be planted hereafter (ഇതമുതലായി), excepting two old jack trees (മൂളഫലംപുലാവ) previously existing in Paṛamba No. 1, and four coconut and one jack tree in Paṛamba No. 2, of which the improvement value has been paid (കുഴിക്കൂറതീർത്ത), although a pre-

---

[1] This is quite a modern phrase. The proper term for a *Kāṇam* deed is *Pāṭṭamōla* or *Pāṭṭōla*. See Glossary and Deeds 17, 23, 31, &c.

[2] *Kuḻikkāṇu kuḍiyirippinna poḻichcheḻuti chārtti.* Literally, for an *improving* (*Kuḻi*) Kāṇam dwelling-house site, having cancelled (*poḻichchu*) and renewed (*eḻuti* = written) and written (*chārtti*).

[3] *Taṛavāḍ Janmam* has now come to signify merely "family property," but the retention of the word *Taṛavāḍ* before *Janmam* points out the direction in which modern ideas on the subject have been derived. All *Janmam* land has descended to the present owners through the ancient Nayar Taravaḍs (*Taṛa* = *Nāyar* village, and *pāḍu* = authority).

[4] Here *Kāṇam* signifies simply money advanced and secured on the land. Compare the use made of the word in Deed No. 4.

[5] The incorporation in the deed of clauses relating to the valuation of improvements is quite a modern practice.

mium[1] (പാട്ടക്കെട്ടുകളി) of Rs. 5-8-0 for 12 years is now collected; if the Puṛappād pāṭṭam payable annually be not paid at stated periods but be allowed to fall into arrears, the same should be paid in one lump (ഒന്നായി), with interest at 12 per cent., whenever I demand it. Written in the hand of Katakkāt Pappu Nāyar on the 19th Dhanu Nyāyar (ഞായറ = solar month) of the year 1057, corresponding to 1st January 1882, with Kuttitāḻat Cheṛunṇi Nāyar and Kannyingāt Appuṇṇi as witnesses (സാക്ഷികളായി).

Registration.		Where situated.				Area.		Boundaries.				Possession.	
District.	Taluk.	Amṣam.	Dēṣam.	Number.	Names of Lands.	East to West.	North to South.	East.	South.	West.	North.	Former.	Present.
Malabar.	Calicut.	Cheṛuvaṇṇūr.	Cheṛuvaṇṇūr.	1	Vaṭṭakandi Paṛamba.	27	38	Innachamkandi Paṛamba.	Atiyarakāvu Paṛamba.	Lane ..	Pathway.	Chellat Govindan Nayar.	Chellat Govindan Nayar.
				2	Tayitōṭṭam Paṛamba.	25	27	Ittamiritū Paṛamba.	Choyichitoḍuka Paṛamba.	Do. ..	Do.		
				3	1 Kandam in Makkaloti Nilath.	15	12	Ummapaḍam Nilam.	Ummapaḍam Nilam.	Ummapaḍam Nilam.	Ummapaḍam Nilam.		

Note.—Translated from a copy received from the Registrar of Malabar.

No. 58.

Karipaṇayam deed (കരിപണയം = mortgage with possession), executed by Mangṅgalaṣṣēri Tekkinkāṭṭil Nārāyaṇan Nāyar, son of Kunchiamma of Mundūr Amṣam and Dēṣam, Pālghaṭ Tāluk, to Ānappāra Purakkal Pāchchi,

---

[1] The tenant's payments here may be summed up thus:—

			RS.	A.	P.
Rent per annum	14 fanams		3	8	0
	4 paṛas paddy at 10 annas ..		2	8	0
Recoupment of premium, with interest at 12 per cent. per annum spread over 12 years.	Principal .. Rs.	5 8 0			
	Interest .. ,,	4 4 7			
	Total ..	9 12 7 / 12 =	0	13	$0\frac{7}{12}$
	Total rent per annum ..		6	13	$0\frac{7}{12}$

The holding is about 1½ acres in extent, so the rent is rather over Rs. 4-8-0 per acre per annum.

daughter of Īḻuvan Vēlu, of Nechchippaḷḷi Dēṣam, Kāvalpād Amṣam, of the said tāluk. One item of land sowing 5 paras and specified in the subjoined schedule being given to (your) possession (കൈയ്യശംതന്ന) as Karipaṇayam (കരിപണയമായി), (I have) this day received 360 fanams, which, with 40 fanams already due, makes under two heads (വകരണ്ടിൽ) a total of 400 fanams, equal to Rs. 114-4-7. For this sum of Rs. 114-4-7 you should, by cultivating (കൃഷിനടന്ന) the land mentioned in the schedule, measure out (വടിക്കേണ്ടും) a pāṭṭam of 33 paras and 5 Iḍangāḻis of paddy, out of which, deducting 22 paras 5 Iḍangāḻis as interest on the money advanced (അർത്ഥപലിശ), (there is left) a balance inclusive of assessment of a pāṭṭam of 11 paras of paddy, which must be annually measured out at my house in my para from 1058 (M.E.) within the 30th Makaram, after being dried and cleaned (വെടിപ്പുവരുത്തി), and a receipt should be taken (by you). Moreover, you should quit and give possession of the land (to me) when the 400 fanams is returned on the day following any Uchchār [ഉച്ചാർ or ഉച്ചാരൽ is the season when leases of land are generally granted and cancelled; ഉച്ചാരൽ = festival in honor of Bhūdēvi's (ഭൂദേവി = goddess of earth) menstruation on Makara Sankrānti (end of January)]. Written in the hand of Nārāyaṇan, the receiver (കൊണ്ടവൻ of the money) on the 29th January 1882, corresponding to 17th Makaram of the year 1057, with the undersigned as witnesses.

District.	Sub-District.	Taluk.	Amṣam.	Dēṣam.	Number.	Name of Land.	Per 6-feet Kōl.		Boundaries.				Possession.	
							East to West.	North to South.	East.	South.	West.	North.	Former.	Present.
Malabar.	Palghat.	Palghat.	Kāvalpād.	Nechchipaḷḷi.	1	One Kandam of 5 paras, out of Manngalaṣṣēri Kūru of 20 paras.	10	30	Mangngalaṣṣēri Kūru Nili Kandam Nilam.	Mangngalaṣṣēri Kūru Aḍa Mari Nilam.	Nili Kandam Nilam.	Canal.	Narayanan Nayar.	Pachchi.

Note.—Translated from a copy furnished by the District Registrar.

APPENDIX XIII.

Mr. GRÆME'S GLOSSARY WITH NOTES AND ETYMOLOGICAL HEADINGS.

INDEX.

LIST OF ABBREVIATIONS NOTED IN THE GLOSSARY.

S.A. = Sadr Adālat.
S.C. = Sadr Court.
M.H.C. = Madras High Court.
M.H.C.R. = Madras High Court Reports.
M.S. Decisions = Madras Sadr Court Decisions.
M.S.C. = Madras Sadr Court.
S.D.C. = South Malabar District Court.
S.S.C. = South Malabar Subordinate Court.
N.D.C. = North Malabar District Court.
I.L.R. Madras = Indian Law Reports, Madras Series.

GLOSSARY.

ADIMA GRANT called a TĪṬṬU.

Aḍima, from Dravidian *aḍi* (= bottom, base, foot), means slavery, feudal dependency. *Tīṭṭu*, from Dravidian *tīnduka* (= to touch, defile), means a writ from a superior to an inferior.

In Malabar there are few castes under the rank of Nāyar who did not, and who do not still, acknowledge a feudal dependence upon some superior lord, and who are not Aḍiyāns or vassals. Persons of this description were not formerly allowed to possess land in Janmam right; and therefore, when a Janmi made over land to a person in the condition of an Aḍiyān, it was called an Aḍima deed or grant, although he might not be his own vassal, and although the proprietor might have received the full Janmam value for the land. The right of proprietorship continued with the Janmi, and the tenant paid him a small sum of money—not more, perhaps, than two fanams annually—by way of acknowledgment of proprietorship. The tenant, however, could not be dispossessed, and the land descended to his heirs, and only reverted to the Janmi on failure of heirs.

The Aḍima grant of a paṛamba or garden was also often conferred by a superior lord, or Tala Uḍaya Tamburān, upon his own Aḍiyān or vassal; but here it was in the feature of an Inām or gift, no consideration having been received for it by the proprietor. An annual trifling tribute of superiority is, however, reserved to the proprietor to prevent the garden being entirely alienated. The garden reverts to the proprietor on failure of heirs on the part of the Aḍiyān and if the Aḍiyān takes a part with the enemies of his patron, the latter may resume the property. Under any other circumstances the Aḍiyān cannot be dispossessed, and he has the right of burial within the garden.

Notes.—1. See *Kuḍima, Changngātam.*

2. In this the land is made over in perpetuity to the grantee, either unconditionally as a mark of favor, or on condition of certain services being performed. The terms Aḍima and Kuḍima mean a slave, or one subject to the landlord, the grant being generally made to such persons. A nominal fee of about two fanams a year is payable to the landlord to show that he still retains the proprietary title. Land bestowed as a mark of favor can never be resumed, but where it is granted as remuneration for certain services to be performed, the non-performance of such services involving the necessity of having them discharged by others will give the landlord power to recover the land. The non-payment of the annual fee will form no ground for ousting the grantee, but it will be recoverable by action. The hereditary property of Native princes cannot be conferred on this tenure, the ruling prince having only the right of enjoyment during life, without power to alienate.—(Proceedings of the Court of Sadr Adalat, No. 18, dated 5th August 1856.)

3. A grant on condition of performing service is irredeemable so long as the grantee is ready and willing to perform the service.—S.D.C. 522 (1876), 113 (1877), 663 (1879).

AḌIMA PAṚAMBU.

Aḍima (q. v.) *Paṛambu* (Dravidian) = higher or dry ground laid out in terraces, all fields too high for irrigation, an orchard, garden, compound.

Is a garden given to a slave (not a Cheṛuman or a person who can be sold), rather a vassal under the lord's particular protection. A certain pāṭṭam is taken sometimes, and sometimes none. Land so given can never be taken away, but remains with the vassal till his death. If he dies without heirs it reverts to the lord paramount. A Vēṭṭuvan or salt manufacturer who had got such a piece of land at Calicut said it was a place where he could be buried. He seemed to consider it a privilege insured to him.

Note.—See *Paṛambu.*

AḌIYĀN.

From Dravidian *aḍi* (= base, bottom, foot), means servant, slave.

Is literally slave both in Tamil and Malayāḷam, and in the Northern Division of Malabar it is applied to the real slaves, but in South Malabar it means generally vassals. Under the old system, where every Tīyan was under a kind of vassalage to some superior, to some patron, to a Tamburān as he is commonly called, the patron was bound to protect him and to redress any petty wrongs he might sustain, and the client or vassal acknowledged his dependent state by yearly presents, and was to be ready with his personal services upon any private quarrel of his patron. This kind of dependency gave the patron no right of disposal of the person of his vassal as a slave, nor did it acquit the dependent individual of a superior obligation to the Rāja or his representatives, the Dēṣavāḻi, and Nāḍuvāḻi, upon a public emergency.

Individuals were often clients of the church, which, by means of its representatives, the Ūrāḷar, was bound to protect them. Even at the present day an individual will immediately say who his Tamburān or patron is, and the yearly presents are still kept up.

Note.—See *Chagngātam.*

ĀḺIPĀḌAM.

From (Dravidian) *āḻi* = (the ocean, the deep) and (Sanskrit) *pāḍam* (a range, especially of rice-fields).

Āḻam means, as in Tamil, depth, lowness, and pāḍam field. The word applies to the lowest rice-lands.

Note.—See *Kandam,*

AḺI ṢILAVU.

Aḻi, properly *aḻu* or *aḻuku* (Dravidian), means the high wall round an orchard. *Ṣilavu,* properly *chelavu* (Dravidian), means expense.

The expense of preparing gardens. It bears the proportion of 20 per cent. to the established valuation of trees, which is settled in making the Kuḻikkāṇam. This being added to the value of the trees, which in most places is half a rupee a coco-nut tree, the proprietor must pay for both, or else the interest of the two sums, according to the usual rate of the place, is included in the Pramānam and deducted from the pāṭṭam.

AMṢAPATRAM or PAKUTI ŌLA.

Amṣpatrām, from Sanskrit *Amṣam* (= share, part) and Sanskrit *Patram* (= a leaf, a letter).

Pakuti Ōḷa, from Dravidian *pakuti* (= division, share) and Dravidian *ōla* (= palm leaf, a writing leaf).

Is a deed of division of hereditary property among relations ; another kind of Paṇaya Ōla Karaṇam for rice-lands ; it is also called Muṛi : the same deed is used for plantations, and it is called in addition Keṭṭi-aḍakkam on account of these words being in the deed, which show that it refers to plantations.

Is a deed under which a Janmi makes over land for money borrowed. The mortgagee pays himself the interest and gives to the Janmi the purapād or residue of the pāṭṭam after deducting the interest, and in some cases the land-tax is also to be deducted. The land is to be restored on payment of the debt without any deduction of Sākshi, and no Polichcheḻuttu is allowed under this deed. The interest is supposed to be rather high in this transaction compared with that of many other land tenures.

ĀNAKKOMBAN.

From Dravidian *Āna* (= elephant) and Dravidian *kombu* (= tusk, ivory).

A species of fine paddy grown in the Pālghat District in low rice-lands, which is ten months in coming to maturity. It is heating. It is generally exported to Coimbatore, where it fetches one-twentieth more than any other kind of paddy.

ANUBHAVAM or Anubhōgam.

(Sanskrit) = enjoyment, usufruct.

A deed of gift of land as a reward for services performed, answering, perhaps, to Inām land. The holder cannot be dispossessed, and the right is hereditary; but if the grantee or any of his descendants die without heirs, the land reverts to the Janmi, and on the succession of heirs the Janmi is entitled to Purushāntaram. In some instances a trifling payment of one or two fanams is made by the grantee to the Janmi in token of acknowledgment of proprietorship. An hereditary grant of Anubhavam of the puṛapād, or residue of puṛapād after deducting mortgage interest, which remains in the hands of a mortgagee, is sometimes made to the mortgagee himself, or to some other person not connected with the land to whom the mortgagee is required to pay it.

Notes.—1. See *Aḍima Kūlichchēkam.*

2. It was customary for princes, when conferring a title on any person, to grant him at the same time sufficient land to enable him to maintain the dignity of his position. Grants under this tenure were also bestowed upon persons for special services rendered, or for the future performance of certain services. The tenant cannot be ejected except where there are conditions imposed and he fails to fulfil them; but, on the other hand, he and his heirs have only the right of enjoyment and cannot alienate their title. A trifling annual fee is generally paid to the landlord to show that he has not surrendered the proprietary.—(Proceedings of the Court of Sadr Adalat, No. 18, dated 5th August 1856.)

APHALAM.

(Sanskrit) = unfruitful, from *a* (Sanskrit negative particle) and Sanskrit *phalam* (= fruit), perhaps from Dravidian *paḻam* (= fruit).

A tree past bearing.

ARECA or Betel-Nut. (*Areca Catechu.*)

The tree = *Kamugu, Kamundu, Kavundu,* or *Kaḻungngu* (Dravidian).
Its fruit = *Aḍakka, Aḍekka* (Dravidian), whence Portuguese *Areca.*

The nut of the betel-nut tree (not the tree itself) in Malayāḻam, whence probably the botanical name areca.

According to Arshad Beg's Settlement of 1783-84 or 959 of the Southern Districts, exclusive of Pālghat—

Total Trees	.. 3,361,195		
Aphalam or Ṣisu	.. 2,161,115		
Productive	.. 1,200,080		
	HOONS	S.	C.
Or about one-third assessable Revenue ..	20,018	0	0

59 productive trees per hoon, or 20 productive trees per rupee.

The number according to the Janmi Pymāish account of 981, furnished by the Collector, Mr. Vaughan, was 4,409,843 ; of this past bearing 1,326,652, pupils 1,376,846, productive 1,706,345. Their revenue of that year, deducting past bearing and pupils, Rs. 58,656 1 qr. $32\frac{3}{4}$ reas ; average assessment per productive tree $13\frac{3}{4}$ reas.

Note.—The number according to the Jamabandi accounts of Fasli 1289 (1879-80) was 8,167,552, of which 1,661,003 were returned as past bearing 3,304,740 as too young to bear, and 3,201,189 as productive. The revenue, assessed on the productive trees alone, was returned as Rs. 81,311-12-0, giving an average of nearly[1] 5 pies per productive tree.

AṬṬIPPETTŌLA or Aṭṭippēṛu.

From Dravidian *Aṭṭi* (= causal of a verb signifying to be close, contiguous to, hence causal form = to come in contact) and Dravidian *pēṛu* (= birth, bringing forth), and Dravidian *ōla* (= palm-leaf, leaf for writing.) The full phrase is *Nīr Aṭṭi pēṛu*, meaning the birthright (pēṛu) obtained by coming in contact (*Aṭṭi*) with *nīr* (= water).

Pēṛ in Malayāḷam corresponds with the Sanskrit word Janmam, which means born, created, acquired, and more generally property. Aṭṭi means to join, mix. These two words united give but an imperfect meaning, and the word nīr is generally prefixed. Nīr-aṭṭi-pēr thus means the Janmam combined with water which is given up. The Janmi reserves no puṛapād (balance of rent after deducting mortgage interest) or anything to himself. He can not, after the execution of this deed, redeem the mortgage, and the relinquishment of the proprietary right is absolute under it. At the time of executing and delivering the deed, the following persons must be present. A Sva-jāti, a person of the same caste ; Bandhu, a relative ; Putran, literally the son, but in Malabar construed to mean the heir, whether a nephew or son ; Narapati, the Rāja ; the writer of the deed ; Tatra Sambandhi, a resident round the spot. In practice the attendance of the Rāja, or the execution of the deed before the Rāja, is dispensed with. It is only necessary that he should be apprized of the transaction. The mortgagee gives two fanams, which is placed in a small vessel of water ; the mortgagor, holding the deed in his hand, pours the water over it, which the mortgagor receives as it falls, and either swallows it, or puts it upon his head, or upon his feet, or upon the ground, according to the relative caste of the two parties. The deed is then delivered to the mortgagee. This deed mentions generally that the full value of the property disposed of has been received, and states the boundaries of it, but it does not specify the amount received.

Notes.—1. See *Janmam* and *Peṛumartham* and *Sthānā-māna-avakāṣam*.

2. The purchaser, in coming into possession, is bound by all obligations which attached to the proprietor. He cannot disturb those who may be holding the property or any portion of it on Kāṇam mortgage, but merely receives the surplus rent produce in place of the former landlord. On the other hand, he comes into all the rights and privileges of the former land-

[1] Correct average = 4 [illegible] pies.

lord, and may pay off Otti mortgages and sell or transfer the property as he pleases.—Proceedings of the Court of Sadr Adalat, No. 18, dated 5th August 1856.)

ĀTTUVEPPU.

From Dravidian *Āṟu* (= river) and Dravidian *veppu* = (placing, planting). Plantations bordering the seashore and rivers.

Notes.—1. One of the classes into which coconut gardens are divided.

2. As matter of fact, such gardens do not always border on the shore or river.

CHANGNGĀTAM.

(Sanskrit) = convoy, guard, income of Rājas from granting such guards, grants of land to persons liable to such service, companion.

Is also a kind of vassalage, and is applied particularly to Nāyars who have placed themselves in a state of dependency upon some Dēṣavāḻi, Nāḍuvāḻi or Rāja. The word Aḍiyān would, with respect to them, be degrading and improperly used. Nāyars have often agreed to give Changngātam or protection-money to some chief of authority, and to make yearly presents in consequence from 4 to 34 fanams to individual patrons, and as high as 120 to the church. The church, again, has often subjected itself to Changngātam money to Rājas to ensure the benefit of their power.

Notes.—1. "Those who desire to proceed thither should first pay a certain sum of money to the king of the country, who will then appoint people to accompany them and show them the way."—*Fah Hian's Travels*, quoted at Indian Antiquary VII, p. 3. "Thither" meant the country called by Fah Hian the "Kingdom of the Dakshiṇa" or of the South.

2. There were four classes of officers about the Rāja, whose posts were not hereditary but within his gift, viz., (1) *Munnaḻippād*, attendants with a daily allowance of three Nāḻis of paddy, youthful attendants: (2) *Āṛunāḻippād*, attendants with double the above allowance; (3) *Pandārappād*, treasury officials; and (4) *Changngātippād* (see heading).—(Gundert's Dictionary.)

3. See *Kuḍima, Kūlichchakkāran, Revenue.*

CHANGNGĀTIKKUṚI.

From Sanskrit *changngāti* (= convoy, guard, companion, friend) and Dravidian *Kuṛi* (= lot, share, lottery, club).

May be construed a season of friendship, a periodical association the lodge of friendship, a society of friends. It was a meeting formerly very common in Malabar among the natives, and still partially kept up, for the purposes of conversation, of discussing any particular subject, of inquiring into the conduct of any individual. It is not, it appears, confined to people of the same caste, but the association was often composed of Nāyers, Tīyars and Māppiḻas. Besides promoting social intercourse, it has a tendency to prudential consequences. It induces economy. Where there is a variety of castes in the society, the entertainer gives to those who are not of his own caste a certain quantity of rice and allows them to dress it by their own people. It is supported by the subscription of the members in the following manner. Suppose there are 25 members; that each contributes 4 fanams monthly, making a total stock for each month of 100 fanams; that the society is limited to 25 months' duration, and every member is obliged to give an entertainment to the party once in the course of this period at his own house. It does not come to the members in regular turn, but is decided by lot, that is, every member places with his subscription a ticket with his name into the deposit, and a ticket is drawn every month by some indifferent person, and the person whose name appears on the ticket drawn gives the entertainment and is entitled to the amount in deposit for the month. The entertainment is calculated to cost at most not more than 10 per cent. of one month's subscription of all the members, and the great advantage is derived from drawing a ticket at an early stage on account of the interest upon the sum to the remaining period; there is no other prize; every member's subscription amounts in the end to the whole principal gain which he can ever make.

The greatest disadvantages to any member are the drawing his ticket towards the close of the duration of the society, the consequent loss of interest on his monthly subscriptions, and the loss of principal expended in the entertainment to the extent of two or two and a half month's subscription.

But these are counterbalanced by his facility of procuring easy loans of money upon the security which the ultimate certainty of attaining a prize affords. The monthly subscriptions in the meantime are small and not felt, and induce a habit of saving which would not otherwise be practised.

The interest upon loans which the members thus procure is to be paid only till the prize comes up. The lender derives no benefit from the chance of its coming up early.

Notes.—1. See *Changngātam.*

2. The *Kuṛi* was of three kinds: (1) *Nelkkuṛi,* where the shares were paid in paddy; (2) *Arikkuṛi,* where the shares were paid in rice; and (3) *Paṇakkuṛi,* where the shares were paid in money.

KUṚI MŪPPAN.

Is the president of the society termed Changngātikkuṛi, whose duty it is to see the money collected, or, in failure, to forfeit to the prize-drawer double the deficient subscription. He is entitled to the privilege of giving the first month's entertainment. The society has of late years fallen into disuse, partly because the European authorities have discouraged it among all public servants as liable to abuse, and partly because it does not enjoy the necessary power to enforce its rules by degradation or other punishment, and members are not to be found who will support it from their own respectability. The contempt of its regulations can only be attempted to be remedied by a tedious, vexatious and expensive appeal to a judicial tribunal—an appeal likely to be more particularly ineffectual from the compact of the parties being rather understood than expressive, founded more upon a sense of honor than upon law or written agreement.

CHANGNGĀTIKKUṚI KALYĀṆAM.

See *Changngātikkuṛi; Kalyāṇam* (Sanskrit) = luck, happiness.

May be termed an association of friendship and pleasure among the natives of Malabar. It is an entertainment given by a respectable native, at which all his friends who are invited present a sum of money and a certain number of coconuts, plantains, betel-leaves and betel-nuts, every man according to his fancy, to the entertainer. The host feeds all those who come and has diversions for the company. An account is kept of what each guest offers, and when these guests in their turn announce that an entertainment is to be given by them, the person who has formerly had the benefit of an entertainment is expected to be present and to make a return at least equal, but in general half as much again, and sometimes double, what he has received.

To any person who evades the invitation and does not send the proper present of money and fruit, a small vessel of arrack and the bone of a fowl are sent in derision to shame him into a more liberal spirit, and he is desired to eat and drink them and to return the money, &c., he formerly received. This, in general, was sufficient to ensure a compliance with the custom.

Note.—Kuṛikkalyāṇam is in some places used to signify *Changngātikkuṛi.* Such associations are still kept up.

CHĀVĒṚ.

From Dravidian *Chāva* (= death) and Dravidian *Ēṛuka* (= to arise, ascend), literally, those who went forth to death.

Or lands granted by Rājas to the families of deceased heroes who fell in performance of solemn vows to fight till death against the enemy. If any escaped this conflict they were excommunicated their caste and obliged to flee the country. The Iḷaya Rāja of Angādipuṛam states that much of his original rājyam in Vullatra was alienated from this cause in his wars with the Zamorin. It appears the private Janmams of conquered states were not respected by the conquerors.

Notes.—1. The name was applied to those persons who, for the honor of the *Vaḷḷuvakōnatiri* or *Veḷḷāṭṭiri Rāja,* elected to run, armed with swords and shields, the gauntlet of the Zamorin's 30,000 spears at Tirunāvāyi in Ponnāni Tāluk every twelfth year.

2. Their ostensible object was to elude the spears and to slay the Zamorin, who, armed with Chēramān Perumāl's sword awaited their onslaught. *Conf.* pp 162-69 of the text.

CHĒṚLĀBHAM.

Chēṛlābham, from Dravidian *chēṛu* (= wet soil) and Sanskrit *lābham* (= gain, profit).

Meaning generally the same as Koḻulābham, but more literally the profit of the earth or soil—the cultivator's share.

Note.—See *Koḻulābham.*

CHEṚUJANMAM.

From *chēṛu* (Dravidian) = small, and *Janmam* (Sanskrit) = birth.

Inferior rights applied to the fees receivable by the carpenter and smith in Malabar.

Notes.—1. See *Janmam*

2. Hereditary rights and perquisites were claimed, within certain defined local limits, by (1) the Kaṇiṣan (astrologer) for feasts, (2) the Āṣāri (carpenter) for dedication of houses, (3) the Taṭṭān (goldsmith) for marriages, (4) the Malayan (musicians and conjurors) for devil feasts, (5) the Vaṇṇān (washerman), (6) the Vēlan (midwife, accoucheur), (7) the Viḷakkattaravan (barber), &c.

CHEṚUMAKKAL.

From Dravidian *cheṛu* = chiru (= small) and Dravidian *makkal* (= children).—(Gundert).

Slaves in general. It is supposed to be derived from chēṛu = soil, and makkal = children: children of the soil, or sons of the earth. Others say from cheṛu, small, and makkal, children, indicating that thev are to be treated as young children by their masters.

Notes.—1. From a census taken in 1857 of the slave population it appeared that they were then distributed as follows:—

1.	Chiṛakkal	13,380
2.	Kōṭṭayam	2,859
3.	Kuṛumbṛanād	16,590
4.	Wynād	16,561
5.	Calicut	14,082
6.	Ērnād	35,419
7.	Waḷḷuvanād	34,902
8.	Pālghat	25,280
9.	Ponnāni	28,668
10.	Cochin	71
	District Total	187,812

2. The bulk of the slaves being located in the ancient *Chēṛanād* (part of the Ērnād Tāluk) and in the neighbourhood of it, it is not unreasonable to suppose they got their name as being the aborigines of *Chēṛanād*, or possibly of the still more ancient kingdom of Chēra.

CHIṚA.

(Dravidian) = enclosure, dam, tank.

A reservoir of water or tank on a smaller scale; it answers to ēri or lke in the Dravida country. In the Pālghat and Temmalapuṛam Districts it is used for cultivation. It is formed by a bank thrown across the higher parts of a tract of rice-lands and resting at each end upon eminences. Cultivation of rice is carried on on land lower than its level; and in the bed of it a kind of rice called Kuṭṭāḍan is sown, which takes nine months to come to maturity. It is sown in Chithri or April, before the commencement of the heavy monsoon, and is cut in Margulli or December, and it shoots its head above the water, the depth of which is often six feet.

COCONUT.

In Malayāḷam *tēngnga* or *tēngngā*, contraction for *tēngngankāyi*, from Dravidian *tekkē* (= south) and Dravidian *kāy* (= ripening fruit).

According to Arshad Beg's Settlement of 1783-84 or 959 of the Southern Districts, exclusive of Pālghat there were—

Coconut trees	2,896,099
Aphalam and Ṣisu	2,162,508
Productive	733,591

or about one-fourth assessable Revenue 36,724-5½ fanams, or twenty trees per hoon, or 7 trees per rupee.

The number according to the Janmi Pymāish account of 981, furnished by the Collector, Mr. Vaughan, was 6,124,367, past bearing 1,792,987, pupils 1,244,440, productive 3,086,939. Their revenue of that year, deducting past bearing and pupils, Rs. 3,15,115-0 qr. 75¼ reas; average of assessment per productive tree $40\frac{13\frac{1}{4}}{16}$ reas.

In talking of the price of coconuts, it is always understood to be the nut without the husk, which latter is sold separately.

Note.—According to the Jamabandi accounts of Fasli 1289 (A.D. 1879-80) the number of coconut trees was 9,519,567, of which 1,310,253 were past bearing, 3,611,506 were not yet come into bearing, and 4,597,808 were productive. The productive trees were assessed at Rs. 3,49,835-11-3, being at the rate of 1 anna 2[illegible] pies per productive tree.

COWLE.

(Arabic) *qabūl* = engagement, cowle.

Notes.—1. A Government cowle for the cultivation of waste land confers a right of entry, and of compensation for improvements, but does not affect the Janmi's right to rent.—S.D.C., 132 (1877), 79 (1878).

3. A Janmi is not at liberty to eject a squatter on waste land who has obtained a cowle from Government, if 12 years have elapsed from the date of entry.—S.D.C., 195 (1878,) 674 (1879).

3. A Government cowle does not confer any right as against a prior occupant.—S.D.C., 47 and 48 (1878).

DASTA BĀKKI.

From Persian *dast* (= balance in hand) and Arabic *bākki* (= remnant, surplus).

A balance of revenue collected from the person due, but not brought to the public credit by the Revenue Officers.

DĒSAM.

(Sanskrit) = region, country, parish.

A village, the same as Taṛa in the Malabar province. In the ancient Hindu histories a kingdom, of which there were 56 in India, is meant by it.

Note.—See pp. 87-90 of the text. The *Dēṣam* and the *Taṛa* were not the same thing. See *Taṛa*.

Dēṣavāḻi.

From *Dēṣam* (q.v.) and Dravidian *vāḻi*, from *vāḻuka*, to live, live prosperously, reign.

Hereditary heads of villages. Before Hyder's conquest some had one, some two or more villages; their places are now supplied by Mukhyastanmār.

The number of Nāyars or fighting men attached to a Dēṣavāḻi was from 25 to 100; if it exceeded the latter number, he ranked as a Nāḍuvāḻi.

Note.—See pp. 87-90 of the Text. He was the military chief, not the civil chief, of the *Dēṣam*.

Dēṣakōyma.

From *Dēṣam* (q.v.) and Dravidian *Kōyma*, modern form of *Kōnma*, from *Kōn* (= king), means sovereignty, authority.

Same as Dēṣavāḻi.

Note.—This word denotes the functions of a *Dēṣavāḻi* which were as follows:—

1. **Dēṣam.**

See *Dēṣam*.

2. **Dēṣādhipatyam.**

From *Dēṣam* (q.v.) and Sanskrit *ādhipatyam* = supreme authority.

3. **Ambalappaḍi.**

From Dravidian *ambalam* (= place devoted for public use or assemblies, a temple) and Dravidian *paḍi* (= a step, bench).

4. **Ūrāyma.**

From Dravidian *Ūr* (= village, town, parish) and Dravidian *vāyma* modern form of *vānma* from vāḻuka (= to live prosperously, reign) meaning authority, office.

Sthānams or dignities.

Ambalappaḍi is the seat of honor, a certain step or degree in a temple to which only particular persons are entitled. The claim to it is derived from ancestry, but the dignity is saleable. It is, however, understood that it cannot be disposed of except to a person of the proper caste and necessary respectability. It is, strictly speaking, confined to Brāhmans, but there have been interlopers of the Samunta caste.

The Ūrāyma is the office to which is attached the general superintendence of the affairs of a temple; a person who has attained the Ambalappaḍi dignity in the village holds invariably also that of Ūrāyma, that is, he is the Ūrāḷan of the temple, but the Ūrāḷan may be such without being an Ambalappaḍi (*sic*).

Dēṣam means that a person possesses in proprietary right the whole property of the village or Dēṣam. He is the janmi or Mutalāḷan of the Dēṣam.

Dēṣādhipatyam is the office held by the Dēṣādhipati or Dēṣavāḻi, which is the political ruler or representative of government in the Dēṣam; of the Dēṣam and Dēṣadhipatyam an individual may be possessed of the one or the other separately. The Dēṣavāḻi was not necessarily proprietor of all the lands of the village. But a person enjoying these four dignities collectively and in the same Dēṣam is esteemed as one who has reached the summit of honor. All the dignities were saleable, either separately or collectively, except the Ūrāyma and the Ambalappaḍi, which went always together, and generally the Dēṣam and Dēṣādhipatyam.

Ambalam equals temple of the first order, called Mahā Kshētram, dedicated to the Hindu Trimurtti. There were 108 principal temples constructed by Paraṣurāma between Gōkarnam and Kannya Kumāri (Cape Comorin), and the one opposite to Mr. Babington's bungalow at Varakkal, near Calicut, is of the number.

Notes.—1. See pp. 87-90 of the Text; also *Taṛa* and *Ūr.*

2. A *Dēṣam* was not synonymous with a *taṛa*. Great confusion has arisen from thinking so.

3. The seat of honor in the *ambalam* is just *outside* the sanctuary. As Brāhmans can enter the sanctuary itself, it was no honor to them to be seated on the *ambalappaḍi*. To be thought entitled to exclusive right to the *ambalappaḍi* was, on the other hand, a source of profit which Brāhmans coveted. The *ambalappaḍi* was originally the seat of the chief man directing the proceedings of any public meeting, such as a temple feast; he was, in short, chairman.

4. *Ambalappaḍi* and *Ūrāyma* were the privileges of the headmen, Kāraṇavar of the *taṛa* (Dravidian *teru* = street, village) or of the *Ūr* (Dravidian = village), along with other privileges, some of which are still observed, for example, *Ūrpaḻḻi*, the special place set apart in the village (*Ūr*) for cutting up the carcases of deer, &c., killed in the village hunt, the headman of the *Ūr* (a *Taṛavāṭṭukāraṇavan*) being entitled to a hind-quarter and other parts of the animal.

EḌAM or IḌAM.

(Dravidian) = place, house, mansion.

Is the distinctive name of a house or palace occupied by a member of the family of the Pālghat Rāja; it is also used sometimes for the house of a Nāḍuvāḻi of consequence in the Pālghat District. In the same part of the country the house of a common man is called a *Vīḍu; Eḍam*, in Tamil means place.

Note.—The use of the word is not confined to the Pālghat Taluk.

ĔLAM.

(Dravidian) = cardamoms.

A thousand rupees a candy the Wynād cardamom sells for.

Note.—The best cardamoms now fetch from Rs. 1,200 to Rs. 1,400 per candy of 700 lb.

EṆṆAM.

(Dravidian) = number, counting.

Counting. It is a term used for the expense of reaping, reckoned 10 per cent. In some places this proportion is given after the paddy is measured out; in others one out of ten sheaves is given in the field.

Note.—The number of sheaves varies: in one part of Chirakkal Tāluk at the present time one out of twelve goes to the reapers. See *Patam*, *Koḻulābham*, *Chēṛlābham*, and *Pandakkāval*.

ETṬUKKONNU and MUPPARA.

Eṭṭukkonnu, from Dravidian *eṭṭu* (= eight) and Dravidian *onnu* (= one),
Muppaṛa, from Dravidian *mūnnu* (= three) and Dravidian *paṛa* (= a measure, bushel).

Meaning one to eight, and three paṛas; it expresses the nature of the land-tax in the Travancore province. On the garden land one in eight (of the pāṭṭam or rent) is said to be taken, and on rice-lands three paṛas (out of ten.)

FANAM.

From Dravidian *Paṇam* = coin, fanam, money in general.

Old Vīrāy or Gold = 4 to a rupee. There are 12½ Malabar pice to one fanam.

New Vīrāy or Gold = 3½ to a rupee. There are 14¼ Malabar pice to one fanam.

Silver = 5 to a rupee, and each fanam worth ten Malabar pice.

Note.—Mr. Græme has omitted mention of the

I. *Rāṣi fanam.*—The most ancient of the indigenous fanams, bearing at the present time a fanciful value. They are of gold, and have the same 14 dots as the gold fanams mentioned above. *Rāṣi* means a sign of the Zodiac, so it is supposed the 12 dots are the 12 signs of the Zodiac, and the two separate dots are the sun and moon. The 12 Zodiacal signs are divided into four good, four middling, and four bad signs, which may account for the appearance of the dots on one side of the coins: the four prolonged dots being the good, the four ordinary-sized ones the middling, and the four tiny dots placed separately in a corner by themselves the four bad signs. The other emblems are not understood.

II. The *Sultāni fanam.*—A coin of Tippu's, which in 1790-92 had fallen in value to 3½ = a rupee.

GARCE.

120 paṛas of 25 Macleod seers, or 3,000 Macleod seers, make a garce. Bombay salt, according to my experiment, weighs 90 lb. the paṛa of salt, so that a garce is 10,800 lb.

GRĀMAM.

(Sanskrit) = village.

Equivalent to Agrahāram in the Carnatic, a Brāhman village. At the time of Paraṣurāma's gift of the country to the Brāhmans, 64 Grāmams were established from Goa to Cape Comorin, 32 from Kānyirote (or Cassergode north to Comorin south); to these were attached all the Sūdra villages.

Notes.—1. See Chapter III. Sections (*a*) and (*b*) of the Text.

2. Mr. Græme here follows the *Keraḷolpatti* tradition, which is unreliable.

GRANDHAVARI.

From Sanskrit *Grandham* = verse, book.

A book formed of the leaves of the Kuḍappana palm or Talipot tree, in which Janmis register their agreements respecting land with their tenants or mortgagees. Where it is kept it is said to be a register which may be safely referred to as authenticating an agreement otherwise doubtful, but it is not kept up so much as it used to be. The Kuḍappana of Malabar does not afford the leaf capable of being so used; the impression of the iron pen goes through and prevents its being written on both sides. The proper kind is only procurable in Travancore and Canara. It is brought for sale. It is much more expensive than that of Malabar. It is also much more durable.

HŌBALI.

(Dravidian) = division of a district.

A term introduced into Malabar by the Muhammadan Government. It is in Malabar a sub-division of a tāluk comprehending several Dēṣams or villages. It corresponds with Māgani in Canara and with Māganum on the Eastern Coast.

Note.—The Muhammadans called their village organization in Malabar the *Taṛa*. See Sir Thomas Munro's Report, Revenue Selections, Vol. I, p. 842. See also *Taṛa* and *Ūr*.

HOUSES.

Different names for them in Malabar according to castes—

Mana	.. Nambūtiripādu's house.
Illam	.. Nambūtiri's house.
Kōvilakam or *Koṭṭāram*	.. Rāja's house.
Iḍam or *Kūṭṭāla* ..	.. Nāḍuvāḷi's house.
Vīḍu	.. Nāyar house.
Pushpōttu or *Pishāram* or *Vāryam*.	Houses of Ambalavāsi or servants of the pagoda, expressive of their caste.
Matham	.. Houses of Chākkyār.
Kuḍi	.. House of Chāliar or weavers.
Pīḍika	.. House of Māppiḷḷa.
Pura	.. House of Tīyan.
Chāḷa	.. The house of a Cheṛuman.
Pura or *chāḷa*	.. The house of a blacksmith, goldsmith, silversmith, carpenter, brazier.

IḌAPĀḌU.

From Dravidian *iḍam* (= place, house of *Nāḍuvāḷis*) and Dravidian *pāḍu* (falling, falling into power, place, rank of officials, &c.), means the authority exercised by the family inhabiting the *iḍam*, who also controlled the pagodas of *Ūrilē Bhagavati* (goddess of the *ūr*, village) and of *Mūvanti kāḷi* (the tutelar deity of Calicut) lying within their limits. Pagodas; 18 should be included in the range of a Kartāva of 3,000 (Nāyars).

Note.—See *Eḍam*.

ILLAKKUṚ.

From Dravidian *Illam* (= a house) and Dravidian *kūṛu* or *kūṛ* (= part share.)

Illam, a house; kūṛ, partition, share. It means the private property of a Rāja which descends to his heirs. He relinquishes this property to his nephew or next heir upon his giving up one official dignity for a higher step. Not that he absolutely gives up all control over it, but this arrangement is made to distinguish and separate it from the public property of the official station he has just held, and to prevent its being claimed by his successor in it.

Note.—See *Kūṛvāḻcha.*

ĪḺAVAN.

From *īḻam*, from *Chingngaḷam, Simhaḷa, Sīhaḷa* = Ceylon.

The name of the Tīyan in the Pālghat and Temmalapuṛam Districts in common parlance, who are aborigines of Malabar; in other places they are only so named in writings.

Note.—The Tīyar or Tīvar (from *tīvu*, corruption of Sanskrit *dvīpu* = an island) are believed not to have been the aborigines of Malabar, but to have come from an island (Ceylon), bringing with them the southern tree (tēng-ngkāy), *i.e.*, the cocoanut. See *Tīyan, Shāṇar, Mukkuvar.*

IṆAKKUMUṚI.

From Dravidian *iṇakku* (= agreement, certificate of agreement) and Dravidian *muṛi*) = fragment, note, bond, receipt).

There are two kinds of deeds of this denomination. A mortgagee making over land to another person in mortgage gives him an Iṇakkumuṛi, or certificate that he has received a sum of money from the second mortgagee and has made over the land to him, and calls upon the Janmi to confirm him in the same tenure which he himself possessed. If this certificate be shown to the Janmi, he has a right to demand Sākshi for the renewal of the deed, but the second mortgagee often withholds the production of the deeds in order to avoid payment of the renewal money. That is also called an Iṇakkumuṛi which a Janmi gives to a mortgagee when he has sold the Janmam right of the mortgaged land to a third person. In it he refers the mortgagee to the purchaser for the future responsibility for the kāṇam money.

Note.—1. Mortgagees may transfer their interest to sub-mortgagees, and the latter come into the enjoyment of the same rights and privileges as the former possessed. A notice should be given to the landlord at the time of such transfer. In an action for the recovery of the property, when an Iṇak has been given, the landlord must recognise and sue the property in possession, but it is only liable to pay the amount which would have been payable to the original mortgagee.—(Proceedings of the Court of Sadr Adalat, No. 18, dated 5th August 1856.)

2. Mr. Græme and the Sadr Court both here use *kānam* as synonymous with mortgage. It is clear that the *Kāṇakkār* had the privilege of selling his holding, independently of the *Janmi*, a most important point. See Chapter IV, Section (*a*) of the Text.

JACK TREE. (*Artocarpus integrifolia.*)

In Malāyaḷam the tree = *pilāvu;* its fruit = *chakka*, whence *Jack.*

Chakkha, = the Malayāḷam name for the fruit of the *Artocarpus integrifolia*, whence is probably derived the name Jack.

Chakka, Mangāy, Taḷ or Tāḷu, Takara = a common saying expressive of the kind of food which the poorer classes of people live upon chiefly in Malabar. Chakka is the Jack, Māngāy the Mango, Tāl or Tāḷu a species of wild Yam with a broad leaf, often cultivated in private gardens, and Takara a species of Dholl. It is called Sāg in Hindustani, and the leaf is eaten boiled. The Jack is eaten boiled, in general mixed with salt, &c.

Note.—According to the Jamabandi accounts of Fasli 1289 (A.D. 1879-80) there were 1,441,034 Jack trees, of which 500,641 were past bearing, 605,640 were too young to bear, and 334,753 were productive. The productive trees were assessed at Rs. 52,337-8-7, or at the rate of 2 annas 6 [illegible] pies per productive tree.

JANMAM.

(Sanskrit) = birth, birthright, hereditary proprietorship, freehold property = the Sanskritised form of the Dravidian *pēṛu* (= birth, birthright).

The landed property of a Janmakkāran or proprietor.

Notes.—1. See Chapter IV, Section (*a*) and *Aṭṭipēṛu.*

2. The purchaser, in coming into possession, is bound by all the obligations which attached to the proprietor. He cannot disturb those who may be holding the property, or any portion of it, on kāṇam mortgage, but merely receives the surplus rent produce in place of the former landlord. On the other hand, he comes into all the rights and privileges of the former landlord, and may pay off Otti mortgages, and sell or transfer the property as he pleases.—(Proceedings of the Court of Sadr Adalut, No. 18, dated 5th August 1856.)

JANMAKKĀRAN OR JANMI OR MUTALĀLAN.

Janmakkāran and *Janmi* = from Sanskrit *Janmam* (q.v.) and Sanskrit *Kāran* (= doer, one who has to do with).

Mutalāḷan, from Dravidian *Mutal* (= beginning, principal, stock, property, money) and Dravidian *āl* (= person).

A landed proprietor. In Malabar there are 44,378, and the same number of estates, and the land assessment being about Star Pagodas 480,000, each estate on an average bears to the whole revenue a proportion of little more than 10 pagodas per annum.—(38th paragraph of the Revenue Board's Minute of 5th January 1818.) This number is taken from the 77th paragraph of Mr. Warden's letter to the Revenue Board of 16th June 1813, and the 33rd paragraph of his letter to the Board of 20th April 1815, which again was taken from the Janm Piymāish accounts of 981, but by mistake the tāluks of Kavāi, Cotiote, and Randataṛa were omitted. The copy of the Janmi Pymāish accounts received from Mr. Vaughan by Mr. Græme makes the number 52,303, which reduces the revenue payable by each to little more than 9 pagodas. It is conjectured (though I have not yet obtained any accounts to prove it) that half the revenue is paid by estates yielding from a thousand to five thousand rupees' assessment, which will make the amount of the assessment payable by the greater proportion of the proprietors very small indeed. Supposing that half the revenue is paid by estates yielding a revenue of a thousand rupees, that will withdraw eight hundred and forty from the number, and the remaining half, viz., 240,000 Star Pagodas, will be to be paid by 52,463 estates or proprietors, which will be between 4½ and 5 pagodas for each. The Board of Revenue have considered the number stated as so many estates, whilst Mr. Warden expressly calls this number so many proprietors, but upon examination I find that neither the one nor the other mode of considering it is strictly correct. That may be called an estate which an individual possesses in the whole province or in a village, and others have denominated single fields estates; but in the Janmi Pymāish accounts is entered as one estate the whole landed property possessed by an individual in one Hōbali comprehending several Dēṣams or villages: the number of estates is therefore either too great or too little, according to the acceptation given to the term. But if it is wished to know what assessment is payable on the whole estate in the province of each individual, this account will not show it. The number of estates is too great. It is only correct with respect to each Hōbali, for many Janmis possess lands in different villages of the same Hōbali, in different Hōbalis of the same tāluk, and in different tāluks of the province, all of which, with the exception of those within the confines of villages, are entered as separate estates. The real number of Janmis is, in consequence, not equal to the number of estates specified. Some individuals are entered ten times instead of one, and very many appear four times. The number cannot therefore be taken at more than 15,000, but for this conjecture there is no document.

Note.—See *Proprietors* and *Perumartham* and *Sthāna-māna-avakāṣam*.

JANMAKKĀVAL.

From *Janmam* (q.v.) and Dravidian *kāval* (= custody, guard, watch).

Is a fee which is given to a kind of headman among slaves for watching a large tract of rice-land and protecting it from cattle. The land may belong to different proprietors, though the watcher is the slave of only one. The fee consists in the crop of a certain portion of every rice-field. The watcher is generally selected from the caste of Palium, which is considered the most trustworthy and attentive, and the watcher goes on such occasion by the name of Kaḷḷāḍi Palium, though the Kaḷḷāḍi is a different caste of slave.

JANMAKKOḺU.

From *Janmam* (q.v.) and Dravidian *koḻu* (= ploughshare, cultivating tenure).

Answering to Moolgainee in Canara. It is a fixed rent which cannot be raised, and the proprietor cannot remove the tenant. It prevails in some few places in the Northern Division of Malabar.

Notes.—1. In this case the land is made over for permanent cultivation by the tenant in return for services rendered. Where the proprietary title is vested in a pagoda, the grant will be made for future services. In some cases land is mortgaged on this tenure, the Kāṇam mortgagee paying the surplus rent produce to the landlord after deducting the interest of the money he has advanced. The tenant has, in North Malabar, only a life-interest in the property, which at his death reverts to the landlord. In the South the land is enjoyed by the tenant and his descendants until there is failure of heirs, when it reverts to the proprietor; except where the land is granted for special services, an annual rent is payable under this tenure. The tenant's right is confined to that of cultivation, but it is permanent, and he cannot be ousted for arrears of rent, which must be recovered by action, unless there be a specific clause in the deed declaring the lease cancelled if the rent be allowed to fall into arrears.—(Proceedings of the Court of Sadr Adalat, No. 18, dated 5th August 1856.)

2. This right reverts to the landlord on failure of tenant's heirs.—High Court Spec. App. 495 (1869)

JANMAKKUḌIYĀN.

From *Janmam* (q.v.) and Dravidian *Kuḍiyān* (= inhabitant, subject, tenant).

May be translated a proprietary inhabitant. It is not uncommonly used to designate the modern Janmakār, who has acquired his property by purchase, in contradistinction to the ancient or hereditary Janmakār.

JANMAPAṆAYAM ŌLAKKARAṆAM OR JANMAPAṆAYAM EḶUTTU.

Janmapaṇayam, from *Janmam* (q.v.) and Dravidian *paṇayam* = (bet, stake, pledge).

Ōlakkaraṇam, from Dravidian *Ōla* (= palm-leaf writing) and Sanskrit *Karaṇam* (= acting, instrument, deed). *Eḷuttu* (Dravidian) = writing, writ.

The Janmakkāran is supposed to have received an additional 10 per cent. on the amount of the Otti, making altogether 30 per cent. beyond the Otti. Under this deed he pledges the Janmam or proprietary right, without relinquishing the actual possession of it by which he is bound not to transfer the Janmam right to another without the consent of the present mortgagee. He has still, however, the power of redeeming the mortgage by paying the debt and the interest of all sums borrowed since the period of the execution of the Otti deed, with the proviso that the interest do not exceed double the amount of the sums so borrowed. The amount of the debt, but not the pāṭṭam, is specified in this deed.

Notes.—1. "This is the last resource short of selling the land altogether. In executing this deed the landlord relinquishes the power to redeem his land, and has nothing left him but the nominal right of proprietorship. By going through the form of casting a few drops of water from his hand he yields up all right of further interference in the land. Nor can he sell his proprietary title to any one but the mortgagee, as he has already made over to him all the rights and privileges possessed by a proprietor. This tenure prevails only in the neighbourhood of Calicut."—S.C. Circular dated 5th August 1856, No. 18.

2. Mr. Græme in his report (paragraph 1553) remarked: "Before the conquest several intermediate stages of mortgage, in the hope of future redemption before land was sold, were common, and its disposal with all this was very rare; but in the present times the intermediate deeds are

dispensed with entirely in Pālghat, and in Calicut the Oṭṭi and Janmam deeds, instead of being as before at different and distant periods from each other, are now very frequently executed on one and the same day, and the property transferred without reservation on the part of the proprietor."

3. The above interpretation of this deed was probably more theoretical than real. It was supposed to be the fifth of the six deeds culminating in *Janmam.*

4. A suit to recover lands granted on a pepper-corn rent is barred after 12 years from the grant.—S.D.C., 368 (1879).

KĀL.

(Dravidian) = foot, leg, stem, pillar.

Literally, leg; figuratively, support. In the Northern Division of Malabar it means the standard tree round which the pepper-vines climb. It applies to trees such as the Moochy wood tree (moorka), which are planted expressly for the support of the vine. A coconut or jack would not be called a Kāl.

KALAMENI.

From Dravidian *Kalam* (= pot, vessel, measure) and Dravidian *mēni* (= body, shape, sample, average).

An average.

KAḶAPPĀD.

From Dravidian *Kaḷam* (= a threshing-floor) and Dravidian *pāḍu* (= falling, falling into power of, rank, nature, measure of space and time).

A term in use in the Waḷḷuvanād Tāluk, and, perhaps, other places to the southward in Malabar. It means a threshing-floor, a house or a place for removing the grain from the straw, whether by threshing, or, as in Waḷḷuvanād, by treading with men. More generally it means a collection of paddy-fields under one manager or cultivator, the produce of which is brought to one threshing-flour.

KĀLĀYI.

(From Dravidian *kāl* = foot, stem, or stubble, and *āyi* (= became) = the second cultivation of a rice-field.

Means rice of a second crop. It implies that one crop must have been cut in Kanni (September and October), and that the second crop is cut in Makaram (January and February). It does not apply to a crop cut in Makaram which had no previous crop.

Note.—Kālāyi Nilam is the opposite of *Arīri Nilam,* which means land on which *Arīri*—a single crop—is raised.

KĀLKUṚA PATINĀṚU.

Kāl (Dravidian) = one-fourth; *kuṛavu* (Dravidian) = deficiency; *patināṛu* (Dravidian) = sixteen.

Quarter less 16 or 15¾ Vīray fanams, which Dēṣavāḷis could receive in fines from inhabitants. If the fine amounted to 16 or above it, it was the right of the Nāḍuvāḻis.

KIRĀNI or Kaṇakkappiḷḷa.

Derivation of *Kirāni* is doubtful. *Kaṇakkapiḷḷa*, from Dravidian *kaṇakku* (= accounts) and Dravidian *piḷḷa* (= child, honorary title).

Writer or Accountant. In Malabar the first used exclusively for Portuguese and half-caste writers, the second is also used for them, but I find it was also the common name for the Rāja's accountants in the Kaḍattanāḍ, Kōṭṭayam (Cotiote), and Chiṛakkal Rājyams.

KĀṆAM.

From Dravidian *kāṇuka* (= to see) means now-a-days possession, mortgage or lease, but originally it meant supervision, protection.

Which, I think, is generally supposed to mean mortgage or pledge, must be construed to be the thing or consideration for which the mortgage or pledge is given, and it seems applicable only to lands, timber trees, and slaves. In Arabic the terms for the different incidents of mortgage are very distinct and precise. Murhoon is the thing mortgaged or pledged; Rāhin is the mortgagee; Moortahin the mortgagor; and Mooblunghi Murhoon the money or consideration which is given for the pledge. Kāṇam corresponds with Mooblunghi Murhoon, or the money given, and Paṇayam with Murhoon, or the thing mortgaged. Paṇayam Eḻuttu is the mortgage writing or deed. Though the pāṭṭam or rent capable of being collected from the lands which is in the possession of the mortgagee is more than sufficient to pay the interest of the mortgage debt, yet it is generally calculated that the value of the pāṭṭam would, if sold, be not more than adequate to pay the principal. If the mortgagee retains more than his fixed share of the pāṭṭam for the payment of the interest of the debt, and neglects to pay the remainder to the Janmakkāran, he forfeits the land, which is instantly resumable by the Janmakkāran. It is supposed that the original intention of receiving the Kāṇam was to secure the proprietor against the imposition or the neglect of the tenant, that it was to be considered that the pāṭṭam was permanent notwithstanding the representations of the tenant, whether true or false, of bad seasons and accidents. The principal of the Kāṇam was not, therefore, more than equal to one year's pāṭṭam, and the proprietor thus provided against failure by having received the pāṭṭam in advance for a year. The introduction of the land-tax and the increasing necessities of the proprietors obliged them to involve deeper in debts and mortgages.

There is a great distinction to be observed between a mortgage and what is called Kāṇam. A mortgage is the thing given for the security of the creditor for money borrowed of him. A Kāṇam is an advance of rent made by a tenant to a proprietor for the security of the latter against failure in payment of the pāṭṭam. It was originally as much the custom for a tenant to have been a long time in possession of land, merely paying the simple pāṭṭam before he advanced money, as for him to acquire possession in consequence only of advancing the pāṭṭam money. The occupancy of the land, in short, sometimes preceded, and sometimes followed, the advance of money.

One of the six Pramāṇams or deeds of mortgage recognized in the Ṣāstra.

Notes.—1. See Chapter IV, Section (*a*) of the Text, and *Pāṭṭam* and *Pāṭṭōla* or *Pāṭṭamōla* and *Proprietors* and *Keikkūli*.

2. Said to be the second of the six deeds culminating in *janmam*.

3. If no period be specified the mortgage is considered to extend to 12 years, and always so where a fee has been paid. The mortgagee has possession, recovering the interest of the money he has advanced from the produce of the land, and paying over the net profits to the landlord. Should he fail in the last respect, the amount is placed to the landlord's credit when the mortgage is paid off, allowance being made, on the other side, for any improvements which the mortgagee may have effected. Failure to pay over the net proceeds regularly to the landlord will not give the latter power to redeem his land before the expiration of the period stipulated (or that of 12 years), unless there be an express condition to that effect in the deed. Any attempt, however, on the part of the mortgagee to defraud the landlord and usurp the property will give the latter that power. Should the landlord desire to raise a further sum of money on the land, and the mortgagee be unwilling to advance it, he may mortgage the property to a third party, who will be entitled to possession on paying off the sum originally advanced by the first mortgagee. The latter, however, has the option of advancing the required sum and remaining in possession if he pleases. Where the land has been mortgaged for a particular period, the landlord cannot interfere until the expiration of such period. Kāṇam mortgages are generally renewed at the end of the period fixed, the landlord receiving a fee; but there is no obligation on either side to renew them unless the landlord and mortgagee should be mutually desirous of doing so. Where the mortgagee discovers that the landlord has acted fraudulently in valuing the produce of the land, he is entitled to have the deed cancelled.—(Proceedings of the Court of Sadr Adalat, No. 18, dated 5th August 1856.)

4. The following are notes of some of the voluminous and conflicting decisions of the Courts on the various points connected with *Kāṇam* and *Kuḻikkāṇam*. The Courts, starting with an erroneous idea as to what *Janmam* was, have, in their endeavours to ascertain customs, been evidently making law instead of merely declaring it, and deciding by it.

(*a*.) *Renewal.*—The payment of *Keikkūli* fees (fine) is merely an accident of the contract, and when the Kāṇam amount has been passed, all necessary acts will be presumed to have been done, particularly when undisputed possession has followed upon the demise.—S.S.C., 5 (1856).

"The payment or non-payment" (of the renewal fees) "is wholly irrelevant to the question of validity of the deed."—S.S.C., 57 and 155 (1855). A suit for money advanced on account of renewal fees is not barred until three years from the date of the refusal to renew.—S.D.C., 69 and 182 (1876). A renewal is the making of a new, not a continuation of an old, contract.—S.S.C., 197 (1855). A contract to renew, of which the mortgagee might claim specific performance, is a sufficient answer to a suit for redemption.—S.D.C., 524

(1876), 644 and 650 (1877), 305, 572, 573 (1879). A tenant may forfeit his right to insist on specific performance of an agreement to renew by denying his mortgagor's title to a portion of the demised property.—S.D.C., 625 (1877). A contract to renew must, if in writing, be stamped, and if the consideration exceeds Rs. 100, and if the proper construction is that the whole amount is to be credited to renewal fees, it ought to be registered under Section 17, Clause 3. Act VIII of 1871. *Aliter*, if part of the consideration is for arrears of rent.—S.D.C., 126 (1876). The execution of the Kāṇam and Kychit deeds and their registration is good evidence of oral agreement to renew.—S.D.C., 333 (1877).

(*b.*) *Incidents.*—A Kāṇakkāran creating a mortgage or *quasi*-mortgage of the Kāṇam holding of which he is not owner "is to me a contradiction in term;" the *quasi*-mortgagee is simply a creditor.—S.S.C., 144. (1855). It is necessary for the security of a sub-mortgagee that he should make known his claims to the proprietor. By not doing so he renders himself liable to have his claim overlooked on a settlement occurring between the proprietor and the superior mortgagee, and for this the proprietor can of course not be held liable.—S.S.C., 103 (1844). A mortgagee cannot, by private arrangement with his mortgagor, prejudice the rights of the sub-mortgagee in possession.—S.D.C., 346 (1878). Sub-mortgagees have no right as against Janmis to hold for twelve years from date of sub-mortgage.—S.D.C., 180 (1851). No sub-kāṇam does exist. The Kāṇam, with all its incidents attached to it, can only be cut out of a right superior to itself, and the only way in which a mere Kāṇakkāran can convey such a right is by selling that which accrued to him from the possessor of a Janmam or Otti right. He can also give his Kāṇam right on simple mortgage.—S.S.C., 234 (1855). The Janmam right can be sold while Kāṇam right is outstanding.—S.S.C., 113 (1858). The contract is not complete till the deed has been properly delivered.—S.D.C., 626 (1876). "No Janmi can, in less than twelve years, demand the restoration of his land by a Kāṇakkāran, except in the case of the breach of express or implied covenants by such Kānakkaran. Such a protection the custom of the country provides against the grasping avarice of proprietors, and it is only the strict preservation of this custom which can prevent this species of tenure from becoming a monstrous fraud, in which the weak will always be the prey of the strong."—S.S.C., 398 (1854). So also in S.S.C., 63 (1855), and M.S.C., 154 (1855). A Janmi has no power to enhance his demands during the currency (12 years) of a Kāṇam lease.—S.S.C., 57 (1853). Kāṇam right is "an incorporeal right over the land, which may or may not be accompanied by physical possession."—S.S.C., 441 (1855). If a Kāṇakkāran has two claims, both must be settled before he can be ousted from the land.—

N.D.C., 125 (1856); M S.C., 22nd April 1858. The Kāṇam amount cannot be apportioned piecemeal on the several parcels of land the possession of which constitutes the Kānakkār's security.—S.S.C., 37 (1854). The Kāṇam amount secured on several parcels of land cannot be apportioned among them: the Kāṇakkāran may resist redemption and recovery till the whole of his Kāṇam claim has been paid.—N.D.C., 380 (1868). So also "my money was advanced on the security of all the parcels, good, bad, and indifferent together, and until I get all back I shall not relinquish any."—N.D.C., 198, 216, 221 (1876); M.H.C., 611 (1877). In a suit by a Janmi for damages for waste, the defendant's liability will depend on whether there has been any injury to plaintiff's reversion.—S.D.C., 116 (1876), 560 (1877). A Janmi cannot attach and sell his Kāṇakkāran's interest for arrears of rent if that interest has already been assigned by private sale.—S.D.C., 335 (1877). A Kāṇam deed is not a lease for more than one year, and is not compulsorily registrable.—S.D.C., 353 (1876). An understanding as to how the increased fruitfulness of trees is to be brought to account in future demises does not make the tenure a permanent one.—N.D.C., 177 (1861). If land is taken back before the expiration of the lease, a portion of the fees paid at the commencement of the lease, proportionate to the time unexpired of the lease, is returned to the tenant, who, however, if guilty of breach of covenant, is not entitled to the return of such proportionate part.—N.D.C., 401 (1873).

(c.) *Mēlkāṇam.*—"When there are two valid equitable titles, he who has got the legal estate shall prevail is a doctrine peculiarly necessary in a country like this." A man should not accept a Kāṇam deed when the land is not in the possession of his demiser without sufficient enquiry into the demiser's title to give him possession, which was held in this case by a previous Kāṇam demisee.—N.D.C., 38 (1860). If the Janmi is unable to give possession, the remedy is by suit against him for return of the money.—2 M.H.C.R., 315. "These acceptors of Kāṇam rights while other rights are outstanding are a pest to the country. The remedy for this hardship is the non-acceptance of Kāṇam rights until it is in the power of the Janmi to deliver the land."—N.D.C., 86 (1860). A first Kāṇakkāran is entitled to the first chance of supplying his Janmi's further needs. If this is not done, and even if, in the course of proceedings in Court, the first Kāṇakkāran denied his Janmi's title, the second Kāṇakkāran has no cause of action for asking a return of the land.—1 M.H.C.R., 13.

Semble: If the first Kāṇakkāran denied his Janmi's title before the date of the second Kāṇam, it would not be necessary to give him the option of supplying his Janmis' needs.—*Ibid.*

A Mēlkānam is not wholly invalid, but will operate as an assignment of the equity of redemption although the time for redeeming may not have arrived.—S.D.C., 484 (1879). Whilst a prior Kāṇam mortgage is outstanding and the document is in the hands of third persons claiming a lien thereon, a renewal of such mortgage is invalid.—S.D.C., 159, 743, 768 (1877). A Mēlkāṇakkāran cannot oust a Kāṇakkāran or his assignee before the expiration of 12 years from the date of the Kāṇam.—M.S.C., 129 (1862).

(*d.*) *Puṛappād.*—Rent tendered and refused, if of the proper amount, exempts the tenant from future claims for that amount.—S.S.C., 157 (1855). In deciding that a Kāṇam tenant allowing the *Puṛappād* to fall into arrears was not liable to be turned out, the High Court pointed out two ways in which the Janmi can recover his puṛappād, viz., (1) by suing for it; or (2) by taking credit for it on paying off the Kāṇam amount after the lapse of 12 years.—1 M.H.C.R., 112. In a suit for redemption of Kāṇam, arrears of rent, the recovery of which is barred by the Statute of Limitations, may be set off against the mortgage money.—S.D.C., 426 (1876), 449 (1877). The principle of this is that the Kāṇam is deposited as security for the rent, and that the mortgagor is entitled to an account of rents and profits.—S.D.C., 285 (1877). When no date is specified for payment of rent in kind the presumption is that the rent is payable in Kanni and Makaram. If the rent for one crop is specified, double the amount may be presumed to be a fair rent for two crops.—S.D.C., 370 (1877). It is usually the rule that 60 per cent. of the rent is payable in Kanni and the rest in Makaram.—S.D.C., 393 (1878). The words "Kāṇam free from the payment of rent" will not enlarge that Kāṇam into an Otti.—M.H.C., 142 (1870).

(*e.*) *Improvements.*—When a Janmi rents a land, he must well know that the tenants cannot live thereon without a house, and, consequently, that they would, in conformity with established usage, build one. If the building is unnecessarily large, or in other respects informal, or not sanctioned, he ought to have put a stop to it; but the idea of making the renters pull it down and carry off the materials, since he tacitly consented to its being built, is absurd.—N.D.C., 55 (1843). The Sadr Court admitted an appeal to try "whether the tenant was entitled to the full value of the house," or "whether he has the option of either removing the materials or receiving only their value," and confirmed the Civil Judge's decree allowing hire of laborers as part of the cost of the house.—M.S.C., 11 (1847). Tenants in North Malabar are entitled to Veṭṭukāṇam, and the law encourages cultivation so much that even trespassers are entitled to it less one-tenth.—M.S.C., 32 (1872); N.D.C., 312, 315 (1873). Rupees 11½ per 100 perukkams (1210 to the acre) was taken as a fair price for converting paṛamba into rice-fields.—N.D.C., 283 (1874). The implied contract to pay for improvements is limited to agricultural leases.—S.D.C., 286 (1876). No compensation is claimable for improvements made prior to the date of the demise, unless specially reserved.—S.D.C., 627 (1877). All reasonable improvements must be paid for.—S.D.C., 156, 161 (1877). It is usual to apportion the compensation for improvements among the sub-tenants.—S.D.C., 170 (1878).

(*f.*) *Forfeiture of Lease.*—The following have been held as reasons—

I. *Sufficient* for cancelling the lease before the expiration of the customary 12 years' period. Failure under improving lease (*Kuḻikkāṇam*, q.v.) to make reasonable improvements.—N.D.C., 68 (1859). Alteration of boundaries.—S.D.C., 75 (1853). Denial of Janmi's title.—2 M.H.C.R., 161. Removal of foundation-stones of a ruined pagoda outside limits of holding, and from possession of which the tenant was specially shut out.—N.D.C., 82 (1844). Neglect to plant trees under improving lease (Kuḻikkāṇam, *q.v.*).—N.D.C., 62 (1875). "Acts to invalidate the lessor's title obviously operate the forfeiture of lease."—S.S.C., 191 (1854); N.D.C., 172 (1861). Destruction of a pond essential to irrigate the lands.—S.S.C., 157 (1855). Cutting down trees without Janmi's permission.—N.D.C., 211 (1859). Fraudulent setting up of a different tenure to that given by the Janmi.—N.D.C., 218, 219, 220 (1859). Failure to cultivate in a husband-like manner under an improving lease (Kuḻikkāṇam, *q.v.*).—N.D.C., 274 (1859). Fraudulent attempt to embarrass the Janmi by a false dispute as to the boundaries of a portion of the holding.—N.D.C., 21 (1861). False claim of right larger than tenant really possessed.—N.D.C., 176 (1861). Denial of Janmi's title by the assignee of a Kāṇam right.—1 M.H.C.R., 14, 445. Neglect to cultivate.—N.D.C., 350 (1870). Cutting down fruitful trees without Janmi's consent.—N.D.C., 386 (1872). Denial of Janmi's title after institution by the Janmi of a suit to oust.—2 M.H.C.R., 109. Express agreement to surrender on demand.—S.D.C., 566, 612, 621 (1876), 204 (1878); M.H.C., 278 (1879).

II. *Insufficient* for cancelling the lease before the expiration of the customary 12 years' period. Burial of a corpse.—N.D.C., 350 (1873). "Non-payment of puṟappād being a breach going only to a part of the consideration, should not in all principle be held to repeal the contract."—N.D.C., 172 (1861). So also in 1 M.H.C.R., 112, and M.S.C., 84 and 111 (1862).

Kāṇakkāran.

From *Kāṇam* (q.v.) and Sanskrit *Kāran* (= doer, or one who has to do with).

Mortgagee; the person who has lent the Kāṇam.

Kāṇam-Puṟam-Kaḍam.

From *Kāṇam* (q.v.) and Dravidian *puṟam* (= the back, outside, beyond) and Dravidian *Kaḍam* (= debt, obligation).

This is an expedient for raising money on land already made over on Kāṇam. It is quite a separate transaction, sometimes taking place at the time of the mortgage, in which case it is referred to in the Kāṇam deed; at other times effected long after the mortgagee has come into possession. In the latter case the fact of the mortgage is alluded to in this deed, and the landlord engages to pay off both the mortgage and the loan together. The loan thus made gives the mortgagee an additional lien upon the property as security for the repayment of the loan. Where the new loan is added to the sum first advanced, and a fresh mortgage-bond is executed, the transaction is treated altogether according to the rules applying to Kāṇam mortgages.—(Proceedings of the Court of Sadr Adalat, No. 18, dated 5th August 1856).

KANDAM.

(Sanskrit) = piece of anything, land.

A division in rice-fields.

Note.—Perhaps this word meant originally a share of the *Taṛa* rice-fields held in common.

Nilam.

(Dravidian) = ground, soil, rice-field.

Which means particularly rice-land; means also a field (answering to a stullum in the Carnatic) having a distinct name, and having many Kandams or divisions of banks for the convenience of irrigation.

Pāḍam.

(Sanskrit) = range, especially of rice-fields.

Ubhayam.

(Sanskrit) = in South Malabar, rice-fields.

Ulpatti.

Sanskrit = birth, origin, rice-fields.

Terms used in Malabar for rice-lands; some of these terms are peculiar to some districts.

Vayal.

(Dravidian) = rice-fields.

A large tract or sheet of paddy land.

KAṆḌI.

(Dravidian) = gap in a hedge or fence, a piece of high ground.

A division used in garden lands only to express one paṛamba or garden. It is used when speaking of the number of gardens in an estate.

KAPPAM.

(Dravidian) = tribute, taxes.

Equivalent to peishcush or tribute. The Rājas of the Northern Districts of Malabar agreed to give to the Bednore Government in 913 M.S. a Kappam of 80,000 rupees.

KĀRĀḶAN.

(Dravidian) = workers, agents, temple servants. Their office *Kārāyma* (ancient, *Kārānmei*).

Is the agent or deputy for the Ūrāḷan, or founder, in the management of the lands of Hindu temples.

Notes.—1. *Kārāyma* right is not proved to be a right of perpetual tenure of land; it is equally consistent that it was a title to the perpetual performance of certain services for which certain payments were demandable.—N.D.C., 142-171 (1859). *Kārāyma right* is unsaleable—M.H.C., 120 (1867)—and indefeasible.—M.H.C., 623 (1874). *Kārāḷar* have no right to succeed Ūrāḷar on these becoming extinct. The right of appointing others "always did, and does still lie with the executive."—N.D.C., 1 (1860).

2. Lands made over by the trustees or managers of pagodas to those employed in performing certain offices therein are conferred on this tenure. So long as they fulfil their duties, the tenants are not liable to be ousted; to maintain an action of ejectment, therefore, it must be shown either that they have neglected their duties, which has rendered it necessary to employ other persons to perform them, or that they have endeavoured to set up a proprietary claim in subversion of that of the pagoda.—(Proceedings of the Court of Sadr Adalat, No. 18, dated 5th August 1856.)

3. For other and more ancient uses of this word, see pp. 110–13 and Chapter IV, Section (*a*) of the Text.

KARAṆAM or PRAMĀṆAM.

Karaṇam (Sanskrit) = acting, organ, instrument, deed; *Pramāṇam* (Sanskrit) = measure, authority, proof, bond.

Generally means bonds and agreements of all kinds.

Note.—The six kinds of *Karaṇams* culminating in *Janmam* were, 1, *Kuḻikkāṇam*; 2, *Kāṇam*; 3, *Otti*; 4, *Ottikkumpuṛam*; 5, *Janmappaṇayam*; 6, *Janmam*.

KARAVEPPU.

From Dravidian *Kara* (= shore, river-side, bank) and Dravidian *Veppu* (= deposit, planting).

Plantations on elevated spots of ground, in contradistinction to Āttuveppu, situated on low ground.

Note.—High-lying coconut gardens are divided in the revenue accounts into three classes of Karaveppu. See *Ūr*. *Karaveppu* gardens are not unfrequently situated on the high banks of rivers and backwaters. See *Āttuveppu*.

KĀṬṬAKKĀṆAM also MŪPPAPPAṆAM.

Kaṭṭakkāṇam, from Dravidian *Kaṭṭa* (= lump, mass, clod) and *Kāṇam* (q.v.); also called *Kashtakkāṇam*, from Sanskrit *Kashtam* (= hard, bad) and *Kāṇam* (q.v.).

Mūppappaṇam, from Dravidian *Mūppan* (= old man, chief) and Dravidian *paṇam* (= money).

Is the acknowledgment or Nuzur paid by a cultivator to a proprietor for land he is allowed to cultivate. It is not an advance which is recoverable.

It is not deducted from subsequent payments to be made, nor is any interest granted upon it; the cultivator pays the full established pāṭṭam besides. Its proportion to the pāṭṭam does not seem niform. It means, literally, clod-money.

Note.—Kaṭṭakkāṇam is the tenure of a simple lessee who deposits in his Janmi's hands a sum of money as security (*a*) for due fulfilment of his lease contract, and (*b*) for payment of rent. It does not carry with it a right to hold for 12 years; the security is returned without interest at the end of the ease.—N.D.C., 18 (1874); S.D.C., 466 (1877).

KAṬṬAVAḌI or KAṬṬAKŌL.

From Dravidian *Kaṭṭa* (= lump, clod) and Dravidian *vaḍi* (= stick, staff), or Dravidian *Kōl* (= staff, rod).

Literally, clod-breaker. The stick in Malabar, with a knob at the end of it, with which men and women break the clods in a field after it has been dug by the mamutty or spade.

KĀṬṬUVĀRAM.

From Dravidian *Kāḍu* (= jungle) and Dravidian *vāram* (= share of produce).

A tax of two fanams upon every individual possessing land in a few Hobalis of the Temmalapuṛam District, where there is no regular Mōḍan cultivation. It was intended as an equivalent for any cultivation which might be carried on in the Kād or jungle.

KAVALPHALAM.

From Dravidian *Kāval* (= custody, protection) and Sanskrit *phalam* (? Dravidian *paḷam*) (= fruit, produce).

Protection fund or compensation for protection.

KEIKKŪLI or ṢHĪLAKKĀSU.

From Dravidian *Kei* (= hand) and Dravidian *Kūli* (= wages) and from Dravidian *Shīla* (= purse) or perhaps Sanskrit *Shīlam* (= conduct, habit, character) and Dravidian *kāsu* (= gold, copper coin).

A fee or fine or Nuzur of so many fanams on a Potippāḍu which the lessee or Veṛumpāṭṭakāran gives to the Janmi or proprietor upon the renewal of his lease. In Kavāi Tāluk two Veḷḷi fanams, the Potippāḍu, is the rate fixed, which, calculating at the rate of $41\frac{1}{2}$ rupees per 1,000 Iḍangaḷis, is supposed to add one-fourth to the Janmi's share in the year in which it is imposed. It is the extent of Shīlakkāsu which any land can afford that seems to give it a value in sale and purchase above its nominal value, or that at which the pāṭṭam is entered in account. Where this proportion is given the lease is only for one year; where it is for four, it is equal to one year's pāṭṭam, that is, the full pāṭṭam is taken once in four years, being an equivalent for Poḷichcheḻuttu, though Keikkūli in the Southern Division answers to Shīlakkāsu in the Northern Division, where the transaction is a simple lease or Veṛumpāṭṭam. It is also applied in the Southern Division to land having already a mortgage upon it. It is taken in lieu of Sākshi, being in general the amount of one year's pāṭṭam.

Note.—See *Kāṇam* and *Pāṭṭōla*.

KEIPPAṆAM.

From Dravidian *Kei* (= hand) and Dravidian *paṇam* (= money).

Note.—Keippaṇam property is property given on marriage (among Māppiḷḷas), which is returnable on termination of the marital state by death or divorce; to the widow if she survive, or to her children if she has died, or to the Taṛavād in absence of wife and children. The widow and children have a life interest independent of the Kāraṇavan.—N.D.C., 60 (1874).

KEIVIDĀ OTTI.

From Dravidian *Kei* (= hand) and Dravidian *viḍā* or *viḍātta* (= without leaving) and *Otti* (q.v.).

Is not a separate deed, but if the two first words are tacked to the Otti deed it becomes a condition that the mortgagee can never be dispossessed, that the land can never go out of his hands, that the mortgage is irredeemable. Kei is "hand" and viḍā is "without letting go."

The following note is by an experienced Native Revenue Officer of the district :—

Notes.—1. This question is not settled as yet. I believe it has been decided both ways. The whole thing turns on the meaning of the expression. Above it is written കൈവിടാ ഒററി, and interpreted accordingly. But some hold that the term is കൈവിട്ടുക ഒററി, and that the meaning is that in Otti of this description the landlord "relinquishes" in favor of the Otti-holder his right, recognized in ordinary Otti cases, of taking from the garden mortgaged (if the property is a garden) a few coconuts and a jack-fruit annually without asking for the permission of the tenant.

2. The balance of authority is in favor of a Keiviḍā Otti being irredeemable. The mortgagee cannot, however, assign.—S.D.C., 578-629 (1878).

3. The landlord in this case relinquishes the power of transferring the property to a third party, and binds himself to borrow any further sum he may require only from the mortgagee. Should the latter decline to advance the amount, the landlord may pay off the mortgage and re-assign the property to another party.—(Proceedings of Madras Sadr Adalat, No. 18, dated 5th August 1856.)

KĒRAM.

Canarese mode of pronouncing *Chēram*.

The Sanskrit name for the coconut fruit. A law is in existence in Malabar, contained in a book called Kēra Kalpam, composed in the Sanskrit language but written in the Malayāḷam character, regulating the mode of planting coconut, betel-nut and jack trees, and the pepper-vine, and of settling the Kuḷikkāṇam.

Note.—Dr. Gundert's view is that *Kēram* is the Canarese mode of pronouncing *Chēram*, i.e., *Chēra* or Malabar, and hence applied to its chief fruit, the coconut palm.

KĪḶĀYIKŪṚUJANMAM or KĪḶĀYIJANMAM.

From Dravidian *Kīḷu* = place below, under;

From Dravadian *Āyi* = became;
Do. *Kūṛu* = part, share, class; and
Sanskrit *Janmam* (q.v.).

A deed in use.

Note.—Means the right to the lower kinds of paṛamba produce when the higher (*i.e.*, *Nālubhayam* or coconut, areca and jack trees, and pepper-vines) belong to another.

KOḌUNGA KATTI.

From Dravidian *Koḍunga* (= bent) and Dravidian *Katti* (= knife).

The knife worn for defence by the Nāyars of Malabar, fastened to a hook attached to a leathern girdle at the back of the body.

Note.—Also called *Āyudha Katti, Veṭṭu Katti, Katti Vāḷ*, Nāyar knife, Māppiḷḷa knife, &c.

KOḶICHCHAL.

(Dravidian) = falling.

Literally, fall. Is an allowance made by inspectors of pepper-vines for the quantity of pepper which is likely to fall off between the period of inspection and the season for plucking.

KŌL.

(Dravidian) = staff, rod, measuring rod.

A pace (a native's), ten of which regulate the distance that ought to be observed in the original planting of coconuts; another is afterwards planted between the two original ones, when they have grown large, in order to supply their place when they decay.

KŌL PEIMĀṢI.

From *Kōl* (q.v.) and Persian *Paimāish* (= measure, survey).

The survey which took place in 983 under Mr. Warden of the rice-lands by actual measurement in cawnies and goolies is so called; all other paimāishes in Malabar have been merely inspections without measurement.

Note.—The result of this *Pymāish* was embodied in what are known in the district as the Hinduvi, *i.e.*, Mahratta accounts. It is the only reliable account in the records, but even in regard to it the details, owing to the changes in names of fields and in holdings, are not always available for references. It refers to wet lands alone.

KOḺULĀBHAM.

From Dravidian *Koḻu* (= ploughshare) and Sanskrit *lābham* (= getting gain, profit).

Koḻu, ploughing; and lābham, profit; or the profit of agriculture. It is the cultivator's share.

Is the cultivator's clear profit after deducting expenses under the name of Vittu Valli, or charges of cultivation. Out of the Koḻulābham is reckoned, indeed, to pay the inconsiderable expense of Ēru Irimbu, or cattle and iron. It is generally supposed that the Koḻulābham is a third of the gross produce (deducting, always, 10 per cent. for reaping), and that the Vittu Valli is another third. It may be so reckoned when the produce is above seven-fold, but within that the Vittu Valli comes to more than a third and encroaches upon the Koḻulābham.

Notes.—1. "Besides the rent there is a cultivator's share, which is very valuable and which affords a comfortable subsistence to a family."—Græme's Report, paragraph 1428.

2. "Taking the pāṭṭam to be four-tenths of the gross produce, the gross produce would be paṛas 19,204,887; to this again may be fairly added 20 per cent. ("the usual deduction," paragraph 1555) for the expense of reaping, for the fees of carpenters, smiths, and other petty proprietors denominated Cheṛu Janmakkār, and for portions of crops given up to slaves for watching, *which are never brought into any calculation of produce* and the gross produce would then be paṛas 23,045,865."—Græme's Report, paragraph 1563.

3. See *Eṇṇam, Patam, Chērlābham, Kuḻiyānkūr, Pandakkāval, Vālli-vittu.*

KOḺUPPAṆAYAM.

From *Koḻu* (Dravidian) = ploughshare, and *paṇayam* (q.v.).

Notes.—1. Under this tenure the mortgagee has only the right to cultivate the land. If no period be specified, the landlord is at liberty to pay off the mortgage whenever he pleases. This tenure prevails in the neighbourhood of Pālghat as well as in North Malabar.—(Madras Sadr Adalat Proceedings, No. 18, dated 5th August 1856.)

2. In absence of a period fixed in the lease, it was held that a *Koḻukkāṇam* lease was for 5 years, which had been the time fixed in the previous lease.—N.D.C., 248 (1877).

KOYILMĒNI or EṆṆIPĀḌU.

From Dravidian *Koyil* (= hire of fruit-gatherer) and Dravidian *Mēni* (= average). And from Dravidian *Eṇṇuka* (= to count) and Dravidian *pāḍu* (= authority).

Different modes in use of valuing or estimating the produce of coconut gardens. Koyilmēni means strictly the number of pluckings, or more generally the number of crops. After deducting the Ṣiṣu or young plants, and the Aphalam or those past bearing, it is estimated what the productive trees will yield with reference as well to their appearance as to the kind of soil—Āttu Veppu, Kara Veppu, Paṣima, &c. (in which they are classed by nature rather than by any public account or any written deed). It is estimated that the tree produces so many crops in the year and so many fruit for each crop. Eight crops (Eṭṭu Koyil) of 7 fruit each (Ēḻu Mēni) are the highest at which a tree is rated in account, making altogether 56 fruit; but it is reported that there is one garden at Calicut whose trees have in general produced 64 fruits each.

The Eṇṇipāḍu is the reckoning of the actual number of fruit growing in a particular year. There is supposed to be great enmity between the Janmi and the Kuḍiyān when this extreme measure is resorted to, and it is not common. When the estimation is fixed to take place, the Janmi gives notice to the tenant that he must not touch the fruit for a year, but allow it to remain on the trees. At the end of the year the Janmi counts the number there actually are, and fixes his pāṭṭam or share accordingly. In the present times the fear of the dishonesty of the tenant, who might make away with many of the fruit before the day of examination arrived is sufficient to deter Janmi from this unpopular mode.

KRISHI.

(Sanskrit) = ploughing, agriculture.

Seems the land under the direct management of proprietors or their stewards, also called Svakāryam Krishi.

KRISHIKKĀRAN.

From *Krishi* (q.v.) and Sanskrit *Kāran* (= doer, one who has to do with).

Steward of Janmi, employed to pay the slaves of the estate and other domestic expenses.

KUḌI.

(Dravidian) = house, hut.

A pair; applied to a slave and his wife in speaking of their price.

KUḌICHILLAṚA.

From *Kuḍi* (q.v.) and Dravidian *chillaṛa* (= sundries).

Tax on houses, shops, warehouses, and implements of the profession of blacksmiths, potters, oilmen, weavers, &c. Persons of these professions pay the house-tax as well as the tax on their implements. The Kuḍichillara amounts in Malabar to a revenue of Rs. 1,10,441-12-9 $\frac{16\frac{1}{4}}{25}$ and consists of the following items, viz., taxes on large houses, on small houses and huts, on upper-roomed retailer shops, on retailers' shops, on petty retailers' shops, on warehouses in the bazaar, warehouses in other places, on oilmen's mills, on carpenters' tools, on blacksmiths' anvils, on silversmiths' tools, on grinders' stones, on sawyers' saws, on weavers' looms, on smiths' hammers, on smiths' shops, on potters' furnace, on brass-smiths' shops, on barber shops, on washermen's stones, on mud-wall bricklayers, on mat-makers' tools, on Pattom or Cheṛumars, on fishermen's nets, on fishermen's boats, on pack-bullocks, on brinjals, &c., on betel-leaf vendors, on grazing lands in Kānattil, on salt godowns belonging to salt-pan proprietors, on coconut safe, on chunam-makers' furnace on Kangany, interest on Sircar land given on Kāṇam, Annakat or fees on tailor acting as barber, on teahtorum; total 37 items composing the Kuḍichillaṛa. Supposing the tax upon the houses of the lower classes to be generally 2 fanams (new Vīrāy) a house, it would take off the tax upon 25,000 houses to reduce the house tax revenue in the sum of 5,000 pagodas or 60,000 fanams.

Note.—The Mohturfa taxes were abolished in 1861.

KUḌIPPAKA or **Kuḍuppu**.

From *Kuḍi* (q.v.) and Dravidian *paka* (= separation, enmity).

Family or house feud or enmity. It is the common term to express the deadly hatred subsisting between two families. If a member of a family has been killed, his relations have been known to steep a cloth in his blood and vow never to lose sight of it till they have avenged his murder by the death of the murderer and the destruction of his habitation.

Note.—It was the custom to burn the body of the slain in the house of the slayer, which was of course also burnt. It was usual, however, to burn only an outhouse.

KUḌIYĀN.

(Dravidian) = inhabitant, subject.

Who pays revenue direct to Government, not less than one hundred and fifty thousand.—(Mr. Warden's letter to Board of Revenue, 16th June 1813, paragraph 77.)

Note.—The number of separate pattas issued or in force in Fasli 1290 (A.D. 1880-81) was 178,790.

KUḌIYĀN KUṚ.

From *Kuḍiyān* (q.v.) and (Dravidian) *Kūṛ* (= share, portion).

Cultivator's share.

Note.—See *Koḻulābham*, &c.

KUḌIYIRIPPU.

From *kuḍi* (q.v.) and (Dravidian) *irippu* (= sitting, residence).

It is consideration of 2 fanams which before the land-tax a tenant used to pay to a proprietor for land taken for building alone.

Note.—1. A *Kuḍiyirippu* tenure carries with it power to build shops if the locality is suitable for the purpose.—N.D.C., 21 (1879). One who has obtained permission to build a house in a paṛamba, but not to enclose any portion of it, is liable to pay rent for use and occupation if he excludes the owner or his assignee from access to the trees.—S.D.C., 367, 382 (1877).

2. The payment was made as a token of fealty to the *Janmi*. The land taken was used for a garden as well as for building purposes.

KUDIYIRUMAPPĀḌU.

From *kuḍi* (q.v.) and (Dravidian) *irikkuka* (= to sit, remain, be in a place), and (Dravidian) *pāḍu* (= falling, falling into one's power, &c.)

Is a muṛi or document by which a Janmi who is entitled to receive puṛappād from a mortgagee assigns over the payment of it to a third person from whom he has borrowed money.

Note.—This is an agreement between a landlord and his creditor, according to which the latter agrees to receive the rent produce of land leased to a tenant in lieu of interest in money upon the sum borrowed by the landlord. Should any dispute arise between the landlord and his tenant, and should the latter in consequence refuse to deliver rent produce according to the landlord's deed of assignment, the creditor can sustain an action only against the landlord.—(Sadr 'Adalat Proceedings, No. 18, dated 5th August 1856.)

KUḌUMANĪṚ or KUḌIMANĪṚ.

From Dravidian *Kuḍuma* (= narrow point, crest, (top) or Dravidian *Kuḍma* (= tenantry) and Dravidian *nīr* (= water).

The terms of the body of this deed [1] are the same as those in the deed of Aṭṭippēr. The difference in the title alone shows a difference in the attributes. The proprietor acknowledges by this deed to have received the full value of the property, and the execution and delivery of the deed are attested by the same formalities as those of the Aṭṭippēr deed. The word Kuḍima,[2] which means the condition or station of tenant, shows that the proprietor has still some proprietary right, and that the mortgagee continues in the relation of Kuḍiyān or tenant. As a tribute of acknowledgment of proprietorship the mortgagee is bound to pay a sum of money, not exceeding two fanams or a half or a whole Tipree of ghee, which, and the periods of payment, are specified in the deed. Under this deed the proprietor has no power of redemption.

Notes.—1. See *Aḍima*.

2. The foot-notes to Mr. Græme's text are by an experienced Native Revenue Officer of the district.

3. In this case the land is made over in perpetuity to the grantee, either unconditionally as a mark of favor or on condition of certain services being performed. The terms Aḍima and Kuḍima mean a slave or one subject to the landlord, the grant being generally made to such persons. A nominal fee of about two fanams a year is payable to the landlord to show that he still retains the proprietary title. Land bestowed as a mark of favor can never be resumed, but where it is granted as remuneration for certain services to be performed, the non-performance of such services involving the necessity of having them discharged by others will give the landlord power to recover the land. The non-payment of the annual fee will form no ground for ousting the grantee, but it will be recoverable by action. The hereditary property of native princes cannot be conferred on this tenure, the ruling prince having only the right of enjoyment during life, without power to alienate.—(Proceedings of the Court of Sadr Adalat, No. 18, dated 5th August 1856.)

4. Kuḍima Janmam is the highest but one of the Malabar tenures ; the land is never recoverable.—N.D.C., 285 (1862).

KŪLICHCHAKKĀRAN.

From Dravidian *kūlichcham* (from *kūli* = hire, wages) = pay of Nāyar militia, and Šanskrit *kāran* (= doer, one who has to do with).

An armed servant or vassal of a Nāḍuvāḻi or Rāja ; he is sometimes paid with land for his maintenance.

Note.—See *Aḍima, Kuḍima, Changngātam.*

---

[1] *Aḍima* is more properly *Service Inam.* It used to be granted in favor of village artisans, washermen, and others who in return for the bulk of the rent of the land were bound to perform certain services. Sometimes it was likewise granted to Cheṟumars and other low caste people to enable them to bury or burn their dead in spots where the latter were not liable to be disturbed.

[2] *Kuḍima* used to be given by big Janmis to their dependents and others as building sites.

KŪLICHCHĒKAM.

Or *Kūlichcham* (see Kūlichchakkāran), from Dravidian *Kūli* (= hire, wages), means besides pay the honorable service of Nāyars, especially in war. Military tournaments formerly in use among the Nāyars.

KŪLICHCHĒKAM or YĀPANA or ANUBHŌGAM.

Kūlichchēkam (q.v.) *Yāpana* (Sanskrit) = livelihood, maintenance, provisions for soldiers. *Anubhōgam* (q.v.).

Corruptly called Chaikavam, the terms used for lands given in free gift, that is, without rent to Nāyars for the performance of military service when required.

Note.—See *Aḍima, Kuḍima, Changngātam, Anubhavam.*

KUḺIKKĀṆAM.

From Dravidian *kuḻi* [= hollow, hole, excavation, pit (for planting fruit trees)] and *kāṇam* (q.v.).

Before the introduction of the land-tax the pāṭṭam used to be settled once in twelve years, and Kuḻikkāṇam allowed for young trees, and a deduction made for those that had gone to decay. This practice was observed even though the garden did not admit of any increase beyond the number originally planted. The tenant's business was to take care of the trees that were standing, but he was under no obligation to replace old ones with young ones without being paid the Kuḻikkāṇam money. Since the tax, wherever the proprietor receives regularly from the tenant the pāṭṭam and takes upon himself the payment of the public assessment, the settlement of the Kuḻikkāṇam and the pāṭṭam is conducted as before; but where the assessment is entered in the name of the tenant, and he only pays to the proprietor the Nikuti Ṣishtam, or what remains after discharging the assessment, the system of Kuḻikkāṇam and pāṭṭam is generally relinquished. The tenant is responsible for the revenue; he gets nothing from the proprietor for improvements, and he enjoys the undivided profits of them. The Kaḍattanād Rāja is said to have made over all his garden lands to his tenants in this way, and no settlement of Kuḻikkāṇam and pāṭṭam has been made between them for many years. The chief condition of it is that the mortgagee is to be paid a certain sum for the trees he may grow in a garden, or the interest upon that sum, to be deducted annually from the pāṭṭam or rent in case the principal is not paid. If the tenant who planted the trees is continued in the lease, the Kuḻikkāṇam money is only given for such trees as bear; but, if he is to be dispossessed for another, the proprietor must pay it for the young trees also. This kind of tenure does not, I think, imply poverty in the Janmi. It is a good arrangement for ensuring the improvement of property by giving the tenant an interest in it. The general price of a coconut tree is from 1 old to 4 fanams from 4 to 8; betel-nut trees 1 fanam, pepper-vine 4 rupees for vines capable of yielding 1 maund, and jack trees from 2 to 16 fanams each.

It is according to the Ṣāstra and to ancient custom to plant coconut trees at the distance of forty feet from each other. It was then the practice to continue the tenant in possession who had planted the trees, but the Māp-

26

piḷḷas being now in the habit of turning out the original tenant as soon as the trees come to maturity and paying off the Kuḻikkāṇam money, the tenants now plant closer than they used to do in order to increase the number of trees upon which they are entitled to the Kuḻikkāṇam.

It is not customary to settle the Kuḻikkāṇam and the pāṭṭam for four or five years after the trees begin to bear. The tenant in this period enjoys the produce free of any payment to the proprietor, which, and the produce of Chāma and the oil-plant for the first two years, make up the expense he has to sustain, as the compensation to him does not come to him till the latter period of his undertaking. A tenant who takes upon himself the planting of trees must possess a certain capital from which he can afford to advance the expense, or, at all events, he must be able to afford to labor unpaid for this period.

The Kuḻikkāṇam rates vary from one to four old gold fanams, or one-quarter to one rupee, but half a rupee is the most prevalent.

Paṇaya-pāṭṭa Kuḻikkāṇam.

See *Paṇayam*, *Pāṭṭam*, and *Kuḻikkāṇam*.

This is a deed[1] of mortgage executed by the mortgagor in favor of the mortgagee for plantations, and differs in no respect from that given for rice-lands, except that it promises to give the Kuḻikkāṇam, or the fixed value of the trees, and the Aḻiva, or the expense of preparing the garden, in conformity with the Dēṣa Mariyāda or custom of the village. In deeds[2] in use in the Northern Division of Malabar the rates of Kuḻikkāṇam for the dfferent kinds of trees are specified. In the Paṇayapāṭṭa deeds, as well for rice as garden lands, the proprietor of the land has a right of Poḷichcheḻuttu, that is, to renew the deeds every twelve years; or, when the Janmi dies, his successor[3] may demand the Poḷichcheḻuttu (or tearing up of old bonds and the making of new), by which he is entitled to a deduction Sākshi and Oppu and Sūchi from the mortgage debt, or to receive the amount of it in hand from the mortgagee. It is understood that the proprietor has not the right of renewal within five or six years after the last renewal. There are two modes of settling the pāṭṭam on plantations, the Kuḻikkāṇam pāṭṭam and the Koyil[4] Mēni pāṭṭam : the first is where the pāṭṭam is fixed at one-fifth or 20 per cent. of the Kuḻikkāṇam or established value of the trees, and the latter is where the produce is estimated and two-thirds of it determined

---

[1] I have already said that Kāṇam sometimes means simply money. I believe Kuḻikkāṇam means digging money or hole-money, *i.e.*, compensation for digging and planting the land. ഴലവ expense.

[2] Sometimes the descriptions of trees in respect of which *alone* improvement value is claimable are likewise specified.

[3] Obsolete.

[4] Koyil = harvesting ; mēni = fold. Koyil mēni = gross produce ? The Kuḻikkāṇapāṭṭam is almost nominal, being fixed at a time when there are perhaps no bearing trees in the paramba. The practice is to lease out on a nominal rent in the first instance, and to continue to collect the same till the trees planted by the tenant have come into bearing. When this is done the custom is to value improvements, make the value a charge (kāṇam) on the paramba, fix a Koyil Mēni Paṭṭam, deduct therefrom the interest on the Kāṇam amount, and divide the residue between the Janmi and Government.

to be the pāṭṭam. Under the Kul̲ikkāṇam tenure the tenant or mortgagee is not answerable for any loss of trees or diminution of produce occasioned by mere neglect in not fencing the premises or not manuring the trees. No remission, however, is made in the pāṭṭam by the Janmi for loss occasioned by this cause. The loss the tenant himself thus sustains is a sufficient punishment to him. If, however, he does a positive injury by cutting down trees without the consent of the Janmi, he is answerable [1] to him for their value; they are the property of the Janmi. The Kāṇam money may be forfeited *in toto*, or in part in proportion to the injury done. He is not, however, responsible for the acts of the sovereign or the visitations of Providence, known by the name of Rājīkam and Deivīkam. A tenant is entitled to the value of the Kul̲ikkāṇam for every succession of trees which he plants, and if he throws up the garden, insisting upon this right, the proprietor must pay, but much depends upon the relative situations of the proprietor and the tenant. If the latter has a good thing of the tenure, or from having no other residence it would be inconvenient for him to remove, he will submit to a modification of the right not quite so favorable to him. For instance, a tenant possesses a garden producing a pāṭṭam of 100 fanams; he plants more trees yielding a further pāṭṭam of 40 fanams. The pāṭṭam being a fifth of the Kul̲ikkāṇam value, he is entitled to 200 fanams for the addition without any deduction for trees decayed of the original number. The loss from this cause being, however, 20 fanams of pāṭṭam, the proprietor deducts it and gives him credit for only 20 fanams in addition, that is, he gives him only 100 instead of 200 fanams to which he was entitled as Kul̲ikkāṇam, but a remission is made for the pāṭṭam of trees decayed, and the future pāṭṭam is fixed at 120 fanams. He has the right to revise the pāṭṭam upon the tenant's demand of Kul̲ikkāṇam for new trees, but if he anticipates an unfavorable result, he will decline any inspection of the trees upon which the pāṭṭam has been settled; he must, at all events, pay the Kul̲ikkāṇam money. If a tenant is obliged to quit a garden on the motion of the proprietor, the proprietor must pay the full Kul̲ikkāṇam of all trees, however young, and the tenant on notice of such a measure frequently introduces young trees for the purpose of getting the Kul̲ikkāṇam money.

The Janmi has no right to revise a pāṭṭam after it has once been fixed, except upon a demand of Kul̲ikkāṇam for new trees, but all this depends a good deal upon the relative circumstances of the parties. Upon every Poḷichchel̲uttu or renewal of bonds the tenant has a right to demand a revision of the pāṭṭam, and if he has suffered from Deivīkam (the visitation of Providence, which comprehends losses by fire, lightning, storms, floods, &c.) or from Rājīkam (the acts of a sovereign), he may claim remission or decline payment of the pāṭṭam. These losses [2] must be supposed to exceed 20 per cent. to come within the extent of these exceptions. Jack and mango trees are exclusively the property of the proprietor, and cannot [3] be cut without his permission. The tenant is entitled to cut down all unproductive coconut and betel-nut trees.

Notes.—1. See *Kāṇam*.

---

[1] Doubtful. *Vide* note below.

[2] Not legally or customarily recognized at present as far as I am aware.

[3] Nor, in my opinion, can the landlord do so without the tenant's consent.

2. The foot-notes to Mr. Græme's text are by an experienced Native Revenue Officer, Mr. P. Karuṇākara Mēnon.

3. The landlord contended that "whenever a Kuḻikkāṇam deed provides for no period, the ryot must give up the land when demanded," and that "if this be not allowed, the ryot (who is merely to receive his Kuḻikkāṇam improvements) and proprietor are placed on the same footing." The tenants contended "that it is not customary to resume paṛambas when no injury or arrear of rent is sustained." It was held that summary ejectment in the manner asked could not be granted.—Malabar Auxiliary Court, 43 (1843).

4. "The law only gives 12 years' possession to a Kuḻikkāṇam tenant."—N.D.C., 33 (1876).

5. In a Kuḻikkāṇam lease there was a clause to this effect: "If you plant these said four fruits and the coconuts bear fruit as is the usage, I will give a taragu, fixing rent after estimate of the produce." Held that the Janmi was entitled to take a full rent after the Kuḻikkāṇam lease was up, that is, after 12 years quiet and sure enjoyment by the tenant, and that the tenant was obliged to give up the land at the end of the 12 years on receiving the value of his improvements.—N.D.C., 98 (1876).

6. A Kuḻikkāṇam lease is not forfeited by failure to pay rent; even though there is an express stipulation in the deed of lease, the tenant has a right to hold for 12 years.—N.D.C., 75 (1875).

7. Where no express period has been stipulated this lease is considered to run for 12 years, otherwise for such period as may have been agreed upon. At the expiration of either of these periods the landlord may either renew the lease to the same tenant, paying him the value of his improvements, which may also be invested as a mortgage, or he may satisfy all the tenant's claim upon the land for improvements, and may let the property to a new tenant. Compensation is allowed for buildings and fruit-producing trees and shrubs of every description. In the event of the tenant failing to reclaim the land, plant trees, and otherwise fulfil the conditions of the deed, he may be dispossessed by the landlord before the expiration of the period specified. The landlord may exercise a similar power in the event of the tenant setting up a fraudulent title to the land.—(Proceedings of the Court of Sadr Adalat, No. 18, dated 5th August 1856.)

8. Under this tenure the tenant binds himself to pay a stipulated rent, as well as to bring new land under culture. Failure in either of these respects, or any attempt to defraud the landlord of his title, will render the tenant liable to ejectment. If no period is named in the agreement the lease will be considered to extend to 12 years.—(Proceedings of the Court of Sadr Adalat, No. 18, dated 5th August 1856.)

9. A tenant cannot be disturbed under this tenure for 12 years, or during the period, if any, stipulated, unless he attempts to set up a claim subversive of the landlord's rights. Possessing a pecuniary interest in the property, he cannot be dispossessed for neglect to improve it.—(Proceedings of the Court of Sadr Adalat, No. 18, dated 5th August 1856.)

10. The customary payment for improvements was meant as payment for the *Janmi's* share of produce not as payment for the cultivator's interest in the land. See Chapter IV, Section (*a*) of the Text.

KUPPA MANYAL.

From Dravidian *Kuppa* (= heap of dirt, sweepings), and Dravidian *Manyal* (= saffron, yellow dye).

The Anotta or *Bixa orellana*. There is a great abundance of it growing wild at Quilandy, about 15 miles north of Calicut, without any kind of cultivation. The natural color of the juice of the seed, which is used as a dye, is yellow, for which purpose it is exported to Bombay. It is so easily procurable that no stock is laid in for exportation, but the coasting merchants pick it up as they find it growing in the lanes about Quilandy. The seeds are carried off without any preparation. They are used in Malabar as beads in necklaces by the Māppiḷḷa women and are called Mulla. The tree grows in hedges with little or no care within the precincts of the town of Tellicherry.

KŪṚVĀḺCHA.

From Dravidian *Kūṛ* (= share) and Dravidian *vāḻuka* (= to live, live well, reign).

Is the step or throne which the Rājas of Malabar ascend. It answers to Puttum in Tamil and to Musnud Tukht in Persian. Kūṛ is share and Vāḻcha is the management or government, implying that a Rāja has come to the possession of the share of rank to which he is entitled by his seniority.

Note.—The term was always used in speaking of the share of Government entrusted to a subordinate prince of the ruling family.

KUṬṬĀDAN or MUNDAKAM.

A species of paddy sown within the bed of tanks in the Pālghat District. It is sown in the middle of Chittree (April), when there has been a little rain, and it grows afterwards during the monsoon in water, and is not cut till the middle of Tye (January), making a period of nine months for its growth.

The name of a rice which has only one crop in the year, and that crop is only cut in Makaram (January and February).

The names of paddy crop sown in Kumbham (February and March) and is eleven months before it comes to maturity. After the ploughing there is no expense of cultivation. The smallness of the expense of cultivation is mentioned as a proof that the Valli cannot be regulated by the number of mēni produce.

Note.—The two names are not generally applied to the same kind of paddy; the former kind grows in salt marshes—planted April, reaped January. The latter is a rice of slow growth, reaped about January.

KŪṬṬAM.

(Dravidian) = junction, assembly.

A collection of houses, consisting of 500 or 600 persons, six necessary for a Kartāvu of 3,000.

Notes.—1. See pp. 131, 132 of the text. The *Kuṭṭam* was evidently the "*Six hundred*" of Deeds Nos. 3 and 4, Appendix XII.

2. The Kūṭṭam answered many purposes, *e.g.*, *Niḻalkūṭṭam*, assembly under shade of a tree to discuss Taṟa affairs, &c.; *Paḍakūṭṭam*, for war; *Nāyāṭṭukūṭṭam*, for hunting; *Yōgakkūṭṭam*, for meditation; *Nāḍu-kūṭṭam*, for arbitration.

3. In the Laccadive Islands there are periodical kūṭṭams for killing the rats which infest the coconut trees. Any one absenting himself is fined.

4. The Honorable Mr. Hudleston has suggested that the *Koot* organization which gave so much trouble in Canara in 1832-33 was probably identical with the *Kūṭṭam* of Malabar.

KUTTIKKAṆAKKŌLA.

From Dravidian *Kutti* (= stake, peg to mark limits) and Dravidian *kaṇakku* (= accounts), and Dravidian *Ōla* (= palm-leaf, writing).

A kind of memorandum or register written upon the Karimbana palm or palmyra leaf, in which is recorded the Janmakāran's Pramāṇams or deeds with his tenants and the amount of the pāṭṭam share.

KUTTIKKĀṆAM.

From Dravidian *Kutti* (= stake, peg, stump) and *Kāṇam* (q.v).

Is the privilege of half a rupee or one rupee (according to local custom) to which every proprietor of a forest is entitled for every tree cut within the limit of his property. It means literally, stump money.

Note.—This is an arrangement by which the landlord assigns on mortgage a tract of forest land, receiving a stipulated fee for every tree felled by the mortgagee; the entire number of trees to be cut down, and the period within which they are to be felled, being expressly fixed in the Karār entered into between the parties. The mortgagee usually makes an advance and agrees to pay the balance by instalments. The non-payment of the stipulated instalments does not render the mortgagee liable to dispossession unless there be special clause in the agreement to this effect. The instalments may be recovered by action, but the mortgagee remains in possession during the period stipulated.—(Proceedings of the Court of Sadr Adalat, No. 18, dated 5th August 1856).

KUTTINELLU or VĒLINELLU.

From Dravidian *Kutti* (= peg, stump, stake, in a fence) and Dravidian *vēli* (= hedge, fence) and Dravidian *nel* (= rice).

Hedge grain; a contribution formerly made by Janmakārs for keeping up fences against cattle, half of which contribution was taken and consolidated with the land revenue in 975 M.S. in the tāluk of Kavāi. It amounted to 16 Iḍangaḻis for every 100 of seed, or 8 of which were incorporated with the land revenue.

KUTTIVĀṢI.

From Dravidian *Kutti* (= peg, stake, stump of a tree, hence what remains, balance) and Dravidian *vāṣi* (= excess, difference).

With the soft *t* it may be called the Nuffur Bakee, or balance against individuals.

KŪVA.

(Dravidian) = arrowroot.

The Malayāḷam name for the arrowroot that grows in Malabar. It grows without cultivation, and is commonly eaten by the poorer classes boiled in water and mixed sometimes with teire (curds), and salt.

Note.—The different kinds in Malabar are *Ānakkūva*, elephant arrowroot; *Channakkūva*, Costus speciosus; *Nyettikkūva*, Curcuma augustifolia, *Manyakkūva* and *Malankūva*, Kœmpferia; and *Manyalkkūva*, Curcuma longa.

MACLEOD SEER.

Macleod seer is 25 to a paṟa of salt, or 3,000 to a garce. Of the Madras seers there appear to be 4,800 to the garce in measuring salt.

MADHYASTANMĀR.

Plural of Sanskrit *Madhyastam* (= neutral person, mediator, arbitrator).

Arbitrators answering to Panchāyat, though the latter term is not known in Malabar. *Dharmakartā* is also used.

Note.—The *Kāraṇavar* of the *Taṟa* answered to the village Panchāyat of Eastern districts. See *Taṟavāṭṭu Kāraṇavar*.

MĀLIKĀNA.

(Persian) = what is due to the *Mālik* or proprietor when set aside from the management of his estate, allowances to deposed Rājas.

Which is a Bengal term implying the fee or privilege of the proprietor, and was originally applied to the allowance made to the Bengal Zemindar in concluding the permanent settlement; means in Malabar the fifth or 20 per cent. of a fixed revenue of their former countries which the dispossessed Rājas of Malabar receive from the Company.

Note.—The allowances are calculated on the revenue of 1800-1.

MAṆIYĀṆI.

(Sanskrit) = manager of estate on behalf of the Janmi.

POḶUTTIKKĀRAN.

A Malayāḷam corrupt form of—

PRAVRATTIKKĀRAN.

From Sanskrit *Pravratti* (= occupation, business) and Sanskrit *kāran* (= doer, one who has to do with).

Stewards or managers for Janmis or proprietors on estates or fields kept under their own direct management.

Note.—The officers who collect the revenue from ryots in Cochin and Travancore are called *Pravrattikārs*.

MANNĀṬṬAPPAN.

From Dravidian *Mannāḍi* (= immigrant landowners in Pālghat) and Dravidian *appan* (= father).

A caste of Veḷḷāḷars or cultivating Sūdras residing in certain Hōbalis of the Pālghat Tāluk, who are said to have come from Kāngayam in the Coimbatore province, and who are now so intermixed with the Nāyars as not to be distinguished from them except when a Tīyan addresses them and gives them this appellation instead of Nāyar. In Kāngayam they are called Mannāḍi.

MĀPPIḶḶA.

From *Mā*, that is, Sanskrit *Mahā* (= great) and Dravidian *piḷḷa* (= child, honorary title).

A tribe of Mussulmans in Malabar whom Europeans call Māppiḷḷas. They are supposed to be descendants of the Arabs who first settled on the Malabar Coast, and in some families the inheritance by nephews, instead of sons, is observed, the same among the Nāyars, but generally the succession is by sons. Some derive the name from Mā, mother, and piḷḷa, son, implying that they are the sons of their mothers, but that their fathers are unknown in consequence of the promiscuous intercourse between the first Arab settlers and the Native women of Malabar. Others, from Makkal, daughter, and piḷḷa, son, literally, but meaning son-in-law, that is, son to the man whose daughter he has married. Makkalpiḷḷa is usually pronounced Māppiḷḷa. Makkalpiḷḷa is the common word for son-in-law in Tamil. Mokhaee-piḷḷa, or people from Mokhaee, as Mocha is usually pronounced, is another derivation. The Rājas, in writing to a Māppiḷḷa, designate him Jōnakan, and they are often called Jōna Māppiḷḷas. The Nestorian Christians are called Nassrāṇi Māppiḷḷas. The number of Māppiḷḷas in Malabar, according to an account taken in 1807, amounts to 172,600.

Notes.—1. Dr. Gundert's view is that *Māppiḷḷa* was an "honorary title given to colonists from the West, perhaps at first only to their representatives." The name is not confined to Muhammadans.

2. The number of Māppiḷḷas (Muhammadans) in Malabar at the census taken in 1871 was 546,912.

MARICHAM.

(Sanskrit) = pepper.

The Sanskrit name for the pepper. The Hindustani word *mirch* is evidently derived from it.

MARYĀDA.

(Sanskrit) = limit, boundary, custom.

Which in Tamil means honor, respect; signifies in the Malabar province the custom, the usage, and corresponds exactly with the Hindustani word māmool.

MĒLKKŌYMA.

From Dravidian *mēl* (= above) and Dravidian *kōnma* or *kōyma* (= royal authority).

Note.— *Mēlkkōyma* was the right the sovereign power possessed over property of which the ownership was in others. Malabar Rājasnot now being sovereigns have no longer Mēlkkōyma rights.—N.D.C., 118 (1861).

MĒNAVAN or MĒNŌN.

From Dravidian *mēl* (= above), and Dravidian *avan* (= he).

Is the accountant or register, and answers to Karnam and Kaṇakkapiḷḷa

(Conicapoly). The appellation is generally, if not always, confined to an accountant of the caste of Nāyar.

Note.—The accountants of Amṣams (parishes) are now styled *Mēnōns.*

MĒNI VILACHCHAL.

From Dravidian *Mēni* (= body, shape, sample, average article), and Dravidian *viḷachchal* (= produce of corn).

Means in one case the number of fold. If you ask the Mēni Viḷachchal, or produce of an extent of land requiring so many paṛas of seed to sow it (in a single crop), it is usual to state the Viḷachchal, or produce, of the best crop, and not the aggregate of the different crops. For instance, the first crop may produce 8 paṛas, the second 10, and the third 6 : instead of saying 24, the answer would be 10.

It means also the gross produce. The number of fold produced from one paṛa of seed land (or land which requires one paṛa to sow it for a single crop) is about 5 $\frac{14}{16}$ in the province of Malabar upon applying the total gross produce (15,571,268 paṛas) to the total seed sown (2,638,163 paṛas) according to the accounts rendered by the Janmakārs in 981. The assessment being proposed to be regulated on the principle of deducting seed and the same quantity under the name of Vittuvalli or expense of cultivation, and also one-third for the cultivator, and dividing the remainder in the proportion of 6 in 10 to the Sircar and 4 in 10 to the Janmi, the Government assessment comes to 1 $\frac{8\frac{1}{2}}{16}$ of a paṛa for every paṛa sown, or about 26 $\frac{6}{16}$ per cent. of the gross produce.

Note.—The distribution of wet land produce, according to the scheme drawn up by Mr. Rickards and approved by Government (1803-4), is known as the *Viḷachchal mēni pāṭṭam* (q.v.) scheme.

MĒNNŌKKI.

From Dravidian *mēl* (= above), and Dravidian *nōkkuka* (= to look at, view, look after).

The common name formerly for accountants in the Kuṛumbranād and Polwye and Pyūrmala Districts, and in the Kartāvus or lordships of Vaḍakkampuṛam, and Kiḷakkampuṛam, or the Northern and Southern Divisions of the Calicut District.

MŌḌAN and PUNAM.

Mean generally high lands where a particular kind of paddy is capable of being cultivated, and where the oil-plant and millet and toor are also planted. In the Northern Division that land only is called Punam in which there is a great deal of underwood, and which can only be cultivated once in six years ; and that Mōḍan which is high land, but not overgrown with wood, and capable of being planted with coconut, &c., trees ; but in the Southern Division Mōḍan is the only name and Punam is not known. The Punam is never ploughed, but always dug. The plough could not make its way through the roots of the underwood. The seed is sown, or rather placed in the holes dug, dry and not sprouted.

Rice sown on high orchard land.

Note.—*Mōḍan* cultivation is now assessed at a uniform rate of 12 annas per acre in the low-country tāluks, and *Punam* cultivation at rates varying from 8 annas to 12 annas per acre. The assessment is imposed only on the breadth of ground annually occupied.

MRIGAM NĀLKKĀLI.

Mrigam (Sanskrit) = quadrupeds, wild animals. *Nālkkāli* (Dravidian) = quadrupeds, tame animals.

Four-footed animals. In the Southern Districts of Malabar a permanent allowance has, by ancient custom, been made by proprietors in fixing the pāṭṭam for estimated losses by animals, whilst in the Northern Districts no allowance was made for this and other items, such as Vēli Nellu; but the proprietors take upon themselves the expense of protecting their fields from cattle and pay it out of their pāṭṭam, each contributing so much to one or more persons appointed to watch a particular tract.

MŪḌA.

(Dravidian) = load, bale.

Means, literally, a fastening, or bundle, or package. It is applied to the packages in a circular form, like a Dutch cheese, fastened with whisps of straw, in which rice is made up in the south of Malabar and Canara. It is uniformly of the same size, containing 25 Macleod seers. In the Sea Custom accounts the Mūḍa of rice is reckoned at 81 lb. and of paddy at 55 lb.

MUKHYASTHAN.

From Sanskrit *mukhyam* (= chief, principal) and Sanskrit *stham* (= staying).

Is quite a modern term, introduced since Hyder's invasion, in lieu of the Taṛavāṭṭukārar or heads of villages. Though it may be derived from the Sanskrit word Mukhyam or chief, it is doubtful whether Mukhyastan, which was unknown in Malabar, was not an imitation of the Persian word Mokhtusir, which was common in the Mysore durbar, and means a person of authority, a chief.

Note.—Mr. Græme, contrary to other observations made by him, here alludes to the *Taṛavāṭṭukārur* as being the heads of villages. See *Taṛa* and *Ūr*, and *Madhyastanmār* and *Taṛavāṭṭu-kāraṇavar*.

MŪKKĀTAVĀḺI.

From Dravidian *mūnnu* (= three) and Dravidian *Kātam* (= about five English miles, a league), and Dravidian *vāḻi* (= ruler).

The limit of the jurisdiction of a Kartāvu of 3,000 men, extending to 3 Kātam.

MUKKUVAR.

From Dravidian *mukkuka* (= to dip, immerse, plunge) and Dravidian *avar* (= they).

A tribe of fishermen in Malabar whom Europeans call Mucquas; their number, according to an account taken in 1807, was 12,369.

Note.—" Said to be immigrants from Ceylon with Īḻavar " (q.v.)—*Gundert.*

MUḶḶUVALLI.

From Dravidian *muḷḷu* (= thorn) and Malayāḷam *valli* (= proper subsistence given in kind to slaves or day-laborers).

Literally, thorn expense, the expense of taking care of plantations. It is synonymous with Aḻi Ṣilavu.

MŪNNU or NĀLU MĒNI NILAM.

Mūnnu (Dravidian) = three ; *Nālu* (Dravidian) = four ; *Mēni* (Dravidian) = average ; *Nilam* (Dravidian) = rice-field.

A paddy-field requiring only one paṛa of seed and capable of producing three and four fold.

MŪṚI.

(Dravidian) = a fragment, note, bond, receipt.)

A receipt.

MUTIRA.

(Dravidian) = horsegram.

Horsegram, answering to Koḷḷu in Tamil, Kooltee in Hindustani.

NĀḌUVĀḺI.

From (Dravidian *Nāḍu*) = the country, a (province) and Dravidian *vāḻuka* (= to live, to live well, rule).

He was not considered a Nāḍuvāḻi who had not at least 100 *Nāyars* attached to his range; any number below that ranked a person as a Dēṣavāḻi.

Notes.—1. See *Dēṣam* and *Taṛa*, and *Kūṭṭam*.

2. Mr. Græme is here referring to the modern idea of a *Nāḍuvāḻi*. In ancient times the *Nāḍ* was the territory of the Six Hundred, of the *Kūṭṭam*, of the *Kāṇakkār*, supervisors, protectors, Nāyar militia.

NĀLUBHAYAM.

From Dravidian *nālu* (= four) and Sanskrit *ubhayam*) = garden produce in North Malabar).

Means the four products, and is applied in the Northern Division of Malabar to the produce, collectively, of the coconut, the betel-nut, the pepper and the jack tree.

Note.—The fifth in degree of importance was the *Kodi*, betel-leaf vine.

NAMBIYĀR.

Honor, plural of Dravidian *nambi* (= a title among Nāyars).

A caste of Nāyar ; the caste is distinguished by this termination to their name.

NAMBŪTIRI or NAMBŪRI.

From Dravidian *Nambuka* (= to trust, confide) and Sanskrit affix *tiri* (= *tiru* = *srī* = blessed, fortunate).

A Brāhman of Malabar.

NĀYAN, plural NĀYAR.

(Sanskrit) = leader, in honorific plural, lord ; in ordinary sense, soldiers, militia.

A caste of Hindus in Malabar classed among the Sūdras ; their number, from an account taken in 1807, was 156,283. Among Nāyars nephews, and not sons, are entitled to succeed to property. This material point being established, the law of shares among relations follows in other respects the general Hindu law of succession. There are some Nāyar families in Travancore who circumcise. The origin of this custom does not seem clearly known. There is some faint tradition that there was a forcible, but partial, circumcision of natives of Malabar by people from Arabia long before Hyder's invasion. The word Nāyar has much resemblance to the Gentoo word Nāyadu, to the Canarese and Tamil Nāyakkan, and to the Hindustani Naig; all titles of respect, applied in the manner that Sāhib is at the end of a name.

NIKUTI CHĪṬṬU.

NIKITI or NIKUTI, from Arabic *nagdi* (= ready-money) or Canarese *nigadi* (= instalment) or Sanskrit *nīti* (= right, proportion, law, justice), means the land-tax payable in money introduced by the Muhammadans (Mysoreans).

CHĪṬṬU (Dravidian) = note, bill.

A document given by the Sircar to every person who is to pay the Nikuti or public revenue showing the annual amount of Nikuti he is to pay.

NIKUTI ṢISHṬAM.

Nikuti (q.v.) *Ṣishṭam* (Sanskrit) = balance.

Is where the Kuḍiyān gives to Janmakār in pāṭṭam whatever remains in the pāṭṭam after paying the Nikuti.

Different ways in which it is settled in the districts south of the Kōṭṭa river, viz.:—

Suppose in the Sircar accounts the land is entered at .. .. paras	25	seed.
that according to the rate of assessment fixed in the time of Arshad Beg, viz. .. gold fanams	3	
the assessment is originally .. gold fanams	75	
to which is added 1 in 10 augmented in the time of the Rājas, and become the permanent assessment	7½	
The Total Assessment is ..	82½	
Suppose the total pāṭṭam to be .. .. paras	100	
an agreement has passed between the Janmakār and Kuḍiyān that the grain shall be valued at gold fanam	1	
Total Gold Fanams	100	
The Sircar assessment is to be deducted	82½	
There remains Nikuti Ṣishṭam to be given to the Janmakār	17½	

Kāṇam is to be deducted when there is any.

Another way—

The total pāṭṭam is	fanams	100
The interest is to be deducted upon 200 fanams principal of Kāṇam or debt at the rate of ½ in 10.		10
There remains		90
of which 2 in 10 is to be given to the Janmakār or.		18

NIKUTI VITTU.

Nikuti (q.v.). *Vittu* (Dravidian) = seed.

Is the quantity of seed assessed in the time of Hyder by the Huzzur Nikuti accounts. It is in contradistinction to the Vittu, which is the seed required to sow the land for one crop.

Note.—In Wynād also the actual seed sown is not always shown in the accounts.

NĪRMUTAL.

From Dravidian *nīr* (= water) and Dravidian *mutal* (= property, money).

Is a compound of Nīr, water, and Mutal, property; figuratively it means that additional property or security is acquired to the mortgagee by a pledge given by the proprietor that he will perform the ceremony of giving water to the mortgagee. It is a kind of mortgage, without possession, of the additional right which the act of giving water confers. After the execution of this deed, the proprietor cannot transfer the land to another without the express consent of the mortgagee. It is still, however, in his power to redeem the mortgage by payment of the debt. At this stage of the mortgage the proprietor has generally received 10 per cent. upon the sum specified in the deed of Otti in addition to that which he had received under the deed of Ottikkumpuṛam. The amount of the debt, but not the pāṭṭam, is specified in this deed.

Note.—When the landlord requires to borrow a still further sum on the security of land assigned to an Otti mortgagee to whom he has already executed an Ottikkumpuṛam deed, he is bound first to apply to such mortgagee, and if the latter should consent to make the required advance, the landlord gives him a Nīrmutal document, by which he makes over to him all but the right of water. Such further advance is recoverable with the amount of the original mortgage, the Otti claim being, in fact, merged in the Nīrmutal deed. In this case, as in that of an Ottikkumpuṛam transaction, if the mortgagee decline to make the advance, the landlord may obtain it from a third party, who satisfies the claim of the original mortgagee and comes into possession. In any of the three cases last mentioned the landlord is at liberty at any time to pay off the mortgage and redeem his property.—(Proceedings of the Court of Sadr Adalat, No. 18, dated 5th August 1856).

NŌKKICHĀRTTA or NŌKKIYEḶUTTA PEIMĀṢI.

From Dravidian *Nōkki* (= having looked) and Dravidian *chārtta* (= assessed) or Dravidian *Eḷutta* (= written). *Peimāṣi* = (Persian) *Pymāish*.

Terms in use for survey. The latter seems to have been introduced only in Tippu's time. The surveys, except what was made by Mr. Warden in 983, are not to be understood as meaning an actual measurement of the land by square feet, but merely a calculation of the quantity of seed necessary for sowing with respect to paddy, or an inspection of the number and a valuation of the produce of trees with respect to orchards.

OART.

Used in the Commissioners' correspondence of 1793 for garden. The Portuguese word is Horta, and its origin is evidently from Hortus.

OPPU.

From Dravidian *okka* (= together, all), means agreement, and hence a signature as the mark of agreement.

Is the signature. A fee upon one of the parties signing a new mortgage-deed respecting land.

OTTI.

From Dravidian *Otta* (= one, single), hence *ottuka* (= to step aside, make room for another) and *otti* (= the stepping aside to make room for another, or, perhaps, the substitution of one thing for another.)

In former times the Otti deed was scarcely ever executed before the Pāṭṭōla deed. It was the consequence of the mortgagor becoming involved in a greater degree than when he first incurred the debt to the mortgagee. It is a deeper stage into debt. In the present times it is very usual for persons to borrow to that extent at once, without going through the preliminary step of Paṇaya Pāṭṭam to render it necessary to execute the Otti deed.

In this deed the amount of the debt only is specified and not the pāṭṭam or rent. In this stage of mortgage the interest of the debt is equal to the annual pāṭṭam, and the mortgagee pays no pāṭṭam to the proprietor. It is also called Veppu (in Pālghat) and Paliṣa Maḍakku (in Neḍunganād and Waḷḷuvanād), which latter term is expressive of this characteristic feature.

The mortgagor under this deed and under the subsequent deeds, which indicate advanced stages of the mortgage, is not entitled to Poḷichcheḻuttu and its concomitant advantages, Sākshi, &c., &c.

He is considered to have already received two-thirds of the value of his mortgaged land, and to be entitled to one-third more before he has relinquished his proprietary right.

Though this and other deeds have certain defined rules, it must not be understood that they are rigidly observed with respect to the proportion to the whole estimated value of the Janmam or proprietary right which should constitute it to be one kind of deed or another, but the particular sums to be given will be exceeded where the quality of the land and the great demand on the part of others may render the mortgagee apprehensive of losing possession, and in other cases the Janmi may not get so much as is supposed in these explanations.

Under this deed, as the proprietor receives no rent from the land, he must be considered to have lost all interest in it, and to be wholly inefficient for the purpose of improving it; he is no longer even a pensioner upon it.

Notes.—1. This tenure gives the mortgagee possession and the entire produce of the land, the landlord merely retaining the proprietary title and the power to redeem. Where no period has been stipulated, the landlord may pay off the mortgage at any time. The principal alone is repayable, the mortgagee recovering the interest of his money from the produce of the land. If the landlord be desirous of raising a further sum and the Otti mortgagee refuse to advance it, the money may be received from a third party and the mortgage transferred to him. But the original mortgagee has a right to be first consulted.—(Proceedings of the Court of Sadr Adalat, No. 18, dated 5th August 1856.)

2. The following are some of the decisions of the Courts. An Otti holder, like a Kāṇakkāran, forfeits his right to hold for 12 years by denying his Janmi's title.—2 M.H.C.R., p. 161. An Otti holder is entitled to the first chance of supplying his Janmi's deeds for further loans.—M.S.C., 17 (1860); M.S. decisions (1860), p. 249. The words "Kāṇam free from the payment of rent" will not enlarge that Kāṇam right into an Otti right.—M.S.C., 142 (1870). Until the Otti holder refuses to purchase it the Janmam right cannot be sold to another person.—S.S.C., 344-358 (1855). The offer to sell the Janmam right must be "at a reasonable rate."—N.D.C., 64 (1859). A Janmi can at any time call on an Otti holder to purchase the Janmam right, and, on his refusal, he can sell his rights to whom he pleases. M.S.C., 30 (1857). To grant land on Janmam to a third party without the Otti holder's consent is directly at variance with the general usage of the country.—S.D.C., 135-155 (1854). The Otti holder is entitled to the refusal of the opportunity of making a further advance.—M.S.C., 17 (1860) and 1 M.H.C.R., p. 356. The right to hold for 12 years probably attaches to an Otti.—N.D.C., 28 (1862); M.H.C., 380 (1862). The difference between a Kāṇam and an Otti pointed out: the latter includes (*a*) the right of pre-emption of Janmam, and (*b*) Janmi's right is reduced to a mere pepper-corn rent.—M.H.C., 101 (1862).

DRAVYAM.

(Sanskrit) = object, movable property, money.

The amount of Otti received by the Jaṇmi when giving his property under the tenure of Otti.

OTTIKKUM PUṚAMĒYUḶḶA KĀṆAM.

(Literally) the Kāṇam which is in addition to the Otti.

May be considered the third stage of mortgage. The mortgagor has borrowed 10 per cent. more than the sum he had received when he executed the deed of Otti. The deed specifies the amount of debt with this addition, and makes no allusion to the pāṭṭam. The mortgagor is as little entitled to Poḷichcheḻuttu, Sākshi, and Sūchi under this as under the deed of Otti.

If the mortgagor should pay off the mortgage debt, he must also under this deed, and under all the deeds executed at subsequent stages of the mortgage, pay the interest of the additional 10 per cent. from the time he borrowed it, with this qualification, that it do not exceed double the amount of the principal from which it sprung.

Ottikkumpuṛam means above or beyond the Otti.

Under this deed the mortgagor has still the power of transferring the property to another or recovering the possession for himself by redeeming the debt.

The addition to the Otti deed which makes this deed called Ottikkum-puṛam is not necessarily limited to 10 per cent. The mortgage retains this denomination till it becomes deep enough to be classed under Nīrmutal.

The amount of the debt, but not the pāṭṭam, is specified in this deed.

Note.—When the landlord wishes to obtain a further sum he applies to the Otti mortgagee, and on receiving it executes this deed to him, in which he binds himself to repay the amount at the same time that he pays off the mortgage. The mortgagee must always have the option of making such further advance, but if he decline, the landlord may apply to a third party and assign the property to him, the latter paying off the claim of the original mortgagee.—(Proceedings of the Court of Sadr Adalat, No. 18, dated 5th August 1856.)

PALIṢA.

(Maḷayāḷam) = interest on money, distinct from interest on rice (= Polu, or Paliṣa).

Interest. The subjoined are the denominations of the different kinds of Paliṣa and the meaning of them in the Southern Division of Malabar, not including Pālghat and Temmalapuṛam, where the Janmakār's and tenants' pāṭṭam rate is one gold fanam for 2 paṛas. In the Northern Division it is generally 2 silver fanams for 1 paṛa, but in Kavāi alone it is 1 silver fanam for 1 paṛa. The terms of interest which in this table indicate so many years' purchase for the Southern Division generally have not the same meaning in the Northern Division or in the Pālghat and Temmalapuṛam Districts of the Southern Division, for which there ought to be a separate table.

Rice Lands.

Names for the different species of Interest.	Number of Iḍangalis to be given as Interest a year for every Fanam.		Amount of the Interest a year on a principal of 100 Fanams.		Number of Iḍangalis established from ancient usage as the average price per Fanam.		Number of Iḍangalis according to this rate per 100 Fanams.		Centage Interest on the Principal.		Number of years' purchase or number of years in which the Simple Interest or the Paṭṭam will equal the Principal.	
	PS.	YS.	PS.	YS.	PS.	YS.	PS.	YS.	FS.	AS.	YRS.	MOS.
No. 1. Makaṇi (lit. 1/16) Paliṣa.	0	1/16	0	6¼	1 or	10	100 or	1,000	0	10	160	0
,, 2. Arakkal (lit. ⅛) Paliṣa.	0	⅛	1	2½	1	0	100	0	1	4	80	0
,, 3. Kal (lit. ¼) Paliṣa.	0	¼	2	5	1	0	100	0	2	8	40	0
,, 4. Ara (lit. ½) Paliṣa.	0	½	5	0	1	0	100	0	5	0	20	0
,, 5. Mukkal (lit. ¾) Paliṣa.	0	¾	7	5	1	0	100	0	7	8	13	4
,, 6. Ner (lit. full) Paliṣa.	0	1	10	0	1	0	100	0	10	0	10	0

The Mākāṇi Paliṣa is a hundred and sixtieth part paid in interest for the principal,			whether in paddy lands or plantations.
The Arakkāl Paliṣa is one-eightieth	do.	do.	
The Kāl Paliṣa is one-fortieth	do.	do.	
The Ara Paliṣa is one-twentieth	do.	do.	
The Mukkāl Paliṣa is a thirtieth or one-third	do.	do.	
The Ner Paliṣa is a tenth	do.	do.	

Remarks.—No. 1. May be explained to be an interest of one-sixteenth of every Iḍangaḷi pāṭṭam for every fanam borrowed, or (taking the settled price of 10 Iḍangaḷis a fanam) one hundred and sixtieth part of the principal, or 160 years' purchase, or $\frac{5}{8}$ per cent. This explanation applies to the Paliṣa upon paddy-fields. In plantations it is customary to refer its relation to every 10 fanams borrowed. A Mākāṇi Paliṣa is one-sixteenth, to be paid in interest of one fanam pāṭṭam for every ten fanams borrowed. Its centage, number of years' purchase, and proportion to the principal, are the same as in paddy lands.

No. 2. (Blank).

No. 3. After deducting the proportion for the assessment, this rate of interest prevails in some places.

No. 4. After deducting the proportion for the assessment, this rate is the most prevalent.

No. 5. Not in use before the introduction of the land assessment, but now in some places it prevails inclusive of the Nikuti.

No. 6. Not in use before, but now is in use inclusive of the assessment. When the assessment is half the pāṭṭam, the Nēr Paliṣa, including the Nikuti, is equivalent to the Paliṣa exclusive of the Nikuti.

Plantation.

Names of different species of Interest.	Amount of the Interest a year for every 10 Fanams borrowed.		At this rate amount of the Interest a year on a principal of 100 Fanams.		Centage Interest on the Principal.		Number of years' purchase or number of years in which the Simple Interest or the Paṭṭam will equal the Principal.	
	FANAMS	AS.	FANAMS	AS.	FANAMS.	AS.	YEARS.	MONTHS.
Makaṇi ($\frac{1}{16}$) Paliṣa ..	0	1	0	10	0	10	160	0
Arakkal ($\frac{1}{8}$) Paliṣa ..	0	2	1	4	1	4	80	0
Kal ($\frac{1}{4}$) Paliṣa	0	4	2	8	2	8	40	0
Ara ($\frac{1}{2}$) Paliṣa	0	8	5	0	5	0	20	0
Mukkal ($\frac{3}{4}$) Paliṣa ..	0	12	7	8	7	8	13	4
Ner (full) Paliṣa ..	1	0	10	0	10	0	10	0

TIKAPPALIṢA.

From Dravidian *Tikayuka* (= to become full, complete) and *Paliṣa* (q.v.).

With respect to plantations has the same meaning as Nēr Paliṣa in regard to rice-lands. It is the full interest or 10 per cent., that is, it is 10 fanams given in purchase for every fanam paṭṭam (rent). It is the highest interest on land recognized by custom ; any excess above it would be usury.

28

Kadamvāypa.

From Dravidian *Kaḍam* (= debt) and Dravidian *vāypu* (= growth).

Rate of interest observable in loans of money, in contradistinction to the interest on land mortgage loans, which is much lower, but in Ēṛnād and Vellātra many Janmakārs have been obliged to borrow part of the money upon which their land is mortgaged on the terms of the Kaḍamvāypa.

PALIṢA MAḌAKKAM.

From *Paliṣa* (q.v.) and Dravidian *Maḍakkam* (= return).

Used in Pālghat.

The chief feature of this deed[1] is that the interest of the money borrowed is equal to the value of the pāṭṭam in the possession of the mortgagee, and in this respect it exactly resembles the Otti deed. In it, however, the pāṭṭam is specified (which is not the case in the Otti deed) as well as the amount of the debt.

It is rather more favorable to the Janmakār than the Otti deed, because, as long as the mortgage has not reached the point of Otti, the Janmakār is at liberty[2] to raise his terms, and the specification of the pāṭṭam gives him the means of doing it. Under the Otti deed the knowledge of the pāṭṭam is lost in former deeds, and the proprietor, it is well known, has no right to more than half as much again as he has already received. He has already got two-thirds of the whole value of the Janmam.

Notes.—1. See *Otti.*

2. The foot-notes to Mr. Græme's text are by an experienced Native Revenue official.

PAḶḶIYĀL, or Paḷḷiyāli, or Paiḷḷnyāyal, or Paḷḷimanyāyal.

Paḷḷimanyāyal, from Dravidian *Paḷḷi* or *Paḷḷam* (= pit, hole, excavation) and Dravidian *Nyāru* or *Nāru* (= what rises above ground, young plant fit for transplantation).

The highest stage of Ubhayam, a low rice-land; it corresponds, I think, with the *bill* of Canara. The paṛamba may be called the high land which is not artificially irrigated.

In one kind of Paḷḷiyal or Paḷḷimanyāyal or Potta there is no cultivation. It only answers for sowing seed to be transplanted to lower lands.

Note.—Paḷḷimanyāyal was originally land excavated for rearing rice plants for transplantation.

PĀḶPAṚAMBU.

From Dravidian *Pāḷ* (= an empty, void, desolate, waste place) and Dravidian *Paṛambu* (= high ground, orchard, garden).

A destroyed garden.

PAṆAYAM.

From Dravidian root *paṇ* (= to exchange, buy, bet) = bet, stake, pledge, mortgage.

In speech this deed is often designated the Toḍu Paṇayam deed with

---

[1] Otti and Paliṣa Maḍakkam are one and the same, at present at all events.

[2] The distinction is scarcely maintained at the present time.

reference to its character, which corresponds with the *Tore Udawoo* deed of Canara.

By this deed the Janmi engages to pay a certain interest for money borrowed, or, in failure thereof, to make over to the Paṇayakkāran or mortgagee certain lands therein named.

In some cases the term for repayment of the principal is specified, in others it is omitted; but it is supposed the mortgagee has a right to be put into possession of the land if the mortgagor do not pay upon the demand of the mortgagee.

If the Janmi decline putting the mortgagee into possession in failing to pay the interest, the mortgagee is in the habit of bringing an action for the recovery of the principal and interest by any means, whether by the sale of the mortgaged land alone or by the sale of other property belonging to the Janmi; and the Judicial Courts, it is said, pass their decisions conformably to this principle.

If the Janmi, upon failing to pay the interest, were immediately to put the mortgagee in possession, the latter, it is thought, would have no right to sue for recovery of the debt by any other means.

Under this deed the Janmi has properly no right to dispose of the Janmam in the mortgaged land without the consent of the mortgagee; but if any transfer of the kind should be clandestinely made, may insist upon the purchaser paying his demand or placing him in the possession of the land.

Where a mortgagee is placed in possession under this deed, he is to pay to the Janmi the residue of the pāṭṭam after deducting the mortgage interest.

Under this deed there is no right of Poḷichcheḻuttu, Sākshi, Oppu, and Sūchi.

Notes.—1. The land is here pledged as security for the repayment, with interest, of certain sums advanced, but the lender has no right to interfere in the management of the property. In some cases it is stipulated that on failure on the part of the borrower to pay the interest, the lender shall be placed in possession of the land. Where such stipulation exists, the lender can sustain an action for possession; in other cases he must sue for the recovery of the principal and interest of the loan, the land being liable in the event of the money not being paid.—(Proceedings of the Court of Sadr Adalat, No. 18, dated 5th August 1856).

2. The tender of the mortgage amount makes the person to whom tender is made responsible for rent from date of tender.—M.S.C., 134 (1857). A simple mortgagee has no claim to improvements.—S.D.C., 338 (1877).

3. This deed was evidently a mortgage without possession of the land interest pledged.

Paṇaya Eḻuttukāran.

From *Paṇayam* (q.v.) and *Eḻuttukāran* (Dravidian) = writ, or deed-holder.

A creditor of a Janmi, to whom the actual possession of the estate is not consigned, but to whom the Janmi has engaged to consign it in failure of payment by a certain time. It depends upon the terms of the deed whether the land becomes in the possession of the mortgagee or not.

PANDAKKĀVAL.

From Dravidian *Pandal* (= temporary shed of leaves) and Dravidian *Kāval* (= custody, guard, watch).

A watching fee, consisting of the crop of a certain portion of the field, which a slave receives from his master for his trouble. Kāval is watching, and Pandal is the awning or cover under which the slave sets to watch.

Note.—See *Koḻulābham*, and *Eṇṇam* and *Patam*.

PANḌĀRAM.

(Dravidian) = treasury, government.

Term commonly used in Malabar for expressing the Government.

PĀNḌI.

(Dravidian) = the Southern Tamil country with Madura as capital.

The name given to a tribe of Christian fishermen and palanquin-bearers on the Malabar Coast, whom I have seen at Cannanore. They are supposed to have come from the southernmost part of the Malabar Coast, viz., Travancore, and, perhaps, from the Tinnevelly province originally.

PAṆIKKAR.

A kind of Master of Arts, formerly held in great respect in families as teachers of the use of arms and of martial exercises of all kinds.

The agent having jurisdiction either in a village or in a Hōbali on the part of the Kartāvu, or lord of the Nād or district, to whom intermediate references are made from the Aḍiyāns or vassals of the Kartāvu.

PAṚA.

(Dravidian) = a drum, a rice measure.

In the Malabar province means generally ten of the measure next in quantity to it, that is, ten Iḍangaḻis or Dangālis, whatever may be the quantity of the latter. It is nearer to the mercal than to any other measure at Madras.

The standard paṛa which appears in Mr. Græme's statements of assessment contains ten Macleod Iḍangaḻis each Iḍangaḻi being four Calicut Nāḻis and 3,000 Iḍangaḻis a garce.

A Paṛa of Seed Land.

The quantity of seed necessary to sow an extent of land. The quantity varies according to the quality of the land. Major Macleod, in report to the Revenue Board, 18th June 1802, states the average of various experiments from measurement near Calicut made it $\frac{13}{100}$ parts of a cawny, or 7,488 square feet. The lowest rent by these trials was Madras fanams 27 cash 40, and the highest, star pagodas 1 fanam 24 cash 68 per cawny. One paṛa of seed will in some places produce thirty and in others only five fold. I calculate that a paṛa of seed land is seldom more than one-sixth of a cawny or 9,600 square feet, and seldom less than one-ninth or 6,400 square feet.

Note.—See *Viṭṭupād*.

PAṞAMBU.

(Dravidian) = high, dry ground, orchard, garden, compound.

May be considered the high land, whether cultivated with Mōḍan rice, the oil-plant, the chāma (*Panicum miliaceum*), or coconut and other trees, which is not capable of being inundated or irrigated artificially, and it does not apply exclusively to garden land as I at first thought it did.

TOḌI or TŌṬṬAM.

(Dravidian) = garden.

Terms used for gardens and plantations.

PAṢUMA or PAṢIMA.

(Dravidian) = freshness, softness, richness of soil.

RĀṢI.

(Sanskrit) = (a heap) with Dravidian *Kūru* (= class), means poor, light soil.

Terms used for distinguishing the qualities of lands, viz., Paṣima is the first, Rāṣi Paṣima the second, and Rāṣi the third sort.

PATAM.

(Dravidian) = share of reapers.

It is a term used for the expense of reaping, reckoned 10 per cent. In some places this proportion is given after the paddy is measured out, in others one out of ten sheaves is given in the field.

Note.—See *Eṇṇam*, *Koḻulābham*, and *Pandakkāval*.

PĀṬṬAM.

Probably from Dravidian *pāḍu* (= falling, falling into one's power, place, situation, order, office, rank of officials and of princes, &c.), hence probably meaning the share of the produce of land due to officials and princes, and latterly to Janmis or other proprietors of land. It was probably at first written as *pāṭṭa-vāram* (= the *pāḍ's* share (*vāram*) of the produce).

The fixed proportion agreed to between a Janmi and cultivator to be given to the Janmi as his share or rent; this proportion is usually paid in kind for rice cultivation and in money for plantations.

In settling the pāṭṭam of coconut trees it has, in most places in Malabar, been the custom to give 20 per cent. of the kuḻikkāṇam money, that is, of the value of the trees. Where the cultivator has demanded immediate payment of the value, the pāṭṭam has almost everywhere been settled at two-thirds of the estimated produce. 7½ rupees has been the general price almost everywhere in the central Southern Districts, at which the produce has been commuted between the proprietor and tenant in settling the pāṭṭam. At Tellicherry, Kaḍattanāḍ, Kōlattunāḍ and Kavāi the rate is 10 rupees. The Māppiḷḷa proprietors along the coast frequently, however, take their pāṭṭam in kind and dispose of it to the best advantage.

Note.—See "*Vāram*," and note to cl. (*i*) of Deed No. 3, App. XII. See also Chapter IV, Section (*a*) of the Text. The *kuḻikkāṇam* money was the value not of the trees, as Mr. Græme asserts, but of the *Janmi's* share of the produce of the trees, the *pāṭṭam* in fact. It would never have paid any one to have planted a garden and to have undertaken to pay as annual rent one-fifth of the value of the trees, but one-fifth of the value of the *Janmi's* share of produce (*pāṭṭam*) was a very moderate annual rent.

PĀṬṬAKKĀRAN.

From *Pāṭṭam* (q.v.) and Sanskrit *Kāran* (= doer, one who has to do with).

The tenant on a simple lease without any mortgage incumbrance.

Note.—The tenant simply yielded up the whole of the *Janmi's* share of the produce, that is of the *pāṭṭam*. It was the *pāṭṭam* which was not encumbered by mortgage—not the land.

KĀṆI.

(Dravidian) = something to be seen, gift.

Is an allowance, or offering, or tribute, of one Poti of paddy for every Poti of seed-land, which the cultivator makes to the proprietor in Wynād, answering to the Nikuti Ṣishtam of other tāluks. Rāmasvāmi, formerly Tahsildar of Wynād, says the Poti is given for every Poti seed of assessment, which is different from the Poti seed-land and answers to the *Nejja moodre* in Canara.

Synonymous with Pāṭṭam and Vāram, and is used in the Wynād country for the landlord's rent.

VĀRAM.

(Dravidian) = share in general, landlord's share, rack-rent, chiefly of rice-lands (pāṭṭam of trees).—(*Gundert*).

The proportion given to the proprietor by the cultivator from the produce of his land. This proportion is not fixed, but depends on the actual produce, and the proprietor receives either half, or more or less, according to their agreement, which is made with respect to the quality of the land.

Note.—*Pāṭṭam* was probably originally *pāṭṭa-vāram*. In the ancient system certain individuals held the *Vārakōl* (share-staff) and distributed the produce. See Deed No. 3, App. XII. *Conf. Nakachchal.*

VĀRAM PĀṬṬAM.

See *Vāram* and *Pāṭṭam*.

Though in general these two words are synonymous to express the landlord's share of the produce on all kinds of land—Vāram being used in the Northern and Pāṭṭam in the Southern Districts of Malabar—it appears that Vāram is used in the districts south of the Kōṭṭa river in a more limited way, that is, it is confined to mean the landlord's share arising from lands producing Mōḍan or hill paddy and Till only, and no other descriptions of land.

Note.—Doubtful if this is so now.

VEṚUMPĀṬṬAM.

From Dravidian *veṛu* (= empty, bare) and *pāṭṭam* (q.v.).

Simple rent unencumbered with mortgage interest.

Notes.—1. The following are a few of the Civil Courts' rulings:—Veṛumpāṭṭakkār are entitled on eviction to the value of improvements, whether these have been effected with or without the knowledge of the Kāṇakkār or Janmi. This is an ordinary usage in the country.—S.D.C., 40 (1854). A tenancy expressed to be for one year is not necessarily determined at the end of the year. If the tenant remains in possession he holds as a tenant from year to year.—S.D.C., 400 (1877), 437 (1878). Although it is not open for a tenant to deny his lessor's title, it is open to him to show that the title has ceased.—N.D.C., 413 (1861), 73 (1862); S.D.C., 172 (1877). A lessee is debarred from disputing that his lessor had no title.—S.S.C., 366 (1854). *Semble*: Lessor's transferee's lack of title.—M.S.C., 103 (1859). Encroachments by a tenant on adjoining waste are for the benefit of the landlord.—S.D.C., 438 (1877), 559 (1877). A tenant cannot of right claim remission on account of loss by drought.—S.D.C., 60 (1878), 133 (1878).

2. This lease runs only for a single year, unless otherwise specified. At the end of the year the landlord is at liberty either to renew the lease or to let the land to another tenant; but he cannot, under any circumstances, disturb the tenant in his enjoyment until the year has expired. Where the lease is for a specified period, the tenant cannot be ejected during that period unless he endeavour to defraud the landlord or allows the rent to fall into arrears. In either of these cases, however, an action of ejectment will lie against the tenant.—(Proceedings of the Court of Sadr Adalat, No. 18, dated 5th August 1856.)

Note.—See Chapter IV, Section (*a*) of the Text. The records of the Courts having been searched it is believed that no suits of ejectment were in reality brought before 1856, or at any rate before 1822. The *Janmi* used to oust an obnoxious tenant *by selling his interest in the land* before 1856.

VITTA PĀTI PĀṬṬAM.

= literally, pāṭṭam equal to half the seed sown.

Where it is half (of seed sown).

VITTŌḶAM PĀṬṬAM.

= literally, pāṭṭam equal to seed sown.

Where it is equal (to seed sown).

VITTIRAṬṬA PĀṬṬAM.

= literally, pāṭṭam equal to double the seed sown.

Where the pāṭṭam is double the seed sown.

IRUNĀḺI PĀṬṬAM.

= literally, pāṭṭam of two Nāḻis.

That is, two Nāḻis out of four which make an Iḍangāḻi. It is used to express an equal division of the crop between proprietor and tenant, a mode of settlement which is seldom practiced in Malabar, and which is only made for the year. It has the same meaning as Vāram on the Coromandel Coast.

MĒNIPPĀṬṬAM.

From Dravidian *mēni* (= average) and *pāṭṭam* (q.v.).

Means the pāṭṭam or rent of a given extent of land derivable from the aggregate of the different crops, whilst the Viḷachchal mēni, or gross produce, refers only to the best crop, in common parlance, though not in account.

Michchavāram or Michchāram.

From Dravidian *micha* (= height, above) and *vāram* (q.v.).

The balance of pāṭṭam or rent after deducting mortgage interest. It is the same as Puṛappāḍ.

Mēlvāram.

From Dravidian *mēl* (= what is above, above) and *vāram* (q.v.).

The tax upon the pāṭṭam or vāram which was levied by the Rājas in the Northern Districts of Malabar before Hyder's time to pay the tribute of the Bednore or Ikkaree Rāja. The Chirakkal Rāja states it amounted to 2 in 10; in some places it is said to have been 3 in 10, or 30 per cent. of the pāṭṭam.

Maṛupāṭṭam.

From Dravidian *maṛu* (= other, next, back again) and *pāṭṭam* (q.v.).

Is the counterpart of the Pāṭṭam Pramāṇam which the Janmi keeps by him, and may be referred to as a document in failure of the Grandhavari.

It is written upon the Karimbana palm or palmyra leaf.

Munpāṭṭam.

From Dravidian *mun* (= priority in time or place, first) and *pāṭṭam* (q.v.).

Note.—No condition of 12 years' enjoyment attaches to a *Munpāṭṭam* lease.—S.D.C., 215 (1878).

Pāṭṭachchīṭṭu.

From *Pāṭṭam* (q.v.) and Dravidian *chīṭṭu* (= a note, bill, bond).

A receipt.

Note.—It is not a receipt, as Mr. Græme says, but a lease given by the proprietor to the tenant. The counterpart is *Māṛupāṭṭam* (q.v.).

Pāṭṭamāḷi or Pāṭṭāḷi.

From *Pāṭṭam* (q.v.) and Dravidian *āḷi* (= a holder).

Is a subordinate officer attached to a Hindu temple, subject, generally, to the Ūrāḷan or to his *locum tenens* the Kārāḷan. Generally speaking the office is hereditary, but the Ūrāḷan may procure his dismissal for any crime by representation to the Rāja or the reigning authority.

The hereditary Karaṇam or register of a Nāḍuvāḷi. The fixed or permanent writer. It is not applied to registers of Dēṣavāḷis or others.

Pāṭṭōla or Pāṭṭamōla.

From *Pāṭṭam* (q.v.) and Dravidian *Ōla* (= palm-leaf, deed).

Is a deed executed by the mortgagor in favor of the mortgagee, making over certain rice-land to the possession of the latter in consideration of money received, called Kāṇappaṇam. In the deed the amount of the debt is specified, the whole number of paṛas pāṭṭam which the land yields, the number of paṛas which are to be deducted[1] for the interest of the debt, and

[1] Among deductions is likewise the equivalent in paddy of the amount of assessment on the land in cases in which the tax is agreed to be paid by the mortgagee.

the remaining number of the paras pāṭṭam of rice in the husk, called purappād, which are to be paid to the Janmi. It describes the particular kind of paṛa in which the residue is to be paid, and that it is to be delivered at the house of the proprietor. The deed states that the Kāṇam money received is equal to the pāṭṭam, by which is to be understood that the amount of the principal does not exceed the annual pāṭṭam, and it is said that the original intention of the proprietor receiving an advance was merely that of securing himself against the tenant failing in the payment of his pāṭṭam. The necessities of the proprietors in aftertimes drove them to borrow far beyond their annual incomes. Though not specified in the deed, it was formerly customary to give from 3 to 5 per cent. on the amount of the principal to the proprietor upon making out this deed as a fee [1] under the name of Oppu or signature, and further the mortgagee had to give 2 per cent. under the denomination of Sūchi, or the point of the iron style used for writing the deed. This was given where the Janmi's established Paṭṭōlakkāran or register was employed, but the fee was less where the mortgagee appointed a person for the occasion. Altogether the Oppu and Sūchi are supposed not to have exceeded 5 per cent. on the amount of the debt in general. But these payments [2] have been for some time discontinued in practice in most places; they have only reference to a state of things in which the interest of the mortgage debt bore little proportion to the annual rent yielded by the land in the possession of the mortgagee, and are too excessive to be applicable to the altered circumstance of the interest of debts being equal to the pāṭṭam receivable by the mortgagee. With respect [3] to this deed it is understood that if the mortgagee insists upon payment of the mortgage debt, the mortgagor has a right to deduct from the principal from 10 to 20 per cent.,

---

[1] At present the rates differ with different Janmis. In some cases these are *ad valorem*, more frequently they are fixed. Other fees are usually paid now-a-days, such as fee to attesting witnesses, and small presents to the mortgagor's relatives.

In the case of the Zamorin and his Kōvilakams the fines and fees ordinarily levied are the subjoined:—

(1) Avakāṣam, at so much per paṛa, or fanam, Janmapāṭṭam. The rate varies from 8 to 12 annas.

(2) Twenty per cent. on ditto under the name of "Aduppatha."

(3) Stalat chilavu (expenses on the spot), that is, fees to local Karyastans.

(4) Tiruveḻuttu vaḻivāḍu, *i.e.*, the signature fee.

(5) A fee to the agent of the Janmi, who, under a Power of Attorney, admits execution of the documents before the registering officer.

[2] I dare say they were when paddy was so cheap that the Michchāram received in kind hardly enabled the Janmi to meet the Government demand.

[3] I am not aware that where a mortgagee demands money, any deduction in Kāṇam is allowed. The Janmi is not liable to refund fees Within the last few years a practice has been introduced by certain Janmis of inserting a clause in the Kāṇam deed whereby the mortgagee is deprived of his right of holding for 12 years if he keeps rent in arrear or does any act to the prejudice of the Janmi. Sometimes it is provided that the land shall be surrendered *on demand*. In all these cases the mortgagee is entitled to the refund of a fraction of the fines and fees whereof the denominator is 12, while the numerator is the number of years out of 12 which still remain to run out. The Janmi, however, takes care to mention in the document only *a portion* of the fines, &c., actually received by him, and when it is remembered that only a certain fraction of the *principal* is claimable, and not interest thereon, the hardship this practice works on the tenant becomes clear.

the rate depending upon local custom, under the name of Sākshi, and he is under no obligation to return the fees of Oppu and Sūchi which he has received. If the mortgagor refuses payment upon demand, the mortgagee has a right to withhold the whole of the pāṭṭam yielded by the land in his possession until his claim is satisfied, or he may mortgage the land or sell his interest in it to another. He has no claim upon any other but the particular property mortgaged belonging to the mortgagor, or any right of causing the arrest of the mortgagor. If the mortgagor of his own accord tenders payment of the mortgage debt contrary to the wish of the mortgagee, he must pay the full amount without any deduction for Sākshi, and if the mortgagee has not held possession for three years, the mortgagor must return to him the Oppu and Sūchi fees which he has received. If the mortgagee [1] under this deed fails to pay the proprietor the purappād or residue after deducting the mortgage interest from the pāṭṭam, he forfeits all claim to the debt, and the proprietor has a right to demand restitution of the land. The Polichcheḻuttu claimable under this deeds seems intended as an equivalent for the tenant's profit, named Chērlābham, which he has derived from the land. On the demise [2] of the tenant it is a fine of entry to his successor. The amount of it and the frequency of its renewal seem to depend upon the quality of the soil and the quantity of Chērlābham which has been enjoyed by the tenant. The latter is generally ascertained by the competition of neighbours who offer better terms to the proprietor. In the Northern Division the practice of Ṣīlakāsu, or taking one year's pāṭṭam once in three or four years, or a quarter or a third of the pāṭṭam every year, as an equivalent for the Chērlābham, has prevailed in lieu of Poḷichcheḻuttu.

Notes.—1. See *Kāṇam* and the notes of judicial decisions appended thereto.

2. The foot-notes to Mr. Græme's text are by an experienced Native Revenue official of the district.

PAṬṬAN.

Corruption of Sanskrit *bhaṭṭam* (= a class of foreign Brāhmans). Honorific plural = *paṭṭar*, applied as a caste name.

Is the foreign Brāhmaṇ, not an aboriginal of Malabar. In the Pālghat and Temmalapuṛam Districts they are the chief money-lenders and traders.

PATTINNU RANDU.

(Dravidian) = literally, two in ten.

Is where the Kuḍiyān pays only 2 in 10 of the pāṭṭam to the Janmi, whatever the Nikuti may be, and the difference between the Nikuti and what remains is his profit and loss.

PEPPER-VINE.

By a vine in the public accounts is meant the standard tree supporting a number of pepper-vines, or as many pepper-vines as there may be clinging

---

[1] At present the law, except in the cases mentioned in Note 4, is, I believe, that the Janmi shall sue for rent from time to time, or set off the accumulated rent against the Kāṇam money at the end of the 12 years.

[2] This is obsolete now.

to a standard tree are reckoned as one. The vine of assessment, again, the Nikuti valli, is as many vines as produce a certain quantity of pepper; these are counted as one assessment-vine; the quantity is 15 Iḍangāḻis of pepper in the Southern Division.

Notes.—1. The 15 *Iḍangāḻis* were of green pepper, which would turn out about 6 *Iḍangāḻis* of dry pepper.

2. The pepper-vine assessment was abolished in 1806-7, and an export duty levied instead. This continued till 1874-75.

PERPETUAL LEASE.

Notes.—1. A perpetual lease is an absolute alienation of the land subject to a perpetual obligation of paying the quit-rent, but failure to pay the quit-rent will certainly not justify resumption of the land.—S.S.C., 405 (1854), 10 (1855).

2. A perpetual lease is irredeemable, but usually not assignable.—S.D.C., 188 (1877), 29 (1878), 374 (1878), and 236 (1879).

PEṚUM ARTHAM or AḺUKIYA AṬṬIPPĒR.

From Dravidian *Peṛum* (from *peṛuka* = to bring forth, to obtain, acquire, get) and Sanskrit *artham* (= aim, scope, object desired, gain, wealth, riches, money), and from Dravidian *Aḻukuka* (= to rot, decay) and *Aṭṭippēr* (q.v.).

- Is a deed under which the Janmi has received the full value of the property mortgaged and is not entitled to any, the smallest, share of the pāṭṭam, or even the smallest token of acknowledgment of proprietorship, but he withholds the ceremony of giving water that he may retain the empty title of Janmi.

Notes.—1. This tenure approximates closely to that of Otti, the mortgagee being in possession and enjoying the whole produce. The peculiarity of this transaction is that the sum advanced, which is always the full marketable value of the land for the time being, is not mentioned in the deed; and the landlord, in redeeming his property, does not repay the amount originally advanced, but the actual value of it in the market at the time of redemption. In other respects the same rules that apply to Otti mortgages are applicable to this also. Deeds of this kind are in use only at Pālghat and Temmalapuṛam.—(Proceedings of the Court of Sadr Adalat, No. 18, dated 5th August 1856.)

2. *Peṛum Artham* is a mortgage under which, when the mortgagor redeems, the mortgagee is entitled (before restoration of the mortgaged land) to be paid its market value at the time of redemption, not the amount for which the land was mortgaged.—1 I.L.R., Madras, 57.

3. *Query*: Was *Janmi*, as Mr. Græme says, an empty title after his share of the produce of the land had been thus mortgaged? It is contrary to all reason to think so. The *Janmi* still retained his "*water contact birthright*" (*Nīr-aṭṭi-pēṛu*), with various privileges attached to it. See *Aṭṭipēru*, *Janmam*, *Sthāna-māna-avakāṣam*.

PHALAM.

Sanskrit, probably from Dravidian *paḻam* (= ripe fruit), fruit especially of trees, result, produce.

Fruit, profit, compensation. Under the name of Kāval-phalam or compensation for protection the Zamorin in 933 M.S. levied a general tax of one quarter of a Vīrāy fanam upon every paṛa of seed-land specified in Pramāṇams or deeds.

A bearing tree.

Note.—It was in parts of Pālghat only that the Zamorin levied the tax.

PODI-CHĒṚU.

Poḍi, dust; *Chēṛu*, mud; alluding to the different states in which land is before and after the rains. The seed without preparation is sown in the dry land and the sprouted seed on the wet.

POḶICHCHEḺUTTU.

From Dravidian *poḷikka* (= to break open, undo) and Dravidian *Eḻuttu* (= writing).

A deed on the periodical renewal of leases, a new bond.

Literally, tearing (of documents). Is the remission or donation which the mortgagee makes periodically to the Janmi upon the amount of the debt and upon renewing the mortgage-bond. It was formerly renewed once in twelve years, the cycle in use before the present Malabar era, and generally speaking may be reckoned 2 in 10 upon the principal, but every family has its peculiar custom. At present the twelve years are not observed, but it depends on circumstances. The former principal is not reduced in the new bond; for instance, it might have been 1,000 fanams, and the Kāṇakkāran gives one or two hundreds to the Janmi ready money, but the 1,000 are brought into the new bond. It is not receivable when the mortgage has arrived at that stage which is called Otti, nor is it payable upon Kaḍan Vāyppa mortgage.

POTIPPĀḌU.

From Dravidian *poti* (= a measure) and Dravidian *pāḍu* (= falling, subjection, nature, measure of space, time).

Poti is a measure equal to 30 Iḍangāḻis, Potippāḍu is an extent of land which requires this quantity of seed to sow it.

POTIPPATTU.

From *Poti* (q.v.) and Dravidian *pattu* (= ten).

KAVATTU NEL.

From Dravidian *Kayattuka* (= to increase, raise) and Dravidian *nel* (= unhusked rice).

The tenth of the seed, the tax which pagodas used to receive from the Kuḍiyān's share in some Hōbalis in the Kavāi Tāluk. It seems to have been consolidated with the Sircar assessment upon the Company's first survey, and no adequate compensation provided for the pagodas.

PRABHU.

(Sanskrit) = lord, prince, chief of Nāyar militia.

A military chief or leader of a large force.

PRAMAṆI.

(Sanskrit) = chief, influential person.

Village arbitrators in the time of the Rājas, respectable inhabitants.

PRAVRITTIKKĀRAN.

(Sanskrit) = man of business. Often corruptly written Parputty or Parbutty.

The native collector of the revenue of a Hōbali or sub-division of a tāluk or district, of which there are in general from 9 to 15 to a district. It is rather a modern term, substituted for the ancient term of Pravrittikkāran.

PROPRIETORS.

It has been supposed (Mr. Warden's letter to the Board of Revenue, 16th June 1813) that there are 44,378 proprietors [1] in Malabar, the average revenue of whose estates is 480,000 pagodas, and that there are about 150,000 individuals who pay revenue direct to Government, whose payments do not exceed $3\frac{3}{16}$ pagodas each; that almost the whole [2] of the Janmam property is vested in pagodas and other religious establishments, and that about three-fourths of the land are held under foreclosed mortgages. This information is founded upon the account given in by the landed proprietors in 981 or 1805-6; but it has not been adverted to that an immense number of proprietors possess estates in several districts and different Hōbalis. The account of 981 was made out by Hōbalis, and a proprietor who has estates in many Hōbalis appeared separately in the account of each Hōbali, or perhaps three or four times in the account of a district, though properly he should only have been entered once. The number of proprietors is therefore swelled beyond all proper proportion, and their actual number is not supposed to exceed 15,000. The number of persons paying revenue direct is much exaggerated from the same cause, though the payment is certainly in very great detail and the number is no doubt very large who pay within one rupee. I have only, however, been able to see Hōbaliwar accounts, and many individuals have to pay in several Hōbalis of a district. There are no accounts to show how much each individual pays in each district. It has been stated that almost the whole of the Janmam property is vested in the pagodas and other religious establishments. Much of this property must, however, be considered to belong to individual Brāhmans to

---

[1] One-twentieth of them only pay revenue to Government.

[2] This was, *perhaps*, the state of things at the time this was written, but it is *not* at present, although Mr. Chattu Nambiār states that Dēvasvam lands form not less than one-third of the Malabar lands. There is probably some truth in the complaint, so frequently preferred of late, that the Ūrāḷars of Dēvasvams are converting into private (*i.e.*, Taṛavad) janmam lands belonging to the pagodas. It is however, I believe, well known that *all* Dēvasvams are not public institutions. Many are strictly private property. It is considered a great point to own a Dēvasvam, and many janmis, until quite recently, had a tendency to set apart for their Dēvasvam lands till then their Taṛavad property. Others, again, used to do the same in order to guard against lands being sold by posterity (it being considered sinful to dispose of pagoda property, but apparently not to misappropriate the produce thereof) or held responsible by Courts for debts contracted by the owners of the Dēvasvams.

whom the whole landed property is said at one time to have appertained. Taking the number of proprietors at 15,000, each estate may be reckoned to give 32 pagodas revenue, but it is conjectured that half of the whole revenue is due from estates yielding from 1,000 to 5,000 rupees assessment, though the proprietors do not themselves hold the lands in their possession or pay the assessment, the mortgagees being the occupants and paying the revenue. The mortgaging system has been considered injurious, because the mortgagee in possession could not improve his land without the risk of being dispossessed, without affording to the proprietor the temptation to demand more or to transfer possession to another; but it must be recollected that the proprietor cannot dispossess a mortgagee without foregoing the benefit which would be derivable to him if the mortgagee himself were to require payment of a deduction of 20 per cent. from the mortgage debt under the name of Sākshi; that it is not customary to alter a pāṭṭam long established upon an average estimate; that every fresh demand on the part of the proprietor for an increased rent diminishes his and strengthens the rights and interests of the mortgagee in the land, gives the latter an additional mortgage interest and an improved prospect of becoming the ultimate proprietor. By the gradual operation of this system the greater part of the mortgagees have indeed already become the virtual proprietors of the land. It seems to have been considered that lands were expressly and for the first time made over to mortgagees to [1] discharge an existing debt contracted from causes unconnected with the occupation of the land; but the fact is, I believe, that the money was almost invariably borrowed from tenants who were previously in possession. The origin of these loans seems to have been that the tenant should give a year's rent (pāṭṭam) in advance to the proprietor, either as a necessary security for payment or as a bonus for the profit he was allowed to enjoy, and the extravagance or necessities of the proprietor induced them to continue to borrow till the rights and interests of the mortgagee in the land became stronger than those of

---

[1] I do not believe that *in former times* the Kāṇam money was borrowed in order to discharge debts, for it will, I am sure, be found on investigation that in every case, without exception, the existing Kāṇam on any given land might have been borrowed on a mortgage of a *portion* of it. The fact is, I believe, that the money was received rather as security for rent. In short Kāṇam originally was not *mortgage* but was *lease*. *Otti* was mortgage. A janmi who assigned land on Otti did so because he was pinched for money. Of this, however, further on.

A "Kāṇam" is probably equivalent to the Roman *emphyteusis*, under which the tenant possessed the right of enjoying all the fruits, and disposing at pleasure of the thing of another, subject to the payment of a yearly rent to the owner (*dominus*). The idea of a 12 years' holding is quite modern. Indeed it originated, I believe, with Mr. Holloway, who, taking Kāṇam as equivalent to *emphyteusis*, is said to have substituted Vyāḻavaṭṭam or *jubilee*, and thence argued that under Kāṇam demise the tenant was entitled to hold for a Vyāḻavaṭṭam or 12 years.

The meaning of the term Kāṇam is not clear. It is said by some to be "small fee," "usufruct," the word being of Persian origin. The root may perhaps be "കാണുന്നു" to see, and the meaning, meaning "money secured on the land," *i.e.*, seen, visible, or mentioned in the deed ("കാണപ്പണം") as opposed to "കാണാപ്പണം," invisible money, *i.e.*, not secured on the land. The latter term is widely used in respect of renewal fees. Generally the word Kāṇam is used as meaning money, as in Kuḻikkāṇam, Veṭṭukāṇam, Tusikāṇam, &c.

the proprietor. The inherent principle of redemption which the mortgage of Malabar is described to possess, and which applies strictly to the Kāṇam tenure alone, is accountable for by the Chērlābham or cultivator's profit from the soil, which the proprietors have allowed them to possess independently of the deduction from the pāṭṭam on account of the mortgage interest. This is the origin of the Poḷichcheḻuttu, the Sākshi, which may be considered fines for the renewal of leases, of 10 and in some places 20 per cent., according to local custom and the degree of profit enjoyed by the tenant. Mr. Warden says truly that "The variety and number of the mortgage tenures, till they reach the deed which for ever alienates the janmam, affords the most conclusive evidence that can be adduced of the tenacity with which the ancient landholders clung to the janmam right." They may also be considered as the result of a circumspect and jealous[1] precaution on the part of the mortgagees, who, whenever they accommodated the necessities of the janmi, did not fail at the same time to add gradually but strongly to their securities for the ultimate acquisition of the proprietary right, for every step of the different mortgages involved a condition which increased the difficulty of transferring the land to any but the mortgagee.

Notes.—1. The foot-notes to Mr. Græme's text are by an experienced Native Revenue official of the district, Mr. P. Karuṇākara Mēnon. As regards the derivation of *Otti* the derivation shown in its proper place in this Glossary seems preferable; and as regards *Kāṇam*, the original meaning (supervision, protection) is fixed by Deeds 3 and 4, Appendix XII.

2. The number of Paṭṭadārs in Fasli 1290 (A.D. 1880-81) was 178,790.

3. See Chapter IV, Section (*a*) of the Text. The fact that the *chērlābham* or *koḻulābham* (*q.v.*), the cultivator's share of the produce, was "possessed independently of the deduction from the *pāṭṭam* on account of the mortgage interest" by the cultivator should have suggested to Mr. Græme that the thing which the *Janmi* mortgaged under *kāṇam, otti,* &c., was *not the soil itself,* but the *Janmi's* interest in the soil, his share of produce, the *pāṭṭam* in short. And this should also have suggested to him—that the *Janmi* had only a limited interest *in the soil*—that the *Janmi* was a co-proprietor *of the soil* not the *dominus* thereof.

PUKIL.

A crop.

PUNJA.

(Dravidian). The name of a rice which is always cut in Mēḍam or Eḍavam (April and May). It may be the only crop of the season, for some

[1] This is easily accounted for if Kāṇam is assumed to have been security) for rent. Under Kāṇam, then, the mortgagee (I use the word because it is convenient) used to enjoy large profits, and he could not well impose conditions on the janmi. When however, the latter became needy and assigned land on Otti, the profits to the tenant became smaller and he naturally demanded at least greater permanency of title. And here I may attempt to derive the term Otti. I believe it is derived from "ഒററൽ" (which see in Dr. Gundert's Dictionary). The verb is "ഒററുക," *i.e.*, to secure (fish) in an "ഒററൽ." The Otti holder secures the land to a certain extent, for the janmi cannot sell away to another without first giving the Ottidar the refusal.

lands only admit of one, or it may be the second or the third, but it must be the crop that is cut in Mēḍam or Eḍavam to entitle it to the appellation of punja.

PŪTTĀḌA.

From *pū* (Dravidian) = flower.

In the Northern Division of Malabar this species of rice is sown upon paṛamba land, whilst the kind of rice sown on lands overgrown with wood, which requires to be dug rather than ploughed, is called Punam.

REAS pronounced RAIS.

An imaginary coin introduced into the public accounts of the Malabar province, since the Company became possessed of it, from the Bombay Presidency. There are 100 of them to a quarter or 400 to one Bombay rupee.

REVENUE.

Different sources of the former revenues of Rājas in Malabar, viz. :—

Ankam.

(Dravidian) = fight, duel, battle-wager.

Was as high as 1,000 fanams or 250 rupees ; was only leviable by the Rāja. It was the money which he received as umpire between two combatants under the system of battle-wager. These quarrels arose from private feuds and were meant to wipe off stains cast upon an individual's honor. A preparation and training for twelve years preceded the battle in order to qualify the combatants in the use of their weapons. They were not necessarily the principals in the quarrel, generally their champions. They undertook to defend the cause they had espoused till death. It was indispensable that one should fall.

Battle-wager or trial by single combat was a source of considerable revenue to the Rājas in former times, for each combatant was obliged to deposit with the Rāja a certain sum of money. Women were the chief origin of the quarrels which occasioned these combats. They were confined to the Nāyars. They were thought necessary to prove or disprove the charge of seducing women under particular protection. It was not indispensable that the parties themselves in the quarrel should be the combatants. Champions were admitted, and, in general, substituted. The champions settled all their worldly affairs before the onset of the combat, for it was unavoidable that one must fall. A notification of twelve years took place before the day of combat.

Chunkam.

(Dravidian) = toll, custom.

Customs—land and sea—upon imports and exports. By some said to be only 2½ and 3 per cent., and by others as high as 10. Nāḍuvāḻis were also entitled to inland customs.

Ēḻa.

(Dravidian) = fine, penalty, exacting presents.

The systematic usurpation of the estates of such neighbouring Rājas or

Nāḍuvāḻis or other chiefs as might be incapacitated from poverty or other cause from governing. The Ṣāstra says the peculiar duty of a king is conquest.

KŌḺA OR CHĀRĀDĀYAM.

KŌḺA.

(Dravidian) = violence, forced contribution, extortion.

CHĀRĀDĀYAM.

From (? Dravidian) *chār* (= confidant, third person) and Sanskrit *ādāyam* (= gain, income).

Forced contributions levied by Rājas for particular emergencies according to the circumstances of the individuals.

TAPPU.

(Dravidian) = blunder.

Fines levied by Nāḍuvāḻis and Dēṣavaḻis from their inferiors, and by Rājas from them, for accidental unintentional crimes.

PIḺA.

(Dravidian) = slip, fault, fine.

Fines levied in the same manner for intentional crimes, according to the magnitude of the crimes and the circumstances of the individuals. It might be a total confiscation of property.

PURUSHĀNTARAM.

(Sanskrit) = the next generation, succession duty.

Literally, the death of the man. Sums varying from 120 to 1,200 fanams, levied by Rājas from Nāḍuvāḻis, Dēṣavāḻis, heads of commercial corporation, from the holders of lands in free gift or under conditional tenure, and generally all persons holding sthānam, mānam, or official dignities in the State. They also, in common with other Janmis or private proprietors, levied Purushāntaram from their tenants as a fine of entry upon the decease of a proprietor or tenant. It has been supposed that the Rājas were entitled under the head of Purushāntaram to a certain share of the property of deceased Māppiḷḷas, but the prevalent opinion is that there was no fixed proportion, and that it was not levied generally upon all Māppiḷḷas, but was confined to individuals possessed of wealth and holding situations or privileges dependent upon the will or favor of the Rāja. The Purushāntaram was sometimes enjoyed by the Dēṣavāḻi and Nāḷuvāḻi, instead of the Rāja, according to the extent of right and authority which was granted or usurped, and on all occasions they were exclusively entitled to the Purushāntaram of their own private lands.

PULAYĀṬṬA PEṆṆA.

(Dravidian) = lewd, adulterous women.

Pulayāṭṭa-peṇṇa, or degraded women, were a source of profit to Rājas; outcastes, not exclusively, but chiefly of the Brāhmān caste, they were made over to Rājas to take care of. As a compensation for their maintenance and for the trouble of preventing their going astray again, the family of the outcaste were in the habit of offering to the Rājas as far as 600 fanams or Rs. 150. The Rājas then disposed of them for money, but their future condition was not exactly that of a slave. They were generally bought by the coast merchants called Chetties, by whom they had offspring, who came to be intermarried among persons of the same caste, and in a few generations their origin was obliterated of the ramifications of new kindred into which they had been adopted.

PONNARIPPU.

(Dravidian) = (*pon*) gold, (*arippu*) sifting.

Ponnarippu, the sifting of gold, or, generally, gold dust, was considered a royalty and the perquisite of the Rājah or the Nāḍuvāḻi as the case might be.

ATTAḌAKKAM OR ATTĀLAḌAKKAM.

From Malayāḷam *attam* (= extremity, end) and Dravidian *aḍakkam* (= subjection, possession, enjoyment).

Under the name of Attaḍakkam the Rāja was entitled to the property of a Nāḍuvāḻi, or Dēṣavāḻi or an Aḍiyān (vassal), or any person who held lands in free gift, dying without heirs; and no Datt Swikāram or adoption could be valid without his sanction. A Nāḍuvāḻi and Dēṣavāḻi enjoyed the same privilege with respect to persons in the same manner dependent upon them.

AḌIMAPPAṆAM OR TALAPPAṆAM.

From *Aḍima* (q.v.) and Dravidian *tala* (= head) and Dravidian *paṇam* (= money).

Aḍimappaṇam was the yearly payment of 1 and 2 fanams which every Aḍiyān was obliged to pay to his Tamburān or patron, whether he was Rāja, Nāḍuvāḻi, Dēṣavāḻi, or other great man.

CHANGNGĀTAM.

(See note on this word in its proper place in the *Glossary*.)

Whenever a person wished to place himself under the special protection of a man of consequence, he paid from 4 to 64 fanams annually for Changngātam, or companionship or association, making sometimes an assignment on particular lands for the payment. It was meant for the maintenance of a kind of honorary sentinel, a belted official peon of the present times, whom the patron furnished to the person who sought his protection, but this implied also a necessity for the patron to assist with a stronger force if required in his defence.

RAKSHĀBHŌGAM.

(Sanskrit) = *Raksha*, protection, and *bhōgam*, enjoyment, hire.

Rakshābhōgam payments were much to the same extent and for the same purposes. It implies an engagement of protection generally without being limited to any specific aid in the first instance.

KĀḺCHA.

Verbal noun, from Dravidian *Kāṇuka* (= to see), means perception, offering, gift.

Note.—Compare *Kāṇam*.

(Answering to Nuzzur) or presents of from 2 to 1,000 fanams, according to the circumstances of the parties, of congratulation and condolence were made to Rājas and Nāḍuvāḻis by all ranks of people on occasions of the ascension of Rājas to their pattam or throne; of the opening of a newly-built palace, a marriage, a birth, the ceremony of placing rings on a child, and a death in the family of Rājas and Nāḍuvāḻis.

Aḍinynya Urukkal or Wrecks.

From *aḍinynya* (Dravidian) = touched bottom, drifted ashore, and *urukkal* (Dravidian) = vessel, ship.

Rājas alone were entitled to shipwrecked vessels or Aḍinynya Urukkal.

Chērikkal or private domains.

From Dravidian *chēri* (= assemblage, village), and, perhaps, Dravidian *kāl* (= foot, stem, quarter, place in general).

And they besides possessed extensive private domains in proprietary right, whether by purchases, lapses, or escheats, called Chērikkal.

Eimmula.

From Dravidian *ei* (= 5) and Dravidian *mula* (= udder).

Mummula.

From Dravidian *mu* (= 3) and Dravidian *mula* (= udder).

Chenkōmbu.

Literally, red (chem) horn (kombu).

Kaṇṇaḍappuḷḷi.

Literally, eye spotted.

Ānappiḍi.

Literally, elephant-catching.

Pūval.

Literally, spot or speck tail.

Kombu.

(Dravidian) = horn, ivory.

Kuṟaka.

(Dravidian) = the quarter, horn, thigh of an animal.

Vāl.

(Dravidian) = the tail of an animal.

Tōl.

(Dravidian) = the skin of an animal.

Kiṇattil-panni.

Literally, pig (fallen) into a well.

Rājas and Nāḍuvāḻis were besides entitled to *Eimmula* and *Mummular*, cows having 5 or 3 dugs; to *Chenkombu*, or cattle that had destroyed a man or any animal; to *Kaṇṇaḍappuḷḷi*, cattle having a white spot near the corner of the eye; *Ānappiḍi*, elephants caught; *Pūval*, a buffalo having a white spot at the tip of the tail; *Kombu*, the tusks of an elephant killed; *Kuṛaka*, the leg of a deer, wild hog, or other eatable wild animal; *Val*, the tail of a tiger; *Tōl*, its skin; and *Kiṇattil panni*, a hog fallen into a well.

MODERN LAND REVENUE.

The revenue in rice-lands, applying the existing professed rates of assessment per 100 paṛas to the average value, as fixed by Mr. Græme, of the *actual pāṭṭam as rendered by the Janmis in* 981, is Rs. 84 3 qrs. 52 reas per cent. in the Southern Division, and Rs. 72 1 qr. 15½ reas in the Northern Division of the pāṭṭam, or for the whole province Rs. 82 0 qr. 1¼ reas.

RICE.

According to Arshed Beg's Settlement of 1783-4 or M.E. 959 of the Southern Districts, exclusive of Pālghat:—

Total paṛas sowable	743,031	
Deduct fallow	38,386	
Sowable land	704,645	
	HOONS	F.
Revenue	231,481	4

Seed of rice sown, 3 paṛas per hoon or 1 paṛa per rupee.

RICE LANDS.

There are 231,114 cawnies of rice-land in the Malabar Province, with the exception of Wynād, according to the survey by measurement in 983, and according to Mr. Warden's abstract accompanying his report to the Revenue Board of 16th June 1813, of which 149,143 yield only one crop, 59,720 cawnies produce two crops, and 1,031 cawnies produce three crops; but deducting 24,214 cawnies for waste and for pagoda and other Ināms, there were remaining assessable to the revenue cawnies 209,899, of which 149,143 produce one crop only, 59,727 two crops, and 1,031 three crops. According to the Janma Pymaish accounts of 981 each cawny gives 67 standard paṛas and 3¼ Iḍangāḻis gross produce, and 5 rupees 42½ reas assessment, if the total revenue of 980 is applied to the total cawnies.

Note.—The rice-lands of the district are now supposed to measure, including Wynād, 393,411 acres, and excluding Wynād 366,466 acres, equivalent to 277,140 cawnies. The total revenue on the rice-lands is Rs. 11,65,921 or Rs. 2-15-5 per acre.

ROBBIN.

Is what in the English correspondence is understood by a mūḍa of rice. I cannot discover its origin.

SĀKṢHI.

(Sanskrit) = witnessing, evidence.

Means renewal or confirmation connected with Poḷichcheḻuttu; 2 in 10 is given for Sākshi upon the renewal of a mortgage-deed.

Note.—See *Pāṭṭōla*, *Poḷichcheḻuttu*.

SALT.

From Fasli 1216, the first year of the monopoly, to the end of Fasli 1227—

	S.PS.	F.	C.	S.PS.	F.	C.
The highest gross revenue				72,269	2	54
Deduct purchase price ..	23,169	22	39			
Deduct charges	2,127	19	64			
				25,296	42	23
Remaining highest net revenue				46,972	5	31
The average gross revenue				54,477	0	0
Deduct average purchase price.	17,739	0	0			
Deduct average charges ..	2,590	0	0			
				20,338	0	0
Remaining average net revenue				34,139	0	0

	GARCE.	M.	SEER.
The highest quantity sold in any year ..	2,563	84	11
Of which was exported out of Malabar ..	346	151	3

In Bombay the price rarely exceeds 2 rupees per ton. In 1821 it had risen to 6 and 7.—(*Bombay Gazette*, 18th April 1821.) A ton is 2,240 lb.; a Madras garce of Bombay salt (reckoning a paṛa at 90 lb. and 120 paṛas to a garce) is 10,800 lb. or 4 tons and 1,840 lb. The price of a Madras garce at 2 rupees a ton is therefore 9 rupees 2 quarters and 57 reas. The usual price at which Bombay salt has been bought in Malabar has been 13 rupees a coomb or 39 rupees a garce at Cannanore, Tellicherry, and Mahé, 42 at Calicut, and 45 at Ponnāni.—(Mr. Warden's report of 3rd October 1828). At 7 rupees a ton the price is Rs. 33 3 qr. the Madras garce.

According to a letter from Government to the Revenue Board, of 20th March 1820, the present average consumption of salt in all the territories under the Madras Presidency may be taken at 25,000 garces; reckon them at Rs. 112 the garce, monopoly selling price, they will come to 27,90,000 rupees; but reckoning 30 per cent. for prime cost and charges, the net revenue will be Rs. 19,53,000, or between 5 and 6 lakhs of pagodas. In this calculation there is nothing authenticated but the number of garces sold.

Note.—The annual average importations of salt for the five years preceding the introduction of the excise system was 4,239[1] garces. Since the introduction (1877) of the excise system the annual average importation has been 3,016 garces, *i.e.*, 19 garces of Government salt, 2,596 garces of duty prepaid salt, and 401 garces of foreign salt.

[1] Government salt, 3,956 garces; duty prepaid salt, 243 garces; foreign salt, 40 garces; total 4,239 garces.

SALT PANS.

The owners of salt pans in Malabar used before the monopoly to employ laborers for the manufacture of salt, or to let the pans out on rent or pāṭṭam. The pāṭṭam was not fixed for a length of time together as on rice-lands, but depended upon the annual produce. It is generally supposed to have been a third, leaving two-thirds to the manufacturer.

SHĀNĀR.

The name by which Tīyars or toddy-drawers are called in the Temmalapuram and Pālghat Districts, who are not aborigines of Malabar, but come from the districts to the east of the ghāts.

Note.—See *Īḻuvar* and *Tīyar*.

ṢISHT-BĀKKI.

From Sanskrit *Ṣishtam* (= remainder) and Arābic *bākki* (= surplus).

A balance of revenue uncollected from the person from whom due, in contradistinction to Dast-bākki, a balance collected but not brought to the account of Government.

ṢIṢU or TEI.

Ṣiṣu (Sanskrit) = young animal or plant. *Tei* (Dravidian) = shoot, young tree.

A young plant.

SLAVES.

Amount, taken in 1807, to 96,368.

Note.—In 1857, when the last census of slaves was taken, the number was found to be 187,812, of whom 148,210 had up to that time remained with their former masters. See *Cheṛumakkal.*

STHĀNA-MĀNA-AVAKĀṢAM.

From Sanskrit *Sthānam* (= standing, place, situation, rank) and Sanskrit *Mānam* (= honor, rank) and Sanskrit *Avakāṣam* (= title, claim, right).

Dignity and emoluments of a public situation.

Note.—This probably denoted the true position of a Janmi or holder of the "*water contact birthright*" (*Nīr-aṭṭi-pēru*). See *Aṭṭipēṛu, Janmam, Peṛumartham.*

ṢŪDRAN, plural ṢŪDRANMĀR.

(Sanskrit) = the fourth caste in the Hindu system.

Who according, to the Ṣāstram, are the fourth class of Hindus, are a particular caste of Nāyars in Malabar, whose duty it is to perform ceremonies or Karmam in Brāhman families on the birth of a child, &c.

Note.—Nāyars generally do now style themselves as Ṣūdras.

SVARŪPAM.

(Sanskrit) = one's own shape, image, idol, dynasty.

Means descent, family, race, house, answering to Vamṣam. The Calicut

Zamorin Rāja's family is called the Nāyaririppu (or vulgarly, Neḍiyirippu) Svarūpam, that of the Kaḍattanād Rāja is the Porḷātiri Svarūpam, that of the Chiṛakkal Rāja, Kōlattiri or Kōla Svarūpam, that of Kōṭṭayam or Cotiote the Puranāṭṭukara or Puṛāṭṭara Svarūpam, that of the Kuṛumbṛanād the Kuṛumbarātiri or Kuṛumbiyātiri Svarūpam. The Waḷḷuvanād Rāja is the Ārngngōṭṭu Svarūpam, the Cochin Rāja is the Perimbaḍappu Svarūpam, the Travancore Rāja is the Trippa or Trippāppu Svarūpam.

SVARŪPAKKŪṚ.

From *Svarūpam* (q.v.) and Dravidian *Kūṛu* (= part, share).

Office, dignity, and Kūṛu, share, partition, allotment. It means the property attached to the official rank of a Rāja.

SVARŪPAM.

See *Svarūpam*.

Head of a family. Ten necessary for a Kartāvu or lordship of 3,000 men.

TALA UḌAYA TAMBURĀN.

Literally = the head-possessing lord.

The Kartāvu or superior lord of a vassal.

TANḌU.

(Sanskrit) = palanquin hanging on silk cords.

An open palanquin, which in the Malabar Province is also called Manchal, and which Englishmen call Manchil. The attainment of the rank of Vāḷum-puḍavum is indispensable to qualify any person, whether a common man or a Rāja, to ride in a palanquin.

TAṚA.

(Dravidian) = foundation, mound, ground, village, quarter. Similar to Tamil and Malayāḷam *teru,* Telugu *teruvu,* Canarese and Tulu *teravu.*

A village. The same as Dēṣam in the Malabar Province.

Note.—See *Ūr* and *Dēṣam.* This and not the Dēṣam was the true village of Malabar, that is, it was the *Nāyar* village or unit of organization for civil purposes among the *Nāyars.* *Conf.* p. 88 of the text.

TAṚAVĀḌU.

From *Taṛa* (q.v.) and Dravidian *pāḍu* (= falling, falling into one's power, place, situation, rank, authority).

A house or family.

Note.—Compare *pāṭṭam.* Dr. Gundert defines the term as a house chiefly of noblemen, ancestral residence of landowners, a family. The term was applied only to the families of authority in the *Nāyar* village (Taṛa).

TAṚAVĀṬṬUKĀRAN OR PRAMĀṆI.

From *Taṛavāḍu* (q.v.) and Sanskrit *Kāran* (= doer, one who has to do with), and Sanskrit *Pramāṇam* (= measure, authority).

In every Dēsam four householders or Taṛavāttukārar possess a certain hereditary sthānam or dignity which points them out as the proper persons to apply to whenever a marriage, a death, a religious ceremony or dispute takes place. They are sometimes called Pramāṇi, or principal inhabitants, and latterly, under the Company's Government, Mukhyastanmār. They did not possess the Kōyma or controlling authority in the Dēsam, but were a kind of arbitrators. When a dispute could not be settled by their mediation it went to the Dēsavāḻi.

Names of former heads of villages.

Note.—Mr. Græme, contrary to previous notes, here states correctly, if Taṛa be submitted for Dēsam, the position of the *Taṛavāṭṭukkārar*. The *Dēṣavāḻi* was usually one of the *Taṛavāṭṭukārar* of his taṛa or village. See *Madhyastanmār* and *Mukhyastan*.

TARIṢU.

(Dravidian) = waste rice-land.

TINGALPPAṆAM.

From Dravidian *tingal* (= the moon) and Dravidian *paṇam* (= money).

General monthly levy on all classes of the inhabitants. One of the contributions levied in Malabar by the Rājas.

TIPPAḺI.

Is the same as Naḻi, a measure of which 4 go to a Iḍangāḻi. It is supposed that in Malabar a man has enough to eat if he has 1¾ Tippaḻis of rice and ½ Tippaḻi of conjee a day, or 1 Iḍangāḻi of paddy of 4 Calicut Nāḻis. There are many in a starving condition who get less, and many affluent who eat more.

TIRUVĀTIRA NYĀTTUTALA.

From *Tiruvātira* (= the sixth asterism, including Betelgeuze) and Dravidian *Nyāttutala* (= the time of a constellation).

Nyāttutala is a period of fourteen days. It is in the fourteen days commencing with about the 7th of Mithunam (June) that there must be constant rain for the proper growth of the pepper; the failure of this season may cause a difference of produce of perhaps 25 per cent.

TĪYAN.

Formerly written *Tīvan*, that is, islander (from Sanskrit *dvīpam*).

Toddy-drawer and cultivator of land. Upon asking a number of Brāhmans and Nāyars assembled at Calicut whether Tīyars were included among the Ṣūdraṣ of the Ṣāstra they professed ignorance, and said they must refer to the Ṣāstra. Their number, according to an account taken in 1807, was 128,045.

The Tīyan woman (Tīyatti) wears no cholee, or any cloth thrown over her shoulders and neck. Her body down to the waist is entirely exposed.

Notes.—1. See *Īḻuvan, Shānar.*

2. This caste now numbers 527,928 (Census, 1871).

TOBACCO.

Average annual consumption 1,500 candies of 640 lb., or 1¾ per head in the whole population.

TOḌUPPAṆAYAM.

From Dravidian *Toḍuka* (= to touch, feel, come into contact with) and *Paṇayam* (q.v.).

A deed in use.

***Notes.*—1. The land is here pledged as security for the repayment with interest of certain sums advanced, but the lender has no right to interfere in the management of the property. In some cases it is stipulated that no failure on the part of the borrower to pay the interest, the lender shall be placed in possession of the land. Where such stipulation exists the lender can sustain an action for possession. In other cases he must sue for the recovery of the principal and interest of the loan, the land being liable in the event of the money not being paid.—(Proceedings of the Court of Sadr Adalat, No. 18, dated 5th August 1856.)**

2. Another term for the same deed is *Chūndippaṇayam* (Dravidian *Chūnduka* = to point at).

TŪṢIKKĀṆAM.

From corruption of Sanskrit *Sūchi* (= a needle, iron style) and *Kāṇam* (q.v.).

Is the fee to the writer of a new mortgage-deed. This and the Oppu may amount to 7 per cent., sometimes more, sometimes less.

UḶA-PAṚAMBU.

***Uḷa* for *uḷavu* (Dravidian) = tillage, and *Paṛambu* (q.v.).**

Ploughable or arable highland by which the hill rice cultivation, or Mōḍan paṛamba, is distinguished from the plantations, which are more properly called paṛamba.

***Note.*—Applied to land made over temporarily for use.**

UṆḌAṚUTI.

From Dravidian *Uṇṇuka* (= to eat) and Dravidian *āṛuti* (end); literally, therefore, it means having eaten and ended, that is, the property is enjoyed until the money advanced has been fully recovered with interest.

Uṇḍaṛuti means a settlement[1] (of the debt) by the enjoyment of the profits by the usufruct. It is a species of mortgage which seems to answer to the Vivum Vadium, where the mortgagee holds the estate till the rents and profits repay the sum borrowed; with this exception, that the pāṭṭam or rent is previously determined, and it is therefore known beforehand in how many years the debt will be liquidated, and the mortgagee is under no necessity of rendering to the proprietor an account of the produce of the estate.

In this deed the pāṭṭam being first determined and specified, whether in rice or garden lands or in grain or money, a provision[2] is made out of it

---

[1] *Uṇḍaṛuti* is, I conceive, a lease. The full rent for the term of the lease is paid in advance. In fixing the rent, of course the tenant will take care to see that only the *present worth* is offered and paid. An Uṇḍaṛuti lessee is never entitled, as a matter of right, to cancel the lease. In any case he would get back no interest for the reason just advanced.

[2] Not that I know of.

to the mortgagee for the interest of the debt at the rate agreed upon, and a further provision for such a share of the pāṭṭam as shall, within a certain time, repay the principal. If the mortgagee relinquishes the land before the expiration of the time and claims the debt, the mortgagor may take credit for the amount which the mortgagee has received, during the period he has been in possession, out of the fund allotted towards the discharge (not of the interest, but) of the principal, and from the remainder he is entitled to deduct 23 per cent. for Sākshi and Sūchi. The mortgagee having undertaken the responsibility of the management, this deduction is considered a just fine for his breach of engagement.

Example.

	PANAMS.
The amount of the debt is	100
The annual pāṭṭam is	10
The interest to be received by the mortgagee at 5 per cent. is	5
The share of the pāṭṭam to be received by the mortgagee towards the discharge of the principal is per annum	5
Which will thus be paid in 20 years.	
The mortgagee has enjoyed possession, say, 8 years, when he wishes to throw up; he has therefore received	40
Which, being deducted from the original sum, leaves	60
A deduction of 23 per cent. from the latter sum on account of Sākshi and Sūchi amounts to ..	13⅘
Leaving the balance to be paid to the mortgagee ..	46⅕

It has been[1] said that the mortgagee does not receive the Koḻulābham or cultivator's profit, but according to my inquiries he is entitled to it.

The interest under the Uṇḍaṟuti deed is greater than that under the principal deeds of mortgage which have their rise from the Kāṇa Janma Maryāda. It is generally 10 per cent.

Though it affords the means of early liquidating the debt, it is considered in a less friendly light by the mortgagee in general than the Paṇaya Pāṭṭōla deed. It is true he recovers his money, but what he receives annually is probably expended annually, and at the end of the specified period he does not become the laird of the land. It is a mere mercantile speculation which does not add to his dignity. The old proprietor, on the contrary, prefers this kind of tenure; for though he suffers deprivation for a period, he is ultimately restored to his station of proprietor of the soil.

Notes.—1. The foot-notes to Mr. Græme's text are by an experienced Native Revenue official.

2. The tenant is much in the same position as a Kāṇam mortgagee having possession and recovering the interest of his money from the rent produce of the land. Instead, however, of making over the surplus pro-

[1] Major Walker's treatise on Mortgages.

duce to the landlord, he places it to his credit in account, to be applied to the reduction of the principal. As soon as the principal is in this manner repaid, the mortgagee must restore the land to the proprietor.—(Proceedings of the Court of Sadr Adalat, No. 18, dated 5th August 1856.)

3. *Uṇḍaṛuti* is a species of mortgage, the nature of which is to absorb the principal amount in the profits of the mortgaged property till it is reduced to nothing.—N.D.C., 25 (1874).

ŪR or KARA.

Ūr (Dravidian) = village, hamlet. *Kara* (Dravidian) = shore, bank, hamlet.

A collection of houses in different directions, a number of which constitute a Dēṣam. Houses are generally built round a tract of paddy land, and, according to their bearings, are named Vaḍakku kara (a collection to the north), Tekku kara, and so forth. The Ūrus or Karās have no separate boundaries and no distinct names, but are comprehended in the Dēṣam.

Notes.—1. See *Taṛa* and *Dēṣam.*

2. These were probably congeries of houses inhabited by husbandmen, cultivators, subordinate to the *Dēṣavāḻi* in military, and to the *Taṛavāṭṭu Kāranavar* in civil, matters.

ŪRĀLAN.

From *Ūr* (q.v.) and Dravidian *āḷ* (= person, able person). Their office *Ūrānma* or *Ūrāyma.*

May be considered the patron or founder of a pagoda, whether established in the time of Paraṣurāma or in more recent times by Brāhmans or Rājas.

Notes.—1. When the pagoda is itself the property of the family, by the custom of Malabar the lands attached thereto are alienable as any other private possession.—M.S.C., 64 (1861). A sale of *Ūrāyma* right is invalid. —N.D.C., 34 (1874). Lands attached to a pagoda cannot be alienated by the whole body of *Ūrāḷar.*—N.D.C., 102 (1843). *Ūrāḷar* cannot sell their rights.—7 M.H.C.R., 210; 1, I.L.R., Madras I, 235.

2. See *Dēṣam.*

VAKACHCHAL.

From Dravidian *vakayuka* (= to divide).

The share of 2 in 10 in the pāṭṭam, in kind, which the Rājas used to receive in the northern districts, before Hyder's conquest, from all but the pagoda lands, after which, in 953, the Huzzur Nikuti or the basis of the present assessment was established. The Vakachchal is said to have been introduced first in 907, when the Ikkery or Bednore Government first invaded Malabar.

VAKACHCHA(L)KKĀRAN.

From *Vakachchal* (q.v.) and Sanskrit *Kāran* (= doer, one who has to do with).

The collector of the share (of the pāṭṭam). He held the situation under the Rājas formerly nearly corresponding to the Pravartti of the present day.

Note.—See *Pravrittikkāran* and *Vāram.*

VAKKU.

(Malayāḷam) = hemp. From *Vala* (Dravidian) = net, hence *Valkkuka* or *Vakkuka* = to catch fish and *vakku*, the material used for lines.

Hemp. It is sown in paṛamba land, but it is supposed to thrive best in the land called Paḷḷiyāl, which has a sufficient command of water without being too low. The cultivation of it has extended of late years in consequence of the encouragement given to it by the canvas manufactory at Beypoor, but in the Kiḷakkampuṛam and Vaḍakkampuṛam and Pōlnād Districts there is an ancient prohibition against its culture, as there is against that of ginger and against the use of buffaloes for ploughing, said to have been issued by a Rāja of these districts, from whom the Zamorin Rāja usurped them, and who has since become the Kaḍattanād Rāja.

VALLI and VITTU.

Valli from *val* (Dravidian) = strong, means proper subsistence given in kind to slaves or laborers. *Vittu* (Dravidian) = seed.

Is the charges of cultivation, and with Vittu or the seed is called Vittu-valli. As the hire of labor applies only to slaves, Kūli or Cooly is the term when free men are employed. Vittu-valli comprehends the expense of ploughing, of digging, of sowing, of manuring, of weeding, and of threshing. (On the Eastern Coast the paddy is trod by bullocks, in Malabar by men.) The Valli is reckoned to amount to a third of the gross produce (deducting always 10 per cent. for reaping), but where the produce falls short of seven-fold the Valli exceeds this proportion. It must be paid, it is supposed, out of the Koḷulābham or the cultivator's profit.

Mr. Rickards, in his proposed settlement for Malabar, recommends the quantity of seed sown and an equal quantity for charges to be deducted on account of Vittu-valli from the gross produce, and the different shares to be determined on the remainder. The proportion to the gross produce varies according to the quality of the soil and its estimated produce. (See the account given by the Janmis to Mr. Rickards in 978.) The lowest sort of land in this statement is supposed to produce three-fold only, which is $33\frac{4}{10}$ per cent., the highest thirty-fold, which is only $3\frac{4}{10}$ per cent. of the gross produce for Vittu-valli.

Note.—See *Koḷulābham, &c.*

VĀḶUM-PUḌAVUM.

Vāḷ (Dravidian) = sword. *Puḍavu* (Dravidian) = double cloth.

Is a certain rank conferred upon Rājas and Nāḍuvāḷis, the external ceremony of which is conferring a sword and some cloth. To a Rāja the ceremony is performed by a Nambūripād Brāhman, and to a Nāḍuvāḷi by a Rāja. Money is given on these occasions by the person upon whom the honor is conferred.

VĀLUMĒL KOḌI.

Literally = colored tip of the tail.

A buffalo having a white tip to the tail, belonging to individuals, became the property of Dōsavāḷis in former times as one of their privileges.

VANŌKKI.

Perhaps from *Vānam* (Dravidian) = sky, and *nōkkunnu* (Dravidian) = to look, observe, meaning crops dependent on the sky, rain-fed.

Same as Punam and Mōḍan.

VARGE.

A word used in the early records of Malabar. From the Portuguese word Varja, and means field or meadow.

VASTU and VASTU-MUTAL.

Vastu (Sanskrit) = substance, matter, thing, property, weighty action, provender. *Mutal* (Dravidian) = beginning, blossom, principal or capital, stock in trade, property, money.

Means generally the landed property of an individual; to include the personal property it is necessary to say Vastu-mutal.

VEḶḶAKKĒḌU.

From Dravidian *veḷḷam* (= water) and Dravidian *kēḍu* (= destruction, loss, damage).

Loss by flood. In fixing the pāṭṭam for the Kuḍiyān remission is allowed on this account.

VEYILKKĒḌU.

From Dravidian *veyil* (= sunshine) and Dravidian *kēḍu* (= destruction, loss, damage).

Injury by heat or drought. In fixing the pāṭṭam in Malabar permanent allowance appears to have been made on this account.

VIḶACHCHAL MĒNI-PĀṬṬAM.

Viḷachchal, from Dravidian *viḷa* (= vegetation, crop), means produce of corn, ripe crop. *Mēni* (Dravidian) = body, shape, sample, average. *Pāṭṭam* (q.v.).

Is the pāṭṭam deducible from taking, according to Mr. Rickards' proposed settlement, two-thirds of the Viḷachchal or gross produce of the Janmi Pymāish account of 981, after deducting a quantity equal to the quantity of seed sown, and one-third for the cultivator's share. In the Malabar Province, with the exception of Wynād, it amounts to standard paṛas 6,210,562 and 5 Iḍangāḻis. It is to be distinguished from the Veṛumpāṭṭam of the same account, which is the quantity stated by the Janmis to be actually receivable by them from their tenants. It amounts to standard paṛas 5,910,375 and 3 Iḍangāḻis. The Viḷachchal-mēni-pāṭṭam with respect to gardens is two-thirds of the gross produce according to Mr. Rickards' proposed settlement.

Note.—See *Pāṭṭam* and *Koḻulābham*.

VĪḶUMPAḌI.

From Dravidian *vīḻuka* (= to fall) and Dravidian *paḍi* = measure, at the rate of, according to).

Is a mode of agreement in practice between the Janmi and Kuḍiyān in Kiḻakkampuṛam and Vaḍakkampuṛam of the Calicut Tāluk.

Suppose that in the Sirkar accounts the land is entered as requiring to be sown upon it	20 paṛas.
The original assessment of Arshad Beg at 3 gold fanams per paṛa make ..	60 gold fanams.
To which being added 1 in 10 the increase by the Rājas	6 do.
Total ..	66 do.
Then suppose that the total pāṭṭam is.	100 paṛas.
That the interest upon 400 gold fanams lent by Kuḍiyān to the Janmi be deducted	20 do.
There remain ..	80 do.
Which, at the rate of agreement between them, is	80 fanams.
From this deduct the assessment ..	66 do.
There remains to be paid by the Kuḍiyān	14
But it is agreed that the Kuḍiyān shall pay on the number of paṛas fixed as interest the same proportion of assessment as the Janmi pays upon the whole land; this upon 20 paṛas makes	13¼ gold fanams.
Which being added makes as the amount which the Kāṇakkāran is to give to the Janmi	27½ do.

It has above been explained to mean the proportion of the public assessment which a Kāṇakkāran agrees to pay out of his share of the produce in common with the Janmi. Refers also to a mode of levying the assessment in Waḷḷuvanād, &c., tāluks on Mōḍan and hill produce. For instance, the permanent jamma under these heads being in any village considered to be 100 fanams, an annual inspection of the produce takes place, and 2 in 10 being assumed as the Sirkar share, this share is valued at a higher or lower rate on the different lands as may be necessary to bring the jamma exactly to 100 fanams. As a farther illustration, the Sirkar share of the produce might, in one year, be 100 paṛas; one fanam would accordingly be fixed as the rate for 10 Iḍangāḻis. In another year the Sirkar share of the produce might be only 80 paṛas; the rate would then be a fanam for every 8 Iḍangāḻis. In both cases the total amount would be equal. Vīḻumpaḍi means generally proportion, ratio, rate.

VIRIPPU.

(Dravidian) = bedding, crop cut in August and September.

The name of a rice which has only one crop in the year, and that crop is only cut in Kanni (September and October).

VITTUPĀḌU.

From Dravidian *vittu* (= seed) and Dravidian *pāḍu* (= falling, falling into power of, rank, nature, measure of space and time).

Answers to Verripadoo in Tamil and Beenjivurree in Hindustani. It means seed-land, that is, the quantity of seed which any land requires to sow it for a single crop. That is, suppose a land takes 10 paṛas to sow it or one crop and that it yields three crops. It would altogether require 30 paṛas for the different crops, but it would be called only a 10-paṛa Vittupāḍu.

A specific superficial extent in cawnies or acres is not to be ascertained merely by the quantity of seed required to sow any land, because bad soil requires a larger, and good soil a smaller, quantity to sow it in the same extent of land.

Note.—See *One Paṛa Seed Land.*

VYĀḺAVAṬṬAM.

From *vyāḻam* (Sanskrit) = the planet Jupiter, and *vaṭṭam* (Dravidian) = a circle; means the cycle of Jupiter, about 12 years.

A cycle of 12 years, to which all transactions in Malabar had reference previous to the establishment of the present Malabar era,—renewal of leases, bonds, and rent of gardens. Each year of the cycle was named alternately from the 12 signs of the Zodiac, and as months were distinguished in the same way, the name of the month and the name of the year might often be the same in a deed.

Note.—The word *āṇḍu*, in the Jews' Deed (No. 1) and in the old *Kāṇam* Deed (No. 4) printed in Appendix XII, signified this cycle of Jupiter, or a cycle of 60 years.

VYAVAHĀRAMĀLA.

From Sanskrit *vyavahāram* (= dealings, usage, practice of Courts, lawsuit) and Sanskrit *māla* (= garland, wreath, necklace).

A book containing the law of division of produce between the cultivator and proprietor, without allusion to any assessment which did not at that time exist.

Note.—As matter of fact, the *Vyavahāramāla* is more taken up with judicial matters than with matters agricultural.

APPENDIX XIV.

A.—ANJENGO FACTORY AND RESIDENCY.

List of Chiefs and Residents.

Factory established in	1684
John Brabon, Chief about	1710
Alexander Orme, do.	1723
Hezakiah King, do.	1729
William Wake, do.	1735
The factory records extant commence from 1st August	1744

—	Date of assuming charge.	Date of retirement.	Remarks.
Chiefs.			
R. Bouchier ..	....	1st February 1750..	Was Chief on 1st Aug. 1744.
T. Byfeld	2nd February 1750..	5th March 1751.	
T. Hodges	5th March 1751..	7th April 1752.	
W. Hornby, acting ..	8th April 1752..	14th May 1752.	
G. Scott	15th May 1752..	27th March 1757.	
I. Spencer	28th March 1757..	12th September 1758.	
C. Crommelin ..	13th September 1758..	20th April 1759.	
I. Whitehill ..	21st April 1759..	8th September 1769..	Died at Anjengo.
W. Taylor, acting ..	8th September 1769..	9th December 1769.	
P. E. Wrench ..	10th December 1769..	16th February 1774.	
S. Ewart, acting ..	17th February 1774..	23rd March 1774.	
N. Slackhouse ..	24th March 1774..	12th February 1776..	The Chiefship was now reduced to a Residency.
Residents.			
G. Bigger, acting ..	13th February 1776..	31st December 1776.	
J. Torlepo	1777..	8th December 1780..	Diary missing.
J. Morley	9th December 1780..	10th December 1781.	
J. Hutchinson, acting	11th December 1781..	22nd March 1782..	Mr. Hutchinson was appointed Cochin Commissioner, but in five months he returned to Anjengo and died there.
Do. confirmed.	23rd March 1782..	24th February 1796.	
I. T. Dyne, acting ..	25th February 1796..	17th July 1796.	
J. Hutchinson ..	18th July 1796..	11th October 1797.	
I. T. Dyne, acting ..	12th October 1797..	22nd February 1798.	
G. Parry	23rd February 1798..	3rd September 1803.	
A. W. Handley ..	4th September 1803..	1st July 1808..	Died at Anjengo.
I. T. Dyne, acting ..	1st July 1808..	27th October 1808.	
I. Smee	28th October 1808..	27th December 1809.	
R. Coward	28th December 1809..	10th December 1810..	Factory abolished and Anjengo transferred to the Political Resident, Travancore.

B.—TELLICHERRY FACTORY AND RESIDENCY.

List of Chiefs and Residents.

——	Date of assuming charge.	Date of retirement.	Remarks.
Chiefs.			
Robert Adams ..	....	10th March 1728..	Chief.
John Braddyll ..	10th March 1728..	17th December 1732.	
Stephen Law ..	17th December 1732..	27th February 1739.	
William Wake ..	27th February 1739..	8th November 1742.	
William Jeynson ..	8th November 1742.	8th February 1743..	Provisional.
John Geekie ..	8th February 1743..	20th January 1746.	
George Dudley ..	20th January 1746..	13th May 1747.	
William West ..	13th May 1747..	20th May 1748..	Provisional.
Robert Rawdon ..	20th May 1748..	31st October 1748..	Died.
Thomas Byfeld ..	31st October 1748..	17th January 1750.	
Thomas Dorrill ..	17th January 1750..	3rd January 1754..	Suspended.
John Sewell and Thomas Hodges.	} 3rd January 1754..	13th March 1754..	Supravisors.
Thomas Hodges ..	15th March 1754..	13th February 1762..	Chief.
William Hornby ..	13th February 1762..	30th April 1764.	
Thomas Byfeld ..	30th April 1764..	28th September 1765..	Died.
Harry Huet ..	28th September 1765.	13th November 1765.	
James Ryley ..	13th November 1765.	13th January 1767.	
William Hornby ..	13th January 1767..	10th December 1768.	
Daniel Draper ..	10th December 1768..	10th January 1770.	
Rawson Hart Boddam	10th January 1770..	4th March 1776..	Chiefship reduced to Residency.
Residents.			
William Ashburner ..	4th March 1776..	7th March 1777.	
Richard Church ..	7th March 1777..	22nd January 1781.	
Samuel Stedman and Michael Firth.	} Factors in charge to May 1781.		
William Freeman ..	21st May 1781..	18th January 1784..	Chiefship restored.
Chiefs.			
Richard Church ..	18th January 1784..	14th February 1785.	
J. Beaumont	14th February 1785..	5th June 1786.	
William Page and George Paterson.	} Factors in charge to 24th November 1786.		
William Lewis ..	24th November 1786..	24th December 1789.	
Robert Taylor ..	24th December 1789..	27th July 1794..	Factory abolished.

C.—SUCCESSION OF COMMISSIONERS, SUPRAVISORS, PRINCIPAL COLLECTORS AND COLLECTORS IN THE PROVINCE OF MALABAR.

Names.	Designation.	From	To	Period.	Remarks.
				Y. M. D.	
W. G. Farmer, Esq. Major Alexander Dow	Commissioners for inspecting the countries ceded by Tippu Sultan.	18th March 1792	11th September 1792		
W. G. Farmer, Esq. William Page, Esq. Major Alexander Dow	Do. do.	12th Sept. 1792	17th December 1792		
W. G. Farmer, Esq. J. Duncan, Esq. W. Page, Esq. Charles Boddam, Esq. Major Alexander Dow	Do. do.	18th Dec. 1792	11th October 1793		
W. G. Farmer, Esq.	Supravisor of the Province of Malabar.	18th March 1793	25th February 1794		
James Stevens, Esq.	Do. do.	25th February 1794	24th December 1794		
A. W. Handley, Esq.	Ag. do. do.	24th Dec. 1794	17th May 1796		
T. Wilkinson, Esq. Lieut.-Colonel A. Dow A. W. Handley, Esq. Robert Rickards, Esq.	Commissioners for executing the office of Supravisor and Chief Magistrate of the Province of Malabar.	18th May 1796	2nd August 1796		
T. Wilkinson, Esq. Lieut.-Colonel A. Dow Robert Rickards, Esq.	Do. do.	3rd August 1796	24th February 1797		
James Rivett, Esq. T. Wilkinson, Esq. Lieut.-Colonel A. Dow Robert Rickards, Esq.	Do. do.	25th February 1797	14th April 1797		
J. Rivett, Esq. Richard Torin, Esq. Lieut.-Colonel A. Dow Robert Rickards, Esq.	Do. do.	15th April 1797	25th April 1797		
John Spencer, Esq. Robert Torin, Esq. Lieut.-Colonel A. Dow Robert Rickards, Esq.	Do. do.	26th April 1797	19th September 1797		

John Spencer, Esq. Major-General Hartley Richard Torin, Esq. Robert Rickards, Esq.	Do. do.	20th Sept. 1797	30th October 1797		
John Spencer, Esq. Major-General Hartley J. Smee, Esq.	Do. do.	1st Nov. 1797	13th May 1798		
John Spencer, Esq. Major-General J. Hartley Joshua Uthoff, Esq. J. Smee, Esq.	Do. do.	14th May 1798	December 1799		
John Spencer, Esq. J. Smee, Esq.	Do. do.	January 1800	22nd February 1800		
John Spencer, Esq. J. Smee, Esq. Lieutenant Joshua Watson	Do. do.	22nd February 1800	9th March 1800		
J. Spencer, Esq. J. Smee, Esq. Major A. Walker	Do. do.	10th March 1800	30th September 1801		
Major Macleod	Principal Collector	October 1801	March 1803	2 7 0	
Robert Rickards, Esq.	Do.	March 1803	Do. 1804	1 0 0	
Thomas Warden, Esq.	Do.	Do. 1804	December 1816	12 10 0	
James Vaughan, Esq.	Do.	December 1816	January 1826	9 2 0	
William Sheffield, Esq.	Do.	January 1826	February 1831	5 1 0	
A. F. Huddleston, Esq.	Do.	February 1831	August 1832	1 6 0	
F. F. Clemenston, Esq.	Do.	August 1832	February 1839	6 7 0	
W. E. Underwood, Esq.	Ag. do.	February 1839	October 1839	0 9 0	
E. P. Thompson, Esq.	Ag. do.	November 1839	February 1840	0 3 0	
H. V. Conolly, Esq.	Collector	February 1840	September 1855	15 7 0	Assassinated 11th September 1855, 8-30 P.M.
T. Clarke, Esq.	Ag. do.	September 1855	October 1856	1 0 0	
W. Robinson, Esq.	Ag. do.	October 1856	May 1858	1 8 0	
P. Grant, Esq.	Ag. do.	June 1858	April 1862	3 11 0	
G. A. Ballard, Esq.	Collector	May 1862	25th March 1869	6 9 25	Appointed Resident, Travancore and Cochin.
E. C. G. Thomas, Esq.	Ag. do.	March 1869	27th August 1869	0 6 3	

C.—SUCCESSION OF COMMISSIONERS, SUPRAVISORS, PRINCIPAL COLLECTORS AND COLLECTORS IN THE PROVINCE OF MALABAR—(*Continued*).

Names.	Designation.	From	To	Period.	Remarks.
				Y. M. D.	
A. McC. Webster, Esq. ..	Collector	27th August 1869 ..	1st April 1870 ..	0 7 4	
A. MacGregor, Esq.	Do.	8th April 1870 ..	20th March 1876 ..	5 11 12	Appointed Resident, Travancore and Cochin.
W. Logan, Esq.	Ag. do.	6th June 1875 ..	20th March 1876 ..	0 9 15	
Do.	Collector	21st March 1876 ..	6th February 1878 ..	1 7 16	
D. Buick, Esq.	Ag. do.	7th February 1878 ..	8th May 1878 ..	0 3 1	
W. Logan, Esq.	Collector	9th May 1878 ..	21st April 1879 ..	1 1 12	
C. W. W. Martin, Esq. ..	Ag. do.	22nd April 1879 ..	4th May 1879 ..	0 0 13	
G. MacWatters, Esq. ..	Ag. do.	11th June 1879 ..	22nd November 1880 ..	1 5 0	
W. Logan, Esq.	Collector	23rd November 1880 ..	3rd February 1881 ..	0 2 11	Appointed Commissioner, Malabar Land Tenures.
G. MacWatters, Esq. ..	Ag. do.	4th February 1881 ..	19th April 1882 ..	1 2 15	
C. L. B. Cumming, Esq. ..	Ag. do.	20th April 1882 ..	23rd June 1882 ..	0 2 3	
W. Logan, Esq.	Collector	24th June 1882 ..	11th November 1882 ..	0 4 17	
L. R. Burrows, Esq. ..	Ag. do.	12th November 1882 ..	18th January 1883 ..	0 2 6	
W. Logan, Esq.	Collector	23rd January 1883 ..	27th April 1883 ..	0 3 4	Appointed Acting Resident, Travancore and Cochin.
C. A. Galton, Esq.	Ag. do.	28th April 1883 ..	12th October 1884 ..	1 5 14	
V. A. Brodie, Esq.	Ag. do.	13th October 1884 ..	21st November 1884 ..	0 1 9	
W. Logan, Esq.	Collector	22nd November 1884 ..	....	....	

APPENDIX XV.

Proclamation.

The Government of Fort St. George having received information through various channels that great inequalities exist in the present revenue jamabundy of the province of Malabar, transmitted orders some time back to the Principal Collector to frame by survey and assessment a new jamabundy upon improved principles founded on a liberal consideration of the relative rights of the Sirkar, of the proprietor and cultivator. Those orders the Principal Collector has now determined to carry into immediate and due execution.

It is well known to be considered a just system of assessment for the Government to derive its land revenue from the *pāṭṭam* (or net rent) payable by the cultivator's tenant to his proprietor.

To establish a fixed rule by which the *pāṭṭam* shall be calculated and ascertained, it must be in the recollection of every one that the principal Malabar Rājas, Head Nambūtiris and Mukhyasthans in each district were some months ago assembled by summons at Calicut, and, after the most patient inquiry into the mode by which the *pāṭṭam* was usually rated, it was found that a variety of systems prevailed, which might chiefly be ascribed to the existing inequalities in the revenue in the different districts in the province.

In order to rectify such errors and establish a permanent revenue by which one ryot shall neither be more heavily nor more favorably assessed than another, it became obviously convincing and desirable to all parties that one uniform system should obtain in estimating the *pāṭṭam* on which the Sirkar revenue was to be fixed.

Having fully and deliberately discussed the many points connected with so material a question and pretty accurately ascertained the customs which in former times regulated the *pāṭṭam* on lands and gardens generally throughout the province, the aforesaid Rājas, Head Nambūtiris and Mukhyasthans at length unanimously concurred in certain fixed principles whereby to determine the Sirkar revenue, which they [1] recorded and authenticated by their several signatures.

Those being the very principles which the Right Honorable the Governor in Council had formally and finally confirmed and ordered to be adopted in framing the new assessment of Malabar, they are now hereunder written and hereby published for the information of all its inhabitants.

First—On wet or rice grounds after deducting from the gross produce the seed and exactly the same quantity for expenses of cultivation and then allotting one-third of what remains as *koḻu-lābham* (or plough profit) to the *kuḍiyān*, the residue or *pāṭṭam* is to be divided in the proportion of six-tenths to the Sirkar and four-tenths to the *janmakkār*;

---

[1] *Treaties, &c.*, ii, CCXLII—CCXLIII.

Secondly—On *parambu* or orchard lands one-third of coconut, supary, and jack-tree produce being deemed sufficient for the *kudiyān*, the remainder or *pāṭṭam* is to be equally divided between the Sirkar and *janmakkār*; and,

Thirdly—On dry grain lands (which are very scantily cultivated in Malabar) the Sirkar's share is to be half of the *janmakkār's vāram* on what is actually cultivated during the year.

The assessment on the pepper produce will be fixed upon hereafter.

The new paymash on the preceding principles has in the first instance been entrusted to the execution of the several Subordinate Collectors, to whom the necessary orders have been issued.

As the present mode of assessment has been acknowledged to be fair and moderate, it is expected that the *janmakkārs* will render a true and faithful account of the *pāṭṭam* of their estates at the cutcherries of the Subordinate Collectors, who on their parts will take care that every assistance shall be given by the local revenue servants in each district as the *janmakkārs* belonging to it might want to obtain information from their tenants relative to the existing state of their landed property. A form will be likewise given to the several *janmakkārs* by order of the Sub-Collectors, agreeably to which the required accounts are to be drawn out.

After these accounts are all delivered in, a rigid scrutiny will be made and the fullest means devised to ascertain their accuracy. The true result will then be submitted for the approbation of the Board of Revenue and Government, under whose sanction the Principal Collector will visit each district for the purpose of granting sealed and signed *pattas*, or assess notes to the several *janmakkārs* and other inhabitants, specifying the correct annual revenue they are to pay to the Company's Government.

The Principal Collector therefore confidently expects that, without making themselves liable to punishment by any act of palpable fraud or deception, the inhabitants will willingly and readily render exact accounts of their property, in order that all their apprehensions might be dissipated by the early establishment of an unalterable assessment.

(Signed) T. WARDEN,
Principal Collector.

CALICUT,
21*st July* 1805.

APPENDIX XVI.

Average annual price of Unhusked Rice (Paddy), 1,000 Macleod seers, from 1860 to 1880, calculated at the rate of 4½ seers of Rice to 10 of Paddy.

Years.	Chirakkal.	Kottayam.	Kurumbranad.	Wynad.	Calicut.	Ernad.	Walluvanad.	Palghat.	Ponnani.	Cochin.	District generally.
1	2	3	4	5	6	7	8	9	10	11	12
	RS. A. P.	RS. A. P.	RS. A. P.	RS. A. P.	RS. A. P.	RS. A. P.	RS. A. P.	RS. A. P.	RS. A. P.	RS. A. P.	RS. A. P.
1860	60 11 8	56 3 7	62 5 1	52 8 3	55 7 2	57 9 4	46 0 9	53 8 4	55 6 0	57 15 1	55 12 4
1861	56 2 10	48 3 9	62 5 1	55 4 7	51 10 10	57 9 4	52 0 3	53 8 4	49 4 1	57 5 7	54 5 6
1862	59 9 4	50 3 3	60 11 4	54 7 5	53 10 0	57 9 4	42 10 9	51 12 5	50 10 4	52 15 7	53 6 9
1863	60 3 7	55 12 6	56 5 11	67 8 2	58 14 5	55 12 11	36 5 11	42 0 7	57 4 8	59 11 8	55 0 0
1864	60 11 5	69 7 10	63 8 3	76 8 1	63 13 2	55 0 11	38 14 5	50 11 11	59 13 0	61 15 10	60 0 10
1865	60 8 5	67 12 3	66 15 1	91 13 3	65 11 11	58 2 10	39 11 0	52 4 3	61 0 7	66 2 1	63 0 2
1866	76 9 9	79 10 11	76 1 3	102 15 5	79 10 7	70 14 9	51 10 10	53 11 10	70 5 9	72 2 2	73 6 1
1867	59 3 4	58 14 4	61 12 3	85 4 6	63 0 4	49 9 5	38 9 2	46 10 5	52 8 3	56 13 0	57 3 8
1868	53 7 9	52 8 0	57 1 3	75 8 10	63 7 1	47 14 1	43 4 2	51 10 10	54 8 4	58 2 0	55 12 0
1869	59 5 2	58 11 9	63 12 4	64 7 6	62 1 6	54 5 10	57 5 4	51 8 7	54 15 0	55 8 10	58 3 5
1870	51 11 0	56 14 1	60 3 4	56 9 10	56 4 2	47 3 4	58 8 10	49 1 3	49 13 3	51 8 0	53 12 6
1871	46 7 7	45 4 6	48 15 1	51 12 2	45 5 0	38 15 5	45 2 5	38 6 6	44 4 0	50 5 10	45 4 8
1872	51 4 9	40 12 8	52 13 6	61 0 9	50 5 8	53 3 5	50 0 3	44 15 4	46 1 9	49 6 6	50 12 10
1873	51 6 10	53 15 0	51 13 4	70 11 5	48 4 10	47 14 4	51 5 5	45 14 10	46 7 4	49 14 10	51 13 5
1874	60 1 4	62 0 5	60 4 1	71 12 7	60 6 3	55 15 5	58 2 11	53 8 8	54 3 9	59 7 4	59 9 7
1875	56 8 7	57 0 11	54 8 9	66 12 1	55 5 1	56 15 6	58 0 6	50 13 6	50 8 6	54 12 0	56 2 2
1876	59 8 8	62 13 11	63 4 3	80 12 5	59 2 2	57 8 11	64 1 4	58 1 11	57 9 4	60 12 6	62 5 11
1877	75 9 0	79 6 9	77 10 5	112 6 0	73 12 0	78 9 4	75 4 3	84 7 10	72 0 1	77 13 8	80 11 2
1878	80 1 3	77 10 8	79 7 2	101 11 1	78 11 11	81 8 4	73 13 1	77 8 7	74 11 10	78 9 4	80 6 1
1879	76 12 10	70 3 10	70 9 4	83 0 1	68 9 3	72 14 1	67 0 1	65 13 11	64 4 3	69 7 11	70 13 10
1880	58 14 8	61 2 5	58 3 10	72 12 8	56 9 4	55 1 10	54 11 3	51 13 8	48 2 9	58 7 2	57 9 7
Total ...	1,274 15 9	1,273 13 4	1,308 10 11	1,555 11 1	1,268 2 3	1,210 6 8	1,102 10 11	1,128 1 6	1,172 14 10	1,259 4 11	1,255 7 6
Averages { Of the 21 years.	60 11 5	60 10 7	62 5 1	74 1 3	60 6 3	57 10 3	52 8 2	53 11 6	55 13 8	59 15 6	59 12 7
Averages { Do. dear do. ...	71 12 0	70 0 7	68 9 5	89 15 11	67 14 10	72 6 8	62 15 11	67 15 3	64 10 2	69 9 1	70 1 9
Averages { Do. cheap do. ...	56 4 9	53 10 0	56 9 9	62 2 3	53 8 7	53 0 4	44 10 3	49 4 4	50 7 2	55 2 8	54 9 11
Mr. Graeme's commutation rates (as per column 15 of enclosures 1, 3, 5, 7, 9, 11, 13, 15, 17, 19, 21, 23, 25, 27 and 29 to his report of 14th January 1822).	Kavai. RS. A. P. 27 2 11	Kotiote. RS. A. P. 30 15 11	Kadattanad. RS. A. P. 33 0 1	Mr. Graeme's inquiries did not extend to Wynad.	Calicut. RS. A. P. 23 10 6	Ernad. RS. A. P. 18 4 11	Walluvanad. RS. A. P. 14 12 5	Palghat. RS. A. P. 17 5 5	Bettattnad. RS. A. P. 19 15 6	Mr. Graeme's inquiries did not extend to Cochin.	...
	Chirakkal. RS. A. P. 31 0 0	Tellicherry. RS. A. P. 30 14 6	Kurumbranad. RS. A. P. 25 4 2			Chernad. RS. A. P. 18 10 6	Nedunganad. RS. A. P. 12 4 10	Temmalapuram. RS. A. P. 16 11 0	Chavakkad. RS. A. P. 18 2 8		

APPENDIX XVII.

Average monthly price of Unhusked Rice (Paddy), 1,000 Macleod seers, from 1860 to 1880, calculated at the rate of 4½ seers of Rice to 10 of Paddy.

Months.	Chirakkal.	Kottayam.	Kurumbranad.	Wynad.	Calicut.	Ernad.	Walluvanad.	Palghat.	Ponnani.	Cochin.	District generally.
1	2	3	4	5	6	7	8	9	10	11	12
	RS. A. P.	RS. A. P.	RS. A. P.	RS. A. P.	RS. A. P.	RS. A. P.	RS. A. P.	RS. A. P.	RS. A. P.	RS. A. P.	RS. A. P.
January	58 9 2	57 15 0	59 0 8	68 10 9	57 0 9	56 7 0	51 10 6	50 6 6	53 11 11	57 7 1	57 1 6
February	58 11 8	57 13 4	59 15 7	66 9 4	56 15 7	54 13 1	51 13 2	53 13 10	54 7 7	57 6 5	57 3 10
March	60 11 4	58 2 5	62 0 3	67 1 1	59 7 4	57 5 3	52 10 8	55 0 9	55 9 9	58 5 1	58 10 2
April	61 11 9	60 1 11	62 0 6	69 7 8	60 12 4	57 2 5	52 11 2	56 3 4	57 5 6	57 10 5	59 8 4
May	61 14 8	61 9 9	62 3 6	71 5 4	61 2 0	58 0 3	52 14 6	56 14 1	57 4 5	61 6 11	60 7 7
June	65 0 8	62 5 11	63 7 6	75 13 2	62 13 0	60 15 11	57 15 4	58 3 6	58 14 0	62 5 1	62 12 7
July	60 14 10	62 12 11	65 0 2	79 9 1	65 13 0	66 2 4	57 0 9	57 4 0	59 10 10	63 4 5	63 12 0
August	63 4 4	63 3 8	66 0 5	80 11 10	64 0 10	64 8 9	56 15 6	59 1 3	60 8 2	65 2 5	64 5 9
September	60 1 10	61 15 11	64 6 9	79 7 6	60 11 7	56 6 10	53 8 8	50 4 6	53 10 3	61 13 10	60 4 0
October	60 3 10	62 8 8	61 11 11	79 4 7	59 9 0	50 13 1	44 13 0	47 3 3	52 13 4	59 5 2	57 13 5
November	57 14 9	60 8 8	61 0 9	77 10 7	58 8 8	52 14 0	46 10 3	48 13 6	52 2 5	57 15 9	57 6 9
December	59 5 10	58 13 7	60 13 4	73 4 0	57 12 8	56 1 8	51 6 2	51 5 1	54 1 9	57 7 1	58 0 9
Total ...	728 8 8	727 15 9	747 13 4	888 14 11	724 10 9	691 10 7	630 1 8	644 9 7	670 3 11	719 9 8	717 6 8
Averages: Of the 12 months.	60 11 5	60 10 7	62 5 1	74 1 3	60 6 3	57 10 3	52 8 2	53 11 6	55 13 8	59 15 6	59 12 7
Averages: Do. dear do.	62 9 3	62 6 10	64 11 9	78 12 1	62 8 9	62 6 10	54 13 3	56 10 5	58 11 9	62 12 11	62 5 2
Averages: Do. cheap do.	59 6 1	58 14 6	61 1 10	69 6 4	58 3 8	55 3 11	49 4 3	49 9 9	53 12 9	57 15 0	57 15 6
Mr. Graeme's commutation rates (as per column 15 of enclosures 1, 3, 5, 7, 9, 11, 13, 15, 17, 19, 21, 23, 25, 27 and 29 to his report of 14th January 1822).	Kavai. RS. A. P. 27 3 11	Kotiote. RS. A. P. 30 15 11	Kadattanad. RS. A. P. 32 0 1	Mr. Graeme's inquiries did not extend to Wynad.	Calicut. RS. A. P. 22 10 6	Ernad. RS. A. P. 18 4 11	Walluvanad. RS. A. P. 14 12 5	Palghat. RS. A. P. 17 5 5	Bettattnad. RS. A. P. 19 15 6	Mr. Graeme's inquiries did not extend to Cochin.	...
	Chirakkal. RS. A. P. 31 0 0	Tellicherry. RS. A. P. 30 14 6	Kurumbranad. RS. A. P. 25 4 2			Chernad. RS. A. P. 18 10 6	Nedunganad. RS. A. P. 12 4 10	Temmalapuram. RS. A. P. 16 11 0	Chavakkad. RS. A. P. 18 2 8		

APPENDIX XVIII.

Statement showing the price of 1,000 *Macleod seers of Gingelly-seed*, 1861–81.

Years.	Chirakkal.	Kottayam.	Kurumbranad.	Wynad.	Calicut.	Ernad.	Walluvanad.	Palghat.	Ponnani.	Cochin.
	RS. A. P.	RS. A. P.	RS. A. P.	RS. A. P.	RS. A. P.	RS. A. P.	RS. A. P.	RS. A. P.	RS. A. P.	RS. A. P.
1861	..	156 4 0	260 6 8	..	145 13 4	..	..	..	..	..
1862	..	161 7 4	260 6 8	..	161 7 4	..	..	..	..	156 4 0
1863	..	156 4 0	260 6 8	..	151 0 8	..	..	..	..	161 7 4
1864	..	177 1 4	260 6 8	..	171 14 0	..	..	..	..	161 7 4
1865	..	182 4 8	239 9 4	..	161 7 4	..	..	..	..	177 1 4
1866	..	218 12 0	239 9 4	..	213 8 8	..	..	..	..	182 4 8
1867	..	223 15 4	239 9 4	..	187 8 0	..	..	..	..	229 2 8
1868	..	161 7 4	239 9 4	..	..	..	..	..	..	171 14 0
1869	..	135 6 8	239 9 4	..	156 4 0	..	..	..	..	145 13 4
1870	..	197 14 8	239 9 4	151 0 8	171 14 0	..	..	..	..	166 10 8
1871	203 2 0	151 0 8	239 9 4	151 0 8	166 10 8	166 10 8	125 0 0	156 4 0	..	161 7 4
1872	187 8 0	145 13 4	239 9 4	130 3 4	..	166 10 8	125 0 0	156 4 0	..	156 4 0
1873	218 12 0	151 0 8	239 9 4	156 4 0	..	197 14 8	125 0 0	156 4 0	177 1 4	145 13 4
1874	197 14 8	166 10 8	239 9 4	156 4 0	..	197 14 8	125 0 0	156 4 0	166 10 8	125 0 0
1875	208 5 4	130 3 4	239 9 4	177 1 4	..	197 14 8	125 0 0	156 4 0	156 4 0	125 0 0
1876	234 6 0	177 1 4	239 9 4	177 1 4	..	229 2 8	125 0 0	187 8 0	156 4 0	156 4 0
1877	218 12 0	296 14 0	239 9 4	177 1 4	..	229 2 8	187 8 0	187 8 0	281 4 0	166 10 8
1878	218 12 0	239 9 4	239 9 4	156 4 6	..	265 10 0	125 0 0	187 8 0	281 4 0	281 4 0
1879	187 8 0	213 8 8	239 9 4	156 4 0	..	265 10 0	125 0 0	187 8 0	239 9 4	239 9 4
1880	161 7 4	166 10 8	239 9 4	125 0 0	..	125 0 0	125 0 0	187 8 0	197 14 8	177 1 4
1881	..	..	197 14 8	125 0 0	..	..	..	..	182 4 8	166 10 8
Total ..	2,036 7 4	3,609 6 0	5,072 14 8	1,838 8 8	1,687 8 0	2,041 10 8	1,312 8 0	1,718 12 0	1,838 8 8	3,453 2 0
Average ..	203 10 4	180 7 6	241 9 1	153 3 5	168 12 0	204 2 8	131 4 0	171 14 0	204 4 6	172 10 6

APPENDIX XIX.

Statement showing the price of Coconuts and Arecas for twenty years from 1862 *to* 1881.

Years.	Chirakkal.		Kottayam.		Kurumbranad.		Wynad.		Calicut.		Ernad.	
	Price of 1,000 green Coconuts.	Price of 1,000 green Arecanuts.	Price of 1,000 green Coconuts.	Price of 1,000 green Arecanuts.	Price of 1,000 green Coconuts.	Price of 1,000 green Arecanuts.	Price of 1,000 green Coconuts.	Price of 1,000 green Arecanuts.	Price of 1,000 green Coconuts.	Price of 1,000 green Arecanuts.	Price of 1,000 green Coconuts.	Price of 1,000 green Arecanuts.
	RS. A. P.	RS. A. P.	RS. A. P.	RS. A. P.	RS. A. P.	RS. A. P.	RS. A. P.	RS. A. P.	RS. A. P.	RS. A. P.	RS. A. P.	RS. A. P.
1862	23 0 0	1 6 8	26 0 0	0 13 4	25 0 0	0 8 0	53 13 4	1 8 0	19 0 0	1 8 0	25 0 0	1 6 0
1863	25 0 0	1 3 10	21 8 0	1 1 1	25 0 0	0 8 0	47 8 0	1 8 0	22 0 0	1 8 0	23 8 0	1 4 0
1864	22 1 4	1 6 6	22 0 0	1 1 2	30 0 0	0 9 7	46 10 8	1 10 0	21 0 0	2 0 0	20 0 0	1 4 0
1865	20 0 0	1 0 0	26 8 0	1 1 1	30 0 0	0 9 7	56 10 8	1 10 0	20 0 0	1 8 0	22 0 0	1 8 0
1866	22 0 0	1 6 5	39 8 0	1 14 2	45 0 0	0 9 7	56 10 8	1 10 0	24 0 0	2 4 0	32 0 0	3 0 0
1867	35 0 0	3 8 0	30 0 0	2 2 0	35 0 0	0 9 7	55 8 0	1 8 0	30 0 0	2 0 0	30 0 0	2 4 0
1868	30 0 0	2 0 0	24 8 0	1 3 0	30 0 0	0 9 7	45 6 8	1 8 0	30 0 0	2 0 0	28 0 0	1 12 0
1869	20 4 0	1 4 1	20 8 0	1 3 2	26 0 0	1 0 0	42 14 8	1 8 0	22 0 0	1 10 0	27 0 0	1 12 0
1870	20 4 0	1 4 1	33 8 0	1 8 6	30 0 0	0 8 0	49 2 10	2 15 8	21 0 0	1 12 0	25 0 0	1 12 0
1871	18 8 4	0 12 8	24 0 0	0 13 7	25 0 0	0 8 0	46 4 9	1 14 5	30 0 0	1 12 0	24 8 0	1 10 0
1872	19 0 0	0 11 2	16 0 0	0 13 0	30 0 0	0 8 0	35 8 7	1 12 10	19 0 0	1 4 0	25 0 0	1 8 0
1873	17 13 9	0 13 10	24 0 0	1 8 6	32 0 0	0 8 0	38 8 0	1 10 0	17 0 0	1 0 0	25 8 0	3 0 0
1874	23 10 6	0 8 0	23 8 0	2 0 0	32 0 0	0 8 0	40 0 0	1 15 0	19 0 0	1 0 0	30 0 0	4 0 0
1875	34 0 0	1 0 0	22 0 0	1 3 2	35 0 0	0 8 0	42 0 0	1 15 0	19 0 0	1 0 0	30 0 0	3 0 0
1876	23 8 0	0 12 10	23 0 0	2 8 9	30 0 0	0 8 0	44 2 5	1 15 0	22 0 0	1 8 0	29 0 0	2 8 0
1877	33 0 0	2 13 7	35 0 0	1 10 6	28 0 0	0 8 0	50 4 3	2 0 0	21 0 0	1 8 0	27 8 0	1 12 0
1878	33 4 0	2 0 0	32 0 0	1 9 7	26 0 0	0 8 0	52 11 0	1 8 0	33 0 0	1 8 0	25 0 0	1 8 0
1879	21 8 0	0 9 10	20 0 0	1 0 0	23 0 0	0 8 0	41 12 1	1 8 0	27 0 0	1 8 0	24 0 0	1 8 0
1880	19 0 0	0 12 0	18 8 0	1 8 0	20 0 0	0 9 7	34 9 6	1 0 0	20 0 0	1 4 0	18 0 0	1 0 0
1881	18 0 0	0 12 0	..	..	18 0 0	0 9 7	37 8 0	1 6 0	17 0 0	1 4 0	..	..
Total ..	478 13 11	26 1 6	482 0 0	26 10 7	575 0 0	11 3 1	917 10 1	33 13 11	453 0 0	30 10 0	491 0 0	37 4 0
Average ..	23 15 1	1 4 10	25 5 11	1 6 5	28 12 0	0 8 11	45 14 1	1 11 1	22 10 5	1 8 6	25 13 6	1 15 4

Statement showing the price of Coconuts and Arecas for twenty years from 1862 *to* 1881—(Continued).

Years.	Walluvanad.		Palghat.		Ponnani.		Cochin.		Chavakkad.*	
	Price of 1,000 green Coconuts.	Price of 1,000 green Arecanuts.	Price of 1,000 green Coconuts.	Price of 1,000 green Arecanuts.	Price of 1,000 green Coconuts.	Price of 1,000 green Arecanuts.	Price of 1,000 green Coconuts.	Price of 1,000 green Arecanuts.	Price of 1,000 green Coconuts.	Price of 1,000 green Arecanuts.
	RS. A. P.	RS. A. P.	RS. A. P.	RS. A. P.	RS. A. P.	RS. A. P.	RS. A. P.	RS. A. P.	RS. A. P.	RS. A. P.
1862	32 8 0	1 12 0	30 0 0	0 14 0	28 0 0	Information not available.	26 5 4	1 11 0	28 4 0	0 14 9
1863	30 0 0	1 0 0	30 0 0	0 14 0	25 0 0		24 2 8	1 5 4	28 12 0	1 4 9
1864	12 8 0	0 6 5	30 0 0	0 14 0	25 0 0		20 13 4	1 7 8	39 0 0	1 14 4
1865	30 0 0	1 4 0	30 0 0	0 14 0	25 0 0		23 10 8	2 6 4	40 0 0	2 1 7
1866	50 0 0	2 8 0	35 0 0	0 14 0	25 0 0		34 9 4	3 12 0	41 0 0	4 14 5
1867	37 0 0	1 15 0	35 0 0	0 15 0	25 0 0		31 15 9	2 12 2	39 4 0	2 4 9
1868	30 0 0	1 12 0	35 0 0	0 15 0	28 4 0		28 6 9	1 2 2	39 0 0	1 14 5
1869	25 0 0	1 8 0	35 0 0	0 15 0	26 5 0		27 1 6	1 11 9	38 0 0	1 8 0
1870	25 0 0	1 8 0	35 0 0	0 15 0	26 6 0		25 3 7	2 13 2	38 8 0	1 11 2
1871	25 0 0	1 8 0	30 0 0	0 15 0	22 0 0		25 13 4	1 9 8	35 0 0	2 12 9
1872	20 0 0	1 0 0	30 0 0	0 14 0	16 11 8	3 8 0	25 0 0	1 6 6	23 0 0	1 3 2
1873	20 0 0	1 0 0	30 0 0	0 14 0	20 15 0	3 12 0	26 0 0	4 0 0	25 0 0	1 0 0
1874	30 0 0	1 0 0	30 0 0	0 14 0	22 9 8	4 0 0	31 8 0	6 0 0	27 0 0	1 4 9
1875	35 0 0	1 0 0	30 0 0	0 14 0	22 12 8	3 4 7	31 0 0	2 8 0	32 0 0	2 14 4
1876	35 0 0	1 0 0	30 0 0	0 14 0	22 13 8	3 0 0	29 0 0	2 12 0	31 12 0	1 14 4
1877	30 0 0	1 8 0	30 0 0	0 14 0	29 10 0	3 8 0	28 0 0	1 8 0	33 4 0	1 8 0
1878	27 8 0	1 0 0	30 0 0	0 14 0	32 4 4	3 0 0	26 0 0	1 8 0	36 2 0	1 9 7
1879	27 8 0	1 0 0	30 0 0	0 14 0	23 12 4	1 8 0	25 0 0	1 8 0	31 8 0	1 0 9
1880	25 0 0	1 0 0	30 0 0	0 14 0	18 15 4	1 0 0	25 0 0	2 0 0	22 2 0	1 3 2
1881	..	..	..	..	..	..	..	..	19 4 0	1 6 4
Total ..	547 0 0	24 9 5	595 0 0	16 15 0	466 7 8	26 8 7	514 10 3	43 13 9	647 12 0	36 5 4
Average ..	28 12 8	1 4 8	31 5 1	0 14 3	24 8 10	2 15 2	27 1 5	2 4 11	32 6 2	1 13 1

* Chavakkad is separately shown as a place noted for coconut produce.

APPENDIX XX.

List of the Mālikhāna Recipients of Malabar and of the Amounts of their Mālikhānas.

Family Names and Titles.	Malikhana per annum.			Total amount of Malikhana received by each Family.		
The Calicut or Nediyirippa Family.	RS.	A.	P.	RS.	A.	P.
Manavikrama Sāmutiri Mahārāja Bahadur (The Zamorin).	69,663	4	0			
Do. Ēralpad Raja	15,000	0	0			
Do. Munnalpad Raja	7,000	0	0			
Do. Edattralpad Raja	5,000	0	0			
Do. Neduttralpad Raja	4,500	0	0			
Ambadi Kovilagam Tamburatti	4,000	0	0			
Putiya Kovilagam Valiya Tamburatti	9,000	0	0			
Padinyāra Kovilagam Valiya Tamburatti	9,000	0	0			
Kiḻakka Kovilagam Valiya Tamburatti	9,000	0	0			
Total ..				1,32,163	4	0
The Chirakkal or Kōlattiri Family.						
Raja Rāja Varmma Raja	12,475	0	2			
Tevaṇankott Kovilagam Udhaya Varmma Raja ..	1,593	12	0			
Tevaṇankott Kovilagam Kunyi Amma Rani ..	1,400	0	0			
Kaviṇisseri Kovilagam Ravi Varmma Raja	2,993	12	0			
Padinyāra Kovilagam Kunyandi Amma Rani ..	1,496	14	0			
Do. do. ..	1,496	14	0			
Chenga Kovilagam Ravi Varmma Raja	170	13	3			
Udhayamangalam Mittale Kovilagam Kēraḷa Varmma Raja.	500	0	0			
Total ..				22,127	1	5
Kadattandd Porḷḷātiri Family.						
Porḷḷatiri Māna Varmma Valiya Raja	13,801	0	0			
Do. Sankara Varmma Iḷaya Raja	4,000	0	0			
Do. Valiya Rani	600	0	0			
Āyanchēri Kovilagam Valiya Rani	4,020	0	0			
Edavalatta Kovilagam Valiya Rani	4,020	0	0			
Total ..				26,441	0	0
Kurumbranād Kurumbiyātiri Family.						
Ramamangalatta Kovilagam Vira Varmma Raja ..	4,000	0	0			
Mutirakkal Kovilagam Valiya Tamburatti	420	0	0			
Do. Cheriya Tamburatti	180	0	0			
Mallissēri Kovilagam Tamburatti	480	0	0			
Do. Vira Varmma Raja	600	0	0			
Koḷappatta Kovilagam Valiya Tamburatti	144	0	0			
Total ..				5,824	0	0

List of the Mālikhāna Recipients of Malabar and of the Amounts of their Mālikhānas—(Continued).

Family Names and Titles.	Malikhana per annum.	Total amount of Malikhana received by each Family.
Kottayam Family.	RS. A. P.	RS. A. P.
Tekka Kovilagam Kēraḷa Varmma Rāja	1,250 0 0	
Do. Amma Rani	500 0 0	
Padinyāra Kovilagam Lakshmi Rani	1,750 0 0	
Kiḻakka Kovilagam Sankara Varmma Rāja	1,650 0 0	
Do. Kēraḷa Varmma Rāja	750 0 0	
Total ..		5,900 0 0
Beypore Family.		
Kēraḷa Varmma Valiya Rāja	1,725 14 4	
Rāma Varmma Iḷaya Rāja	276 11 5	
Vīran enna Rāja Rāja Varmma Mūnnām Rāja ..	223 1 2	
Gōda Varmma Nalām Rāja	151 10 3	
Valiya Tamburātti	85 7 11	
Manayatt Kovilagam Tamburātti	142 13 0	
Nediyāl Kovilagam Tamburātti	142 13 0	
Panangāt Kovilagam Tamburātti	142 13 0	
Putiya Kovilagam Tamburātti	142 13 0	
Total ..		3,034 1 1
Parappanād Family.		
Valu Putiya Kovilagam Rāja Rāja Varmma Rāja ..	3,085 11 6	
Do. Kunyakkutti Tamburātti ..	1,028 9 2	
Total ..		4,114 4 8
Vaḷḷuvanād Family.		
Vallabha Rāja	16,415 1 7	16,415 1 7
Pālakkād Family.		
Sekhari Varmma Valiya Rāja	13,898 4 6	
Do. Iḷaya Rāja	2,857 3 3	
Do. Valiya Rani	137 2 3	
Naduviledam Kunchu Achchan	517 13 9	
Iḷaya Achchan Edattil Kombi Achchan rendam Dharmma Achchan.	517 13 9	
Kiḻakka Konikkal Edattil Kombi Achchan . ..	170 13 9	
Total ..		18,099 3 3
Kavaḷappāra Nāyar Family.		
Valiya Nāyar	4,567 10 3	4,567 10 3
Payyormala Nāyar Family.		
Avinyatt Nāyar	4,058 4 2	
Kuttāḷi Nāyar	1,766 12 10	
Total ..		5,825 1 0
Puḻavāyi Nāyar Family.		
Maṉṉiledattil Nayar	1,610 9 2	1,610 9 2

***List of the Mālikhāna Recipients of Malabar and of the Amounts of their Mālikhānas*—(Continued).**

Family Names and Titles.	Malikhana per annum.			Total amount of Malikhana received by each Family.		
Pālakkād Nāyar Families.	RS.	A.	P.	RS.	A.	P.
Kongāttil Valiya Nāyar	1,044	13	1			
Edattara Valiya Nāyar	1,031	6	4			
Mannūr Valiya Nāyar	976	12	8			
Total ..				3,053	0	1
Iruvaḻināḍ Nambyār Families.						
Kiḻakkedatta Kunhi Sankaran Nambyār	1,191	9	6			
Mīttangott Kunnummal Nārāyani Amma	595	12	9			
Kāmpratta Kunhi Krishnan Nambyār	791	9	6			
Kāmpratta Kunyi Pārvati Valiya Amma	400	0	0			
Chandrotta Kunyi Komappan Nambyār	315	0	0			
Do. Mādhavi Amma *and* Kunyi Chantu Nambyār.	280	12	9			
Nārangoḻi Kunyi Sankaran Nambyār	835	15	0			
Do. Ramatta Tāvaḻi Kunyappa Nambyār ..	278	10	4			
Do. Puttalatta Tāvaḻi Kunyappa Nambyār ..	278	10	4			
Do. Mallissēri Tāvaḻi Kunyi Lakshmi Amma .	278	10	4			
Kariyātt Vālōḻi Edattil Kunyi Krishnan Valiya Nambyār.	724	10	0			
Do. do. Tachchormman Govindhan Nambyār.	362	5	0			
Do. do. Kunnummal Nārāyana Nambyār.	362	5	0			
Total ..				6,695	14	6
Kurungōtt Tadam and Poyyappram Nāyar Families.						
Kurungōtt Tadattil Putiya Vīttil Rayiru Nāyar ..	350	3	2			
Do. do. Kunyi Chāttu Nāyar.	150	0	0			
Do. Trikkeikkal Cheriya Kunyi Raman Nāyar.	75	13	4			
Do. Putiya Vittil Uppātti Amma *and* Kunyi Chāttu Nāyar *and* Kunyi Mādhavi Amma *and* Kunyi Rāman Nāyar.	244	7	4			
Kurungōtt Tadattil Koderi Madhattil Kunyi Krishnan Nāyar.	116	7	4			
Do. Taḻa Kurungōtt Kunyi Pārvvati Amma, Kunyi Lakshmi Amma.	107	2	4			
Do. Vishnumangalam Kunyi Pārvvati Amma *and* Kunyi Madhavi Kettilamma and Kunyi Pārvvati Amma.	178	1	8			
Poyyappratta Rāmar Nāyar	155	9	7			
Do. Devaki Amma *and* Kunyi Amma ..	50	0	0			
Total ..				1,427	12	9
Grand Total for the District ..	....			2,57,297	15	9

APPENDIX XXI.

CHIRAKKAL TALUK.

By Chuppu Menon, B.A.

Position, Boundaries, Area.—This taluk formerly comprised the taluks of Kavāyi and Chirakkal. It is the most northerly taluk of the district. Boundaries: *North*—South Canara; *East*—Coorg; *South*—Kottayam taluk; *West*—the Arabian Sea. Its area is not accurately known, there having been no regular survey of it by the professional department. For the census of 1881 the area was taken to be 648 square miles. About 150 square miles may be said to be under cultivation.

Physical Aspect.—The terraced character of the laterite formation is nowhere more conspicuous than in the Chirakkal taluk, and more particularly in that portion of it lying to the north of the Valarpaṭṭanam river. These laterite terraces are, as a rule, unproductive, but where they break off in abrupt cliffs the soil is extensively cultivated with coconut and jack and pepper. The flats also lying between the laterite terraces are thickly peopled and every inch of available ground is occupied. Along the coast, the beach, except at Mount Deli and again to the south of Cannanore, is low and sandy. Inland, the outlying spurs of the Ghat mountains are covered with scrub jungle, and even the Ghats themselves are in great part also covered with scrub, the heavy forest having disappeared before the axes and fires of the thriftless *punam* cultivators.

Population and Houses.—The population, according to the census of 1881, was 272,669 as against 257,377 in 1871, showing an increase of 15,292 or 5·9 per cent. on the number returned in the latter year. The Hindu population numbered 207,909, and there were 60,154 Muhammadans, 4,507 Christians, and 99 persons belonging to other classes. The males were to the females as 132,715 to 139,954, and the density of population was 421 per square mile. The total number of houses in the taluk was 54,005, of which 44,250 were occupied and the rest unoccupied.

Sub-divisions of Taluk for Administrative Purposes.—The taluk is sub-divided, for purposes of revenue administration, into 43 amsams or villages, each of which is as usual placed under an adhikari (village head) aided by a menon (accountant) and a petty staff of peons. Groups of amsams are assigned to officers, designated Deputy Tahsildars, and these latter exercise criminal jurisdiction likewise over the area under their control. There are two Deputy Tahsildars, located one at Taliparamba and the other at Cannanore, whose territorial jurisdictions extend over 10 and 9 amsams respectively; and the Tahsildar, who has general revenue charge of all the amsams and special magisterial charge of 24 of them, has his head-quarters at Cannanore. The Tahsildar and Revenue and Magisterial establishments generally work under the Sub-Collector.

Public Establishments.—In addition to the village and taluk establishments above specified, there are two District Munsifs' Courts, situated at Taliparamba and Chōva,[1] usually designated the District Munsifs' Courts of Kavāyi and Cannanore respectively, and there are also four sub-registry offices, located at Palayangādi, Taliparamba, Cannanore and Anjarakandi.

The details of the several public establishments in the taluk are given below:—

[2] 1. Brigadier-General commanding the Western District, comprising Malabar and Canara, with the offices of the Deputy Assistant Adjutant and Quarter-master Generals' and Medical Departments, Cannanore.
2. Cantonment Magistrate and his establishment, Cannanore.
3. Civil Surgeon, Cannanore, and Medical subordinates, Cannanore.
4. Superintendent, Central Jail, and his establishments, Cannanore.
5. Chaplain, Cannanore, and church servants, Cannanore.
6. District Munsifs at Taliparamba and Cannanore.
7. Tahsildar, two Deputy Tahsildars, Taluk Sheristadar, Revenue Inspectors and other subordinate revenue staff.
8. Sea Customs Superintendent and Port Conservator, Cannanore, and his subordinates.
9. Two Inspectors of Police, one at Taliparamba and the other at Cannanore, with station-house officers and men.
10. D.P.W. Supervisor, Cannanore sub-division, and his subordinates.
11. Sub-Registrars of Assurances at Palayangādi, Taliparamba, Cannanore and Anjarakandi.
12. Officers of the Postal and Telegraph departments.
13. Sub-Inspector and other subordinates of the Salt and Abkari department.
14. Local Fund Overseer and his subordinates.
15. Municipal establishment, Cannanore.
16. Inspecting Schoolmasters and teachers.
17. Vaccinators.

Towns.—Cannanore (lat. 11° 51′ 20″ N., long. 75° 21′ 45″ E.), which is the head-quarters of the taluk, is a straggling town situated on the sea coast. It consists of two detached portions, locally known as the old town, or Cannanore proper, and the cantonment. Between the two, and commanding the old town, lies Fort St. Angelo, an old-fashioned fort built of laterite and standing on a rocky promontory surrounded on three sides by the sea. The fort is held by the British troops located in the cantonment. It has a dry ditch on the landward side and flanking bastions. The greater part of the outworks was demolished some years ago. The fort has a flag-staff with a mast-light for the use of mariners. Adjoining the fort is the brigade parade ground, which is very extensive, and has on its outskirts the barracks of the European regiment, the Anglican, German, and Roman Catholic churches, the European cemeteries, the powder magazines, the Commissariat office, and the little village of Barnacherry. This esplanade is used for parade and other military purposes. At a short distance north from the brigade parade ground lies another esplanade used by the Native Infantry regiment. On

---

[1] Since transferred to Cannanore.

[2] The head-quarters and a portion of the British Infantry regiment stationed at Cannanore were transferred from Cannanore to Wellington and Malabar annexed to the newly constituted "Southern District" (G.O., No. 7124, dated 15th November 1886, Military, and Board's Proceedings, No. 62, dated 18th January 1887,) since this article was sent to press.

its outskirts lie the camp bazaar, the depository of the arms of the native regiment and their lines, and a bazaar known as "Thekki" bazaar, used by the native troops. The public buildings at Cannanore present no marked features. They consist of Commissariat offices, Deputy Assistant Adjutant and Quartermaster Generals' offices, the Tahsildar's and Sub-Registrar's offices, civil and military dispensaries, postal and telegraph offices, and the Government school. The chief places of resort for travellers are the Esplanade Hotel, the travellers' bungalow, and the mussafarkhana, the latter two belonging to the Cannanore Municipality.

Cotton fabrics of different descriptions are manufactured at Cannanore, chiefly by the mercantile branch of the German Mission. About 3 miles north of the fort is the Central Jail, at a place called Utayan Kunnu; and the court-house of the District Munsif, Cannanore, is located at Chōva,[1] a suburban place about 3 miles to the south-east of the fort. The Central Jail is built on the system of blocks of cells radiating from a central watch tower. There is an extensive garden attached to it, in which is situated the Superintendent's house. The jail can accommodate 829 prisoners.

The Municipal Act (X of 1865) was introduced into Cannanore by the notification of Government, dated 24th June 1867, but its operation was suspended over the area included in what are called "kirar limits," owing to the protest made by Sultan Āḷi Raja of Cannanore. His objection was, however, overruled by the Madras Government,[2] and the area temporarily excluded was brought within the operation of the municipal enactment in June 1873. The municipality now comprises portions of Puḷati and Elayavur amsams, and has an area of about 4 square miles. Its population, according to the census of 1881, was 26,386, of whom Hindus numbered 10,656, Muhammadans 11,617, Christians 4,087, and other classes 26. The males were to the females as 13,046 to 13,340. The number of houses within the municipality was 5,981, of which 1,943 were returned as "unoccupied" at the recent census. The income of the municipality from all sources of revenue amounts to about Rs. 19,000 on an average. The following table shows how the funds are raised and spent:—

CANNANORE MUNICIPALITY.

Receipts.

	1884-85.
	RS.
Opening balance ..	1,202
Rates on houses and lands ..	8,391
Taxes on arts ..	2,788
Taxes on vehicles and animals ..	1,414
Registration of carts ..	536
Tolls ..	3,100
Licenses ..	115
Assignments by Government ..	799
Fees and fines ..	631
Endowments, &c. ..	71
Miscellaneous ..	740
Total Receipts ..	19,787

[1] Since transferred to Cannanore.

[2] G.O., dated 21st June 1873, No. 264, Political.

Charges.

	1884-85.
Grant I.	RS.
New works—Sanitary and miscellaneous repairs	..
Communications	781
Buildings	88
Sanitary and miscellaneous	222
Establishment	180
Tools and plant	..
Grant II.	
Municipal schools	..
Results grants	2,502
Schools on the combined system	314
Inspection (contribution)	100
Miscellaneous	..
Grant III.	
Hospitals and dispensaries	3,285
Medical college	100
Sanitary inspection	102
Vaccination	317
Registration of births and deaths	142
Conservancy	6,570
Grant IV.	
Lighting	832
Choultries	..
Avenues and watering roads	20
Miscellaneous	819
Grant V.	
Supervision and management	2,209
Refunds	272
Balances	932
Total Charges	19,787

Villages or Important Places.—*Payyannur,* which is the northernmost amsam of the taluk, contains, *inter alia,* the desams of Kavāyi and Payyannur, both of which are of some importance. The former is situated on an island and contains the bungalow of that name which stands at the frontier of the district. There is a large mosque, and an old redoubt built many years ago, probably by the French. Payyannur lies two miles to the south-east of Kavāyi and possesses an ancient temple dedicated to god Subramaniya. The image is said to have been consecrated by Parasu Rama. The *mandapam* is elaborately sculptured and the temple is surrounded by a strong wall. The place is celebrated as having been the seat of the "Payyannur Gramakkars" whom Parasu Rama is said to have specially favoured, and whose descendants still follow the marumakkatāyam law of inheritance, unlike the other Brahmans of the district. There is still extant a poem entitled the Payyannur Pattōla, described by Doctor Gundert as "certainly the oldest specimen of Malayalam composition which I have seen," and of which he gave a very interesting account in a paper contributed to the Madras Journal of Literature and Science (No. XIII-II, pp. 14-17). "The language," continues Doctor Gundert, "is rich and bold, evidently of a time when the infusions from Sanskrit had not reduced the energy of the tongue, by cramping it with hosts of unmeaning particles." "The legend of Payyannūr, N. Lat. 12° 5' near Kavāi."—"Nilakēsi, a woman of good family, an inhabitant of a place called Sivapêrûr (Trichur ?), a town famous for female beauty, could not obtain a son though married to several men. She resolves, therefore, to do penance by wandering about as a beggar, and comes to the famous emporium, Cachilpatnam (near Mt. Deli), where the chief of the place, a merchant named Nambu Chetti, or Chombu Chetti, enters into conversation with her, advises her to perform certain vows, and then takes her to his palace as his lawful wife. A son is born and receives the name of Nambūsari Aren, and a feast of rejoicing is celebrated on the 41st day on the plain of Payyannūr. At that time Nilakēsi's brothers happened to go up the coast in a ship. They hear the music and disembark to see the play, but as they climb up a wall of the temple some spectators expostulate with them. They call themselves Culavanier (merchants), who cannot be expected to know the customs of the place, and appeal to the chief. He comes, but applies his rod to the head of one, a scuffle ensues and the strangers are killed.

"Nilakēsi, when acquainted with the murder of her brothers, leaves the palace and her son, and again wanders forth begging. The son grows up and is instructed by his father in all the arts of trade and ship-building (given in interesting detail, full of obsolete words). The ship being at length launched and manned with *Vappūrawas* (?) *Pandias, Chonakas, Chōlias,* and also with one *Yavanaka,* the merchants start fearlessly on a voyage, first to Pūmpatna round Mt. Eli, then passing the *māla* (—Dives) into the *Tanipunulāru* (river) to the town of *Pūvenkāpatna,* proceed further on to the Cavēri, from whence they sail into *another sea and to other shores* till they reach the *Gold mountains* (Ponmala), where they exchange all their cargo for *gold,* return and land their goods in *Cachilpatnam,* store them in a new magazine, and dismiss the mariners with their shares. After this, when the father and son are amusing themselves with playing chess, a female devotee is announced who is not satisfied with alms, but wants to see the young merchant. Then follows a long and mysterious conversation. She invites him urgently to be present at a night feast of a woman at Payyannūr. He promises, but cannot afterwards persuade his father to give him leave, who fears a plot and danger, but the son persisting in importuning him, and at last, prostrating himself, he consents.

"'I swear by thee, O Father! I must go.' Father: 'I have opposed thee to the utmost, but now I must not prevent thy going—thou goest far away like dying men. *Strong guards* (*or companions*) are now required—take the *children* of the *Gôvâtala chetti* of *Anjuvannam* and of the *Manigrama* people, who, together with ourselves, are the 4 (classes of) colonists in the 4 towns.'

"They took of the 4 classes of colonists, *the sons* (*or servants*) *of the town lord in that country,* 14 companions, a noble household, not to be outwitted (or defeated) *by any in this country* (and, says the son), 'though I should be dragged by the foot I shall return (to-morrow) to Cachilpatnam, nor shall this eye sleep (to-night).'

"Upon this, the father advises them to take some merchandise along with them in the ship as for a fair, and the poem, evidently a fragment, closes in the 104th sloka with an enumeration of wares, replete with obscure terms free from any anachronisms.

"I believe that the people of Anjuvannam and Manigramam here mentioned as belonging to *yonder* country can only mean Jews and Christians (or Manicheans), who, for commerce sake, settled also beyond the Perumāl's territories. It would be interesting to know who the 2 other classes are. In the meantime the existence of 4 trading communities in the old Kērala seems to be proved, and the നാലുചെരി of the first Syrian document receives some elucidation from this incidental allusion." Gundert in M. J. L. S., XIII-II., 14-17.

Taliparamba, which is the seat of the local Deputy Tahsildar's and Sub-Registrar's offices and of the court of the District Munsif of Kavāyi, has an area of 5,938 acres and a population of 8,363 souls. It has a bungalow and a mussafarkhana close to the Deputy Tahsildar's office, and is celebrated for two of the most ancient and important temples in North Malabar, known as Taliparamba and Trichchamparam temples. The former is dedicated to *Siva*, and is a magnificent structure covered with brass plates and surrounded by a high laterite wall. On the bank of a tank attached to the temple is a building on which is a granite slab bearing an inscription; and another, dated K.A. 954 (A.D. 1778), is to be seen at the foot of a banyan tree in front of the temple. The former is to the effect that the bathing house was finished in Kollam Ándu 700 (A.D. 1524). The temple has many sculptures and some fine *gopurams* (towers) which were, however, destroyed by Tippu. It is said to be of very great antiquity, to which the architecture in parts bears witness. There is a large and important mosque here and an old mud fort. On the south side of the road leading to Kuppam is a sculptured figure of a village goddess. Four rock-cut sepulchres were excavated some time ago near the travellers' bungalow, one of which had a circle of massive laterite blocks ranged round it. These caves consist of a small chamber with a domed roof and entrance. In the centre of the dome is a hole to the upper air closed with a slab. The celebrated temple at Trichchamparam is dedicated to Krishna, and there is another at Kanjirangott dedicated to Siva. In the former an annual utsavam (ഉത്സവം) or festival, commencing on the 22nd Kumbham and ending on the 6th Minam, is performed, and on the last-named day a large concourse of people from all parts of the district, estimated from 15,000 to 30,000, are said to assemble. The Trichchamparam is supposed to be a corruption of Srì Sambaram (ശ്രീശംബരം), so called after the great rishi of that name who did penance there, propitiated the god, and in his honor consecrated the image.

Mādāyi or *Paḻayangādi*, about 14 miles north north-west of Cannanore, is a Mappilla village of some importance situated on the right bank of a fine river and is a place of trade. Boats of a large size come up to it. Here is a small redoubt, also a bungalow for the reception of travellers, and in the middle of the village is a handsome mosque bearing an inscription in Arabic commemorating its building in Hijira 518 (A.D. 1124). There is another inscription stating that a tank was constructed by a Hindu. The grave of an Arab, who died several years ago, also exists. In the hamlet of Paḻayangādi is an old tank known by the name of the "Jewish tank" near which stands the old Eḻi palace of the Kōlattiri Rajas.

The tank was probably constructed by a colony of Jews or "Yavanas." There is also a Hindu temple close to the Madayi bungalow.

Ettikulam, a small village lying a mile to the south of Mt. Deli or Eḻi mala, where the sea forms a small bay, is inhabited by Mappilla merchants who supply Cannanore and Tellicherry with firewood. On a small hill stretching into the sea is a redoubt strongly built but overrun with shrubs. It was probably built by the Portuguese to protect their trade on this coast, and it subsequently passed into French and then into English hands. There is an insignificant mosque almost on the summit of Mt. Deli frequented on certain days by numbers of Māppillas. It is infested with monkeys.

Irukkur, a large Māppilla town with some mosques, and lying south-east 25⅞ miles from Kavāyi, is a place of note, being on the high road from the coast leading through the Pudiya Chūram or Huggel pass towards Coorg and Mysore. It is on the right bank of the Valarpattanam (Beliapatam) river and can be reached by small river boats at high tides. During the rains a great deal of timber and bamboos in rafts are floated down to Valarpattanam and other places for sale and for the construction of small crafts.

Sirukkandhapuram, a Māppilla bazaar with a mosque, has a dense population in its vicinity. It is on the right bank of the northern branch of the Valarpattanam river, which is navigable as far as this for small boats. The bazaars or store-houses contain the produce of the hill cultivation which is here collected and sent down by water to the towns on the sea coast.

Valarpattanam (Beliapatam, called, it is said, after the Raja Valabham, who built it), situated 5 miles north north-west of Cannanore, is a small trading town composed of a street of shops and large houses. It is on the left bank of a magnificent river which discharges itself into the sea 4 miles to the south-west of it. The banks are fringed with coconut and other trees.

Chirakkal is famous as being the residence of the Raja of Chirakkal, who has a Kōvilakam or palace at this place on the south side of a reservoir of fresh water of considerable dimensions, estimated to be 1,042 feet in length and 492 feet in breadth. Half a mile on the west of the high road, a street is formed by weavers and other castes, and on a height south-west of the palace are to be seen the remains of a redoubt.

Other places and religious institutions of minor importance are described in the following table :—

Name of amsam.	Name of religious or other institutions for which the place is celebrated.	Descriptive remarks.
Chuḻali .. .. ചുഴലി.	Vayital mala .. .. വയിത്തൽമല.	A very high hill. Previous to the invasion of Tippu it appears that there was a wealthy tribe of Kshetriyas called Vayital Kovvanmar (കൊവ്വന്മാർ) who owned temples and property in the amsams of Eramam, Chuḻali, Kuttūr, Kuttiyéri, &c., below the ghat. In course of time they found rivals in the influentia. Nambiyars of Chuḻali, who waged war against and exterminated them.

Name of amsam.	Name of religious or other institutions for which the place is celebrated.	Descriptive remarks.
Kannileri .. .. കാഞ്ഞിലെരി.	Payyávúr temple .. .. പയ്യാവൂരക്ഷെത്രം.	Image of Siva in the hunting costume of Kiráthan—Tiled building. Tradition says that Siva, in order to try the inflexibility of Arjuna's penance, attacked and threw him away, but that from where he fell he made the image of Siva and began to worship, which greatly pleased the latter deity.
Pattuvam .. .. പട്ടുവം.	Pattuvatt temple .. .. പട്ടുവത്തകാവു.	Image of Bhagavati—Tiled roof. Cases in which parties agreed to abide by oaths are sent here for the purpose of oaths being taken.
Kunhimangalam .. കുഞ്ഞിമംഗലം.	Ramanthali narayam Kannúr temple. രാമന്തളി നരയംകണ്ണൂര ക്ഷെത്രം.	Image of Shasthâv—Thatched building—Is an old temple on the western slope of Mount Deli and close to the sea. Contains Vatteḻuttu inscriptions which have not yet been deciphered. Is supposed to contain valuable medicinal plants.
Cherukunnu .. .. ചെറുകുന്ന.	Cherukunnu temple .. ചെറുകുന്നക്ഷെത്രം.	An important temple with tiled roof in North Malabar—Has an image of Bhagavati (Annapûrnéswari). Tradition says that the temple was constructed by Parasu Rama and that the deity came from the north near Benares. There are seven old temples here. On the west side of the hill on which stands the temple of Kunnúr Matilakam is a rock-cut cave.
Moraya .. .. മൊറായ.	Katamperi temple .. കടമ്പെരിക്ഷെത്രം.	Image of Chulali Bhagavati—Tiled. Contains some carved figures. Has a fine tank.
Kayaralam .. .. കയരളം.	Velath temple .. .. വെളത്തക്ഷെത്രം.	Images of Vishnu, Ganapathi, and Siva. There are two arikovils of which one is tiled and the other thatched. There is an inscribed slab broken, in the temple, said to be in Dévanágari character.
Kuttiyattúr .. .. കുററിയാററൂര.	Kuttiyattúr temple .. കുററിയാററൂരക്ഷെത്രം.	Image of Siva. Srikovil is tiled and the rest thatched. In the gate of the temple is a stone bearing an insciption not as yet read—in characters stated to be unknown.
Maniyúr .. .. മണിയൂര.	1. Maniyûr temple .. മണിയൂരക്ഷെത്രം.	Image of Subramaniyan. Srikovil tiled and the rest thatched. On the northside of the trench surrounding the temple is a stone having an inscription "in unknown characters" on its four sides.
	2. Kanhirattu Jamath mosque. കാഞ്ഞിരാട്ടജമാത്തപള്ളി.	Tiled—believed to be once a Hindu temple and converted into a mosque.
Chirakkal .. .. ചിറക്കൽ.	Kalariváthukkal temple .. കളരിവാതുക്കൽക്ഷെത്രം.	Image of Bhagavathi—Tiled—supposed to be originally a *Kalari* (gymnasium) of Patuviláyi Nayar, but subsequently fell into the possession of Chirakkal Raja.

Name of amsam.	Name of religious or other institutions for which the place is celebrated.	Descriptive remarks.
Alikot .. .. അഴിക്കൊട്.	Perinthra kovil, Kottaram. പെരിന്ത്രകൊവിൽ കൊട്ടാരം.	This is the residence of an agent of Taliparamba Devaswam and is noted for a peculiar custom locally observed. There is a big tract of field known as "Olıkôt vayal," the ownership of which is supposed to vest in *Perinthra Kovilappan.* There is no image of this god. At the time of sowing and harvesting the crop in that locality, the Devaswam agent goes in procession and sows or cuts with his own hand, and unless this is done, no one can carry on any operation. A fixed portion of the produce is also assigned to the Devaswam, and this assignment is known by the name of Kangani.
Etakad .. .. എടക്കാട.	Oorpaḻéchi temple .. ഊർപ്പഴെച്ചികാവ.	Image of Siva in the hunting costume of Kiráthan and of Vettakkorumakan. Srikovil and surrounding buildings have copper roof and the rest tiled. This is a very important temple.
Makréri .. .. മക്രെരി.	Peralasseri temple .. പെരളശ്ശെരിക്ഷെത്രം.	Image of Subramaniyan. Srikovil tiled and the rest thatched. Supposed to have great power of curing poison.

Anicuts—Canals.—Neither dams nor canals of irrigation are to be met with. There is, however, one canal of communication usually known as the Sultan's Canal between the river of Paḻayangādi and a branch of another which runs north and joins the Kavāyi immediately to the south of the town of that name. It is three miles in length, cut through low paddy ground. It was executed at the expense of the Bībi of Cannanore with the object, it would appear, of having a safe inland navigation from Nileshwaram in South Canara to Kakkad 2 miles to the north-east of Cannanore. It is now shallow and impassable during the dry season.

Minerals, Industries and Manufactures.—Laterite is met with in abundance. Some coarse cotton cloths are made at a few places in the interior by rude appliances. At Cannanore there is an excellent weaving establishment under the supervision of the German Mission. In the Central Jail, Cannanore, carpentry and other works are carried on.

Kunhimangalam is noted for its brass works, chiefly lamps.

Trigonometrical Station.—Mount Deli, in Kunhimangalam amsam, lies in latitude 21° 01′ 37·04″ and longitude 75° 14′ 40·51″ and belongs to Lambton's series.

ANJARAKANDI AMSAM.

By V. Chappu Menon, B.A.

Anjarakandi or *Ancharakandi* (literally 5½ sections or desams) is an interesting amsam belonging to the Chirakkal taluk, and situated about 8 miles north north-east of Tellicherry, and is administered in a peculiar manner: It has no paid adhikári or other village officers, and is held by the family of Mr. Murdoch Brown on a lease of 99 years granted by the Honorable Company on the 30th April 1817. The lease consequently falls in on the 29th April 1916. The circumstances which led to the grant of this lease were as follows :—

In 1797 the Honorable East India Company opened out at this place, then known as Randattara, a plantation of about 1,000 acres for the cultivation of special products, such as coffee, pepper, cinnamon, nutmeg, cassia, cotton, sugarcane and sandalwood plants, and appointed Mr. Murdoch Brown, who had originated the scheme, to be the "overseer and manager" of the estate. Mr. Brown was a merchant at Mahé, who, on the fall of that settlement in 1793, had entered the Company's service. The terms of agreement were that—

(1) The plantation was to be undertaken and carried on solely and entirely on behalf of the Honorable Company.

(2) Any special products suggested by the Company's agents were to be planted in the manner desired, full accounts of receipts and expenditure being furnished.

(3) If the scheme sketched out for the carrying on and management of the plantation were disapproved by the Court of Directors, then the concern was to be undertaken by Mr. Brown on his own account, the Company being reimbursed within three calendar months after such intention shall have been announced, the principal and interest of money expended on the plantation provided, however, that the possession of the ground occupied by the plantation be secured to him and to those concerned with him at a reasonable rent to be rated according to the custom of the country.

(4) In the event of the contingency referred to in clause 3 occurring, that is, if the plantation be carried on by Mr. Brown on his own private account, the whole produce of pepper, coffee and cotton, and all such articles as shall be produced thereon, shall be wholly and exclusively tendered in sale to the Honorable Company's agents, the Honorable Company paying for the same, viz., pepper at Rs. 50 per candy of 640 lb., coffee at Rs. 8 per bale of 20 lb. and other articles at such prices as Government may deem their qualities and species entitled to. This agreement was signed by Mr. Murdoch Brown on the 31st December 1797.

In 1799, the Court of Directors, who disapproved of the project, ordered the transfer of the plantation to Mr. Brown in accordance with the terms of his agreement; but there was some difficulty in arranging the transfer which was effected by the Principal Collector, Major William MacLeod, only in the year 1802. In 1803 the plantation was almost wholly destroyed by the Palassi (Pychy) rebels, and this again complicated matters. After some years of correspondence, it was settled in 1817 that a lease of the estate for 99 years should be granted to Mr. Brown, and this was accordingly done subject to the following terms :—

(1) Mr. Murdoch Brown binds himself, his heirs and assigns to the payment of an annual revenue amounting to Rs. 2,257-2-0 by such kists or instalments as the Collector might from time to time direct.

(2) When a new survey of the land revenue of Malabar shall take place, Mr. Brown or his representatives shall pay the new revenue on the estate at the same rates as the same species of land and productions of the district shall be assessed.

(3) It shall be lawful for Mr. Brown to purchase, with the consent of the inhabitants who occupy and pay revenue on the 918 acres of land included within the plantation estimated to comprise 2,000 acres of arable land, all or any part of the said 918 acres, the purchases being duly registered in the Collector's office or in the Zilla court.

(4) It shall be lawful for the Honorable Company to prohibit Mr. Brown from purchasing occupied lands from the said inhabitants, but in that case he will be granted an equal extent of unoccupied arable land (not exceeding 918 acres) in the vicinity at the time of such prohibition being signified to him.

(5) At the expiration of the lease it shall remain, at the option of Government, to resume the lands thus leased on repaying to the lawful owner the sums paid to the natives for their janmam kudimanir rights and the products on them, when purchased.

(6) Whereas Mr. Brown did in 1802 offer and agree to pay for the purchase of the said plantation the amount expended on it until then by the Company with certain deductions agreed to by Government: and whereas the destruction of the buildings and nearly all the productive vines and coffee trees in 1803 by the rebels from Cotiote put it out of his power to fulfil his agreement and necessitated a reference to the Court of Directors for their final decision as to the amount of remission to be granted to him, it is further declared that Mr. Brown, who has already paid two instalments of Rs. 10,000 each, does bind himself, his heirs, executors and assigns to pay such further sum in final discharge of his debt as the Court of Directors may determine, deducting therefrom the value of the goods delivered to the Company's Commercial Resident in Mahé agreeably to the account furnished to the Principal Collector in 1802.

(7) Mr. Brown shall at all times conform to all lawful orders issued to him under the authority of Government or its officers.

Agreeably to the above provision, clause 2, a survey took place in 1820-25 by the Commissioner, Mr. Græme, and the Collector, Mr. Vaughan, and this was followed in 1833 by another under the Collector, Mr. Clementson. The assessment for Fasli 1294 (1884-85) was as follows:—

	RS.	A.	P.
Wet	781	10	10
Dry	1	10	3
Bhagayet	1,374	9	7
Inam jodi	39	15	3
Total ..	2,197	13	11
Abkari revenue on Katti and Chatti	71	6	4
Local cess	292	9	6
Grand Total ..	2,561	13	9

The estate of Anjarakandi consists of five tarras or dēsams of—

1. Muringéri,	4. Anjarakandi,
2. Mámba,	5. Pâlêri,
3. Kamayatt,	

together with a strip of land situated on the opposite side of the Anjarakandi river in Kottayam taluk bounded by the dyke of ten feet in height constructed in the year 1800 for the defence of the plantation and containing about 40 acres of land. The total area of the amsam is 3,382 acres, or a little more than 5¼ square miles, and it has a population of 4,155 souls, of whom 2,064 are males and the rest females. The Hindus number 3,609, Muhammadans 518, and Christians 28. The number of houses occupied is 711 and unoccupied 93.

The collection of revenue is made by Mr. Brown, who also exercises petty judicial powers usually inherent in the village head. The late Mr. F. C. Brown was appointed by Government to be an Honorary Magistrate of the First Class, and the High Court was also moved to issue in his name a Commission of the Peace. (*Vide* G.O., No. 1315, dated 14th September 1865.)

Mr. Murdoch Brown, son of Mr. F. C. Brown, was appointed by Government, in 1869, to be an Honorary Magistrate in the Chirakkal taluk with the powers of a Subordinate Magistrate of the Second Class (G.O., No. 52, dated 12th January 1869). The only paid public establishment at Anjarakandi is that of the Sub-Registrar of Assurances at that station.

CANNANORE—KIRAR TERRITORY.

By V. Chappu Menon, B.A.

This is a tract of land about 2,364 acres in extent in Cannanore belonging to the Māppilla Raja of Cannanore and which is held by his family under an agreement entered into with the British Government, as already described in Vol. I.

The judicial administration of the Kirar territory is conducted by the officers of the British Government. The raja is merely permitted to collect rents on the lands comprised within the Kirar limits, and has no power to interfere with the collection of special rates chargeable under the municipal or fiscal law. His palace is situated in what is called the old town of Cannanore, and is known as the Arakkal palace. A lamp is kept burning throughout the day and night in one of the rooms in the palace, the belief being that if extinguished the prosperity of the house would be destroyed. The maladministration of the Laccadive Islands belonging to the raja led to endless outbreaks and defiance of authority on the part of the islanders, and the revenue due to him was threatened with extinction. The peishcush due to Government also fell into arrears, and the Government of India therefore assumed the management of the islands till such time as the arrears remained unpaid and a better system of administration has been introduced into them. A detailed account of the islands is given separately.

The temples and mosques within the Kirar territory are shown below :

Names.	Descriptive remarks.
1. Thayil temple തയ്യിൽക്ഷേത്രം. ..	Image of Vishnu. Srikovil roofed with copper plate. The rest tiled.
2. Jamath mosque ജമാഅത്തപള്ളി. ..	A very important mosque roofed with copper plates. There are several small mosques within the town.
3. Thayil church തയ്യിൽപള്ളി. ..	Roman Catholic chapel—Tiled building.
4. Khajana Kōṭṭa ഖജാനക്കോട്ട. Chutikōṭṭa ചൂട്ടിക്കോട്ട Katalai Kōṭṭa കടലായിക്കോട്ട. Avera Kōṭṭa അവേരക്കോട്ട.	These are names of certain forts that existed within Kirar limits. All of these are now in ruins and have in some cases been converted into lands for cultivation.

The peishcush due by Sultan Aḻi Raja of Cannanore, according to the engagement dated 28th October 1796, is Rs. 15,000 per annum.

N.B.—The exact amount appearing in the Revenue accounts is Rs. 15,000-0-11, payable in three equal instalments—the first on the 15th of Dhanu (8th December), the second on the 15th of Medam (6th April), and the third at the end of Chingam (15th September).

An abatement of 1,500 star pagodas, equivalent to Rs. 5,250, was allowed by the Court of Directors in 1822 as compensation for the loss of the Amin Dīvi Islands attached to the South Canara District.

THE LACCADIVE ISLANDS.

By V. Chappu Menon, B.A.

Position and Extent.—The Laccadives (*Laksha Dwīpa*—"The hundred thousand islands," also called the Dīvi or Amindīvi Islands) consist of a group of islands off the Malabar Coast lying between 8° and 12° N. lat. and between 72° and 74° E. long. The northern portion of the group is attached to the collectorate of South Canara, and the southern portion, which is otherwise known as the Cannanore Islands, is attached to the Malabar district. The approximate area, population, and other particulars regarding the latter group are given below :—

Islands.	Distance from Calicut.	Area in square miles.	Population.	Number of houses.	Dependent islets.
	MILES.				
Agatti	218	1¼	1,375	302	(1) Parali, (2) Bangara, (3) Tinnakara, (4) Kalpitty.

Islands.	Distance from Calicut.	Area in square miles.	Population.	Number of houses.	Dependent islets.
	MILES.				
Kavaratti	195	$1\frac{1}{3}$	2,129	314	(1) Pitti, (2) Seuhelipar, consisting of Valiyakara and Cheriyakara.
Androth	139	$1\frac{2}{3}$	2,884	407	*Nil.*
Kalpeni	149	1	1,222	213	(1) Cheriyam, (2) Thilakka, (3) Pitti.
Minicoy (*Menakâyat*).	243	$1\frac{3}{4}$	3,191	524	(1) Viringilli.
Total ..	..	$7\frac{1}{3}$	10,801	1,760	

All the dependent islets are uninhabited, with the exception of Viringilli, which is used occasionally as a hospital for the small-pox patients of Minicoy.

Physical Aspects.—The topographical features of all the islands are very simple and almost identical. Each is contained within a coral reef stretching in a general direction from north to south and lies just within the eastern side of the reef, whilst on the western side a more or less extensive lagoon intervenes between the shore and the reef. Androth is, however, an exception to this rule, in that it has no lagoon worthy of the name and lies east and west instead of north and south. Outside the reef on one side the sea deepens abruptly beyond the reach of ordinary sounding tackle (on the east side, save in the case of Androth where it is on the south), and on the other the coral shoal slopes gradually away for some distance till a depth of about 20 fathoms is attained, when ordinary soundings again suddenly cease and reveal the existence of a stupendous submarine precipice. The water in the lagoon is generally so still that in the worst weather coir or coconut fibre may be soaked without danger of being washed away. The surface of the islands is almost flat, the small inequalities that exist being either of artificial origin as in Androth and Kalpeni, or in some few instances of the nature of sand dunes. The elevation is nowhere more than a few feet above the level of the sea. The crescent-shaped form of the body of the island is due to the more perfect development of the eastern and protected side of the coral formation. The same feature characterises all these shoals and leads to the theory[1] that they rose to the surface in the form of circular or oval shallow basins, and that, under the protection of the shoal, the eastern rim gradually developed itself towards the centre and formed an island. This theory is strengthened by the fact that on some of the islands this gradual increase towards the lagoon is still going on. The receding tide leaves the outer edge of the reef nearly dry, and the tide water passes out of the lagoon by two or three breaches in the outer rim, which are sufficiently large to admit the light native craft into the natural harbour formed by the lagoon and varying in depth from a few inches to several fathoms at low tide.

Soil and Products.—The soil is generally poor, consisting solely of white coral sand and extending for the most part to a depth of only a few feet,

[1] *Note.*—Mr. Darwin's theory that the coral insect by its ceaseless labours slowly formed the land as the island mountain tops as slowly sank in the ocean, is the one that best fits all the known facts. The coral insect, it seems, cannot work at greater depths than between 20 to 30 fathoms.—W.L.

at which depth a substratum of coral limestone is met with. In most of the islands also there are spots where the soil is almost entirely composed of loose coral stones. The islands are covered with vegetation, the luxuriance of which under such unfavorable circumstances is apparently due to the favorable climatic influences of their insular situation and to the fact that the coral free stone substratum underlying the islands is porous. In all the islands fresh water is to be found at a depth varying from 5 to 8 feet, but it is affected by the tide, rises and falls several inches, and is not as a rule very wholesome. The chief products are coconuts, limes, which grow luxuriantly in favourable situations, bread-fruit, dry grains and vegetables—the latter two only to a very limited extent.

There are cattle and goats in some, and fowls in all, of the islands. Rats are unfortunately numerous, and prove very destructive to the coconut plantations. Turtles, both of the green and of the tortoise shell-bearing species, are common, particularly the former, and fish, in great variety and of most astonishingly bright colors, are abundant. The sea slug (*holothuria*), which passes its time in taking in and discharging large quantities of sand, is also plentiful. Shell fish too are abundant, particularly the cowry, and conch shells are not uncommon.

In birds, the islands are singularly defective. The golden plover, the whimbrel, and one or two varieties of cranes visit the islands during their migrations, and owls have been imported to slay the rats.

People.—The people belong, without exception, to the Muhammadan faith, but they are organised after the Hindu fashion into three simple classes or castes—

(1) *Kārnavar* (*doers, agents*), consisting of the families of principal people who monopolise the boat-owning.

(2) *Mālumis*, subdivided into—
   (*a*) *Mālumis* proper (pilots or sailors), and
   (*b*) *Urukārs* (boat people), employed formerly as common sailors, but now in various avocations, and

(3) *Mēlachēris* (climbers), who are the tree-climbers and toddy-drawers and universally dependants of the higher classes.

Notwithstanding their form of religion, monogamy is universal, and the women appear in public freely with their heads uncovered, and in Minicoy take the lead [1] in almost everything, except navigation. Their language is Malayāḷum, which is usually written in the Arabic character, except in Minicoy where Mahl [2] with a mixture of corrupt Malayāḷum is spoken. The inhabitants, more especially those of Minicoy, are bold seamen and expert boat-builders. The condition of the various classes and their ordinary avocations are described in the separate notices of the islands.

History of the Islands.—The ancient history of the islands is involved in obscurity. Tradition says that the principal islands were settled about 1,000 years ago by people from the coast. The first occupation is attributed to an accident, but considerable voluntary immigration also appears to have taken place. The accident referred to was as follows :—

"A tradition is preserved among them that their forefathers formed part of an expedition from Malayāḷa, which set out for Mecca in search [3] of their

[1] *Conf.*, Vol. I, p. 287. [2] *Conf.*, Appendix XI. [3] *Conf.*, Vol. I, p. 241.

apostate King, Chēramān Perumāl, and was wrecked on these islands. The inhabitants certainly remained Hindus long after their first settlement and were probably converted to Islam not more than 250 or 300 years[1] back. They retain some of the general distinctions of caste as well as the law of succession in the female line with certain local modifications. This law is still adhered to on the island of Amindīvi, where distinctions of caste and a more numerous population have been obstacles to the gradual change by which the custom of regular parental descent is supplanting the local law of Malabar on the islands of Kadamat, Kiltan and Chetlat of the Canara portion of the group; in the southern islands, still under native management, the old custom is more rigidly observed."—(Robinson.)

Some of the principal inhabitants claim descent from the Nāyars and even the Nambūtiris of Malabar. The Mēlachēris are apparently the descendants of Tīyyars and Mukkuvars (fishermen) of the coast. The early administration of the islands appears to have been of a purely patriarchal type, conducted by a Mundyāl, Mudutāl or chief inhabitant, and the heads of the principal families. It continued till nearly the sixteenth century, and in no way differed from that prevailing on the mainland. Society was organised by castes having hereditary functions to perform in the body politic, and indeed the archaic form of organisation appears to have been better maintained in these isolated islands than on the mainland. The land in particular appears to have formed a portion of the common stock of the community—and, at the present time even, the idea of ownership *of the soil* has very imperfectly taken hold of the minds of these islanders. Minicoy, though the population is Mahl, is no exception to this rule, and so little has the idea of property *in the soil* taken root, that it is customary *even now* for a man to plant a coconut tree in his neighbour's backyard if his neighbour neglects this duty and if space is available. The trees growing on the soil are, however, strictly considered to be private property, and the islanders have marks which enable them to distinguish one man's trees from those of another. The islanders embraced Muhammadanism at some period subsequent to the thirteenth century, owing, as is supposed, to the preaching of Mumba Mulyaka, an Arab teacher who first appeared in the island of Amēni. He met with opposition at the outset, which was, however, overcome by his demonstration of miracles and supernatural powers. Androth, which was the scene of his first success, contains his grave and shrine and has always been looked upon as a holy island. The islanders were probably always more or less dependent on the princes of the Kōlattiri family and the admirals of their fleets, the progenitors of the Māppiḷḷa house[2] of Cannanore.

The Portuguese made a settlement on the island of Amēni, but were shortly afterwards (about A.D. 1545) exterminated by poison owing to the intrigues of the Kōlattiri princes. About 1550, the Kōlattiri Raja, who no doubt found the islands to be, after the advent of the Portuguese, an irksome possession, conferred them, it is said in Jāgir, with the title of Áḻi Raja (Raja of the deep or sea), on the head of the Cannanore family, the stipulated

---

[1] *Note.*—The islanders probably became Muhammadans at a somewhat earlier period than this. The change of faith was probably contemporaneous with the rise of the Mapiḷḷa house of Cannanore (*conf.*, Vol. I., p. 360 foot-note).

[2] *Conf.*, foot-note, Vol. I, p. 360.

peishcush being either 6,000 or 12,000 fanams. It is said that this tribute continued to be paid, but probably with more or less irregularity as the fortunes of the two houses waxed or waned, by the house of Cannanore to the Kōlattiri princes till the middle of the eighteenth century. The Bednur invasion and subsequently that of Hyder Ali led to the dismemberment of the Kōlattiri kingdom and to the independence of the Cannanore house, who retained the exclusive possession of the islands as allies of Hyder Ali and Tippu Sultan. The island of Minicoy appears to have been a more recent acquisition by the Cannanore family from the Sultan of the Maldives and the people probably never acknowledged fealty to the Kōlattiri princes.

The islanders state that it was surrendered by them to the Cannanore house on condition of protection being afforded to them against the Kōttakkal[1] Kunyāli Marakkārs, the famous Malayāli pirates, who used to harry the island periodically.

In 1786 the inhabitants of the group attached to the South Canara district revolted, in consequence of the rigorous enforcement of the coir monopoly, and transferred their allegiance from the Cannanore house to Tippu Sultan. In 1799, when Canara fell to the East India Company, these islands, which had been attached by Tippu Sultan to his Kacheri of Mangalore, were not restored to the Bibi of Cannanore, but a remission of 1,500 pagodas, equivalent to Rs. 5,250, was conceded instead in 1822. The Cannanore islands became at the disposal of the Company by the storming of Cannanore towards the end of 1791, and were further ceded with Tippu's entire dependencies in Malabar by the Treaty of Seringapatam in 1792. This southern or Malabar group of islands, along with Cannanore itself, are still held by the Cannanore family at a peishcush of Rs. 15,000 (less the remission above mentioned), alleged to be one-half of the profits derived from the trade with the islands and from the lands at Cannanore—a tribute which, though adopted only provisionally at the time of the first settlement, has remained unaltered to the present time. The Malabar islands have, in recent years, been twice sequestrated for arrears of revenue, and at the present time are under the direct management of the Collector of Malabar.

Fiscal Administration.—The sources of the revenue derived from the islands during their administration by the raja comprised—

(1) The monopolies of coir, coconuts, cowries, tortoise-shell, holothuria, and ambergris.

(2) Confiscations, escheats, naziranas, pilot customs, and fines for criminal offences and for evasions of fiscal restrictions.

Besides these, there were several other cesses levied by Mukhyastans, the Pandāram or fiscal agents of the raja and the kāzi, in matters falling within their respective provinces. But these, which were for the most part discretionary and unauthorised, have been given up or discontinued. The only monopolies now recognised are those of coir, cowries, tortoise-shell, holothuria, and ambergris. The two last named have almost died out, and yield no revenue to the Pandāram exchequer.

Coir Monopoly.—By far the most important item of revenue is the monopoly of island coir. The earliest form in which this assessment was collected was by the exaction of a tithe of the produce on exportation from the islands

[1] *Conf.*, Vol. I, p. 12 and p. 332 foot-note.

as well as by the collection of a tithe of rice brought in exchange. For two centuries this, with certain royalties, constituted the whole revenue of the group. In 1765 the right of purchase of coir by the Pandāram was first introduced, when the market value of that article was 60 to 70 rupees per candy, and the price to be paid by the Pandāram was fixed at Rs. 30 per candy payable in rice at a fixed rate of Rs. 2¼ per mūda, supposed to contain 50 Calicut seers, whilst the average price of rice was Rs. 1-12-0 per mūda. The tithe duty on coir was transferred to Cannanore and charged as an import duty; the tithe duty on rice imported into the islands was also retained. From these sources the profits were for a time enormous, and this system was pursued until 1826.

In 1827 the price of coir suddenly fell from Rs. 60 to Rs. 20 or less, but considering the profits derived from the coir monopoly for so many years previously, the Government held with regard to their Canara islands that they could not fairly call on the islanders to share in the loss by low prices, and no change whatever took place in the Government islands. In the Cannanore islands, on the other hand, the nominal price payable to the islanders was reduced from Rs. 30 to Rs. 22 subject to the same deductions as before (viz., 10 per cent. import duty on coir, 10 per cent. export duty on rice and 1 per cent. on account of sundry expenses), and to further aggravate the evil, the commutation price of Rs. 2¼ per mūda of rice was maintained, notwithstanding the fact that the market price at that time was only Rs. 1½.

In 1832 a further reduction was made in the rate of payment for coir which was fixed, irrespective of the market or any other money rates, at 5¾ mūdas of rice for a candy of coir subject to the usual deductions of 21 per cent. The price obtained by the islanders for their coir thus dwindled down to about Rs. 6-6-0 per candy. It was alleged by some of the islanders, who represented their grievances to Government, that, besides the starvation rate allowed to them on their coir, they were subjected to further and considerable hardships and losses, because—

(*a*) Their coir was dried[1] again and beaten in bundles at Cannanore with a view to reduce its weight.

(*b*) Deductions were made on account of old debts which were never proved to their satisfaction.

(*c*) The raja's agents exacted presents.

(*d*) There was considerable delay in settling the accounts and allowing the vessels to return to the islands.

All these charges were of course denied by the raja and his agents, but the fact remained that the islanders were driven into open defiance of his authority and refused to import any coir into Cannanore. These complaints, as well as the large arrears of peishcush left unpaid by the Cannanore house, induced Government to interfere in the interests alike of the raja and of the people, and the islands were on the last occasion attached and brought under Government management on the 3rd April 1875. The monopoly rates at which the islanders have been paid since 1st January 1878 for their coir are as follows:—

---

[1] The islanders, as recent experience shows, sometimes damp their coir to give it more weight. The temptation to do this must have been irresistible, when their produce was being paid for at a starvation rate.

(*a*) First sort coir per candy of 560 lb., Rs. 6 *plus* four sacks or eight mūdas of rice, nominally equivalent to Rs. 22 in all, but actually rising or falling above or below that sum according as the price of a mūda of rice rises above or falls below Rs. 2 per mūda.

(*b*) Second sort coir do., Rs. 4 *plus* $3\frac{1}{2}$ sacks or 7 mūdas of rice, nominally equivalent to Rs. 18 in all.

(*c*) Third sort coir do., Rs. 4 *plus* $2\frac{1}{2}$ sacks of rice, nominally equivalent to Rs. 14 in all. Each sack contains 100 Calicut seers of 65 tolas of rice each. The rates are very nearly the same as those prevailing on the Canara islands.

This arrangement is advantageous to the islanders because it secures to them payment for their coir yarn in the article (rice) in which payments are made for its manufacture at the islands, and the money payment in addition enables the islanders to purchase other articles of consumption. The islanders are (as in justice they ought to be, so long as such a faulty revenue system remains in force) protected against a falling market for their produce and a rising market for rice; and as matter of fact, the price of rice having risen of recent years, the islanders have been receiving for their coir yarn better prices than they could have obtained in the open market.

The following statement shows the revenue from the coir monopoly during five years ending with Fasli 1293. The figures represent actual sales, including in some cases the balance of coir yarn of previous year. For convenience, fractions of candies and rupees have been omitted.

Islands.	Fasli 1289 (1879-80).		Fasli 1290 (1880-81).		Fasli 1291 (1881-82).		Fasli 1292 (1882-83).		Fasli 1293 (1883-84).	
	Weight.	Value.	Weight.	Value.	Weight.	Value.	Weight.	Value.	Weight.	Value.
	CANDS.	RS.	CANDS.	RS.	CANDS.	RS.	CANDS.	RS.	CANDS.	RS.
Agatti ..	294	9,396	290	8,790	454	13,339	268	7,804	269	11,257
Kavarathi ..	439	13,984	391	11,890	579	16,907	431	12,851	443	18,567
Androth ..	517	16,454	466	13,942	679	19,989	493	23,774	454	19,069
Kalpeni ..	189	6,002	217	6,583	323	9,500	256	7,350	272	11,383
Minicoy ..	11	390	10	481	4	120	24	669	22	924
Total ..	1,450	46,226	1,374	41,686	2,039	59,855	1,472	52,448	1,460	61,200

The revenue fluctuates with the season and with the varying conditions of the coir market, and cannot be relied on. Sometimes the monopoly results in losses to the island administration. The coir monopoly does not exist in the island of Minicoy. A sort of Kārāyma or fixed rent, at the rate of 15 palams or 5 lb. of coir on each tree confiscated and allowed to remain in the management of the family from whom the property was seized, is exacted in some of the islands. The Kavaratti islanders chiefly noticed this as one of their grievances.

Coconut Monopoly.—In 1826 a coconut monopoly was established in the islands according to the same system as existed in regard to the coir. It has, however, since been abolished. During the continuance of the monopoly, people turned to the manufacture of jaggery which was free; but whereas in Agatti the toddy was not plentiful, they betook themselves to the manufacture of oil. Almost all the revenue derived from coconuts is now obtained from Minicoy; it amounted in Fasli 1293 (1883-84) to Rs. 20,394. The produce, however, included a portion of the stock of the previous year and was unusually large.

Cowry Monopoly.—It is not known at what period this monopoly was commenced. The fisheries were carefully preserved for the Pandāram and could not be undertaken without permission. This permission is, however, not required now except when people proceed to any part of the islands where there is danger of theft of Pandāram coconuts. When fished, the whole must be delivered under heavy penalties to the Pandāram. They were received originally by measure in exchange for rice, the earliest rate being two seers of rice for one seer of cowry. In 1826, when the price of coir fell, the cowry rate was reduced to one seer of rice for one seer of cowry. When this change tended to diminish the supply, the rice rate was raised from one to one and a half seers. The present price is 4 annas a seer of cowries, which weighs nearly two pounds. The monopoly is a failure. In Fasli 1293 there were purchased 11 candies, 10 maunds, 27 lbs. of cowries at a cost of Rs. 871-5-1 and these realized on sale only Rs. 448-4-7.

Tortoise-shell.—Green turtles are found in considerable numbers on the shoals and in the lagoons of the islands, and are valuable for their blubber. The tortoise-shell yielding species is comparatively rare. Up to 1815 the rate was 10 to 15 seers of rice for each tortoise-shell according to its size, and this was raised afterwards to Rs. 6 per lb. with a view to hold out sufficient inducement to the people to prosecute the fishing. The present rate is Rs. 2 per lb. In Fasli 1291, 11½ lbs. were purchased from the islanders at a cost of Rs. 23, and realized on sale Rs. 57-8-0. As cowries and tortoise-shell are not important sources of income to the islanders, there were no serious complaints about the inadequacy of the remuneration paid to them by the raja.

Holothuria (*Bēche-de-mer* of commerce).—The manufacture of *bēche-de-mer* appears to be somewhat recent and to have given rise to some successful speculation. The Pandāram claimed it as a royalty and preserved all holothuria, either manufacturing the *bēche-de-mer* on its own account or renting the fishing to coast merchants. Mr. Underwood, in 1882, found that "the trade in the Atta or sea-leach (*bēche-de-mer*) has not quite died out. Men do not come over from the mainland as in former days and hire labour to catch them. Some of the more industrious islanders go and pull them off the rocks and out of the sand and cure them. They are sent to Mangalore in the ōdams and thence shipped to China."

Ambergris.—Very little of this article is found on the islands, but when found it is considered to be a royalty.

Morinda Citron and Lime Monopoly.—The Morinda citron of Androth and the lime of Kavaratti were formerly articles of monopoly. The former used to be monopolised at one-fourth of its value and the latter gathered by the Pandāram agents, a good portion being taken as the Pandāram share and sent to Cannanore or made into pickles. The tax was abolished with the sanction of Government, conveyed in their order of 23rd February 1880.

Salt and Tobacco Monopoly.—On the introduction of salt and tobacco monopoly on the coast they were imitated in the Cannanore islands. The raja made considerable profit by this; but of late it has fallen into disuse, and the people now supply themselves. The free supply of salt to the islanders was recognized by Government in February 1880.

Pilot Customs.—The people of the group are skilful pilots. They used to pilot crafts from the coast till they cleared the group of islands, and also to Arabia. A nazirana, at the rate of Rs. 3-8-0 on a voyage of the former description and of Rs. 7 on the latter, was exacted. This has now been given up.

Other naziranas used to be exacted as follows :—

First.—Rs. 300 to 500 on succession of the heir to the office of kāzi, which is hereditary.

Secondly.—Rs. 100 to 300 on occasions of titles or dignities being conferred on principal personages. These titles had local privileges attached to them and implied power to levy certain contributions, such as pick of fish, &c.

Thirdly.—Rs. 4 to 11 on occasions of interviews or audiences of the raja.

Fourthly.—Payments for permission to wear ornaments. Formerly toddy-drawers, too, had to pay cesses under the name of naziranas towards the support of the public servants, although the trade in jaggery manufactured by them was free. All these have since been given up.

Bread-fruit trees have been assessed with the sanction of Government, conveyed in February 1880.

Waste Land.—The raja claims all waste lands as Pandāram or crown property. The claim has been acquiesced in to a large extent by the people. The ideas of the islanders in regard to property *in the soil* have been only slowly developing in recent years. Originally, the land was the common stock of the community and the administration is now engaged in dividing it among the people. The waste lands claimed by the raja are given on application to any one who will undertake under a cowle [1] or written agree-

---

[1] The form of cowle at present in use is as follows :—

Agreement between ________ on behalf of the Collector of Malabar and ________ of ________

I, ________, hereby lease to you ________ and I ________ hereby take on lease from you ________ the Pandaram land described at the foot of this document on the following terms :—

1. Whereas there are now standing on the said land the following trees :—

Coconuts.		Bread-fruit.	Limes.
Tei			
Kili			
Maram			
Phalam			
Aphalam			

I, ________, agree to pay rent for the same as specified below, viz. :—

(*a*) In ________ of coir of the best sort made in the island and at this rate in each year till ________.

ment to cultivate them within a certain time, and all improvements made become the sole property of the cultivator. When the land has been all thus settled, it will probably become possible to abolish the trade monopolies with their irksome restrictions, and to throw the island trade open.

General and Judicial Administration. — Very little is known about the ancient administration of the islands. The administrative machinery of each island consisted of a kāryakār (raja's agent), one accountant and three or four Nadapāls (village runners), the latter number having been subsequently reduced to two. These officers were under the immediate orders of Cannanore, and were seldom controlled in their work by the personal visits of either the raja or his principal kāryakārs. They were entrusted with the administration of petty police and civil justice, the maintenance and protection of the monopolies, the collection of revenue and the management of the Pandāram property.

The kāryakārs were aided in their work by mukhyastans or principal men who sat with them in committee in the adjudication of all matters. The mukhyastans were invested with certain dignities and privileges and had their office hereditary in their families. Their presence was necessary

---

(*b*) In ____________ of coir of the sort above said and at this rate in each year till ____________.

(*c*) In ____________ of coir and at this rate in each year until the undermentioned paimash is made.

2. I, ____________, further agree that within three years from the date of this lease the said land shall be cleared, and shall thenceforwards be kept clear, of jungle and planted up with coconuts, in such a manner that there may be at no time less than one plant for every ____________ perukams, exclusive of the land occupied by buildings.

3. Paimashes shall hereafter be made at such intervals as may be fixed with the sanction in writing of the Collector of Malabar, acting under the general or special orders of the Government of Madras, and at each paimash the rent to be thenceforwards paid by me shall be calculated at the rate of ____________ on each tree found to be in bearing at the said paimash.

4. I further undertake that I will not erect any mosque or bury any human body in the said land.

5. I, ____________, under the authority vested in me by Government through the Collector of Malabar undertake that no rent shall be demanded from you, your heirs, representatives or assigns on account of any trees hereafter planted by you or them on the said land until the expiration of ____________ years from the date of this lease.

6. I, ____________, further undertake that (subject to your punctually paying the stipulated rent, and otherwise complying with the terms of this agreement) you, your heirs, representatives or assigns shall not be ousted until the expiration of forty years from the date of this lease, nor after the termination of the lease, until you are paid the compensation provided for in the next succeeding paragraph. But with the sanction in writing of the Collector acting under the general or special orders of the Government of Madras, this contract may for any special reason be terminated after one year's notice in writing has been given to you. In this case you will be entitled to compensation as provided in paragraph 7 together with a further sum amounting in all to 15 per cent. of such compensation.

7. I further undertake that if you, your heirs, representatives or assigns are ejected on the expiration of your lease, or for non-payment of rent or for any other sufficient reason, you or they shall be paid compensation for all valuable trees of whatever description you or they have planted during the lease at rates to be fixed with the sanction in writing of the Collector of Malabar, acting under the general or special orders of the Government of Madras, or by a person appointed by him as arbitrator.

to constitute the kachēri for the transaction of business and they exerted considerable influence over the islanders. This form of patriarchal administration was suited to the rude state of society on the islands, but corruption and its concomitant baneful influences were rampant, and goaded the islanders into open rebellion and resistance of the Cannanore authority.

All cesses, customs and contributions due to the Pandāram and local servants, judicial fines and penalties for breaches of fiscal rules, &c., were secured by attachment and confiscation of the defaulter's property and where they could not be fully recovered they were carried into the accounts as debts against the family and realized whenever opportunity offered. Evasions of payments were also punished by fines and imprisonment. There were no prescribed rules of procedure in regard to trials or judicial proceedings and matters of importance were referred to Cannanore for orders. It was supposed that records had been kept of all such proceedings, but they were stated to be not forthcoming when demanded of the Raja by the Collector.

---

8. You, your heirs, representatives and assigns are at liberty to dig wells and tanks, to erect buildings (other than mosques) and to dwell on the land.

9. On you, your heirs, representatives or assigns being ejected you shall be at liberty to remove the said buildings, and shall be allowed one month so to do; subject to a lien thereon for any rent which may be due.

10. You shall not be entitled to receive any sum as compensation save and except in the manner provided in paragraphs 6 and 7.

11. Until the next paimash, the rent shown in paragraph 1 (*a*) and (*b*) as payable by you in coir shall at your option be payable in money at the rate of ____________ per ____________

12. You ____________________ shall be at liberty to relinquish the land after giving a year's notice in writing to the Collector of Malabar, but in this case you will not be entitled to any compensation for improvements.

13. If you, your heirs, representatives or assigns lease the land or any portion of it to a sub-tenant, the sub-lease shall be in writing and registered, and such sub-tenant shall not during the remainder of the currency of this lease, be ousted from possession of the land, except with the sanction in writing of the Collector of Malabar acting under the general or special orders of the Government of Madras, and then, only on compensation being paid to the sub-tenant at full market rates for all improvements made by him.

14. In the event of the rent being allowed by you to fall into arrears, it will be collected by the attachment and sale of your moveable property.

Name of Island.	No. of plot on Survey Map.	Measurement in 6 feet Koles.		Area.	Boundaries.			
		N. & S.	E. & W.		N.	E.	S.	W.

There was no distinction between criminal offences and those constituted by commercial and fiscal arrangements, and the same summary proceedings were resorted to in all matters.

It has been affirmed that offences of a heinous nature happily never occurred on the islands, and it is possible that this might have been the case. Some years ago the murder of a child alleged to have been committed with a view to obtain her jewels was stated to have occurred in the island of Kavaratti, and it was believed that the perpetrator's house was "plundered" by the inhabitants in an organised body,[1] the jewels and a boat were sold and the proceeds given to the victim's family. A plantation of 8 or 10 trees was also carried to the Pandāram account.

It is curious that this form of rough and ready justice was most frequently employed for the punishment of the offence of sorcery. In the adjudication of petty civil disputes oath, arbitration and ordeal were freely employed, and oaths in the name of the raja and on the Koran were considered peculiarly solemn. The kāzi also exercised jurisdiction over matters falling within his province.

The islands form one of the scheduled districts and no written law has yet been extended to them. Nor is there, so long as the islands remain under the direct administration of Government officers, much necessity for the introduction of written laws, which in the case of such archaic forms of society only lead to the breaking up of the bonds on which society rests, and to the consequent multiplication of chicanery, fraud, and other too numerous evils. When society has become more complex, written laws must of course follow; but meanwhile the enlightened despotism of the officers of Government, founded on justice and good conscience, is a form of administration which the islanders thoroughly appreciate and which they have as yet shown no wish to have changed.

Since the last sequestration of the islands, in April 1875, for arrears of peishcush due by Sultan Āḻi Raja of Cannanore, the administration of the islands has been improved in several ways. The islands have been periodically visited by Covenanted European officers and a small staff of clerks, and the grievances of the people have been fairly and equitably dealt with both on the spot as well as on the mainland. One amin with a gumasta (clerk) to assist him, and paid fairly well, has been appointed for each island, and has been authorized to try petty civil and criminal cases of a nature which do not involve any intricate or nice questions beyond the ken and intelligence of this class of officers. Their powers extend to a sentence of imprisonment not exceeding 15 days and of fine not exceeding Rs. 15, and the trial is conducted with the aid of two or more assessors selected in turn from the list of chief men in each island. A number of volumes of the Registration Department usually in use on the coast have been sent to the islands, and the amins have been directed to copy into them wills and other documents relating to divorce and other important transactions in the island. The present establishments on the islands are as follows:

---

[1] The *Kūṭṭam* (see Glossary) was no doubt a rough but most effective instrument of justice in such cases. The community simply rose and plundered (as in this instance) the guilty individual and his family, reducing them to beggary.

Islands.	Amins.		Gumastas.		School-masters.		Peons.		Total.	
	No.	Salary.	No.	Salary.	No.	Salary.	No.	Salary.	No.	Salary.
		RS.		RS.		RS.		RS.		RS.
Agatti ..	1	20	1*	15	..	..	2	8	4	43
Kavaratti ..	1	20	1*	12	..	..	2	8	4	40
Androth ..	1	20	1	7	1	15	2	8	5	50
Kalpeni ..	1	20	1*	10	..	..	2	8	4	38
Minicoy ..	1	25	1	15	..	..	3	13½	5	53½
Total ..	5	105	5	59	1	15	11	45½	22	224½

* Does also the duty of schoolmaster.

The islands were attached on the first occasion for arrears of peishcush due to Government under orders issued on the 7th September 1854, but from circumstances beyond control there was some delay in carrying them into effect. The islands of Androth, Kalpeni, Kavaratti and Agatti were taken charge of on the 9th November 1854, and the island of Minicoy on the 22nd March 1855, but there was resistance in the last-named island owing to the intrigues of the house of Cannanore, and this was not finally overcome till after the visit of Mr. Thomas in the early part of 1858. The islands were released from attachment on liquidation of arrears in 1861. The attachment on the second or last occasion took place on the 3rd April 1875.

The names of officers who have from time to time visited some or all of the islands are as follows :—

Name of officer.	Designation.	Date of visit.	Remarks.
Lieutenant Bentley ..	....	1795 ..	To institute enquiries as to the condition and resources of the islands.
Mr. (afterwards Sir) William Robinson.	Head Assistant Collector.	1847 ..	To afford relief to the islanders who were in distressed circumstances after the great storm of April 1847.
Mr. E. C. G. Thomas.	Special Assistant Collector.	1856 ..	To inspect and report on the islands after their sequestration by Government for arrears of peishcush.
	Do. ..	1858 ..	To investigate the cause of the mutinous spirit exhibited by the people of Minicoy and to bring them to a sense of allegiance to Government.
Mr. W. Logan	Sub-Collector ..	1869 ..	To report on the condition of the islands, their administration and remedial measures for establishing order and good government.
Mr. J. B. Spedding ..	Do. ..	February 1873.	To ascertain whether the arrangements suggested in Mr. Logan's report had been carried out by the raja and his agents.

Name of officer.	Designation.	Date of visit.	Remarks.
Mr. H. M. Winterbotham	Special Assistant Collector.	February and March 1876.	To dispose of island matters on the spot and to submit proposals for the administration of the islands.
	Do. ..	December 1877 and January and February 1878.	Do. do.
Mr. V. A. Brodie ..	Do. ..	January to March 1880.	For disposal of ordinary island matters.
Mr. W. G. Underwood ..	Do. ..	November 1881 to February 1882.	
Mr. A. C. Tate	Do. ..	January to March 1884.	
Mr. G. W. Dance ..	Head Assistant Collector.	December 1884.	To appoint a competent Amin at Minicoy.
	Do. ..	January 1885.	For the disposal of ordinary island matters.
Mr. W. Logan	Collector.	January 1887.	Do. do.
Mr. G. W. Dance ..	Head Assistant Collector.		

AGATTI ISLAND.

Position and Extent.—The island of Agatti, situated in Lat. 10° 51′ 30″ N. and Long. 72° 28′ E. and lying about 35 miles north-west of Kavaratti, is the most westerly of the Laccadive group. In formation it somewhat resembles Kalpeni. Like that island, it lies north-east and south-west, and has on its western side a fine lagoon. The coral shoal upon which it stands is between 6 and 7 miles in length and from 3½ to 4 miles in breadth. On the east, the reef is situated close to the beach and beyond it the water deepens rapidly; whilst on the west, the reef trends outwards so as to enclose the lagoon, which at its broadest point is more than two miles wide, and in this direction beyond the reef the slope of the coral shoal is very gradual. Besides the main island, the reef also encloses the small uninhabited island of Kalpitti situated to the south of Agatti proper and separated from it by a narrow and shallow channel. The main island is long and narrow, being nearly 5 miles in length, whilst its greatest breadth is under 1,000 yards. The southern portion consists of a long narrow strip averaging for more than 2 miles of its length little over 100 yards in width. The total area of the two islands is 716 acres or nearly $1\frac{1}{8}$ square miles, Agatti comprising an extent of 688½ acres and Kalpitti 27¼ acres. At a distance of about 5 miles to the north lie the uninhabited islands of—

1. Bangara (115 acres),
2. Tinnakara (76¾ acres),
3. Parali (10 acres),

but these, though situated upon what is no doubt an extension of the Agatti coral shoal, are enclosed by a separate range of reefs and the channel between is deep.

There are two entrances into the lagoon navigable by the island vessels, viz., one situated close in shore at the north-western extremity of the island, and the other on the west side of the lagoon. The former is the passage ordinarily used by the island vessels, but the latter is the largest. At high water, there is in this passage about 7 feet of water and inside the lagoon a depth of several fathoms is obtained. As the lagoon is fairly free from coral rocks its navigation is easy.

Soil and Products.—The soil is comparatively sterile. About two-thirds of the island are under coconut cultivation and the rest is waste, but there are no large jungles. The lands claimed by the Pandāram are of small extent and as the cultivation is very imperfect and the quality of the soil poor, only a small revenue is obtained from them in this island. Some attempts have been made to form a *tōttam* (artificial low land) for the cultivation of cereals, but the extent is trifling and the quality very poor. The only grain raised is a sort of vetch (*payar*), but the quantity is small. The islanders also cultivate sweet potatoes and plantains to a small extent, and there are a few bread-fruit trees, lime trees, one areca palm and betel vines. A plant called Ittala grows in Bangara, from the root of which a sort of tapioca is obtained used as diet for invalids. The fauna and flora of Agatti are the same as in the case of Kalpeni and Androth, save that in this island and in Kavaratti there are no crows.

Animals.—The islanders possess 110 cattle and 46 goats and the usual domestic fowls. One islander introduced a pair of rabbits from the coast a few years ago and they seem to thrive well. The sea products are the same as those of Kalpeni. Fish of many kinds is abundant and the inhabitants are very expert fishermen.

People, their Customs and Occupation.—This island is a mēlachēri or low caste island, but the division of the people into castes according to occupations that exist in the other islands is also found here, viz. :—

(*a*) Kārnavars (principal inhabitants),
(*b*) Urukārs or sailors, and
(*c*) Mēlachēris or tree-climbers.

In disposition the inhabitants are the most enterprising and energetic, and are also very hospitable and cheerful. Both in person and in their habits they are very cleanly. The language differs slightly from that of the other northern islands and bears a closer resemblance to Tamil in interrogative suffixes. Thus they use "â" for "ō" as the interrogative affix, *e.g.*, "orangiyâ," did you sleep? Of the men belonging to the two lower classes only about half permanently reside in the island. The others go and settle on the coast, either in Malabar or Canara, as topee-makers (capmakers), and as the price obtained for a topee varies from Rs. 5 to Rs. 15, this is a pretty profitable employment. As this occupation deprives the kārnavar (or headmen) to a large extent of the personal services of their dependents, it is not very popular amongst them. Besides topee-making those who settle on the coast are in the habit of chanting the koran at private houses, for which they get their food and a small present.

Population, Sanitary Condition and Medical Aspects.—The population of the island, according to the census of 1881, was 1,375, of whom 672 were males and the rest females. In 1848 the population numbered 1,545.

The houses are built much in the same style as those of Androth, but they differ in two important respects. First, there is no central hall off which all the rooms open, and, secondly, the back verandah is within and not outside the outer wall of the building. As in Androth, the walls are built of quarried slabs of coral free stone, but these are not kept in position by posts. As they whitewash the outer walls of their houses, they have a cleaner and brighter appearance than in any of the other islands. The doors and barred windows also are usually painted black or green, and in respect of ventilation they are superior, as they are built with eaves, and the rooms have barred windows. The people also pay more attention to conservancy than those of the other islands, and all house-refuse is collected in one spot and either used for manuring the coconut trees or burnt from time to time.

No epidemic has visited the island of late years, and the only prevailing complaints are eye-diseases and skin-diseases.

Education.—Secular education is more neglected here by the people than in Androth.

Out of 30 boys, with whom a school was established in 1878, only 11 appeared for examination in 1880. There are four mosque schools, at which about 60 boys and girls of the better classes are taught the koran.

Religion and Mosques.—The people are, as in other islands, exclusively Muhammadan. The number of mosques in 1880 was 27, of which 19 had cemeteries attached to them. The number of mosques in 1848 was 35.

Manufactures and Trade.—The manufactures and trade of this island are the same as in other islands and call for no special notice. The number of boats owned in 1876 was 121, of which 18 were large and the rest small. The total number prior to 1847 was 68.

Survey and Cowles.—The survey of the island has been completed and a portion of the Pandāram lands has been granted on cowle or lease.

Sub-divisions of the Island.—The island is divided into three cheries or sub-divisions, viz., 1. Edacheri, 2. Vadakancheri and 3. Tekkancheri.

General remarks.—In June 1880, a British steamer, named the "Mahableshwar," was wrecked on the reefs of this group of islands.

KAVARATTI ISLAND.

Position and Extent.—This island is situated in Lat. 10° 34′ N. and Long. 72° 57′ E., and so is distant about 74 miles from Kalpeni and 35 from Agatti. The coral shoal is the least extensive of any. The length of the island from north-east to south-west is about 3½ miles and its greatest breadth about three-quarters of a mile. The area is 865½ acres or about 1⅓ square miles. As usual the island is situated just within the reef on the east, whilst on the west there is a lagoon which at its widest part is about half a mile broad. At the southern end it would appear that there was formerly a separate island, but it is now connected with the main island by a narrow strip of land about 50 yards wide. The islets attached to Kavaratti are—

1. Pitti.
2. Seuheli or Seuhelipār composed of { (a) Valiyakara. (b) Cheriyakara.

The former, a mere sandbank on a coral limestone foundation, lies about 15 miles to the north-west of Kavaratti and is frequently visited by the people of that island and by those of Agatti and Amēni for fishing purposes. A pile of stones with a stout post in the centre has recently been put up as a landmark to attract the attention of mariners. The tides here run strong and there is often great difficulty in landing owing to the surf.

About 37 or 40 miles to the south-west of Kavaratti lies the coral shoal of Seuheli or Seuhelipār. It is composed of Valiyakara (big shore) at the northern extremity of the lagoon and of Cheriyakara (little shore) at its southern extremity. These two islets were formerly the common property of the Kavaratti islanders, but were many years ago confiscated by the Pandāram. As in Bangaram and Tinnakara the coral substratum is imperfect in both islets so that no fresh water is procurable; but for the same reason the soil is exceptionally damp and fertile.

Valiyakara is completely overrun with jungle, throughout which scattered coconut trees occur. Unlike the jungle in the other islands it contains no screw-pine whatever. In the centre there are large trees of various kinds, the most common being a species of banian (*Ficus Indica*). At the eastern and western extremities, the jungle becomes smaller and is composed of a species of shrub resembling the Rhododendron called Kanni by the islanders. On the north the shore is composed of coral rock and the vegetation overhangs the water. On the other shores the beach is sandy.

Cheriyakara lies east and west and has an extreme length of three-quarters of a mile. Its breadth at the widest point does not exceed a quarter of a mile. The area is 81¾ acres. The beach is generally sandy and the lagoon in its immediate neighbourhood is very shallow, especially on the south and east where large sand flats are left dry at low tide. Unlike Valiyakara it contains no jungle worthy of the name. The island is covered with coarse long grass and a kind of small shrub. There is a well the water of which though brackish is occasionally used for cooking and drinking purposes. Near the centre and at about 100 yards from the eastern shore there is an extensive shallow pond and marsh of stagnant water surrounded by a dense fringe of small shrubs. It serves no useful purpose whatever and might be filled up.

Soil and Products.—The soil of Kavaratti is poor and is unsuited for the cultivation of cereals or vegetables. Beans, plantains and brinjals and a few areca palms, tamarind trees and betel vines are, however, grown; but the extent of cultivation is very limited and is hardly worth the name. The people depend almost entirely upon their coconut cultivation which covers nearly the entire island. A leaf disease formerly affected many coconut trees. There are a considerable number of bread-fruit and lime trees; the timber of the former is used for ship-building and by the toddy-drawers for making wooden vessels to hold toddy.

Animals.—The number of cattle and goats in 1880 was 137 and 193 respectively. The chief sea-products, besides fish, are cowries, tortoise and turtle. The latter is captured chiefly for its oil. The lagoon adjacent to Seuheli affords excellent fishing. People, who visit Seuheli for fishing purposes, are allowed to pluck the coconuts required for their use free of payment. This privilege has existed for a long time.

People, their Customs and Occupation.—The same division of the inhabitants into classes or castes exists here as in Androth, but all castes claim to be janmis. A few who immigrated from other islands at the time of the great storm in 1847 are dependents of the Koyas; some of the lower classes are topee-makers like those of Agatti. Mōlachēris are called Thandēls at Kavaratti. The people are as a rule quarrelsome and litigious; the Malumis are more numerous and influential than the same class on other islands.

Population, Sanitary Condition and Medical Aspects.—The population of the island, according to the census of 1881, was 2,129, of whom 1,030 were males and the rest females. The number in 1848 was 2,060. The houses along the west coast of Kavaratti are built in a row and in close proximity to each other. On the east and south coasts they are scattered here and there and are built in the same fashion as those of Androth. The health of the island has of late been good. In 1039 M.E. (1863-64 A.D.) about 700 people are supposed to have died of cholera.

Education.—A Malayāḷam school started at Kavaratti was closed for want of pupils. The number shown in the census report of 1881 as "instructed" and under "instruction" is 513.

Religion and Mosques.—The inhabitants are exclusively Muhammadans. The number of mosques in 1848 was 51. At Seuheli there is a mosque of rude construction and the tomb of a pious Tangal held in much veneration by the islanders. Many miracles are ascribed to him, and it is especially common to invoke his aid in storms or when distressed by adverse winds. The islanders say that when in a storm they make a vow to visit the shrine of this saint the sea at once goes down and the winds become favourable.

Manufactures and Trade.—The manufactures of this island consist mainly of coir-yarn. The number of boats owned by the islanders in 1876 were 30 large and 126 small vessels.

Pandāram Lands and Income therefrom.—In this island as elsewhere the body of the island is the common property of the people. Over a part, however, the Pandāram asserts exclusive claims on the ground that it was formerly waste land and therefore the property of the raja. The claims were resisted by the people and gave rise to great discontentment and opposition on their part.

The Pandāram income is derived—

1st. From the trees on the Pandāram Pak (forbidden ground) to the south of the island which comprises about one-fourth of the total area. It is cut off from the body of the people's plantation by an old wall probably thrown up while it was really waste, and as such no entry could be made on this land without a pass from the raja's agent.

2nd. From the trees on pādipādi (half and half) lands, the produce of which is equally divided between the Pandāram and the tenants.

3rd. From Nāttagatta Karāyma, a fixed rent on escheated trees in various parts of the island.

4th. From Chuttu Karāyma, a fixed rent arbitrarily assessed on all trees growing within 40 koles (kole = 30 inches) of the sea-shore.

All these lands have been granted to tenants on cowle with the exception of Chuttu Karāyma lands, the rents of which were relinquished in favour of the occupants of the adjacent holdings. The tax on lime trees was remitted, and the bread-fruit trees were brought under assessment.

Sub-divisions of the Island.—The inhabited portion of the island is divided into four chēris, viz. :—

1. Mēlachēri or Mōchēri on the north-west coast.
2. Tekkechēri on the east coast.
3. Porakechēri to the south.
4. Pallichēri on the south-west shore.

Porakechēri is separated from Mōchēri and Pallichēri by a small valley which was apparently excavated formerly for grain cultivation.

ANDROTH ISLAND.

Position and Extent.—This island, which is the largest of the northern group of the Cannanore islands, is situated in Lat. 10° 48′ N. and Long. 73° 57′ E. It is about 139 miles from Calicut and differs in its formation from all the other islands of the group in that it lies east and west and has hardly any lagoon. The coral shoal upon which it is situated is of considerable extent, but the coral crops up to the surface only in the immediate neighbourhood of the land, the reef being hardly anywhere above sixty yards from the beach, and on the east the beach and reef are coincident. The greatest length of the island from south-east to north-west is about 3½ miles, and the greatest breadth, which is at about the centre of the island, is 1¼ miles. The area is 1,067⅘ acres or about 1⅔ square miles. The coast line is scarcely at all indented, so that the island forms a regular oval figure. The surface is generally a level plain, elevated but a few feet above the sea, but here and there it is varied by mounds formed mostly of the heaped-up material excavated in forming the "Tottam" or arable land. The highest mound is probably not 40 feet above the sea and the average elevation not more than 7 or 8 feet.

Soil, Products.—The soil is comparatively superior to that of other islands save perhaps parts of Kalpeni. It is richest in the centre and west parts and poorest on the south-east, where it is largely mixed with coral stones varying in size from small pebbles to considerable boulders. The Pandāram or crown lands comprise about one-fourth of the area of the island, and are scattered throughout the holdings of the islanders. They have been acquired by escheat or confiscation and contained, according to Sir William Robinson's report, about 20,000 coconut trees prior to the great storm of 1847. The chief Pandāram possessions are the East and West Valiya Pandarāms which are comparatively in a neglected condition. The holdings of the islanders are well stocked with coconut trees. The chief produce of the island is coconuts; but dry grains, such as raggi, varagu, and millet, yams, sweet potatoes, bread-fruit trees, plantains, limes, areca palms and betel vines are also grown to a limited extent.

Animals.—The number of cattle and goats is larger in this island than in any other and amounted in 1880 to 208 cattle and 418 goats. The only other domestic animals are fowls and cats. There are several species of rats which commit great injury to coconut plantation. The crow is the only wild bird that breeds on the island, but it is visited by various kinds of sea birds and also by migratory birds, such as the golden plover, the smaller curlew and the cuckoo. As there is no lagoon, the turtle and tortoise are very scarce, and from the absence of extensive shallow coral banks, the same is the case with cowries and other shells. Fish also are not plentiful, but there is a small species of octopus, called by the islanders *appallu*, which when roasted is esteemed a great delicacy.

People, their Customs and Occupation.—The people of the island fall under three main classes, viz.:—

(1) Kārnavar (*doers, agents*), sub-divided into Kārnavar proper and Thanakapirantha Kudiyāns.

(2) Mālumis (*pilots and sailors*), sub-divided into (*a*) Mālumis proper, (*b*) Urukārs.

(3) Mēlachēris (*tree-climbers*).

The first class of Kārnavars is composed of the rich ōdam (vessel) owners and Panchayatkārs (arbitrators). The male members of this class are also distinguished by the title of Koya—a religious dignity. The island Kārnavans, Amin and Kāzi, all belong to this class. The Thanakapirantha Kudiyāns are less wealthy and cultivators. The second class or the Mālumis are, as the name implies, sailors. They are generally Paṭṭa Kudiyāns, *i.e.*, partly independent and partly dependent on the higher classes. The only difference between the Mālumis proper and the Urukārs appears to be in the names. The third class, Mēlachēris, are servants and toddy-drawers (the name signifies one who works aloft).

These are generally Adima Kudiyāns or serfs of the Kārnavars, but they are at liberty to change their employers. Intermarriage between the two classes of Kārnavars is free and unrestrained, and lately it appears that the *jusconnubium* (right of intermarriage with Kārnavars) has been accorded to the second class, but it is still withheld from the third class or Mēḷachēris, intermarriage with whom is punished by the exclusion of the offender from his or her caste. The marriage is, however, deemed a valid one.

The islanders compare favourably in physique with the people of the coast and in their customs and habits closely resemble the Māppiḷḷas of North Malabar. The men of the upper classes wear jackets and head gear, but the Mēlachēris or lowest classes wear neither the one nor the other. Contrary to what is the usage on the mainland, the women do not cover their heads and are not kept in seclusion. The women are generally very untidy and dirty.

The people are, as a rule, quiet in their disposition, but the complexities of the Muhammadan rules of inheritance and marriage and the existence, side by side, of the Makkatāyam and Marumakkatāyam rules give rise to frequent litigation. The men are comparatively indolent, but the women are engaged from morning till dark in cooking, pounding rice, beating, unravelling and twisting coir-fibre, carrying loads, boiling toddy in order to make jaggery, &c.

It is somewhat difficult to define what is the occupation of the Kārnavar class, as they rarely do any thing save bullying their dependents or quarrelling among themselves ; occasionally they do a little cultivation and fishing, and those who have ōdams (vessels) superintend the repairs and accompany the ōdam on the voyage to the coast where they do all the buying and selling, only rendering an account upon the return of the ōdam to the island.

The dependents of the Kārnavar caste serve for nothing in their master's ōdam (boat), or, when he has none, in the ōdam in which he sails or sends his goods. The Kudiyān must also ship the produce of his trees, &c., in the master's ōdam, or through him in the ōdam in which the master ships his own goods, and 20 per cent. of the goods he so exports is appropriated by the master as freight. The *tōttam* or arable land is sometimes cultivated by the master, but most is given over to Kudiyāns (dependents) on the share-and-share-alike system.

The income of the Kārnavar class, who are all landholders and many of them ōdam-owners, is thus derived from the following sources:—

(1) From the produce of parambas retained in their own hands.
(2) From the export and sale of the goods worked up by the females of the family.
(3) From the freight paid them by their Kudiyāns on the goods they export. Where the Kārnavan is also the ōdam-owner he gets the whole 20 per cent.; when he is not, he usually gets freight for his own goods and those of his Kudiyāns at the rate of 10 per cent. in the ōdam of another and the other 10 per cent. of the exports of his Kudiyāns is alone appropriated by him.
(4) From the rent (half the produce) of their arable lands.
(5) Kudiyāns are also bound to give the Kārnavan a share of the fish they catch when fishing in his boat and to make presents on the occasion of weddings and other festivities in the Kārnavan's family.
(6) Some of this class also make tours on the mainland giving themselves out to be priests and often return to the island with large sums collected from the faithful of the places they visit.

The second class or Mālumis are sailors and are engaged in exporting the produce of the island to the mainland in the Kārnavars' ōdams; some of them also possess fishing boats and small ōdams of their own, in which they make voyages to the coast, and this has excited the jealousy of the Kārnavar class, who look upon them as interlopers and rebels. There is thus ill-feeling between the two classes.

The Mēlachēris or the third class are the hardest working population of the island. They alone climb trees and so pluck the nuts and draw toddy from the trees in the possession of the higher classes. For plucking nuts, a small percentage is given them as hire, and the toddy which is drawn twice a day is given every other day to the Kārnavan, *i.e.*, half goes to the Mēlachēri and half to the Kārnavan. Besides their profession of toddy-drawing, they have to do ōdam service for their lords, and they also work in the *tōttam* and go fishing. A few coast people who have settled in the island are silversmiths and jewellers.

Population, Sanitary Condition and Medical Aspects.—The population of the island previous to the great storm of 1847 was 2,576; in 1876 it was 2,629. According to the census of 1881 it numbered 2,884 souls, of whom 1,412 were males and 1,472 were females. A large number of people perished during the storm of 1847, and it is believed that the number that remained in the island, omitting those who emigrated to the other islands, did not exceed 900. The island has now thoroughly recovered itself from the disastrous effects of 1847.

The sanitary condition of the island, although more satisfactory than that of the rest is, as might be expected, very backward. There is no conservancy, and house-refuse is allowed to accumulate in the house-yards until it becomes objectionable, when it is collected and occasionally burnt. Rarely it is placed as manure in the pits in which young coconut-plants are planted. Water-supply is good, there being as a rule a well attached to each house. The wells consist of a pit about 5 feet square and about 5 feet deep with steps leading down one side to a similar pit at the bottom cut through the coral substratum. From these wells, which are never dried up, excellent water is obtained. Some of the mosques and better sort of houses have also small tanks similarly constructed attached to them. These are used for bathing purposes only, but the sea is the chief resort for this purpose. There are no wells for purely cultivation purposes.

The houses are built with thin slabs quarried from the coral free stone substratum, the size of the blocks averaging about 5 to 6 feet in length, 2 feet in width and 4 inches in thickness. These are placed lengthwise on their edges and the walls so formed are plastered to give them stability. The houses are ill-ventilated and are in some cases so dark that a stranger requires to be shown about with torch or other light. The higher and lower clases are opposed to vaccination, but several children have been operated on, and a beginning has been made. There are two native physicians in the island. They purchase the necessary medicines from native physicians on the coast. There is hardly any medicinal plant to be found there. The most prevalent diseases are fever, rheumatism, consumption, dysentery, itch and ophthalmia.

Education.—The upper classes do not seem to be wanting in intelligence, but they are very indifferent to education, whilst the lower classes from the state of the subjection in which they are held are rude and ignorant. Most of the members of both sexes belonging to the former class can read the koran character, but the number that can read Malayāḷam is comparatively limited. The number shown in the census return of 1881 is 89. A school was started by Mr. Winterbotham in 1878 with a nominal roll of 36 boys, but this number had dwindled away to 14 in 1880. The plan of combining mosque schools and secular schools is being tried.

Religion and Mosques.—All the people of the island profess Muhammadanism. There were 30 mosques in 1880, of which 28 had grave-yards attached.

Manufactures and Trade.—The only manufactures carried on in the island are the manufacture of coir-yarn and that of jaggery. Shark fins are cured for exportation in small quantities, but the curing of *holothuria* has been entirely given up. Jaggery is prepared from *meerah* (as the sweet toddy drawn from the coconut palm is called) by a process of evaporation. In order to prevent fermentation, in place of rubbing the collecting pots with *chunam* (lime water) as is done on the mainland, the Mēlachēris are in the habit of putting in them small coral limestone pebbles which answer the same purpose, and to this cause is attributed the peculiar sweet taste of the island toddy. When the *meerah* has become semi-fluid, which it does after about two hours boiling, various articles are usually mixed with it in order to flavour it, such as rice, raggi flour and the scrapings of tender coconuts, &c. It is then taken off the fire and allowed to cool, when it forms a solid but sticky mass. This the women mould into balls (Pindika) of from 1 lb. to 2 lbs. in weight, which they wrap up in bread-fruit tree leaves, and in this form it is exported. At Calicut a price of about two annas per pound is obtained. Jaggery is used by Māppiḷḷas in the preparation of the Calicut "alva," a very popular sweetmeat amongst them. Ambergris, which was mentioned by Sir William Robinson as a product of Androth, was found by Mr. Brodie only in the possession of one islander.

The principal exports from the island are, as in all other islands, coir-yarn, coconuts, with and without husk, jaggery and pindika (a kind of sweetmeat) and a little vinegar, lime-pickle and shark fins. The imports are rice, salt, areca-nuts, betel, curry-stuffs, cooking utensils, both earthen and metal, implements of husbandry, clothes and occasionally cattle and ornaments. Teak, mango-wood and bamboos are also imported and used in repairing the ōdams and small boats. As Androth is the nearest island to the coast, many ōdams from other islands call there for water, &c., both on their way to the mainland and when returning. The usual coast markets visited by the islanders are Calicut, where they sell their goods, and Mangalore where they usually purchase their supplies. Occasionally they also call at Tellicherry and Cannanore. The number of boats possessed by the islanders in 1880 as contrasted with the numbers in 1876 and 1848 is given below :—

Year.	Large coast-going vessels.	Small boats and fishing crafts.	Total.
1848	31	152	183
1876	32	130	162
1880	40	162	202

Survey and Cowles.—The demarcation and survey of the Pandāram lands in Androth have been completed and most of the lands granted on cowle.

Sub-divisions of the Island.—The island is divided into four sub-divisions or *chēris*, viz. :—

(*a*) Edachēri,
(*b*) Mēchēri,
(*c*) Kīchēri, and
(*d*) Chēmachēri.

The last *chēri* is situated upon the southern shore and separated from Edachēri by the *tōttam* or garden. Formerly these *chēris* were political and revenue sub-divisions, but now that all matters are decided by the Amin with the assistance of the Kārnavars, regardless of the chēri to which the latter belong, and the Mūppans and the Nadapals are abolished and the revenue administration directly committed to the Amin, these sub-divisions have lost all importance. There are no islets attached to Androth for administrative purposes.

KALPENI ISLAND.

Position and Extent.—The island of Kalpeni lies about 44 miles due south from Androth in Lat. 10° 7′ N. and Long. 73° 55′ E., and is thus the most southerly of the northern group or Laccadives proper. The coral shoal upon which it stands is very extensive, being about 8 miles in length and 3½ to 4 in width. Besides the main island (Kalpeni proper), which alone is inhabited, there are two small rocky islands to the south-west, called respectively Thilakka and Pitti, separated from the mainland

38

and each other by narrow channels and a long narrow island called Cheriyam, about 1½ miles to the north of the main island. These four islands together form a figure resembling a bottle with an elongated neck (Cheriyam and the north of Kalpeni) running from north by east to south by west. The extreme length from the north point of Cheriyam to the south point of Kalpeni is about 7 miles, and the greatest width about three-quarters of a mile. The total area of the group is 650 acres or just over 1 square mile. On the east, the reef forms the shore line of Kalpeni and Cheriyam and on the south lies but a short distance from the beach. On the west it trends outward so as to enclose a magnificent lagoon of still water over 7 miles in length and from 2 to 2½ miles broad at its widest point. The entrance, distant some 4 miles from the landing place, is good; but although the lagoon attains a depth of over three fathoms in many places its navigation is rendered very intricate and difficult by numerous coral rocks that rise in many instances to within a foot or so of the surface at low-water. As there are no waves, no breakers disclose their presence, but in daylight their situation is easily discernible. On the east the coral shoal slopes rapidly away. On the west beyond the reef, the slope is so gradual that the bottom can be seen for a considerable distance. The channels between the various islands are at low water very shallow, and the islanders can easily pass on foot from one to another, and it was from these shoals (particularly that between the main islands and Cheriyam) that cowries, of which this island used to export the largest quantity, were usually gathered.

	ACRES.
Kalpeni	494½
Cheriyam	129⅜
Thilakka	12¾
Pitti	13⅛
Total ..	649⅞

The main island is about 3 miles long. For the first two miles of its length from the north it consists of a long strip increasing in width from about 50 yards at its northern extremity to about 400 yards at the termination of the big north Pandāram, after which it suddenly bulges out, attaining its greatest width in a few hundred yards. Only this southern portion is inhabited, as it is only here that good drinkable water is procurable. No drinkable water is found in the other small islands. All the uncultivated portion of the main island and the attached islets are covered with a dense jungle of screw pine, &c., in many parts of which scattered coconut trees occur. Perhaps the most remarkable feature in the topography of the island, the general level of which is very low, is the natural sea-bank of coral stones along the east and south-east shore. This bank is supposed to have been cast up by the sea at the time of the great storm in 1847. As it is about 12 feet high and 60 feet in width at the base, it forms a grand natural barrier against the recurrence of such a disaster. It is a peculiarity of this island that the coral substratum is wanting, or at least not so solidified into a layer of limestone rock as in the other islands.

Soil and Products.—The soil appears to be very good in the central and southern portions of the main island, but the smaller islands of the group are very rocky and though covered with luxuriant vegetation, the coconut trees growing in them are not very productive. Along the east shore of the main island also there is a long strip about 50 yards wide, so stony that its cultivation would be very difficult and probably unproductive. Besides land suited to the cultivation of the coconut palm, this island contains, like Androth, a considerable plot of low arable land adapted to the cultivation of a few coarse grains. In the tōttam (as the arable ground is called) the same coarse grains are cultivated as in Androth, but the area devoted to the cultivation of plantains is more extensive than in the latter island. The plantains are very productive and are stated to require no watering. The bread-fruit also appears to grow more luxuriantly in this island than in any other, and whole groves of it occur everywhere throughout the inhabited portion of the island. A few areca palms, one tamarind tree, lime bushes, and betel vines are also cultivated. The wild almond tree and punnan (a tree used for masts), found occasionally in the jungle, furnish fairly good timber, but the islanders usually import what they require. On the whole Kalpeni may be said to be one which nearly produces the food-supply necessary for the support of its inhabitants, and this is clearly shown by the fact that they export a large quantity of the produce of the *tōttam* (grain, plantains and sweet potatoes), fish, oil and dried fish to the other islands (mainly Kavaratti), getting in exchange coconuts, young plants, jaggery and coir.

The three islets mentioned above, as well as the greater portion of the main island, which together comprise about three-fourths of the entire extent, are claimed by the Pandāram. Cultivation is most backward in these parts. The inhabitants are extremely lazy and a considerable portion of the islands is therefore covered with jungle. The tōttam alone is well cultivated.

Disaster of 1847.—On the 15th April 1847 a violent hurricane visited the island of Kalpeni and caused most woeful injury to life and property. It commenced at about 8 P.M. at the season of spring tides and passed on to Androth which it reached between 12 and 2 A.M. of the 16th. It then arrived at Kiltan, one of the islands attached to the South Canara district, and after that gradually subsided. The following extract taken from the Proceedings of the Board of Revenue, dated 2nd August 1849, gives a clear idea of the dreadful catastrophe :—

"The sea rose and flooded the whole but across the narrower part of the mainland; it seems to have had tremendous velocity. All the trees, with the very soil, and between 50 and 60 houses, were washed into the ocean with upwards of 200 persons, while along the whole length of the shore a flood of loose coral has been deposited over the island which will render a considerable tract quite unserviceable until it has decomposed and become soil. Across the broader parts of the island the water was not so destructively rapid, but so complete was the inundation that the first impression of the islanders was that the whole shoal was sunk. The water filled the *tōttam* with salt water, killing all vegetation and drowning many persons. It was, in consequence, last year quite waste. Over the eastern bank of the tōttam a flood of loose coral stones was poured, which has filled up and destroyed a part of this useful land. Many wells and tanks were filled with sand and stones, and the fresh water in all of them was spoilt. The inundation was probably more destructive than the wind, and has shaken the confidence of the people in the stability of the islands greatly. The storm lasted for about an hour in all its violence.

"Then a sudden lull and the wind soon sprung up briskly from the westward and the flood subsided, leaving the islands in the most perfect state of desolation.

"Of the 348 houses standing before the storm, not one escaped. Many were so entirely washed away as scarcely to leave vestiges of their foundation. All were unroofed and otherwise damaged. All the mosques, 29 in number, were injured, and nearly the whole of them at the time of Mr. Robinson's visit were lying in a state of ruin.

"The population of Kalpeni, prior to the hurricane, is reckoned at 1,642 souls. Of these, 246 were drowned or washed away during the storm, far the larger proportion being women and children. One hundred and twelve perished in the ensuing five months from famine or from the diseases engendered by unwholesome and insufficient food, 376 escaped to the coast during the monsoon, thus leaving in the island 908, of whom nearly four-fifths are women and children.

"The plantations in the island have been entirely destroyed; out of upwards of 105,000 full-grown coconut trees, the number before the storm, 768 only are now standing; the total number of trees, young trees and plants which have survived, scarcely exceeds 10,000. This is only the main island Kalpeni; the state of the adjoining islets, Thilakka Pitti and Cheriyam, is even more disastrous. The other trees—bread-fruit, banana and betel-nut—are likewise all lost. More than a third of the trees destroyed are Pandāram or the Beebee's property.

"The hurricane reached Androth between 12 and 2 A.M. of the 16th April, five or six hours later than at Kalpeni. The tide was then happily low, so that only a small part of the island was inundated, and the results of the visitation, though sufficiently deplorable, were less disastrous than those experienced in the latter islands."

Animals.—The domestic animals that existed in the island in 1880 consisted of 94 cattle and 64 goats and the usual fowls and cats. In sea products Kalpeni is peculiarly rich. The ayacura (seer fish), tarandi (skate), shark, appal (Bombay duck), flying fish (paramīn) of two sorts, sword-fish and many other large fish are caught in abundance. The turtle, killed for oil but not for eating, is very common, and the tortoise pretty frequent. As might be expected from the great extent of the coral shoals and of the lagoon, shell-fish of many kinds are most abundant. One or two sorts are occasionally gathered for food, but the cowries are what were chiefly gathered formerly for export and are much more abundant in this island than in any other.

People, their Customs and Occupation.—In physique the inhabitants of Kalpeni appear decidedly inferior to those of the other islands. They are also the most ignorant and superstitious, the most bigoted and the dirtiest, both in person and habits. The men are the laziest, and it was with great difficulty that they were got to do some cooly work during the periodical visits of the officers to the island. Nearly all the work is done by the women, and, besides their usual work, the women of the Mēlachēri class have, on the return of the ōdams from the coast, to carry the bags of rice, &c., from the vessels to the houses of the consignees, receiving one seer per bag as cooly. The sailor class arrogate to themselves the reputation of being the best mālumis (pilots), but this pretension is ridiculed by the other islanders. The generality of the people are poor, all the wealth and influence being confined to a few of the Kārnavar class who keep the others well under subjection. The Kārnavar class claim to have derived their descent from the Nambūtiris or Brahmans of Malabar, and their houses are generally distinguished by the word *illam*—the appellation in Malabar peculiar to the houses of Nambūtiris. The other islanders are considered to be of Sudra or Nāyar extraction and the distinctions of caste still survive amongst them. Every one, male or female, over about 10 years of age, carries a pouch containing betel, tobacco, &c. The superstition of the islanders and their fear of ghosts is such that they hardly venture out of their homes after dark.

Population, Sanitary Condition and Medical Aspects.—The population of the island had been reduced by the storm of 1847 to about 450. In 1876 it numbered 1,029 and at the census of 1881 it amounted to 1,222, of whom 604 were males and the rest females. The sanitary condition of the island is most defective. The bad smell emanating from the accumulation of refuse matter is so powerful that no stranger can pass through the house-yards of even the wealthiest without his olfactory nerves being grievously offended. The dwelling houses are constructed differently from those in other islands for want of building stones. To form the walls two parallel rows of stakes are driven into the ground about 6 inches apart and the intervening space filled in with suitably sized stones obtained from the beach. When this space has been well and tightly filled up, the wall so formed is plastered on both sides, and when this plaster dries the stakes are removed. A second and thicker layer of plaster is then applied which completes the outside wall upon which the roof is placed. As in Kavaratti all the houses are enclosed with fences and the entrances secured by tatty screens. In the yard of each, also, there is usually a small shed in which the women, who are more secluded in this island than in the others, work. Some houses have also two out-houses, used as kitchen and room for receiving visitors, attached to them. There is no native physician in the island, but the gumasta has the credit of being the best. He only uses castor-oil and some made-up medicines he gets from the coast, and has never had any training.

Education.—A school was established in 1880 at the desire of the islanders. It is hoped that it may improve. The number of persons capable of reading, according to the census of 1881, is 221.

Religion and Mosques.—The people are exclusively Muhammadans. There are 16 mosques in all, of which 7 are supposed to belong to the Pandāram. The number of mosques in 1847, according to Sir William Robinson, was 29.

Manufactures and Trade.—The coir-yarn is the chief manufacture of the island. It is generally of an inferior quality. The number of boats belonging to the islanders in 1880 was 16 large vessels and 70 small boats. The corresponding numbers in 1876 were 15 and 68.

Survey and Cowles.—The survey and demarcation of the island have been completed. A portion of the Pandāram lands has also been granted on cowle.

Sub-divisions of the Island.—The island is divided into 4 sub-divisions or chēris, viz., (1) Vadakkanchēri, (2) Tekanchēri, (3) Kichēri, (4) Mēchēri. The islets attached to it have already been mentioned above.

General Remarks.—There is not in this island the same amount of ill-feeling between the Kārnavan and the Kudiyān as exists to a greater or less extent in the other islands. It appears that only 10 per cent. of the

Kudiyān's produce is deducted as freight. Probably this explains the absence of disputes between Kārnavar and Kudiyāns. Eight Ipecacuanha plants were planted by Mr. Tate during his visit in 1884.

A large English steamship, named the "Amelia," was wrecked upon the reef of Kalpeni in April 1880.

MINICOY ISLAND.

Position and Extent.—The island of Minicoy is situated in Lat. 8° 17′ N. and Long. 73° 19′ E. and is distant about 243 miles from Calicut. Though a dependency of the Cannanore family and so classed with the Laccadive group, it is situated about midway between the Laccadives proper and the Maldives, and the inhabitants belong to the latter race and speak Mahl. Its extreme length from north-west to south-east is 6 miles, 1 furlong, 56 yards, and its greatest breadth 4 furlongs, 12 yards. The area is 1,120 acres or 1¾ square miles. The island is long and narrow and in shape somewhat resembles a crescent, the convex of which faces east, whilst on the west there is a magnificent lagoon. The northern portion of lagoon is deep and not very difficult to navigate. To the south of the main island, and separated from it by a channel about one-fourth of a mile wide, is a small island called Viringilli to which small-pox patients are transported to prevent the epidemic from spreading in the village.

Soil and Products.—Though the soil has every appearance of being fertile, yet the cultivation upon which the islanders almost entirely depend is that of the coconut palm, with which the whole island is more or less planted up. In the Pandāram plantations there is a considerable amount of jungle interspersed with coconut trees. The wealthier islanders possess gardens which are secured against depredators by strong fences and locked gates. The late Amin, Āli Mālikhan, made a garden in which plantains, pumpkins, brinjals, beans, chillies, cucumbers, limes and betel vines were found to thrive excellently. There is also one small mango tree. No grain is cultivated, save a few plots of cholum. The jungle contains many trees, of which the banian and wild almond are the chief. The jungle products are much the same as in other islands. The Ittala plant, already mentioned as found in Bangaram, is also very common. The only marine product which calls for remark[1] is the maas fish (Bonito), of which large quantities are annually cured and exported chiefly to Ceylon.

Animals.—The number of cattle and goats in the island is very small; there were only one of the former and ten of the latter in 1880. It is alleged that cattle cannot be bred in the island, as they are killed by mosquitoes and a kind of poisonous grass. The few to be found on the island are imported for slaughter at religious ceremonies.

People, their Customs and Occupation.—The inhabitants are divided into four classes, viz. :—

1. Mālikhans, corresponding to the Kārnavar of the other islands.
2. Mālumis (pilots).
3. Takkaru (sailors and boatmen).
4. Mēlachēris, or kohlus as they are called (tree-climbers).

---

[1] *Conf.*, Vol. I, footnote p. 286.

The boat-owners and holders of valuable property from the Pandāram upon a light quit-rent belong to the first class. The Mālumis and Takkarus are sailors, and the Kohlus tree-climbers and servants. The late Amin, Āli Mālikhan, was the most influential man in the island, and, besides maintáining strict order, used to insist on a certain amount of respect being paid to him by the other islanders. In the island, he and the gumasta alone wore jackets as a mark of distinction, all others being prohibited from doing so whilst in the island, though out of it, *e.g.*, in Calicut, other Mālikhans are in the habit of dressing somewhat gaudily. Amongst the women also sumptuary distinctions prevail, the lowest class being strictly prohibited from wearing silver or gold ornaments. In personal appearance and in their dress, manners and customs they differ considerably from the inhabitants of the other islands. They are much smaller in stature, darker, and have very round faces. In disposition they are quiet and obliging.

The customs of the islanders are in many respects remarkable and bear no trace of having been introduced from Cannanore. One which is without parallel amongst any society of Mussalmans is that the men are monogamous. The custom forbidding men to have more than one wife at a time is so strong that even the late Amin, influential as he was, dared not break through it when he wanted a second wife. Some of the men appear to be anxious that this custom should be abrogated by Government interference; but the women, in spite of the number of spinsters amongst them, will not hear of it. The women appear in public freely with their heads uncovered and take the lead in almost everything except navigation. In fact they seem to have as much freedom as there is in European countries. Enquiry into their civil condition (*e.g.*, whether they are married or unmarried) is regarded as an unpardonable affront. Unmarried men may converse with maidens, and courtship is a recognised preliminary to marriage. The girl's consent is in all cases necessary, and the Kāzi will not perform the ceremony unless he has sent two mukris to ascertain that she is willing. After marriage the wife remains in her mother's house, a very convenient custom where the men are mostly sailors absent from the island a great part of the year. Three or four couples find accommodation in the same chamber, each enveloped in long cloth mosquito curtains. If the daughters are numerous they leave the parental roof in order of seniority, and the houses erected for them become their property. The men have no right of ownership over houses. Every woman in the island is dressed in silk. Their gowns fit closely round the neck and reach to the ankles. The upper classes wear red silk and ear-rings of peculiar fashion.

The Mēlachēri women are restricted to the use of a dark striped silk of a coarser quality. Every husband must allow his wife at least one candy of rice, two silk gowns and two under-cloths a year. He also presents her on marriage with a fine brass betel pouch (brought from Galle) and a silver ornament containing receptacles for lime and tobacco and instruments of strange forms intended for cleaning the ears and teeth. The husband retains the power of divorce, and it is not the custom of the island to pay dower. Bathing tanks are set apart for the use of the women, and men are not allowed to intrude on that part of the island behind the village where the women congregate of a morning to prepare the coconut husks for the manufacture of coir.

Population, Sanitary Condition and Medical Aspects.—The population, according to the census of 1881, numbered 3,191, of whom 1,412 were males and the remaining, 1,779, were females. In 1867, three vessels were lost in a cyclone at Calcutta, and it is estimated that the number of men that perished then was 120. The sanitation of the island is excellent. The houses of the people are built close to each other in rows. The rows run parallel to each other from the beach inland or east and west and are eight in number, each of which has a distinct name. One long cross road and several smaller lanes intersect the village. The walls of the houses are of undressed stone and plastered as in Kalpeni, but the style of architecture is quite different. Each has a long verandah running throughout its whole length off which the various rooms open. In front is a small yard which is fenced or walled off from the street and the entrance protected by a neat tatty screen. The houses of the wealthy have kitchens and store-houses attached to them, and also wells inside their yard. The poorer classes get their water from public wells in the streets or from the well of the nearest wealthy man. Some wells have also been sunk in the uninhabited parts of the island for public convenience, to each of which there belongs a long stick with a coconut shell cup at the end to draw water with. The wells are all square in shape and the sides built up and plastered ; the water obtained from them is excellent. There are also six large built tanks with parapets and steps used for bathing purposes. The village is in good order as regards conservancy and the streets are daily swept.

The custom of the islanders in regard to sanitation and the interment of the dead is valuable and most beneficial. There are three separate burying grounds in remote parts of the island for persons who die of small-pox, cholera and leprosy. The precaution of separating lepers is maintained ; on the appearance of the disease, the sufferer is called before the Kāzi, and if the leprosy is pronounced to be contagious, he is expelled to the north of the island where a place is set apart for the purpose. A hut is built for him and he exists on supplies of food and water which his relatives bring at intervals and leave on the ground at a safe distance. There is a boundary line beyond which lepers are not permitted to proceed. The islanders have a horrible superstition that in the night time goblins may be seen clawing at the leprous parts, and the leper habitation seems to be generally regarded with dread. The poor patients receive only occasional treatment during the visits of the European officers ; small-pox patients are invariably transported to the island of Viringilli to prevent the disease spreading in the village, but if it becomes epidemic, those attacked are allowed to remain and be treated in their own houses. The health of the island is fairly good, but there is a very unwholesome practice among the people who, in order to protect themselves from mosquitoes, sleep on cots surrounded by thick linen curtains, thus inhaling accumulated foul air. In the evening swing-cots are used to keep off the mosquitoes.

Education.—There are hardly more than three individuals in the island who can speak or read Malayāḷam. The language spoken is Mahl, and there is therefore great difficulty in communicating with the islanders. The majority of the upper classes and a few of the Mēlachēris have learnt the koran character in the mosque schools, and many of the men of the upper classes have picked up a knowledge of Hindustani and Tamil in the course of their voyages to Ceylon and the Bay of Bengal.

Religion, Mosques and Cemeteries.—The inhabitants are exclusively Muhammadans. There are about 20 mosques and 26 cemeteries. The cemetery at Viringilli is used for small-pox patients who die there and for those who perish at sea, whatever be the cause of death. The reason given in the latter case is that the disease being unknown, it is safer to bury the bodies at a distance. There is also a small ground to the south on the main island in which are buried those who die on the maas-boats, as also Kohlus who, taking up a temporary residence in the big south Pandāram to draw toddy, die there. Near here is the grave of a holy man to whom prayers are offered to quell the raging of the sea. Deceased violent lunatics are buried to the north at a place called Runnagatta. The lepers have their own cemetery within the limits of their holding. In all cases the Mukri and sextons of the Jamāth mosque go and perform the prescribed rites and give decent sepulture.

Manufactures and Trade.—The manufactures of Minicoy are the same as those of other islands. The coir is a little dark in color but much finer in quality than that produced in the other islands. This is due to the coconut husk being allowed to grow hard and woody before being soaked for fibre.

The nuts are not gathered from trees but are allowed to ripen and fall on the ground. Maas-fish is cured and exported largely to Ceylon. In 1876 there were 8 large and 33 small vessels. The former increased to 9 in 1882. Of these, two go to the coast, the Maldives and Ceylon, and the others to the Bengal side. There are 11 maas-boats, to one of which every one in the island belongs. Men get a share of the fish in addition to their wages. The maas-boats are excellently built, with deep keels, fine lines, and a large allowance of beam. They carry a large square mat sail with a linen try-sail behind it. They are nicely finished off and painted and go very fast under sail. The islanders are skilful sailors.

The sides of the boats are of coconut and probably do not last long. The islanders have a very good assortment of ship-building tools and are very well skilled in their use. The Pandāram had three vessels, of which one, which could not be repaired except at an enormous cost, was sold by public auction at Beypore in 1883. The other two vessels are still in the island. The customary rates of payment to the crew of the Pandāram vessel are as follow:—

In the case of small vessels each sailor gets on the day of embarkation 50 coconuts, 4 lbs. of jaggery and 4 lbs. of rice. This is about the equivalent of Rs. 1-8-0. During the voyage he gets 1 lb. of rice and two coconuts a day. The tindal gets twice and the mālumi four times the allowance of a sailor. When the larger vessel sails, each sailor receives 100 coconuts, 28 lbs. of jaggery and 22 lbs. of rice on embarking and rations as above.

Pandāram Lands, their Tenure and General Remarks.—The land is the property of the community, and is managed by the *Pandāram, i.e.*, the Government. Private property *in the soil* is unknown, but improvements, such as houses, coconut and other trees, &c., belong to the persons who make them. The Mālikhāns or chief men state that their forefathers voluntarily surrendered the island to the Cannanore Raja on his undertaking to protect them against pirates. Every tree in the inhabited part of the island has the mark of its owner cut upon it, so that disputes respecting the ownership of trees have been very rare.

The principal sources of revenue are—

(1) Valiyapāṭṭam or pāṭṭam payable by certain Mālikhāns.
(2) *Attiri-pāṭṭam* or sea-shore *pāṭṭam*.
(3) *Pāṭṭam* on tōttam or garden.
(4) Poll-tax at the rate of 20 lbs. of coir per male and 5 lbs. per female. The families of Mālikhāns, one married female in each house, all unmarried adults and toddy-drawers are exempt from this tax.
(5) Sugar-tax in the nature of a poll-tax on toddy-drawers.
(6) Cowrie monopoly.
(7) Produce of the Pandāram trees.
(8) Tax (in rice) on large vessels trading with Bengal.
(9) Tax (in maas-fish) on fishing boats.
(10) Hire of Pandāram boat at 14 per cent. on fish taken.

There is no coir monopoly in this island, and this fact explains chiefly the absence of disaffection towards the raja.

Divisions.—The island is demarcated into nine large blocks—

(A) The great north Pandāram.
(B) North Moiluth grant.
(C) Leper settlemeut.
(D) South Moiluth land.
(E) Mālikhān land.
(F) Central Pandāram.
(G) Attiri Pandāram (containing most of the village site).
(H) Eastern block (containing rest of the village tōttams and Pandāram plots).
(I) Great southern Pandāram.

NOTE.—The village (blocks G and H) is divided for purposes of administration into *attiris* (sea-shore or male assemblies) and *varāngis* (female assemblies). Of the latter, there are ten, which lie in order from north to south, thus :—

1. Bodu, 2 Kudahē, 3. Punghilōlu, 4. Alūdi, 5. Sōtivaḷu, 6. Kandamātu, 7. Hanimagu, 8. Oḷikoḷu, 9. Digu, 10. Koḷu. The *attiris* correspond in name to the *varāngis* except that No. 7 lies inland from No. 6, and the head-man of No. 6 having charge of the *attiri*, that is, sea-shore, is head-man of both Nos. 6 and 7. To each *varāngi* there is a head-woman. The *Malumi* (pilot) and *Mālikhān* (chief men) castes are independent of these *attiri* and *varāngi* organisations, which are formed exclusively of the two lower castes, *viz., Takkarus* (sailors) and *Mēlachēris* (tree-climbers), and which exist for the *public* services (male and female) of the community. Each *attiri* and *varāngi* has a special place of meeting, and the sexes being told off to certain well-defined services, there is no clashing of authority. The head-men control all the men and youths of their *attiris*. The head-women exercise authority over all females and over boys until the latter are old enough to join in the services performed by the males of the *attiris*, that is, till they are about 7 years of age. The different castes are located in the village thus :—

Name of *Varāngi.*	Households of				Total.
	Mēlachēris (tree-climbers).	*Takkarus* (sailors).	*Malumis* (pilots).	*Mālikhāns* (chief men).	
1. Bodu	96	..	..	..	96
2. Kudahō	..	54	6	1	61
3. Punghilōlu ..	..	60	..	3	63
4. Alūdi	..	29	6	4	39
5. Setivaḻu	..	43	5	4	52
6. Kandamatu ..	..	15	2	2	19
7. Hanimagu ..	..	30	3	2	35
8. Oḻikoḻu	..	45	8	1	54
9. Dugu	47	10	4	..	61
10. Koḻu	64	16	2	..	82
Total ..	207	302	36	17	562

Each *attiri* has a number of maas-fishing boats. The owner of the boat gets 14 per cent. of the catch of fish, the rest is divided equitably among the *attiri*.

Lighthouse.—A fine lighthouse, constructed by the Trinity House Board, has been recently erected at the south end of the island in block I. The light was first exhibited on the 2nd February 1885.

KOTTAYAM TALUK.

By V. Chappu Menon, B.A.

Boundaries, Position and Area.—The Kottayam taluk, which comprises the old taluks of Kottayam and Tellicherry, is bounded on the north by Chirakkal, on the east by Coorg and Wynād, on the south by Wynād and Kurumbranād, and on the west by the sea. It lies immediately to the south of the Chirakkal taluk and resembles the latter in its general features.

Area.—462 square miles, of which 80 square miles may be said to be under cultivation.

Population.—The population, according to the census of 1871, was 143,761, which in 1881 rose to 165,775, showing an increase of about 15 per cent. The males were to the females as 81,345 to 84,430. The Hindus numbered 124,099, Muhammadans 39,825, Christians 1,842, and other classes 9. The population is most dense towards the coast.

The number of houses occupied in 1881 was 25,646 and of those unoccupied 6,200.

Sub-division of the Taluk for Administrative Purposes.—The taluk is divided into 28 amsams of which 16 are under the charge of the Tahsildar for magisterial purposes and the remaining 12 under the Deputy Tahsildar, Kuttuparamba. The taluk head-quarters are at Tellicherry.

Public Establishments.—The various public establishments existing in the taluk are specified below :—

1. District Court, North Malabar, Tellicherry.
2. Sub-Collector and Joint Magistrate's Court, Tellicherry.
3. Civil Surgeon, Tellicherry.

4. Assistant Superintendent of Police, Tellicherry.
5. Sub-Court, North Malabar, Tellicherry.
6. District Munsif's Court, Tellicherry.
7. Tahsildar and his establishment, Tellicherry.
8. Deputy Tahsildar, Kuttuparamba.
9. Sea Customs Superintendent and Port Conservator, Tellicherry.
10. District Registrar, Tellicherry, and Sub-Registrars of Kuttuparamba and Panur.
11. Police Inspectors, Tellicherry and Kuttuparamba, with station-houses at Kallāi, Chavassēri, Iritti, Kannavam, Kuttuparamba, Kasba, Nagaram and Panur.
12. Postal and Telegraph offices at Tellicherry.
13. Inspector of Salt and Abkāri Revenue, North Malabar.
14. Teachers of the Brennen High School and other educational institutions.
15. Local Fund Supervisor, Tellicherry sub-division.
16. Deputy Inspector of Vaccination, North Malabar.
17. Municipal establishments.

Towns.—Tellicherry (Lat. 11° 44′ 53″ N., Long. 75° 31′ 38″ E.), which is the head-quarters of the taluk, was constituted a municipal town under Act X of 1865 with effect from 1st November 1866 (*vide* notification of Government, dated 13th September 1866, and G.O., dated 13th September 1866, No. 925).

The boundaries of the town are—

North.—Eranjoli river as far as the old bridge on the Coorg road.

East and South.—The Eranjoli old road as far as the Tiruvangād kovil large tank, and the cross road thence to Kodapalli kunnu on the sea-shore.

West.—The sea.

The town extends from the Koduvalli bridge on the north to the small hill in the Mailanjanmam amsam on the south; from the sea-shore on the west to the river on the east. The distance north to south is 3 miles and east to west 1¾ miles. The area is about 4 square miles and the population, according to the census of 1881, was 26,410, of whom 15,488 were Hindus, 9,149 were Muhammadans, 1,765 were Christians, and 8 belonged to other classes. The males were to the females as 12,939 to 13,471. The number of houses occupied was 3,426, and of those unoccupied 2,118.

The municipal town comprises at present the whole of the Tellicherry amsam and portions of Tiruvangād and Mailanjanmam amsams. In 1880 a portion of the Nittur amsam was added to the municipality, but was excluded in 1884 as it did not derive much benefit from the municipal administration. In March 1884, proposals for the incoporation of the remaining portions of the Tiruvangād and Mailanjanmam amsams were sanctioned by Government, but the order was subsequently cancelled on the representations of the inhabitants of the locality. The receipts and charges on account of the Tellicherry Municipality for the year 1884-85 are subjoined :—

TELLICHERRY MUNICIPALITY.

Receipts.	1884-85. RS.
Opening balance	179
Rates on houses and lands	11,419

	1884-85.
	RS.
Taxes on arts	4,057
Taxes on vehicles and animals	793
Registration of carts	46
Tolls	2,183
Licenses	100
License tax	..
Assignments by Government	200
Contribution from Local funds	1,050
Fees and fines	190
Endowment, &c.	1,200
Miscellaneous	6,467
Advances recovered	..
Total	27,884

Charges.

Grant I.

New works— Communications	..
Buildings	..
Sanitary and miscellaneous	..
Repairs—communications	2,182
Buildings	123
Sanitary and miscellaneous	67
Establishment	608
Tools and plant	..

Grant II.

Municipal schools	6,163
Results grants	543
Schools on the combined system	448
Inspection	150
Miscellaneous	..

Grant III.

Hospitals and dispensaries	4,437
Medical college	..
Sanitary inspection	..
Vaccination	584
Registration of births and deaths	344
Conservancy	5,585

Grant IV.

Lighting	1,488
Choultries	123
Travellers' bungalows	..
Miscellaneous	576
License tax	..
Police	..

Grant V.

Supervision and management	3,050
Advances recoverable	50
Refunds	152
Balances	1,211
Total	27,884

Tellicherry is a healthy and picturesque town, situated upon a group of wooded hills running down to the sea, and protected by a natural breakwater of rock. The citadel or fort, still in excellent preservation, stands to the north of the town and was used as a district jail till the latter was abolished on 1st June 1885. The buildings in the fort are now intended for public offices. The fort is built of laterite in the form of a square with flanking bastions on the south-east and north-west corners. The south-east bastion has also a cavalier bastion above it. On the north is another bastion situated on a cliff overhanging the sea, and separated from the main work by a space of about 150 yards. The immediate precincts of the fort were further protected by a strong wall of which portions still remain loopholed for musketry and with flanking towers at intervals. The native town lies to the south; the principal street runs parallel to the coast, and is a mile in length. A white dioptric light, exhibited from a small masonry tower on the fort wall, 70 feet above high water, marks the harbour.

The East India Company established a factory at Tellicherry in 1683 to secure the pepper and cardamom trade; and on several occasions, between 1708 and 1761, the Company obtained from the chiefs of the Kōlattiri family and other local chiefs, not only grants of land in and near Tellicherry, but some important privileges, such as the right to collect customs, administer justice, &c., within the lands so granted.

Hyder's invasion of Malabar narrowed the Company's operations for a time, and in 1766 the factory was reduced to a residency. From 1779 to 1782 the town withstood a siege by Hyder's General, Sirdar Khan; on the arrival of relief from Bombay under Major Abington, the enemy was severely handled in a sortie and the siege was raised. In the subsequent wars with Mysore, Tellicherry was the base of operations for the ascent of the ghats from the west coast. After the peace, the town became the seat of the Superintendent of North Malabar and of the Provincial Court of Circuit.

The various public offices existing in the taluk have been already noticed.

The following edifices which exist in the town deserve mention. They are—

(1) The civil dispensary built partly with subscriptions raised by Dr. Ross, a former Civil Surgeon of the station, and partly with funds supplied by Government.

(2) A Protestant church (the foundation of which was laid by Lord Napier in 1869), raised with funds left by the late Master Attendant, Edward Brennen, Esq.

(3) A church of the German Mission.

(4) A Roman Catholic church over a century old.

(5) A large Māppiḷḷa mosque called Orta (in Portuguese, garden) Pally (ഓടത്തിൽപള്ളി) built by a very opulent Māppiḷḷa, Chovakkāran Mussa, the site being the Government garden, hence the name.

(6) Another mosque of some note, that of the Cutch Muhammadans, built by the late Āli Hāji Sett, a rich merchant of this town, whose descendants are still trading here.

(7) A Hindu pagoda in Tiruvangād dedicated to Sri Rama, an incarnation of Vishnu, and commonly called "Brass Pagoda" owing to its being covered with brass sheeting instead of tiles, and of which the walls and gopurams are in a state of disrepair.

(8) A high school, also built with funds left by Mr. Brennen and known as the Brennen High School.

(9) Another school in charge of German Missionaries built with money provided by a Parsee by name Kasroo—a grandson of Darashoo Cursetjee, an old Parsee merchant of this place.

(10) A terrace made by the late Vice-President, Mr. Overbury, with municipal fund and which presents an agreeable appearance commanding an excellent view of the sea, and is now much resorted to by town people, especially in the evening. There are also a travellers' bungalow and two chattrams, one of which was built by the Municipality and the other by the Government. There is also another chattram, built and endowed by Moyan Kunhi Raman Nāyar, who was once a ward under Government, and intended for Hindu travellers.

Of the private dwelling houses which are of some note, there are only two deserving mention here. One of these at Mōrakkunnu was built by Mr. James Stevens, and the other at Pallikkunnu by Mr. Thomas Harvey Baber, both first Judges of the late Western Provincial Court.

There are two large tanks within the town, the largest at Tiruvangād, measuring 250 feet by 340, belongs to the Tiruvangād temple, and the other measuring 150 feet by 150, near the High school, was sunk by the late Mr. Baber, and goes by his name.

There is no hotel here, but there is a club for Europeans situated close to the fort.

Other institutions of minor importance in the town are noted below :—

1. Lekshmi Narasimham temple (ലക്ഷ്മി നരസിംഹക്ഷേത്രം), roofed partly with copper and partly with tiles belonging to the Konkani Brahmins.
2. Old Jamāth mosque (പഴയജമാത്ത പള്ളി).
3. Mattāmprath mosque (മട്ടാമ്പ്രത്തപള്ളി).
4. Lower bazaar mosque (താഴെ അങ്ങാടിപള്ളി).
5. Trikkayil temple dedicated to Siva (തൃക്കയിൽക്ഷേത്രം).
6. Ayyalath palli (അയ്യലത്തപള്ളി).
7. Seydarpalli (സെയ്യാർപള്ളി).

Nos. 1 to 4 are in Tellicherry amsam, and Nos. 5 and 6 in Tiruvangād amsam, and No. 7 in Mailamjanmam amsam.

Kutaḷi amsam—about 12 miles north north-west of Tellicherry, contains a bungalow known as Chalot Bungalow and a petty bazaar. It is on the high road from Cannanore to the Pudiachuram pass into Coorg.

Pattanur amsam—has nothing worthy of note, except perhaps a Vishnu temple called Nayikkali (നായിക്കാലി).

Chāvassēri amsam—about 4 miles north north-east of Paḷassi, has a Māppiḷḷa bazaar and a palace to the north of it. It contains the Kallur temple and Palot mosque, and also a small bungalow and chattram.

Veliyambra amsam—contains the village of Iritti, which has a bridge of that name in course of construction. It contains Kuyimbil (കുയിമ്പിൽ) temple and Uliyil (ഉളിയിൽ) mosque.

Muḷakunnu amsam—contains a fort called Harischandra Kōtta on the Purali mala hill, near this is a rock-cut cell. There are two temples known as Mulakunnu (മുഴക്കുന്നു) and Tillangiri (തില്ലങ്കേരി) and a mosque called Pālayil (പാലയിൽ).

Gannavam amsam—is a hilly tract containing an area of 41,440 acres, or about 65 square miles. It has a travellers' bungalow and a mussaferkhana and two religious institutions, one (Muntemparamba temple മുണ്ടേംപറമ്പ ക്ഷേത്രം) belonging to the Hindus, and the other (Āralathpalli ആറളത്ത പള്ളി) belonging to the Māppillas. The Iritti bridge is on the boundary of Gannavam and Veliyambra amsams.

Manattana amsam—about 28 miles from Tellicherry and 8 from Kannoth, was once a military post. There is a redoubt on the summit of a low hill in good order but overrun with trees and shrubs. It is the largest and most hilly tract in the taluk, and has, according to the census of 1881, an area of 106,000 acres, or about 165 square miles, and a population of 4,365 souls. There is a temple of great celebrity called Tricharumanna at Kottiyur, (തൃച്ചെറുമന അപ്പെങ്കിൽ കൊട്ടിയൂർ ക്ഷേത്രം) dedicated to Siva, and although situated in a wild woody tract, it has an annual festival in April-May attended by about 50,000 people. The nearest inhabited place to Kottiyur is Manattana, about 8 miles distant from it. The road from Manattana to Wynād passes through this village. At Nitumpoyil, there exists a chattram for the use of travellers. There is also a mosque called Kolayat (കൊളയാട്ട പള്ളി).

Kannavam amsam—is a large hilly tract about 14 miles north-east of Tellicherry, and was formerly a military post. Here is a small redoubt on a hill in ruins. There is a good bungalow for travellers and a substantial stone bridge thrown over a small river by a battalion of pioneers employed in Wynād, in 1822-23. There is a celebrated pagoda known as Totikalam (തൊടീക്കളം) temple about one mile north-north-west of Kannoth, where, in the month of Vrischigam, Tiyyars bring tender coconuts as offerings to the deity. There are three rock-cut caves in Totikalam, said to be paved with bricks. There is also a mosque in the amsam known as the Kannoth mosque. At Kannoth there was a rich janmi known as Kannoth Nambiyar, who joined the rebellious Palassi (Pyche) Raja of Kottayam, and who disturbed the peace of the taluk for a series of years. He eventually fell into the hands of the authorities and was hanged on the hill near the bungalow, his estate being declared escheated to Government in 1805. The property known as Kannoth escheat is of large extent and lies in Kannoth and Manattana amsams. It has mostly been dealt with by the escheat department, and has a portion of it planted up with teak trees. The area of the tract is variously estimated. The Tahsildar of Kottayam once put the area at 375 square miles, but forty square miles is a very moderate estimate not taking into consideration the increased superficial area caused by the mountainous character of the locality. The forests are peopled by Kurichiyars—a class of jungle tribes who raise various products in them. The forest has been notified for reservation under the Madras Forest Act V of 1882.

Palassi amsam—was the seat of the Raja known in Malabar history as the Pychy (Palassi) Raja of Kottayam who carried on warfare against the East India Company for a long time, and who was finally killed in 1805, his whole estate being confiscated to Government. There is a small fort which is now in ruins. The two temples in this amsam are Perincheri (പെരിഞ്ചേരി)

and Mattanūr (മട്ടന്നൂർ). Mattanūr is painfully interesting as being the scene of the terrible tragedy enacted there in 1852, wherein a whole family of Brahmans, consisting of 18 souls, were most cruelly butchered by Māppiḷḷa fanatics.

Kandamkunnu amsam—is the seat of the Kuttuparamba Deputy Tahsildar's office, and contains also a Sub-Registrar's office, a Police station, a Mission school, a public bungalow and an old fort now in ruins. There is also a large maidan in the possession of Government and a street inhabited by buffalo-herdsmen. It lies on the high road to the Periah pass. The Merumpoya bridge, over the river of that name, is situated in this amsam. There are also the (1) Nirveli (നീർവ്വേലി), (2) Mananteri (മാനന്തേരി) and (3) Ramapuram (രാമപുരം) temples, and (4) Merumpoya (മെരുമ്പായി) mosque and (5) Muriyat (മുര്യാട്) mosque.

Patuvilai amsam—contains two Hindu temples known as Kallayi (കല്ലായി) and Patuvilai (പാട്ടുവിലായി) and two mosques called Kallāi and Vengatti.

Dharmatam amsam.—Dharmatam (literally a place of charity) is a small island close to Tellicherry and contains a redoubt on the top of an elevated place and also an old rock-cut cave. There was here one of the earliest Muhammadan mosques now demolished. The place was ceded to the Honorable East India Company in 1734, was seized by Revi Varma, Raja of Chirakkal, in 1788, but was retaken in 1789. There are two Hindu temples called Melur (മേലൂർ ക്ഷേത്രം) and Andalur (അണ്ടല്ലൂർ കാവു), a Christian church and a Jamāth mosque. There is also a Trigonometrical survey station here.

Pinarayi amsam—contains an old palace belonging to the Raja of Kottayam and the Paraprath (പാറപ്രത്ത) mosque.

Mailanjanmam amsam—contains a mosque called Seydarpalli and two small rock-cut sepulchral caves like those at Taliparamba.

Katirur amsam—about 4 miles north-east of Tellicherry, was formerly the seat of the Tahsildar and subsequently of the District Munsif. It had a palace built by the Pychy (Paḷassi) Raja. There are (1) Katirur temple (കതിരൂർ ക്ഷേത്രം) with a nice tank attached to it, (2) Chirumpa kavu temple (ചിറുമ്പകാവു), (3) Talath (തായത്ത) mosque, (4) Telayilat (തെലായിലാട) mosque, and (5) two rock-cut caves.

Kottayam—also called Kottayakam and Kottangādi, is a large village about 7 miles north-east of Tellicherry, and contains the palaces of the Kottayam Rajas and the houses of several wealthy Māppiḷḷas. It is celebrated for a fine temple known as Trikayikunnu (തൃക്കയിക്കുന്ന) and a big tank close to it. The rebel Pychy (Paḷassi) Raja belonged to one of the branches of the Kottayam family. There are three mosques called (1) Kottayath Jamāth mosque (കൊട്ടയത്ത ജമാത്ത പള്ളി), (2) Mutiyanga Jamāth mosque (മുതിയങ്ങ ജമാത്തപള്ളി), (3) Cheruvancheri mosque (ചെറുവാഞ്ചേരിപള്ളി).

Panur amsam.—Panur, about 7 miles from Tellicherry, was formerly the seat of a District Munsif and has now a Police station and a Sub-Registrar's office. It is a populous Māppiḷḷa village and contains a bazaar. There are the ruins of an old fort and a rock-cut sepulchral grave, the latter in Kannampalli dēsam. The chief religious institutions are Kutteri temple (കുറ്റേരി അമ്പലം) and Panur mosque (പാനൂർപള്ളി).

Puttur amsam—is a jungly tract and contains Pullanhot (പുല്ലാഞ്ഞോട)

temple and Kallil (കല്ലിലെപള്ളി) mosque; also two rock-cut caves in Kolavallur dēsam.

Triprangottur amsam—is a jungly tract and contains the Vishnu temple known as Kotantram velli temple (കോടന്ത്രം വെള്ളിക്ഷേത്രം) and the Katavattur mosque (കടവത്തൂർപള്ളി). Both have thatched roofs.

Panniyanur amsam—contains the temples known as Kottarattil Ampalam (കൊട്ടാരത്തിൽ അമ്പലം) and Kilaketath Ampalam (കിഴക്കെടത്ത അമ്പലം).

Peringalam amsam—about 8 miles from Tellicherry, contains a rock-cut cave on the top of a hill. There are also a rock-cut cave with two pillars and four caves in the amsam. The Menapratt (മെനപ്രത്ത) and Anniyārath (അന്നിയാരത്ത) temples and Peringalathur (പെരിങ്ങളത്തൂർ പള്ളി) mosque are the only religious institutions of note. At Kanakamala there is a small spring which is considered sacred, and in which people bathe on certain days in the year.

Olavilam amsam—contains Olavilath Tadathil (ഒലവിലത്ത തടത്തിൽ) temple and Tottathil (തൊട്ടത്തിൽ) mosque.

Kallayi amsam—contains two caves cut out of laterite, also Parimatam temple (പരിമഠം) and Kallai mosque.

Karyad amsam—contains Pallikunil temple (പള്ളികുന്നിൽ അമ്പലം) dedicated to Vettakorumakan.

Mountains, Hills and Forests.—The line of ghats to the eastward, the crest of which forms the boundary dividing Kottayam from Coorg and Wynād, are lofty, some of the peaks being about 4,000 feet above the level of the sea. The valleys formed by the slopes are extensive and covered with dense forests. The Kanaka mala is a lofty ridge stretching west from the ghats, the slopes from it approaching within 10 miles of the coast due east of Tellicherry. Purali (പുരളി) mala, situated centrically, is a long ridge about 6 miles in length east and west unconnected with the ghats. It is covered with wood and bamboos to the summit. In the north-east portion several table-lands covered with wood, apparently flat, rise abruptly from the cultivated valleys. The country, 8 miles in a parallel with the coast, is composed of open ridges between the cultivated valleys. A few of the eminences are wooded. There is very little flat land in the district beyond a belt along the coast about Tellicherry and the cultivated valleys. The whole of the eastern portion is one dense wood with a few cultivated spots to the foot of the ghats. In the small island of Dharmapatam the only flat ground is that under wet cultivation and marsh; the rest is undulating ground falling in cliffs towards the sea. Opposite to it is a rocky island called Grove Island with some wood surrounded by rocks. About half a mile to the west of Tellicherry is a ridge of rocks which affords some shelter for craft. The description of the Kannoth forest belonging to Government will be found in the Notice of the Wynád Forests.

Soil and Productions.—The soil in some parts towards the coast is brown and sandy; on the rising grounds in the interior it is rich and gravelly; the cultivated valleys a brown loam; towards the mountains and in the forests it is rich and black.

The productions are rice of different kinds, coconut, betel, areca-nut, cardamom, pepper in great quantities and dry grains of sorts. Kottayam is celebrated for its pepper crops.

Minerals.—Iron is to be found in some parts, but it is not worked.

Manufactures.—Cloths of an inferior sort are made in several amsams. In Nittur, a suburb of Tellicherry, weaving is carried on by the Basel Mission weaving establishment. Arrack, jaggery, oil from copra and other nuts are manufactured. Copper vessels are manufactured at Tellicherry and at Mattanūr in Paḷassi amsam.

Fairs and Markets.—Fairs are held at almost all the temples where people resort for public festivals or worship. Kottiyur is one of the most important of the pagodas in this respect. A festival is held there in April-May every year which attracts thither great trade.

Bungalows and other Public Buildings.—There are three travellers' bungalows in the taluk at—

1. Kannoth in Kannavan amsam,
2. Gannoth in Gannavam amsam, and
3. Kuthuparamba.

Mussaferkhanas are provided at—

1. Nedumpoyil in Manattana amsam.
2. Chālōt in Kudali amsam.
3. Chāvassēri.
4. Iritti in Veliyampra amsam.
5. Gannoth in Gannavam amsam.

Trigonometrical Station.—At Dharmapaṭṭanam.

—	°	′	″
Lat. N.	11	45	59·76
Long. E.	75	30	09·82

KURUMBRANĀD TALUK.

By C. Kunhi Kannan.

Position, Boundaries, Soil and Area.—The Kurumbranād taluk is bounded on the *north* by the Kottayam taluk, on the *east* by the Wynād taluk, on the *south* by the Calicut taluk, and on the *west* by the Arabian Sea. The soil of the interior is generally red and much impregnated with laterite, which gradually assumes a rich loam in parts cultivated with paddy, whilst towards the coast it is brown loose earth.

The Kurumbranād taluk comprises the old taluks of Kadattanād and Kurumbranād.

The area of the taluk, according to the census returns of 1881, is 538 square miles. This is only an approximate calculation as accurate figures are not available, the district not having been surveyed. Of this extent about 175,613 acres, or about 274 square miles, are under cultivation. The demand of land revenue for fasli 1295 (1885-86) was Rs. 2,13,565, giving an average of Rs. $1\frac{1}{4}$ nearly per acre of cultivated area.

Population.—The population of the taluk, inclusive of floating population as ascertained by the census of 1881, was 261,024, being 129,394 males and 131,630 females. The population returned by the census of 1871 was 244,166. The population of 1881 may be classified as follows :—

Hindus	196,383
Muhammadans	64,245
Christians	394
Others	2
Total ..	261,024

which give an average of 485 persons per square mile.

Education is backward in the taluk as will appear from the fact that under the head of "instruction" the census returned 7,944, "instructed" 20,206, and "illiterate including not stated" 232,874 persons.

There were 56,471 houses (48,440 occupied and 8,031 unoccupied) in 1881 against 45,597 houses in 1871. The average number of persons per occupied house in 1881 was 5·4.

Division of Taluk for Administrative Purposes.—The taluk comprises 57 amşams each with an adhikāri on Rs. 5¼, a menon on Rs. 6 and two peons on Rs. 3 each *per mensem.*

Prior to 1866 there were 63 amşams in the taluk, but in that year 6 amşams were transferred to the Calicut taluk. The names of these amşams will be found in the Note on the Calicut taluk.

The old Kadattanād taluk comprised 21 hobalis and the old Kurumbranād 10 hobalis. As already observed, these two taluks were amalgamated into the present Kurumbranād taluk.

Government Establishments of different kinds maintained in the taluk, and where located.—The taluk kachēri of Kurumbranād, including the Sub-jail and Police station, is at Badagara, where there is also a District Munsif's Court and a Sub-Registrar's office. The District Board maintain a middle school, a dispensary on a small scale, a travellers' bungalow and a mussafer-khana at Badagara.

There are two other District Munsifs' Courts in the taluk, one at Nādāpuram in Kummangōd amşam, 9 miles north-east of Badagara, and the other at Payanād in Quilandi, 14 miles south of Badagara. There is a Deputy Tahsildar's kachēri at Quilandi. There are Sub-Registrars at Nādāpuram, Payōli, Quilandi, Naduvannūr and Kuttiyādi. There are combined Post and Telegraph offices and Sea Customs offices at Badagara and Quilandi. There are Police stations at Chōmbāl in Aḻiyur amşam, Nādāpuram in Kummangōd amşam, Badagada Payōli in Iringatt amşam, Quilandi in Viyūr amşam, Tiruvaḻḻur, Kuttiyādi, Pērāmbra, Naduvannūr and Iyād.

Short Descriptive Notices of Towns, &c.—There are no Municipal towns in Kurumbranād. Kadattanād is one of the ancient chieftainships (nāds) into which Malabar was formerly divided. It stretches from the sea coast up the western declivity of the Western Ghats. The level tracts near the sea are very fertile. The eastern hilly parts are well wooded and contain indigenous cardamom plants. The petty State is said to have been founded in 1564 by a Nāyar chief who inherited it in the male line from the Tekkelankūr (southern regent) of the Kōlattiri kingdom.

Badagara (Vadakkēkara = the north bank) is the chief town in the taluk. According to the census of 1871, there were 1,037 houses with a population of 7,718 souls in Badagara amşam. At the census of 1881, there were 1,643 houses and a population of 8,336 persons. Of these 3,849 are Māppiḷḷas. Badagara is situated on the sea coast at the northern extremity of the Elattūr-Badagara backwater and on the trunk road from Calicut to Cannanore, 30 miles from the former and 12 miles south of Tellicherry. There is a fort at Badagara which originally belonged to the Kōlattiri Rajas, and it is said to have been acquired by the Kadattanād Raja in 1564. On passing into the possession of the Mysoreans it was made the chief export customs station on the coast. In 1790 it was taken from Tippu by the English, and having been restored to the Kadattanād Raja, it was converted by him into a Brahman feeding-house, which was afterwards transferred to the Paravantala temple in Badagara amsam. The raja has since built a thatched house in the fort. The fort is 246 feet square with bastions at each corner, and immediately west of it is a tank 168 feet long and 144 feet broad.

Badagara is a straggling but busy Māppiḷḷa town with several irregular streets or lanes. On the beach there are several substantial store-houses. There is a Jamātt mosque here as well as minor mosques. The Jamātt mosque is 114 by 42 feet. In Paravantala dēṣam in Badagara amṣam is a well 66 feet in circumference and 42 feet deep. This well is said to have been jumped across by Tachchōḷi Odēnan, the hero of a folk song noted in North Malabar.

In Badagara amṣam, Paravantala dēṣam, there is a temple dedicated to Subramanyan. It is 76 feet long and 56 feet broad. Attached to the temple is a tank 72 feet square. The temple, said to be an ancient institution, was renewed by the Kadattanād Raja about the year 1864. The roof of the shrine is covered with copper plates. The raja maintains a Brahman feeding-house here.

In Kuttipuram amṣam, 10 miles to the north-east of Badagara, is the fortified palace of the Kadattanād Pōrlātiri Valiya Raja, and in Purameri amṣam, 8 miles from Badagara, is the Pōrlātiri Iḷaya Raja's house. The remaining two branches of the raja's family live in Āyanchēri Kōvilakam and Edavalatt Kōvilakam in the same amsam.

Kōṭṭakkal, 3 miles south of Badagara, is a sea customs sub-port subordinate to Badagara. It was once a large town inhabited by Māppiḷḷas. There is a mosque of some note on the southern bank of the river at Kōṭṭakkal. Kōṭṭakkal was formerly the stronghold of a Māppiḷḷa pirate called Kunhāli Marakkār, who committed depredations in the surrounding country which are described in a folk song. Hardly any vestige of the stronghold now remains.

The Sacrifice Rock is opposite the Kōṭṭakkal sub-port in Lat. 11° 29′ 45″ N., Long. 75° 31½ E., bears S. ½ E. from Tellicherry 5¼ leagues, and is distant 4¾ miles from the land opposite; it has a white aspect, 40 feet in height, and is discernible 3 and 3½ leagues from a large ship, the deck being elevated 15 or 20 feet above water. It is called Veḷḷiyānkallu or the white or silvery stone by the natives of Malabar. This rock or island is steep all round, having 12 and 13 fathoms close to it, 16 fathoms 2¾ miles outside, 10 fathoms within it, to 7 fathoms about midway between it and the mainland in a very good channel. Ships passing through the inside channel ought to give the point a berth of 3 miles by borrowing towards the rock; and in working should heave the lead quick, if they come under 6 fathoms standing in shore. Passing outside Sacrifice Rock in the night, ships should not come under 16 or 17 fathoms water.

Nādāpuram is a rising Māppiḷḷa town in Kummangōd amṣam 9 miles from Badagara. The amṣam has a population of 5,328 souls. The recent establishment of a Munsif's Court has increased the importance of this place. There is a Jamātt mosque here, which is 104 by 33 feet in size.

At Kuttiyādi, which was once a strong military post, 17 miles from Badagara, there is an old redoubt as well as a small Māppiḷḷa village. The Kuttiyādi Ghat begins here. There is a Sub-Registrar's office and a Police station here. There is also a Jamātt mosque, 53 by 27 feet.

The Kuttiyādi Pass, in the Western Ghats, leads from Kurumbranād taluk into Wynād. It is steep and only practicable for foot-passengers and beasts of burden. The Kuttiyādi river is navigable from Badagara up to 30 miles. Large quantities of timber are floated down the river to Elattūr in Calicut, and to Badagara.

In Ponmēri amṣam, 5 miles from Badagara, is a Siva temple which is 124½ feet by 87 feet. It is sculptured. The roof of the shrine is covered with copper. There is a granite slab at the eastern entrance with an inscription in unknown characters. The temple is very old and was destroyed by Tippu's soldiers.

In Edachēri amṣam, 5 miles from Badagara, is Vēngōḷi temple in which Ganapati is worshipped. It is 70 by 53½ feet. The Kadattanād Rāja maintains a Brahman feeding-house here. Not far from the temple to the north there is a Bhagavati temple called Kaḷiyāmpaḷḷi temple. It is 97 feet long and 86 feet broad. There is an inscription on a slab in unknown characters.

In Muttungal amṣam, Veḷḷikuḷangara dēṣam, 4 miles north of Badagara, there is a Siva temple, 54 by 41 feet. Outside the temple, there is a slab with inscription in an unknown language. At Kārshkād in this amṣam, there is a Muhammadan mausoleum over the grave of one Siti Kōya, who is alleged to have migrated to Malabar from Arabia about 200 years ago. The mausoleum is held in great veneration by Māppiḷḷas, who flock to it in large numbers from different parts and make offerings.

In Vēḷam amṣam, 12 miles south-east of Badagara, there is a reservoir of fresh water locally known as Tura, which is 1,080 feet long by 218 feet wide. There is a similar Tura in Kuttiyādi amṣam, which is 684 feet by 72 feet with a depth averaging 22 feet. These are fabled to have been excavated by the Pandus in pre-historic period.

Chōmbāla in Aḷiyūr amṣam is a Basel Evangelical station. The mission was started there in 1849, and the number of church members in the colony on the 1st January 1885 were 309. There is a girls' orphanage here, which was transferred from Cannanore in 1872. A branch weaving establishment has existed here since 1883. There are three schools for boys and girls with an average attendance of about 200 pupils. The Chōmbāla Mission has an out-station at Badagara and Mūvarātt. The station at Quilandi, opened in 1857, is subordinate to the mission at Calicut. The congregation at Quilandi numbers 68.

In Mēlati amṣam, 10 miles from Quilandi, there is a Siva temple known as Kīḷur, which has its shrine roofed with copper. The temple is 93 by 70 feet. In the month of Vrischikam (November-December), a festival is celebrated here with great pomp. During the festival an important cattle market is held close to the temple over a large area. Divers other articles also find ready sale here on the occasion. More than 60,000 head of cattle are brought here from different parts of the district and Coimbatore, &c., and more than 10,000 people assemble during the festival.

Quilandi, the head-quarters of the Deputy Tahsildar, is in Viyyūr amṣam. There are besides a District Munsif's Court, Sub-Registrar's office, Sea Customs office, a combined Post and Telegraph office, Police station, Subsidiary jail, travellers' bungalow and mussaferkhana at Quilandi. The population of the amṣam in 1871 was 10,367 and in 1881, 10,259. In 1881 there were 2,095 houses against 1,757 in 1871. Of the former, 1,752 were occupied and the rest unoccupied.

Quilandi was a large flourishing port and town, of which many substantial buildings remain. It had also the advantage of being in the neighbourhood of the Kollam mud bank resembling those at Alleppey and Narakkal. Towards the close of the last century, the port was suddenly destroyed by a cyclone.

It was close to Quilandi (Capocate) that Vasco da Gama's fleet first cast anchor in 1498. Close to the seaport on the north is one of the nine original Muhammadan mosques established on the Malabar Coast by Malik Ibn Dinar. The mosque (recently renewed) is at Kollam, sometimes called northern or Pantalāyini Kollam. This mosque appears to have been built in imitation of one at Mecca. The dome is covered with sheets of copper which Arab vessels passing down the coast never failed in former days to salute, and all Muhammadan seamen offered up prayers on coming abreast of it. Three festivals are annually celebrated in the mosque. In Kollam, there is a Jamātt mosque in which there are three granite slabs containing inscriptions.

In the town of Quilandi there is an old mosque 130 by 70 feet. It is very high, having three storeys. The Government have granted lands yielding annually Rs. 1,800 for the support of this mosque. A brief account of the circumstances of this endowment will not be uninteresting.

The mosque appears to have been founded in 1779 by Saiyid Abdulla Bin Saiyid Ahamad Hadi. In 1780 voluntary engagements were entered into by the Muhammadan and Hindu merchants of different villages in Tinnevelly, by which they bound themselves to pay for the mosque a trifling fee upon each man's load or bullock load of merchandise which passed through their respective villages. A payment analogous to this was also in due course secured in Malabar in behalf of this mosque. The above collection was continued until 1803 when Regulation XII of that year put a stop to the practice.

In 1810, Saiyid Ali Hadi, the founder's son, brought to the notice of Government the difficulties experienced in regard to the up-keep of the mosque by the enforcement of Regulation XII. An enquiry was instituted into the matter in 1826 which eventually resulted in the grant of an allowance of Rs. 1,800 per annum, payable by monthly instalments, for the support of the mosque and establishment, and an additional payment down of Rs. 2,000 for repairing the mosque (G.O., dated 29th February 1828). The mosque was described by the Sub-Collector. Mr. Wheatley, to be a magnificent structure affording accommodation to travellers and to a largely attended school where instruction was imparted to Muhammadan youths. It was also stated that pilgrims to Mecca and visitors from Arabia were entertained here. The Government consequently directed the allowance to be continued as long as the institution was kept up on a proper footing and found to be beneficial to that portion of the public which had been accustomed to resort to it for lodging, entertainment or religious purposes.

In their despatch of 15th June 1831, the Court of Directors approved the grant and the proviso laid down for its continuance, and observed that what was intended was a degree of utility not altogether disproportionate to the allowance made. The Inam deed pertaining to this confirmed the grant to the present Inamdar for the purposes of the Inam as long as he continues to be loyal.

In 1841 Government withdrew from all connection with religious institutions, and in 1846 the Government accepted the Collector's proposal to make over to the Quilandi mosque as Sarvamānyam certain escheated farms in Ērnād producing a net revenue of Rs. 1,800 per annum. In 1848, 199 pieces of paddy fields and nursery plots and 16 gardens measuring in all 306 cawnies, 828 koles, and assessed at Rs. 1,176-10-1 with proprietor's share of Rs. 623-5-11 aggregating Rs. 1,800 were made over to the Inamdar. These lands lie in the amṣams of Manjēri, Kārakunnu, and Trikalangōd in Ērnād taluk. The Inamdar now squeezes from his tenants more than Rs. 3,200 per annum.

A festival is annually performed in the month of *Ramuḷḷan* on Mayath Kunnu (grave-yard hill) in Kollam. There are several ancient tombs on the hill, some of them with inscriptions.

In Kollam dōṣam is the Vishārī Kāvu temple, dedicated to Bhagavati and Siva. The roof of the Bhagavati shrine is covered with copper. The temple is 93 by 84 feet. The Dasra festival is celebrated here with pomp in Kanni (September-October), and in the month of Mīnam (March-April), a festival takes place for 8 days which attracts many pilgrims and calls into being in its neighbourhood at Kannādikkal a fair for divers articles aggregating in value about Rs. 10,000.

The temple possesses inam lands in the amṣams of Viyūr, Mūdādi Tiruvangūr, Arikkuḷam, Kiḻariyur and Mēlur, the revenue of which amounts to Rs. 343.

There is a tank 920 feet by 502 feet at Kollam.

There are inscriptions in illegible characters in the minor temples of Maralur, Pantalāyini and Taliyil in Viyūr.

In Edakkara amṣam, 10 miles from Quilandi, there is a hill called Vallikkāt-Mittal Kunnu crowned by a small shrine. There is a perennial flow of water from the top of the hill which is considered to be tīrtham or holy water and to which a large number of pilgrims flock in the month of Tulām (October-November). In Veḷur dēṣam, Manikottaparamba, there is a hat-stone 36 feet in circumference on an upright stone about 3 feet high and 4 feet thick. There was a similar circular stone in the same compound which has fallen from its prop.

In the neighbourhood of these hat-stones there is a stone-cut cave with a central column and raised platforms on sides similar to those found elsewhere in the district.

Naduvannūr is an important village and was the head-quarters of the old Kurumbranād taluk. It has a population of 3,386 souls, of whom 2,616 are Hindus and 770 Muhammadans. There is a Sub-Registrar's office here as well as a Police station. There is also a travellers' bungalow. A market is held every Saturday.

In Kārayād amṣam, Tiruvangur dēṣam, 6 miles from Quilandi, there is a Siva temple called Tiruvangur perched on a rock-hill called Kāppa mala. There are sculptures in the temple. It is 109 feet by 63 feet. The Sivarātri festival is celebrated here annually in the month of Kumbham (February-March). On the north and south of the temple as well as within the precincts of the temple, there are as many as nine *quasi* tanks varying from 6 to 60 feet in circumference, excavated on the top of the rocky hill which are never dried up. They are esteemed for ablutions. On a granite rock at the temple there is an inscription in unknown characters.

In Meppayūr amṣam, Eravattūr dēṣam, there are two ponds known as Narikkilāpuḻa and Tiyarapuḻa. The former is 600 feet long and 90 feet broad and the latter is almost as broad. They are used for washing. A local legend imputes their excavation to the Pāndavas.

In Pāmpiri dēṣam of the same amṣam is a garden called Kudakottiparamba, in which there is a hat-stone 30 feet in circumference supported by an upright column about 3 feet high and about 5 feet thick. The circular stone is a little damaged on one side. This is 9 miles north-east of Quilandi.

Payōli in Iringatt amṣam is a rising town. The population of the amṣam is 3,408, being 2,508 Hindus, 892 Muhammandans and 8 Christians. There is a Sub-Registrar's office at Payōli and a Police station as well as a travellers' bungalow on an eminence overlooking the river. A weekly market on every Monday is held here. There is a lock at Payōli on the canal which connects the Akalapuḻa backwater with the Kuttiyādi river, and thus provides an uninterrupted line of inland navigation from Elattūr in Calicut to Badagara. Fees are levied on boats passing the lock. Payōli is 10 miles from Badagara and 11 from Quilandi.

The rivers of the taluk are—

1. The Kōṭṭakkal or Kuttiyādi river.
2. The Mahé or Mondole river.
3. The Naduvannūr river.

A list of ferries in the taluk is subjoined :—

Second Class.

1. Mūrāt kadavu.

Third Class.

2. Kanayankōd kadavu.	10. Perinchēri kadavu.
3. Puramannāli kadavu.	11. Māniyan kadavu.
4. Nirattukuḷi kadavu.	12. Puḻakandi kadavu.
5. Chittāni kadavu.	13. Idinja kadavu.
6. Kūniyott kadavu.	14. Kōtta kadavu.
7. Muttunkal kadavu.	15. Chenthodi kadavu.
8. Kayippratt kadavu.	16. Thorashēri kadavu.
9. Puliyapuḻa kadavu.	17. Akalāpuḻa kadavu.

Third Class—continued.

18. Nelliyādi kadavu.	22. Thorāya kadavu.
19. Nadēri kadavu.	23. Chāttanātt kadavu.
20. Annala kadavu.	24. Kuniyil kadavu.
21. Ollūr kadavu.	

Fairs and Markets.—A weekly market is held at Badagara every Tuesday, at Nādāpuram every Thursday, at Payōli every Monday, at Kōkkallūr, close to Iyad Police station, every Wednesday, at Naduvannūr every Saturday.

Trigonometrical Survey Station.—There is a Trigonometrical survey station on Nādāpuram hill in Kunnummal amṣam, 16 miles from Badagara, as well as one on Puramala hill in Mūtādi amṣam, 5 miles from Quilandi.

Dams and Anicuts.—There is a dam at Pūlayād for the exclusion of salt water from the paddy cultivation lying above the dam. There is also a dam at Kāttāmpalli in Panangād amṣam.

Ayyanikkad dam is an old one between Uḷḷiyēri and Arikkuḷam amṣams. These dams are intended for the protection of cultivation and revenue.

Archæology.—Reference has already been made to the rock-cut cave and hat-stones in Edakkara amṣam, and a hat-stone in Meppayūr amṣam.

In Mūtādi amṣam, Muchukunnu dēṣam, in the valley of Valiyamala hill, there are two caves. One is large, being 66 feet long and 36 feet wide. At the western end of the cave is a circular pit 9½ *koles* in circumference and 1½ *koles* deep.

In Mullipād dēṣam, Cheruvannūr amṣam, 9 miles south-east of Badagara, there is a small rock-cut cave not yet excavated.

On the eastern side of the temple in Kaḷiyāmveḷḷi, in Edachēri amṣam, 6 miles north north-east of Badagara, there are some inscriptions.

On the eastern side of the temple in Veḷḷikuḷangara in Muttungal amṣam, 4 miles north of Badagara, there are some inscriptions. There is an old fort in Érámala amṣam.

An old Siva temple in Iringannūr, 8 miles north-east of Badagara, is fabled to have been founded by a rishi.

There is a small rock-cut cave in Koḻukkallūr dēṣam of Kārayād amṣam, 18 miles south-east of Badagara. There is an inscription on a granite rock at the temple of Tiruvangāra.

Kāvuntara, 12½ miles south-east of Badagara, 3 miles west of the bungalow at Naduvannūr, there is a deserted ruined temple. Close to the temple in the yard of a house is a stone with an inscription said to be illegible, and there is another on one of the steps of the tank belonging to the temple.

Kiḻariyūr is 15 miles south south-east of Badagara. There are two rock-cut caves here.

In the mosque at Kollam on the edge of the bath is a granite slab, broken, bearing an inscription in Vaṭṭeḻuttu characters. It is dated K.A. 684 (1508 A.D.).

Meppayūr, 10 miles east south-east of Badagara. In the grove attached to the Elavattara temple of Durga are some "sculptured images." A channel on the south side of the Malamangalam temple is fabled to have been excavated by the Pāndavas and is said to contain treasure. In Kāyalāt are to be seen a dolmen and two menhirs, and in Kiḻapaḻiyūr are a dolmen and five menhirs. In Pampiri dēṣam are two stone circles already referred to. Funeral urns of pottery have been found here.

Panangād, 18½ miles east south-east of Badagara. A ruined and deserted temple, on the eastern wall of the porch of which is an inscription in unknown characters. There is an old ruined fort here

Ponmēri, 5 miles north-east of Badagara. In the Si... temple is an ancient inscription on a broken slab in unknown characters. The temple is very old. It was destroyed by Tippu's soldiers.

Viyyūr, 10 miles south of Badagara. In the Maralūr temple there is an inscription. There is another in the Pantalāyini temple and one in the deserted temple of Talayil.

Mahé and the adjoining Aldees.

The French settlement of Mahé is situated in Lat. 11° 41′ 50″ N., and Long. 75° 34′ 25″ E. to the south of the mouth of the river Mahé with a roomy harbour whose rocky bar admits vessels up to 70 tons. Vessels may anchor off Mahé in 5 fathoms, with the flag-staff east north-east and 2 miles from shore.

Mahé consists of two portions, the one lying on the left bank of the river at its junction with the sea, the other lies inland on the opposite side of the river, and is a narrow strip of land touching at one point the small river which debouches at Tellicherry.

The population in 1871 was 8,492. The present population is 8,383, of whom 191 are Christians, 6,340 Hindus, and 1,852 Māppiḷḷas. The superficial area of Mahé proper restored to the French on the 23rd February 1817 was 1,445 acres, being 1,329 acres of lands under cultivation and 116 acres of public lands. It is about 4 miles to the south of Tellicherry. The restitution of the outlying aldees (villages) of—

(1) Chālakkara,
(2) Paḷḷūr,
(3) Chembra and
(4) Pandakkal,

or what is collectively called Nālutara, on 14th November 1853, enlarged the possession to 5 square miles in extent.

The dēṣams constituting the settlement are—

(1) Valiyangādi.
(2) Pūrakkal.
(3) Mundōkkil.
(4) Manchakkal.
(5) Chūdikkōtta.
(6) Valavil.
(7) Pūḷiyil.
(8) Mattāmmal.
(9) Ōdattinakam.
(10) Vaḷappinakam.
(11) Chālakkara.
(12) Paḷḷūr.
(13) Chembra.
(14) Pandakkal.

Mahé was at first a place of considerable importance and trade, but afterwards, having fallen so frequently into the hands of the English, the settlement and its trade suffered; and in 1782 its fortifications were not only razed to the ground, but the town was almost entirely burnt. Most of the chief buildings in Mahé are picturesquely situated on the bank close to the river mouth. The site is hilly, but densely covered with coconut trees. Mahé is celebrated for the fertility of its soil and the salubrity of its climate. It is in charge of a Chef de Service subordinate to Pondicherry. There is a Roman Catholic chapel to which a large number of devotees are annually attracted from different and distant parts on the occasion of a festival on the 15th of October every year. There are three boys' schools and one girls' school. There is also a British Post office and a long wooden bridge maintained by the Malabar District Board across the Mahé river. The coast road from Beypore to Tellicherry and Cannanore passes through Mahé.

There is a temple called Kiḷakkē Puttalatt Bhagavati temple of note in Mahé. Here a festival takes place every year in Kumbham (February-March), when more than 5,000 people assemble from different places in North Malabar.

Close to Mahé, at Kallāyi in British territory, there is a British Sea Customs Superintendent. Round Mahé there are four land customs chowkies with a preventive police establishment for guarding the frontier against the smuggling of dutiable goods, such as liquor, arms, ammunition, and military stores, opium and salt.

Of the four outlying aldees or villages restored to the French, Chālakkara, Paḷḷūr and Chembra formed the demesne of the Nambiyārs of Iruvaḷinād and Pandakkal of Kurungōtt Nāyar, and the four villages together constituted the amṣam of Nālutara in Kottayam taluk. In obedience to Extract from Minutes of Consultation, the Board of Revenue, in their Proceedings, dated 28th September 1846, directed the delivery to the French Government of the villages of Chālakkara, Paḷḷūr, Chembra, Pandakkal, as also the three detached points called Fort St. George and the great and small Kallāyi. These were accordingly handed over by Mr. J. D. Robinson, Head Assistant Collector, to Monsieur Hayes, Chief of Mahé, on the 14th November 1853. The boundaries of the four villages were—

East.—Part of Panniyanūr, Peringaḷam, Oḷavilam and Kallāyi amṣams.

West.—Tiruvangād and Kallāyi amṣams.

North.—Poniyam river and part of Panniyanūr amṣam.

South.—Part of Oḷavilam and Kallāyi amṣams.

Of the three detached points which communicate with each other—

North.—The strip of Kallāyi lying between them and Vera Kunnu.

South and south-west.—A strip of Kallāyi amṣam intervening between them and Mahé river, and a portion of Tellicherry.

East.—A mosque and precipice.

West.—A portion of Tellicherry road and a strip of Kallāyi amṣam intervening between them and Kanien Kunnu.

WYNĀD TALUK.

By V. Chappu Menon, B.A.

Boundaries, Area and Population.—The Wynād taluk which forms part of the table-land of Mysore originally consisted of three divisions known as North Wynād, South Wynād and South-East Wynād, comprising seven, six and three amsams respectively. The North and South Wynād divisions still appertain to the Malabar district, but the south-east portion, consisting of the amsams of Nambalakod, Munnanad and Cherankod, was transferred to the Nīligiri district with effect from 31st March 1877 (Fort St.

George Gazette, dated 13th March 1877). This article is confined to the notice of the Malabar-Wynād, Mr. A. E. C. Stuart who has been engaged for some time in the settlement of forests and of escheat claims in Wynād having, with the sanction of Government, undertaken the preparation of a special manual for the entire tracts known at present as the Nīligiri-Wynād and the Malabar-Wynād.

The Malabar-Wynād is bounded on the north by Kottayam and Coorg, on the east by Mysore, on the south by the Nīligiri district and Ērnād, and on the west by Calicut and Kurumbranād.

Area.—999 square miles, of which 80 square miles may be said to be under cultivation.

Population.—According to the census of 1881, the population numbered 88,091 souls, of whom 76,898 were Hindus, 9,056 were Muhammadans, 1,983 were Christians and 154 belonged to other classes. The males were to the females as 49,661 to 38,430. The number of houses occupied was 8,666 and of those unoccupied 3,982.

Physical Aspects.—Wynād is an elevated and exceedingly picturesque mountainous plateau. It is generally rugged and broken and has some of the largest mountain peaks in the district. The central portions consist of ranges of low hills of easy slopes, covered with grass and low bamboo jungle, while the eastern parts are fairly open and flat and merge insensibly into the table-land of Mysore. The Nīligiri-Kunda range abuts on the south-east corner of the taluk, while the Bramagiri hills on the north separate it from Coorg. The average height of the plateau above sea-level is 3,000 feet, though many of the mountain peaks are over 5,000 feet, *e.g.*, Vāvūl mala (Camel's Hump), the highest peak in the taluk, is 7,677 feet; Vellera mala, 7,364 feet; Bānasūr, 6,762 feet; and Bramagiri peak, 5,276 feet.

Mountains and Forests.—The table-land of Wynād is composed of low ridges with innumerable valleys running in all directions; the only space which is of a more level surface is about Porakudi, Panamaram and Ganapativattam, in the south-east. The eastern portion is under heavy forest and few hills appear. The whole of it is undulating. The ghats from the Periah pass towards the Tāmarassēri pass and 11 miles to the east are lofty consisting of immense peaks, from 5,000 to 6,000 feet and occupy a large surface. To the north of Manantoddy (5 miles) is a lofty ridge branching off from the ghats and north of it (4 miles) is the famous mountain of Bramagiri. This ridge forms the limit common to Coorg and Wynād and between these two ridges lies the valley of Tirūnelli. In the interior are several detached hills of considerable elevation. The following are the principal mountains :—

(1) The Bālasūr or Bānasuran mala (ബാണാസുരൻ), called after the giant Bānasuran who is supposed to have built a fort on its summit.
(2) Bramagiri, supposed to be the abode of the god Brahma, and which would make a splendid sanitarium.
(3) Chambra mala (ചമ്പ്രമല).
(4) Tala mala (തലമല).
(5) Tariyōtt or Terriōte mala (തരിയൊട്ടുമല).
(6) Vāvūl mala (Camel's Hump).
(7) Elampileri mala (ഏളമ്പിലെരിമല).

The forests in Wynād are very valuable. A note on them prepared by the District Forest Officer, Mr. Rhodes Morgan, will be found at the end of this paper.

Rivers.—The important rivers in the taluk are—

(1) The Kabbani which has its principal sources in the Western Ghats. They take their rise in the valley of the high mountains north-west and north-east above the Tāmarassēri pass. Several streams, such as the Kalpetta, the Manantoddy and the Bavalli join this river, which when united drains nearly the whole of North and South Wynād.

(2) The Chola or Solayar, one of the main tributaries of the Beypore river which leaps down in a magnificent cataract from the crest of the hills close to the Choladi pass into the Nilambūr valley.

(3) The Manantoddy puḷa which has its sources in the mountains between Bānasūr peak and the summit of the Kuttiyādi and Periah passes and joins the Kabbani near the famous Fish Pagoda.

(4) The Panamaram puḷa.

(5) The Kunnattu puḷa (കുന്നത്ത) in Vayitiri amsam.

(6) The Putusseri puḷa (പുതുശ്ശേരി) in Kurumbala amsam.

(7) The Kanayamcheri puḷa (കണയഞ്ചേരി) in Etannatassakur amsam.

(8) The Alatur puḷa (ആലത്തൂർ) in Ganapathi Vattam amsam.

Nos. 4 to 8 united join the Manantoddy river near the Fish Pagoda and form the upper waters of the Kabbani.

The Rampur and the Moyar rivers chiefly drain the South-East Wynād.

Passes.—The main passes uniting the low country with the taluk are—

(1) The Smugglers' pass from Dindimal to Manatana.

(2) The Periah pass descending on Kannavam in Kottayam taluk.

(3) The Ellacherum pass (Cardamom Mountain pass) leading to Kuttiyādi in Kurumbranād taluk.

(4) The Kuttiyādi pass also descending on Kuttiyādi.

(5) The Tariyōtt pass likewise leading to Kuttiyādi.

(6) The Tāmarassēri pass into Calicut taluk.

(7) The Choladi pass leading into the Nilambūr valley.

(8) The Kārkūr pass into the Ērnād taluk.

Nos. 2, 6 and 8 are broad roads open for cart traffic. No. 3 is only available for horse or pack-bullocks. The remaining are minor passes, used only by foot-passengers.

History.—The traditionary history of Wynād is very obscure, but the following account of it has the merit of having been in vogue in the early years of British rule.

The country was formerly held by a line of Vedar Rajas ruling the Vedars (wild hunters), and thus much is probably correct, for Wynād has been the last refuge and is still the home of many aboriginal tribes, Kurumbars, Kurichiyars, Panniyars, &c., driven up probably from the low country of Malabar.

In the times of the Vedar Rajas a man of the Kshatriya caste called the "Cumbala Raja" (? Kumbla) came to Wynād from the north with a view to visit the Tirūnelli shrine. He was taken prisoner and carried before the

Vedar Raja, who insisted, before permitting him to depart, on his marrying one of the daughters of the kingly Vedar line.

Being a Kshatriya he would not consent to marry into the Vedar tribe, but as the Raja was inexorable he at last agreed on the condition that the ceremony should be carried out in accordance with Kshatriya customs. This was allowed and a delay occurred while marriage pandals and other preparations were being made.

Taking advantage of this delay, the imprisoned Raja communicated with the Kshatriya Rajas of Kottayam and Kurumbranād in the low country, and these princes, with their forces, put in an appearance on the wedding day. The Vedar Raja was besieged in his fort; the fort was taken, and the Vedar Raja and most of his people were slain.

The intended bride of the "Cumbala Raja" was given, it is said, in marriage to one of the Nambiar caste who was entrusted by the Kottayam and Kurumbranād Rajas with the government of the country.

The allied Rajas next consulted, it is said, how to divide the country so as to avoid disputes. To this end they set out in different directions and agreed to make the place where they should meet the boundary. This plan failed, as may well be conceived by any one who has even now-a-days tried to find his way through the elephant grass and tangled swamps with which Wynād abounds.

The Kottayam Raja then generously gave up all his claims to the country to the Kurumbranād Raja, stipulating only that if posterity failed the latter the country should come to him and his posterity.

An ascetic with matted hair, who had been one of the attendants of the Cumbala Raja, settled down, it is said, in Wynād, and his daughter was afterwards married to a Kottayam Raja. It is not said what became of the other attendant who is described as a Sudra Vellāḷan. Subsequently the Kottayam and Kurumbranād families fell out, and by the time the British raj was established, the Kottayam family was supreme in the taluk.

It is unnecessary to detail here the events of the Paḷassi (Pychy) Raja's rebellion and death, as these have been treated fully in Vol. I.

The attainder passed on him and his heirs in Wynād deserves, however, a few remarks.

On the 16th June 1805, Lieut.-Colonel McLeod offered rewards for the apprehension of the Paḷassi (Pychy) Raja and eleven of his principal adherents, and "also made known that all the estates and property belonging to the described rebels is confiscated from this date." The rebel leader and five of his followers were killed on the 30th November 1805. The sentence of forfeiture pronounced on the 16th June 1805 has never been effectively carried out, though from time to time attempts have been made to ascertain the exact limits of the "Pychy escheats" with a view to the assertion of the rights of the State therein. The consequence has been that many of the lands in Wynād—the janmam property of the Pychy rebels and therefore the property of the State by forfeiture—have been usurped by fictitious janmis, whose claims are now being investigated. The decisions arrived at in the various claims preferred and investigated will be carried out at the new revenue settlement of the tract about to be commenced.

Sub-divisions of the Taluk for Administrative Purposes.—Wynād originally comprised eleven hoblis consisting of thirteen amsams, the latter being subsequently increased to 16 by the creation of Peria, Vayitiri and Cherankod amsams. The names of the hoblis and of the ancient and modern amsams are shown below:—

Ancient Hoblis.	Old Amsams.	Modern Amsams.
		North Wynād.
1. Muthornad (മൂത്തോർനാട).	1. Edavaka Ārathara (എടവക ആറതര). 2. Thondernad Anjuthura (തൊണ്ടർനാടഞ്ചുതറ).	1. Peria (പെരിയ). 2. Edavaka (എടവക). 3. Thondernad (തൊണ്ടർനാട).
2. Porunnanur (പൊരുന്നന്നൂർ).	3. Porunnanur (പൊരുന്നന്നൂർ).	4. Porunnanur (പൊരുന്നന്നൂർ).
3. Nallurnad (നല്ലൂർനാട).	4. Nallurnad. (നല്ലൂർനാട).	5. Nallurnad (നല്ലൂർനാട).
4. Ellurnad (എളളൂർനാട).	5. Ellurnad (എളളൂർനാട).	6. Ellurnad (എളളൂർനാട).
5. Wynad (വയനാട).	6. Anjuthara Kuppatod (അഞ്ചുതറകുപ്പത്തോട). 7. Puthadi Ārthara (പുതാടി ആറതറ).	7. Kuppatod (കുപ്പത്തോട). *South-Wynād.* 8. Puthadi (പുതാടി).
6. Kurumbala (കുറുമ്പാല).	8. Kurumbala (കുറുമ്പാല).	9. Kurumbala (കുറുമ്പാല). 10. Vayitiri (വൈത്തിരി).
7. Edanatassakur (എടനാടസ്സുകൂറ).	9. Edanatassakur (എടനാടസ്സുകൂറ).	11. Edanatassakur (എടനാടസ്സുകൂറ).
8. Muppainad. (മൂപ്പയിനാട).	10. Muppainad (മൂപ്പയിനാട).	12. Muppainad (മൂപ്പയിനാട).
9. Ganapativattam (ഗണപതിവട്ടം).	11. Ganapativattam (ഗണപതിവട്ടം).	13. Ganapativattam (ഗണപതിവട്ടം).
		South-East Wynād.
10. Munnanad (മൂന്നനാട).	12. Munnanad (മൂന്നനാട).	14. Munanad (മൂന്നനാട). 15. Cherankod (ചെരങ്കൊട).
11. Nambolakod (നമ്പൊലക്കൊട).	13. Nambolakod (നമ്പൊലക്കൊട).	16. Nambolakod (നമ്പൊലക്കൊട).

Pulpalli dēsam which formed part of the Kuppatod amsam was transferred to Puthadi amsam in 1884 under Board's Proceedings, dated 9th August 1884, No. 2754.

The tāluk was formerly under the Sub-Collector, Tellicherry, who was replaced by the Deputy Collector on the creation of that class of officers on the 12th August 1859. Its civil jurisdiction vested in the Deputy Tahsildar, Vayitiri, and the Deputy Collector, Manantoddy, until 1879, when a separate Munsif's Court was established at Vayitiri for the entire tract (*vide* notification in the Fort St. George Gazette, dated 28th January 1879, page 112). The seven amsams of North Wynād forming the Tahsildar-Magistrate's jurisdiction are subordinate to the District and Sessions Court, Tellicherry, for judicial purposes; whilst those of the South Wynād forming the Deputy

Taheildar's charge are subordinate to the District and Sessions Court, Calicut, (*vide* notifications in the Fort St. George Gazette, dated 2nd January 1863, 3rd March, and 15th October 1886). Until recently, the District Munsif, Vayitiri, was subordinate only to the District Court, Calicut, but in the Government notifications, dated 3rd March and 15th October 1886, already quoted, he was placed in subordination to both the North Malabar and South Malabar District Courts. The District Munsif is generally invested with first-class magisterial powers with a view to presiding at the Bench of Honorary Magistrates for South Wynād.

The following are the principal public offices:—

(1) The Deputy Collector and Magistrate located at Manantoddy.
(2) The Tahsildar and Sub-Magistrate located at Manantoddy.
(3) The Police Inspector located at Manantoddy.
(4) The Deputy Tahsildar and Sub-Magistrate located at Vayitiri.
(5) The Police Inspector located at Vayitiri.
(6) The District Munsif located at Vayitiri.
(7) The Sub-Registrar, Manantoddy, under the District Registrar, Tellicherry.
(8) The Sub-Registrar, Vayitiri, under the District Registrar, Calicut.
(9) Combined Postal and Telegraph office at Vayitiri.
(10) Other Post offices at Manantoddy, Kalpetta, Tariyōtt, Sultan's Battery and Mēpadi.
(11) Police stations at Manantoddy, Oliyot, Koroth, Panamaram, Kalpetta, Vayitiri, Mēpādi, Tariyōtt, Sultan's Battery and Periah.
(12) Sub-Assistant Conservator at Manantoddy and his subordinates.
(13) Local Fund Supervisors and Sub-Overseers at Vayitiri and Manantoddy.
(14) Local Fund Middle School at Manantoddy.
(15) Vaccine staff for North and South Wynād under the control of the Deputy Inspectors of Tellicherry and Calicut circles respectively.
(16) Hospitals at Vayitiri and Manantoddy in charge of Apothecaries; the latter being supervised till August 1886 by a European medical officer, who drew a special allowance of Rs. 150 per mensem from Government.
(17) Bench of Magistrates, North Wynād.
(18) Do. South Wynād.

Manantoddy—in Vemom dēsam of Ellurnād amsam, is the head-quarters of the Deputy Collector and of the Tahsildar of Wynād. It contains, in addition to public offices, a hospital, a travellers' bungalow, a chattram in Buffalo street *and another at Bavalli* and a middle school, and is the centre of some trade. A weekly market is held here on Sundays. There was formerly a cantonment at this place on a low flat hill, consisting of a small redoubt, an artillery shed, a range of officers' quarters, place-of-arms, hospital, &c. The important religious institutions in the Ellurnād amsam are—(1) Tirūnelli temple (തിരുനെല്ലിക്ഷേത്രം), (2) Trichaleri temple (തൃച്ചലേരിക്ഷേത്രം), (3) Valliyurkāva (വള്ളിയൂർകാവു), the famous Fish Pagoda (Vol. I., p. 540), (4) the Roman Catholic church. There is a Protestant cemetery at Manantoddy and another at Vayitiri. Tirūnelli and Trichaleri are considered most sacred places, and a short account of the origin of the temple at the former locality is given below :—

Trūnelli temple (literally the temple having the sacred nelli tree) lies in a valley of the mountains to the south of the Bramagiri peak. It is known by three different names, viz., (1) Tirūnelli temple (തിരുനെല്ലിക്ഷേത്രം), (2) Āmalaka temple (ആമലകക്ഷേത്രം), and (3) Sidha temple (സിദ്ധക്ഷേത്രം). It is believed to have been dedicated by Brahma to Vishnu known as Dēva Dēvēsan (ദേവദേവെശൻ) and Tirūnelli Perumal (തിരുനെല്ലിപെരുമാൾ). The mythological origin of the temple is as follows :—

Once upon a time when Brahma was enjoying one of his periodical peregrinations, he happened to be delighted beyond measure with this place with a grove of most beautiful trees and plants, of flowers and foliage among which stood a nelli tree (*Phyllanthus emblica*), on which was seen the image of Vishnu with four hands bedecked with numerous fine jewels. The image immediately vanished from sight. Being overtaken with grief and surprise at this sudden disappearance, Brahma engaged himself in deep contemplation, when the image reappeared and he heard the following words uttered by an invisible being : "The image that thou hast seen is that of Vishnu, the excellence of this place draws and keeps him here." Convinced of these divine utterances, Brahma made a temple, consecrated Vishnu therein and entrusted its keeping to two pious Brahmins of the Āmalaka village. The Brahma ordained that visits to, and prayers at, the temple would remove the sins committed though they were for generations, and secure paradise, and that the performance of prayers and ceremonies would lead to the translation of the spirits of the departed, who have not obtained salvation, to the "Pithurloka" (regions of blissful spirits) wherein to enjoy eternal happiness. This blessing, pronounced by the Brahma, is believed in by Hindus, and pilgrimages are therefore undertaken to the shrine.

In connection with the temple there are seven holy water fountains, which are—

(1) Pāpa-nāsini (പാപനാശിനി), literally extinguisher of sins, (2) Panchathirtham (പഞ്ചതീൎത്ഥം), (3) Irnamochini-thirtham (ഋണമോചിനിതീൎത്ഥം), (4) Gunnika-thirtham (ഗുണ്ണികതീൎത്ഥം), (5) Satā-vinnu (ശതവിന്നു), (6) Sahasravinnu (സഹസ്രവിന്നു), (7) Varāham (വരാഹം).

There is a rock called Pinnapara (പിണ്ഡപ്പാര) where offerings to the spirits of the departed are made, and this rock is supposed to be the bone of an asuran (demon) named Palana-bhedi (പാഷാണഭേദി), who was killed by Vishnu and who at the time of his death prayed to that deity that his body might be converted into a rock extending from Tirunelli to Gaya and divided into three parts fit for the performance of offerings for the departed, viz., at (1) Tirunelli representing his foot, (2) Godaveri representing the middle part, and (3) Gaya representing the head.

Offerings at any of these three places are supposed to have special benefits in producing happiness and in the propitiation of the spirits. For the safe guarding of the temple four shrines have been created, viz., the shrine (1) of Durga at the east, (2) of Siva at the south, and (3) at the west and (4) of Subramaniam at the north. These four shrines are supposed to represent (1) Valliyurkāva temple (വള്ളിയൂൎക്കാവ), (2) Trichaleri temple

(തൃശ്ശിലേരി,) (3) Tricharakunnu temple (തൃച്ചറകുന്ന), and (4) a temple said to exist in the Brahmagiri mountains.

There are some old copper plate grants in this temple in the Vatteḻuthu (വട്ടെഴുത്ത) character which have not yet been deciphered.

In the dēsam of Ārattuthara (literally a place of bathing the idol), in Ellurnād amsam, is situated the Valliyurkāva temple, at which a festival takes place annually, when an immense concourse of people assemble and live in small booths built from materials obtained on the spot. Feeding the mahseer and other carp which abound in the pool of the river lying close to this shrine is considered meritorious, and hence the popular name of the "Fish Pagoda" by which it is generally known to Europeans.

Vayitiri—in the amsam of the same name, is the seat of the District Munsif and of the Deputy Tahsildar. It contains likewise the offices of the Sub-Registrar and the Police Inspector and is a place of some importance. The Bench of Magistrates for South Wynād meets at Vayitiri. There is a Hindu temple known as Kunnath ampalam now in ruins. There is also a Roman Catholic chapel in fair condition and a chattram. About a mile to the south-west of the village lies the Pukkote lake, a natural sheet of water among hills, the only thing of the kind of which the district can boast. On the picturesque bank of the lake the European planters of the district have built a club, and there is a large store adjoining it.

Lackadi—in the same amsam, lies at the head of the Tāmarassēri ghat pass and contains a bungalow, a chattram and the ruins of the old Mysorean stockade (Lekkiti-kōtta), from which it derives its name.

Periah—in the amsam of the same name, is about 19 miles from Manantoddy and lies on the road to Tellicherry. It is celebrated for its cardamom cultivation, and has a travellers' bungalow, a chattram and a Police station.

Nallurnād.—Payingātiri, in Nallurnād amsam, is a Brahman village of some note, and is about two miles from Manantoddy. The amsam contains a mosque known as Pallikkal Angadiyil palli (പള്ളിക്കൽഅങ്ങാടിയിൽപള്ളി) and a bazaar.

Kuppatōt.—*Panapuram* or *Panamaram* (literally the place of palms) in Kuppatōt amsam was once a strong military post consisting of an extensive square mud fort with a sepoy place-of-arms and other buildings; but the whole of it is now in ruins.

It contains now a Māppiḷḷa bazaar and a Police station.

Putati.—*Putati* and *Purakati*, in Putati amsam, are places of note. At the former is a temple known as Arimula Ayyappan temple, on the east wall of the mandapam of which is an inscription, dated K.A. 922 (A.D. 1746), in a mixture of four languages. There is a Canarese inscription on a stone which belonged to the Pātiri temple, but is now in the possession of Pātiri Manjaya Gavundan. In the hamlet of Pakkam is a free standing stone.

At Kaniyampatta, in the Putati amsam, there is a bungalow belonging to the District Board.

Porunnanur amsam contains the bazaar known as Kellur (കെല്ലൂർഅങ്ങാടി), and also three mosques called (1) Kellurangadi palli (കെല്ലൂർ അങ്ങാടിപള്ളി), (2) Palanchana angadi palli (പഴഞ്ചന അങ്ങാടിപള്ളി) and (3) Kandattvayal palli (കണ്ടത്തവയൽപള്ളി).

Tondarnād.—*Korom* or *Koroth* in Tondarnād amsam is a place of considerable trade chiefly in the hands of the Māppiḷḷas. It contains a travellers' bungalow, a Police station, two Hindu temples known as Tondarakōtta (തൊണ്ടറകോട്ടക്ഷേത്രം) and Bhagavati Kāvu (ഭഗവതികാവുക്ഷേത്രം), and two mosques called Koroth angadi palli (കോരൊത്ത അങ്ങാടിപ്പള്ളി) and Koroth putiya palli (കോരൊത്തപുതിയപള്ളി).

Etannatassakur.—*Kalpatta* alias *Kalpatti*, in Etannatassakur amsam, is a place of some note from its being the residence of some Brahmans and Chettis. It is on the high road from the Tāmarassēri pass, and contains a bungalow and a chattram.

Tariyōtt—is another place in the same amsam of some note, and contains a chattram.

Ganapativattam—(literally the circle or range of the god Ganapati), otherwise known as Sultan's Battery from the fact that Tippu Sultan had a fort here, is a village of little importance. There was a British regiment stationed here in the early part of the present century. On the hill known as Nālapāt chāla kunnu is a stone having an inscription in old Tamil on two sides. It has not yet been read. There is another on the *Dipastambha* (lamp post) at the Ganapati temple, and a third on a stone standing in the north court of the Māriyamma temple. In the hamlet of Kitanganat are twelve dolmens, a menhir and three carved stones.

Muppainad—contains a small fort and a pagoda of some importance, dedicated to Vēttakorumakan. The Devaswam is usually known as the Mūttīl Devaswam. In the hamlet of Mūttīl are 22 dolmens, and in Chingēri 2.

Christian Churches and Cemeteries.—There are two Roman Catholic chapels in the taluk, one at Manantoddy and the other at Vayitiri, also a Protestant chapel at Chundale and a temporary edifice at Vayitiri used for divine service by the Protestant community. At Vayitiri the service is performed by the Chaplain of Calicut, and at Manantoddy by the Chaplain of Cannanore. At the latter station there is no separate building, the service being performed in the Local Fund school-house. There are two Protestant cemeteries, one at Manantoddy and the other at Vayitiri, which are in good condition. The Roman Catholic cemeteries are not secured by proper walls.

Bungalows and Chattrams.—There are bungalows at (1) Periah, (2) Koroth, (3) Manantoddy, (4) Lakkidi, and (5) Sultan's Battery, and chattrams at (1) Periah, (2) Manantoddy, (3) Bavalli, (4) Kalpetta, (5) Tariyōtt, (6) Lakkidi, (7) Vayitiri, and (8) Sultan's Battery.

Mines, Minerals and Manufactures.—Iron ore may be obtained in several parts, but none of it is manufactured. The principal rocks, which are gneisses, granites, &c., are traversed by quartz reefs, which are frequently auriferous, but they are found chiefly in South-east Wynād. The favourable reports on the auriferous character of the Wynād fields led to several companies being formed for working gold, and although several blocks of estates were purchased for this purpose, no operations are now being carried on in Malabar-Wynād. The collapse of the mining industry, which at one time promised to be so important, told seriously on the other, and ordinary pursuits, such as the planting of coffee and other products. The jungle tribes from a remote period used to work gold from the sands of rivers which are sometimes mixed with gold particles. This practice has now fallen into desuetude.

Soil and Productions.—The soil in the cultivated valleys is a fine rich brown, on the heights it is mostly red mixed with gravel. Towards the east and the woody tract it is almost black and rich from the accumulation of dry leaves and other matter. The productions are generally different kinds of rice, horse-gram and other dry grains, castor and other oil seeds and sugar-cane, from which latter, jaggery to a very limited extent is manufactured. Since 1840, the cultivation of coffee has occupied the attention of European planters and proved for a long time highly remunerative. Owing, however, to leaf-disease and other causes, the industry began to languish, and hopes are now centered in tea and cinchona plantations as well as in coffee.

The taluk produces very little pepper and no coconuts nor areca-nuts, though a few trees of each may be seen. Cardamoms are produced in great plenty between the Periah and Kuttiyādi passes, and are considered to be of a superior quality. Small quantities are also obtained on the slopes of the mountains forming the Tāmarassēri valley above the pass. Large quantities of honey and bees' wax are obtained from the forests and rocks among the mountains. These useful articles find a ready sale in the seaport towns, from whence they are exported. Some tobacco is produced, but only in small quantities and for private consumption.

Inams.—The inams granted in the Wynād taluk are the following:—

(1) Pūmalathalachil Bharadēvata (goddess) temple in Kuppattot amsam, Rs. 96-10-4.

(2) Pallimalamma Bhagavati (goddess) temple in Tondernad amsam, Rs. 11-6-0.

The inams granted in the above amsams are intended to defray the expenses attending the usual ceremonies in the temples.

Cattle and other Animals.—Cattle and buffaloes are numerous and are sometimes a source of mischief to planters. Sheep and goats are almost unknown except such as are imported for food. The taluk abounds with deer (sambur) and wild pigs. Elephants and bison are also to be found in the ghat forests. Tigers are fairly numerous, and panthers abound to such an extent as to be an intolerable nuisance to any one with pet dogs.

A peculiar practice of spearing tigers and panthers obtains among the Chettis in Ganapativattam, Muppainad and Putati amsams. When a kill takes place, the beast of prey is quietly allowed to gorge itself with beef, and under such circumstances it lies up in the first favourable sheltering cover it finds. Word is sent round the country and the people bearing nets and spears quietly assemble at the spot. If the patch of jungle in which the animal has lain up is of small extent, the nets are immediately run up round it and fastened to stout stakes driven into the ground. The nets are of ordinary thin rope, and, when stretched, are about 5 feet high. Ordinarily, however, the matter is not so easily arranged, but the probable course of the animal after it is roused is usually well known, a piece of likely jungle is selected and three sides of it are beforehand netted in. Scouts are posted, the animal is then disturbed, and as soon as it enters the netted space, the fourth side is immediately closed with nets, the workers being protected by the spearmen while this ticklish operation is in hand. The animal thus netted rarely escapes, the netted space is gradually reduced in size by clearing away brushwood and eventually the animal is confined in a space measuring some 18 or 20 yards in diameter. The aid of the village deity is invoked, and the huntsmen armed with spears challenge the animal to combat at the time pronounced by the oracle to be favourable for action. The ground where the so-called combat is fought is called Narikandi (tiger-ground), and people sometimes have to await the oracular revelations for four or five days. At the hour appointed, the animal is enraged by every sort of device: when its first low muttered growls are heard, the spearmen surrounding the net in an unbroken phalanx shout in response; the growls gradually become louder and more continuous, until at last breaking into short and sharp savage grunts, the maddened animal delivers a charge full at the net when the spearmen half mad themselves from arrack and excitement receive it on their spear points. Several such charges are usually delivered before the animal receives its death thrust.

The skin of a tiger or panther thus slain is never removed either for obtaining rewards from Government, or for sale, but the carcass is hung on a horizontal bar and there allowed to rot.

Fairs and Markets.—Weekly markets are held on Sundays at Vayitiri and Manantoddy. A large fair is held for five days at Valliyūr Kāvu (fish pagoda) during the annual festival; markets are also held at Kalpetta, Tariyōtt, Mōpādi and Sultan's Battery.

Climate.—The climate of Wynād is much cooler than the low country, being about 3,000 to 4,000 feet above the level of the sea. The thermometer during the cool weather is as low as 60°, but during the months of March, April and May, it rises to 84° and sometimes higher. On the whole, it is considered unhealthy, owing chiefly to defective water-supply and the prevalence of malaria. Manantoddy is, from a climatic point of view, better than Vayitiri, and has comparatively an open country around it. From October to January the climate may be said to be fairly dry, cool and salubrious; from February to May hot land-winds blow and fever is prevalent; from June to October rain falls with short intermissions, and though the temperature is lower and fever less general than in the preceding months, dysentery, diarrhœa and rheumatism are common. The average rainfall of the taluk for three years is given below:—

Months.	Manantoddy.			Vayitiri.		
	1882.	1883.	1884.	1882.	1883.	1884.
	INCHES.	INCHES.	INCHES.	INCHES.	INCHES.	INCHES.
January	·30	..	..	·82	..	..
February	..	..	..	..	..	..
March	·95	2·31	..	1·12	5·27	·10
April	2·91	2·75	2·62	5·76	5·82	5·51
May	4·29	2·74	1·80	8·16	7·05	1·47
June	47·06	21·47	12·20	88·56	43·77	18·35
July	84·68	38·41	21·94	118·20	64·53	39·30
August	14·98	30·46	31·51	34·35	54·34	55·05
September	9·89	4·83	9·58	16·34	12·30	18·56
October	7·87	7·57	5·87	12·70	17·90	5·90
November	2·68	2·26	2·96	4·52	3·80	7·19
December	..	1·69	·12	·20	3·05	1·52
Total ..	175·61	114·49	88·60	290·73	217·83	152·95

Trigonometrical Stations.—There is but one survey station to be preserved and annually reported on (Board's Proceedings, dated 28th July 1886, No. 1706).

Name of G.T.S. Station.	Situation.	Series.	Modern values.	
			Latitude.	Longitude.
			° ′ ″	° ′ ″
Narikod	Vayitiri amsam.	Modern ..	11 32 26·88	76 01 21·07

Traffic Registry Stations.—Two stations for registering the traffic with Mysore were opened in December 1880 at Bavalli and Sultan's Battery. The statistics of trade for 1885-86 are given below :—

Imports into Malabar from Mysore.

Articles.		*Viâ* Bavalli.		*Viâ* Sultan's Battery.		Total.	
		Quantity	Value.	Quantity.	Value.	Quantity.	Value.
			RS.		RS.		RS.
Animals, living, horses	No.	1	22	5	113	6	135
Do. cattle	,,	737	4,444	523	4,008	1,260	8,452
Do. sheep and goats.	,,	4,856	17,339	5,523	18,445	10,379	35,784
Do. other sorts ..	,,	56	14	207	341	263	355
Chinese and Japanese ware ..	Val.	..	35	..	..	..	35
Coffee	Mds.	203	1,097	694	10,895	897	11,992
Cotton twist and yarn, Indian ..	,,	..	..	1	40	1	40
Do. piece-goods, Indian ..	,,	130	9,635	133	6,986	263	16,621
Do. do. European ..	,,	41	2,608	4	280	45	2,888
Dyeing and colouring materials —Turmeric	,,	24	188	17	100	41	288
Earthenware and porcelain ..	Val.	..	130	..	423	..	553
Fruits and nuts, coconuts ..	No.	1,500	48	30,200	843	31,700	891
Do. all other kinds	Mds.	2	10	..	..	2	10
Grain and pulse, wheat	,,	7,752	13,907	6,924	14,597	14,676	28,504
Do. other spring crops.	,,	3,015	4,163	2,638	6,903	5,653	11,066
Do. rice not in the husk	,,	347	1,427	4,642	21,844	4,989	23,271
Do. rice in the husk ..	,,	35	37	69	69	104	106
Do. other rain crops ..	,,	11,508	15,757	21,953	33,296	33,461	49,053
Leather, manufactures of ..	Val.	..	270	..	50	..	320
Liquors	,,	..	10,237	..	..	..	10,237
Mats	,,	..	248	..	241	..	489
Metals and manufacture of metals,—Brass and copper ..	Mds.	29	1,222	37	1,578	66	2,800
Do. —Iron	,,	1	8	1	12	2	20
Oils	,,	865	9,817	652	7,394	1,517	17,211
Provisions, ghee	,,	29	813	3	72	32	885
Do. other kinds	,,	1,419	4,109	630	1,843	2,049	5,952
Salt	,,	..	..	65	136	65	136
Saltpetre, &c., other saline substances	,,	..	..	172	112	172	112
Oils, mustard	,,	93	314	4	15	97	329
Do. gingelly	,,	6,929	30,901	130	510	7,059	31,411
Do. other oil seeds	,,	18	100	175	489	193	589
Do. other seeds, other kinds ..	,,	440	1,293	191	588	631	1,881
Spices, other sorts	,,	629	2,811	325	2,122	954	4,933
Sugar, unrefined	,,	980	4,186	2,952	15,998	3,932	20,184
Do. refined	,,	20	205	9	93	29	298
Tobacco	,,	11	102	138	1,156	149	1,258
Wood, timber	,,	942	2,032	109	125	1,051	2,157
Wool, piece-goods, Indian ..	,,	97	2,585	391	10,275	488	12,860
Do. European ..	,,	2	55	2	121	4	176
All other articles of merchandise. { Unmanufactured	Val.	..	5,806	..	6,860	..	12,666
All other articles of merchandise. { Manufactured.	,,	..	2,015	..	1,558	..	3,573
Total ..		..	1,49,990	..	1,70,531	..	3,20,521

Exports from Malabar to Mysore.

Articles.		Viâ Bavalli.		Viâ Sultan's Battery.		Total.	
		Quantity.	Value.	Quantity.	Value.	Quantity.	Value.
			RS.		RS.		RS.
Animals, living, cattle	No.	19	235	..	..	19	235
Coffee	Mds.	..	..	70	1,236	70	1,236
Cotton, raw	,,	6	50	..	..	6	50
Cotton manufacture, piece-goods, European	,,	107	6,050	..	...	107	6,050
Fibrous productions, other fibres manufactured	,,	10	72	..	..	10	72
Fruits and nuts, coconuts ..	No.	5,900	216	..	..	5,900	216
Do. all other kinds	Mds.	11	170	..	..	11	170
Grain and pulse, wheat	,,	33	72	..	..	33	72
Do. rice, husked ..	,,	33	93	..	..	33	93
Do. rice, unhusked.	,,	1,246	1,256	1,126	1,139	2,372	2,395
Gums and resins	,,	4	33	..	..	4	33
Hides and skins, hides of cattle.	,,	79	1,029	33	426	112	1,455
Do. skins of sheep and goats.	,,	76	977	41	465	117	1,442
Leather, unmanufactured ..	Val.	..	..	..	313	..	313
Metals and manufactures of metals,—Brass and copper ..	Mds.	8	400	..	..	8	400
Do. —Iron	,,	214	3,445	..	..	214	3,445
Oils	,,	1,802	10,275	76	439	1,878	10,714
Provisions, other kinds	,,	24	160	1	3	25	163
Salt	,,	15,320	38,925	2,620	4,702	17,940	43,627
Seeds, other seeds, other kinds..	,,	49	630	..	..	49	630
Spices, betel nuts	,,	21	573	..	..	21	573
Do. other spices	,,	15	622	..	..	15	622
Sugar, refined	,,	9	110	..	..	9	110
Do. unrefined	,,	1	6	..	..	1	6
Tobacco	,,	11	126	1	11	12	137
Wood, timber	,,	1,279	2,565	64	275	1,343	2,840
Wool, manufactured piece-goods, Indian	,,	4	160	..	..	4	160
All other articles of merchandise. { Manufactured.	Val.	..	153	..	98	..	251
All other articles of merchandise. { Unmanufactured ..	,,	..	1,000	..	1,300	..	2,300
Total ..		..	69,403	..	10,407	..	79,810

WYNÃD FORESTS.

By Rhodes Morgan, Esq., District Forest Officer.

General Description.—The whole of the Wynãd plateau must have been covered at no very remote period with dense forest, the greater portion of which, more especially in the centre of the taluk, has been swept away by the system of cultivation known as "*Tuckle*" or *punam* in Malabar, leaving a fringe of deciduous teak forest all along the eastern frontier, from whence it extends into the province of Mysore. On the north and west, the steep declivities of the Western Ghats, covered with a primeval growth of evergreen forest also escaped destruction.

The deciduous forests occupy a zone extending from 11° 58′ Lat. on the north to 11° 35′ Lat. on the south, and between 75° 59′ and 76° 33′ East Long. The evergeen forests clothe the slopes of the Western Ghats on the west, and of the Dindimal and Bramagiri ranges on the north. These ranges run out at right angles to the Western Ghats and form buttresses of that great chain of mountains.

The deciduous forests contain the most valuable timber trees, such as teak, rosewood, iynee (*Artocarpus hirsuta*), venghay (*Pterocarpus marsupium*), ven-teak (*Lagerstræmia microcarpa*) and a host of others, and produce many valuable articles of commerce, of which wax, honey, resin, turmeric, zedoary and myrabolans are the principal. They are more or less open, and there is little undergrowth, except in one or two tracts where fire has been artificially excluded. Thousands of acres are covered with a growth of coarse grass from 4′ to 8′ high. Where the soil is richer, and the growth of trees denser, there is an undergrowth of low scrub, consisting of *Lea-Helicteres*, *curcuma*, &c. Many trees grow to a great size, yielding as much as 300 cubic feet of timber occasionally; but the average contents of the trees are about 40 cubic feet.

In the evergreen forests, the trees are lofty, and the growth very dense. There is little or no undergrowth, except in patches, where a dwarf Pandanus is common. These forests have a gloomy aspect, and the sun rarely penetrates them except where some tree has fallen from old age, or has been up-rooted by some storm.

The most valuable trees are the red and white cedars, the wild jack, the poonspar, and the ironwood. Cardamoms are the principal product; they are extensively cultivated, and also grow spontaneously. Bees' wax, dammer, rattans and pepper are the only other products much collected at present, though resins, kino, gamboge, &c., abound, but have no market value.

Past History.—When Wynād was taken from Tippu Sultan by the British, the Paḻassi (Pychy) Raja, a petty chieftain in possession, rebelled against the British, was conquered and shot. His forests and other possessions were then escheated. For years no real effect was given to the order of escheat, and many forests were usurped possession of by various persons. In the year 1859, a Forest Department was formed and an officer, Mr. Hunter, sent down to work the Wynād. At that period, the Collector administered the forests and sold timber, on what is known as the stump-fee system, *i.e.*, any person paying a certain sum per tree was allowed to cut it down and remove it. In the case of teak, this stump-fee was Re. 1 per tree.

The forests were worked on the native system for many years, no efforts were made to improve them, and trees were indiscriminately felled where found, whatever their age might be.

In 1878 all felling of living teak was stopped, and the Forest Department turned its attention to the utilisation of the wind-fallen and dead trees which were being annually destroyed by fire.

In 1882, the Forest Act was introduced, and immense progress has been made in the scientific treatment of the forests.

Present Condition of Forests.—The deciduous forests have been divided into 14 blocks, of which six are reserved forests, two are under reservation, and six blocks are reserved lands.

The evergreen forests have been divided into three blocks; all at present are under reservation. The annexed statement gives particulars of all these blocks, and their areas.

Of the reserved forests, three—Bēgur, Kurchiyat, and Rampūr—have been demarcated with posts and cairns, and two others will be demarcated before this year has ended.

They are all under special fire protection under rule 8 of the rules under section 26 of the Forest Act; but only one (Bēgur, area 15,366 acres) is fire-traced, and systematically patrolled in the fire season. Gradually complete protection will be extended to all the others.

The Bēgur Forest has been divided into 8 compartments, and a working scheme will be prepared for it shortly. At present, as already stated, only dead wood is being removed.

All the forests have been roaded, and about 80 miles of such roads exist at present; but these roads are all more or less primitive.

The timber in the forests is squared, with much skill, by aboriginal tribes, on contract. They are paid three-fourths of an anna per cubic foot; when felled, the logs are hauled by elephants into depôts, and are from thence carted to the banks of the Kabbani river and floated to Mysore. In the dry weather, logs are carted the whole way to Mysore; but such transport is so costly as to be almost prohibitive. There are eight elephants and ten buffaloes altogether maintained for the haulage of timber in the forests.

Numerous buildings have been erected, and still more will shortly be erected for the establishment employed to work the forests, which consists of—

1 District Forest Officer.	1 Ranger.
1 Sub-Assistant Conservator.	3 Foresters.
	20 Forest Guards.

The members of the establishment are constantly being changed, owing to the excessive malariousness of the forests in the dry weather, which wrecks the very strongest constitutions in a few months.

List of Reserved Forests and Reserved Lands with their areas, &c., in Wynād.

Number.	District.	Taluk.	Amsams.	Name of Forest.	Area in Acres.
				Reserved Forests.	
1	Malabar.	Wynad.	Ganapathi vattam ..	Kuppādi	7,337·44
2			Do. ..	Kurchiyat	18,053·86
3			Do. ..	Rampūr	18,854·67
4			Do. ..	Nūlpoya	3,613·28
5			Do. ..	Mavanhalla	12,576·64
6			Ellurnad	Bēgūr	15,365·92
				Total ..	75,801·81

List of Reserved Forests and Reserved Lands with their areas, &c., in Wynād—continued.

Number.	District.	Taluk.	Amsams.	Name of Forest.	Area in Acres.
				Reserved Lands.	
1	Malabar—*continued.*	Wynād—*continued.*	Ellurnad	Kudrakōte	43,764
2			Pūtati	Padri	34,385
3			Tondernad	Periah cardamom forest	13,440
4			Periah	Chappāram	112
5			Do.	Panniyatta	150
6			Ganapathivattam ..	Palapattur	1,538
7			Do. ..	Vengūr	3,013
8			Do. ..	Chedleth (excluded portions in) ..	960
9			Do. ..	Karapur	1,825
10			Do. ..	Kallur	5,230
11			Do. ..	Excluded portions of Trans-Beni ..	7,459
12			Ellurnad	Botanical Garden, Manantoddy ..	21
				Total ..	101,897

KANOTH FOREST.

Attached to the Wynād Sub-division there is an extensive tract of forest known as the Kanoth forests. It is situated in the Kottayam taluk, at the base, and partly on the western slopes of the Western Ghats. The area of these escheat forests has been approximately computed at 375 square miles. Of this enormous tract, a very small portion (some 40 square miles) is in the hands of the Forest Department, the rest has not been settled yet.

These forests were escheated from the Kanoth (Kannavath) Nambiar, one of the principal adherents of the rebel Paḻassi (Pychy) Raja. In 1883, the management of the tract was transferred to the Forest Department, and immediate steps were taken for its conservation and improvement.

It is inhabited by an aboriginal tribe known as Kurichiyars, who had for years previously carried on the destructive system of "Punam" cultivation (known in Wynād as "Tuckle"). The whole forest, with the exception of a few patches near the crest of the ghats (3,500′ elevation), had been ruthlessly hacked to pieces. The present growth is from 3 to 7 years of age, and consists principally of a multitude of worthless pollards and crooked coppice shoots.

It has been demarcated and surveyed, and 31 miles of the northern boundary have posts and cairns erected as well. It is now under reservation. At the conclusion of the settlement, the aboriginal inhabitants will be removed, and settled elsewhere, and works started for the improvement of the growth.

Nurseries have been established, and large quantities of *ficus elastica* seed obtained from Assam and planted, and numerous seedlings raised. Mahogany and bamboo seedlings are also being raised to plant out clearings.

There are four small experimental teak plantations made in 1876–78, which, however, are not so forward as could be wished, having been seriously injured, when young, by an attack of borer. Teak is, however, indigenous and promises yet to be a success.

CALICUT TALUK.

By C. Kunhi Kannan.

Position, Boundaries, Soil and Area.—The Calicut taluk occupies a central position in the district. It is situated in Lat. 11° 15′ N., and Long. 75° 50′ E. It is bounded on the north by the Kurumbranād and Wynād taluks, on the east by the Wynād and Ërnād taluks, on the south by the Ërnād taluk, and on the west by the Arabian Sea. The soil about the seaboard is brown or white sand; in the interior it is red with gravel approaching in certain parts to a mixture of red and brown.

The approximate area of the taluk, according to the census report of 1881, is 339 square miles. Of this about 68,057 acres or 106 square miles are cultivated.

The demand on account of land revenue in the fasli year 1295 (1885-86) was Rs. 1,29,814, giving an average of Rs. 1⅞ per acre of cultivated area.

Population.—The population of the taluk, including floating population, according to the census of 1881, is 205,962 (103,669 males and 102,293 females) against 189,734 as ascertained by the census of 1871. Of the former, which gives an average of 456 persons per square mile, 149,843 are Hindus, 52,942 Muhammadans, 3,126 Christians and 51 "others." Under the head of education, the census of 1881 returned 6,384 persons as "under instruction," 18,721 as "instructed" and 180,857 as "illiterate including not stated"—a state of things which shows that education has not reached the masses. There were in the taluk 39,450 houses in 1881 against 36,479 in 1871. Of the former, 34,751 houses were occupied and 4,699 unoccupied. The average number of persons per occupied house is 5·7.

Division of the Taluk for Administrative Purposes.—The taluk comprises 41 amṣams, each having an adhikāri on a salary of Rs. 5¼ per mensem, a menon on Rs. 6, and two peons on Rs. 3 each. But in the Nagaram amṣam, in which the capital of the district stands, there are two menons on Rs. 6 each and four peons on Rs. 3 each, whilst in the Panniyankara amṣam, which has the largest revenue in the taluk, there are 3 peons.

In 1860, when the taluks of the district were re-organized, there were only 35 amṣams allotted to Calicut taluk. But in 1866 six amṣams in the Kurumbranād taluk, namely—

1. Nediyanād,
2. Kīḷakkōtt,
3. Maṭavūr,
4. Annassēri,
5. Naṭuvallūr,
6. Nanminda,

which were nearer to Calicut than the head-quarters of Kurumbranād, were transferred to the Calicut taluk under the orders of Government, dated 5th September 1866, No. 2362.

Government Establishments maintained in the Taluk.—As the capital of the district all the important offices are located in the town of Calicut. They are—(1) the Collector's office including the District Board's office, Assistant or Temporary Deputy Collector's office, the Treasury Deputy Collector's office, the Currency office, the Treasury and Press, the District Forest office, and the District Board District Engineer's office; (2) the District and Sessions Court[1] of South Malabar including the Sub-Court and the District Munsif's Court; (3) the office of the District Superintendent of Police; (4) the office of the District Medical and Sanitary officer; (5) the office of the Executive Engineer, West Coast division; (6) the Deputy Tahsildar's and Town Magistrate's Court including the Sub-Jail; (7) the Telegraph office; (8) the Post office; (9) the Port office; (10) the office of the Superintendent of Customs; (11) the Police station; (12) the District Jail; (13) the Government college; (14) the District Registrar's office; (15) the Branch Bank of Madras and (16) the office of the Assistant Commissioner of Salt and Abkāri Revenue.

The Tahsildar's office including the Sub-Jail is on a hill at Chevayūr about four miles east of the town of Calicut. There is a Sub-Registrar's office at Chevayūr as well as at Tāmarassēri in Kedavūr amṣam, about 19 miles from Calicut on the road to Vayitiri. There are Police stations at Ellatur, Naduvattam (Beypore), Kunnamangalam, and Tāmarassēri, Kannipáramba, Chevayūr and Putupādi.

Short Description of the Town.—The Towns Improvement Act X of 1865 was extended to Calicut on the 3rd July 1866. The limits of the town for the purposes of the Act were—

West,—Sea;

North,—Road from the sea north of the barracks, past Rock Hall and East Hill, to the Conolly Canal at Kāraparamba;

East,—Road from Kāraparamba to Kakōdi bridge to intersection of the road running south near Florican Hill, and on to its intersection with the Calicut to Tāmarassēri road—thence by said road to the canal—thence the canal to its intersection with the water-course dividing the Komeri dēṣam from the Vaḷayanād dēṣam of the Vaḷayanād amṣam, thence eastward along the line of the said water-course and the northern boundary of the Vaḷayanād dēṣam to the foot of the Pokkunnu Hill—thence south-east along the foot of the hill, and from the hill along the eastern boundary of the Vaḷayanād dēṣam to the backwater at Attupurathu paramba—thence returning by the backwater to the Māngāvu bridge, and from the bridge along the canal leading to the Beypore river to the portion of it called Kotta Pota, where the canal turns eastward;

South,—Thence turning to the west along a foot-path leading to the Mammaḷḷi road, and from the road to the Tiruvachira or tank, and thence to the sea, keeping along the southern boundary of the Panniyankara dēṣam of the Panniyankara amṣam;

including within those limits houses and premises wholly or in part within 100 yards of the outside of any boundary road—

---

[1] The Zilla Court at Calicut was established in 1803. It was abolished in 1843 to make room for a Civil Court for which was substituted a District Court under Act III of 1873.

1. Panniyankara (portion).	5. Vaḷayanād (portion).
2. Nagaram (all).	6. Edakkād (do).
3. Kasaba (do).	7. Kōttūḷi (do).
4. Kachchēri (do).	

Act X of 1865 (Municipal) was in force until 1871 when it was repealed by Act III of 1871, which again was replaced by Act IV of 1884. The extent of the Municipal town is approximately 13 square miles.

The sources from which the municipal income is derived are—

(*a*) An annual tax on arts, professions, trades and callings, and on offices and appointments at the rates specified in the Act;

(*b*) An annual tax on lands and buildings not exceeding 7½ per cent. on the annual value of such lands and buildings;

(*c*) A half-yearly tax on vehicles with springs, palanquins and animals at rates not exceeding those specified in the Act;

(*d*) A half-yearly tax on carts and other vehicles without springs at a rate not exceeding Rs. 2 for each half year in respect of every such vehicle; and

(*e*) Tolls on vehicles and animals entering the Municipal limits at rates not exceeding those prescribed in the Act.

The purposes to which the funds raised under the Act are applied are—

(*a*) The construction, repair, and maintenance of streets and bridges and other means of communication;

(*b*) The construction and repair of hospitals, dispensaries, lunatic asylums, choultries, markets, drains, sewers, tanks and wells, the payment of all charges connected with the objects for which such buildings have been constructed, the training and employment of medical practitioners, vaccinators, the sanitary inspection of towns and villages, the registration of births and deaths, the lighting of the streets, the cleansing of streets, tanks and wells, and other works of a similar nature;

(*c*) The diffusion of education, and with this view the construction and repair of school-houses, the establishment and maintenance of schools either wholly or by means of grants-in-aid, the inspection of schools and the training of teachers;

(*d*) Other measures of public utility calculated to promote the safety, health, comfort, or convenience of the people;

(*e*) The payment of salaries, leave allowances, pensions, gratuities, and compassionate allowances to servants employed by the Municipal Council; and

(*f*) The payment of all expenses specially provided for by the Act, but not included under the preceding clauses, (*a*) to (*e*).

The revenue of the Calicut Municipality during the official year ending 31st March 1886 was Rs. 56,925, and expenditure during the period was Rs. 48,294.

The population of the Municipal town of Calicut, according to the census of 1881, was 57,085 (30,009 males and 27,076 females) against 48,338 returned by the census of 1871. The latter figure cannot be considered as accurate, inasmuch as it embraced the population of the amṣams of Nagaram, Kasaba and Kachchēri only, which are wholly included within the Municipality. The census of 1881 includes the population of the above three amṣamṣ as well as of such parts of Edakkād, Panniyankara, Vaḷayanād and Kōttūḷi amṣams as are within the Municipality.

The population of the town is classified as follows :—

Hindus	33,875
Muhammadans	20,257
Christians	2,909
Others	44

There are 10,152 houses in the town, being 8,540 occupied and 1,512 unoccupied. The average number of persons per occupied house is 6·7. The density of population is 4,391 per square mile.

There is a Protestant church called the St. Mary's Church at Calicut, which was built in June 1863. Before its erection the Anglican community held Sunday service in a portion of the Collector's office. There is an old European cemetery close to the beach and not far from the new Custom house, where there are several graves and tombs—the earliest inscription goes back to the seventeenth century. The tomb built by the friends of Mr. Conolly, the Collector of Malabar, who was assassinated by Māppiḷḷas, is in this cemetery.

The history of the Roman Catholic Church, Calicut, which is interesting, is briefly as follows :—

In 1513 A.D., a treaty was concluded between the Portuguese and the Zamorin, in which the latter allowed the former to erect a factory at Calicut to which was attached a chapel.

On the 4th of March 1724 a Portuguese man-of-war, called Mater de Deos, anchored in the Calicut roads, and its commander, Pedro Guedes de Magalhaens, effected a treaty on behalf of Pedro Mascurenhas, Coude de Somdomil, the Portuguese Viceroy and Captain General of India, with the Zamorin in the presence of Mons. Andre Molandin, chief of Moye (Mahé), who became surety for the execution of the treaty. By this the Zamorin undertook, *inter alia*, the erection of "a church of stone and mortar with a parochial house, vestry, porch and a belfry having a bell weighing 150 lb." This treaty was, it appears, engrossed on a copper plate, which, it is said, remains in the possession of the Portuguese Government at Goa to this day.

Towards the close of the year 1724, Mons. Molandin named above informed the authorities at Goa that the Zamorin had deposited 17,000 fanams as the price of a bell to be cast at Goa, that the building of the church had been commenced and that the Zamorin had in the presence of the Vicar, Bernado da Sa, given a moor merchant, Bamacheri Isumali, as surety to pay all further expenses for the completion of the work. About 1725, the church was completed, dedicated to "Mater de Deos," and the Zamorin granted a garden in perpetuity for the support of the church.

The church management went on smoothly till the invasion of Malabar by Hyder Ali in 1766. In that year the Portuguese Vicar and Factor waited on Hyder Ali and obtained an order to Madye, Raja of Coimbatore and Governor of Calicut, for the payment of 2,420 fanams annually to the

Vicar of the church. Hyder Ali also ordered that the rent and revenue or benefits of the landed property should not be appropriated.

In 1775 the church, which was then under the immediate jurisdiction of the Archbishop of Cranganore and Cochin, was repaired.

The Mysorean Government continued its payment to the church till 1781, when Sirdar Khan, Tippu's fouzdar, stopped the allowance. But the Vicar raised the revenue from the glebe lands till 1788, when a Brahman named Daxapaya came as Tippu's Revenue Collector of Calicut, and demanded from the Vicar, Gabriel Gonsalves, the church revenues and imprisoned him; but the Vicar effected his escape with the connivance of Arshed Beg Khan, Tippu's fouzdar, and fled to Tellicherry.

The Vicar returned to Calicut and resumed possession of the church lands in 1792, when Malabar came under the East India Company. But the Company "had caused 500 coconut trees belonging to the church to be cut down" as they had rendered "the English Factory close and unhealthy and impeded also the sight of the flagstaff." The Vicar therefore applied in March 1793 to the Malabar Commissioners for "a just indemnification and for permission to collect the rent on houses built on church ground agreeably to immemorial custom and privileges as per the Zamorin's grant engraved on copper plate still preserved at Goa."

The Vicar's petition was repeated to Mr. Farmer, the Supravisor of Malabar, who wrote to the Bombay Government showing an account of the annual rents of the church lands and allowances made by the former Governments and stating that he has since October 1793 paid Rs. 50 *per mensem* to the Vicar, and adding "that the collections formerly made by the Padre will now be made by the Company, in which by the increasing number who flock to our Government there will be a progressive increase."

On the 24th December 1793, the Bombay Government agreed to allow the Padre Rs. 50 "for his own maintenance expenses, for the servants and repairs of the church"—an allowance which has been continued to this day.

Although it would appear that the rents of all the glebe lands were to be collected by the East India Company as proposed by Mr. Farmer in 1793, yet it is said that the church records up to 1825 shew that a large extent of lands obtained by endowments and legacies remained with the church and was leased by the Vicars. In 1835, Vicar Leornad Arclino de Casta stated that "on the acquisition of the country by the English a part of the land was taken possession of by them with the view of answering certain public ends, and a commutation in money at the rate of Rs. 50 per month was granted for the support of the curate as well as other expenses of the church."

In 1838, by the Bull of Pope Gregory XVI, this church, along with other churches on the Malabar Coast, was placed under the jurisdiction of the Archbishop of Verapoly. In 1850 this church, with other churches in Malabar and Canara, was placed under the Carmelites.

In 1862 an orphanage and asylum was started. For completing the building the Madras Government paid Rs. 2,000 in 1875 and Rs. 1,500 in 1882.

The Carmelite Mission established a convent and girls' school and a school for boys in lieu of the old parochial school. These schools are now in a thriving condition. The boys' school was up to the end of 1884-85 aided from Municipal funds, but in 1885-86 it was recognised as a poor European school for which grant-in-aid is paid from Provincial funds. The strength of the boys' school on the 31st March 1886 was 172, whilst that of the girls' school was 94.

In December 1878 the Malabar and Canara Portuguese Missions were, by the Bull of Pope Pius IX, placed under the jurisdiction of the Jesuits, under whom it remains.

In 1878 another charitable institution was attached to the Roman Catholic Mission at Calicut, denominated the Society of St. Vincent de Paul. It has since been divided into two branches—St. Mary's conference and St. Francis Xavier's conference. The poor and helpless of every creed are here assisted in their temporal necessities.

There is a small Roman Catholic chapel called the Chapel of the Holy Cross at Calicut on the road to Wynād, about two furlongs north of the Mānānchira tank. It was a thatched chapel until last year, when it was substantially built by a member of the Roman Catholic congregation.

There is also a Basel Mission church at Calicut. The history of the Mission is briefly noted below :—

In May 1842 the Mission was established by the Rev. J. M. Fritz. In the same year, two Malayāḷam schools and a Tamil school were opened. One of the former was raised to the standard of a high school in 1879.

In 1845 a girls' orphanage was opened, and in connection with it female education commenced. This institution existed until 1882, when it was amalgamated with that at Chōmbāla in Kurumbranād taluk.

In 1854 the erection of the Basel Mission church at Calicut was commenced, and it was on 20th December 1855 used for the first time.

The Basel Mission cemetery is about a mile to the north of the church in a compound which lies between the trunk and the Wynād road.

In 1855 a carpenter's workshop and a weaving establishment with six looms were opened. In the former, Christians and Heathens are employed, and in the latter the number of workmen exceed 100.

In 1868 a mercantile mission shop was opened. It is the only shop at Calicut, which fully meets the demand of the public. In 1874 the mission started tile works. Here machines of German make are used for manufacturing tiles after the European fashion, for which there is an ever-increasing demand. The tile works furnish employment for more than 150 persons both Christians and Heathens. Here it must be noted that these industrial establishments are entirely of a charitable character.

In 1876 a caste girls' school was opened in Calicut, and in 1883 a congregation girls' school with nearly 100 pupils was also started.

There are seven Hindu temples of note in the town of Calicut. They are—

1. The Taḷḷi temple.
2. Tiruvannūr temple.
3. Varakkal temple.
4. Bilāttikuḷam temple.
5. Arikkodi Kāvu.
6. Kokkōḻikōtt temple.
7. Bhairāgimadham temple.

The Taḷḷi temple is in kasaba amṣam in a locality of the same name in the heart of the Calicut town close to the Zamorin's old palace. The temple is a very ancient one, and is 218 feet long from east to west and 270 feet broad from north to south. It is dedicated principally to Siva, though Vishnu, Bhagavati, Ganapati and Ayyappan are also worshipped. The temple contains sculptures of a high order as well as paintings intended to perpetuate Hindu religious legends. Attached to the temple is a tank in pretty good preservation with laterite steps. The tank is 240 feet long from east to west, and 349 feet broad from north to south, and is used for bathing purposes. Close to this is a tank known as Kandamkuḷam, also used for washing. It is 349 by 140 feet. Taḷḷi is densely populated by Brahmans, Nāyars and others. A festival is celebrated for a week annually in the month of Mēdam (March-April) at the Taḷḷi temple.

The Tiruvannūr temple is in Panniyankara amṣam, 2½ miles from the town in a dēsam (hamlet), from which the temple derives its name. Originally the name appears to have been Tirumunnūr (the holy three hundred). The Zamorin lives near the temple. His Putiya (new) Kōvilakam (palace) branch is also located at Tiruvannūr, another branch called the Padinhārē Kōvilakam is in Vaḷayanād amṣam, Mānkāvil dēṣam, and a third one, called the Ambādi Kōvilakam, is in kasaba amṣam. The chief object of worship in this temple is Siva, though Vishnu, Ganapati and Ayyappan are also collaterally worshipped. This temple is a very ancient one, is elaborately sculptured, and contains paintings. The newly erected gateway is interesting, being in style precisely similar to the *bastis* at *Mudabidri* in South Canara erected by the Jains. The temple is 246 feet long from east to west and 198 feet wide from north to south. The Zamorin maintains a Brahman feeding-house at Tiruvannūr.

The Varakkal temple is in Edakkād amṣam and is 96 feet long from east to west and 66 feet broad from north to south. It is on an eminence, and is dedicated to Bhagavati, Ganapati, Ayyappan and Dakshinamūrtti. It is fabled that the image in this temple was placed by Parasu Rāma with his own hands. The temple contains sculptures. The dasra festival is celebrated annually with great eclàt in this temple. Thousands of people congregate here for the performance of ancestral obsequies on the occasion of new moon in the month of Tulam (October-November).

On this day all married men among the native community in Calicut are, by custom, expected to go to their wives' houses with presents in the shape of sweetmeats, plantains, &c., on pain formerly of having their marriages dissolved, a custom perpetuated in a couplet which runs when translated as follows:—

"Failure to visit on the occasion of Varakkal new moon, entails forfeiture of relationship." വരക്കൽ വാവിന്ന വന്നില്ലെങ്കിൽ, ബന്ധു മുറിഞ്ഞത അടയാളം.

There is a tank attached to the temple for washing purposes which is 228 feet long from east to west and 390 feet broad from north to south.

Bilāttikuḷam temple is in kachēri amṣam, in which Vēttakarumakan is worshipped. It is 24½ feet long from east to west and 19½ feet broad from north to south. A festival is celebrated here for forty days in December and January.

The tank attached to the Bilāttikuḷam temple is 378 feet from east to west and 150 feet from north to south, and is used for washing purposes.

The Arikkodikāvu temple is in kasaba amsam in which Bhagavati, Ayyappan and Andimahākāḷan are worshipped. The temple is 120 feet long from north to south and 108 feet broad from east to west. In the month of Kanni (September-October) a festival lasting for 10 days is celebrated here. The Kokkōḻikōtt temple is also in kasaba amṣam dedicated to Siva. It is 120 feet long and 84 feet broad.

The Bhairāgimadham temple is in nagaram amṣam in which Siva, Pārvati, Ganapati and Hanumān are worshipped. It is in the very heart of the Calicut town behind the southern row of the main big bazaar. It is in the possession of the Bhairāgis, a set of ascetic gowda Brahmans who emigrated from Northern India. It is a small temple being only 20 by 12 feet.

There are no less than 40 mosques in the town of Calicut. The most important of them are the two Jamātt mosques, Shēkkindē Paḷḷi and Paḻaya Paḷḷi. Besides these there are several other suburban mosques.

The two Jamātt mosques lie on either side of the big tank known as Kuttichira in the middle of the Māppiḷḷa quarters in Calicut. The one on the south of the tank is 144 by 114 feet, and the other on the north is 115½ by 64½ feet. The Kuttichira tank is 410 feet long north to south and 210 feet wide east to west. It is built in laterite and is used for washing purposes.

Shēkkindē Paḷḷi (mosque) is 48 by 32 feet and is looked upon with much reverence by Māppiḷḷas. It is said to have been built over the grave of a Māppiḷḷa named Sūppikkāvittil Shaikh Māmu Kōya, who by his piety approached in sanctity in the opinion of Māppiḷḷas to that of a Saiyid. He is said to have died more than 300 years ago. This mosque is constantly resorted to by Māppiḷḷas for the adjustment of civil and other disputes by the test of oath.

Paḻaya Paḷḷi which is 56 by 30 feet is looked upon as an ancient institution as its name indicates.

The West Hill barracks, built on an eminence commanding a good view of the sea and the surrounding country, lie in Edakkād amṣam within the Municipality. A detachment of European soldiers is garrisoned here. The detachment was first stationed at Calicut in 1849 owing to frequent Māppiḷḷa outrages. It was removed to Malapuram in 1851, but again brought back on the assassination of Mr. Conolly, the Collector of Malabar, on the 12th September 1855 in his bungalow on the West Hill.

The Light-house at Calicut was built in February 1847. It is a column of laterite in chunam, 102½ feet high, and the white dioptric fourth order light is visible in clear weather at 14 miles. The Calicut port bears from Sacrifice Rock south-east distant 20 miles. Vessels should anchor in 5 fathoms mud. The merchants find it more convenient, when the sea breezes are strong, to load from the beach 1 or 2 miles to the north of the light-house, where there is always less surf than opposite the town. Large Kotiyās and Pattimars are built on the beach 1½ miles south of the light-house, by the entrance of the Kallai river or creek, where the shore is also smooth, being partially protected by the Coote reef. There is a patch of rocky ground with 4 fathoms least water, having 6 fathoms mud, all around it, bearing west north-west distant 3¾ miles from the light-house. This is supposed to be the shoal discovered by Captain Hogg of the "Juliana." Calicut reef, on which the sea breaks in one part almost always where there is only two feet at low water, is of irregular outline. This shoal-patch of two feet is in its centre, and bears from the light-house south south-west ½, west 1¼ miles, and is distant 6 cables' lengths from the nearest shore abreast. The southern extremity of this reef (which is generally called the Coote reef after the late East India Company sloop-of-war Coote which was lost there) lies 2 cables' lengths to the south of the centre breakers. To the south and east of the reef, the bottom is soft mud. There is a considerable extent of anchoring ground for small coasting craft in 2 and 2½ fathoms at low water, partially protected from north-west winds by the reef. A red buoy to mark the western extreme of this reef, as a guide to small coasting vessels, was moored two cables' lengths west by north from the most shallow part. Seaward of the reef are numerous dangerous rocky patches, but none have less than two fathoms on them. This foul ground extends more than two miles off shore. One patch of 13 feet at low water bears south-west ¾, west 1¾ miles from the light-house, and another with a similar depth south south-west ½, west rather more than two miles. It is high water on full and change at Calicut and Beypore at 12 hours 15 minutes; springs rise little more than 4 feet, but extraordinary tides as much as 5 feet; neaps rise 2½ feet. Calicut south-west shoal bears from the light-house about south-west by west 2½ miles. On the northern extremity of this shoal, with the light-house bearing east north-east, are rocks in 4 fathoms, and on its western edge rocks in 4½ fathoms. Over the centre of the shoals are numerous rocky heads, with 3 fathoms on them, and 3¾ to 4½ fathoms between them. These are the rocks on which the "Juliana" first struck when Captain Hogg anchored in 5 fathoms, light-house bearing east north-east. On the inner or eastern side of the shoal was 4 fathoms clear ground, with the water decreasing gradually towards the shore. When there is any sea on, it breaks, and may generally be seen. On the outer edge are rocks in 3½ fathoms with 2 and 2½. The remains of the "Juliana" lay in 3½ fathoms south-west, ¾ south, about 1¾ miles from the light-house. There is said to be another dangerous ledge, bearing west from the light-house, from 1½ to 2¾ miles distant. On the northern side of this shoal, with the light-house east ¾ south are 4 fathoms, and on the southern side with light-house east ¾ north 4 fathoms; on the western extremity 4¾ fathoms. Ships approaching from either the south or the north intending to anchor, ought not to come inside of 8 fathoms till the light-house bears east by south, then steer for the anchorage. The best anchorage in Calicut roads is, during the north-east monsoon, in 5½ fathoms, with the light-house about east by south. This is a convenient berth for the new screw-pile pier. The best distinguishing mark for Calicut in the morning is the house amongst trees on the hill more than 2 miles north of the light-house; in the afternoon, the white column of the light-house shows well 10 miles off. The Camel's Hump, or Wavulmullay, over 7,000 feet above the sea level (the culminating peak of the Wynad mountains which stand 20 miles west of the Nīlgiri range) bears from Calicut light-house north-east by east ½, east 23½ miles. It may be seen in clear weather, as soon as a vessel is on the bank of soundings. In the hazy weather of March and April, it is frequently indistinct from the anchorage off Calicut. The southern extremity of the mountain range is rather abrupt, the mountains thence receding far to the east.

The District jail at Calicut was formerly situated close to the French Loge at Calicut. The jail was removed to a hill about two miles from the beach to the east on 17th November 1869, when buildings were erected at a cost of Rs. 92,393. On the 31st December 1885, there were 200 prisoners in the jail.

The pier at Calicut was built in 1871 at a cost of Rs. 64,000. It is close to the new customs office, about half a mile north of the light-house. The pier is 400 feet long, and barges drawing from 3 to 6 feet of water are employed at the T end for the importation and exportation of goods. The pier went out of order in 1883, when, with the permission of Government, a company of local merchants, designated the Calicut Pier and Warehouse Company, Limited, to carry on the business of warehousemen and to levy cranage and other dues and tolls, was started with a capital of Rs. 5,000, which was utilized for repairing the pier.

A Telegraph office was opened at Calicut in September 1856. It is now held in a rented building adjoining the Captain's tank to the south of the Roman Catholic church in close proximity to the District Court premises.

The Post office at Calicut is also held in a private building rented for the purpose. It is not far from the Telegraph office.

There is a club for Europeans on the beach which was started on the 8th February 1864. Connected with the club is a station library maintained by subscriptions.

The hospital and dispensary at Calicut was opened in October 1845, under the auspices of Government. It was transferred to the Municipality when it was instituted at Calicut. It is now kept up at Municipal expense supplemented by a grant from the District Board. The dispensary has an endowment of Rs. 13,000 collected by private subscriptions and invested in Government securities yielding Rs. 520 per annum as interest.

The lunatic asylum at Calicut was established on 20th May 1872 at a cost of Rs. 39,250. It is about 2½ miles east of Calicut on the road to Chevayūr. It is built on a hill called Kutiravattam. On the 31st March 1885, there were 149 lunatics in the asylum.

The Municipality maintains a public bungalow and a mussaferkhana in the town. These are in the neighbourhood of the Mānānchira tank, which is a reservoir of excellent drinking water. It has laterite steps on four sides. It is 420 feet east to west, and 488 feet north to south.

A few yards to the south-east of this tank is another called Mutalakuḷam. It was originally octagonal in shape, but has by time become dilapidated resulting in the change of its original form. It was included in the premises of the Zamorin's old palace which lay contiguous to it. The compound on which the Zamorin's old residence stood, called the Kōttaparamba, immediately adjoins the tank on the south. The installation of the Zamorin takes place to this day in this Kōttaparamba, divided by the Beypore road into the eastern and western portion. The spot where the ceremony takes place is marked by an upright granite pillar in the eastern portion.

To the east of the Mānānchira tank is a small parade ground originally provided for the detachment stationed at Calicut, but now used by the Volunteers and Police. The Head-quarter Police office faces this open ground on the east; and the new office of the Collector and District Magistrate is about to be built on its southern limit.

Besides the Mānānchira tank there is another immediately south of the

Roman Catholic church called the Captain's tank, which is 244 by 237 feet. It is in a state of good preservation, though the water is not used for drinking purposes.

In Panniyankara amṣam there are two large tanks called Nilōttachira and Tiruchira used for washing, which are respectively 260 by 166 and 630 by 360 feet in size. There are many more tanks in the town which need not be specially enumerated.

Two newspapers are published in Calicut town. One in English entitled the Malabar and Travancore Spectator, and the other the Kēraḷa Patrika in Malayāḷam. A monthly Malayāḷam periodical called Parōpakāri, edited by a Muhammadan, is also published at Calicut.

There are at present three registered public presses at Calicut in addition to the Government Press. They are the Spectator Press, Vidya Vilāsam Press and James' Press. A press is also maintained at Kāraparamba by a European firm which is used more by the firm than by the general public.

In 1885 the European and Eurasian inhabitants of Calicut organised themselves into two companies of Volunteer Rifles. These companies and others located at Tellicherry, Wynād and Cochin, with a section at Pālghat and numbering altogether about 300 men, were amalgamated into the "Malabar Volunteer Rifles" under a Major Commandant with head-quarters at Calicut.

The French have a *Loge*[1] in Calicut "Occupèe par un gardien." The *Loge* consists of 6 acres on the sea-shore about half a mile north of the Calicut Light-house and adjoins the old district jail site. The exact facts connected with the foundation of the French factory are involved in doubt. It was apparently obtained by the French from the Zamorin, but there is nothing to lead to the supposition that the Zamorin had ever conceded to them anything more than mere commercial privileges within the limits of the *Loge*. The Zamorin appeared to have exercised fiscal and judicial authority within its limits—an authority which neither Hyder Ali nor Tippu Sultan ever bestowed on the French after the Zamorin's power ceased.

Beyond the fact that the landed property and houses are untaxed, there is nothing to distinguish the *Loge* from the rest of Calicut. It is doubtful what rights the French Government has in it. As it has been altogether omitted from the treaty of Versailles, dated the 3rd September 1783, it has been held that the French had no sovereign rights in it. The *Loge* was restored to the French on 1st February 1819.

In the first capitulation of Mahé made by Monsieur Louet, Commander-in-Chief of the French garrison at Mahé, and signed on the 10th February 1761, it was agreed in article 9 that "the French factory at Calicut shall be suffered quietly to enjoy the privileges of neutrality observed there."

Industries and Manufactures.—In the town of Calicut a weaving establishment and tile works are maintained by the Basel Mission. Soda water machines are worked by two Parsi merchants. Coffee and ginger curing is undertaken by several European and Native firms and traders. A Bombay

---

[1] The name of "loge" or "comptoir" is given to factories or isolated establishments comprehending one house with the adjacent grounds where France had the right to have her flag flying and to form factories, &c. (Pharoah and Co.'s Gazetteer of 1855.)

merchant has opened a large coir manuafctory close to the south beach road, about a mile south of the old Custom house, at which more than 100 persons are daily at work in dressing fibre and twisting coir.

The Malabar Spinning and Weaving Company, Limited, was started in November 1883, with a capital of Rs. 6,00,000. The buildings are in course of construction, and the Company have not started business yet. The premises are in Panniyankara amṣam.

Railway Stations, Roads, Bridges, Canals, &c.—The Madras Railway, which had its terminus at Beypore, will shortly be extended to Calicut. The line has been formed and rails laid and the station is in course of construction in the heart of the town. The line, it is expected, will be open for traffic in the course of a year.

The aggregate length of roads maintained by the Municipality is 52 miles.

There is a very extensive street of bazaars known as the big bazaar extending inland from the beach in an unbroken line about a mile in length. Several narrow cross-streets lead from the main one.

There is a temporary wooden bridge over the Kallāi river. It will be replaced by the railway iron bridge which is so designed as to suit the local traffic as well. Near this bridge is a Government timber depōt, where teak and saplings, from the Nilambūr plantations, are floated down and stored.

The Conolly canal connects the Kallāi with the Ellatūr river and thus provides an uninterrupted line of water communication from Beypore to Badagara, a distance of 37 miles. A list of ferries in the taluk is given below:—

First Class.

1. Mammaḷḷikadavu.
2. Chāliampuḻa (Beypore ferry).
3. Kōrapuḻakadavu.

Second Class.

4. Elamaramkadavu.
5. Ūrakadavu.
6. Arapuḻakadavu.
7. Ōlashērikadavu.

Third Class.

8. Chakkumkadavu.
9. Irupuḻinyikadavu.
10. Kūlumadamuku *alias* Puttanangādikadavu.
11. Irupuḻinyi Mokkakadavu.
12. Teyyattinkadavu.
13. Kūliyatamokkakadavu.
14. Manakadavu *alias* Kuttankadavu.
15. Puttekadavu.
16. Paḷḷikadavu.
17. Parayangōtkadavu.
18. Manantalakadavu.
19. Mukkuvarkandikadavu.

Fourth Class.

20. Pulikkalkadavu.
21. Purakātirikadavu.
22. Putukkātkadavu.
23. Putiyōttilkadavu.
24. Parambilkadavu.
25. Cheruvattākadavu.
26. Māvaḷikadavu.
27. Chettukadavu.
28. Kurungōtkadavu.
29. Kudattāyikadavu.
30. Kakkōdikadavu.
31. Tōttattilkadavu.
32. Tondinmēlkadavu.
33. Attiyanmoḻikadavu.
34. Kannanchinnanpālam.
35. Kunnattukadavu.

In Edakkād amṣam is a small Māppiḷḷa village known as Putiyangādi (new bazaar), about three miles from Calicut town. Here lives the Māppiḷḷa priest, called Putiyangādi Tangal of pure Arab extraction. There is a

Jamātt mosque here said to be more than 130 years old, 72 by 30 feet in size. A festival is celebrated here annually. Though a small Māppiḷḷa hamlet, Putiyangādi possesses eight mosques.

In Panniyankara amsam there is a locality called Gōmukham (cow's face) on the sea-shore where Hindus resort for ablutions as a place of sanctity on occasions of new moon and eclipse.

In Cheruvannūr amṣam at Mammaḷḷi, about seven miles from Calicut, there is a coffee-curing establishment under European management.

There is in this amṣam an important Hindu temple called the Cheruvannūr temple dedicated to Siva, Subramanyan, Ayyappan, Ganapati and Dakshinamūrtti. The roof of the shrine is copper plated. The temple is sculptured. On a beam is a comparatively recent Malayāḷam writing that the temple was built by the Uralars. The temple is 99 by 44 feet in size, and a festival is celebrated annually for 41 days called Mandala Viḷakku in December and January.

In this amṣam are the Marakkāt works once noted for its iron manufacturies.

Beypore is a small town in an amṣam of the same name. It was formerly known as Vaypura and Vada Parapanād. Tippu Sultan named the town "Sultan patnam." It lies between Lat. 11° 10′ N., and Long. 75° 50′ 30″ E. According to the census of 1871, there were 1,102 houses; the population was 6,214. In the census of 1881 there were 1,119 houses with a population of 6,739 souls. Though many attempts have been made to utilize the great natural advantages of its position, it was not until 1858, when Chālliyam Island, on the opposite bank of the river, was made a terminus of the Madras Railway, that the town became of importance. Tippu selected it as the site of the capital of Malabar, but hardly a vestige of its short-lived importance has survived. In 1797 saw mills, in 1805 a canvas factory, in 1848 iron works and, later still, ship-building works were started here, but all from one cause or another have failed. In 1858 the railway created the present town, and Beypore is every year becoming busier. But the extension of the railway to Calicut is likely to result in the reversion of Beypore to its old state of a fishing village.

The Beypore bar admits crafts of 300 tons to the river, and at low spring-tides, gives soundings of 12 to 14 feet and at high tides from 16 to 18 feet.

In Beypore amṣam there are four Kōvilakams called—

1. Manayatt kōvilakam,
2. Nediyāl kōvilakam,
3. Pudia kōvilakam,
4. Panangāt kōvilakam,

belonging to the family of the Beypore branch of the Parappanād family. There is also a Hindu temple containing sculptures and dedicated to Siva, Ganapati and Bhagavati with a laterite built tank and a Brahman feeding-house. The temple is 180 by 138 feet. There is a travellers' bungalow as well as a Sea Customs office here.

There is a place of sanctity for Hindus on the sea-shore in this amṣam, called Kōtēsvaram for purposes of ablution on occasions of new moon or eclipse.

In Vaḷayanād amṣam there is an ancient temple called Srīvaḷayanād temple. The roof of the shrine is copper plated. It is 192 feet long by 144 feet broad. There are elaborate sculptures on the gōpuram. The temple belongs to the Zamorin. An annual festival lasting for 8 days is celebrated in this temple in the month of Makaram (December-January), when the image of Bhagavati worshipped in the temple is taken in procession round the temple on an elephant's back with great pomp.

At Tāmarassēri, in Kedavūr amṣam, there is a palace belonging to the Kōttayam Raja. Close to it is a tank which is 240 by 144 feet. It is not in a state of preservation, but there are indications of its having been built in laterite. As stated elsewhere, there is a Sub-Registrar's office here as well as a chattram maintained by the District Board. At Putupādi, in this amṣam, there is a chattram kept up by a native landlord. There is also a comfortable little hotel for Europeans travelling to and from the Wynād planting districts. Tāmarassēri ghaut is much used for the export of coffee from Wynād.

In Kanniparamba amṣam, there is a temple dedicated to Siva, Vishnu, Ganapati, Ayyappan and Dakshinamūrtti. It is 132 feet square. It is a very ancient temple so much so that it is fabled to have been founded by Kannwa Rishi commemorated in the Maha Bharata.

In Kanniparamba amṣam, there is on the rocky pinnacle of a hill a pit which is four *koles* square and half a *kole* deep, from which, according to native popular belief, holy water gushes out daily in the morning in the month of Edavam (April-May) for a nāḻika (20 minutes), when it miraculously becomes dry. It is also said that the holy water begins to flow on the occasion of Sivarātri festival in Kumbham (February-March). Pilgrims aggregating 3,000 in number assemble on this hill on such occasions. This hill has been noticed in Ward and Connor's memoir.

Fairs and Markets.—At Kāramparamba, in Kachēri amṣam, a weekly fair is held on every Monday, when more than 1,000 persons resort to it from rural parts. A weekly fair on every Sunday is held in Manāssēri amṣam and at Kedavūr every Tuesday.

In the town of Calicut, the Municipality maintains two important markets. There are also several petty markets in the town licensed by the Municipality.

Archæology.—Kaulanur dēṣam in Annassēri amṣam, 8 miles north of Calicut, there are two rock-cut caves. In Kannankara dēṣam there are three menhirs and a stone circle.

In Nagaram amṣam, in Machchindō mosque, is a slab let into the wall, having an inscription in Arabic, Canarese and an unknown language. It is much injured by time and weather.

In Chevayūr, 3 miles north-east of Calicut, exists a sepulchral rock-cut cave; an erect pillar stands in the middle of the main chamber. The hole at the top of the cave was covered by a block of stone which hid it from sight. Several pots and parts of a sword were found in it.

In Iringallur amṣam, 3 miles east of Calicut, there is a dolmen, in the dēṣam of Kottul, there are four such dolmens, and in Kayilamatham one. They are all surrounded by stone circles.

In Kanniparamba, 11 miles east of Calicut in the hamlet of Kalpaḷḷi, there is a toppikal or hat-stone. In Atuvātu and Māvūr, there is a menhir in each, and in Palangāt. a rock-cut cave.

In Karipuram temple, in Payipalasseri dēsam, Kiḷakkōtt amṣam, 15 miles north-east of Calicut, there is an inscription in old Tamil on a slab.

In Koduvaḷḷi amṣam, 16 miles north-east of Calicut in Chorgotūr dēṣam in the temple, is a granite slab with an inscription in old Tamil. There is also a menhir here as well as in Manapuram dēṣam. In the temple at the latter dēṣam, there is an inscription in old Tamil on a granite slab. In Kōvūr amṣam, 5 miles from Calicut, in Velliparamba dēṣam, a cave was discovered in the back-yard of a private house. It was opened and closed again by the house owner.

In Padinhāttummuri amṣam, 6½ miles north of Calicut, a number of very interesting rock-cut caves were excavated, from which a quantity of pottery was unearthed. An account of the place with two plates of engravings was published in Vol. VIII of the Indian Antiquary. The articles found in the cells were sent to the Madras Museum.

In Puttūr amṣam, 12½ miles east north-east of Calicut, in the temple in the Chōkūr dēṣam, there is an inscribed granite slab with an old Tamil inscription. In the dēṣam of Ketayantūr is a dolmen and a rock-cut cave, and in Chōkūr dēṣam there is a menhir.

In Talakuḷattūr amṣam, 8 miles north of Calicut, there is an old temple with an illegible inscription on a stone.

In Vaḷayanād amṣam, 2 miles east south-east of Calicut, in Konneri dēsam, there is a rock-cut cave now filled up.

Trigonometrical Survey Station.—Pokkunnu in Vaḷayanād amṣam is the only Trigonometrical Survey station in the Calicut taluk.

Dams and Anicuts.—In Kārannūr amṣam, there is a dam known as the Mūḷiyār nada, which is constructed for the protection of cultivation.

At Putiyachira on the road to Chevayūr, there was some time back a lock in the Conolly canal for the protection of cultivation from the influx of salt water. It is not now repaired as the water traffic is of more importance. The Conolly canal passes through the amṣams of Kasaba, Kōṭṭuḷi, Kachchēri, Edakkād, Kārannūr, Makkada and Elattūr, and connects the Kallayi with the Elattūr river.

ĒRNĀD TALUK.

By V. Chappu Menon, B.A.

Boundaries.—This taluk comprises the two old taluks of Ērnād and Chēranād. It is bounded on the north by Calicut and Wynād, on the east by the Nīlgiri district, on the south by Walluvanād and Ponnāni, on the west by the sea.

Area.—811 square miles, of which 140 square miles, or about one-sixth of the whole extent, may be said to be under cultivation. The remainder consists of waste lands and hilly tracts.

Population.—The total population, according to the census of 1881, was 296,143, of whom 148,521 were males and 147,622 females. Distributed according to sects, the population stands as follows :—

Hindus	145,451
Muhammadans	149,987
Christians	699
Other classes	6

This taluk contains the largest number of Muhammadans usually denominated Māppiḷḷas, comprising, as it does, a ratio of 23 per cent. of the entire Māppiḷḷa population in the district.

The total number of houses in the taluk in 1881 was 60,596, of which 54,415, or about 90 per cent., were occupied and the rest unoccupied.

Physical Aspects.—The country is overrun with woods, hills, and mountains. The eastern portion comprehending the Nilambūr valley formed by the ghats and the Kunda mountains and the Wāvūl range extending to Chekkunnanmalai (ചെക്കുന്നമല), a high saddle-hill north-east of Ariakode contains teak and other timber in almost inexhaustible quantities and it is mostly from this valley that the largest timber is obtained. The central portion is here and there flat with mountain ridges running in different directions. The western portion, with the exception of a few miles from the coast, which is flat, is undulating intersected in all directions by extensive valleys of wet cultivation.

Mountains and Hills.—The most remarkable hills are—

(1) The Wāvūl range.

(2) The Chekkumalai or Chekkunnan hill, containing a Trigonometrical Survey station.

(3) The Pantalur hill whose ridge separates the Ĕrnād from Walluvanād taluk.

(4) The Ūrothmala hill which formed the boundary of the old Chēranād taluk and which contains likewise a Trigonometrical station.

Forests.—Ĕrnād taluk furnishes most valuable timber trees. Various exotics, such as mahogany and rubber trees, castilloa, hevea and ipecacuanha, are being planted and experimented with, and some of them have thoroughly been acclimatized and established there. At Nilambūr, these experiments and plantations are under the management of the District Forest officer located at that station. The following is a list of forests which are under the control of this officer :—

Number.	Name of Forest.	Situation.		Area in square miles.	Whether Government or leased forest, and if leased, from whom.
		Taluk.	Amsam.		
1	Karimpoya Reserve	Ĕrnād.	Nilambūr ..	6·18	Government Forest.
2	Amarapolam do.	Do.	Do. ..	0·77	Do.
3	Chathamborai do.	Do.	Do. ..	1·09	Leased from Naduvatti or Wandur Nambūdiripad.
4	Nellikutta do.	Do.	Do. ..	2·99	Leased from the Zamorin of Calicut.
5	Valluvasheri block comprising—				
	(1) Pokode	Do.	Do. ..	1·18	Leased from Trikkallur Devasam.
	(2) Panangode	Do.	Do. ..	1·41	Do.
	(3) Valluvasheri ..	Do.	Do. ..	1·45	Do.

Number.	Name of Forest.	Situation.		Area in square miles.	Whether Government or leased forest, and if leased, from whom.
		Taluk.	Amsam.		
6	Nilambūr block comprising—				
	(1) Trovallikava . ..	Ērnad.	Nilambūr ..	8·37	Leased from Trikkallur Devasam.
	(2) Anwakod	Do.	Do. ..		
	(3) Edakod	Do.	Mambat ..		
	(4) Ellanjeri	Do.	Nilambūr ..		
	(5) Ramalūr	Do.	Do. ..		
	(6) Mulataranna ..	Do.	Do. ..		
7	Erambadóm	Do.	Do. ..	·90	Leased.
8	Kanakut	Do.	Do. ..	1·04	Leased from Trikkallur Devasam.
9	Muriat	Do.	Do. ..	2·75	Do.
10	Karieu	Do.	Do. ..	1·48	Do.
11	Mangalasseri	Calicut.	Manasheri ..	·01	Do.
12	Ambalakandy	Do.	Pannikod ..	·001	Do.
13	Arimbracutta	Ērnad.	Urangattiri.	·50	Do.
14	Puthalatha and Chittarikkal.	Calicut.	Manasheri ..	·01	Do.
			Total ..	30·13	

The Nilambūr teak plantations were first suggested in 1840 by Mr. Conolly, Collector of Malabar, who described their object as being "to replace those forests which had vanished from private carelessness and rapacity—a work too new, too extensive, and too barren of early return to be ever taken up by the native proprietor." Great difficulty was at first encountered in getting the seed to germinate and many expedients were resorted to. These proved entirely unsuccessful. In 1843 Dr. Róxburgh suggested the method of sowing the seed at the beginning of the rains in shaded beds lightly covered with earth and rotten straw, and this system, which proved a success, is now pursued with slight modifications suggested by experience. The first attempt at planting was made in 1842 and was followed in regular succession under the able management, first of Chathu Menon, the native conservator, who for 20 years carried on the operations, and of Mr. Ferguson, whose skilled and unremitting attention during the long tenure of his office from 1863 to 1883 has brought the plantations to their present pitch.

The "Memorandum on the Conolly Teak Plantations," prepared by Mr. Atholl McGregor in 1877 (printed at the Travancore Government Press), and Lieut.-Col. Beddome's "Report upon the Nilambūr Teak Plantations," printed at the Government Press, Madras, in 1878, contain most valuable information in regard to the Nilambūr forests. An extract from the former publication is printed at the end of this paper.

Rivers.—The following are the principal rivers in the taluk :—

1. *The Beypore river* (also called the Ponpuḷa or Gold river) which rises in the mountains south of the Naduvattam pass, and after meandering through Wynād, rushes down the ghats into the Nilambūr valley, receiving in its devious windings before reaching Nilambūr (*a*) the Kalakkampuḷa, (*b*) the Karkurpula, (*c*) the Sholayar or Cholayar on its right bank and (*d*) the Karimpuḷa on its left bank. The last named is a formidable river fed by numerous streams rushing down from the crest of the Nīlgiri and Kunda mountains. The union of these streams now forms one considerable

river, which runs north of Nilambūr, and after receiving in its serpentine windings and course several streams, such as the Kūrampuḷa and the Kudirapuḷa, discharges itself finally into the sea at Beypore. The river is navigable all the year round up to Ariakode, but boats go up with ease to Nilambūr during the monsoon, and smaller boats proceed even further up to Edakara, about 8 miles north-east of Nilambūr. The distance from Calicut to Ariakode *by land*, according to the Route-book, is 27 miles ; from Ariakode to Edavanna 8 miles ; from Edavanna to Nilambūr 8 miles ; from Nilambūr to Edakkara 8 miles ; and from Edakkara to Nādagani 10 miles.

2. *The Kadalhundi* (*Kadal-tundi*) *river* rises in the southern slopes of the Kunda mountains, enters the taluk near Chāppanangadi, meanders westerly with many serpentine windings, and after flowing *viâ* Tirurangādi, empties itself into the sea at Kadalhundi. One branch of the stream joins the Beypore river opposite to the place of that name and forms the island of Chāliyam. Like other rivers in Malabar, the Kadalhundi river is known by different names in the different parts of its course, *e.g.*, at Malapuram, it is called the Ânakayam river ; at Tirurangādi, the Tirurangādi river, &c. The bed of the river is exceedingly narrow and rocky with high banks fringed with wood and groves of areca and other palms at intervals. Teak and other timber, also rafts of bamboos are floated down to the coast to the depôts at Beypore and Kallai near Calicut.

Sub-divisions of the Taluk for Administrative Purposes.—The taluk is divided into 52 amsams, of which 35 are under the magisterial jurisdiction of the Tahsildar-Magistrate and 17 under the Sub-Magistrate of Tirurangādi.

Previous to the revision [1] of the taluk establishments by Mr. Pelly, there were 2 taluks, designated Ērnād and Chēranād, but in the year 1860 they were amalgamated, a Deputy Tahsildar being appointed for the Chēranād division.

The taluk of Ērnād was along with Waḷḷuvanād and the magisterial charge of Chēranād entrusted to Mr. Collett, the Assistant Collector and Magistrate, under Collector's proclamation, dated 12th November 1849. He remained in charge till April 1854, when he was appointed Special Assistant Collector and Magistrate and latterly Sub-Judge, Calicut. In 1856 Mr. E. C. G. Thomas was appointed Special Assistant and was succeeded by Mr. A. MacGregor under the orders of Government, communicated in G.O., dated 20th October 1863, No. 1902. The Special Assistant was transferred to Coimbatore for employment on the Nīlgiris and the office was revived, on the recommendation of Mr. MacGregor after the Kolattur outbreak, by G.O., dated 11th October 1873, No. 1629. A further reconstitution took place in 1886, whereby the Special Assistant was placed in the revenue charge of Ērnād and Calicut taluks and in the magisterial charge of Ērnād and portion of Waḷḷuvanād (*vide* G.O., dated 15th February 1886, No. 126). The Divisional Magistrate's head-quarters are at Malapuram in Ērnād taluk.

Public Establishments.—The various offices located in the taluk are the following :—

(1) The Special Assistant Collector and Magistrate at Malapuram.
(2) The Tahsildar and his establishment at Manjēri.
(3) The Deputy Tahsildar and his establishment at Tirurangādi.

---

[1] G.Os., dated 1st October 1860, No. 1751, and 3rd November 1860, No. 2038.

(4) The District Munsif of Ērnād at Manjēri, and of Chēranād at Parappanangādi.
(5) Assistant Superintendent of Police at Malapuram.
(6) Inspector, Special Police force at Malapuram.
(7) Inspectors of Police at Manjēri, Malapuram and Tirurangādi and Police stations at—

Manjēri.	Kondotti.
Edavanna.	Ariakode.
Nilambūr.	Tirurangādi.
Wandur.	Parappanangādi.
Pandikad.	Chāliyam.
Malapuram.	Feroke.
Kottakal.	

(8) District Forest Officer and his establishment at Nilambūr.
(9) Sub-Registrars of Manjēri, Malapuram, Wandur, Kondotti and Tirurāngādi.
(10) Government Telegraph office at Malapuram and the Railway Telegraph offices at Beypore and Parappanangādi.
(11) Post offices at Manjēri, Malapuram, Nilambūr, Kondotti, Parappanangādi and Beypore.
(12) Local Fund middle school at Manjēri.
(13) Local Fund hospitals at Manjēri and Nilambūr.
(14) Local Fund Supervisor and Overseers.
(15) Vaccine staff.
(16) Military detachment at Malapuram.
(17) Marine office at Beypore (Chāliyam) under the charge of the Port officer, Calicut.

Towns and other places of importance.—There are no municipal towns constituted under the Act in the taluk. The places of importance are described below:—

Manjēri—in the amsam of the same name, is the head-quarters of the taluk and is the seat of the Tahsildar, the District Munsif and the Sub-Registrar of Assurances. There are a Local Fund hospital, a public bungalow, a middle school and a chattram at this station. A weekly market is held which is generally well-attended. About a quarter of a mile to the south-east of the taluk is a pagoda called Srimuttra Kunnu *alias* Kunnath Ampalam, dedicated to Durga and situated on a low hill, and immediately below it is the residence of the Manjēri Karnamalpād. In the east wall of the temple is an inscription, dated K.A. 827 (A.D. 1651), stating that Mana Vikrama built a matam. There is another near a well to the north, dated K.A. 833 (A.D. 1657), by the same man.

It was this temple that was seized by the gang of Māppiḷḷa fanatics under Attan Kurikal in 1849, and Ensign Wyse, who lies buried on the taluk cutchery hill was killed in an attempt to take the temple from the fanatics. There are several large dolmens, menhirs and rock-cut caves in this amsam.

Nilambūr—which is about 16 miles from Manjēri, is an important station for timber traffic. It is the seat of the District Forest Officer who has charge of the extensive Government teak plantations, and contains a hospital, a Police station, a public bungalow and a Post office. The District

Forest Officer is also a Special Magistrate for the trial of offences under the conservancy clauses of the Police Act.

The Nilambūr and Amarampalam Tirumalpads who own extensive forests reside in the Nilambūr amsam. There are two temples, one dedicated to Vettakkorumakan and the other to Siva. There is an inscription on a block of gneiss rock in the Cherupuḷa river about 1½ miles below the junction with the Karimpula, known as "Eltu Kallu" or Eḷuttu Kalla, and used to determine the boundary between two janmis. The stone is in the middle of a forest far from any habitation, and the inscription is only visible in extremely dry weather, being below the ordinary low water level. There are numerous dolmens and menhirs and rock-cut caves in the amsam. Gold washing was carried on formerly at Nilambūr and the gold so obtained was called channam.

Etakkara—on the river side 8 miles to the east of Nilambūr on the road to Nīlgiris, is an extensive plain of black rich soil, supposed to be once thickly populated judging from the remains, which are still visible, of ruined temples, houses, tanks, wells, &c. It is now covered with dense jungle, which is well stocked with game. The place is feverish at certain times of the year. There is a public bungalow for the accommodation of travellers going by the Kārkūr pass.

Wandur—in the amsam of the same name, is 12 miles from Manjēri and is the seat of a Sub-Registrar of Assurances, who is also a Special Magistrate. There is a Police station, also a good public bungalow which was once largely used by passengers travelling by the Sispara or Chichchippara route to the Nīlgiris. The road has fallen into disuse and is not now properly maintained. There is a mosque at this place ; also a Siva temple.

Pandikad—in the amsam of the same name, is 8 miles from Manjēri, and has a Police station, a small public bungalow and a weekly market. Iron ore is obtained to some extent in these parts.

Mambat—in the amsam of the same name, contains a Māppilla bazaar and is a place of timber trade.

Edavanna—in Tiruvali amsam, is a rising Māppilla town on the Nilambūr river about 8 miles from Manjēri and has considerable timber trade. There is a mosque at this station, also a temple at Tiruvali about 2 miles from the Edavanna bazaar.

Ariakode—in Iruvetti amsam and about 11 miles from Manjēri, is a small Māppiḷḷa town pleasantly situated on the south bank of the Beypore river, and has considerable timber trade. There is a Police station and a good bungalow built on a hill about half a mile from the village, for the accommodation of travellers going to Nīlgiris *viâ* the Kārkūr pass. The scenery about the place is charming and plenty of easy shooting is available in the neighbourhood. There is a mosque at this station.

Trikkallur or Trikkalliyur—in Urangāttiri amsam, is celebrated for a Siva temple standing on elevated ground. It was in this temple that Kutti Assan and eleven other Māppiḷḷas made a determined stand against the Police and the Military from the 27th to 29th December 1884. The temple was captured and the fanatics slain after breaking open the loopholed barricaded doors with dynamite. The temple owns large property managed by Kirrangat Ashtamurti Nambūdiripād of Vallappuḷa amsam, in Waḷḷuvanād taluk. Opposite the temple stands the Churoth mosque, in which the fanatics prayed before taking post in the pagoda. The Māppiḷḷa inhabitants of the amsams of Urangāttiri, Mappram, Chikod, Iruvetti and Tiruvāli were fined for this outrage under the provisions of the Māppiḷḷa Outrages Act XX of 1859.

Chembrasseri amsam.—Iron ore is found in this amsam, which is one of the biggest in the taluk.

Kottakal—in the amsam of the same name, is 14 miles from Manjēri and is the seat of the Kilakke Kovilakam Rajas, one of the three branches of the Zamorin's family. There are here the old fort, called Venkatakotta and a small bungalow built by the Raja for the accommodation of visitors. A weekly fair is held, at which areca-nut, arrow-root flour and ginger form the principal articles of trade. The Military camping ground at Klari is only 2 miles from this place.

Malapuram—(literally mountainous place) in Kiḷumiri amsam, is a healthy military station about 7 miles from Manjēri and 31 miles from Calicut. It is the seat of the Special Assistant Collector, of the Assistant Superintendent of Police and the Special Police force and of the Sub-Registrar of Assurances. It contains, likewise, Post and Telegraph offices, a public bungalow, a D. P. W. halting shed, barracks for European troops, a chapel, two Christian cemeteries, a small bazaar, and a weekly market well-attended. Tippu had a fort here, which is now in ruins. Near the barracks there are good recreation and camping grounds for the troops. Malapuram is the centre of the country which has been fruitful in Mappiḷḷa fanatical outbreaks, and in consequence of two risings in 1841 and 1843, native troops were sent here; but as they proved useless during the outbreaks of 1849 and 1851, a detachment of European troops has been stationed here since 1852.

A description of the boundaries of the Military Cantonment for the European barracks at Malapuram will be found printed at page 172 of the Fort Saint George Gazette, dated 22nd February 1853.

The detachment was augmented and officers' quarters built since the Kolattur outrage of 1873. On more than one occasion, special Police corps[1] were raised in Malapuram to deal with local outrages, but in the lull which followed the passing of the Māppiḷḷa Outrages Act, the work was transferred to the regular constabulary.[2] A special Police force has again been postod here since 1885.

At a short distance from the Malapuram barracks is the Malapuram mosque, which is a tiled building and is of some importance. An annual festival, called Nērchcha is held here usually in the month of Kumbham, supposed to be in commemoration of the death of 40 Māppiḷḷas who fell in an encounter with the neighbouring Hindu landlord, Para Nambi's followers. There are three Hindu temples in the amsam, known as (1) the Tripuranthakan temple near the barracks, (2) the Mannur Siva temple and (3) the Channath Siva temple. The sacred places of Muhammadans, in addition to the Malapuram mosque, are (1) the Hajiyar Palli and (2) Sayyid's Jarum (സെയ്യുന്മാരുടെജാറം).

---

[1] *Vide* extracts from Minutes of Consultation, dated 16th May 1854, No. 352.

[2] G.O., dated 4th May 1860, publishod in the Fort Saint George Gazette of the same date.

Kondotti—in Kolattur amsam (17 miles from Calicut), is an important Māppiḷḷa town on the road to Calicut and contains the office of the Sub-Registrar who is also a Special Magistrate. There are besides a Police station, a Post office, and a public bungalow. It is the residence of the Kondotti Tangal who is the Muhammadan high priest of the section of Māppiḷḷas known locally as Kondotti Kayikkars. There is a shrine here called *Kondotti-thakkiya*, which is supposed to have been built in 948 M.E. (A.D. 1773) by the then Tangal, named *Muhammad Shāha* and in which lie interred his remains. A Nērchcha is performed here annually in the month of Mīnam. The Tangals have been loyal to the British Government and their loyalty has been rewarded by the grant of a personal inam to the extent of Rs. 2,734 per year (*vide* G.O., dated 12th October 1865, No. 2474), and by permission to keep seven pieces of cannon (*vide* license granted by the Government of India, under date the 15th September 1885, No. 43, forwarded with Madras Government G.O., dated 29th September 1885, No. 2617, Mis.). There are two mosques at this station which are largely attended.

Ūrakam-Melmuri contains the Ūrōth hill which was used as a heliographic station in February 1885 during the disarming operations then in progress. On the top of the hill stands the Tiruvarchchanam Kunnu temple dedicated to god Sankara Narayanan. The Ponmundam fanatics in May 1885 tried to occupy this hill after the murder of Cheruman Kutti Kariyan and his family on the 1st May 1885, but had to leave it for want of water. The celebrated Mattattūr mosque is situated in this amsam.

Tirūrangādi—(literally Tiru=sacred, ūr=village, angadi=bazaar or the place of bazaar in the sacred country of Chēranād) in Trikkulam amsam, is the seat of the Deputy Tahsildar, of the Sub-Registrar of Assurances and of the Police Inspector of that division, and contains a Post office, a bazaar and a well-attended weekly market. The town, which consists of long and crooked streets, lies on the south bank of the river and has nothing remarkable about it, save that there are a jamāth mosque which is attended by a large congregation and a Hindu temple dedicated to Siva. There are the remains of a fort dismantled several years ago. In the vicinity of this fort, a decided victory was gained by General Hartley over Tippu's troops in 1790 (Vol. I, p. 473).

And it was in the same neighbourhood that Colonel Humberstone defeated and slew Mukhdam Ali, one of Hyder Ali's Generals on 8th April 1782 (Vol. I, p. 436). It is curious that the only two pitched battles fought in Malabar between the Mysoreans and the British took place on the same battle field.

Mampram lies directly opposite to Tirūrangādi, on the north bank of the river, in Kotuvayur amsam, and contains the mukhām or tomb of a great Tangal buried there. It is on this account a place of considerable pilgrimage. The history of the Tangal who lies interred there is as follows :—

In the early part of the 18th century a Tangal named Sayyid Hussain Ibn Alabi Jiffiri Tangal, who is supposed to have come from Arabia, settled at the place called Mampram or Mampuram which was then an extensive waste. It was reclaimed and planted with coconut trees for the growth of which the soil appears to be admirably adapted. He lived in a house called Taramal, and died in the month of Shāban in the Hejira 1169, leaving a daughter named Fāttima. In the fifth year after his death, there arrived at Mampram his nephew (sister's son) and son-in-law (Fāttima's husband) named Sayyid Alabi Ibn Muhammad, whom in his lifetime the Māppiḷḷas served with the utmost devotion and whom after his death they have deified. His first marriage with Fāttima was not fruitful, and he married, as his second wife, a woman from the Putiamaliakal house in Calicut.

His next marriage was with a woman of Quilandi, by whom he had, among others, Sayyid Fazl usually known as Pūkkoya who was banished with his relatives beyond India on the 19th March 1852. Sayyid Alabi's fourth wife was a woman of Ponmundam in Ponnāni taluk, who bore him a daughter. The mukhām or shrine intended and used primarily as a receptacle for the dead bodies of the principal Tangals is a rectangular building constructed on very solid foundations, and divided into large hall-like rooms. The building has upper storeys, in one portion there are three and in the other two storeys. The second floor of one of the rooms stands on a higher elevation than that of the other ; and over it an upper floor stands, the circular wall of which is capped by the dome. On the foundation floor of the domed hall are laid 9 coffins, including in them those of Sayyid Alabi who died in 1019 M.E. (Hejira 1260), and his uncle and those of their nearest deceased relatives. The other hall is the place where verses from the Koran are read for the salvation of the souls of the deceased persons.

The shrine was built over the grave of his uncle by Sayyid Alabi in the third year after his arrival at Mampram or in the 8th year after the uncle's death. The space in the interior, which was originally of lesser dimensions than the foundation, was found not sufficient to allow of walking on it after the nine bodies had been buried there. A certain Karachi merchant out of gratitude to Sayyid Alabi for his having been miraculously saved by the latter in a shipwreck at sea, had the room extended at his own expense so as to cover the entire space on the foundation. The dome having gone out of repair in recent years, it is now being put up anew and furnished by Putiyamāligayil Sayyid Abdulla Koya of Calicut, out of contributions for the purpose made by his co-religionists. This shrine has been frequently visited by Māppiḷḷa fanatics for the purpose of invoking the Varkkaths (blessings or aid) of the great Tangal buried there, previously to the execution of their designs. And it is also largely resorted to by other Muhammadans and by Hindus to invoke the great Tangal's aid in any enterprises in which they are interested.

Parappanangādi (literally the bazaar place in the Parappanād raj) is a small Māppiḷḷa village about 4 miles from Tirūrangādi and is the seat of the Chēranād Munsif's Court. It contains likewise a Post office, a Police station and the Railway station of the same name. The palace of the Kshatriya family of Parappanād Rajas is situated at a short distance from the Railway station. It is from this family that the consorts of the Ranis of the Travancore family are usually selected. Pepper, ginger, salted fish and areca-nut form the chief articles of trade and are exported in large quantities. The Munsif's Court-house and the Railway station though usually known by the name of "Parappanangādi" are really located within the limits of the Netuva amsam.

Ferokh or (as Malayâlis write it) *Paramukka* (written also Ferokabad in military department Route book), in Nallur amsam contains a Police station and an important weekly market to which people from Calicut resort for the purchase of poultry, provisions, &c. Half a mile south-west of it on an elevated spot are the ruins of Ferokabad commanding two beautiful reaches of the Beypore river which flows immediately to the north of the fortress. It was planned by Tippu whose intention it was to make it the capital of Malabar, but his troops were driven out of it in 1790 before the design was fully carried out. He compelled a large portion of the inhabitants of Calicut to settle here, but on the departure of his troops they returned to their former abode. The ferry at Ferokh is called the Mammalli ferry. The railway now in course of extension to Calicut passes through this place. An iron bridge on cylinders is being carried across the Mammalli (Beypore) river, and the bridge is to carry ordinary traffic as well as the railway. A railway station is also proposed at this locality. Two miles above the Mammalli ferry on the Èrnâd or south bank of the river lies Chăttamparamba, a laterite hill containing numerous tombs of a long forgotten generation, some of them excavated from the laterite rock and others in the shape of huge earthen pots buried beneath the surface. From some of these the interesting beads depicted in the illustrations at pages 180-81 of Vol. I have been taken. Some of the beads are of agate with designs on them which take one back to the times of the Buddhists. The pottery, which is found in abundance in these tombs, is of a very varied character and quite different to anything manufactured in recent times.

Châliyam in Palanchannûr amsam (erroneously called Beypore, which is a contiguous amsam on the north bank of the river in the Calicut taluk) is an island formed by the Kadalhundi and Beypore rivers, and by the sea on the west. It is about ten miles in circumference. It is the present western terminus of the Madras Railway and contains a hotel, two public chattrams, a Police station, Post office, Marine flagstaff, a Protestant chapel and cemetery, a mosque and a petty bazaar. The travellers' bangalow and the Beypore Sea Customs office lie on the northern side of the Beypore ferry in the Calicut taluk. The Railway station has a flower garden and a small park kept in neat order by the railway company.

There is a rocky islet lying to the southward of the entrance to the Beypore river and connected with the mainland by a groyne. This islet contains two mounds, a northern and a southern one, and the Port Officer, Calicut, made excavations round the base of the former and discovered the remains of what appeared to be the remains of a fortress. Captain Gillham states as follows :—

"There is now no question or doubt but that the masonry was the commencement of foundations for a very formidable fortress for the protection of the entrance to Beypore river. The walls being the strongest on the west and north-west and north angles where the foundations were 13 feet across and from 2 to 3 feet deep, commencing on coarse sand and shelly bottom. The portion comprised between the south-west angle of the mound round by east to the north angle is of cut laterite stone built in chunam, and from the north angle to the south-east angle round by east, the foundations are cuttings and levellings on the upper surface of the laterite rock, with small portions of concrete and masonry levellings in places. From the fact of the foundation having been commenced on sandy soil, together with the fact that when excavations were being made into the base of the north mound, a considerable quantity of red soil was found, has led me to the opinion that the mounds on the islet are not natural, but artificially made from soil carried to the islet from the mainland."

The Port officer also dug three wells with the object of ascertaining whether fresh water was obtainable on the isle. Of these three, two yield perfectly pure water, but the third proved brackish. It is likely that the foundations of the fortress discovered formed part of Tippu Sultan's project for protecting his projected city at Ferokh.

Kadalhundi and *Nirumkayitha kōtta* in Vallikunnu amsam are small hamlets of some note. The former contains a Māppiḷḷa bazaar and the latter the important temple known as Nirumkayitha kōtta dedicated to god Ayyappan. The temple has a copper sheet roof and stands on the slope of an elevated hill. On the top of the hill called Melkotta there is a deity which persons proceeding to the Nirumkayitha kōtta temple go up to worship. The place is infested by monkeys, supposed to be a portion of the army with which Rama conquered Ceylon, left here by him on his return from his expedition.

The following temples and mosques which are not described above deserve notice :—

(1) *Manjēri Amsam.*—(1) Arizhayi Siva temple, (2) Pantalur temple, (3) Manjēri mosque.

(2) *Trikkalangōt Amsam*—contains the Trikkalangōt temple dedicated to Vettakorumakan and certain inscriptions in Vatteḻuthu and five dolmens. The celebrated Karikkatt temple, dedicated to Subramania, also exists here.

(3) *Ponmala Amsam*—contains the important Ponmala temple and the Ponmala mosque.

(4) *Intiannur Amsam*—contains a temple, dedicated to Ganapathi and Siva.

(5) *Kottakkel Amsam*—contains (1) Kottakkel Siva temple, (2) Pandamangalam Vishnu temple, (3) Vēttakkorumakan temple.

(6) *Netiyiruppu Amsam*—contains Pūlikkad Bhagavathi temple.

(7) *Aḻinjilam Amsam*—contains (1) Pariapuram temple, dedicated to Subramania, (2) Palakkel Bhagavathi temple, (3) Karumaken kāvu temple, (4) Ariyil Siva temple.

(8) *Nallur Amsam*—contains the Nallur Siva temple which is of some importance.

(9) *Chelembra Amsam*—contains (1) Vennayur Vishnu temple, (2) Itavaḻikkel Ganapathi temple, (3) Tiruvangat Siva temple.

(10) *Karat Amsam*—contains Virali kāvu temple.

(11) *Puthur Amsam*—contains Cherukunnath Bhagavathi temple, the deity of which is supposed to have come from the temple of that name in North Malabar.

(12) *Valluvambram Amsam*—contains Pullanur mosque.

(13) *Netuva Amsam*—contains Pisharikkel kāvu temple *alias* Puthiarayara Nallur temple, dedicated to goddess Mūkambika.

Christian Churches and Cemeteries and scattered Tombs.—There are Roman Catholic and Protestant chapels at Malapuram and at Chāliyam (Beypore). There are also cemeteries at each of these stations. The scattered tombs in the taluk are the following:—

(1) Tomb near the District Forest office at Nilambūr bearing the following inscription—"To the memory of Samuel Robert Clogstoun, Lieutenant in the 23rd Regiment, M.N.I. He was born on the 26th January 1824 and drowned in the Chellambore river (Nilambūr) near this spot on the 13th August 1843. Generous, high spirited and of great promise; he died deeply regretted. His brother officers, in testimony of esteem for his worth and sorrow for his early death, have erected this tomb."

(2) Tomb of Ensign Wyse, who died at the hands of Māppiḷḷa fanatics in 1849 in Manjēri amsam close to the District Munsif's Court, bears no inscription.

(3) Tomb of Mary Elliot in the Valakkāt coffee estate, in the jungly wilds of the Silent Valley in Chembrasseri amsam.

Soil and Productions.—The soil of the western portion of Ērnād and on the heights, is red laterite intermixed with gravel; in the valleys of cultivation, it is a rich brown free from gravel, so also in the cultivated tract in the interior. The dense coconut belt usually not more than 4 miles wide extending along the coast, runs up for 12 or 15 miles into very nearly the heart of the taluk about Malapuram, and the soil in these parts seems to be singularly well adapted to this tree and to other vegetable productions, among others, the pineapple which nowhere flourishes better than in these richly cultivated low-lying valleys in Ērnād. In the forests and mountains, the soil is a rich black mould owing to the constant falling of decayed leaves and rotten wood. Granitic gneiss is conspicuous on the face of the ghats and the mountains to the east where it is seen to form a perfect barrier. The productions generally are rice of various sorts, and several species of dry grain and pulses; pepper is produced but not in such abundance as in the tracts along the coast. The areca palm is cultivated extensively about the central parts and grows luxuriantly on the banks of all the rivers; it is, however, scarce to the east of Nilambūr. Timber of many descriptions, also bamboos, honey and bees' wax are obtained from the forests.

Inams.—A list of inams of various descriptions granted in the taluk is appended.

No.	Name of Inamholder.	Amsam in which Inam lands are situate.	Amount. RS. A. P.	Remarks.
	Devadayam (or Inams granted for temples).			
1	Kapilkarimkali kshetrom	Nilambūr ..	1 3 3	For the expenses attending the usual ceremonies in the temple.
2	Chementala Bhagavati kshetrom	Do. ..	18 8 5	
3	Wandur Siva kshetrom.	Wandur ..	7 10 3	

No.	Name of Inamholder.	Amsam in which Inam lands are situate.	Amount.			Remarks.
			RS.	A.	P.	
	Devadayam, &c.—cont.					
4	Punapalei Siva kshetrom	Wandur ..	6	0	11	For the expenses attending the usual ceremonies in the temple.
5	Chatengam Kulangara Vishnu kshetrom ..	Do. ..	3	11	9	
6	Karikat kshetrom ..	Do. ..	20	0	0	
7	Do. ..	Irimpuli ..	28	13	3	
8	Irimbuli Vishnu kshetrom	Do. ..	5	7	9	
9	Mutrakunnu kshetrom.	Do. ..	32	2	6	Do. and for entertainments given to Brahmins.
10	Karikat kshetrom ..	Trikalangode ..	19	1	1	For expenses attending the usual ceremonies in the temple.
11	Meladatha kshetrom ..	Do. ..	33	4	0	
12	Mutrakunnu kshetrom.	Manjēri ..	1,112	7	10	Do. and for entertainments given to Brahmins.
13	Arupiraya Siva kshetrom	Do. ..	28	12	3	For expenses attending the usual ceremonies in the temple.
14	Vakethodi Karinkali kshetrom	Do. ..	35	8	5	
15	Tiruvidaikal kshetrom.	Do. ..	14	2	4	
16	Orinadatha Siva kshetrom	Do. ..	14	11	2	
17	Pantalūr Bhagavati kshetrom	Do. ..	63	3	8	
18	Potiyātu kshetrom ..	Melmuri ..	13	4	8	Do. and for entertainments given to Brahmins.
19	Kurumangote Iyyappan kshetrom	Pandikad ..	2	6	6	For the expenses attending the usual ceremonies in the temple.
20	Naduvatha kshetrom ..	Do. ..	9	3	6	
21	Nechiparambeth Tripurandakan kshetrom.	Kilmuri ..	31	4	8	
22	Ulanam Siva kshetrom.	Neduva ..	19	1	9	
23	Chiramangalath Vettakkorumakan kshetrom.	Do. ..	19	12	0	
24	Tirumāndhan kunnu Bhagavati kshetrom.	Porur ..	7	1	5	
25	Talaparamben kshetrom.	Kotuvayur ..	12	5	6	
26	Mutuvelūr Bhagavati kshetrom	Kulimanna ..	37	11	6	For the expenses attending the usual ceremonies in the temple.
27	Mannūr kshetrom ..	Vallikunnu ..	98	13	4	
28	Nerumkaithakotta temple	Do. ..	311	6	4	
29	Do. ..	Palenchennur ..	9	6	10	
30	Trikkolam kshetrom ..	Trikkolam ..	13	1	2	
		Total ..	2,029	12	0	
	Dharmadayam (or Inams granted for charitable purposes).					
31	Cherukuticheri karapram chattram ..	Mapprom ..	2	9	6	For the expenses attending the entertainments given to Brahmins.
32	Do. ..	Chikōd ..	18	6	2	
33	Kēraladhiswarapuram kshetrom	Neduva ..	125	0	5	
34	Do. ..	Nannembra ..	5	1	0	
35	Do. ..	Valakulam ..	18	8	8	
36	Trikandiyur chattram.	Do. ..	2	11	5	
		Total ..	172	5	2	

No.	Name of Inamholder.	Amsam in which Inam lands are situate.	Amount.	Remarks.
	Religious Institutions (or Inams granted for mosques).		RS. A. P.	
37	Malapratha Ajiyara Palli mosque ..	Kilmuri ..	0 10 9	For defraying the expenses for lights.
38	Mampad Vali Jamath Palli mosque ..	Mampad ..	7 5 10	
39	Mampad Cheria Jamath Palli mosque..	Do. ..	14 13 2	
40	Ariakode mosque ..	Iruvetti ..	6 15 1	For the expenses attending the Vilakkatiyantram festival.
41	Tannur Daraka Palli mosque	Nannembra ..	109 12 10	
42	Quilandi mosque ..	Trikkalangode.	191 14 11	For the support of the Quilandi Palli mosque.
43	Do. ..	Manjēri ..	745 13 2	
44	Do. ..	Karakunnu ..	862 3 11	
45	Mamprathа Palli mosque	Kotuvayur ..	2 0 4	For defraying the expenses for lights.
		Total ..	1,941 10 0	
	Personal (or Inams granted for special services).			
46	Kondotti Tangal ..	Kulimanna ..	143 5 3	These inams were confirmed in 1865 to Ishtiyak Shah, the Kondotti Tangal, so long as he continues true and loyal to the Government.
47	Do. ..	Chikōd ..	1,125 2 3	
48	Do. ..	Kolattūr ..	318 7 3	
49	Do. ..	Karipur ..	263 3 11	
50	Do. ..	Olakara ..	35 8 7	
51	Do. ..	Kavannūr ..	58 13 9	
52	Do. ..	Chirukavu ..	13 3 2	
53	Do. ..	Nediruppu ..	32 0 3	
54	Do. ..	Urangattiri ..	73 13 1	
55	Do. ..	Iruvetti ..	251 14 8	
56	Do. ..	Chengara ..	135 15 3	
57	Do. ..	Arimbra ..	283 1 2	
		Total ..	2,734 8 7	
		Grand Total ..	6,878 3 9	

Mines, Minerals and Manufactures.—Iron ore is found in different parts of the taluk, chiefly in Chembrasseri and Pandikād amsams, but very little of it is actually worked. Gold ore is found in the beds of the rivers and streams running down from the ghats into the Nilambūr valley. One of the principal branches of the Beypore river is called the Ponpula or gold river from an idea that a large portion of that mineral is washed down the stream during the rains. The manufactures in the taluk are of little moment and consist of some cloth of an inferior quality. The cloths formerly famous as shaleeats appear to have derived their name from Chāliyam, the present terminus of the Madras Railway, but the art of weaving them appears to have been lost. Oils from coconut and castor, coir on the sea coast, jaggery and arrack from toddy are manufactured almost everywhere.

Bungalows and Chattrams.—There are bungalows at (1) Kondotti, (2) Ariakod, (3) Etavanna, (4) Nilambūr, (5) Etakkara, (6) Wandur, (7) Malapuram, (8) Pandikād, (9) Manjēri; and chattrams at (1) Manjēri and (2) Karimpula.

The bungalows at Pandikād and Manjēri are under the supervision of local fund overseers.

Railway Stations.—In the Ērnād taluk there are railway stations at Chāliyam (erroneously called Beypore) and Parappanangādi and one proposed to be built in connection with the extension to Calicut at Ferokh.

Fairs.—There are fairs at—

(1) Manjēri,
(2) Malapuram,
(3) Kottakal
(4) Wandur,
(5) Vatapuram,
(6) Pandikād, and
(7) Ferokh.

Trigonometrical Stations.—The survey stations to be preserved and annually reported on are named below (Board's Proceedings, dated 28th July 1886, No. 1706):—

Name of G. T. Station.	Situation.	Series.	Modern values.	
			Latitude.	Longitude.
			° ′ ″	° ′ ″
Chekkunnu	Urangāttiri.	Modern.	11 15 27·71	76 08 22·58
Urōt mala	Urakam Melmuri.	Do.	11 05 15·73	76 03 05·60

MEMORANDUM ON THE CONOLLY TEAK PLANTATIONS AT NILAMBŪR, ĒRNĀD TALUK, MALABAR DISTRICT.

By Atholl MacGregor, M.C.S., late Collector of Malabar.

The Nilambūr Teak Plantations were first suggested in 1840 by Mr. Conolly, Collector of Malabar, who described their object as being "to replace those Forests which have vanished from private carelessness and rapacity—a work too new, too extensive, and too barren of early return to be ever taken up by the native proprietor."

Great difficulty was at first encountered in getting the seed to germinate, and many expedients were resorted to. It was argued that in the natural forest the hard outer covering of the seed was destroyed by the annual fires, and it was sought to effect the same object by covering the seed with a light coating of dry grass and setting fire to it. Soaking in water was also tried. In the one case the heat destroyed the vitality of the seed, and in the other the seed rotted. Removing the husk by hand was also tried, it being suggested that it was only the seeds in the forest which happened to be cleaned by white-ants that germinated.

The transplantation of self-sown teak saplings had been simultaneously tried, but whether from injury to the trees in removal, or from attempting to grow too much under shade, or too near mature teak that had already exhausted the surface soil so far as regarded the constituents of teak, this also proved a failure, and Mr. Conolly, in a letter of 4th August 1842 reported that of 30,000 seeds sown none had come up, and that of 10,000, saplings transplanted more than half had died. Recourse was next had to a Mr. Perrotet, a French gentleman, Superintendent, Botanical Gardens at Pondicherry. His advice was to plunge the seed in water nearly boiling, and to uncover the roots of old stumps and cut them in places in order to cause the development of shoots; this experiment came no nearer success.

The true method appears to have been first suggested by Dr. Roxburgh at the end of 1843. He advised sowing the seed at the beginning of the rains in shaded beds lightly covered with earth and rotten straw. The present method is given in an appendix, and it will be seen that 30 years have added little to the knowledge acquired in 1844—for except that the seed is sown 2 months before the rains, and artificially irrigated so as to give it an additional start the method is substantially the same.

Writing in 1845, Mr. Conolly described the experiment as at an end, and success achieved owing to the extraordinary healthy appearance of the young seedlings, 50,000 of which were raised in May, June, and July 1844.

The marginal statement gives the area planted annually arranged in periods of 10 years.

Years.	Acres.	Years.	Acres.	Years.	Acres.
Up to 1844	31	1853	55	1863	81
1844 ..	63	1854	92	1864	121
1845 ..	61	1855	100	1865	56
1846 ..	100	1856	79	1866	128
1847 ..	118	1857	36	1867	118
1848 ..	182	1858	42	1868	145
1849 ..	134	1859	39	1869	53
1850 ..	132	1860	39	1872	235
1851 ..	147	1861	86	1873	86
1852 ..	38	1862	50	1874	84
10 years.	1,006	10 years.	617	10 years.	1,107
Yearly average	100		61		110

The years 1870 and 1871 are not represented, operations having been carried on elsewhere. The statement shows that up to 1874 the area planted in this section aggregates 2,730 acres, or an average of 91 acres per annum for the 30 years.

The Nilambūr valley is of the shape of a horse shoe, and is elevated about 400 feet above sea level. The hills surrounding it on three sides rise in the direction of Sissapāra on the S. E., and the Camel's Hump on the N. W. to 8,000 feet, while to the N. E., the plateau of S. E. Wynād, which closes it in on that side, does not attain an average elevation of more than 3,000 feet. The semi-circle of hills overhangs one vast amphitheatre of valleys of denudation converging on Nilambūr, and a great part of the Valley, including almost always the river bank to a distance of several hundred yards, is an alluvial deposit of enormous depth; the rocks are described by Mr. King as gneiss of quartzo-felspathic or quartzo-horn-blendic variety. The rainfall is about 120 inches, falling chiefly between June 1st and November 1st. The temperature in shade ranges from 80 to 90 throughout the year, and there is a singular absence of high wind all the year round.

Rainfall on slopes of surrounding ghats is probably over 200.

The rivers are navigable by rafts up to January, and below Mambāt, the most westerly point of the Plantation, the navigation is so easy that the largest rafts can be managed by one man. The river which drains the valley empties itself into the sea at Beypore, and 4 miles from the mouth of the river a navigable canal communicates with another river which traverses the heart of the Calicut Bazaar, the best timber market on the west coast. This river is connected with the Calicut roadstead by a bar always open, so that the cost of conveying timber from the Plantations alongside ship may be regarded as at a minimum.

A good cart road is carried from Calicut through Nilambūr up the Kārkūr Ghat to S.E. Wynād, whence the main line is carried on to Mysore, with branches on the north to the Devala gold fields and South Wynād, and on the south to the Ouchterlony Valley and to Ootacamund. The road skirts the plantations for 6 miles, having bridges over the two large rivers.

The climate of Nilambūr is tolerably healthy throughout the year. The months of March, April and May are the fever months, but with due precaution fever is seldom [1] contracted at Nilambūr itself.

Forests in Malabar are chiefly private property and the great bulk of the land in the Nilambūr valley is the property of the Nilambūr Tirumulpād, a wealthy landowner not likely under any circumstances to sell land, still less for the purpose of instituting a local industry of a character to compete with his own agricultural and timber operations for the limited supply of local labour. The plantations owed their existence to the accident that one of the many religious bodies holding temple lands happened to be in want of funds and to own blocks of land scattered here and there in this valley, many of which constituted the very best sites for planting that could have been selected had the whole area been available to choose from.

In considering, however, the difficulties which had to be contended with, it is necessary to regard as occupying a prominent position, the jealousy of a local Janmi of overpowering influence whose house and pagoda formed the only point of social attraction in what was otherwise a jungle.

At first, operations were confined to the narrow strips of river bank, west of Nilambūr, and when in 1853 these appeared to be exhausted, a point to the east, further up the river was selected, and became the scene of the operations of that year as well as of 1855 and 1856. The mistake was, however, made of including in the planted area several laterite hills over which the trees signally failed.

Accordingly attention was again turned to the lands down stream, and in the vicinity of the earlier plantations on the north bank land was found yielding sites for 1857–1862 inclusive, of fair quality, some being very good. In 1860, however, exploration had been set on foot further up stream than had hitherto been attempted, *i.e.*, above the junction of the Shurly River with the Karimpuḷa or main stream. Here there were found several pieces of land included in the Government Estate, with first-class soil and water carriage which formed a compact block adapted for further extension on a larger scale. In 1863 Mr. Ferguson arrived, bringing the knowledge of a forester trained in the extensive plantations of Perthshire, and operations were vigorously prosecuted for the ensuing 7 years, *i.e.*, from 1863–1869, by which time 619 acres had been planted in this quarter. The area of suitable land here having been exhausted, the experiment was made of further extending at Nellikutta, 10 miles up stream and near the

[1] The whole establishment has suffered badly in the current season.

base of the hills, and here in 1870 and 1871 rather more than 100 acres were planted.

The site, however, proved so unhealthy that it was abandoned owing to loss of life and invaliding among the establishment. Fortunately at this time an opportunity presented itself of acquiring by purchase a block of land containing some superior planting sites, and almost surrounded by Government land planted or in forest. Here operations have been carried on since. In order to make up for the break of continuity caused by the plantings of 1870 and 1871 having been carried out at a site that had to be abandoned, 235 acres were planted in 1872 so as to bring up the average to 80 acres for the 3 years, which average was maintained during 1873 and 1874.

During these last two years operations had been carried on simultaneously at the newly-acquired site at Āmarapālam, so as to open up a different source of labour-supply through the village of Vandūr, and create a basis of operations for further extension at the Karimpuḷa site. It is, however, not advisable to go further into these particulars, but to confine observations to the area already described, amounting to 2,730 acres, the object of this paper being to investigate the actual position of the undertaking, with reference to the ascertained survey areas.

To determine the success of the enterprise the questions to be asked are: What have the plantations cost? What do they now return? What are they likely hereafter to return?

Taking as a basis the calculations made in 1872 at the suggestion of Major Pearson, and adding the subsequent cost, the total outlay on the plantations is Rs. 2,29,000,[1] of which since 1863 a sum of Rs. 1,01,000 has been recouped by thinnings, leaving the net cost Rs. 1,28,000. The opponents of planting, however, maintain that up to the period when interest is returned the cost must include compound interest at 4 per cent. on the original outlay.

As a matter of pure calculation of financial results this must be conceded, without, however, admitting that on the showing of absolute profit thus computed is to depend the question of whether a certain portion of the Forest Revenue is to be returned to the land in view to reproduction of timber.

If the net expenditure of each year is taken and calculated up to 1874, at compound interest, the debt against the plantations amounts to Rs. 2,35,000.[1]

This includes payments for land, viz., in 1840 for lease from Pagoda Committee Rs. 9,000 and in 1871 for Chetumboria planting site Rs. 5,000.

To estimate fairly the position, annual extensions must be kept out of sight, and the capital account closed. In 2 or 3 years there would be no very young plantations unable to take care of themselves and entailing, therefore, heavy expenditure. The future outlay will then be restricted to fire-tracing, clearing parasites, watching and thinning out of saplings.

A third of the existing establishment might be debited to the plantations, leaving the remainder to be divided between the natural forest operations, and extension of plantations on new site.

---

[1] Labour has cost 4 annas a day for many years. In the earlier years the cost was less. It may be roughly estimated that at present rates planting costs Rs. 30 an acre—felling, burning, pitting, planting, and once weeding, nurseries and establishment being included.

Altogether an annual expenditure of Rs. 5,000 would probably suffice.

An annual revenue from thinnings of Rs. 10,000 would thus cover the upkeep, and pay 4 per cent. current interest on the actual outlay; and the question is, do the facts lead to anticipate a steady income of this amount?

The actuals derived from the sale of thinnings have been as under:—

	RS.
1863	12,044
1864	1,216
1865	16,776
1866	9,307
1867	15,647
1868	500
1869	9,516
1870	4,173
1871	5,583
1872	843
1873	7,378
1874	11,162
12 years ..	94,144
Per year ..	7,845

The period from 1868 to 1872, inclusive, shows a falling off. This may be partly accounted for by the fact that in the first year or two, owing to previous neglect of thinning, the return may have been abnormally large.

A further explanation will be found in the fact that at about 10 years of age a plantation begins to yield profitable thinnings, and that if the old years' figures be scrutinized, it will be observed that the years that supplied annually to each of these 5 years a plantation for the first time yielding profitable thinnings were those in which a marked diminution in the average area of extension is apparent. Thus the acreage planted, 1858–1862 inclusive, was only 256 acres, or an average of about 50 acres compared to an average of 100 in the earlier period.

During the next 10 years, on the other hand, the annual acreage that will come under thinning each year is 110, and when in addition to this, allowance is made for older plantations requiring thinning for a 2nd and 3rd time, there seems a fair ground for anticipating a gradual increase of income from this source.

The following table shows the classification of thinnings for the market:—

Class.	Average Diameter.	Average Length.	Estimated yield.
	INCH.	FEET.	RS. A. to RS. A.
Superior	3½ to 4	30 to 40	1 0 to 4 0
1	2½ to 3	30 to 45	1 0 to 2 0
2	2 to 3	30 to 40	0 12 to 1 4
3	1½ to 2	20 to 35	0 6 to 0 12
4	1 to 1½	15 to 30	0 1 to 0 8

During the last few years some saplings have been annually brought to market realizing from Rs. 5 to 10 each. This class must undoubtedly increase in number rapidly, as the plantations increase in age; and here a few remarks may be appropriately introduced as to the system that has hitherto guided the selection of trees for thinning. The idea of revenue has been entirely and most wisely ignored, the number removed being decided solely with reference to requirements of space and light, inferior trees being invariably, if possible, removed in preference to superior.

The original planting may be reckoned as giving 1,100 trees to the acre, of which a considerable number never make any show, being dwarfed in the first 3 or 4 years by exceptionally vigorous neighbours, or perishing from other causes.

The first thinnings are not worth removal. The trees remaining per acre at 10, 20, and 30 years may be roughly stated at 750, 500 and 150 respectively.

Thus each tree in a 30 years' old plantation represents a selection, partly natural, partly in accordance with principles of forestry of 1 in 7.

The further reduction that will ensue is a matter of somewhat uncertain conjecture; but, if a final crop is taken at 80 years old, a clean cut being then made, block by block, it is estimated that the trees would be of a size to admit of not more than 50 to the acre, so that 100 trees per acre would be obtained from a 30 years' old plantation before the final crop was taken—timber that would be suitable for minor building purposes, for sleepers and for bridge work of a certain class.

The finding of a market for the ordinary thinnings of the classes before noted is an important consideration, and on the success with which the thinnings are brought to market at the right period and judiciously disposed of, the income from this source greatly depends.

There is a limit to the extent to which this class of materials can command a local market, and it is only the exceptional demand at Calicut that has hitherto admitted of so large an income being obtained. Calicut is a great *entrepôt* for the trade of the Persian Gulf and Arabian Ports, and a demand for poles and minor building materials is naturally great from these rainless regions, not to mention the demand for materials so suitable as these are for the rigging of Native craft.

As years advanced, of course, the numbers of the thinnings of the smaller classes would decrease ; but, on the whole, it is probable that taking into consideration the increase in the larger timber annually removed, the revenue would at least maintain itself at 10,000, and thus simple interest and working expenses be secured till the final crop was realized. It is even likely that this amount may be largely exceeded, and any excess will be so much towards extinguishing the debt.

Captain Seaton, whose estimate is the most careful and business-like of any I have yet seen, calculated the final crop at 100 acres a year, of 50 trees to the acre and 50 cub. ft. to the tree, and taking the rates realized at Rs. 1, $1\frac{1}{2}$ and 2 a cub. ft. he shewed a profit of Rs. 40 per tree, or 2 lakhs annually.

The figures given in this report show that the average area planted annually for the 30 years has been 91 acres, and from this a deduction is necessary to cover spaces, where from some cause or another there has been failure, or where hereafter failure may occur. Looking at the long period of time that is to elapse, the area may, from this cause, be reduced nearly 25 per cent., say to 70 acres. The yield per tree of 50 cub. ft. seems a moderate estimate, considering that exceptionally fine trees might now be pointed out in parts of the older plantations containing more than half that quantity.[1]

Supposing the average price to be 1—8, a net profit of Rs. 40 leaves Rs. 35 for expenses, or 11 annas a cub. ft. This, if applying merely to felling and floating, is excessive, as it is well known that inferior woods, fetching no more than 4 and 5 annas a cub. ft. in the Calicut market, are profitably removed from forests further up the same rivers, and consequently more expensive to work.

Establishment charge, too, would dwindle to a very small figure per cub. ft. over such extensive operations.

It is doubtless safe to allow a wide margin in such calculations, but here there is sufficient to cover not only large excess in cost of operations but also a falling off in the number of trees per acre or in the price realized.

Regarding this last it seems very improbable that at such a distant date, when it may be presumed the natural supply of timber in the market will have so much diminished, an average rate of Rs. 1½ per cub. ft. will not be realized by teak of the clean, straight, sound growth, for which the Nilambūr Valley teak is celebrated, a character which in the plantations promises to be fully maintained.

Colonel Beddome's apprehension that the quality of the timber will be found in a considerable degree inferior in the market to Ānamala teak does not seem well grounded,[2] especially when the absence of heartshake and the economy of working secured by straight growth is considered. A comparison of the conditions under which the two classes of timber can be brought to market shows what a hopeless disadvantage the Ānamala teak labours under.

Speaking of the latter, in a letter dated 14th May 1875, No. 128 (G.O., Madras Government, Public Works Department, 6th July 1877), Captain Campbell Walker observes that he doubts whether Rs. 1½ a cub. ft. for timber delivered in Coimbatore leaves any profit to the department, and Colonel Beddome, under date 19th April 1876 (*vide* same proceedings), wrote that it was very evident that those rates could not be remunerative or even cover working expenses.

In other words, the Ānamala teak, despite its excellent quality, can scarcely be brought to market for the market value owing to the absence of perfect water communication between the forests and market depôt. Hitherto the use of teak generally for bridge work has been on the west coast greatly discouraged by the difficulty of securing with certainty and with no very long notice a large number of beams of the necessary scantling, and hence either inferior sorts of timber are used or iron girders imported.

---

[1] Mr. Stanbrough, Assistant Conservator, took measurements in 1874, and calculated on them an average of 1,500 cub. ft. per acre of timber in the plantations of 1844–1853, inclusive—the maximum of a year being 2,500 and minimum 1,350. Further measurements and calculations are desirable.

[2] Here and there natural teak trees have been left standing, to the great detriment of saplings planted near them. They are from time to time felled, and a batch of such logs was seen by Colonel Morgan, Conservator of the Mudamala Teak Forest, and Mr. Douglas, Conservator of the Ānamalas, while inspecting in 1872. A fair sample of the batch was judged by these two competent authorities to be some 60 years old, and to contain 50 cub. ft. of timber worth, from its even growth and quality, Rs. 2 a cub. ft. in the market depôt, to which Rs. 5 or 6 would suffice to transport it.

With these compact areas to work on, and the great number and uniformity of growth of the trees, it may be fairly expected that teak for bridge work will be much more extensively used when the plantations begin to mature their crop.

It must be freely admitted that all calculations of this nature are liable to error, but making all allowances it seems impossible to resist the conclusion that eventually the result of the plantations must be to contribute to the wants of the country an immense stock of useful material, realizing such a revenue as fully to reimburse the State for their outlay even after compound interest for the unproductive period is allowed. This result must be deemed a satisfactory outcome of the exertions of Mr. Conolly, the zealous pioneer of the enterprise, of the late Chāttu Mēnon, the native Conservator, who for 20 years carried on the operations, and of Mr. Ferguson, whose skilled and unremitting attention during the last 14 years has brought the plantations to their present pitch.

Appendix.

A.—MEMORANDUM ON GROWING SEEDLINGS FROM TEAK SEED, PLANTING OUT, &c.

By Mr. J. Ferguson, Deputy Conservator of Forests, Nilambūr.

1. Collect seed from trees with a clear stem free from decay and of vigorous growth ; February the best month to collect in.

2. *Preparation of Nursery Beds.*—Select good free soil, dig 12 inches deep, removing weeds, roots, and stones. When caked, the soil should be reduced to a fine mould, and the nursery levelled ; line off beds, 3½ feet wide and one foot space betwixt each bed and its fellow, then raise an outer edging round each bed, 3 to 4 inches high ; beds when thus finished will be about 2½ feet wide between the edgings, and 120 seers of seed will suffice for 150 feet in length of the above-sized beds ; sow from 10th to 15th April ; before sowing steep the seed forty-eight hours in water, then sow and cover with a thin covering of fine soil, nearly ¾ inch, then cover with straw to retain the moisture ; betwixt the soil and straw a few very small twigs without leaves to prevent the straw from being washed into the soil by water ; which, if allowed, is apt to destroy the young seedlings on its (the straw's) removal. Water daily copiously, say a common earthen pot of water to each two running feet in length of bed, less or more, according to free soil, or otherwise ; in this way the seed will germinate in from 10 to 15 or 20 days, or more, according to freeness of soil ; water less as the plant strengthens, but keeping up sufficient moisture till the monsoon sets in from the 1st to the 3rd week in June, when the plants will be from 4 to 8 inches high and ready for planting out permanently.

3. The site for planting should be selected and felled in December, allowed to dry till March, fired, then cross cut, piled, and burned off, and after the soil is softened by the rains, line and mark off the pits the required distance apart ; from 6 to 7 feet answers well, the pits dug from 10 to 12 inches square, and equal depth and filled in as dug with earth slightly raised around tops.

4. *Planting.*—The seedling should be put well down in the pit, taking care the tap root is not twisted and turned up (to prevent which the tap root is shortened to 6 inches as lifted from the bed); when planting the cooly inserts his hand the required depth perpendicularly, taking out the soil and putting the seedlings with the other hand (as above without twisting or turning up the root), putting back the removed soil and pressing it firmly round (without damaging) the plant, and this prevents its being wind waved before taking root.

5. Planting should take place after the soil is well saturated with rain; from the 10th to 30th June and 8th July is the best season, as afterwards the seedling's tap root rapidly swells like a carrot and does not throw out fibrous roots, nor establish itself either so quickly or so well as before that state of growth.

When the planting cannot be finished by the 8th of July, the small vigorous seedlings, which continue to germinate up till August and will even germinate after twelve and fourteen months in the beds, should be selected in preference to the larger and more robust with the carroty roots.

Note by the Officiating Inspector.

I am informed by the Conservator of Forests, Southern Division, Bombay, that he has tried transplanting Teak Seedlings in the nursery before planting out, with the best results, and as this plan mitigates the difficulty to which Mr. Ferguson refers with regard to the long carroty roots, it appears worthy of trial where circumstances admit. The Conservator of Forests, Southern Division, Bombay, has promised a memorandum on the subject which will be circulated on receipt.

(Signed) C. WALKER, Capt.,
Offg. Inspector of Forests.

Ootacamund,
26th March 1874.

B.—MEMORANDUM ON PLANTING EXPENSES.

By Mr. J. Ferguson, Deputy Conservator of Forests, Nilambûr.

Cost per acre of Planting Natural Forest.

	RS.	A.	P.
Weeding undergrowth preparatory to felling	2	0	0
Felling	5	0	0
Firing the jungle as first felled	0	4	0
Cross cutting remains of first burn	3	8	0
Piling and burning off clear	10	0	0
Lining, marking, pitting and planting out	3	8	0
Weeding and hoeing round the plants	2	8	0
Second weeding	1	4	0
Third weeding	1	4	0
Fourth weeding	1	4	0
Teak seeds 2 parrahs	0	8	0
Preparing, sowing and watering nursery beds	3	0	0
Contingencies	2	0	0
Total ..	36	0	0

Cost per acre of subsequent Maintenance.

——	2nd year.	3rd year.	4th year.	5th year.	6th year.
	RS. A. P.	RS. A. P.	RS. A. P.	RS. A. P.	RS. A. P.
First weeding	2 8 0	1 8 0	1 0 0	0 12 0	0 12 0
Second do.	2 8 0	2 4 0	1 12 0	1 4 0	1 4 0
Third do.	2 8 0	2 0 0	1 4 0	1 0 0	....
Fourth do.	2 8 0	....	....	....	....
Pruning	0 4 0	0 8 0	0 8 0	0 12 0	0 12 0
Total ..	10 4 0	6 4 0	4 8 0	3 12 0	2 12 0

The above rates are for plantations formed from old natural forests, and should meet all charges on ordinary soil exclusive of superintendence.

If the soil is very fine, and has been previously cropped more than once, the cost of felling and burning will be reduced, but the cost of weeding will be increased for the 1st, 2nd, and 3rd years, but as the plants begin to cover the ground the undergrowth decreases considerably.

If the plantations are intended for first-class timber the thinning should begin from the 6th or 7th year.

Notes.

The memorandum on the Conolly Teak Plantations at Nilambūr, by Mr. Atholl MacGregor, the late Collector of Malabar, in 1874, does not seem to have included the operations carried out at Nellikutta, Amarapālam, &c., which lie at some distance from Nilambūr itself. Of course, at the period, viz., 1874, when the memorandum was drawn up, about three-fourths of the existing acreage of plantations had been finished, and almost all of this acreage was confined to the Nilambūr, Valluvashēri, and Chatamborai blocks all situated close to Nilambūr. The account of expenditure and revenue of these selected areas only has been given in the memorandum, whilst that recorded below treats of the whole plantation.

The system worked out and the figures adopted in the report No. 104 of 20th April 1878, by Colonel Beddome in reference to G.O., No. 2846, dated 24th September 1877, differ greatly from those adopted in Mr. MacGregor's memorandum, and they embrace the whole plantation.

Colonel Beddome's system has accordingly been adopted and the annual figures are recorded below up to date in the forms therein prescribed.

The following figures are quite accurate, having been regularly adjusted year by year from the annual audited accounts, and it is with the Conservator of Forests' approval that they are here shown :—

Area planted annually arranged up to date.

Years.	Acres.	Years.	Acres.	Years.	Acres.	Years.	Acres.
1842	31	1853 ..	56	1863 ..	81	1873 ..	141
1844	105	1854 ..	92	1864 ..	122	1874 ..	160
1845	61	1855 ..	100	1865 ..	57	1875 ..	161
1846	111	1856 ..	79	1866 ..	129	1876 ..	149
1847	119	1857 ..	36	1867 ..	119	1886 ..	* 108
1848	183	1858 ..	43	1868 ..	145		
1849	135	1859 ..	40	1869 ..	54		
1850	132	1860 ..	40	1870 ..	74		
1851	147	1861 ..	174	1871 ..	46		
1852	39	1862 ..	50	1872 ..	208		
10 years.	1,063	10 years.	710	10 years.	1,035	5 years.	719
Yearly average.	106	..	71	..	103	..	145

A.—*Statement showing actual expenditure under "Natural Forests" and "Plantation Proper" with ⅓ and ⅔ B. "Establishment" charges respectively up to 31st March* 1886.

Year.	Expenditure. Natural Forest. Mortgage, moiety of kuttikanam paid to Janmis.	⅓ of B. "Establishment" charges.	Charges on timber.	Total.
1	2	3	4	5
	RS. A. P.	RS. A. P.	RS. A. P.	RS. A. P.
Up to 1884-85 ..	1,10,326 11 2	74,978 10 0	70,065. 0 11	2,55,370 6 1
During 1885-86	3,062 13 10	4,185 9 4	11,487 5 1	18,735 12 3
Total up to 31st March 1886..	1,13,389 9 0	79,164 3 4	81,552 6 0	2,74,106 2 4

Year.	Expenditure—*continued*. Plantation Proper. Floating teak saplings.	Plantation charges.	⅔ of B. "Establishment" charges.	Total.	Grand Total of columns 5 & 9.
	6	7	8	9	10
	RS. A. P.	RS. A. P.	RS. A. P.	RS. A. P.	RS. A. P.
Up to 1884-85 ..	70,129 4 10	2,08,798 15 5	1,49,957 3 11	4,28,885 8 2	6,84,255 14 3
During 1885-86 .	10,849 7 3	5,986 11 2	8,371 2 9	25,207 5 2	43,943 1 5
Total up to 31st March 1886..	80,978 12 1	2,14,785 10 7	1,58.328 6 8	4,54,092 13 4	7,28,198 15 8

* This is teak coppice with mahogany standards. Planted *vide* G.O., No. $\frac{1222}{F.\ 175}$, dated 4th November 1885; not surveyed.

B.—*Statement showing actual receipts under "Natural Forests" and "Plantations Proper" up to 31st March 1886, greater part of the Miscellaneous receipts forming refund of moiety of Kuttikānam or Stump Fee which properly refers to timber, two-thirds of the item has therefore been shown under "Natural Forests" and one-third under "Plantation Proper."*

Year.	Receipts.											
	Natural Forests.											
	Timber.			Bamboos.			Two-thirds, Miscellaneous.			Total.		
1	2			3			4			5		
	RS.	A.	P.	RS.	A.	P.	RS.	A.	P.	RS.	A.	P.
Up to 1884-85	3,06,169	4	6	17,455	14	5	5,401	5	10	3,29,026	8	9
1885-86	18,709	2	2	2,062	0	5	401	5	4	21,172	7	11
Total ..	3,24,878	6	8	19,517	14	10	5,802	11	2	3,50,199	0	8

Year.	Receipts—*continued.*											
	Plantation Proper.									Grand Total of columns 5 and 8.		
	Teak saplings.			One-third, Miscellaneous.			Total.					
	6			7			8			9		
	RS.	A.	P.	RS.	A.	P.	RS.	A.	P.	RS.	A.	P.
Up to 1884-85	3,18,354	13	11	2,700	10	11	3,21,055	8	10	6,50,082	1	7
1885-86	59,766	8	10	200	10	8	59,967	3	6	81,139	11	5
Total ..	3,78,121	6	9	2,901	5	7	3,81,022	12	4	7,31,221	13	0

For the purpose of showing the valuation of plantations in the annual Code form No. 60, the total of column 7 in statement A above, viz., Rs. 2,14,786, has been adopted at the suggestion of the Conservator of Forests, as charges debited under A-VIII (*d*) in accordance with the Code, para. 239. The amount, viz., Rs. 3,78,121 of the corresponding column 6 in statement B above, is the total revenue realized up to date from the thinnings, and this deducting the actual cost, viz., Rs. 2,14,786, shows a surplus revenue of Rs. 1,63,335 in favor of the plantations.

In the absence of any record of the revenue and expenditure under "Plantation proper" with 4 per cent. compound interest up to date, it had to be worked out from the very beginning, and the following are the results obtained. In making the calculations to avoid tedious multiplication figures, fractions of 100 above 50 have been treated as 100, and fractions of 100 amounting to 50 or less have been omitted.

I.

	RS.
Plantation outlay from commencement up to date calculated at 4 per cent. compound interest is	4,11,285
Plantation revenue from commencement up to date calculated at 4 per cent. compound interest	5,20,734
Surplus revenue in favor of plantation ..	1,09,449

II.

Grand total of the expenditure as per column 10 of the statement A above	7,28,199
Grand total of receipts as per column 9 of the statement B above	7,31,222
Surplus revenue in favor of the division ..	3,023

III.

Grand total of expenditure with 4 per cent. compound interest recorded up to date	12,86,640
Grand total of revenue with 4 per cent. compound interest recorded up to date	10,66,253
Balance against the division ..	2,20,387

It will be advantageous here to quote para. 58 of Colonel Beddome's report above referred to.

"The two following statements show all expenditure (establishment and working charges) and all receipts up to date. Mr. MacGregor, in his report which is only down to 1874, estimates all charges and receipts on the surrounding forests which are really part and parcel of the land handed over for planting, and he excludes the sale-proceeds on timber cut in these tracts and on timber cut on the tracts actually planted; he also only debits a certain portion of the establishment charges (*i.e.*, one-third) against the plantations. This does not appear to me the proper way to treat the question. Certain tracts of forests are taken up by Government for planting, and the felling and sale of the timber removed from the portions planted and the treatment as forest of such portions not adapted for planting are all necessarily part of the same transaction and cannot be treated separately. By the terms of the agreements we pay 30 per cent. on the net proceeds of all jungle timber cut off plantation sites, and 50 per cent. on the same cut in the "natural forests," and a stump fee of 1 rupee on all teak and blackwood trees cut in the natural forest, so that to these operations two-thirds of the pay of establishment are also debited; there is a loss instead of a profit; so that Mr. MacGregor's plan is a little in favor of the plantations although there is not much difference, but it leads to complication."

The two statements referred to by Colonel Beddome in the above-quoted paragraph of his report are in much the same forms in which the statements A and B above given have been prepared, the only difference being that in A and B the revenues and charges debitable respectively to "natural forests" and "plantations" have been at the suggestion of the Conservator of Forests more clearly brought out.

The following table shows the present classification of thinnings for the market with their estimated yield shown against each item :—

Classification.	Quarter girth on centre.	Average diameter at butt end.	Average length.	Estimated yield.	Remarks.
	INCHES	INCHES.	FEET.	RS.	
Superior large saplings ..	5 and more.	..	30	5	
Do. small	..	7	30	3	
1st class	..	6	27	2	
2nd do.	..	5	25	1	
3rd do.	..	4	20	$\frac{3}{4}$	
4th do.	..	3	15	$\frac{1}{2}$	
5th do.	..	$2\frac{1}{2}$	12	$\frac{1}{4}$	
6th do.	..	..	..	$\frac{3}{8}$	Dry saplings.
7th do.	..	..	..	$\frac{1}{16}$	Crooked do.
8th do.	..	..	..	$\frac{1}{8}$	Butt ends of broken saplings of the first four descriptions.

The following tabular statements C to E are in connection with the preliminary working scheme for five years' thinning of the teak plantations, framed by the Conservator of Forests when he inspected the division in October 1885. This has been recorded in detail in his inspection report embodied in Board's Proceedings, No. $\frac{3263}{F.\ 659}$, dated 30th November 1885. The system has been adopted during the year and the result is yet to be decided.

C.—*Statement showing approximately the number of trees which should be removed and left standing in the Teak Plantations during quinquennial periods from the* 11*th to* 61*st year of growth.*

Age.	Number remaining at each period.	Number to be removed during each period.
1 to 11 years	* 1,100	300
End of 11th year ..	800	200
Do. 16th do. ..	600	200
Do. 21st do. ..	400	150
Do. 26th do. ..	250	130
Do. 31st do. ..	120	10
Do. 36th do. ..	110	10
Do. 41st do. ..	100	10
Do. 46th do. ..	90	10
Do. 51st do. ..	80	10
Do. 56th do. ..	70	10
Do. 61st do. ..	60	10

* *N.B.*—Trees planted per acre (allowing for casualties unreplaced, roads, and other unplanted spaces).

D.—*Statement showing the Plantation blocks with their area and approximate number of trees per compartment and per acre.*

Name of block.	Compartment.	Year of planting each compartment.	Area of each compartment. Acs.	C.	Total number planted in each compartment.	Total number thinned up to and for 1884-85.	Balance number standing in each compartment.	Number of trees standing per acre.
I. Áyiravillikáva	1	1842 ..	30	93	11,214	8,278	2,936	94
	2	1844 ..	27	35	25,920	21,378	4,542	166
	3	1852 ..	38	57	37,201	29,761	7,440	193
	4	1853 ..	34	71	37,200	14,908	22,292	642
		Total ..	131	56	111,535	74,325	37,210	..
II. Edaköd	1	1844 ..	30	65	12,228	9,579	2,649	86
	2	1845 ..	28	14	34,750	16,404	18,346	653
	3	1846 ..	44	78	46,418	21,661	24,757	553
	4	1847 ..	54	61	52,000	26,220	25,780	472
	5	1848 ..	82	15	63,000	46,368	16,632	202
	6	1849 ..	44	58	42,200	25,647	16,553	371
	7	1850 ..	49	67	40,800	26,049	14,751	297
	8	1851 ..	147	19	123,960	67,485	56,475	384
	9	1857 ..	36	14	38,800	19,665	19,135	529
	10	1860 ..	39	56	41,680	23,897	17,783	450
	11	1861 ..	86	05	83,700	54,567	29,133	339
	12	1862 ..	50	11	45,900	31,010	14,890	297
		Total ..	693	63	625,436	368,552	256,884	..
III. Rámalúr	1	1844 ..	4	93	4,435	2,922	1,513	307
	2	1850 ..	16	40	12,000	6,275	5,725	349
		Total ..	21	33	16,435	9,197	7,238	..
IV. Elanjëri	1	1845 ..	33	19	38,214	24,585	13,629	411
	2	1846 ..	65	84	55,285	34,961	20,324	309
	3	1849 ..	89	95	61,680	42,558	19,122	213
	4	1850 ..	66	15	54,700	32,864	21,836	330
	5	1858 ..	42	79	43,460	25,125	18,335	428
	6	1859 ..	39	84	38,800	22,877	15,923	399
		Total ..	337	76	292,139	182,970	109,169	..
V. Aruvaköd	1	1847 ..	29	29	25,000	19,317	5,683	194
	2	1848 ..	84	34	67,800	37,344	30,456	361
		Total ..	113	63	92,800	56,661	36,139	..
VI. Múlatmanna	1	1847 ..	34	63	30,000	24,492	5,508	159
	2	1848 ..	16	04	10,000	6,295	3,705	231
	3	1853 ..	20	89	18,700	13,187	5,513	274
		Total ..	71	56	58,700	43,974	14,726	..

D.—*Statement showing the Plantation blocks with their area and approximate number of trees per compartment and per acre*—continued.

Name of block.	Compartment.	Year of planting each compartment.	Area of each compartment. ACS.	C.	Total number planted in each compartment.	Total number thinned up to and for 1884-85.	Balance number standing in each compartment.	Number of trees standing per acre.
VII. Panangōd	1	1854 ..	92	33	85,200	51,080	34,120	369
	2	1855 ..	100	32	104,314	60,702	43,612	435
	3	1856 ..	79	26	93,000	49,619	43,381	546
	4	1863 ..	81	25	71,220	42,750	28,470	350
	5	1864 ..	40	57	36,320	21,871	14,449	356
		Total..	393	73	390,054	226,022	164,032	..
VIII. Āmarampalam	1	1861-68	87	44	88,000	31,407	56,593	647
	2	1873 ..	42	39	43,500	8,880	34,620	817
	3	1874 ..	69	03	73,000	..	73,000	1,058
	4	1875 ..	60	91	60,000	..	60,000	985.
	5	1876 ..	149	00	146,872	..	146,872	986
		Total..	408	77	411,372	40,287	371,085	..
IX. Valluvashēri	1	1864 ..	81	14	70,543	24,686	45,857	565
	2	1865 ..	56	63	55,133	24,252	30,881	545
	3	1866 ..	128	64	120,140	53,022	67,118	522
	4	1867 ..	118	63	103,000	59,791	43,209	364
	5	1868 ..	145	40	104,250	62,439	41,811	370
	6	1869 ..	53	56	52,000	17,044	34,956	..
		Total..	584	00	505,066	,241,234	263,832	..
X. Nellikutta	1	1870 ..	74	23	75,000	19,068	55,932	753
	2	1871 ..	46	00	59,460	13,424	46,036	1,001
		Total..	120	23	134,460	32,492	101,968	..
XI. Chātamborai	1	1872 ..	207	56	235,000	50,488	184,512	889
	2	1873 ..	99	08	85,361	26,474	58,887	594
	3	1874 ..	91	46	84,000	13,955	70,045	766
	4	1875 ..	100	00	65,000	..	65,000	650
		Total..	498	10	469,361	90,917	378,444	..
XII. Arimbrakutta	1	1843 ..	..	..	13,550	700	12,850	..
	2	1844 ..	..	..	8,539	500	8,039	..
		Total..	..	..	22,089	1,200	20,889	..
			61	68	..	..	..	375
Chāliyapuram Mangalashēri ..	3	1844 ..	..	..	3,850	1,591	2,259	..
Pozhayi Mangalashēri ..	4	1844 ..	..	..	20,050	2,039	18,011	..

E.—*Preliminary working scheme for thinning*

Series.	Edakód, Acres 693·63.		Elanjéri, &c., Acres 675·84.			Panangód, Acres 393·73.	
Year.	Compt. No. and Year.	Acreage.	—	Compt. No. and Year.	Acreage.	Compt. No. and Year.	Acreage.
1885-86 ..	(8) 1851	147·19	Āyiravillikāva ..	(2) 1844	27·35	(3) 1856	79·26
	(10) 1860	39·56	Aruvakōd ..	(2) 1848	84·34	..	..
			Mūlatmanna ..	(1) 1847	34·63	..	..
Total ..	..	186·75	..	..	146·32	..	79·26
1886-87 ..	(7) 1850	49·67	Aruvakōd ..	(1) 1847	29·29	(2) 1855	100·32
	(9) 1857	36·14	Āyiravillikāva ..	(1) 1842	30·93	..	..
	(2) 1845	28·14	Do. ..	(4) 1853	34·71	..	..
			Mūlatmanna ..	(2) 1848	16·04	..	..
Total ..	..	113·95	..	..	110·97	..	100·32
1887-88 ..	(4) 1847	54·61	Elanjēri	(1) 1845	33·19	(4) 1863	81·25
	(1) 1844	30·65	Do.	(2) 1846	65·84	..	..
			Ramalūr	(1) 1844 (2) 1850	21·33	..	..
			Mūlatmanna ..	(3) 1853	20·89	..	..
Total ..	..	85·26	..	..	141·25	..	81·25
1888-89 ..	(3) 1846	44·78	Elanjēri	(3) 1849	89·95	(1) 1854	92·33
	(5) 1848	82·15	Do.	(5) 1858	42·79	..	..
	(6) 1849	44·58					
Total ..	..	171·51	..	..	132·74	..	92·33
1889-90 ..	(11) 1861	86·05	Elanjēri	(6) 1859	39·84	(5) 1864	40·57
	(12) 1862	50·11	Do.	(4) 1850	66·15	..	..
			Āyiravillikāva ..	(3) 1852	38·57	..	..
Total ..	..	136·16	..	..	144·56	..	40·57
Grand Total ..	..	693·63	..	..	675·84	..	393·73

NOTE.—For convenience of arrangement, the whole plantations have been divided into six circles on blocks, and *Nellikutta* includes the Nellikutta, Āmarampalam, Mangalasheri and other small outlyime

NILAMBÚR,
22*nd March* 1887.

the Plantations during the next five years.

Valluvashéri, Acres 584·00.		Chatamborai, Acres 498·10.		Nellikutta, Acres 590·68.			Total.
Compt. No. and Year.	Acreage.	Compt. No. and Year.	Acreage.	—	Compt. No. and Year.	Acreage.	
(5) 1868 (a)	33·94	(1) 1872 (a)	100·00	Nellikutta ..	(1) 1870 ..	74·23	..
(b)	79·08	..	..		(2) 1871 ..	46·00	..
	..	..	..			..	..
..	113·02	..	100·00	..	..	120·23	745·58
(5) 1868 (c)	32·38	(1) 1872 (b)	107·56	Amarapālam ..	(3) 1874 ..	69·03	..
(4) 1867 (b)	77·32	..	..	Do. ..	(4) 1875 ..	60·91	..
..	..	..	..	..	..	..	..
..	..	..	..	..	..	..	..
..	109·70	..	107·56	..	..	129·94	672·44
(4) 1867 (a)	41·31	(2) 1873	99·08	Amarapālam ..	(1) 1861-68	87·44	..
(6) 1869 (a)	39·36	..	..	Do. ..	(2) 1873	42·39	..
(6) 1869 (b)	14·20	..	..	..	..	..	..
..	..	..	..	..	..	..	..
..	..	..	..	..	..	..	..
..	94·87	..	99·08	..	..	129·83	631·54
(3) 1866 (a)	32·30	(3) 1874	91·46	Mangalashēri, &c.	(1),(2),(3), &	61·68	..
(3) 1866 (b)	96·34	..	..	..	(4), 1843 &	..	..
..	..	..	..	..	1844	..	..
..	128·64	..	91·46	..	..	61·68	678·36
(1) 1864 ..	81·14	(4) 1875	100·00	Amarapālam ..	(5) 1876 ..	149·00	..
(2) 1865 ..	56·63	..	..	..	..	..	..
..	..	..	..	..	..	..	..
..	137·77	..	100·00	..	..	149·00	708·06
..	584·00	..	498·10	..	..	590·68	3,435·98

series, of which *Elanjēri* includes the Elanjēri, Āyiravillikāva, Aruvakōd, Mūlatmanna, and Rāmalūr blocks.

(Signed) G. HADFIELD,
District Forest Officer,
South Malabar.

WALLUVANĀD TALUK.

By P. Karunakara Menon.

Boundaries.—The Tālūk is bounded on the north by Ernād Tālūk and a portion of Nīlgiris district, on the east by Coimbatore district, on the south by Palghat Tālūk, Cochin State and Ponnāni Tālūk, and on the west by the Ponnāni and Ernād Tālūks.

Area.—According to the figures adopted for the census of 1881, the total area of the Tālūk is 963 square miles; 137,417 acres or about 214 square miles of which are under cultivation, and 273,454 acres cultivable, while 3,000 acres represent the extent of hills and forests, and other lands not cultivable.

Soil.—The soil is chiefly red loam, except where black alluvial clay is found in the valleys.

Topography.—The Tālūk extends along the foot of the Western Ghauts, many spurs of which run into it, *e.g.*, in the amsams of Tūvūr, Tiruvaḷamkunnu, Kōttopādam, Arakurushi, Tenkara, Kumaramputtūr, Kalladikkōd, &c. A part of the Arakurushi amsam lies east of the ghaut and is known as the Attappādi valley which contains the head waters of the Bhavāni river. The area of the valley is estimated at about 200 square miles. The whole of it as well as the spurs and slopes of the ghaut are covered with valuable timber and other trees, and abound in elephants, bison, tigers, sambur, &c. There are also several detached hills in the Tālūk, such as Pāṇakkōdan mala, the Avunhikkádan mala, the Chirattamanna mala, the *Anangan mala*,[1] &c. The whole Tālūk may be said to be one series of hills and dales, the latter being cultivable with paddy, while the borders of the former are covered with gardens containing jack, areca, and various other trees, in the midst of which stand the houses of the people. These hills are covered with scrub jungle or grass, and afford pasturage for cattle and thatching material for the houses of the poorer classes.[2] The principal rivers are the Ponnāni or Wālayār river which forms the southern boundary of the Tālūk, the Malappuram or Anakkayam river which forms the northern boundary and the Mannarghāt or Tūtha river, a tributary of the Ponnāni river. All these streams are perennial and are largely used for floating timber in rafts from the hills to the coast during the rainy season and are also passable for small boats for several miles except in the hot season.

The subjoined table gives the rainfall of the Tālūk for a series of years:—

---

[1] The origin of this word Anangan is interpreted in two ways—(1) picturesque (the sanscrit word Anangan being a synonym for cupid), (2) without limbs (the sanscrit word signifying അൻ = without, and അംഗം = limbs) meaning that the hill is one single elevation without arms.

[2] In the Nenmani hills experimental coffee cultivation is carried on.

Years (Faslis).	July.	August.	September.	October.	November.	December.	January.	February.	March.	April.	May.	June.	Total.
	IN.	IN.	IN.	IN.	IN.	IN.	IN.	IN.	IN.	IN.	IN.	IN.	IN.
1288 ..	22	29	27	22	3	1	..	..	3	1	20	11	139
1289 ..	26	15	6	12	9	..	..	..	..	2	9	27	106
1290 ..	19	6	2	4	8	..	..	..	..	..	2	4	45
1291 ..	22	17	4	6	5	..	..	..	..	4	12	32	102
1292 ..	45	14	9	17	11	1	..	..	5	3	6	27	138
1293 ..	31	16	4	11	11	3	..	..	..	2	3	17	98
1294 ..	21	18	12	13	7	..	..	..	1	..	10	45	127
1295 ..	33	18	5	25	3	4	..	..	..	3	10	16	117
Total ..	219	133	69	110	57	9	..	..	9	15	72	179	872
											Average per year ..		109

From all these it may easily be concluded that the climate is not very healthy, fever is present more or less throughout the year and is the chief prevailing disease. In the months of January, February and March generally a sort of malarious fever prevails throughout the taluk, sometimes, attended with serious results.

Population.—The total population, as per last census is 308,102 against 292,482 in 1871. Of this number 153,236 are males and 154,866 females. Hindus number 225,075, Muhammadans 82,883, Christians 142 and "Others" 2. The average population per square mile is 320, but in reality it is far greater, inasmuch as Attappādi valley in Arakurushi amsam and the portion of the Tālūk along the foot of the ghauts is very thinly peopled; while a great part of the Tālūk is not at all inhabited.

The total number of houses in 1881 was 57,220, of which 52,644 were occupied and 4,576 unoccupied. There were 55 occupied and 5 unoccupied houses in every square mile, and on an average 5·9 persons in every occupied house. As elsewhere in the district, all houses stand in detached "compounds," except in the case of towns and bazaars, where they are built in the form of streets. The bulk of the people are occupied in cultivating the soil.

Particulars of Occupation.	Males.	Females.	Total.
Professional	4,319	553	4,872
Domestic	536	691	1,227
Commercial	3,065	708	3,773
Agricultural	62,958	20,785	83,743
Industrial	23,564	18,363	41,927
Indefinite and non-productive	58,794	113,767	172,561
Total ..	153,236	154,867	208,103

The figures in the above table against "agricultural" shows the largest number as compared with the other Tālūks of the district.

The language spoken is Malayāḷam, except in the case of foreigners. In the Attappādi valley, however, the inhabitants, who are quite ignorant and without any education, speak a form of Canarese.

Administrative Divisions.—For purposes of administration the Tālūk is divided into 64 amsams, each having an Adhikāri who collects the tax and is also Village Magistrate and Munsif, and who has under him an accountant (menon) and a couple of peons, except in one instance (Arakurushi amsam) in which the number of peons is four. There is of course a Tahsildar with the powers of a Magistrate of the 2nd class, whose head-quarters are at Perintalmanna and who is assisted in his revenue work by a Deputy Tahsildar stationed at Cheruplassēri and usually invested with 2nd-class magisterial powers.

Cultivation, &c.—The staple produce is rice, though areca, jack, and plantains are also grown largely and coconuts on a small scale. The areas under the several crops are returned as follow:—

	ACRES.
Nanja	78,815
Gardens	23,116
Punja	35,486

"Punja" represents upland cultivation, such as mōdan, punam, gingelly, &c. The areas under each crop vary considerably from year to year, according to the nature of the season and other circumstances.

Particulars of Revenue.—The subjoined statement shows the Revenue of the Tālūk from various sources for a series of years:—

Particulars.	Fasli 1288.			1289.			1290.			1291.		
	RS.	A.	P.	RS.	A.	P.	RS.	A.	P.	RS.	A.	P.
1. Land Revenue ..	2,43,480	4	8	2,41,095	1	11	2,43,119	14	2	2,43,058	5	0
2. Service Fund ..	20,768	1	10	20,777	2	2	20,781	4	2	20,787	7	4
3. Local Fund ..	30,743	8	1	30,440	1	6	30,748	0	8	37,480	11	11
4. Abkari	13,140	0	0	13,104	15	7	7,087	8	0	8,475	12	0
5. Stamp	24,512	2	0	36,043	5	0	32,906	12	0	33,358	14	0
6. License Tax ..	4,232	8	0	566	8	9	1,795	0	0	1,660	0	0
7. Miscellaneous ..	24,116	8	4	64,807	10	3	57,487	1	1	1,17,381	5	6
8. Special Fund ..	10,098	0	1	7,789	0	0	6,809	0	0	3,502	12	6

Particulars.	1292.			1293.			1294.			1295.		
	RS.	A.	P.	RS.	A.	P.	RS.	A.	P.	RS.	A	P.
1. Land Revenue ..	2,43,054	1	7	2,45,715	8	7	2,44,190	1	7	2,45,064	4	4
2. Service Fund ..	20,788	0	0	20,801	14	8	20,807	0	3	20,807	10	8
3. Local Fund ..	30,841	8	11	31,151	12	1	30,990	13	1	30,995	10	11
4. Abkari	11,712	8	0	11,943	10	5	8,300	0	0	10,770	0	0
5. Stamp	30,507	10	0	29,632	3	0	35,047	9	0	36,879	8	0
6. License Tax ..	1,575	0	0	2,040	0	0	1,950	0	0	2,095	0	0
7. Miscellaneous ..	51,739	14	1	52,585	10	3	51,331	5	5	50,314	2	9
8. Special Fund ..	5,939	0	0	8,060	0	0	11,209	8	1	10,932	0	8

Roads.—The Tālūk is intersected by 17 main roads:—

The most important of these is road No. 7 from Palghaut (*viâ* Parli) Pattāmbi, &c., to Ponnāni, which enters the Tālūk at the south-eastern corner and traverses its whole length along the southern boundary, a distance of 24 miles. Next in order comes road No. 6 from Calicut to Palghaut *viâ* Kondōtti and Malapuram; the total length of it in this Tālūk is 39 miles.

The Madras Railway passes through the Tālūk nearly parallel to road No. 7. Pattāmbi, Shorannur, Ottappālam and Lakkidi are Railway stations in the Tālūk. Pattāmbi is the nearest station to the head-quarters of the Tālūk from which it is distant 14 miles. The Deputy Tahsildar's station (Cheruplasseri) is about 13 and about 12 miles respectively by road from Pattāmbi and Ottappālam, while Shorannur and Lakkidi are farther off.

The subjoined list gives information regarding the principal festivals in the Tālūk :—

No.	Name of festival.	Probable No. of persons attending.	Duration.	Locality.
	Hindus.		DAYS.	
1	Tirumāndha Kunnath Pūram ..	8,000	15	Angādipuram.
2	Cheruplassēri Utsavam	2,000	8	Cheruplasseri.
3	Mulayankāvil Baghavati temple Kūtu Pūram	2,000	45	Kulukalūr.
4	Muthassiarkāvil Tālappoli	1,000	23	....
5	Mundakōt Kurusi Cheriya Mulankutkāvil Kūtu Pūram ..	1,000	23	Mundakōt Kurusi.
6	Mullanhūr Kāvil Bharni Vēla ..	1,000	1	Mulanhūr.
7	Tinakatūrkāvil Tālappoli Pūram.	2,500	2	Do.
8	Ariankovil Kūttū Pūram	3,000	21	Kunattara.
9	Srikurumbakāvil Uchcharal Vēla	1,500	1	Kulappalli.
10	Mannārkatt Pūram	4,000	8	Arakurussi.
11	Pariānampatty do.	3,000	7	Mūtedath Madamba.
12	Panankumsikāvil do.	2,500	8	Chettallūr.
13	Karimpuzha Utsavam	1,000	7	Karimbuzha.
14	Tiruvallayanatt Baghavati do ..	1,000	7	Do.
15	Nalussiri Baghavatikāvil Pūram.	1,200	7	Ellampulāssēri.
16	Tiruvegapuram Sivarātri ..	2,000	14	Naduvattam.
17	Tūtakkal Pūram	2,000	25	Do.
18	Cherambatta Pūram	1,000	7	Chalavara.
	Mussulman.			
1	Vettattūr Kappil Nercha ..	2,500	8	Vettattūr.

The following statement gives the particulars of weekly fairs or markets held in the Tālūk :—

No.	Name of fair.	Amsam in which held.	Day of the week.	Distance from taluk head-quarters in miles.	No. of people assembling.	Principal articles brought for sale.
1	Mangata	Mangata ..	Sunday ..	6	100	Betel leaf and nuts, curry stuffs and sundry miscellaneous articles.
2	Kulattūr	Kulattūr ..	Friday ..	8	200	
3	Tiruvegapuram ..	Natuvattam ..	Monday ..	14	400	
4	Cherupulassēri ..	Cherupulassēri ..	Wednesday ..	10	500	

No.	Name of fair.	Amsam in which held.	Day of the week.	Distance from tāluk head-quarters in miles.	No. of people assembling.	Principal articles brought for sale.
5	Vaniamkulam ..	Kūnattara ..	Thursday ..	20	5,000	Betel leaf and nuts, curry stuffs and sundry miscellaneous articles and cattle, ginger (dried), &c.
6	Ottappālam ..	Chunangād ..	Saturday ..	21	400	Miscellaneous do.
7	Pattāmbi ..	Netrimangalam..	Tuesday ..	14	600	Do.
8	Pattirippala ..	Perūr	Sunday ..	30	500	Do.
9	Srikrishnapuram..	Srikrishnapuram..	Tuesday ..	16	200	Do.
10	Mannārkād ..	Arakurussi ..	Saturday ..	18	500	Do.
11	Alallūr	Arakparamba ..	Thursday ..	10	200	Do.
12	Angādipuram ..	Perintalmanna ..	Sunday ..	head-quarters.	1,500	Do. and iron, cloths, vegetables, oils, coconut, &c., &c.

Chief Towns or Villages.

Perintalmanna.—Chiefly inhabited by Māppiḷḷas is the head-quarters of the Tālūk. There is also a Munsif Court, Sub-Registrar's office, Post office and a school; six miles from Perintalmanna is Mankata, the seat of the Waḷḷuvanād Raja, who enjoys a Malikhāma of Rs. 13,400 from Government.

Angādipuram.—Has a beautiful temple called Tirumāndhān kunnu situated on the top of a hill. In the well-known Māppiḷḷa outrage of 1849, the insurgents occupied this temple and were shot in the vicinity. In memory of two privates of H.M.'s 94th Regiment who fell in the action, the Waḷḷuvanād Raja, the owner of the temple, has caused a tomb to be erected over their graves in the compound of the public bungalow. The tomb bears the inscription shown in the margin. The following tradition is told of the origin of this temple.

> Within this tomb rest the remains of James Hart and Thomas Blake, late privates in the Grenadier Company H. M.'s 94th Regiment. They fell in action on the 4th September 1849 while gallantly contesting with a band of fanatic Māppiḷḷas at a temple near Angadipuram, the property of Raja of Waḷḷuvanad who has caused this tomb to be erected in memory of the departed and as a small return for the services rendered him on that day by their surviving comrades of the Grenadiers.

The site of the temple was originally a forest. A female of the Cheruma caste while lopping the branches of a tree happened to sharpen her knife on a stone close by. Whereupon the stone began to bleed. This news was carried to one Kāttilāmittath Nambūdiri, who believing in the sanctity of the stone, cleared the jungle around, while another (Chenamkandath) Nambūdiri cleared the ground and a third, Pandalākkōtt Nambūdiri, erected a pandal over the stone and commenced to make pujas and eventually a temple was erected at the spot.

There is an important mosque also in the place known by the name of Puthanangadi Palli about 3 miles west of the Tālūk cutcheri. The mosque has an inscription in Arabic engraved on planks and set up in the walls explaining the benefits of erecting a mosque. This Palli consist of two separate buildings close to each other. Originally there was only a single building, but another was built close by subsequently for the following reasons given by tradition.

Karuvāyūr Mussad, the prime minister of the Walluvanād Raja, took oath to pull down the original mosque. On the other hand one Mūrikunnan Pokar Mūppan also took oath that he would take off the head of the Mussad if he were to pull down the mosque, and exhibit the same for public view on the spot as a sign of revenge (പൊന്തലകൂത്തൂ) and also that two mosques shall be erected in the place of one. The Mussad and Mūppan both accomplished their respective aims. Hence the presence of two mosques now in the same compound adjoining each other.

Mannārkātt.—This is a jungly place. Horns, honey and wax are obtained abundantly and cheap. This place took its importance as the centre of commerce in olden times. The different products of the Attappādi valley are brought down here and taken to various places.

Karimpozha.—This is the seat of the Eralppād or second Raja of the Zamorin family. The celebrated Hindu author, Thunchath Ezhuthassan, lived here. There are a number of families of Chettis who manufacture thin cloths of the patterns peculiar to natives (male and female) of Malabar and similar in kind, though inferior in quality, to those manufactured in Tinnevelly. The cloth is known by the name of "Karimpula Pávu."

Cherupulasseri.—There are the Deputy Tahsildar's office, Sub-registry office, a school and a Post office here. There is also a temple called "Ayyappan Kavu."

Vaniamkulam.—Has the most important fair in the district. Cattle, grains, nuts, fish (dried), cloths of various sorts and curry stuffs are obtainable at the fair. Elephants and horses are also brought here for sale at times.

Police.—The following is the list of Police stations in the taluk :—

Name of station.	Amsam in which situated.	Remarks.
1. Angātipuram ..	Perintalmanna	Head-quarters of the taluk.
2. Kulattūr	Kulattūr	8 miles from do.
3. Melattūr	Melattūr	10 do. do.
4. Alallūr	Arakparamba	12 do. do.
5. Mannārkatt ..	Arakurushi	18 do. do.
6. Cherupulassēri ..	Cherupulassēri	Head-quarters of the Deputy Tahsildar Magistrate.
7. Srikrishnapuram ..	Srikrishnapuram	8 miles from do.
8. Koppam	Vilayūr	7 do. do.
9. Pattāmbi	Nētirimangalam	10 do. do.
10. Cheruvannūr ..	Mundamuka	14 do. do.
11. Ottappālam ..	Chunangad	11 do. do.

Religious Institutions.—The following is the list of religious institutions in the Tālūk :—

Name of institution.			Amount of Inam grant from Govern-ment.	Amsam in which situated.
			RS. A. P.	
1. Tirumandhankunnu	temple	..	222 6 11	Angātipuram.
2. Andimahakālan	do.	..	9 0 0	Kalladipatta.
3. Kallaribhagavati	do.	..	5 8 0	Vilayūr.
4. Chunangad	do.	..	10 0 0	Chunangād.
5. Tekkekavil Gurutirāman	do.	..	2 0 0	Do.
6. Panamanna Sankaranārāyana	do.	..	17 0 0	Do.
7. Vēttekorumakan	do.	..	1 0 0	Srikrishnapuram.
8. Pariyānampatta Bhagavati	do.	..	6 8 0	Mutedath Madamb.
9. Kōdarmanna	do.	..	2 0 0	Srikrishnapuram.
10. Vēttekorumakan	do.	..	0 8 0	Eledath Madamb.
11. Parizhakatt	do.	..	0 8 0	Do.
12. Cherukēttpulam Siva	do.	..	1 8 0	Kūnattara.
	Total	..	277 14 11	
Sattram.				
1. Chunangātt sattram	..	..	516 2 8	Immovable property paying the revenue is granted.

Trigonometrical Survey Stations.

Name of G.T.S. stations.	Series.	Modern values.		Remarks.
		Latitude.	Longitude.	
		° ′ ″	° ′ ″	
1. Prānakōd H.S. ..	Modern.	10 58 46·65	76 20 01·31	In Chettallur amsam about 7 miles from head-quarters.
2. Anangamalei H.S.	Do.	10 49 10·90	76 25 49·66	In Chunangād amsam 16 miles from head-quarters.

List of Charitable Institutions in the Tālūk.

Name of institution.			No. of persons fed daily.	Amount of Inam grant, if any.
				RS. A. P.
1. Angādipuram	sattram	..	60	..
2. Pattāmbi	do.	..	15	..
3. Mannārkkātt	do.	..	15	..
4. Srikrishnapuram	do.	..	25	..
5. Karimpuzha	do.	..	50	..
6. Cherupulassēri	do.	..	35	..
7. Chunangad	do.	..	30	516 2 8
8. Ottappālam	do.	..	35	..
9. Andimahakalan	do.	..	20	..
10. Tūtakkal	do.	..	20	..

PALGHAT TALUK.

By P. Karunakara Menon.

Position.—This is the easternmost Taluk of the District and lies between 10° 25′ and 10° 55′ N. Lat. and between 76° 27′ and 76° 55′ E. Long. It formerly comprised the Taluks of Palghat and Temmalapuram which were amalgamated into one in 1861.

Boundaries.—*North*, Walluvanād Taluk; *east*, Coimbatore and Pollachi Taluks in the Coimbatore District and Cochin State; *south*, the Native State of Cochin; *west*, the Cochin State and Walluvanād Taluk.

Area.—The Taluk not having been yet fully surveyed the exact area is not known; but, for the purposes of the census of 1881, it was taken to be 613 square miles.

Soil—Topography.—The District not having been surveyed the true nature of the soil too is not known, but speaking in general terms it may be described as black loam. This Taluk is singularly diversified and interesting in its physical aspect, especially towards the hilly tracts along the Coimbatore and Cochin frontiers. The most striking feature in its configuration is the extensive gap historically known by the name of the "Palghat Gap," in the otherwise unbroken great range of the Western Ghauts, about 25 miles across and more than 6,000 feet lower than the hills on its north and south and lying on the meridian of 76° 45′ E. and between the parallels of 10° 33′ N. and 10° 52′ N. This remarkable opening with the lofty Nīlgiri Hills and the Ānamalas on either side, overtopping the ranges by several thousand feet, the numerous projecting off-shoots of the main chain separating the Taluk from the neighbouring Coimbatore District with their heavy forests, extensive ravines and jungles stretching westwards the forest-clad uplands and the gradually succeeding flat rice fields fringed with high palmyra groves and the numerous mountain torrents and small rivers: all combined give an enchantment to the scenery. Almost all these extensive and valuable forests are private property, except the two Government forests known by the names of the "Chenat Nāyar" and the "Wālayār" Reserves. The former of these two reserve forests is a block of hill forest which originally formed portion of the Chenat Nāyar escheat, while the latter comprises the "Varalapadi" and "Pūlāmpāra" forests which were purchased by Government some years ago with the special object of supplying the Madras Railway Company with wood-fuel. The Chenat Nāyar and the private heavy forests in the Taluk, all contain more or less valuable trees, among others, teak and blackwood; while cardamom, honey, gum, &c., constitute the chief minor produce which is collected in the case of the private forests by the resident jungle tribes and generally bartered in the plains for the necessaries of life. The Government forests are under the charge of a Ranger stationed at Palghat, who is assisted in his work by 7 forest guards. Of the rivers intersecting the Taluk the most important are the Kalpāthi locally called the Nōḻanadi) the Kannādi and the Kollangōd (locally designated the Gāyathrinadi) rivers. The first two rivers uniting near Parali take the name of the Ponnāni river or *Bhārathapuḻa* and the last, viz., the Kollangōd river joins the Ponnāni river a little farther on. The Kalpāthi river has its source at a place called Chentāmarakulam in the hills north of Wālayār where the stream forms the boundary between the Malabar and Coimbatore Districts, while the other two are said to rise in the Kollangōd bluff or the Malaya mountains being the north-western extremities of the Ānamalas.

Climate, Health and Meteorology.—During the dry season the climate is very hot, but during the rains it is pleasant and healthy. From November to February a strong east or land-wind blows almost incessantly through the Palghat Gap which makes the weather very trying. The water supply generally is satisfactory and the health of the people, as a rule, good. The prevailing diseases in the Taluk may be said to be small-pox and fever. The Wālayār and other forests are malarious. Cholera makes its appearance occasionally.

Population.—The census of 1881 revealed a total of 342,454 inhabitants distributed over 56 amsams and dwelling in 60,351 houses. Classified according to religion, there were 306,662 Hindus, 32,330 Muhammadans and 3,462 Christians. The density of the population was per square mile 559 per amsam 6,115 and per house 5·7. The number of houses returned as unoccupied was 12,234. Of the total population the number of males was 165,311 and of females 177,143. The percentage of increase in population, as compared with 1871, was in respect of males 3·82 and in that of females 6·31 or 5·09, of both sexes. The appended statement shows the classification of the people according to their various occupations :—

Professional	5,090
Domestic	1,526
Commercial	7,097
Agricultural	93,841
Industrial	51.477
Independent	183,423
Total ..	342,454

Sub-Divisions of the Taluk for Administrative Purposes.

Revenue and Magisterial.—The unit of administration is as elsewhere the amsam, of which there are 56 in the Taluk, each being under an Adhikāri assisted by a Menon and, except in one or two instances, by two peons. The Adhikāris exercise also, as elsewhere, civil powers in respect of petty suits for sums of money not exceeding Rs. 20 and criminal powers in respect of petty cases of theft and assault, arising in their respective amsams. The Tahsildar, assisted by a Deputy Tahsildar to whom are assigned certain specified amsams, has the general revenue charge of the Taluk. These two officers likewise exercise magisterial powers, the Deputy Tahsildar over the area constituting his division and the Tahsildar specially over the remaining portion of the Taluk. The former has his head-quarters at Ālathūr and the latter at Palghat. This Taluk with its adjoining Walluvanād Taluk, forms a separate revenue division designated the "Head Assistant's Division" placed under the charge of a Head Assistant Collector and Magistrate, whose head-quarters are at Palghat.

Judicial, Civil.—There are two Munsif's Courts in the Taluk located at Palghat and Ālathūr respectively, and also a Sub-Judge's Court which is stationed at the former place.

Registration.—For registration purposes the Taluk is divided into 4 sub-districts designated the Palghat, Ālathūr, Koduvāyūr and Mankara sub-districts, the Sub-Registrars' offices being located at Palghat, Ālathūr, Pudunagaram and Parali respectively. The Koduvāyūr Sub-Registrar exercises also magisterial powers in respect of nuisance cases arising within the Pudunagaram town.

Police.— For Police administration, the Taluk is divided into two divisions each placed under an Inspector whose head-quarters are at Palghat and Ālathūr respectively.

Railway Stations.—The Madras Railway enters the Taluk at Wālayār through the remarkable Palghat Gap of the Western Ghauts. Its length in the Taluk is about 30 miles. The stations are as follow :—

1. *Wālayār*—15½ miles east of Palghat.
2. *Congecode* —8½-miles do. do.
3. *Palghat.*—This place is specially noted for trade in timber which from the Mannārghāt forests, the Chenat Nāyar, Government Reserve and the adjoining private forests, is largely brought to the depôts belonging to Government and private merchants and then exported by rail to various parts of the other districts in the Presidency, and also to other places.
4. *Parali.*—5¾ miles west of Palghat. There is a Sub-Registrar's office and a distillery here, and about 3 miles from the place there is a Police station and also an estate, called the *Mankara Nāyar* estate under the Court of Wards, which was assumed charge of on 3rd December 1877.

IMPORTANT TOWNS AND VILLAGES.

Palghat—[Pāla + kādu, a jungle of pāla (*echites scholaris*) trees]—is the chief inland town in the District and a Municipality, and in respect of population stands next to the Calicut town in the district and 14th out of a total number of 227 towns as defined by the last census in the Madras Presidency. The business part of the town lies about 3 miles south of the Olavakod or Palghat Railway Station and this, with its suburbs comprising the Municipality, covers an area of more than 9 miles and includes portions of Koppam, Puthūr, Yākkara, Akathēthara, Kāvalpād, Vadakkunthara and Kannādi amṣams. According to the last census, the total population of the place, is 36,339 classified into 30,424 Hindus, 4,854 Muhammadans and 1,061 Christians. The male population returned is 17,673 and the female 18,666. The following statement compares houses, population and municipal revenue of the place during the 10 years previous to the last census :—

—	Houses.	Population.	Revenue.
1871	5,561	30,752	17,507
1881	6,081	36,339	15,725
Increase or decrease	520	5,587	1,782

On the whole the town has an interesting appearance. Next to the big bazaar (also called *Chathurangapetta*) referred to, the most busy division of the place is *Sultanpetta.* Through this passes the main thoroughfare, by the side or in the vicinity of which are situated the chief public buildings of the place, viz., the Municipal school, the District Munsif's Court, the Head Assistant Collector's dwelling house and his office, the Sub-Judge's Court, the Municipal and Post office, the Roman Catholic Church, the Municipal hospital with its beautifully laid out garden, and the Protestant Church. Here is also situated an old massive fort built of granite slabs and laterite pieces wherein are located the Taluk Cutcheri, the Sub-Registrar's office and the Police station. In-patients as well as out-patients are largely treated in the hospital referred to, the total number of beds available for in-patients being 16 ; 8 for males and 8 for females. There is also an Assistant Police Superintendent's office here. The trade is chiefly in tobacco, food-grains, particularly, the dry grains, oil of all sorts, and various kinds of cloths. Timber is largely exported by rail. The place is specially famous for trade in *Pullupāya* (grass mats), generally known by the name of *Palghat mats* and may also be said to be the centre of tobacco trade in the District. The Brahman community called *Pattars* almost all belong to this Taluk. There are no less than 19 separate settlements or grāmams of this community within the Municipal limits. They are as follow :—

1. Kalpāthi.
2. Paḻaya Kalpathi.
3. Chāthapuram.
4. Govindarājapuram.
5. Vaidyanādhapuram.
6. Komarapuram.
7. Lakshminārayanapuram.
8. Mukka.
9. Chokkanādhapuram.
10. Pūttamkurshi.
11. Sōkaripuram.
12. Rāmanādhapuram.
13. Tārakād.
14. Vatakkumthara.
15. Nūrni.
16. Nellisheri.
17. Thondikulam.
18. Pallipram.
19. Tirunilayi.

Of the numerous Hindu temples attached to these grāmams, the most important is the *Kalpāthi* Siva temple. A car festival, lasting for three days, is annually celebrated here in November, which gathers together a large crowd of people belonging not only to the various parts of this District but also to the neighbouring Cochin State and Coimbatore District. Besides this, there are also two places deserving notice, one within the municipal limits and the other in the neighbouring Elappalli amṣam, both of which are held in high estimation and largely resorted to by the people. The so-called holy places are respectively named *Mukkai* and *Rāmasara thirdham.* The former is the place where the three mountain streams called the Pālayār, Malayār and Wālayār unite and take the name of the Kalpāthi river; while the latter is popularly believed to have been created by Rama, the hero of Ramayana, at the instance of his brother Lakshmanan in the days of their temporary retirement to the jungles for the purpose of bathing in the Ganges water.

Ālathūr—[ālam+oor, meaning the city of ālam trees, (ആലം) *Dalbergia* used to make mortar], the head-quarters of the Deputy Tahsildar of Alathūr, is an important village situated in Kattusseri amsam about 13 miles from Palghat on the road from there to the Cochin frontier *viâ* Vadakkancheri. The place contains a District Munsif's Court, a Sub-Registrar's office, a Police station, a Post office and a Middle class school. There is also a small bazaar and a travellers' bungalow here. In the vicinity of the place lies the "Ālathūr" Hill or "Vēḷumalai," one of the Trigonometrical Survey stations in the District, it contains a somewhat large cave and a natural spring higher up, which is never dry. There is also a ruined Hindu temple here. It is popularly believed that the cave was formerly inhabited. The existence of portions of walls dividing the cave into compartments of hearths and a small mill, all seem to support this tradition. There is a mosque and a Roman Catholic Church here. They are tiled buildings and 140 and 107 feet in extent respectively. In the adjoining Vatakkēthara amṣam there is a Syrian Christian Church known by the name of the *Melarkōtt Palli*. This too is a tiled building about 210 feet in extent. The total population of the amṣam is 3,517, of whom no less than 2,883 are Hindus. Of the remainder, 556 are Muhammadans and the rest Christians.

Vadakkancheri—[vadakku + cheri, means the northern village that is on the northern side of the hill-ranges separating the Taluk from the adjoining Cochin State]—is one of the chief Muhammadan villages in the Taluk, situated in the amsam of the same name about 7 miles south-west of Ālathūr. The amṣam is hill-bound on its south and west. There is a travellers' bungalow and a Police station here. There is also a small bazaar which is chiefly inhabited by Muhammadans who have a mosque about 102 feet in extent. The building is tiled. The place contains also a small Roman Catholic church. This and the adjoining Kannanūr pāttōla amsam are noted for the manufacture of coarse cloths of various kinds. Trade in the minor produce of the hills and also in timber is largely carried on here. An important Hindu temple named "*Tirunara*" is situated in the vicinity. This is held to be of great antiquity, and the tank or spring popularly known by the name of *Brahmakundam* attached to the temple is held in great reverence by the people, believing it to be, as the name implies, a place where "Brahma" performed *yāgam* or sacrifice. A handful of earth taken from the bed of this sacred tank is believed to be essential to the performance of sacrifices by Nambūtiri Brahmans. The total population of the amsam is 11,496, classified into 9,141 Hindus, 1,611 Muhammadans and 744 Christians.

Kollangōd—is an important village in Padinhārathara amṣam, situated about 12 miles south of Palghat. Hindus are the predominating race in the amṣam, who represent 3,978 or 97 per cent. out of a total population of 4,104 ; of the remaining 125 are Muhammadans and 1 Christian. The place contains a Police station and a travellers' bungalow and was formerly noted as being the seat of a petty chieftain named the *Venganaṭṭ Nambidi*, who reigned in these parts of the Taluk before the administration of the district passed into British hands. The present representatives of this ancient family have their residence here. There is an important Hindu temple named the *Kachankurushi Temple* here, dedicated to Vishnu. It is 264 feet in length and 180 in breadth. The *Srikovil* and the *Nālambalam* are both tiled, and the *mandapam* and the surrounding wall of the *Srikovil* painted all over with figures representing the various incarnations of *Vishnu*. As a preliminary step to the performance of a *yāgam* or sacrifice by any Nambūtiri Brahman in the district, it is said that the intended sacrificer ought to come first to this temple and receive from the hands of the

Venganatt Nambidi, the moon-plant (*cynanchum acidum*) the black wood (*mimosa catechu*) and the skin of a black antelope all of which are required for the purpose. Six and three miles respectively from this temple on the hills (*Tenmala*), separating the Taluk from the neighbouring Cochin State, there are two natural springs called the *Govindathirdham* and the *Sīthakundu*. Both of these are held in veneration and resorted to by the people. The origin of the former sacred spring is popularly ascribed to *Devendra* while in respect of the latter the tradition current is that it was created by *Sīta*, wife of Rama, the hero of *Ramayana*, for the purpose of her bathing in *Ganga*, the water of the Ganges, during the time of their sojourn in those parts in the days of their retirement to the jungle for holy purposes.

Pudunagaram—[Pudu + nagaram, means new town]—is the most important and thickly inhabited Muhammadan village in the Taluk. It is situated in Koduvāyūr amsam about 6 miles south of Palghat. In respect of total population this amsam stands next to only the Palghat municipality while in that of Muhammadan population alone it ranks first in the Taluk. The total population is 14,030, classified as follows:—Hindus 8,855, Muhammadans 5,149 and Christians 26. The place contains a Police station and also a *Jamāth mosque* (Jama musjed). It is a tiled building 240 feet in length and 180 in breadth. The Koduvāyūr Sub-Registrar's office is located here. He is invested with magisterial powers to try petty cases of nuisance occurring in the village.

Pālathulli—is a village in the amṣam of the same name, situated about 8 miles south-east of Palghat. It is chiefly inhabited by Chettis. The place is one of the chief centres of cattle trade in the District. The cattle are exported from the adjoining Coimbatore District, especially from the Pollachi weekly market. The amṣam contains a total of 5,861 inhabitants, of whom 5,293 are Hindus, 561 Muhammadans and 7 Christians.

Hindu Temples.—The most important Hindu temples in the Taluk are—

1. *Kallēkkulam* alias *Ēmūr Bhagavathi temple.*—In Akathethara amsam. Dedicated to *Jaladurgha*. The roof of the Srikovil is covered with copper sheeting. The other portions are tiled. The temple is 132 × 114 feet in extent.
2. *Kalpāthi.*—In Puthur amsam. Dedicated to *Siva*. The Srikovil is covered with copper sheeting. The other buildings are tiled. The temple is 288 × 120 feet in extent.
3. *Madappallikāvu.*—In Yākkara amṣam. Dedicated to *Vanadurgha*. Tiled. 156 × 138 feet in extent.
4. *Kāchamkurussi.*—In Padinhārathara amṣam. Dedicated to *Vishnu*. Tiled. 264 × 180 feet in extent.
5. *Pallāvur* or *Tripallāvur.*—In Pallāvur amṣam. Dedicated to *Siva*. Tiled. 500 feet in extent.
6. *Tripālūr.*—In Vateketara amṣam. Dedicated to *Siva*. Tiled. 532 feet in extent.
7. *Kongād.*—In Kongād amṣam. Dedicated to *Bhagavathi*. Tiled. 192 × 150 feet in extent.
8. *Tirunaṛa.*—In Vadakkancheri amsam. Dedicated to *Siva* and *Vishnu*. Partly tiled and partly thatched. 250 feet in extent.

9. *Tiruvālathūr.*—In Tiruvālathūr amsam. Dedicated to *Durgha*. The Srikovil is covered with copper sheeting. The other buildings are tiled. 366 × 330 feet in extent.

10. *Kotamba.*—In Tiruvālathūr amsam. Dedicated to *Subramanyan*. Terraced roof. 132 × 126 feet in extent.

Fairs and Festivals.—Some of the most important festivals celebrated and the fairs held on such occasions in the Taluk are shown below :—

Names of fairs and festivals.	Month held.	No. of days lasting.	No. of persons attending.
1. Kalpāthi car festival	November.	3	
2. Tiruvalathūr utsavam	Nov. & Dec.	9	
3. Kotamba car festival	Jan. & Feb.	3	
4. Kongād puram festival	Mar. & April.	8	
5. Thachamkurushi utsavam	April & May.	10	
6. Kodavayūr car festival	Dec. & Jan.	2	
7. Pudukulangara kavu vela	Mar. & April.	1	About 7,000
8. Parakkatt kavu *alias* Kavasseri puram.	Do.	1	About 12,000
9. Tripalūr navarathri utsavam ..	Sept. & Oct.	9	

Travellers' Bungalows.—There are four travellers' bungalows in the Taluk which are named below :—

1. Palghat, 3 miles from the Olavakod Railway Station.
2. Ālathūr, 13 miles from Palghat.
3. Vadakkancheri, 20 miles from Palghat.
4. Kollangōd, 12 miles from Palghat.

Weekly Markets.—The trade of the Taluk is carried on by means of permanent markets in the Palghat town and a few other places and of weekly markets, the most important of which are as follow :—

1. Pālathulli in Pālathulli amsam held on Sundays.
2. Kongād in Kongād do. ,, Mondays.
3. Alathūr in Kattisseri do. ,, Wednesdays.
4. Vadakkancheri in Vaddakkancheri } ,, Thursdays.
5. Para .. .. }
6. Palghat .. .. ,, Fridays.

The chief articles of export are the various kinds of food grains, tobacco, Palghat mats and various kinds of coarse cloths manufactured in Vadakkancheri and certain other parts of the Taluk, while the chief articles of import are tobacco and various kinds of cloths, spices and cattle. The Pālathulli market may be said to be the chief centre of cattle trade in the District, while the Kongād market is also noted for the same.

Trigonometrical Survey Stations.—There are two Trigonometrical Survey stations in the taluk. They are—

Name.	Latitude.	Longitude.
1. *Kurachimala* S.	10° 47′ 10·15″	76° 39′ 29·61″
2. *Ālathūr* H. S.	10° 37′ 30·07″	76° 34′ 26·80″

PALGHAT FORESTS.

By Rhodes Morgan, Esq., District Forest Officer.

There are four tracts of forests which have been under the management of the Forest Department in the Palghat Range since 1883. The most important of these is the Chenat Nayar forest, which escheated in the early years of the century to Government. The area of this forest is 15,205 acres, of which 12,253 acres are forest, and the balance, 2,952 acres, grass land and sheet-rock. These forests are situated in a rocky range of hills connected with the Western Ghats, which rise to a height of 5,000 feet (Elival peak). On the lower slopes, *i.e.*, up to 1,000 feet elevation, the forests are deciduous, above that, evergreen. The principal trees in the lower zone of deciduous forest are teak (almost exterminated), rosewood, venghay, venteak, irul, &c. The evergreen forests contain white and red cedar, iynee, poonspar, ironwood, &c.

The lower slopes are very malarious, but the open grass lands higher up are above fever range.

There is a forest rest-house on Karimala, at an elevation of about 4,000 feet and another, at the base, near Dhoni. The forests are worked on the "Jardinage" or selection—felling system, the only one feasible in a forest where any felling of blocks might result in serious landslips, and would end in the ruin of the forest. There is very little soil on these hills, which are composed of solid gneiss.

A small quantity of timber is now removed annually, not exceeding 15,000 cubic feet, the forest having been very recklessly worked in former years, and the more valuable trees almost exterminated. This forest has been surveyed and demarcated with cairns of stones and posts.

The second forest is situated at Wālayār on the line of rail. The area of this forest is 3,017 acres, of which 2,600 acres is productive, the rest being barren rock. The forest has been divided into two blocks and ten compartments, and each compartment further sub-divided into sub-compartments. It is worked for fuel for the supply of the railway, and teak poles. The "coupes" are worked on a rotation of ten years, the produce being sold to contractors. A working scheme of this forest has been prepared. It is fenced in, and fire protected annually, and cattle are rigidly excluded. There is a special forest pound for stray cattle.

The remaining two forests are situated in the Walluvanād taluk. They are known as the Panakadan forest in the Tiruvalam dēsam and the Silent valley. The first of these is situated on a small rocky hill of about 1,000 acres in extent. The trees in it are deciduous and the growth average, the villagers in the neighbourhood having been in the habit of pollarding the trees for manure for their paddy fields. In 1883, this was put a stop to and a forest guard appointed to look after this forest, which is very isolated. There are a few small hills in the neighbourhood and a considerable tract on the slopes of the ghats, the ownership of which has not been determined yet. Panakadan hill is Reserved Land, and is under special fire protection. It is intended shortly to notify it as a reserved forest.

The Silent Valley is an enormous tract of mountain forest and grass land situated on the western slopes of the Khoondahs, and is most inaccessible. It is roughly supposed to cover an area of over 70 square miles.

The forest on it is all evergreen, and the principal trees the same as those usually found in such forests in Malabar, viz., poonspar, iynee, ironwood, red and white cedar, wild jack, &c. These forests yield cardamoms, dammer, rattans, &c. The timber is not worked on account of the inaccessible nature of the locality. This forest will shortly be notified for reservation.

PONNĀNI TALUK.

By P. Karunakara Menon.

Position and Boundaries.—This is the southernmost taluk of the district proper. It formerly comprised the three taluks of Betatnād, Kūtnād, and Chāvakkād, which were amalgamated into one in 1861. The boundaries are *north*, Ērnād taluk ; *east*, Waḷḷuvanād taluk and the native State of Cochin ; *south*, the native State of Cochin ; *west*, the Arabian sea.

Area.—The district not having been surveyed, the exact area is not known. The approximate area, according to the census of 1881, is 258,154 acres or nearly 404 square miles. The extreme length of the taluk from north to south along the coast is 64 miles, while its width ranges from 3 to 20 miles in different parts.

Soils and Topography.—The scenery in comparison with that of the two neighbouring taluks of Ērnād and Waḷḷuvanād, is flat and uninteresting, especially along the coast, while inland, low hills clothed sometimes with scrub jungle, but generally with grass and flat rice-fields interspersed with groves of coconut, areca-nut, jack and various other trees surrounding the dwelling houses of the inhabitants, constitute the principal varieties of the landscape. The soil along the coast is poor and sandy, the only redeeming feature being that this open sea-board is fringed with groves of coconut trees. There is no granite in these parts, but in the interior parts the formation seems to be gneissic, traversed by granite veins, which generally prevails in the two adjoining taluks referred to.

Inland Water Communication.—The most striking feature of the taluk is perhaps the series of lagoons or backwaters lying in a zigzag direction along the coast and affording, with the connecting artificial canals, an easy inland water communication. It extends southwards from the Tirūr Railway station to Ponnāni, Chāvakkād and Cochin and thence into the Cochin and Travancore States. The total length of this system of inland water navigation from the Tirūr Railway station to Cochin is 93 miles (of which 77 lie in the taluk) as detailed below : Tirūr to Ponnāni section 16 miles ; Ponnāni to Chāvakkād section 17 miles ; Chāvakkād to Cochin section 60 miles. The boats in general use both for cargo and for passengers are the common country (dug-out) boats and they are manned generally by two men and will hold from 5 to 20 persons. The maximum charge per mile for a boat is 2 annas, and the average speed attainable 2¼ miles an hour. Transit can be effected by day and by night. No cabin boats are available in the taluk. Now and then, one of them passes through it from Cochin to Tirūr. Its average speed is 5 miles an hour, the charge for a boat varying from 3 to 5 and more annas per mile according to size. Owing to want of sufficient water in some parts of the canals connecting the backwaters, the speed in the case of the country boats is diminished, while that in the case of large cabin boats is entirely obstructed during the hot season in certain parts of them. In addition to the aforesaid chain of backwaters, the taluk is intersected by the Ponnāni river and a few other minor streams. Timber from the Ānamalas and the Mannārghat forests is largely floated down the river during the rainy season to the timber depôts at Ponnāni, belonging to local merchants as well as to the Cochin sirkar, for export to foreign places. There are also two large shallow lakes in the taluk. One of them the "Viyyattil" lake is situated about 3 miles east of Ponnāni and the other familiarly known as the "Trichūr" lake is about the same distance east of Chētwāi and 8 miles from Chāvakkād. They are respectively connected with the backwaters communicating with the sea at Veliyangōd and Chētwāi. Protected by strong artificial dams from tidal influence the beds of both the lakes are to a considerable extent cultivated with paddy after the monsoon. The "Viyyattil" lake lies entirely in this taluk, while the greater portion of the "Trichur" lake belongs to the Cochin State. The average extent of such cultivation and the amount of the revenue derived in the former are acres 7,920 and Rs. 10,865, respectively, and in that of the portion of the latter belonging to this taluk, acres 2,292 and Rs. 2,960.

River.

Lakes.

Climate.—The climate along the coast, generally, is temperate more or less throughout the year, while in the interior parts adjoining the taluks of Ērnād and Waḷḷuvanād, it is very hot in the months of April and May.

Meteorology.—The subjoined statement shows the rainfall in the taluk in inches for eight years (1878-85):—

Year.	January.	February.	March.	April.	May.	June.	July.	August.	September.	October.	November.	December.	Total.
1878 ..	..	..	..	10	10	39	23	32	18	9	5	1	147
1879 ..	..	..	2	2	25	17	21	14	6	9	9	5	110
1880 ..	..	..	1	9	6	22	26	5	3	5	6	..	83
1881 ..	..	..	..	..	3	11	10	15	5	4	10	..	66
1882 ..	..	..	..	1	15	30	32	9	9	12	8	..	119
1883 ..	..	..	3	2	18	24	25	16	4	9	10	1	112
1884 ..	..	..	..	..	3	26	20	16	12	8	8	..	93
1885 ..	..	..	3	1	5	37	29	15	4	15	4	3	115
												Total ..	840
												Average ..	105

Health. Water-supply.

The health of the people, as a rule, is good. The water supply is also good, especially towards the interior parts, but it is unsatisfactory in the towns of Ponnāni and Tānūr.

Sanitation.

The conservancy of the chief towns is looked after by a staff consisting of 1 Sanitary Inspector, 1 maistry, 13 sweepers and 1 totti, paid from Local Funds. The Inspector, with his head-quarters at Ponnāni, supervises the work of the whole staff which is distributed as follows:—Ponnāni, 4 sweepers and 1 totti; Betatpudiyangādi, 3 sweepers; Tānūr, 1 maistry and 3 sweepers; the remaining 3 sweepers being attached respectively to the three fish curing yards situated at Ponnāni, Veliyangōd and Tānūr.

Population.—In the matter of population this taluk ranks first in the district. The total population (inclusive of the floating population) was, according to the census of 1881, 392,654, of whom 194,150 were males and 198,504 females. Classified according to race, Hindus predominated; next came the Muhammadans and lastly the Christians, the number returned under each class being 231,402, 146,868, and 14,363 respectively, or 59, 37, and 4 per cent. of the total population. The number of persons shown as belonging to other classes was 21.

Increase when compared with that returned by the census of 1871.

The percentage of increase in the population as compared with that returned by the previous census of 1871 was 4·77 in respect of males and 4·78 in that of females; the total increase in both the sexes being nearly 4·78. The average density of population to the square mile was nearly 972, and in this matter this taluk ranked second in the district, the first being Cochin. The proportion of males to females was in the ratio of 496·5 to 503·5 in every 1,000.

Houses.—There were 78,148 houses in all. Of these 70,625 were occupied and the remainder 7,523 unoccupied, the average number of persons per house amounted to about 5·6.

General Condition of the People.—The people generally are poor. There are a few rich and many indifferently off. The subjoined statement shows the number of persons following the various occupations as returned by the last census (1881):—

Classified according to occupation.

Professional	5,750
Domestic	1,306
Commercial	8,696
Agricultural	88,509
Industrial	65,652
Indefinite	222,741
Total ..	392,654

Incidence of the Imperial License Tax.—The incidence of the Imperial License Tax for the past official year 1885-86 was as follows:—

Trade Dealing, Industry.	No. of persons charged.	Amount of assessment.
Money lending	103	1,520
Cloth bazaar	6	90
In paddy	5	90
In coconuts	5	50
In coconut oil	5	50
In rice	2	20
In fish	2	20
In salt	2	20
In tobacco	2	20
In timber	2	20
Boat rent	1	10
Miscellaneous	3	30
Total ..	138	1,940

Sub-Divisions of the Taluk for Administrative Purposes.—For executive purposes this taluk is split up into 73 amsams. As elsewhere, the revenue work of each amsam is carried on by the Adhikāri assisted by the Menon and a couple of peons. The Adhikāries likewise exercise civil and criminal jurisdiction, their civil powers extending to suits for money not exceeding Rs. 20 in amount, and the criminal to petty cases of assault and theft arising in their respective amsams. The Tahsildar, whose head-quarters are at Ponnāni, has the general revenue charge of the taluk. He is assisted in his work by two Deputy Tahsildars stationed at Betatpudiyangādi and Kuttingal, to whom are assigned 21 and 28 amsams respectively.

Amsams.

General Revenue charge.

Over these amsams they also exercise criminal jurisdiction, while the Tahsildar has the special magisterial charge of the remaining portion of the taluk. The taluk forms a separate revenue charge, designated the "Southern Division" under a General Duty Deputy Collector exercising also magisterial powers who has his head-quarters at Ponnāni.

Agriculture.—The staple produce of the taluk is coconuts, though paddy is also largely cultivated. The subjoined statement gives the acreage under each head in fasli 1295 :—

Acreage under each head.

——		Government.	Inam.
		ACRES.	ACRES.
Wet Lands	Nanja	71,137	3,625
	Punja	13,782	21
Garden	.. .. ..	57,872	1,881
	Total ..	142,791	5,527

Thus the total area under cultivation is 148,318 or 232 square miles, or a little more than 57 per cent. of the total area of the taluk (taking it to be about 404 square miles)—the extent under garden being 40 per cent. of the total area under cultivation.

The following table shows the demand roll of assessment for the same fasli :—

Demand roll of assessment.

Amount of Patta.	No. of holdings.	Assessment.		
		RS.	A.	P.
Under Rupees 10 ..	31,076	82,263	8	2
Rs. 10 under Rs. 50 ..	5,240	1,07,195	10	7
Rs. 50 do. 100 ..	684	47,105	5	0
Rs. 100 do. 250 ..	316	45,461	14	2
Rs. 250 do. 500 ..	52	16,553	14	1
Rs. 500 and more ..	15	12,236	2	11
Total ..	37,383	3,10,816	6	11

Revenue.—The subjoined statement shows the revenue of the taluk derived from different sources for a series of the 8 Fasli years, 1288–95 :—

Year.	Land Revenue.	Local Fund.	Village Service Fund.	Abkari.	Stamp.	Special Fund.	License Tax.	Lan Rever Miscel ous
	RS. A. P.	RS. A. P.	RS. A. P.	RS. A. P.	RS. A. P.	RS. A. P.	RS. A. P.	RS.
1288 ...	3,06,549 15 8	40,382 5 6	19,729 12 9	7,540 8 0	59,344 0 0	278 5 6	3,577 0 0	7,926
1289 ...	3,08,525 5 0	40,100 14 3	19,470 15 7	7,177 4 0	91,537 0 0	248 9 6	1,250 0 0	2,637
1290 ...	3,08,042 5 0	40,016 3 11	19,367 12 11	8,045 9 4	88,868 5 0	232 4 0	1,940 0 0	2,677
1291 ...	3,09,254 6 4	40,165 15 2	19,445 4 2	5,513 14 8	86,396 7 0	357 14 6	1,730 0 0	4,184
1292 ...	3,09,195 11 9	40,219 6 8	19,459 10 9	7,492 0 0	81,146 9 0	300 12 8	1,645 0 0	3,386
1293 ...	3,09,240 5 7	40,229 1 3	19,353 2 10	8,900 0 0	86,431 3 0	324 13 6	1,910 0 0	5,204
1294 ...	3,10,543 3 7	40,384 12 8	19,466 5 1	8,100 0 0	95,909 6 0	399 3 0	1,955 0 0	4,802
1295 ...	3,10,816 6 11	40,372 1 4	19,472 4 11	10,350 0 0	1,02,142 0 0	339 4 6	1,940 0 0	4,532

Note.—The amount shown under the heads Abkari, Stamp, License Tax refers to official years.

IMPORTANT TOWNS OR VILLAGES WITH SHORT NOTICES OF TEMPLES, MOSQUES, CHURCHES, &C., SITUATED IN OR ABOUT SUCH PLACES.

Tānnūr—(a corrupted form of Thānniyūr or Thānni + ūr, meaning the village of Thānni trees, *Terminalia bellerica*, which are still very common here)—is a small town largely inhabited by Māppiḷḷas in Rayirimangalam amsam, situated about a mile west of the Tānnūr Railway station. The streets and the lanes are narrow and generally in a dirty state. It is a seaport, and contains a Travellers' bungalow, a Sea Customs office, a Police station, a Sub-Registrar's office, a Post office and a chattram or mussāfer-khāna, the last three being situated close to one another, a quarter of a mile west of the Railway station, while all the rest lie in different parts of the town. There are four mosques here, of which one is a jamāth mosque (*jama musjid*). It is a tiled building, 186 feet in length and 93 in breadth, having the gate or *gōpuram* covered with copper sheeting. In the same (Rayirimangalam) amsam, about two miles to the south of the town, there is a famous Hindu temple known by the name of *Kēlēswaram* or *Keraladhīswaram* temple dedicated to *Vishnu*. As its name (Kerala + adhiswaran, the governing deity of Keralam or Malabar) implies, it is one of the most ancient Hindu temples in the district. It is about 50 feet in length and 35 in breadth, the *Srīkōvil* or shrine and the *Vātilmadam* or hall being tiled, and the nālambalam or the four wings of the temple thatched. The total number of inhabitants in the amsam is 11,344, no less than 7,037 or 62 per cent. of whom are Muhammadans, while Hindus and Christians number 4,305 and 2 respectively. In the matter of population this amsam stands next to Ponnāni. In the adjoining Pariyapuram amsam, about 2 miles to the north of Tānnūr, there is another temple deserving notice. This is called the *Trikkayikkātt* temple. The deities worshipped here are, Siva, Bhagavati and Ayyappan. It is a tiled building and is about 33 feet in length and 28 in breadth. The figures of *Siva*, *Brahma*, *Vishnu* and *Narasimhamūrthi* are painted on the wall of the Srīkōvil and two sculptures, representing the figures of *Dowasthans* (or door-keepers), are placed in front of the Srīkōvil.

Bettatpudiyangadi.—[Bettat + Pudiya + Angadi, means the New Town in Vettam, which name was given to the place in former days, for, here was the seat of the Raja of Betatnād. This family became extinct and the estate escheated in 1793.] The head-quarters of the Bettatpudiyangādi Deputy Tahsildar, is a village in Talakkād amsam, situated about 3 miles from the Tirūr Railway station along the road from there to Ponnāni.

Muhammadans are the most numerous in the village, the Hindu and Muhammadan population being respectively 3,156 and 3,179, total 6,335. Besides the Deputy Tahsildar's head-quarters, the place contains a Sub-Registrar's office, a Police station and a chattram or mussāferkhāna (now used as a Travellers' bungalow). There is a Post office near the Railway station and a District Munsif's Court and a Local Fund second class middle school about two miles from there on the road to Ponnāni. There are two jamāth mosques (or *jama musjid*) and a minor mosque in the village, the most important of these being the *Pudiyangādi* jamāth mosque, situated in the vicinity of the Deputy Tahsildar's office. This is a grand building about 116 feet in length and 70 in breadth, the roof being tiled and the gōpuram (the main entrance) being covered with copper sheeting. A granite slab on one of the steps of the northern gate bears an inscription. The writing has not yet been read. At the *Vellamassēri* dēsam in the amsam there is a Hindu temple called the *Garudan Kāvu* chiefly dedicated to Garudan (Vishnu's Bird) and such dedications being rare, the temple is regarded with considerable reverence and is also largely resorted to by Hindu population for protection from any *surpapīda* (visitations of serpentine displeasure in the form it is believed of various diseases), the deity being believed according to Hindu purānas to be the natural enemy of serpents. In the adjoining Trikkandiyur amsam there is another ancient and famous temple called Trikkandiyur temple. It is dedicated to *Siva*, and is believed to have been founded by Parasu Rāma. This temple is about 95 feet square. The Srīkōvil is a tiled building, the *nālambalam* being only thatched. There is a big tank attached to the temple lying close to it.

Paronna—[a corrupted form of Paravannūr, so called as being the place of residence in former days of Paravanūr Panikkar, a dēsavāḻi]—is a small Māppilla village lying by the side of the sea in Pachattri amsam about 3 miles to the west of Bettatpudiyangādi. There is a jamāth mosque (*jama musjid*) here. This is a tiled building, 140 feet in length and 58 in breadth The total number of inhabitants in the amsam is 4,243, of whom 1,764 are Hindus, the remainder 2,479 being Muhammadans.

Kodakkal.—[Koda + kal or kallu, meaning umbrella-stone. The place seems probably to have been so called because of the existence of several umbrella-stones in the neighbourhood.] It is a Basel Mission station situated in Triprangōd amsam about 2 miles to the south-east of Bettatpudiyangādi. There is a church, a combined industrial and girls' school and a weaving establishment here. The total population of the amsam numbers 5,393, divided into 2,724 Hindus, 2,398 Muhammadans and 271 Christians. In the neighbourhood of this place are situated some of the most ancient Hindu temples in the district, viz., (1) the *Triprangōd Siva temple*; (2) the *Hanumān Kāvu*; (3) the *Tirunāvāyi Vishnu temple* and (4) the *Chamravattatt Ayyappan Kāvu.* Of these the first two are situated in Triprangōd amsam, while the last two lie in the neighbouring Ātavanād and Pallipuram amsams, respectively. All the temples are considered to be of great antiquity. (1) The Triprangōd (called in Sanscrit Sri + vara + crod) temple is dedicated to Siva and lies about 2 miles to the south of Bettatpudiyangādi. The *Srīkōvil* is a tiled building about 105 feet in length and 75 in breadth. The raised stone foundation of a pillar of the building consecrated to Krishna here bears a long inscription. The writing cannot be deciphered locally. The ceremony of *Sanghābhishēkam* (pouring water on the head of the idol by means of a conch shell, is supposed to be the most acceptable offering to the presiding deity (Siva), and this is performed largely by the people under the honest belief that thereby their life will be prolonged. (2) The *Hanumān Kāvu*, as its name indicates, is dedicated to Hanumān (the monkey chief, deified). The rareness, comparatively, of dedications of temples to this deity, seems to enhance the value of this temple in the estimation of the people. The *Srīkōvil* and the *mandapam* are small tiled buildings, the surrounding wall of the former all over containing paintings of the *dēvās* and of *vyālam*, and it has also two statues of *Dwasthanmār* (door-keepers), placed one on each side of the entrance. (3) *The Thirunāvāyi* (or Shri+naa+yogi+pūra·n) Siva temple seems to have been so called on account of its having been, it is believed, founded by the 9 famous saints. The temple is situated on the northern bank of the Ponnāni river on the road from Bettatpudiyangādi to Trittāla. The place was in former days noted as being the locality where the *Mahamakah Vela* or ceremony was celebrated every 12th year. During the 28 days the festival lasted, the throne of the Zamorin was declared vacant, when a selected number out of the followers of this potentate, and also of the Waḷḷuvanād Rajah, being the rival claimant for the throne (all being well trained for the purpose), fought[1] against each other for it in the interests of their respective masters. The ceremony is said to have been last performed in 1743. The Srīkōvil is a massive tiled building and has two big statues of *Dwasthanmar* as in the case of the Hanumān Kāvu, one on each side of the entrance into it. This place is further famous as containing an institution founded and amply endowed by the Zamorin, where Hindu theology is extensively taught to the Nambutiri Brahman students. This instruction is imparted in a spacious building, called the *Ōththanmar madham*, situated on the opposite side of the river, under the supervision of Tirunāvāyi Vādhyān, the Zamorin's hereditary family priest. Another point deserving notice in connection with this place is the existence of a small temple dedicated to *Brahma*, which is of very rare occurrence. (4) The Chamravattam Ayyappan kāvu, dedicated to *Ayyappan*, is situated on a small island near the Chamravattam ferry on the road from Tirūr to Ponnāni. The Srīkōvil is a small tiled building, but badly in want of repairs. This deity is supposed to possess a specially controlling power over rain, and people hence frequently make small offerings on behalf of this temple for rain when it is wanted and also to stop it when it is not required.

Kuttayi.—[Kutt+aḷi, meaning a junction and a bar, respectively.] It is said that there was here formerly a bar, where the backwaters lying along the coast from Tirūr and Ponnāni united and communicated with the sea. Hence the designation of the place as Kūttāyi. It is a large Muhammadan village, situated by the side of the sea in Mangalam amsam about 4 miles to the south-west of Bettatpudiyangādi. Of the inhabitants, Muhammadans are the most numerous numbering 3,186 out of a population of 5,069, the remainder, viz., 1,883 being Hindus. There is a famous jamāth mosque (or jama musjid) in the village which is a tiled building, being 105 feet in

[1] See pp. 162-69, Vol. I.

length and 48 in breadth. There is also a *Jāram* or mausoleum attached to it called the *Nechchikkāt Jāram*, so named on account of its being surrounded by *nechchi* bushes. It is not known whose remains lie buried here, but it is held in considerable reverence, and is largely resorted to by Muhammadans, especially on the occasion of the annual *Nercha* festival, when the approximate attendance of pilgrims is estimated to be no less than 2,000.

Ponnāni.—[The place is said to have been designated Ponnāni, which is a corrupted form of "Ponnaṇi" "Ponnaṇayam," meaning gold coin, as being the place where the gold coin, called the *Arabikāsu* was first circulated in these parts of the district by the Arab and Persian merchants who possessed the trade between India and the west before the discovery of the sea route to India round the Cape of Good Hope by the Portuguese.] This town, the divisional and taluk head-quarters, is large and populous, situated on the Ponnāni river at its entrance into the sea. It contains also, the Kūtnād District Munsif's Court, the Ponnāni Sub-Registrar's office, a combined Post and Telegraph office, a Local Fund third-class middle school and a hospital and dispensary.

The amsam of Ponnāni of which the town forms a part, contains 12,421 inhabitants, of whom no less than 86 per cent. are Māppiḷḷas. The spiritual head, called the *Makkadum* of the Muhammadan population throughout the district, resides here. There are 27 mosques in the town, of which one is a *jamāth mosque* (or jama musjid), deserving special notice as being also a place where Muhammadan theology is largely taught. The average daily attendance of students, belonging not only to all parts of the district but also to the native states of Cochin and Travancore and even South Canara, who receive instruction in the mosque, is about 400. The mosque is a spacious four-storeyed building, 90 feet in length and 60 in breadth, said to have been built in Hejira 925 (A.D. 1510), by Said-ud-din Makkadum, and stands close to the *jāram* or mausoleum, which contains his own and his successors' remains. Such of the students as attain proficiency in the Muhammadan religion here are called *Musaliyārs*, the Makkadum alone having the privilege to confer that title. This *jāram* is held in great reverence and largely resorted to by the Muhammadan population all over the district. Ponnāni is also a seaport. The principal articles of export are timber, bamboos, coconuts and coir, and the chief imports are salt and rice. Half a mile to the south of the bazaar there is a Travellers' bungalow, while a mile and a half to the east of the town there is a chattram or musāferkhāna. The hospital and dispensary is under the charge of a civil apothecary and has accommodation for 10 in-patients (6 males and 4 females).

About half a mile to the south-east of the town, at Trikkāvu in the adjoining Pallapram amsam, there is an ancient Hindu temple of considerable historical importance. It is dedicated to "*Durghā Bhagavati*," and is believed to have been founded by Parasu Rāma, the demi-god and hero, and made over by him to the Brahman colony at this place, being a sub-division of Sukapuram grāmam, one of his 64 colonies. Tippu is said to have plundered the temple during his invasion of the country, broken the idol into pieces, and used the Srīkōvil as his powder magazine while halting at this place. On the restoration of peace and order in the country, a few of the former owners of the temple who had taken refuge in Travancore on Tippu's approach, returned and discovering in the temple well the broken pieces of the original idol, repaired and repurified it; but later on, being unable to repair all the damages caused to the temple by Tippu, made it over to the Zamorin of Calicut, who seems to have carried out all the necessary repairs in M. E. 1037 (1861 A.D.). Within the precincts of this temple there is another Srīkōvil, consecrated to Vishnu. The history of its foundation is interesting. Tradition has it that in olden days, while a Chetti and a Muhammadan were sailing in their ship laden with merchandise, a violent storm occurred, that they being apprehensive of the loss of their lives, took vows to build a temple and a mosque respectively, in the event of their being able to land safely, and that they having so landed at this place, in fulfilment of their vows, founded this Vishnu temple and the present jamāth mosque in the town. The temple is 112 feet in length and 72 in breadth. Both the *Srīkōvil* and the *Nālambalam* of Dhurgā Bhagavati have tiled roofs. The temple has also a high double-storeyed and tiled gōpuram. There is a large public tank here about 400 feet in length and 300 in breadth. It was in a ruined state formerly, but has now laterite steps all round, these improvements having been carried out by Rāma Kini, a late Tahsildar of this taluk.

Edappal, five miles east of Ponnāni, is a large village situated in the amsam of the same name on the main road from Ponnāni to Palghat *viâ* Trittāla. It is chiefly inhabited by Māppiḷḷas. The total population of the amsam is 6,595. Of this, 4,874 are Hindus, and the remainder Muhammadans. In the neighbouring Vattamkulam amsam, there is an important Hindu temple called the *Sukapuram* [1] temple. It is believed to be of great antiquity and also to have been founded by the hero and demi-god *Parasu Rāma*. It is dedicated to *Dakshināmūrtti* or Siva, and is said originally to have been attached specially to the Nambūtiri Brāhmans of *Sukapuram*, which was one of the 64 *grāmams* or settlements founded by *Parasu Rāma*. Even to this day offerings are invariably made by the Nambūtiris belonging to this grāmam on occasions of marriage or other ceremonies among them, and none who have performed *yāgams* or sacrifices are recognized as such until they are registered at this pagoda. This registration takes place once in 12 years. The *Srīkōvil* or *Garbhagraham* (shrine) of the temple, is a massive laterite structure, 50 feet in length, 45 in breadth and 40 in height, the roof being covered with copper sheeting.

About 6 miles to the north-east of Edappal village and about the same distance in the same direction from the *Sukapuram* temple, there is another famous ancient Hindu temple. It is situated in Chekōd amsam. This also is believed to have been founded by the same hero and demi-god, *Parasu Rāma*, being specially attached to the Nambūtiri Brahman colony of *Panniyūr* [1] (another of the 64 settlements referred to). This temple is a small tiled building, the presiding deity being *Varāhamūrthi* (according to the Hindu purānas the 3rd incarnation of Vishnu). This is the chief temple of the Nambūtiris, designated the *Panniyūr Grāmakkār* of the present day. They are said not to possess the prerogative of studying the Vēdas, having, it is said, been deprived of the same owing to some of their ancestors in ancient days having placed a red hot vessel on the head of the idol of the

[1] Conf. pp. 119-20, Vol. I.

presiding deity of the temple. In front of the temple there are some granite sculptures and also a slab of the same material bearing an inscription in *Vattezhuthu* characters, some of which having now become indistinct, the writing has not been deciphered.

Trittāla.—It is a small village in Kodanād amsam, situated by the side of the Ponnāni river on the road from Ponnāni to Palghat about 17 miles to the east of Ponnāni. The total population of Kodanād amsam is 5,840, of whom 4,877 are Hindus and the remainder Muhammadans. There is a travellers' bungalow and a chattram or musāferkhāna here. It is also the station of a Sub-Registrar. A weekly market is held here. About four miles south of this place are the ruins of a mud fort, 200 yards in length and 176 in breadth. This fort appears to have been at one time the principal place in this tract of country for it has given a name—Kutnād—to the nâd lying south of the Ponnāṇi river, which prior to the reorganisation of Tālūks in 1861 formed the Kutnād Tāluk. About three miles to the north-east of these ruins and by the side of the road from Padinharangādi to Shoranōre, is a small building called *Kāttilmādam* or *Kaittalimādam*, built entirely of granite slabs, and in the form of a Hindu shrine. It is ten feet square and of the same height, having a round dome formed of a single slab. Tradition ascribes its construction to supernatural agency. One popularly received account is that it was intended as the second storey to a pagoda about 4 miles off in Netirimangalam amsam of Walluvanād tāluk on the other side of the river, and a comparison of the shape and size of the existing shrine at the pagoda with those of this curious structure certainly favors this theory.

There is another place in the neighbourhood of Trittāla deserving notice. It is called *Velliyāmkallu* and is situated about a mile down the river from there and on the opposite side of it. It is considered by Hindus as a sacred place as being the spot where the Nambūtiri Brahmin named the Meḻathūr *Akkithripad* is believed to have performed a number of *yāgams* or sacrifices and is hence largely resorted to by them for the performance of the anniversaries of their ancestors on Vāvu (new moon) days occurring in the Malayāḷam months of Tulām and Karkitagam.

Chālisseri is a small village and a bazaar situated on the borders of Kappūr and Kotachira amsams about 6 miles to the south of Trittāla. It is chiefly inhabited by Syrian Christians. This community has a small church here. The place is noted for trade in areca-nuts.

Veliyangōd is a village chiefly inhabited by Māppiḷḷas, situated in the amsam of the same name, about 4 miles to the south of Ponnāni. There is a Police station here and also a Sub-Registrar's office at Andathōd in the adjoining Ayrūr amsam. The total population of Veliyangōd amsam is 6,826, of whom the majority are Muhammadans, numbering 3,771, the remainder being Hindus.

Kōttapadi.—[Kōtta or fort and padi or gate. The place seems to have been so designated on account of its being situated close to the seat named the *Punnathur Kōtta* of one of the feudatory chieftains of the Zamorin in ancient days, known by the name of the Pūnathur Raja.] It is a small village about 3 miles to the north-east of Kūttingal. It is chiefly inhabited by Syrian Christians who have a church here. The place is noted for trade in coconut oil and the rearing of country pigs by the Christians. These animals are generally transported to the Nilgiri hills and other distant places for sale. The present representatives of the above-mentioned chieftain's family still reside here.

Kūttingal, the Chāvakkād Deputy Tahsildar's head-quarters, is a village in Pālayūr amsam lying by the side of the canal from Ponnāni to Cochin, about 17 miles to the south of the former place. The total population of the amsam is 6,296, of whom 3,482 are Hindus, 2,456 Muhammadans and the rest 308 Christians (Syrian). The village also contains a District Munsifs' Court, a Sub-Registrar's office, and a Post office. Half a mile north of the place there is a Local Fund 2nd-class middle school, and half a mile east of Kūttingal, there is a Syro-Roman Catholic church, called the *Pālayur church*, which is noted as being one of the seven original churches of Malabar. The congregation believe that St. Thomas the Apostle preached at the place, and it is noteworthy in connection with the suggestion made at p. 202 of Vol. I, that in immediate proximity to the existing modern church there is a mound with small debris strewn about it, which is still known as the site of the "Jews' church," and which was evidently occupied by a building of some kind in former times. The only relics of any age about the place now are some carved stones, including part of a Siva lingam stone and a wornout Vatteḷuttu inscription, the spoils of a Ṣiva shrine also in the neighbourhood. The modern church is a tiled building, 86 feet in length and 34 in breadth. It is under the See of the Patriarch of Babylon.

In the Pālayur and the adjoining Chavākkād amsams there are also two mosques called after the respective amsams. The former is about quarter of a mile to the east of Kūttingal, while the latter is about a mile to the west of it. They are tiled buildings, 40 and 50 feet in length and 21 and 15 in breadth, respectively. There is also a *jāram* or mausoleum in Pālayūr amsam of some importance containing the remains of one Hydros Kutti [1] who was, it is said, the Commissioner appointed by Hyder Ali, on his conquest of the district, to collect the revenue in these parts of the taluk, but who having subsequently espoused the cause of the people against his master's tyrannies, seems to have incurred that tyrant's displeasure and fallen in battle with the forces sent against him, on the spot where the building now stands. It is held in reverence, and is also resorted to by the Muhammadan population in these parts of the taluk.

Guruvāyūr.—[So designated after the famous temple of Kṛishna located there, which is believed to have been founded, as its name indicates, by *Guru* and *Vāyu*, being, according to the Hindu Purānas, the preceptor of the *Dēvas* and the god of wind, respectively.] It is an important Hindu village, situated in the amsam of the same name, about 2 miles to the north-east of Kuttingal. The amsam has a total population of 6,686 inhabitants, of whom Hindus are the most numerous, amounting to 4,946, the remainder being divided into 527 Muhammadans and 1,206 Christians. The residents about the Guruvāyūr temple are chiefly the higher classes of Hindus, viz., Brahmans and Nāyars. It is one of the most important Hindu temples in the district, and is held in great reverence, and also largely resorted to by the Hindu population (especially by the sick) throughout the district, as well as of the neighbouring native states of Cochin and Travancore. It is surrounded by a high laterite wall and has two lofty

---

[1] See Vol I. p. 667.

gōpurams or entrances, one in the east and the other in the west. On the granite door-frame of the western one there is an inscription which indicates that it was built in 922 M.E. by one Panikkavīttil Ittirāricha Menon Kāriyakkār. A granite slab in the front part of the eastern entrance, too, contains an inscription in Sanscrit verse as noted in the margin. Both the *srīkōvil* (shrine) and the *mandapam* have roofs covered with copper sheetings, while the *nālambalam* has tiled roofs. The temple flagstaff deserves special notice. It is 110 feet in height, having a bell metal covering throughout, save about 9 feet from the top, which has a gold covering. The surrounding wall of the shrine is elaborately painted all over, in illustration of the various adventures of Vishnu as recorded in the *Bhāgavathapurāna*.

ഭൂപാലൈർവ്വന്ദ്യമാനൈഃ കലിമലരഹി
തൈരാജ്ഞിതാൻ പുണ്യലോകാൻ ആരോഃ
ഢും നിഃശ്രേയസം നിജസുകൃതജിതാൻ മിച്ഛ
ന്സോപാനമാർഗ്ഗം തുംഗമൈരന്നതുരമ്യം ഗുരുപ
വനപുരേശാഗ്രതോ ഗോപുരാഗ്ര്യവ്യാജേനാ
ധ്യാത്മം ജാതേഗ്രേ ഛത്രമതിരകരൊമൈഷലാ
ചാരാന്നിധീശഃ

Chittātkara—is a small village chiefly inhabited by Syrian Christians, situated in Brahmakulam amsam about 4 miles to the south-east of Kuttingal. There is a small church belonging to this community here. The total population of the amsam is 4,179, of whom 2,256 are Hindus. Of the remainder, 1,582 are Christians and the rest Muhammadans. The chief articles of trade here, are coconut and coconut oil.

Ēnāmākkal—is anotber village mainly inhabited by Syrian Christians in Venkitanga amsam, about 8 miles to the south-east of Kuttingal and 4 in the same direction from Chittatkara. Here, there is an important ancient Syrio Roman Catholic church. It is a tiled building, about 93 feet in length and 35 in breadth. The total population of the amsam is 6,416, of whom 1,770 are Syrian Christians, the rest being divided into 3,686 Hindus and 960 Muhammadans. The chief articles of trade here, too, are coconut and coconut oil.

Valappād—is a village chiefly inhabited by Syrian Christians, situated in Pallipuram amsam about 17 miles to the south-west of Kuttingal. It contains a Police station and a Sub-Registrar's office. About a mile to the north of the place at Triprayār, in Nāttika amsam, there is a famous ancient Hindu temple. It lies by the side of the inland water communication to Cochin and belongs to the Cochin State. The presiding deity here is Srī Rāma. The temple is 342 feet square, and the roof of the shrine is covered with copper sheeting, the *nālambalam* being tiled. On a granite slab of the wall of the srīkōvil there is an inscription, but it is very difficult to decipher the writing. A granite slab by the side of the eastern entrance, also, bears an inscription in Malayāḷam. The total number of inhabitants in Pallippuram amsam is 4,563, of whom 3,513 are Hindus; of the remainder, 655 are Muhammadans and 395 Christians.

പഴമെഞ്ചെരിപനാടനായതും - തൃപ്രയാററ
മേശത്തും - പെരിങ്ങൊട്ടുമേശത്തും - ആരി
യപൊന്നിമേശത്തും ഊരാളരും കരാളരും
നെട്ടുംകൊണ്ടേവരും കടിമുരിഷാടതിരി.

Edathiruthi—is another Syrian Christian settlement situated in the amsam of the same name about 4 miles south of Valappād. The amsam has a population of 8,886 inhabitants, classified into 6,548 Hindus, 1,293 Muhammadans and 748 Syrian Christians. There is a small church belonging to Syrian Christians here.

Madilagam.—[The place is so called after the name of the temple, called the *Trikkanna* or Trikkata Madilagam temple, which existed there in ancient days and is believed to have been founded by Parasu Rāma for the use of Trikkannapuram grāmam, being one of the 64 Nambūtiri Brahman settlements founded by him. It is said that it was subsequently destroyed by the Dutch who had formerly a settlement at Chētwāi. Traces of the foundations of an old temple are still visible.] It is another Syrian Christian settlement in Pāppinivattam amsam. There is an ancient church belonging to this community here. The total number of inhabitants in the amsam is 5,739, of whom 3,610 are Hindus; of the rest, 1,737 Muhammadans and 392 Christians. The place contains also a mosque, and is situated about 9 miles south of Edathiruthi.

Police.—For purposes of Police administration, the taluk is divided between 3 Inspectors, who have their head-quarters at the Tahsildar's and Deputy Tahsildar's head-quarters respectively. There are 17 Police stations in all, distributed in the three divisions as follows:—

Ponnāni Division.

(1) Veliyangod: In Eramangalam amsam, 5 miles from Tahsildar's head-quarters.

(2) Ponnāni: In Ponnāni amsam, Tahsildar's head-quarters.

(3) Edappāl: In the amsam of the same name 6 miles from Tahsildar's head-quarters.

(4) Chiyyānūr: In Othalur amsam, 10 miles from Tahsildar's head-quarters.

(5) Padinhārangādi: In Kumaranallur amsam, 11 miles from Tahsildar's head-quarters.

(6) Kūtnād: In Kodnad amsam, 16 miles from Tahsildar's head-quarters.

Chāvakkād Division.

(1) Madilagam: In Pappinavattam amsam, 28 miles from Chāvakkād Deputy Tahsildar's head-quarters.

(2) Valappād: In Pallipuram amsam, 17 miles from Chāvakkād Deputy Tahsildar's head-quarters.

(3) Chāvakkād: In Pālayur amsam, Deputy Tahsildar's head-quarters.

(4) Vylathūr: In Vylathūr amsam, 4 miles from Deputy Tahsildar's head-quarters.

(5) Audathod: In Ayrūr amsam, 8 miles from Deputy Tahsildar's head-quarters.

Bettatpudiyangādi Division.

(1) Kūttayi: In Mangalam amsam, 4 miles from Bettatputiyangādi Deputy Tahsildar's head-quarters.

(2) Putiyangādi: In Talakkād amsam, Deputy Tahsildar's head-quarters.

(3) Tānūr: In Rayirimangalam amsam, 6 miles from Deputy Tahsildar's head-quarters.

(4) Kalpagancheri: In the amsam of the name, 6 miles from Deputy Tahsildar's head-quarters.

(5) Vatakkumpuram : In Kattiparutti amsam, 16 miles from Deputy Tahsildar's head-quarters.

(6) Kuttipuram : In Ātavanād amsam, 8 miles from Deputy Tahsildar's head-quarters.

Festivals and Fairs.—The chief annual festivals celebrated in the taluk are shown below. On these occasions fairs are also held ; the most important being the one held on the occasion of the Guruvāyūr Ēkādēsi festival, and for a week or so after it is over. The chief articles charging hands are lasting copper and bell metal vessels of various kinds :—

No.	Name of festival.	Number of days lasts.	In what month.		Approximate number of persons attending.
			Malayalam month.	English month.	
1	Guruvāyūr Ēkādēsi festival.	3 days ..	Vrischigam.	Nov.-Dec. ..	5,000
2	Guruvāyūr Ārāt utsavam.	8 „ ..	Kumbham.	Feb.-March ..	3,000
3	Triprayar Ārāt utsavam.	8 „ ..	Meenum ..	March-April..	2,000
4	Trittala Sivarātri festival.	1 day ..	Kumbham.	Feb.-March...	2,500
5	Trittala Ārāt utsavam ..	7 days ..	Dhanu ..	Dec.-January.	2,000
6	Triprangod Sivarātri utsavam.	1 day ..	Kumbham.	Feb.-March..	4,000
7	Tirunāvaya Ārāt utsavam.	7 days ..	Medam ..	Apl.-May ..	4,000
8	Tirunāvaya Karkataka Vāvu festival.	1 day ..	Karkatakam.	July-August.	5,000
9	Tirunāvaya Thula Vāvu festival.	1 „ ..	Thulam ..	Oct.-Nov. ..	5,000
10	Garudan Kāvu Mandala Vela.	5 Sundays.	1st Vrischigam to 10th Dhanu.	Nov.-Dec. ..	1,000 each day.
11	Trikandiyur Thula Vavu festival.	1 day ..	Thulam ..	Feb.-March..	2,000
12	Kelaswaram Ārāt utsavam.	7 days ..	Vrischigam.	Nov.-Dec. ..	1.000

List of Charitable Institutions in Ponnāni Taluk.

Amsam.	Name of Institution.	No. of persons fed annually at the institution.		Amount of Land Revenue granted as Inam from Government for the institution.	Amount of private donation.	
		Brahmins.	Travellers (Byragies).		In land.	In money
				RS. A. P.	RS.	RS.
Vettam Pallipram..	1. Chamravattam Sattram.	492	41	124 11 1	714	..
Trikkandiyūr ..	2. Vettakarumakan Kāvu Sattram.	36,000	3,600	1,399 14 2	3,100	..
Do.	3. Triprangōd Samūham.	10,125	..	235 2 1	2,000	..
Rāyirimangalam ..	4. Kēralādhiswarapuram Sattram.	.61,200	12,240	2,704 13 4	3,819	..
Talakkād	5. Vellikullangara Ayyappan Kāvu Sattram.	5,250	750	..	575	..
Pariyāpuram ..	6. Ganapathiyankāvu Sattram.	1,260	..	..	55	..

List of Charitable Institutions in Ponnāni Taluk—continued.

Amsam.	Name of Institution.	No. of persons fed annually at the institution. Brahmins.	Travellers (Byragies).	Amount of Land Revenue granted as Inam from Government for the institution.	Amount of private donation. In land.	In money.
				RS. A. P.	RS.	RS.
Nullasseri	7. Peringatt Uttu Sattram.	4,380	1,095	..	60	..
Guruvāyūr	8. Guruvāyūr Sattram ..	29,200	1,095	..	..	..
Do.	9. Tāmarayūr Sattram ..	4,380	..	..	300	..
Vylattūr	10. Alakkal Brahmarakshasan Sattram.	3,650	720	321 0 1	3,270	..
Nāttika	11. Triprayār Sattram.	27,375	3,650	..	..	3,878
Vādānappalli ..	12. Panayamkulangara Sattram of Ullanatt house.	7,300	3,650	..	5,602	..
Do.	13. Panayamkulangara Sattram of Manhallavil house.	2,920	365	..	1,000	..
Kayppamangalam ..	14. Māllikakkal Sattram ..	..	1,825	..	..	228
Ātavanad	15. Tirunāvhya Sattram ..	7,200	720	..	..	660
Unmattūr	16. Kurumhikāvu Sattram.	..	..	..	..	..
Do.	17. Parakulangara Sattram.	900	60	..	300	..
Do.	18. Kodalil Sattram ..	900	..	..	120	1,260
Kōdanād	19. Trittāla Sattram.	9,000	1,080	..	..	..
Parutur	20. Chembalangatt Samūham Kotikunni Sattram.	900	..	48 10 0	300	125
Irumbliam	21. Perashannūr Sattram ..	900	..	..	..	..
Ayirūr	22. Kāttupinath Vettekorumakan Sattram.	2,555	2,160	..	470	225
Iswaramangalam ..	23. Tirumalassiri Kottayil Chavati Sattram.	..	1,800	..	..	1,000
Trikkandiyūr ..	24. Kumaramanglam Subramaniya temple Sattram.	9,150	2,440	..	..	140
Kōktanad	25. Asuramahakalan temple Sattram.	720	..	..	..	..
	Total ..	225,757	37,291	4,834 2 9	21,585	7,516

List of Hindu Religious Institutions in Ponnāni Taluk in connection with which Government have remitted Land Revenue as Inam.

No.	Name of Institution.	Amount of Inam granted.	Date of grant.	Remarks.
		RS. A. P.		
1	Trikāvu Temple in Pallapram amsam.	334 1 0	..	Temples Nos. 3 & 4 originally belonged to the Bettat Rajah, but were afterwards made over to the Zamorin, when the Rajah's estate lapsed to Government.
2	Guruvāyūr temple in Guruvāyūr amsam.	1,428 9 0	..	
3	Triprangod temple in Triprangod amsam.	1,127 0 6	..	
4	Trikandiyūr temple in Trikandiyūr amsam.	2,292 13 0	..	

Weekly Markets.—The subjoined statement shows the weekly markets held in the taluk. There are nine such markets. The majority of the traders being Muhammadans, and Friday being a holy day with them, no markets are held on that day. In all the markets, salted fish seems to be the chief article of trade, while vegetables and other articles are also largely sold :—

Day held.	Where held.	Number of persons attending.
Sunday ..	Trittāla. Close to the travellers' bungalow	2,000
Monday ..	Madilagam. Half a mile south of the bungalow	2,000
Tuesday ..	Andathod. In the neighbourhood of the Veliyangod Police station.	1,000
	Valāncheni. In the vicinity of the Vatakkumbram Police station.	1,500
Wednesday	Kūttingal. Close to the Chāvakkād Deputy Tahsildar's office.	2,500
	Kalpagancheri. In the vicinity of the Police station there..	1,500
Thursday ..	Chalisheri. In the vicinity of the village of the same name.	1,500
Saturday ..	Valappād. Close to the Police station	1,800
	Kuttipurām. Close to the Police station	1,500

Travellers' Bungalows and Chattrams.—There are five travellers' bungalows and four chattrams or musāpherkhānas in the taluk as shown in the following statement :—

Name of bungalow and chattram.	Situation.
Travellers' Bungalows.	
Tanūr	A mile and a half to the west of the Tanūr Railway Station
Ponnāni	In the town of the same name.
Trittāla	By the side of the Ponnāni river at the village of the same name about 4 miles to the west of the Puttambi Railway Station on the road from Palghat to Ponnāni.
Chētwāi	Four miles south of Kūttingal by the side of the Chētwai river (or backwater) on the road from Ponnāni to Cochin.
Madilagam	By the side of the inland water communication referred. About 23 miles south of Chētwai.
Chattrams.	
Tanūr	Two furlongs west of the Tanūr Railway Station.
Bettatputiyangādi ..	Close to the Deputy Tahsildar's office of the place about 2½ miles south-west of the Tanūr Railway Station.
Ponnāni	A mile and a half east of Ponnāni by the side of the road from there to Palghat.
Trittala	Close to the travellers' bungalow.

G. Trigonometrical Survey Stations.—There is only one such station in the taluk. This is called the Kūtnad or Kurungūt hill station situated about a mile to the south of Trittāla in N. Lat. 10° 47′ 32·64″ and Long. 76° 08′ 36·50″. It is in good condition.

European Tombs and Burial Grounds.—There is only one isolated tomb and no European burial grounds exist in this taluk. The former is situated near Trittāla and is in fair condition. It bears the following inscription : "Here rest the remains of Henrietta, the beloved wife of Captain James Falconer, H.M.'s 74th Highlanders. She died at Trittāla on 24th February

1855, aged 35 years. This stone has been placed here by her bereaved husband as a small token of affection."

A tombstone recording the death of the first Dutch commandant of the Dutch fort at Chētwāi who died at that place in 1729 also exists, and has already been referred to in Vol. I., p. 351. The site of this grave is unknown.

Statement showing old tombs or Pandu Kulis existing in Ponnāni Taluk.

Pandu Kulis groups of stones.		Single stones:	
Amsam.	No.	Amsam.	No.
1. Nāgalassēri	1	1. Kappūr	1
2. Ozhūr	1	2. Kumaranelore	1
3. Klari	2	3. Tavanūr	4
4. Vadakumbram	18	4. Alancode	1
5. Mullasseri	3	5. Nāgalassēri	10
6. Annakara	1	6. Triprangōde	1
		7. Kanmanam	5
		8. Mēlmuri	10
		9. Olūr	1
		10. Klari	6
		11. Ponmundam	1
		12. Kattiparuthi	2
		13. Parutūr	1
Total ..	62	Total ..	44

COCHIN TALUK.

By C. Kunhi Kannan.

Cochin was formerly a small place on the bank of a river, but in the year 1341 A.D., certain changes took place in the large backwater between the sea and the Western Ghauts, and whether from cyclone winds, or earthquake, or other cause not now traceable, the island of Vypeen was formed —a circumstance commemorated by an era of its own known as Putuvaippu or Putuveppu, meaning "new deposit." The traditions of Cochin show that violent and uncertain changes have always been experienced in this neighbourhood in exceptional south-west mo nsoons. All along this portion of the coast important changes are quoted. Islands and lakes have been formed; towns and harbours have risen and had their day of prosperity, but have now so completely retired that, after the comparatively small interval of five centuries their former sites and names are not recognizable. Cochin itself was built in the tenth year after Vasco da Gama arrived on the coast, and its advantages being very apparent, the large colonies of white and black Jews and other important portions of the community quitted Cranganore, which from time immemorial had been the head-quarters of trade and the most convenient harbour north of Quilon.

Cochin, which lies between Lat. 9° 58′ 7″ N., Long. 76° 17′ E., is bounded on the *north* by the Native State of Cochin and by the backwater, on the *south* by the Cochin State, on the *east* by the river and the Cochin State, and on the *west* by the sea. In extent Cochin taluk, with its outlying pāṭṭams, is about 1½ square miles. The population of the town of Cochin in 1881 was 15,698 (8,374 males and 7,324 females) against 13,588 in 1871. The population of 1881 was classified as follows :—

Hindus	4,383
Muhammadans	2,942
Christians	8,360
Others	13
Total ..	15,698

of whom 1,262 were "under instruction," 3,240 "instructed," and 11,196 "illiterate, including not stated." In the census of 1881, there were 2,411 occupied and 467 unoccupied houses, giving an average of 6·5 persons per occupied house. The population of Cochin, with its outlying pāṭṭams, was 17,161 in the census of 1881.

The revenue of the Cochin taluk in fasli 1295 (1885-86) was Rs. 14,467.

The Municipal Act was introduced into Cochin in 1866. The receipts of the Municipality during the official year 1885-86 amounted to Rs. 20,479, whilst the charges were Rs. 18,914. The Municipal receipts were chiefly derived from rates on houses and lands, taxes on arts, taxes on vehicles and animals and carts, licenses, income from markets, fees, fines, &c.

The expenditure incurred was for public works, education, sanitation and medical service, supervision and management, and miscellaneous.

There are nine Christian churches in the town of Cochin, two Protestant, six Roman Catholic and one Syrian.

And there are two Hindu temples, Ammankōvil dedicated to Bhagavati and Janārdana Dēvaswam in Amarāvati, belonging to Chetties.

On 31st March 1886 there were 16 schools, middle, primary, aided and unaided, with an attendance of 996 pupils.

The town of Cochin is sub-divided into the following pāṭṭams :—

1. Kōṭṭa.
2. Koṭṭavādu.
3. Vernede garden or Jātika Vaḷappu.
4. Mackenzie Vaḷappu.
5. Tamaraparamba pāṭṭam.
6. Odattakal.
7. St. John pāṭṭam.
8. Tirumala Dēvaswam.
9. Vania Teruvu pāṭṭam.
10. Valiya Pattayatōdu pāṭṭam.
11. Choriya Pattayatōdu pāṭṭam.
12. Veliparamba pāṭṭam.
13. Chulikkal pāṭṭam.
14. Kalvetti.
15. Vypeen.

The outlying paṭṭams subject to Cochin with particulars of their population, &c., are noted below :—

Names.	No. of houses.	Population.		No. of churches.	Remarks.
		MALES.	FEMALES.		
1. Tumbōḷi paṭṭam ..	15	30	34	..	Near Alleppy, about 30 miles S. of Cochin.
2. Attaḷakkad do. ..	2	3	2	..	About 6 miles N. of No. 1.
3. Kaṭṭur do. ..	7	19	19	..	,, 12 ,, E. of No. 2.
4. Manakkōdatt do. ..	21	37	47	1	,, 8 ,, N. of No. 2.
5. Tekkēparampunkara do ..	4	13	10	..	Close to No. 6 in the south.
6. Antony Fernandez do ..	1	4	2	..	About 4 miles S. W. of No. 7.
7. Mundamvēli do. ..	54	119	155	1	About a mile E. of No. 8.
8. Domingo Fernandez Palakkal paṭṭam.	11	28	26	..	,, half a mile E. of Nos. 9 & 10.
9. Teiveppu do. ..	35	77	79	1	South of No. 11 and adjacent to it.
10. Santiyāva do. ..	40	90	94	2	Do. do.
11. St. Louis do. ..	5	15	17	..	About half a mile S. of No. 12.
12. Belicho Rodrigues do ..	1	2	3	..	,, 2 miles S. of No 13.
13. Duvadatt Louis do ..	47	116	120	1	South of Nos. 14 and 15, and contiguous to them.
14. Sondikkal Guvankūr Silva paṭṭam.	1	2	2	..	West of No. 15 and adjacent to it.
15. Hendrick Silva do. ..	42	101	108	..	About 3 miles south of Cochin.
16. Raman Turutta paṭṭam.	10	24	20	..	,, 3 ,, north-east.
17. Palliport hospital paramba.	7	28	21	..	,, 15 ,, north of Cochin.

The town of Cochin, which is situated on the southern side of the entrance of the most considerable river in Malabar, is a place of consequence as a naval depôt. The place was noted formerly for ship building and several ships were built here for merchants of Bombay, measuring from 600 to 1,000 tons. The land in the back of Cochin is all low. Facing Cochin to the north lies the island of Vypeen formed, as already noted, in A.D. 1341. The many old granite Dutch buildings give a picturesque appearance to the town.

Tradition asserts that St. Thomas, the apostle, extended his labours to Cochin in A.D. 52 leaving behind him the colony of Christians now called Nassarānis. It is further said that in the first year of the Christian era the Jews settled on the site of their present colony. Afterwards they established their head-quarters at Cranganore (Kodungallūr), where they remained until driven away in the sixteenth century by the Zamorin's Māppiḷḷas. From copper plates still extant it is put beyond doubt that the Jewish and Syrian churches were firmly established in Cochin State by the eighth and ninth centuries.

In 1530, St. Francis Xavier preached here and made many converts. In 1557, the society of Jesus published at Cochin the first book printed in India. In 1585 Cochin appears to have been visited by the English traveller, Ralph Fitch, who with a band of adventurers came by the way of Alleppo, Bagdad and the Persian Gulf to India.

In 1663 the town and fort were captured from the Portuguese by the Dutch, and the English retired to Ponnāni. The Dutch greatly improved the place and its trade, building substantial houses after the European fashion, and erecting quays, &c. In 1778, Adrian Van Moens completely altered the fort providing it with new ditches and building seven strong bastions.

In 1806 the English blew up the cathedral, destroying at the same time some of the quays, the best houses in the place and the fort. In 1814 Cochin was formally ceded to the English by treaty.

The Protestant church (formerly the principal chapel of the Franciscan monastery, which escaped the general destruction above referred to) is a plain massive building with a nave 142 feet long by 51 feet broad. Its exact age is uncertain ; but from inscriptions on the floor it certainly existed before 1546, and is therefore the oldest European church in India, except perhaps the Calicut church. It contains some curious old Portuguese and Dutch tombstones. The façade of the church was surmounted by an ornamental bronze cross and a weather-cock, 6 feet high, which could be perceived some 10 miles off at sea ; but in 1865 these were pulled down. The building occupied as the Deputy Collector's office was formerly the Roman Catholic convent.

The Custom house is situated on the boundary limits of British and native Cochin. The chief native quarters are Calvetti bazaar, peopled by Māppiḷḷas, and Amarāvati, inhabited by chettis and goldsmiths.

In 1796 a fiscal (Dutch Superintendent of Police, Justice of the Peace and Attorney-General in criminal cases), a criminal and civil court and a court of appeal were constituted at Cochin. The college for the guardianship of orphans and minors (a Dutch institution answering to the Court of Wards), a separate orphan-house, an hospital for lepers at Palliport, and a matrimonial college were also continued. In 1800, Cochin was placed under the Malabar Commissioners ; in 1801, the Cochin Commission was abolished and it was placed under the principal Collector of Malabar.

The establishment at Cochin was afterwards reduced to that of a Principal Sadr Āmin and Joint-Magistrate and of a Tahsildar-Magistrate. The hospital at Palliport, 15 miles north of Cochin, is still maintained.

The present officers of Cochin are a Deputy Collector with the powers of a 1st-class Magistrate and Sub-Judge, a Sheristadar-Magistrate with 2nd-class powers under the Deputy Collector, a Civil Surgeon, a Port officer, an Assistant Superintendent of Sea Customs, and an adhikāri with a menon and two peons. There are a Telegraph office, a Post office, a Police station, a jail, and also a travellers' bungalow maintained by the municipality.

The Cochin light-house is on a small mound which formed the bastion of the old fort to the south of the harbour. It is a white laterite column, on which a fixed white catadioptric fourth order light is exhibited 100 feet above the sea level and seen 15 miles off.

This new light-house is 800 yards to the south-west by west of the port flagstaff, where the old light used to be hoisted on the top of the cathedral tower. The best anchorage in the Cochin roads is from 5½ to 6½ fathoms soft ground, 2 to 2½ miles off shore.

The stream of tide is very strong and its times of change are very irregular, influenced by the evaporation from, or the fall of rain upon, the immense area of backwater, of which the Cochin river-mouth is the outlet. At the anchorage abreast the bar, the ebb sets west north-west, but the tendency of that tide is to the north-west; its racing over the sand-banks on the northern side of the river entrance always produces heavy breakers there, which a ship's boats should avoid. The bar at the river's mouth is a narrow strip of land having 13 feet on it at low water, but the rise and fall being only 3 feet at spring tides, pilots will only take in vessels drawing less than 14½ feet. The bar is marked by two buoys. The best channel does not always remain at the same spot. There is at times a surf on the bar occasioned by the strong ebb running out against the sea breezes when there is any swell outside.

The river inside is deep 7 to 9 fathoms. Repairs to sailing vessels are executed at Cochin.

The parade ground of Cochin occupies the heart of the town beyond the Protestant church. Near the church is the old Dutch cemetery, a small square spot enclosed within high walls. The new burial ground is a mile and half from the town.

There are several jetties erected on coconut piles along the bank of the river, and the number of Chinese fishing nets, especially in Vypeen, is surprising. There is an interesting Roman Catholic church in the island of Vypeen.

The malady most prominently brought under one's notice at Cochin is elephantiasis.

About a mile and a half from the fort, upon the island of Bolghatti, (Pōnhikarō) is the British Residency, a good type of a modern bungalow. The rooms, spacious and well furnished, open into a large and airy verandah, whence the view between the trees and over the wide sheets of water in all directions is most agreeable. The grounds are planted with a variety of trees, and covered with turf.

The Raja of Cochin has a palace at Mattānchēri near Cochin. It is used on State occasions. Immediately adjoining the palace is the synagogue of the Jews, which has a belfry at one end in which a rude clock, said to be more than 200 years old, regulates their time. The floor of the synagogue is paved with very neat porcelain tiles.

Three miles north-west of the town of Cochin is Nārakkal, which owes its importance to a mud bank, which stretches about 2½ miles seaward and is 4 miles long. Within this, vessels can run in the worst part of the south-west monsoon when all other ports on the coast are closed.

Two weekly English newspapers, the Western Star and the Cochin Argus, are published at Cochin, in addition to a Malayāḷam paper designated the Kēraḷa Mittram.

Roads, Canals, &c.—The roads in Cochin lie within the town which is connected with Mattānchōri, in native Cochin State, by a road running almost parallel to the river bank leading to Jews' town.

The Calvetti canal is about 6 miles long. Starting from Calvetti it joins the river up at Kallanchēri. Owing to silting, through navigation is possible only during monsoons.

The water supply of Cochin is bad and the supply of drinking water is brought by boats from Ālwāyi, 20 miles from Cochin.

Industry and Manufactures.—The industry of Cochin is now confined to the manufacture of coir-mats and cordage and of coconut oil. A peculiar kind of coir-screen, intertwined with cuscus, is largely exported.

Dams and Anicuts.—Extensive protective works were carried on at Cruz Milagre where an opening from the backwater into the sea threatened by diminishing the scour on the Cochin bar to impair the value of the harbour.

Archæology.—There are the ruins of an old church in the Municipal garden. In the backwater near the Master Attendant's jetty are to be seen fragments of stone-pillars, archways, &c.

The ruins of the foundation of the Portuguese fort, first built by Albuquerque are traceable along the sea face.

One of the elders of the Jewish synagogue has in his possession the original copper plate deed by which in the eighth century at latest (according to Dr. Burnell) the Jews obtained lands at Cranganore.

On the west side of the Deputy Collector's office at Cochin within the compound are to be seen two broken stones with inscriptions. Many slabs bearing inscriptions are utilized in the town for crossing the side drains into private houses.

Tangaṣṣēri and Anjengo are administratively subject to Cochin.

TANGAṢṢĒRI.

By C. Kunhi Kannan.

Tangaṣṣēri is situated in Lat. 8° 54′ N. and Long. 76° 38′ 15″ E., and is bounded on the *north* and *north-east* by the Travancore territory, and on the *west*, *south* and *south-east* by the sea. In extent it is only 96 acres. In 1871 its population was 1,562, whilst in 1881 it was 1,665 (784 males and 881 females). The inhabitants are almost exclusively Christians, there being 4 Hindus, 2 Muhammadans, 1,658 Christians and 1 other caste.

Tangaṣṣēri adjoins Quilon. It was a Portuguese possession from 1519 to 1661 when it was captured by the Dutch. The fort is built on a headland of laterite jutting into the sea. The length is about 2½ furlongs east and west, and the mean breadth 1 furlong. Portions of the old walls are still visible, as are also the ruins of an old Portuguese tower and belfry. The English Government came into possession of Tangaṣṣēri on the capture of Cochin in 1795. It has been leased to the Travancore Government for an annual rent of Rs. 2,447, which will be referred to hereafter.

In civil judicial matters the people are subject to the District Munsif's Court at Anjengo, which is again subordinate to the District Court of South Malabar. For criminal matters there is a resident Subordinate Magistrate under the immediate orders of the Deputy Magistrate of Cochin. The Sub-Magistrate also exercises the functions of a Sub-Registrar of Assurances.

A bank of hard ground called the Tangaṣṣēri reef extends 1½ miles to the south-west and 3 miles to the west of the Tangaṣṣēri point, and 6 miles along the coast to the northward. The bank should not be approached by vessels under 13 fathoms of water by day or 17 fathoms at night.

The origin of the word Tangaṣṣēri or Changacherry is involved in doubt. Changacherry was the former ruler of Kollam (Quilon), who was dispossessed in 1740 by Travancore. The place might have taken its name from this ruler; "Changa" means conch and the name might imply conch-village. It is also conjectured that the name Tangaṣṣēri or gold village (tangam=gold) owes its origin to the circumstance of a large quantity of gold coins having been put in circulation by the Portuguese who settled there at first and who exchanged them for the goods purchased by them.

Tangaṣṣēri is level, crowded with houses, and very thickly planted with coconut, bread-fruit and other trees. There is no room for the cultivation of paddy or other grains.

Religious Institutions.—There are two sections of Roman Catholics at Tangaṣṣēri, the one owing allegiance to the Goa Mission, and the other to the Propaganda Mission of Verapoly. The church of the latter is very old, having been built, it is said, in 1789. It is 96 feet long by 36 feet broad.

The Propaganda Mission has since 1840 started an English and Vernacular boys' school. A convent was added to the church in 1845 and a girls' school was opened in 1885. Within the church at the foot of the altar lies a tombstone with an epitaph over the grave of the first Vicar Apostolic Bishop.

The church under the Goa Mission was founded in 1841 by the Archbishop elect of Cranganore, Don Manual De Sam Joquim Neves. It was, it appears, originally intended as a chapel for his burial, and built in a garden of his own. He died in 1849, and his body was interred in the centre of the church which is marked by a tombstone bearing an epitaph. This church is now being enlarged. It is 122 feet by 52 feet.

There are two cemeteries in Tangaṣṣēri enclosed within walls. They are separated by the road leading to the flagstaff. One of them is a Protestant graveyard, which is looked after by a gardener on Rs. 5 per mensem.

Tangaṣṣēri is, as already observed, leased to the Travancore State for Rs. 2,447 per annum. The conditions of the lease are the following:—

That "all rents, customs, or jenkums, profits and produce, accruing from the said rented premises of all denominations, whatsoever, are hereby declared to become the sole property of the Travancore Sirkar during the full and entire period of three years.

"That the inhabitants, residing within the limits of the said village of Tangaṣṣēri, of all castes and descriptions, whatsoever, shall continue to be under the protection of the British Government in all cases of a civil or Police nature.

"That with the exception of the introduction of the monopoly of the sales of tobacco and spirits, the Travancore Sirkar or its Agents are prohibited from imposing new taxes, levying unusual duties or arbitrary exactions of any kind on the inhabitants of Tangaṣṣēri, and that an attempt to do so by the Travancore Sirkar, will forfeit all claim to a continuance of the Farm.

"The Police establishment at Tangaṣṣēri are to afford every aid and support to the servants of the Farm in the detection of frauds or attempts to introduce into Tangaṣṣēri any of the articles under Government monopoly.

"The Police will give all aid in securing peaceable execution of revenue processes as far as required and authorized by law so to do."

The lease was last renewed for three years on 10th July 1883.

ANJENGO.

By C. Kunhi Kannan.

Anjengo[1] lies between Lat. 8° 40′ N., Long. 76° 47′ 50″ E. It is bounded on the *north* and *south* by the Travancore State, on the *east* by the Anjengo backwater, and on the *west* by the Arabian sea.

It is only 211 acres in extent. Its population in 1871 was 2,410, whilst in 1881 it was 2,534 (1,240 males and 1,294 females) classified as follows:—

Hindus	1,054
Muhammadans	165
Christians	1,315

Of this number 167 were returned as "under instruction," 216 "instructed," and 2,151 "illiterate, including not stated." In 1871 there were 436 houses, whilst in 1881 there were 517 houses, of which 70 were unoccupied.

Anjengo is divided into two dēsams—the Kōṭṭadilli farm called in Malayāḷam Kodutala, and Vādikkakam or Anjengo proper, including Pūttura.

Kōṭṭadilli is farmed to the Travancore Government for a sum of Rs. 1,450 per annum. The terms of the lease will be adverted to hereafter.

There is a Subordinate Magistrate at Anjengo who has his office in Vādikkakam or Anjengo proper. He exercises magisterial, civil, revenue, and registration powers. He has a small establishment. He is immediately subordinate to the Deputy Collector of Cochin. In civil matters, Tangaṣṣēri is subject to Anjengo.

There is an old European cemetery looked after by a gardener on a salary of Rs. 5 per mensem. It is enclosed within walls. There was a hospital in Anjengo which was abolished in 1880.

Vādikkakam and Pūttura are free from land-tax and duties of customs.

Physical Aspects.—Anjengo has a level surface. The soil is sandy and congenial to coconut trees with which it is planted up. There is very little of paddy cultivation and the outturn is poor. The water supply for drinking is indifferent and scarce.

Churches and Temples.—There are two Roman Catholic churches and two small Hindu temples. One of the churches, St. Peter's, is an ancient one, having very old paintings. It is 115 by 36 feet. It is under the jurisdiction of the Archbishop of Goa; but when there were disputes between the Propagandists and Pedroists, some of the Christians seceded from the latter party and built a small church 42 by 20 feet, dedicated to St. Philomena. In 1850, a reconciliation took place between the two antagonistic sections who submitted themselves to the jurisdiction of the Vicar Apostolic of Quilon.

Of the two temples one Sivan kōvil belongs to the Īḻuvars, in which Siva is worshipped, the other Amman kōvil belongs to Veḷḷāḷas and is dedicated to Sakti. Festivals are celebrated here in Kumbham (February-March) and Mīnam (March-April).

The Fort of Anjengo.—The fort of Anjengo is in Vādikkakam or Anjengo proper. Like Tellicherry it was of use to protect the Hon'ble E. I. Com-

[1] The name is said to be derived from Anchutenga or five coconut trees. The origin of the word continues to be a matter of speculation.

pany's trade at their factory established here in the end of the 17th century. And from this place was spread the English influence on native affairs in Travancore and Cochin, which has already in Volume I been fully described. The fort is 86 yards square. It was built in 1695, the East India Company having obtained permission from the Rāni of Attingal, a village 10 miles north-east of Anjengo, to occupy the site in 1684. A portion of the lower mast of the old flagstaff still stands on the north-western angle of the fort. The fort is now quite deserted.

Though the defects of the situation were from the first apparent, it was hoped that the facilities afforded for the collection of pepper, coir, and calico would compensate for the disadvantages. During the wars of the Carnatic, Anjengo was found of use as a depôt for military stores and as the point from which the first news of outward-bound ships reached Madras. The anchorage off Anjengo under 10 fathams is foul rocky ground, and outside of that depth the bottom is sand and shells. Ships cannot therefore anchor under 10 or 11 fathoms, and the prevalence of considerable surf on the coast particularly to the southward, renders it unsafe for ships' boats to land. In 1792 Anjengo was reported to be in hopeless decline. In 1809 during the hostilities with Travancore its roadstead was blockaded, and in the following year the post of Commercial Resident was abolished and the station made subordinate to the Political Resident at Trivandrum. Robert Orme, the historian, was born here in 1728. He was the son of a physician attached to the Anjengo factory who became afterwards chief of the factory; and here lived Eliza Draper, to whom some of Sternes' letters were addressed.

It has already been stated that Vādikkakam or Anjengo proper was acquired from the Rāni of Attingal. Kōṭṭadilli was ceded to the English on 10th January 1731 under the following circumstances:—

When hostilities commenced between the Kāriyakkār of Attingal and the English at Anjengo, Mr. Walter Brown of the Bombay Council arrived at Anjengo, and it was agreed that as soon as the customary annual allowance to the Rāni was paid all disputes should be laid in oblivion.

Accordingly, the Chief of Anjengo, Mr. Gyfford, with a party of ten persons marched to Attingal to offer presents to the Rāni on 15th April 1721. A few invalids alone were left for the defence of the fort. Though Mr. Gyfford and his party met with a good reception at Attingal, they were all later on treacherously murdered, including Messrs. Gyfford, Burton, Fleming, Cowes and others. After this the murderers made for the fort of Anjengo which was most valiantly defended by Gunner Ince, who repulsed every attempt of the besiegers to scale the walls. He kept the besiegers at bay until succoured by men sent out by Mr. Adams, Chief of Tellicherry. In satisfaction for this outrage, the Raja of Travancore and the Rāni of Attingal granted the gardens of Palatadi and Kōṭṭadilli to the Honorable Company on 10th January 1731. The grant is given below:—

"Towards Cherreungne are the garden of Palatadi and Kōṭṭadilli which were formerly bought by the Commander of Anjengo, but when on 15th April 1721, he and ten other persons went to Atenga to make presents to the Queen, they were killed by the treachery of Pullays and Karikars who seized the money of the Honorable Company. Seeing the loss and damage thus done to the Honorable Company, we have ceded the same gardens to them giving up their revenues and the right of cutting trees and all other privileges which the Company may take and they and heirs may enjoy these gardens without any obstacle or having any obstruction; but we are obliged to ask for a free passage and protection on the part of the Honorable Company. Thus in truth we confirm (the grants) with our signatures to the Commander on the 10th January 1731."

The terms of the lease of the Kōttadilli farm to the Travancore Government are given below:—

That "all rents and taxes with revenue arising from the sale of tobacco, salt and spirits, as well as all other profits and produce whatever accruing from the said rented premises are hereby declared to become the sole property of His Highness the Maharaja's Government.

"That the inhabitants of the farm of Kōttadilli of all castes and descriptions whatsoever shall continue to be under the protection of the British Government and amenable to its authorities in all cases of a police or civil nature and that the British Resident is empowered by the second para. of the Minutes of Consultation of the Government of Fort St. George, No. 90, under date the 25th February 1847, to interfere summarily in all complaints made by the ryots against the Sirkar officers.

"The Police establishment of Anjengo shall afford every aid and support to the Sirkar servants in the detection of frauds, or attempts to introduce into the Kōttadilli farm, any of the articles under Sirkar monopoly and in the collection of the revenue of the village."

Products and Industry.—Coconut is the staple produce. The majority of the people engage themselves in catching fish. They use drag nets. They go out to sea in the height of the monsoon in catamarans to catch fish. The owner of each net has to pay one-third of the price of fish caught every Friday to the church. This rate is called Friday contribution or Veḷḷiyāḻcha Kūru.

Lemon-grass oil and coir yarn are manufactured at Anjengo. The former is distilled on the Travancore hills and exported from Anjengo. The trade in this oil was once great, a dozen bottles of oil fetching as much as Rs. 100. But the trade is now on the wane.

The coir yarn turned out in Anjengo is superior to that made elsewhere on the coast.

Dried fish and hides are occasionally exported to Ceylon, where the majority of Anjengo Christians go to work on the coffee estates.

Anjengo is still noted for its paintings.

Archæology.—There are several old tombstones in Anjengo. The earliest inscription is that raised over the grave of the wife of the Commander of the Fort, John Brabon, in A.D. 1704.

There is uninterrupted inland water communication from Anjengo to Tirūr, a Railway station in Ponnāni taluk, a distance of nearly 200 miles.

MAP
of
MALABAR DISTRICT
PONNANI TALUK
PALGHAT TALUK
COCHIN